WHITAKER'S
OLYMPIC ALMANACK

THE ESSENTIAL GUIDE
TO THE OLYMPIC GAMES

© Stan Greenberg 2003

First published 2000

A & C Black Ltd
37 Soho Square, London W1D 3QZ

ISBN 0-7136-6724-9

The publishers make no representation, express or implied, with regard
to the accuracy of the information contained in this book and cannot
accept legal responsibility for any errors or omissions that take place.

A CIP catalogue record for this book is available from the British Library

Editorial team: Mandi Gomez; Inna Ward; Lauren Simpson
Cover photography: © Getty Images
Internal photography: © Getty Images
Designed by: Fiona Pike
Printed and bound in the EU by: Chiltern Press, Bicester, UK

FOREWORD

Most books about the Olympic Games tend to deal with them in Games order, i.e., starting with Athens in 1896 and following through until the latest celebration. Invariably, they deal with the various sports, breaking them up into those in the Summer Games, and then those in the Winter Games. This is all very well and proper, but it makes things very difficult for the reader or researcher who wants to look up, let's say, the competitor with the most medals, or the oldest to win a gold medal, or the tallest ever competitor. Having been involved in reference work for most of my life, putting things into lists, files and classification systems, it seemed obvious to me that what was required was an Olympic compendium in an alphabetical order – similar to an encyclopaedia. You will find the different celebrations of the Games, whether Summer or Winter, in chronological order, i.e. by year, in a separate section. However, all the various sports, Summer, Winter and Discontinued, plus subsidiary subjects, such as Most Medals, Smallest, Tallest etc., are shown in alphabetical order. It is my opinion that this method of presentation, a unique one I believe, will enable the reader to find the information they require easier and faster than previously possible.

I would like to express my thanks to Keith Greenberg and Paul Sparks for their technical help, and Carole Greenberg for her good humour and understanding. Where contradictions have been found in different sources I have invariably arrived at my own, hopefully correct, conclusion. The political upheavals of the former East European bloc have caused Olympic chroniclers some problems. I have taken my own attitude to such matters and made my own, unusual, medal compilations. However, I have given all necessary data so that readers with different views can reconstruct tables to their own liking if they wish.

Stan Greenberg
London 2003

4

ACKNOWLEDGEMENTS

I am greatly indebted to the original research by
Olympic historians Erich Kamper (AUT), Volker Kluge
(GER), Wolf Lyberg (SWE), Bill Mallon (USA) and Ian
Buchanan (GBR). After extensive research, particularly
by Wolf Lyberg, the International Society of Olympic
Historians (ISOH) has agreed new participation figures.
My main sources have been, in alphabetical order, as
follows:

The Associated Press and Grolier, *Pursuit of Excellence,
The Olympic Story* (1979)
Sandor Barcs (HUN), *The Modern Olympics Story* (1964)
Pat Besford (GBR), *Encyclopædia of Swimming* (1976)
Ian Buchanan (GBR), *British Olympians* (1991)
John Durant (USA), *Highlights of the Olympics* (1961)
Erich Kamper (AUT), *Enzyclopadie der Olympischen Spiele*
(1972); *Lexicon der Olympischen Winter Spiele* (1964);
and *Lexicon der 14,000 Olympioniken* (1983)
Erich Kamper (AUT) and Bill Mallon (USA), *The Golden
Book of the Olympic Games* (1992)
Lord Killanin (IRE) and John Rodda (GBR), *The Olympic
Games* (1976)
Volker Kluge (GER), *Die Olympischen Spiele von 1896 bis
1980* (1981); *Winter Olympia Kompakt* (1992); *Olympia
Guide, Salt Lake City* (2001); *Olympische Sommerspiele I
1896-1936* (1997); *II 1948-1964* (1998); *III 1968-
1984* (2000); *1988-1996* (2001)
Bill Mallon (USA) and Ian Buchanan (GBR), *Quest for
Gold* (1984)
Bill Mallon (USA), *The Olympic Record Book* (1988)

Peter Matthews (GBR), *Track and Field Athletics, The
Records* (1986)
Norris and Ross McWhirter (GBR), *The Guinness Book of
Olympic Records* (1980)
David Wallechinsky (USA), *The Complete Book of the
Olympics* (1984, 1988, 1992); *The Complete Book
of the Summer Olympics* (1996, 2000); *The Complete
Book of the Winter Olympics* (1998, 2002)
Melvyn Watman (GBR), *The Encyclopaedia of Track and
Field Athletics* (1981)

Other experts and organisations whose publications
and personal help have been invaluable include:
Richard Ayling, Howard Bass, Anthony Bijkerk (NED),
Harry Carpenter, Jim Coote, Peter Diamond (USA),
Maurice Golesworthy, John Goodbody, Mark Heller,
Richard Hymans, Peter Johnson, Ove Karlsson (SWE),
Ekkehard zur Megede (GER), Ferenc Mezo (HUN),
Rebecca Middleton, Jan Patterson, Ron Pickering,
Philip Pope, Jack Rollin, Bob Sparks, Stuart Storey,
Dave Terry, John Tidy, Lance Tingay, Martin Tyler,
David Vine, Alan Weeks, Ture Widlund (SWE),
Dorian Williams and Don Wood. The Association of
Track and Field Statisticians (ATFS), British Olympic
Association (BOA), The International Society of Olympic
Historians (ISOH), The International Amateur Athletic
Federation (IAAF), International Olympic Committee
(IOC), International Weightlifting Federation (IWF),
National Ski Federation of Great Britain (NSFGB),
National Union of Track Statisticians (NUTS),
*The New York Times, Sports Illustrated, The Times,
Track and Field News, L'Equipe, USA Today,* and many
national and international bodies and individuals.

KEY TO NOTES IN TABLES

G	= gold or gold medallist	km/h	= kilometres per hour
S	= silver	mph	= miles per hour
B	= bronze	yd	= yards
M	= medallist	m	= metres
W	= wind assisted		

ABBREVIATIONS

All member countries, present and past, have an official
Olympic three-letter abbreviation, used throughout this
book. A list of these can be found under the entry
'Participation, by country' (p.115).

CONTENTS

A CHRONOLOGY OF THE SUMMER AND WINTER OLYMPIC GAMES

ANCIENT GAMES

The Olympic Games originally evolved from legendary conflicts among the Greek Gods and the religious ceremonies held in their honour. Historical evidence dates the Games from about 900 BC, but there is good reason to believe that a similar festival existed four centuries previously. Indeed the modern word 'athlete' is said to derive from Aethlius, King of Elis. The area in which Olympia lies is in the plain of Elis, on the banks of the River Alpheios. It was a successor, Iphitus, who was instrumental in reviving the then faltering concept in the late ninth century BC. He also arranged for the truce (called *ekecheiria*) between the continually warring states of the region which recognised the neutrality and sanctity of Olympia, and which lasted for the period of the Games. The first firm record dates from 776 BC, and the Games were numbered at four-yearly intervals from then. At that time there was only one event, the *stade* race, and the winner, the first recorded Olympic champion, was Coroibis of Elis. The *stade* was 192.27m (210.26yd) long, reputably 60 times the length of the god Heracles's (Hercules) foot. After thirteen Olympiads, in 724 BC, a race of two *stade*, the *diaulus*, was also contested, and in the following celebration the 24-stadia *dolichus*, about 4.5km (2.8 miles) in length, was instituted. In 708 BC came the pentathlon, mythically invented by Jason (of *Jason and the Argonauts* fame). This consisted of a run, standing long jump (with the aid of *halteres*, hand-held weights), throwing the discus and javelin, and wrestling. Eventually chariot racing, running in armour and boxing were included, and in 648 BC the *pankration*, a brutal mix of boxing and wrestling. Numerous variants of these sports appeared over the years, as did also activities of a less sporting nature, such as contests for trumpeters.

Initially contestants wore simple shorts-like garments, but from about 720 BC they competed in the nude, and until 692 BC the Games only lasted for a single day. This was later increased to two days, and in 632 BC to a total of five days, of which the middle three were for actual competitions. For the next six centuries the fame of Olympia spread throughout the known world, and many famous people visited the Games. Victors, in those early days, won only a crown of wild olive leaves, but were often richly rewarded by their home cities or states, and sometimes became very wealthy. Crowd figures were not published but archaeologists have estimated that the stadium at Olympia could hold over 20,000 spectators.

For reasons not fully understood today women, and slaves, were strictly forbidden, under pain of death, to even attend the Games. An exception does appear to have been made for high-ranking priestesses of the most important gods. However, it was possible for a woman to gain an Olympic prize. This was because in the chariot race the chaplet of olive leaves was awarded to the owner of the horses and not the drivers. One of the first women to win an Olympic title in this way was Belistike of Macedonia in 268 BC as owner of the champion two-horse chariot, and an inscription at Olympia refers to Kyniska of Sparta as one of the first such female chariot owners. It is recorded that some women did defy the rules and disguised themselves, but, on discovery, were thrown over a cliff to their deaths. There is a story, perhaps apocryphal, that Pherenice of Rhodes acted as a second to watch her son, Pisidores, win his event. In her excitement she gave herself away, but when it was realised that not only her son, but also her father and brothers had all been Olympic champions, she was pardoned.

Possibly the most famous champion of early times was Leonidas of Rhodes who won the three 'track' events on four consecutive occasions 164–152 BC, making a total of 12 victories — not surpassed since. The first recorded triple gold medallist at one Games was Phanas of Pellene in 512 BC, while the Spartan runner Chionis won the stade in three successive Games 664–656 BC. Other excellent champions included Theagenes of Thassos who won eight titles at boxing, wrestling and *pankration* from 468–456 BC, and Milon of Croton who won six wrestling titles 536–516 BC. Eventually, the very success of the Games gave rise to its downfall. The importance of winning at Olympia, and the reflected glory it bestowed on the winner's birthplace, led cities to hire professionals and bribe judges. With the dawn of the Christian era the religious and physical backgrounds of the Games were attacked. An irreversible decline set in under Roman influence, so much so that in AD 67 a drunken Emperor Nero was crowned victor of the chariot race despite the fact that there were no other entrants (who could blame them) and he did not even finish the course. According to accepted belief, in AD 393 the Roman Emperor Theodosius I issued a decree in Milan, which prohibited the Games. Recent archaeological evidence seems to suggest that the Games may have continued – in some form – for another 100–120 years, but then the ravages of foreign invaders, earthquakes and flooding virtually obliterated the site of Olympia, and the world forgot the glory that once had been.

There was a resurgence of interest in Ancient Greece in the 17th and 18th centuries and references to the Olympic Games in the poems of Pindar and other Greek poets were noted. In Britain the Cotswold Olympic Games were inaugurated in the early 17th century, and in 1850 Dr William Penny Brookes founded the Much Wenlock Olympic Society. At the end of the 18th century, in Germany, the famed founder of modern gymnastics, Johann Guts Muths, had suggested the revival of the Olympic ideal. Some 50 years later a fellow-countryman, Ernst Curtius, who had worked as an archaeologist at Olympia (started by the French in 1829) reiterated the idea in a lecture he gave in Berlin in 1852. In Greece itself Major Evangelis Zappas organised a Pan-Hellenic sports festival in 1859 that attracted a great deal of public support, and which was revived at intervals over the next 30 years.

However, the true founder of the modern Olympic Games is commonly acknowledged to be Pierre de Fredi, Baron de Coubertin, of France. In 1889 he met Brookes of Much Wenlock, and formed his concept of a revived

Games, which he first propounded publicly at a lecture in the Sorbonne, Paris, on 25 November 1892. In the following year, he met with representatives of the top American universities. In June 1894 he convened an international conference, also in the Sorbonne, the outcome of which was a resolution on 23 June, calling for competitions along the lines of the Ancient Games to be held every four years. The International Olympic Committee (IOC) was inaugurated under the presidency of Demetrius Vikelas of Greece with de Coubertin as Secretary-General. The Frenchman had hoped to herald the new century with the first Games in Paris in 1900, but the delegates were impatient. There was strong sentiment in favour of London or Budapest, but, at the instigation of Vikelas, Athens was finally selected and the date set as 1896.

ATHENS 1896

I OLYMPIC GAMES HELD IN ATHENS, GREECE, 6–15 APRIL 1896 (25 MARCH–3 APRIL 1896 ACCORDING TO THE JULIAN CALENDAR)
ATTENDED BY REPRESENTATIVES OF 14 COUNTRIES, COMPRISING 211 COMPETITORS (NO WOMEN).

Although the Greek government was apparently not consulted, and was beset with internal financial and political problems, the Greek public was very enthusiastic. However, it was not until Crown Prince Constantine set up a committee and began organising and collecting funds that the project became feasible, and the prospect of Budapest getting the honour by default faded. The turning point came with the generosity of a Greek businessman, Georges Averoff (formerly Avykeris) who actually lived in Alexandria, Egypt. He offered to pay for the reconstruction of the Panathenean Stadium in Athens at a cost of 920,000 *drachmas* (£36,500 at the 1896 exchange rate). The stadium was initiated and built by the orator Luycurgus, a disciple of Plato in 330 BC. It was rebuilt 500 years later by Herodes Atticus, but had gradually disintegrated and was covered up until 1870 when King George of Greece had arranged for its excavation by a German, Ernst Ziller. The new track measured 33,333m, had very sharp turns, and the competitors ran in a clockwise direction. There was supposed to be a total of 50 events, but the seven rowing competitions were cancelled due to inclement weather in Phaleron Bay.

The opening of the Games coincided with the 75th anniversary of the declaration of Greek independence from Turkish rule. Over 40,000 spectators in the stadium, plus thousands more on the surrounding hills, saw King George I formally open the proceedings. The greater bulk of competitors were from Greece itself. Many athletes entered privately, including holidaymakers, and the British contingent included two employees of the Embassy in Athens. Another member of the British team was an Irishman, John Boland, who was on holiday in Greece at the time and entered the tennis events. He won the singles and, partnering a German, also won gold in the doubles. A French sprinter who insisted on wearing his gloves as he was running before royalty provided a further nice touch of the period.

Not for the last time a gymnast, Hermann Weingärtner (GER), was the most successful competitor, with three first places, two seconds and a third; a Frenchman, Paul Masson, won three cycling events; but perhaps the most outstanding achievement was that of Carl Schuhmann of Germany who not only won three gymnastic events but also won the wrestling title. Another competitor to gain medals in two sports was gymnast Fritz Hofmann (GER) whose total of five placings included a silver medal in the 100m. In shooting, John and Sumner Paine (USA) became the first brothers to win Olympic gold medals, in military pistol and free pistol respectively. Their father had successfully defended yachting's America's Cup some years before, and John Paine's great granddaughter later sculled in the 1996 Games.

The first competition of the modern Olympic Games was heat one of the 100m, which was won, in 12.5sec by the American Francis Lane of Princeton University, thus carving a niche in history for himself. The first gold medallist of modern times was James Brendan Connolly (USA) who won the hop, step and jump (now known as the triple jump). In fact the American team, composed exclusively of college students, dominated events in the stadium, despite arriving only the day before the start of the competitions, having travelled by ship to France and then by train to Greece. Victors actually received a silver medal and a crown of olive leaves; runners-up were given bronze medals and a crown of laurel; no awards were made for third place.

Two new sporting events were introduced at these Games: the discus throw and the marathon. Both were based on Greek antiquity and the hosts were eager to win them. However, the former was taken by Robert Garrett (USA) who had inadvertently practised with an implement much larger and heavier than the one actually used at Athens. The marathon had been proposed by Frenchman Michel Breal, to commemorate the legendary run of a Greek courier, possibly Pheidippides, with the news of a Greek victory over the Persians in 490 BC. He is supposed to have run from the site of the battle, and, after crying out 'Rejoice! We conquer', collapsed and died. To the great delight of the spectators the race was won by a Greek shepherd, Spiridon 'Spyros' Louis, who was escorted into the stadium by Crown Prince Constantine and Prince George.

The oldest gold medallist was Georgios Orphanidis (GRE) in the free rifle contest, aged 36 years 102 days, while the youngest was swimmer Alfréd Hajós (HUN) aged 18 years 70 days when he won the 100m and 1200m freestyle events. A member of the Greek bronze medal gymnastics team was reported to be less than 11 years of age, but some doubt exists about the veracity of this claim. In view of the modern saturation coverage of the Olympics by the media, it is noteworthy to record that the British press gave little space to reports from Athens, despite an earlier complaint in The Times, about the lack of knowledge of the occasion in the country, and Britain's inadequate representation. Nevertheless, the Games were a tremendous success and Greece looked forward to the next celebration, which they also expected to host.

1896 MEDALS

	G	S	B
United States	11	7	1
Greece	10	19	18
Germany	7	5	2
France	5	4	2
Great Britain	3	3	1
Hungary	2	1	3
Austria	2	—	3
Australia	2	—	—
Denmark	1	2	4
Switzerland	1	2	—

PARIS 1900

II OLYMPIC GAMES HELD IN PARIS, FRANCE,
20 MAY–28 OCTOBER 1900
ATTENDED BY REPRESENTATIVES OF 24 COUNTRIES,
COMPRISING 1225 COMPETITORS, OF WHICH 19
WERE WOMEN.

Despite strong Greek pressure for the exclusive rights to organise future Games, Baron de Coubertin won agreement to hold the 1900 Games in Paris, but made a serious mistake in making it part of the Fifth Universal Exposition also being held there. In the event the Games became merely a sideshow to the fair. Numerous internal rivalries within French sport left many of the sports without experienced officials or adequate venues. The track and field events were held on uneven turf at Croix-Catelan, in the Bois de Boulogne, where it is reported that the jumpers had to dig their own pits. Many of the competitors, especially the Americans, had never run on a grass track before. Generally there were few spectators, and even these were nearly reduced in number when the 1896 discus champion threw the implement into the crowd on all three throws. Cricket, croquet and golf made their appearance, and amid the general confusion many competitors, even medal winners, were not aware until much later that they had been competing at the Olympic Games.

France, the host country, had a record-sized team numbering 884, the largest ever entered for the Games. Russia competed for the first time. The Americans were still represented by colleges and clubs, and the decision to have competition on Sunday upset many of those whose colleges were church controlled. Thus the long jump world record holder Myer Prinstein, a Russian-born Jew but under the aegis of the University of Syracuse, a strong Methodist institution, gained a silver medal with his Saturday qualifying round jump (such performances then counted for medals), but had to withdraw from the Sunday final. The eventual winner, Alvin Kraenzlein (USA) set a record of four individual gold medals, a feat never surpassed in track and field at one Games. Also much in evidence was America's Ray Ewry, the standing jump expert, at the start of his fabulous Olympic career, with three gold medals here. Behind him in those standing jumps was countryman Irving Baxter. He had already won the regular high jump and the pole vault, and reputedly became the first athlete of Native American

ancestry to win at the Olympic Games. Athlete Norman Pritchard (GBR), usually, and mistakenly, shown as representing India, won two silvers in the 200m flat and hurdles races, and later became an actor in Hollywood silent films.

Women were allowed to compete for the first time, but not in the major sports, and the first female Olympic competitor (only recently researched) was Helen, Countess de Pourtalès (SUI), in the one- to two-tonne class sailing event in May. The first individual champion was Charlotte Cooper (GBR), who won the tennis singles on 7 July. A unique record was set in the coxed pairs rowing final, in which a small French boy was drafted in at the last moment to cox the winning Dutch crew. His name was never recorded and he disappeared without trace afterwards, but he was no more than ten years old, and possibly as young as seven, in either case the youngest ever Olympic gold medallist. The oldest gold medallist in 1900 was French-born Count Hermann de Pourtalès (SUI) in the one- two-tonne class sailing aged 53 years 55 days. The youngest female champion was Margaret Abbott (USA) in golf aged 20 years 110 days, while the oldest was 31-year-old Helen, Countess de Pourtalès, who was a crewmember for her father.

Press coverage was barely apparent, with many of the events not mentioned at all, and for years afterwards there was much confusion as to the names and nationalities of even the medallists. Thus it was that the first Olympic medals won by Canada, a gold and bronze gained by George Orton, were not 'discovered' for some years, as Orton had been entered by his American university and was billed as an American. Constantin Henriquez de Zubiera (FRA) gained a silver in the tug-of-war, and then a gold medal in Rugby in 1900 – he was Algerian-born and thus the first African and, indeed, black athlete to (a) compete in the Games, (b) win a medal, and (c) gain a gold medal. Even more recently it has been found that the winner of the marathon, Michel Théato (FRA), was actually a Luxembourgeois – in this case the medal tables have not been altered.

1900 MEDALS

	G	S	B
France	27	39	34
United States	19	15	15
Great Britain	17	9	12
Switzerland	6	3	1
Belgium	5	5	3
Germany	3	2	2
Australia	3	—	4
Denmark	2	3	2
Italy	2	2	—
The Netherlands	1	1	4
Hungary	1	2	2
Cuba	1	1	—
Canada	1	—	1
Sweden	1	—	1
Austria	—	3	3
Norway	—	2	3
Czechoslovakia	—	1	2

ST LOUIS 1904

III OLYMPIC GAMES HELD IN ST LOUIS, USA, 1 JULY–23
NOVEMBER 1904
ATTENDED BY REPRESENTATIVES OF 13 COUNTRIES,
COMPRISING 687 COMPETITORS, OF WHICH 6 WERE
WOMEN.

For a time the third celebration seemed likely to go to
Britain, and then to Philadelphia, whilst de Coubertin had
favoured New York. The IOC finally designated Chicago
for these Games, but at the request of President Theodore
Roosevelt, also president of the USOC, the venue was
changed to St Louis to coincide with the World's Fair,
held to celebrate the centenary of the Louisiana Purchase.
Thus again they became merely a sideshow. Held in the
centre of the North American continent, the problems of
distance and travel meant that there were very few
overseas entrants. Indeed, even de Coubertin did not
attend. Thus 85 per cent of the competitors were from
the host country, and, not surprisingly, they won 84 per
cent of the medals. In fact the Games were a virtual
college and club tournament with the New York Athletics
Club (NYAC) beating the Chicago Athletic Association
(CAA) for the track and field team title (a points table was
actually published). It went so far that a German team
applied to enter the gymnastics competition but was
refused because all its members did not belong to one
club. In swimming much was made of the fact that New
York beat Germany and Hungary overall.

DID YOU KNOW?
*In 1904 George Eyser of the United States won three
gold medals in the gymnastics competitions despite
having a wooden leg.*

In such circumstances the Games degenerated into
something of a farce, so that the cycling events, which
had no foreign entrants at all, and included a number of
professional riders, were initially refused official Olympic
status. However, recent scholarship suggests that they
should be included in medal tables and results. So the
unique achievement of Marcus Hurley in winning four
cycling events should now be given due credit. Gymnast
Anton Heida (USA) won five golds and a silver and
became the most successful at these Games.

Under the rather loose controls imposed on most
sports some strange things happened. In the 400-m track
race no heats were held, and all 13 entrants ran in the
final. Rowing events were held over a 1 1/2-mile (2.4km)
course which entailed making a turn. The swimming
events were held over Imperial distances, while the
athletics track (in the grounds of Washington University,
St Louis) measured one-third of a mile in circumference
(536m) and had a 220-yd straightaway, which was quite
an innovation for the visiting Europeans. In the track and
field programme only two events went to non-Americans.
The French-Canadian policeman Etienne Desmarteau
won the 56lb (25.4kg) weight throw. He unfortunately
died the following year of typhoid and a park was named
after him in his home city of Montreal. The ten-event all-
round competition, a forerunner of the decathlon, was
won by Thomas Kiely, who, incidentally, like the silver

medallist in the 2500m steeplechase, John Daly, was an
Irishman. However, as Ireland at the time was part of the
United Kingdom, they have to be taken as representing
Great Britain, despite attempts by 'historical revisionists'
to make it otherwise. The unfortunate Myer Prinstein
redressed his grievance of four years previously by taking
the long jump title, as well as winning the hop, step and
jump. He also placed fifth in both the 60m and 400m
finals. The ever-liberal Prinstein here was representing
the Greater New York Irish Athletics Association
(NYIAA).

The 200m final, uniquely held on a straightaway (i.e.
no turns), was won by Archie Hahn, with all three of his
opponents given a one-yard (0.99m) handicap under the
rules then governing false starts. Joseph Stadler won a
silver medal in the standing high jump, while George
Poage won bronzes in the 200m and 400m hurdles races.
The significance of their performances was that they were
thought to be the first black men to win medals in the
Olympics. Recent research suggests that a French-
Algerian in 1900 pre-dates them. Despite the lack of
foreign opposition the standard in many sports was very
high, and the triple victories of Archie Hahn, Harry
Hillman, James Lightbody, Ray Ewry and swimmer
Charles Daniels were outstanding. Daniels, in winning
three golds, a silver, and a bronze, was the prototype of
the American swimmers who were to dominate Olympic
freestyle swimming for many years.

There was a scandal in the marathon when the first man
out of the stadium, Fred Lorz (USA), was also the first
man back, looking remarkably fresh. It later transpired
that he had received a lift in a car after suffering cramp,
and when the car itself broke down near the stadium he
resumed running – as a joke he claimed. He was banned
for life (but was competing again after only a year) and the
title was awarded to British-born American Thomas Hicks
who had finished in a daze due to being administered
strychnine by his handlers as a stimulant – a practice then
common and allowable. In ninth place was Len Tau (SAF),
in St Louis as part of a World's Fair exhibit, the first black
African distance runner to compete in the Olympics.

The youngest gold medallist was golfer Robert Hunter
(USA) aged 17 years 301 days, while the oldest was the
Reverend Galen Spencer (USA), an archer, aged 64 years
2 days. Another American archer, Samuel Duvall, won a
silver medal aged 68 years 194 days – the oldest American
medallist ever. The oldest female champion was Lida
Howell (USA) in archery aged 45 years 25 days. The
youngest medallist was another archer, Henry Richardson
(USA), aged 15 years 124 days. Another American, Frank
Kungler, won a silver in wrestling, a bronze in tug-of-
war, and two bronzes in weightlifting, to become the
only Olympian to win medals at three different sports at
a single Games.

A final insult to the Games were the Anthropology
Days, during which competitions were held, parodying
the regular Olympic events, for aboriginal peoples, such
as American Indians, African pygmies, Patagonians, Ainus
from Japan, and the like. Finally, in November, with the
Association Football competition won by a Canadian
college over two American teams, the III Olympic Games
came to an end – and many in Europe wondered if the
fledgling movement would recover.

1904 MEDALS

	G	S	B
United States	80	84	84
Germany	4	4	5
Canada	4	1	1
Cuba	4	—	—
Austria	2	1	1
Hungary	2	1	1
Great Britain	1	1	—
Greece	1	—	1
Switzerland	1	—	1
France	—	1	—

ATHENS 1906

THE INTERIM OR INTERCALATED GAMES HELD IN
ATHENS, GREECE, 22 APRIL–2 MAY 1906
ATTENDED BY REPRESENTATIVES OF 20 COUNTRIES,
COMPRISING 826 COMPETITORS, OF WHICH 6 WERE
WOMEN.

After two debacles, in Paris and St Louis, something was needed to revive the flagging Olympic movement and de Coubertin, with some misgivings, agreed a series of four-yearly meetings, interspersed with the main Games, to be held in Athens. Although these had the blessing of the IOC, it was decided that the Interim Games would not be numbered in sequence. This has caused an ambivalence in Olympic historians, when writing about the Games, leading to the ludicrous situation where some of them refuse to include these Games in their narratives, but do include the medals won in their totals. This author considers that as these Games were sanctioned by the IOC, numbered or not, they were genuine Olympic Games, and should be treated as such. In the event, only this meeting of the projected series was ever held. Competitors were housed in the Zappeion, thus predating the first Olympic 'village' by 18 years. Again the Greeks showed their enthusiasm and large crowds, missing for the past ten years, were in evidence. The marble stadium in Athens was full to capacity, and enthusiasm often helped to overcome organisational mishaps.

The 20 countries included the first 'official' American team, selected and sent by the USOC, so ending the practice of colleges, clubs and private individuals entering. Also present was the first ever team from Finland, with the doyen of the famous Järvinen family, Werner, gaining his country's first ever Olympics gold medal. The programme of track and field events was altered by a reduction in the number of sprint and hurdles races, and the addition of a pentathlon and the javelin throw.

There were some excellent performances, especially by some of the 1904 champions such as the perennial Ray Ewry and the New York policeman Martin Sheridan. Another American, with the apt name of Paul Pilgrim, had only been added to the team at the last moment after he had raised the money for his fare privately. He had won a gold medal in 1904 as a member of the NYAC relay team, but in Athens surprisingly won both the 400m and 800m titles, a feat not equalled until 1976.

The new pentathlon event, consisting of a 192m run, standing long jump, discus and javelin throws, and Greco-Roman wrestling, was won by Hjalmar Mellander of Sweden. In third place was his countryman Erik Lemming who also gained bronze medals in the shot and tug-of-war as well as winning the first of three Olympic javelin titles. There was a real surprise in the 1500m walk, which was also the scene of a number of purely chauvinistic decisions by the various national judges. The American distance runner George Bonhag had disappointed in the 1500m and 5 mile runs, and had entered the walk, an entirely new event to him, in a last effort to win a medal. Owing mainly to the excessive number of disqualifications, all the favourites were ruled out, and he won the gold. With all three previous Olympic marathons having been won by the host country, the Greeks were hopeful of continuing the tradition, but despite half of the entrants coming from Greece it was won by William Sherring of Canada, incidentally wearing a trilby hat, by a massive margin of nearly seven minutes. In addition to his medal he was given a goat. The most successful competitor at these Games was shooter Louis Richardet (SUI) who won three gold and three silver medals.

The oldest gold medallist was Maurice Lecoq (FRA) aged 52 years 31 days when he won the rapid-fire pistol event. Youngest was the coxswain of the Italian fours crew, Giorgio Cesana aged 14 years 12 days. The youngest female champion was Marie Decugis (FRA) in tennis aged 21 years 261 days. She and her husband, Max, became the first married couple to win Olympic gold medals. The oldest medallist was fencer Charles Newton-Robinson (GBR) at 52 years 195 days.

Despite the soft cinder track in the stadium, poor facilities for the swimmers at Phaleron Bay, complaints about food and judging decisions, these, since much maligned, Interim Games put the whole Olympic concept back on the path towards de Coubertin's ideal.

1906 MEDALS

	G	S	B
France	15	9	16
United States	12	6	6
Greece	8	11	13
Great Britain	8	11	5
Italy	7	6	3
Switzerland	5	6	4
Germany	4	6	5
Norway	4	2	—
Austria	3	3	2
Denmark	3	2	1
Sweden	2	5	7
Hungary	2	5	3
Belgium	2	2	3
Finland	2	1	1
Canada	1	1	—
The Netherlands	—	1	2
Australia	—	—	3
Czechoslovakia	—	—	2
South Africa	—	—	1

LONDON 1908

IV OLYMPIC GAMES HELD IN LONDON, ENGLAND, 27
APRIL–31 OCTOBER 1908
ATTENDED BY REPRESENTATIVES OF 22 COUNTRIES,
COMPRISING 2035 COMPETITORS, OF WHICH 36
WERE WOMEN.

Originally awarded to Rome the IV Games were re-allocated to London when the Italian authorities informed the IOC during the 1906 Interim Games that they would have to withdraw due to financial problems caused by an eruption of Mount Vesuvius. London formally accepted on 19 November 1906. Nevertheless, they were the most successful held up until then and set the pattern for future Games. Drawing on the expertise of many British sporting governing bodies – such as the Amateur Swimming Association (ASA) founded in 1869, and the Amateur Athletic Association (AAA), founded in 1880 – the organising committee under Lord Desborough went to work. A 68,000-capacity stadium was built in West London for a reported cost of £40,000. (That stated 'capacity' was apparently well exceeded on a number of occasions). It contained an athletics track of three laps to the mile, inside a 660yd banked concrete cycle track. On the grass infield stood a giant (330ft x 50ft, 100m x 15.24m) pool for the swimming events. Rowing was on the Thames at Henley, tennis was held at the All-England Club, Wimbledon, and the new sport of motorboating was on Southampton Water. The sailing competitions took place at Ryde, Isle of Wight, with some on the River Clyde, at Glasgow – the only time that any Olympic events have been held in Scotland. The main competitions took place in July, although the overall programme lasted from April to October. There were 21 sports in all, including four ice skating events. There was also a demonstration sport, bicycle polo, in which Ireland beat Germany 3–1.

Entries were only by nations, as opposed to individuals. This tended to emphasise the nationalism that undoubtedly caused some of the disputes that marred this first truly international sporting occasion. These problems started during the formal opening, by King Edward VII, at what later became known as the White City stadium, on 13 July. Sweden and the United States were upset that their flags had been inadvertently missed from those flying around the stadium. Then Ralph Rose, the American flag bearer, and eventual winner of the shot, refused to dip the Stars and Stripes to King Edward in the march past. The Finnish team would not march behind the flag of Czarist Russia and came in without any banner. Later things got worse as complaints came from all sides, but especially from American officials. They complained about 'fixed' heats, illegal coaching, rule breaking and British chauvinism. The weather was also rather foul, even by British standards, and badly affected cycling and tennis in particular.

All the rancour came to a head in the 400-m event final, in which three of the four finalists were Americans. Prior to the race officials had been tipped off about an American 'plot', after someone overheard them planning how to impede and beat the British favourite, Lieutenant Wyndham Halswelle. In the event the race was declared void, and a re-run, with strings delineating the lanes was

ordered for the next day, and the winner of the disputed race, Carpenter, was disqualified. The other Americans refused to appear and Halswelle gained the gold medal in the only walkover in Games history. One of the runners involved was John Taylor who, as a member of the winning medley relay team, has always been noted as the first black man to win an Olympic gold medal. However, recent research has indicated that an Algerian in the French team of 1900 has that distinction. A more imaginative resolution to a problem, apparently, came in the 110m hurdles. The favourite, Forrest Smithson, an American student of theology, protested against the official decision to run the final on a Sunday, and then proceeded to break the world record with 15.0sec, supposedly carrying a bible in his left hand. While uplifting, the only 'evidence' of this story is a photograph that was obviously staged after the event.

Finally the bitterness reached such a level that it was thought necessary to produce a booklet entitled *Replies to Criticism of the Olympic Games*, which, owing to its rather pompous tone, did little to alleviate the situation. One result of all this was the decision that future control of competitions should be in the hands of the various international governing bodies of the sports and not left solely to the host country.

The previous year the IOC had decided that medals should be awarded for the first three places in all events. There were many excellent performances throughout the Games, despite all the problems. The ubiquitous Ray Ewry, now 33 years old, won his record-breaking ninth and tenth gold medals in the standing jumps, while John Flanagan (one of the so-called Irish-American 'Whales') won his third hammer title. Middle distance runner Mel Sheppard (USA) was a triple gold medallist, as was British swimmer Henry Taylor. Charles Daniels (USA) won the 100-m freestyle to add to his three titles from the last two Games, and set a record of four individual event swimming gold medals that has been equalled, but not beaten, since. The Hungarian swimmer Zoltán von Halmay increased his total medal haul to nine since 1900, a total unsurpassed in the sport until 1972.

The introduction of skating events gave Russia the opportunity to win its first Olympic title, courtesy of Nikolai Panin (actually Kolomenkin), who four years later was a member of the fourth-placed revolver shooting team. Another Olympic first came in the London shooting programme when Oscar and Alfred Swahn of Sweden became the first father and son to win gold medals, with Oscar being the oldest gold medallist at these Games aged 60 years 265 days. The youngest champion was Daniel Carroll (AUS) in rugby aged 16 years 245 days, while the youngest female gold medallist was Gladys Eastlake-Smith (GBR) in tennis aged 24 years 273 days. The oldest female champion was archer Queenie Newall (GBR) aged 53 years 275 days.

Undoubtedly the most famous event in the IV Games was the marathon. Originally the distance was to be about 25 miles (40km), but the start was moved to Windsor Castle, an exact 26 miles (41.8km). Then at the request of Princess Mary, it was moved again to start beneath the windows of the royal nursery in the Castle grounds, making a final distance of 26 miles, 385yd (42.195km). This arbitrarily arrived-at distance was later (in 1924) accepted worldwide as the standard marathon length. The race itself was run in intensely hot and humid conditions, quite the opposite of most of the preceding weather, and was watched by an estimated 250,000 people. The little Italian Dorando Pietri reached the stadium first in a state of near collapse – it has been suggested that his gargling with wine during the race did not react well with the heat. He fell five times on the last part-lap of the track. Over-zealous officials, reputedly, but erroneously, including the famous author Sir Arthur Conan Doyle, helped him over the finish line, thus leading to his disqualification. Doyle was in the stadium, but sitting in the stand reporting the events for a newspaper. On behalf of the second finisher, Irish-born Johnny Hayes, the Americans lodged a protest, which was upheld, and the Italian was disqualified. The wave of public sympathy found expression in the gift of Queen Alexandra to Pietri of a special gold cup.

Great Britain won the greatest number of medals overall, but the United States, as always, was well in front in the centrepiece of the Games, the track and field events. Two sportsmen, Ivan Osiier (DEN) a fencer, and Magnus Konow (NOR) a yachtsman, though unplaced in their events, began Olympic careers which continued until the next Games in London in 1948, setting a record breaking span for Olympic competition of 40 years. Colonel Joshua Millner, winner of the 1000yd free rifle, at least aged 58 years 237 days, was Britain's oldest ever Olympic gold medallist. The youngest British winner in 1908 was William Foster (GBR), in the 4 x 200m swimming relay six days past his 18th birthday.

1908 MEDALS

	G	S	B
Great Britain	56	50	39
United States	23	12	12
Sweden	8	6	11
France	5	5	9
Germany	3	5	5
Hungary	3	4	2
Canada	3	3	9
Norway	2	3	3
Italy	2	2	—
Belgium	1	5	2
Australia*	1	2	1
Russia	1	2	—
Finland	1	1	3
South Africa	1	1	—
Greece	—	3	1
Denmark	—	2	3
Czechoslovakia	—	—	2
The Netherlands	—	—	2
Austria	—	—	1
New Zealand*	—	—	1

* Australia and New Zealand combined as Australasia.

STOCKHOLM 1912

V OLYMPIC GAMES HELD IN STOCKHOLM, SWEDEN, 5 MAY–22 JULY 1912
ATTENDED BY REPRESENTATIVES OF 28 COUNTRIES, COMPRISING 2547 COMPETITORS, OF WHICH 57 WERE WOMEN.

Stockholm finally attained the honour that Sweden had wanted from the very beginning, and Torben Grut designed and built a 31,000-capacity stadium, with a 383m (407yd) track laid out under the direction of Charles Perry, the Englishman responsible for the 1896 and 1908 tracks. Baron de Coubertin had insisted that the number of sports be cut, and now, with only 14, there were high standards of performance and sportsmanship, with few arguments or protests. Boxing was not held, the last time that it has been left out of the Olympic programme. King Gustav V officially opened the Games. One of the rare complaints at these Games was from the Finns, again about competing under the Russian flag. Indeed the triple gold medallist Kolehmainen stated that he almost wished he had not won rather than see the hated flag raised for his victories.

Various innovations included the first use of electrical timing equipment for the running events. Baron de Coubertin had asked for a new event to be introduced, the modern pentathlon, which consisted of five disciplines of different sports. It was dominated by the Swedes but in fifth place was one Lieutenant George S. Patton (USA), later to become a controversial Second World War general. As previously, the American team lived on the liner that had brought them across the Atlantic, ironically named *Finland* – for this was the Games in which the first of the 'Flying Finns', Hannes Kolehmainen, made his appearance, winning the 5000m, 10,000m and 12,000m cross-country. He also set a world record in a heat of the 3000m team race, in which the Finnish team surprisingly did not qualify for the final. Nevertheless, this was the beginning of a domination that lasted into the 1940s. Kolehmainen's race with Jean Bouin of France in the 5000m was one of the most enthralling races ever seen to that time with the Finn winning by a stride in 14min 36.6sec, improving the world record by a margin of 24.6sec. Other track stars were Ted Meredith (USA), gold medallist in the 800m in a new world mark, and Ralph Craig (USA) who took both sprints. Under current rules he would not have won, as he was responsible for three of the seven false starts to the race. He reappeared at the Games, as a reserve yachtsman, 36 years later, in London, when he was given the honour of carrying the American team flag.

In the swimming pool the first of the great Hawaiian competitors, Duke Paoa Kahanamoku, won the 100-m freestyle. The son of Hawaiian royalty, he received his first name as a mark of respect for the then Duke of Edinburgh, Queen Victoria's second son, who was visiting the islands at the time of his birth. He competed in two more Games before becoming a movie star. There was only one cycling event, but it was unique in that it was the longest road race ever held at the Games. It was won by Rudolph Lewis (SAF), who took the 320km (198.8 miles) event in just short of 10½ hours. A great impetus was given to the game of soccer at these Olympics, with 25,000 spectators present to see Great Britain beat Denmark 4–2 in the final. Gymnastics, which like wrestling, was held outdoors, also gained new status.

In wrestling, problems were caused by the extreme length of some of the bouts. In the light-heavyweight final the judges called a halt after the bout had gone on for nine hours and gave both wrestlers a silver medal, with no gold awarded. Even this was surpassed in the middleweight category where the tussle for the silver medal between Asikainen (FIN) and Klein, an Estonian representing Russia, went on for 11hr 40min, a record for the sport. Klein finally triumphed. The first known twins to win Olympic gold medals were the Carlberg brothers, Vilhelm (three) and Eric (two), in shooting, while an even more unusual sibling combination came in the 6-m class yachting when the French winner *Mac Miche* was crewed by the three Thubé brothers.

DID YOU KNOW?

In the 1912 Greco-Roman light-heavyweight wrestling final, the two competitors struggled for nine hours. A draw was declared and both men received silver medals: no gold was awarded. In the semi-final of the middleweight class at the same Games, the competitors wrestled for 11 hours 40 minutes before there was a decision. The winner was too exhausted to contest the final.

However, the star of the Games was undoubtedly Jim Thorpe. Of Irish, French, but mainly Native American ancestry, Thorpe won both the newly constituted athletic pentathlon as well as the decathlon, with consummate ease. Additionally he was fourth in the individual high jump and seventh in the long jump. Thus, it can be said that he actually competed in a total of 17 events. Presenting him with his medals King Gustav V called him 'the greatest athlete in the world'. Thorpe reportedly replied 'Thanks King'. Six months later, a sportswriter for the Worcester Telegram in Massachusetts, Roy Johnson, reported that Thorpe had played minor baseball for money. Owing to the violent amateur/professional dichotomy of the time, perhaps reinforced by American anti-Native American prejudice, Thorpe's medals were taken back and his performances removed from Olympic annals. It seems almost certain that he was ignorant of the amateur laws of the time, and the amount involved was very small. Twenty years after his death in 1953 the American Athletic Union (AAU) reinstated him as an amateur, but the IOC stubbornly refused all entreaties on his behalf. It has been suggested that his cause was not helped by the fact that the President of the IOC from 1952–72 was Avery Brundage, a teammate of Thorpe's in 1912 who had placed fifth (or sixth depending on your view) in the pentathlon. To their credit the runners-up to Thorpe, Hugo Wieslander (SWE) and Ferdinand Bie (NOR) initially refused to accept the gold medals when they were sent them, although their names were inscribed in Olympic annals as winners of the events. Finally, in October 1982 Thorpe, the man who had voted in 1950 as the greatest athlete of the first half-century, was pardoned by the IOC and the medals presented to his family. However, they were in addition to the medals already presented, i.e. the amended result still stands, and two people are reckoned as winners.

DID YOU KNOW?

The oldest ever competitor at the Olympic games was Oscar Swahn of Sweden, who also won a silver medal in the 1920-shooting programme when over 72 years of age. He actually qualified for the next games in 1924, but was

too ill to take part. He had become the oldest Olympic gold medallist ever in 1912, aged nearly 65, when his son, Alfred, was one of his teammates.

The oldest gold medallist at these Games was the ubiquitous Oscar Swahn (SWE) now aged 64 years 258 days, while his teammate, diver Greta Johansson, was the youngest aged 17 years 186 days. Only 40 days older was Isabella Moore (GBR) in the winning freestyle swimming relay team, who became Britain's youngest ever female gold medallist. The youngest male champion was fencer Nedo Nadi (ITA) aged 18 years 30 days. British tennis player Edith Hannam was the oldest female gold medallist aged 33 years 171 days. The youngest medallist was swimmer Grete Rosenberg (GER) in the relay at 15 years 280 days.

At the Stockholm Games the Olympic movement finally 'came of age' and the marvellous efforts of the organising committee under Viktor Balck, later, deservedly, President of the IOC, must take much of the credit. The only unfortunate incident at the Games was the collapse and death of Francisco Lazzaro (POR) during the marathon – ironically it was the first Games that his country had attended. Another new country was Japan, and the Games were beginning to achieve the worldwide support originally envisaged for them.

1912 MEDALS

	G	S	B
United States*	25	18	19
Sweden	24	24	16
Great Britain	10	15	16
Finland	9	8	9
France	7	4	3
Germany	5	13	7
South Africa	4	2	—
Norway	4	1	5
Hungary	3	2	3
Canada	3	2	2
Italy	3	1	2
Australia†	2	2	2
Belgium	2	1	3
Denmark	1	6	5
Greece	1	—	1
New Zealand†	1	—	1
Switzerland	1	—	—
Russia	—	2	3
Austria	—	2	2
The Netherlands	—	—	3

* Adjusted by the re-instatement of Jim Thorpe in 1982.

† Australia and New Zealand combined as Australasia.

ANTWERP 1920

VII OLYMPIC GAMES HELD IN ANTWERP, BELGIUM, 20 APRIL–12 SEPTEMBER 1920
ATTENDED BY REPRESENTATIVES OF 29 COUNTRIES, COMPRISING 2668 COMPETITORS, OF WHICH 77 WERE WOMEN.

When the venue of the VI Games, due in 1916, came to be discussed in Stockholm, three cities were put forward as candidates: Budapest, Alexandria and Berlin. It is said that the latter was chosen in an attempt to avert the war that was then threatening Europe. With the outbreak of hostilities in 1914 hopes of holding the Games virtually disappeared, although the Germans still made preparations for them believing that the war would not last very long. In 1920, although Antwerp was sorely affected by the human tragedy and economic ruin of the conflict, the organising committee under Count Henri de Baillet-Latour, later IOC President, overcame all difficulties to hold the Games. The recent enemies, Germany, Austria, Hungary and Turkey were not invited, but still a record number of countries and competitors attended. These included New Zealand as a separate entity (previously it had been part of the Australasian team), Argentina and Brazil. The Games were opened by King Albert, and the concept of the Olympic oath was introduced, taken by Victor Boin, who had competed in two previous Games, winning medals at water polo, and in Antwerp he gained another at fencing. Another newcomer at these Games was the newly devised Olympic flag, which consisted of five interlaced rings coloured blue, yellow, black, green and red, from left to right. The rings were meant to symbolise the friendship of mankind, with the colours, including the white background of the flag itself, representing all nations, as every national flag contains at least one of these colours.

Unfortunately the 390m running track at the new 30,000-seat stadium was very poor (Charles Perry, the famous British groundsman, had not been able to do much with it) and was badly affected by the persistent rain. Due to the weather and the economic aftermath of the recent conflict, generally crowds were small. The competitors were housed in school buildings, which caused something of a revolt among the American team – though they were much more incensed by the intolerable conditions experienced aboard the old freighter that had brought them to Belgium.

For the first time Finland competed under its own flag, having gained independence in 1917, and they celebrated the occasion by halting the American track and field juggernaut by winning as many athletic gold medals as the United States team. The track star of 1912, Hannes Kolehmainen, made a surprise return to win the marathon. However his mantle had been taken over by another outstanding Finnish runner, Paavo Nurmi, who, although he lost his very first Olympic final, over 5000m to the gassed French war veteran Joseph Guillemot, was at the start of a brilliant career in which he won a record 12 Olympic medals, 9 of them gold, and set 29 world records of one type or another. Britain's Albert Hill, who had fought throughout the First World War, here won the 800m/1500m double, a feat not repeated for 44 years. In addition he also gained a silver medal in the 3000m team race. In second place in the 1500m was Philip Baker (GBR), who later in life, as Philip Noel-Baker MP, was the recipient of the 1959 Nobel Peace Prize – a unique achievement for an Olympian. Charley Paddock retained the 100m sprint title for the United States, delighting the spectators with his spectacular jump finish. Later, after appearing in some movies, he was killed in the Second World War as a Marine Corps captain, and posthumously had a ship named after him. The most successful competitors at these Games were: Willis Lee (USA) who won five golds, a silver and a bronze, and his teammate Lloyd Spooner, who won four golds, one silver and two

bronzes, both as shooting competitors. This sport also produced the first gold medal won by a South American country, when Guilherme Paraense (BRA) took the rapid-fire pistol title. Yet another shooter, the phenomenal Oscar Swahn (SWE) became the oldest ever Olympic medallist with a silver aged 72 years 280 days. Also outstanding was fencer Nedo Nadi (ITA) who won two individual and three team golds. His younger brother, Aldo, added another three to the family total.

Returning to Olympic competition for the first time since 1906, when he had won two golds and a silver, archer Hubert van Innis (BEL) won four golds and two silvers, and was the oldest champion at these Games aged 54 years 187 days. The youngest gold medallist was tiny (1.43m) diver Aileen Riggin (USA) at 14 years 119 days. Indeed she was the youngest Olympic champion ever at the time, but almost lost the honour to Sweden's Nils Skoglund who finished a very close second in high-diving when only three months younger. Riggin won a diving silver four years later and, more unusually, a bronze in the 100m backstroke. The youngest male gold medallist was the Dutchman Franciscus Hin in the yachting aged 14 years 163 days. The oldest female champion was Winifred McNair (GBR) in tennis aged 43 years 15 days.

Swimming was dominated by two Americans, who captured three gold medals each. Ethelda Bleibtrey, who had suffered from polio as a child, won all events open to her, in world record times. The year before she had been arrested in America and charged, under local decency laws, with swimming 'nude' at a public beach, when all she had done was to remove her stockings! Norman Ross won the 400m, 1500m and was part of the winning relay team, and also figured in an unusual incident when he was disqualified in the 100m final for impeding an Australian swimmer. Duke Kahanamoku won the race in world record time. The re-swim was also won by the Hawaiian but in slower time. Another incident, of a more serious nature, occurred in the soccer final when the Czechoslovakian team was disqualified for leaving the field after 40 minutes play in protest at decisions by the British referee. Belgium was leading 2–0 at that point.

Daniel Carroll completed an unique double in the rugby final when he won a second gold medal as part of the United States team. He had played in the victorious Australian team of 1908, but had since emigrated. The tennis events were the stage for one of the greatest players in the game, Suzanne Lenglen (FRA), eventually six times winner of the Wimbledon title. The winner of the single sculls, and, teamed with his cousin, the double sculls, was John Kelly. Earlier in the year the American had been refused entry to the Henley Regatta in England. One report said that it was on the grounds that as a 'bricklayer' he had an unfair advantage over 'gentlemen'. Another, probably more correct report, is that his Philadelphia club, Vesper Rowing Club, had been banned. Ironically, after he had become a millionaire, his son John Jr won at Henley, in 1947, and his daughter, Grace, the film actress, became Princess of Monaco. Coincidentally, these were the first Games at which Monaco participated.

Two winter sports were also held, ice hockey and figure skating, attracting 73 men and 12 women from 10 countries. The latter witnessed the first Winter-event gold medals won by a married couple, the pairs' champions, German-born Ludowika, and Walter Jakobsson of Finland.

On this topic it may be that the first Olympic marriage was that of American diver Alice Lord and high jump champion Dick Landon soon after they returned home. One final note on the subject of matrimonial bliss: it was revealed after the competitions that the ladies skating champion, Magda Mauroy-Julin (SWE) was three months pregnant.

1920 MEDALS

	G	S	B
United States	41	27	26
Sweden	19	20	25
Finland	15	10	9
Great Britain	14	15	13
Belgium	13	11	11
Norway	13	9	9
Italy	13	5	5
France	9	19	13
The Netherlands	4	2	5
Denmark	3	9	1
South Africa	3	4	3
Canada	3	3	3
Switzerland	2	2	7
Estonia	1	2	—
Brazil	1	1	1
Australia	—	2	1
Japan	—	2	—
Spain	—	2	—
Greece	—	1	—
Luxembourg	—	1	—
Czechoslovakia	—	—	2
New Zealand	—	—	1

CHAMONIX-MONT BLANC 1924

I WINTER GAMES HELD IN CHAMONIX-MONT BLANC, FRANCE, 25 JANUARY–4 FEBRUARY 1924
ATTENDED BY REPRESENTATIVES OF 16 COUNTRIES, COMPRISING 258 COMPETITORS, OF WHICH 13 WERE WOMEN.

After skating (1908,1920) and ice hockey (1920) events were held previously as part of the Summer Games, it was finally decided to hold a separate Winter festival. Although initially opposed by the Scandinavian countries, who felt that a Winter Olympics would detract from their own Nordic Games, an 'International Winter Sports Week' was held at Chamonix, France. In 1926 it was accorded the title of Winter Games retrospectively. The French Under Secretary for Physical Education, Gaston Vidal, formally opened the proceedings, and the oath was taken by all the flag bearers, that of France being by a skier, Camille Mandrillon. Seventeen countries marched in the opening ceremony, but Estonia did not have any competitors in the actual competitions. The first ever official Olympic Winter gold medallist was Charles Jewtraw (USA) who won the 500-m speed skating on 26 January, which also made it the earliest gold medal ever won in an Olympic year. It was the only speed skating medal won by a competitor from a country other than Finland or Norway. Clas Thunberg (FIN) won three golds, a silver and a bronze (tied) to dominate the sport. In skiing only the Nordic variety was held as Alpine

skiing was still in its infancy. Norway's Thorleif Haug won three gold medals. He was also, originally, awarded the bronze in the special jumping event, but 50 years later a Norwegian sports historian, Jakob Vaage, discovered that the points had been added incorrectly, and that the fourth placed jumper, Anders Haugen, a Norwegian-born American, had beaten Haug. In place of her deceased father, Haug's daughter presented the bronze medal to the 86-year-old Haugen in 1974. Canada retained its title from 1920 in ice hockey, scoring 110–3 goals against in five matches. At figure skating Gillis Grafström (SWE) gained the second of his three gold medals. He was later to gain even more fame as coach of Sonja Henie (NOR) who, as an 11-year-old competitor in Chamonix, placed eighth and last in the women's skating. Aside from her Olympic successes she was to earn an estimated $47.5 million from her film and ice show activities, making her the richest ever female Olympian. The inaugural four-man bobsleigh contest was won by the Swiss, the first of a record five titles they have won in this discipline. Curling and a military patrol were held as demonstration events.

DID YOU KNOW?

One of the strangest Olympic stories is that of the medal not awarded correctly for 50 years. In the first Winter Games of 1924 held at Chamonix-Mont Blanc, Thorleif Haug of Norway had already won three gold medals in Nordic Skiing. He was then awarded the bronze medal in the ski-jump competition, ahead of the Norwegian-born American, coincidentally named Haugen. Half a century later a Norwegian sports historian discovered that the points had been added up incorrectly and, with Haug deceased, his daughter presented the 86-year-old Anders Haugen with his bronze medal.

The oldest champion was speed skater Julius Skutnabb (FIN) aged 34 years 229 days, and the youngest was Heinrich Schläppi, in Swizerland's four-man bob, aged 18 years 279 days. The oldest medallist was pairs' skater Walter Jakobsson (FIN) aged 41 years 357 days, although it is possible that the Belgian bobsledder, René Mortiaux, was over 42 years. It is of note that Jakobsson and his partner/wife, Ludowika (herself well over 39 years) are the oldest married couple ever to win Winter Olympic medals. Two days before the closing ceremony a meeting established the International Ski Federation (ISF).

1924 MEDALS (WINTER)

	G	S	B
Norway	4	7	6
Finland	4	3	3
Austria	2	1	—
United States	1	2	1
Switzerland	1	—	1
Canada	1	—	—
Sweden	1	—	—
Great Britain	—	1	2
Belgium	—	—	1
France	—	—	1

PARIS 1924

VIII OLYMPIC GAMES HELD IN PARIS, FRANCE,
4 MAY–27 JULY 1924
ATTENDED BY REPRESENTATIVES OF 44 COUNTRIES,
COMPRISING 3092 COMPETITORS, OF WHICH 136
WERE WOMEN.

Originally scheduled for Amsterdam, de Coubertin requested that the Games be transferred to Paris in the hope that the bad image acquired in 1900 could be eradicated. The IOC had taken steps to impose its authority on the staging of the Olympics so that never again could a host country add events as it wished. The Colombes stadium, with a 500m track built in 1909 was enlarged to hold 60,000 spectators. An Olympic village had been proposed but the idea was not carried through, although competitors were housed in huts scattered around the main site. Four of the five 'enemy' countries in the war were included in the record number of nations accepting invitations, but Germany was still not present due to the particularly frosty relations between them and France. Among the newcomers were Ireland, competing separately from Britain for the first time, Romania and Poland. Polish sportsmen had competed previously, but always in the teams of other countries. The Games were formally opened by the President of France, Gaston Doumergue, and were attended by well over 600,000 spectators in total. However, the chauvinism of the French supporters was outrageous at times. The weather was good, in fact sometimes too good – for the 10,000m cross-country event it was reported to be over 40°C and over half of the starters did not finish.

Despite, for the first time, all sports being organised by their international governing bodies and the instigation of Juries of Appeal, there were still many complaints of unfair decisions, notably in boxing. The newly instituted Olympic motto, *Citius, Altius, Fortius*, (faster, higher, stronger) originally composed by Father Henri Didon in 1895, was taken to heart. Numerous records were set, sometimes unexpectedly. The long jump was won by William De Hart Hubbard (USA), with 7.44m. Another American, Robert Le Gendre, had been left out of that event but entered in the athletic pentathlon, during which he broke the world long jump record with 7.76m on the way to winning a bronze medal. Incidentally, Hubbard was the first black athlete to win a gold medal in an individual, as opposed to a team, event.

The track events were dominated by the resurgent Finns and their outstanding stars Paavo Nurmi and Ville Ritola. Nurmi won a then record five gold medals, and American-based Ritola four golds and two silvers. The remarkable Nurmi won the 1500m and 5000m title within 90 minutes on the same day – a unique performance. His other victories came in the 3000m team race and the 10,000m cross-country individual and team events. In this latter event, run in a record high temperature, only 15 of the 38 starters finished, as Nurmi beat Ritola by well over a minute. The statue of him, which stands outside Helsinki stadium, was sculpted in 1925 to commemorate his Paris triumphs. It is interesting to note that the only viable opposition to the 'Flying Finns' came from Edvin Wide of Sweden – but actually he was born in Finland. Two Britons scored upset wins when Harold Abrahams became the first European to win an Olympic sprint title, and Eric Liddell set a world record in taking the 400m crown. Abrahams, who was coached by Sam Mussabini who had also trained Reggie Walker to victory in 1908, later recollected that there were no victory ceremonies and that he received his gold medal in the post some time later. Third in that 100m final was New Zealand's Arthur Porritt, who later became Governor-General of his country. An Oscar-winning film *Chariots of Fire* was made in 1981 with a not too accurate account of the period leading up to the achievements of Abrahams and Liddell.

A unique double was achieved by Harold Osborn (USA), who won the decathlon title and the high jump. In that latter event, Osborn's habit of pressing the bar back against the uprights with his hand as he jumped using the Western Roll technique, led to a change in the event's rules. The rules in another event resulted in a strange set of circumstances when the third finisher in the 400m hurdles was credited with a new Olympic record (also bettering the world mark). This happened because the winner, Frank Morgan Taylor (USA), had knocked down a hurdle, while the second finisher, Charles Brookins (USA), was disqualified for leaving his lane. Thus the eventual silver medallist, third finisher Erik Vilén (FIN) claimed the record. In fourth place was Georges André (FRA) who had taken the oath at the opening ceremony, and who had won a silver medal in the 1908 high jump.

In the pool, Johnny Weissmuller (USA) won three gold medals in freestyle swimming and a bronze at water polo. After more medals four years later, he turned to films, and in the 1930s he became the most famous screen Tarzan of them all. His teammate in Paris, Gertrude Ederle, who had become the youngest person ever to set a world record in 1919 at the age of 12 years 298 days, here won a gold in the relay, and two years later became the first woman to swim the English Channel. Incidentally, this Games was the first to introduce lane dividers in the pool. In rowing another American to gain fame elsewhere was Benjamin Spock, number seven in the winning eight, who later gained renown as a best-selling writer and paediatrician. France came into her own in the fencing and cycling events. In the former, Roger Ducret won three golds and a silver, while in the latter, Armand Blanchonnet won the 188km (117 miles) road race by a near-record margin of over nine minutes. A pointer to the future came in the soccer final, which was won by Uruguay, the first South American country to enter the Olympic football competition.

DID YOU KNOW?

There have always been close links between the Olympic games and Hollywood. One of the first Olympic swimming superstars, Johnny Weissmuller, became a big cinema star in probably the best rendition of the character Tarzan. A 1932 swimming gold medallist, Buster Crabbe, played Buck Rogers and Flash Gordon on the silver screen, and of course, from the Winter Games three-time skating gold medallist, Sonja Henie became one of the most popular film stars of all. Not all sports stars took heroic roles: the 1948 weightlifting silver medallist, Harald Sakata (USA) gained enormous fame as the 'baddie', Oddjob, in the James Bond classic, Goldfinger.

Now aged 45 Alfred Swahn (SWE) won his ninth shooting medal in four Games. His father, the incredible Oscar, had been picked for the team, but at 76 was too ill. However, he and Alfred won a family total of six gold medals, four silvers and five bronzes. The American shooter Carl Osburn gained another silver to raise his individual total since 1912 to 11, comprising five golds, four silvers and two bronzes. Tennis made its last appearance for 64 years, but had an all-star entry with all titles won by Wimbledon champions. One of them, Norris Williams, who partnered Hazel Wightman in the mixed doubles, had been a survivor of the Titanic disaster in 1912. Rugby also disappeared from the Games, leaving the United States as reigning Olympic champions.

DID YOU KNOW?

One of the most remarkable Olympic champions was Britain's Philip Neame. In 1914 he had won the Victoria Cross for bravery in the First World War, won an Olympic gold medal for shooting in 1924, was mauled by a tiger in India – and then married his nurse – led Commonwealth troops in the Libyan desert against Erwin Rommel in 1940, and was knighted at the end of the Second World War.

The oldest gold medallist at Paris was Allen Whitty (GBR), in the running deer shooting aged 57 years 59 days. (There has been some confusion about his age as he falsified his date of birth in order to join the army). The youngest winner at Paris was featherweight boxer Jackie Fields (USA) at 16 years 162 days. The youngest female winner was 400m freestyle champion Martha Norelius (USA) at 14 years 177 days (Recent research has confirmed her as two years younger than originally thought). The oldest female gold medallist was Hazel Wightman (USA) in tennis, aged 37 years 213 days. The United States won the major share of the medals at Paris, but a record number of 30 countries shared in the total.

1924 MEDALS (SUMMER)

	G	S	B
United States	45	27	27
Finland	14	13	10
France	13	15	10
Great Britain	9	13	12
Italy	8	3	5
Switzerland	7	8	10
Norway	5	2	3
Sweden	4	13	12
The Netherlands	4	1	5
Belgium	3	7	3
Australia	3	1	2
Denmark	2	5	3
Hungary	2	3	4
Yugoslavia	2	—	—
Czechoslovakia	1	4	5
Argentina	1	3	2
Estonia	1	1	4
South Africa	1	1	1
Uruguay	1	—	—
Austria	—	3	1
Canada	—	3	1
Poland	—	1	1
Haiti	—	—	1
Japan	—	—	1
New Zealand	—	—	1
Portugal	—	—	1
Romania	—	—	1

ST MORITZ 1928

II WINTER GAMES HELD IN ST MORITZ, SWITZERLAND, 11–19 FEBRUARY 1928 ATTENDED BY REPRESENTATIVES OF 25 COUNTRIES, COMPRISING 464 COMPETITORS, OF WHICH 26 WERE WOMEN.

The decision that the same country should host both Summer and Winter editions of the Games had to be abandoned in 1928, although the principle was still thought to be a sound one. President of Switzerland, Edmund Schulthess, officially declared the Games open, and Hans Eidenbenz, a skier, took the oath. Japan, Holland, Romania and Mexico were making their debuts at the Winter Games. Unseasonal weather threatened the programme – on one day the temperature varied by over 20°C from morning to afternoon. One of the speed skating events had to be cancelled, and in the bobsleighing there were only two runs instead of four.

The cancellation of the 10,000m skating event by the Norwegian referee, particularly caused bad feeling among the American team, as at that point Irving Jaffee (USA) was, surprisingly, leading and seemed likely to retain that lead. Despite vigorous protests by all nationalities no medals were awarded. Perhaps the unfortunate circumstances at Lake Placid four years later provided Jaffee with a measure of rough justice, when he won the gold medal in the 10,000m skating event. In the other events Clas Thunberg (FIN) added two more gold medals to his 1924 haul to amass a total of five golds, a silver, and a bronze; a record for the sport. There was a unique occurrence in the 500m in which two men tied for first place and three men for third, with no silver medals awarded. Another uncommon happening was in the skeleton toboggan race conducted on the famous Cresta Run, where brothers Jennison and John Heaton (USA) gained the gold and silver respectively.

The bobsleigh, which for the first and only time comprised five-man teams, also went to the United States. The driver, William Fiske, was aged only 16 years 260 days, and was then the youngest ever male Winter gold medallist. Also in the team was the oldest gold medallist at these Games, Nion Tucker aged 42 years 182 days. The youngest was Sonja Henie (NOR) taking the first of her three titles aged 15 years 316 days. She was the 'star' of the Games with her interpretation of *The Dying Swan*, which began a whole new era for figure skating. The youngest medallist at these Games was Thomas Doe (USA) in the bob aged 15 years 129 days, while the oldest was his teammate Jay O'Brien at 44 years 361 days. Pair skating witnessed the last appearance of the 1920 champions, Ludowika and Walter Jakobsson (FIN), who were placed fifth, their ages totalling 89 years. The men's skating event gave Gillis Grafström (SWE) his third consecutive gold medal.

In ski-jumping the defending champion Jacob Tullin-

Thams (NOR) was nearly killed, crashing at the end of a 73m jump on a hill designed for considerably shorter jumps. A true Olympian, he reappeared in 1936 to gain a silver medal in sailing. Johan Grøttumsbråten (NOR) won the 18km race and the Nordic Combination title to match Thunberg's two wins. As was becoming a habit, the Canadians easily won the ice hockey tournament scoring a total of 38 goals for and none against. The only demonstration event was a military patrol contest.

1928 MEDALS (WINTER)

	G	S	B
Norway	6	4	5
United States	2	2	2
Sweden	2	2	1
Finland	2	1	1
Canada	1	—	—
France	1	—	—
Austria	—	3	1
Belgium	—	—	1
Czechoslovakia	—	—	1
Germany	—	—	1
Great Britain	—	—	1
Switzerland	—	—	1

AMSTERDAM 1928

IX OLYMPIC GAMES HELD IN AMSTERDAM, HOLLAND, 17 MAY–12 AUGUST 1928
ATTENDED BY REPRESENTATIVES OF 46 COUNTRIES, COMPRISING 3014 COMPETITORS, OF WHICH 290 WERE WOMEN.

After unsuccessfully applying for the Games of 1916, 1920 and 1924, the Dutch were finally rewarded, and built a new 33,000-capacity stadium on reclaimed land in Amsterdam. The size of the running track, 400m, encircled by a cycling track, was then standardised for future Games. The design of the stadium won the architect, Jan Wils, an Olympic prize in the architecture competition. One innovation was the erection of a large results board; others included the release of pigeons at the opening ceremony – to symbolise peace – and the burning of an Olympic flame throughout the period of competitions. The formal opening was conducted by HRH Prince Hendrik, the consort of Queen Wilhelmina who was on a state visit to Norway, although the Queen herself did hand out the medals at the end of the Games. The record number of countries included Rhodesia and Panama for the first time, and Germany made its return to the Olympics in great strength.

After much argument in world sporting circles, and despite the opposition of Baron de Coubertin, women were allowed to compete in track and field, albeit in only five events. World records were set in all five, although there were, reportedly, such harrowing scenes of distress at the end of the 800m that it was then omitted from the programme until 1960. In winning that 800m Lina Radke won the first ever Olympic track and field gold medal for Germany. Her teammate, Anni Holdmann, became the first woman to win an Olympic track race by finishing first in heat one of the 100m on 30 July. Other firsts in the sport were a gold medal for Japan by Mikio

Oda in the triple jump, and the appearance of the first Asian female competitor, his teammate Kinuye Hitomi. The reigning world record holder in the long jump, an event that was not included in these Games, Hitomi remarkably took a silver medal in the 800m.

The Finns again dominated the athletics, although the fabulous Paavo Nurmi only won one gold and two silvers. Looking far older than his 31 years, due to his increasing baldness, the dour Finn offered some light relief when he competed in the steeplechase: unused to the event, he had problems with most of the barriers, and in his heat ignominiously fell into the water jump. Another competitor, a Frenchman, Lucien Duquesne, stopped and courteously helped him to his feet. Obviously grateful, Nurmi uncharacteristically acknowledged and thanked him, and then proceeded to 'shepherd' the French runner for the rest of the race, even inviting him to break the tape first. This Duquesne, to his eternal credit, declined to do. Despite running his fifth distance race in seven days, Nurmi won the silver medal (behind a teammate) in the final. It was later reported that the great Finn had damaged his famous stopwatch in the fall.

The unheralded Canadian youngster Percy Williams took both sprints, and, with Lord Burghley becoming the first member of the British House of Lords to win an Olympic athletic title, and Douglas Lowe (GBR) successfully defending his 800m title, the Americans had a lean time. A pointer for the future was the victory in the marathon of Boughèra El Ouafi, representing France, but an Algerian, and the pathfinder for future great North African distance runners. The American team was under the control of the President of the USOC, Major-General Douglas MacArthur, later in command of the victorious Americans in the Pacific theatre of the Second World War.

In the swimming pool another threat to United States dominance came from the Japanese. In Amsterdam they won their first ever swimming medals, giving an indication of things to come. American honour was saved by Johnny Weissmuller in the 100m and relay. Dorothy Poynton (USA) won a silver medal in springboard diving when only 24 days past her 13th birthday, one of the youngest medallists ever. She won gold medals at the next two Games. There was an unfortunate mix-up in the result of the men's high diving when Farid Simaika of Egypt was initially awarded the gold on the basis of his greater points score. The result was later reversed and the title given to Ulise 'Pete' Desjardins (USA) as the judges had made more first place decisions in his favour. Canadian-born Desjardins had been the first Olympic diver to be awarded a score of ten, in the 1924 springboard event.

Another Egyptian, Ibrahim Moustafa, won the light-heavyweight wrestling title to become the first non-European to take a Greco-Roman event. Not for the first time, or the last, boxing was beset with protests about the standard of officiating. In sailing, Crown Prince Olav, later King Olav V of Norway, gained the first Olympic victory by a member of a Royal household when he was a crew-member of the 6-m yacht Norna (his son, Crown Prince Harald, also competed in Olympic sailing 1964–72, but not with his father's success). In the soccer tournament Uruguay retained its title, beating another South American country, Argentina, in the final. In front of 50,000 people India won the first of their six consecutive hockey gold medals, retaining the title until 1960. Their goalkeeper, Richard Allen, did not concede a single goal in the tournament.

DID YOU KNOW?

Four future kings have competed in the Olympic Games' sailing events – two of them winning gold medals. The future King Olav V of Norway won a gold in 1928, and his son, later Harald V, competed at three Games. The other gold medallist was the future Constantine II of Greece, who gained his victory in 1960. His brother-in-law, Juan Carlos of Spain, competed in the 1972 Games.

A teammate of the Crown Prince in *Norna*, Johan Anker, a champion from 1912, was the oldest gold medallist in Amsterdam aged 57 years 44 days, while the youngest gold medallist and male medallist, also waterborne, was the Swiss pairs cox Hans Bourquin aged 14 years 222 days. The youngest female champion was Elizabeth Robinson (USA) who won the 100-m sprint aged 16 years 343 days, while the oldest woman to win a gold medal was Virginie Hériot (FRA) in the 8-m sailing event aged 38 years 15 days. The youngest medallist was Luigina Giavotti (ITA), winning a silver in gymnastics aged 11 years 302 days – she remains the youngest ever female medallist in Olympic history.

1928 MEDALS (SUMMER)

	G	S	B
United States	22	18	16
Germany	10	7	14
Finland	8	8	9
Sweden	7	6	12
Italy	7	5	7
Switzerland	7	4	4
France	6	10	5
The Netherlands	6	9	4
Hungary	4	5	—
Canada	4	4	7
Great Britain	3	10	7
Argentina	3	3	1
Denmark	3	1	2
Czechoslovakia	2	5	2
Japan	2	2	1
Estonia	2	1	2
Egypt	2	1	1
Austria	2	—	1
Australia	1	2	1
Norway	1	2	1
Poland	1	1	3
Yugoslavia	1	1	3
South Africa	1	—	2
India	1	—	—
Ireland	1	—	—
New Zealand	1	—	—
Spain	1	—	—
Uruguay	1	—	—
Belgium	—	1	2
Chile	—	1	—
Haiti	—	1	—
Philippines	—	—	1
Portugal	—	—	1

LAKE PLACID 1932

III WINTER GAMES HELD IN LAKE PLACID, USA, 4–15 FEBRUARY 1932
ATTENDED BY REPRESENTATIVES OF 17 COUNTRIES, COMPRISING 252 COMPETITORS, OF WHICH 21 WERE WOMEN.

Snow had to be brought over to the United States from Canada by lorries for some of the venues at Lake Placid, and a thaw caused the four-man bob event to be held after the official closing ceremony on 13 February. The Games were opened by the Governor of New York State, Franklin D. Roosevelt, who became President of the United States the following year. Incidentally, Eleanor, his redoubtable wife, took a ride down the bob course. The oath was taken by Jack Shea, who won the 500m speed skating gold later in the day. An Olympic first was achieved in the opening ceremony by the British contingent when female skater, Mollie Phillips carried the British flag. Innovatively, figure skating was held indoors, and drew large crowds, and three speed skating events for women were given demonstration status – 28 years later such events were on the programme proper. Demonstrations were also given of curling and dog sleigh racing; the latter won by Emile St Goddard of Canada.

Not surprisingly the Scandinavians swept the Nordic skiing, but an upset occurred in the speed skating where the Americans and Canadians dominated. It is arguable whether this was more to do with the abilities of the North Americans than with the change of rules that the organising committee had invoked. Instead of the more usual European system of competition in pairs, with the fastest times deciding the medal places, American rules were in force. Under these, mass start races were held, similar to track running, with heats and finals. Lack of familiarity with the tactics employed, often quite physical, put the Europeans at a distinct disadvantage. Indeed, Finland's four-time gold medallist, Clas Thunberg did not even bother to appear at Lake Placid. The Canadians won the ice hockey title for the fourth consecutive time, but only on goal average after three periods of overtime against the United States in the final game.

In figure skating the peerless Sonja Henie (NOR) easily retained her title, but triple champion Gillis Grafström (SWE), now 38, was the victim of an unfortunate accident. During the compulsory figures he collided with a badly positioned movie camera and fell, suffering a mild concussion. This may well have cost him an unprecedented fourth title. The oldest competitor was Joseph Savage (USA) aged 52 years 144 days in the pairs skating. The winners of that title, Pierre and Andrée Brunet (FRA), became the first pair to win both as an unmarried and married couple. In so doing Andrée was the oldest female gold medal winner in Lake Placid aged 30 years 149 days. They later coached American gold medallists Carol Heiss (1960), Hayes (1956) and David Jenkins (1960). In the ladies individual event Cecilia Colledge was Britain's youngest ever Olympic competitor, at any sport, aged 11 years 73 days. She was also the youngest ever competitor in the Olympic Winter Games.

History of a different kind was made by Eddie Eagan (USA) in the four-man bob as a late and virtually untried draftee. As part of the winning team he became the only man to win gold medals in both Summer and Winter celebrations – he was a 1920 boxing champion. The two-man bob was won by the brothers Curtis and Hubert Stevens of the United States); a third brother, Paul, won a silver medal in the four-man event. The oldest gold medallist at Lake Placid was Eagan's bob teammate Jay O'Brien aged 48 years 359 days (he is still the oldest person to win a Winter Olympics gold medal), while Sonja Henie was again the youngest, now aged 19 years 308 days. The youngest male champion was ice hockey player Albert Duncansson (CAN) aged 20 years 134 days.

1932 MEDALS (WINTER)

	G	S	B
United States	6	4	2
Norway	3	4	3
Sweden	1	2	—
Canada	1	1	5
Finland	1	1	1
Austria	1	1	—
France	1	—	—
Switzerland	—	1	—
Germany	—	—	2
Hungary	—	—	1

LOS ANGELES 1932

X OLYMPIC GAMES HELD IN LOS ANGELES, USA,
30 JULY–14 AUGUST 1932
ATTENDED BY REPRESENTATIVES OF 37 COUNTRIES,
COMPRISING 1408 COMPETITORS, OF WHICH 127
WERE WOMEN.

As early as 1920 the United States delegation to the IOC led by William May Garland had applied for either the 1924 or 1928 Games to be held in Los Angeles. Despite trepidation felt over the memory of the 1904 'farce' at St Louis, in 1923, Los Angeles was awarded the 1932 Games. Against further worries of distance and cost of travel were set the advantages of favourable weather and competitive conditions. The announcement by the organising committee that they would subsidise transportation, housing and subsistence costs helped greatly at a time of the Depression, and did much to offset the critics. One source of income was from a new three-cent postage stamp, which depicted a runner, for which the model was the anchor-man of the 1924 gold medal relay team, Alfred Leconey. The concept of an Olympic 'village' came to fruition with the construction of 550 specially designed small houses for male competitors in the Baldwin Hills area. Cowboys who 'rode the fences' strictly guarded the compound around the perimeter, and the strict rule preventing women in the village barred the Finnish team's female cook. Female competitors were put up separately in the Chapman Park Hotel on Wilshire Boulevard. Despite prohibition, the French team was allowed to bring in wine for its own consumption. After journeys often lasting two weeks the foreigners found excellent weather and facilities awaiting them.

The main stadium was the Los Angeles Coliseum, which had begun construction in 1921 and opened two

years later. In 1930 it had been enlarged to hold 101,000 spectators seated, and the track had a new crushed-peat running surface. Also there was the 10,000-seat swimming stadium, the State Armory where fencing took place, the Olympic Auditorium, seating 10,000 to watch boxing, wrestling and weightlifting events, and a specially built wooden track was erected in the world famous Pasadena Rose Bowl for the cycling. Long Beach Harbour was the venue for sailing, and the Long Beach Marine Stadium hosted the rowing. The Los Angeles Museum of History, Science and Art accommodated the fine art competitions. The Games were formally opened by the Vice President of the United States, Charles Curtis, on behalf of President Hoover who was in the middle of an electioneering tour (interestingly, he lost the Presidency the following year, to Franklin D. Roosevelt, who had officially opened the Winter Games at Lake Placid earlier in the year). The oath on behalf of the competitors was taken by an American fencer Lieutenant George Calnan of the United States Navy, who died the following April when the dirigible *Akron* crashed into the Pacific Ocean. Although the number of teams, and the total number of competitors, were lower than at Amsterdam, there were two countries making their Olympic debuts: Colombia and China, both with sole representatives, neither of which achieved any success. However, another small team, Ireland, with only eight men, finished well up the medal table with two gold medals.

At these Games new ideas included the use of photo-finish equipment – the Kirby two-eyed camera – for track races. Although it could accurately provide times to one-hundredth of a second it was only used to decide close finishes, and only a few of the timings have ever come to light. Another innovation was the three-tiered victory stand, with medal awarding ceremonies involving the raising of national flags taking place at the end of each day's events. In boxing the system of having the referee in the ring with the boxers was introduced into the Games for the first time, although it did not settle all arguments in that sport.

As with all such international gatherings there were some unfortunate incidents, but in the main they were of minor importance. Prior to the arrival of teams there was a major 'scandal' when the International Association of Athletics Federation (IAAF) banned the great Finnish runner, Paavo Nurmi, under charges of professionalism: he was accused of accepting unduly large expenses on a German tour. Despite rigorous protests on his behalf, the Finnish Federation finally accepted the ruling although he had already been selected for the marathon and, indeed, arrived with the team in Los Angeles. It seems not unreasonable to suggest that he would have finished a remarkable career with another gold medal. Once the Games were underway, the Finns were also involved in another incident when the runners in the 3000m steeplechase ran an extra lap due to a miscalculation by the lap counter. Happily the error did not appear to have altered the final medal placings. Another minor irritant was the American habit of announcing all the field event results only in Imperial units of measurement, much to the annoyance, and bafflement, of the foreign competitors and spectators. But there were two more serious occurrences, one on the track and one in the swimming pool. The first was when the eventual winner, Lauri Lehtinen (FIN) deliberately blocked the American, Ralph Hill, twice in the final stages of the race, a not uncommon practice in Europe, but one which drew loud booing from the basically partisan crowd. The crowd was quickly quietened by the announcer Bill Henry, whose words; 'Remember please, these people are our guests' have entered Olympic lore.

The second incident was of a much more serious nature when the Brazilian water polo team, after losing 7–3 to Germany, lost their tempers and insulted the referee. They were disqualified from the tournament. On the brighter side was the performance of the outstanding individual of the Games, Mildred 'Babe' Didrikson. (Since her death her family has insisted that the surname should be spelt the Swedish way, that is with an 'e', and not an 'o'). Much to her annoyance she was only allowed to enter three events. She set Olympic records in each of them, winning the javelin and 80m hurdles, and gaining a silver medal in the high jump. Thus she is the only athlete to win medals in individual running, jumping and throwing events. In the high jump there was a strange judgement made, for although Didrikson cleared the same height as her teammate, Jean Shiley, and then tied in a jump-off, the judges decided that her 'Western Roll' style of jump had been performed illegally, with her head preceding her body over the bar, and illogically they placed her second. She later became the world's greatest female golfer under her married name of Zaharias.

Another unusual thing occurred in the 400m hurdles when Irishman Bob Tisdall, who reportedly spent most of the preceding days in bed recuperating from a long and tiring journey, won the gold medal in a time superior to the world record. However, because he knocked down the last hurdle, the world record was given to the runner-up Glenn Hardin (USA). Remarkably, the first four finishers were all gold medallists in the event – Tisdall (1932), Hardin (1936), Taylor (1924) and Burghley (1928).

In the 200m final Ralph Metcalfe was inadvertently made to start about 1.5m (5ft) before the correct place, thus almost certainly costing him a silver medal. As Americans had placed first, second and third, Metcalfe, later an American Congressman, declined the offer of a re-run. The Indian hockey team, while not quite so invincible as previously, set a record score by defeating the United States by 24–1, with Roop Singh scoring 12 goals. Similarly, in the water polo competition, Hungary beat Japan with a record score of 18–0. Nevertheless, the Japanese were particularly noteworthy in swimming, highlighted by their superb 4 x 200m team breaking the world record by a remarkable 37.8 sec.

The oldest gold medallist at Los Angeles was yachtsman Pierpoint Davis (USA) aged 47 years 224 days, while the youngest was 1500m freestyle champion Kusuo Kitamura (JPN) aged 14 years 309 days. The youngest female champion was Claire Dennis (AUS) who won the 200m breaststroke aged 16 years 117 days. The oldest female winner was Lillian Copeland (USA) in the discus aged 27 years 251 days. The youngest medallist was diver Katharine Rawls (USA) 58 days past her 14th birthday. The oldest medallist was Hiram Tuttle (USA) in

the dressage aged 49 years 231 days. As demonstration sports the hosts provided American football and lacrosse. During the closing ceremony the President of the IOC, Count Henri de Baillet-Latour, presented Olympic Merit Awards for Alpinism to Franz and Toni Schmid (GER) for the first climb of the north face of the Matterhorn. Despite all the economic and organisational misgivings the Xth Games were a great success, attended by a total of 1.25 million spectators, and realising a profit of about $1 million.

One last innovation at these Games was the use of two sentences, attributed to Baron de Coubertin, but actually based on words used by the Bishop of Central Pennsylvania, Ethelbert Talbot, in a sermon at St Paul's Cathedral, London on 19 July 1908. Displayed on the scoreboard at every opening ceremony since 1932, the words are: 'The most important thing in the Olympic Games is not to win but to take part, just as the most important thing in life is not the triumph but the struggle. The essential thing is not to have conquered but to have fought well.'

1932 MEDALS (SUMMER)

	G	S	B
United States	41	32	30
Italy	12	12	12
France	10	5	4
Sweden	9	5	9
Japan	7	7	4
Hungary	6	4	5
Finland	5	8	12
Germany	3	12	5
Great Britain	4	7	5
Australia	3	1	1
Argentina	3	1	—
Canada	2	5	8
The Netherlands	2	5	—
Poland	2	1	4
South Africa	2	—	3
Ireland	2	—	—
Czechoslovakia	1	2	1
Austria	1	1	3
India	1	—	—
Denmark	—	3	3
Mexico	—	2	—
Latvia	—	1	—
New Zealand	—	1	—
Switzerland	—	1	—
Philippines	—	—	3
Spain	—	—	1
Uruguay	—	—	1

GARMISCH-PARTENKIRCHEN 1936

IV WINTER GAMES HELD IN GARMISCH-PARTENKIRCHEN, GERMANY 6–16 FEBRUARY 1936 ATTENDED BY REPRESENTATIVES OF 28 COUNTRIES, COMPRISING 668 COMPETITORS, OF WHICH 80 WERE WOMEN.

It is not always remembered that when the Winter and Summer Games of 1936 were awarded to Germany five years previously, Adolf Hitler was virtually unknown.

However, by the year of the Games they were seen by many as a test case of how the German Olympic Committee would react to the demands of the National Socialist government of Germany. There had been much heated discussion around the world as to the advisability of attending these, or the later Summer, Games, due to the racist policies of that government. In spite of this a record entry included teams from Bulgaria, Turkey, Australia, Spain and Liechtenstein for the first time. Chancellor Adolf Hitler declared the Games open, and Wilhelm Bogner, a cross-country skier, took the oath on behalf of competitors. By the end of the competitions, over 500,000 paying spectators had watched the six different sports. These now included Alpine skiing, although the only event was a combination one, for both men and women.

Birger Ruud (NOR) successfully defended his ski jump title, and then caused a major surprise by winning the downhill segment of the men's Alpine combination. By dint of a 5.9sec margin of victory in the slalom segment the title went to Franz Pfnür (GER) and Ruud fell back to fourth place. In the women's event there was a similar situation when the downhill race was won by 16-year-old Laila Schou Nilsen (NOR) who, a year later, broke five world speed skating records. She had entered the skiing in the absence of any other such events for women. In the slalom, Christl Cranz (GER), who was eventually to win 12 world skiing championships, won by the quite astounding margin of 11.3sec and took the overall gold medal, Nilsen gaining the bronze.

The top medal winner was speed skater Ivar Ballangrud (NOR) with three golds and a silver. Contrary to the Lake Placid conditions of four years earlier the racers competed under European-style rules with pairs of skaters racing against the clock. Instead of the four gold medals the Americans had won in 1932, here they only gained a solitary bronze. Sonja Henie (NOR) won her third consecutive figure skating title, to add to her ten world championships, and then went off to Hollywood, followed sometime later by the 16th-placed British woman Gladys Jepson-Turner, who gained cinematic fame as Belita, and 17th-placed Vera Hruba (TCH). The British caused a major upset by winning the ice hockey, with a team containing mainly British-born Canadians. Also in this competition was Rudi Ball, one of only two athletes of Jewish origin selected by Germany in 1936. A bronze medallist in 1932, he was especially requested to return from his exile in France – the hosts hoping to offset criticism of their attitude to Jewish competitors by this act.

A most unusual double nearly came the way of Ernst Baier (GER) who won the pairs skating, but only came second in the men's singles. It was still the best such double placing ever. His pairs partner, Maxi Herber was the youngest gold medallist aged 15 years 128 days, and sister and brother Ilse and Erik Pausin (AUT), the pairs silver medallists, were the youngest ever couple to gain a medal in the event, their ages totalling a mere 32 years 307 days. The oldest gold medallist was Carl Erhardt (GBR) one day past his 39th birthday in the ice hockey final. The demonstration events were German curling and the military patrol.

1936 MEDALS (WINTER)

	G	S	B
Norway	7	5	3
Germany	3	3	—
Sweden	2	2	3
Finland	1	2	3
Austria	1	1	2
Switzerland	1	2	—
Great Britain	1	1	1
United States	1	—	3
Canada	—	1	—
France	—	—	1
Hungary	—	—	1

BERLIN 1936

XI OLYMPIC GAMES HELD IN BERLIN, GERMANY, 1–16 AUGUST 1936
ATTENDED BY REPRESENTATIVES OF 49 COUNTRIES, COMPRISING 4066 COMPETITORS, OF WHICH 328 WERE WOMEN.

These Games were awarded to Berlin just prior to the rise to power of Adolf Hitler and the National Socialist (Nazi) Party. Abhorrence of Germany's policies under this government led many countries, not least the United States, to propose a boycott, but the President of the USOC, Avery Brundage, was strongly in favour of participation, and won the day. In Germany itself the notorious Heinrich Himmler was opposed to the Games being held, but Josef Goebbels convinced Hitler that they would present tremendous propaganda opportunities. Political overtones overshadowed the Games until the last moment when Spain withdrew owing to the outbreak of the civil war there.

The original intention had been to enlarge the stadium that had been built for the aborted 1916 Games, but Hitler decreed that a brand new 100,000-capacity stadium should be built. The architects were Werner and Walter March, whose father had designed the 1916 stadium. However, recent research has indicated that, according to Albert Speer, Hitler had expressed his displeasure with the finished stadium, and that Speer instigated some finishing touches, to placate him. It seems that the Fuhrer envisaged that after his final victory, all future Games would be held in this stadium. Other fine stadia and halls were erected, plus a magnificent 'village' of 150 buildings for the competitors. Sailing events were held at Kiel on the northwest coast. At the instigation of Carl Diem, the main organiser, a torch relay was inaugurated to bring the sacred Olympic flame from the Temple of Zeus at Olympia – where it was lit by 'priestesses' Koula Pratsika and Aleka Katseli, who handed it to a Greek runner, Kyril Kondylis, the first of 3331 runners. The flame crossed seven countries (3187km, 1980 miles) in ten days. The last runner into the stadium to light the cauldron was athlete Fritz Schilgen. Chancellor Hitler formally opened the Games, as a specially commissioned 16½-ton bell was rung and thousands of pigeons set free. As the massive German contingent, 348 strong, entered, the giant airship *Hindenburg* flew overhead.

The German team, with full government backing, was probably the best-prepared team ever in the Games. As a sop to foreign criticism it contained one athlete of Jewish origin, Helene Mayer, persuaded to return from America with the promise of full 'Aryan' classification. Ironically she placed second in the foil to the Hungarian Jewess, Ilona Elek, with another Jewish fencer in third. Perhaps even more ironic, at the opening ceremony the 1896 marathon victor, Spiridon Louis attired in national dress, presented Hitler with an olive branch – signifying peace – from Olympia. In the teams' march-past a number of them gave the Nazi salute, but the United States and Great Britain to their credit and to the annoyance of the crowd, merely made the traditional 'eyes right'.

The famous composer Richard Strauss conducted the music for the ceremony. An indication of the future came with the first ever use of television at the Games, with a closed circuit system to special halls in the city. Very high sporting standards were reached at these Games, and at the forefront of the record breaking were the ten black members of the American track and field team. Anathema to the German propaganda machine, which dubbed them 'Black Auxiliaries', they won seven gold, three silver and three bronze medals – more than any other national team, including their own white teammates. Outstanding among them was Jesse Owens with four gold medals, in the 100m, 200m, long jump, and as a member of the 4 x 100m relay team. In second place in the 200m was Mack Robinson, whose brother Jackie was the first black major league baseball player. It should be noted that the majority of fans did not share the German government's attitude toward Owens and he was in tremendous demand by autograph hunters.

Much has been written about Hitler refusing to meet and congratulate Owens and the other black gold medallists. In fairness it should be realised that after he had made a point of personally greeting the German victors on the first day, he was rebuked for the practice by the President of the IOC, Henri de Baillet-Latour, who informed him that only IOC-designated people performed such duties in an Olympic stadium. After that he refrained from further congratulatory meetings, although it is reported that he met all German medallists in private. Thus, if he did snub anybody, it would have been the only black winner on the first day, high jumper Cornelius Johnson.

Other track highlights included the superb sprinting of Helen Stephens (USA), the decathlon victory of teammate Glenn Morris, later to be a screen Tarzan, and the 1500m world record by Jack Lovelock (NZL). This last event was considered by many to have been the highlight of the Games. The Finns took all three places in the 10,000m as well as the first two places in the 5000m and steeplechase, Volmari Iso-Hollo successfully defending his title in the latter. Outstanding in the pool were the Dutch women led by Hendrika Mastenbroek, who personally won three golds and a silver. The winner of the women's springboard diving, Marjorie Gestring (USA), became the youngest ever female gold medallist, and the youngest ever individual event champion, aged 13 years 268 days. The oldest gold medallist at Berlin was Friedrich Gerhard (GER) in the dressage team, aged 52 years 20 days. The youngest male champion was fencer Edoardo Mangiarotti (ITA), aged 17 years 124 days, while the oldest female champion was gymnast

Friedl Iby (GER) at 31 years 128 days. In taking the bronze medal in the 200m breaststroke, Inge Sørensen (DEN) became one of the youngest ever Olympic medallists aged 12 years 24 days.

Robert Charpentier (FRA) won three gold medals in cycling, in which Toni Merkens (GER) won the 1000m sprint despite being fined, but not disqualified, for obstruction in the first race. In wrestling, Kristjan Palusalu of Estonia matched the achievement of Ivar Johansson (SWE) in 1932 by winning titles in both freestyle and Greco-Roman styles. Interestingly, the list of gold medallists at Berlin includes the name *Nurmi*, but in this case it was the name of the horse ridden by Ludwig Stubbendorff (GER) to his easy victory in the tough three-day event. Of the 14 teams that started, only four finished with sufficient scorers. These included Great Britain, whose final placer, Captain Richard Fanshawe, gained his team the bronze medal despite numerous penalty points incurred resulting from having to chase his horse for 4km (2.5 miles) before remounting.

In the single-handed Olympia class sailing, the bronze medal went to Peter Markham Scott, son of the tragically killed Antarctic explorer, and later himself a world-famous naturalist. Canoeing and basketball made their official debuts, with the inventor of the latter, Dr James Naismith, on hand to see the United States team begin its remarkable sequence of victories. At the end of the Games Leni Riefenstahl produced the magnificent film *Olympische Spiele*, which although criticised as propaganda, is still the best documentary record of an Olympic Games. In addition to their traditional awards, gold medallists were given oak tree seedlings. Forty years later research by the USOC indicated that at least 16 of the trees were still alive and well.

1936 MEDALS (SUMMER)

	G	S	B
Germany	33	26	30
United States	24	20	12
Hungary	10	1	5
Italy	8	9	5
Finland	7	6	6
France	7	6	6
Sweden	6	5	9
Japan	6	4	8
The Netherlands	6	4	7
Great Britain	4	7	3
Austria	4	6	3
Czechoslovakia	3	5	—
Argentina	2	2	3
Estonia	2	2	3
Egypt	2	1	2
Switzerland	1	9	5
Canada	1	3	5
Norway	1	3	2
Turkey	1	—	1
India	1	—	—
New Zealand	1	—	—
Poland	—	3	3
Denmark	—	2	3
Latvia	—	1	1
Romania	—	1	—
South Africa	—	1	—

Yugoslavia	—	1	—
Mexico	—	—	3
Belgium	—	—	2
Australia	—	—	1
Philippines	—	—	1
Portugal	—	—	1

ST MORITZ 1948

V WINTER GAMES HELD IN ST MORITZ,
SWITZERLAND, 30 JANUARY–8 FEBRUARY 1948
ATTENDED BY REPRESENTATIVES OF 28 COUNTRIES,
COMPRISING 669 COMPETITORS, OF WHICH 77 WERE
WOMEN.

In 1936 the Winter Games of 1940 were initially awarded to Sapporo, Japan, but as a consequence of the Sino-Japanese conflict they were re-allocated to St Moritz. Due to some disagreements the IOC transferred them again in June 1939 to Garmisch-Partenkirchen, Germany, at the same time deciding that the 1944 meeting should be held at Cortina d'Ampezzo, Italy. The Second World War then upset these plans, and in 1946 a postal vote of IOC members relocated the 1948 Games in St Moritz, as Switzerland, being neutral, had been virtually untouched by the war. Chile, Denmark, Iceland, Korea and Lebanon competed for the first time in these Winter Games, but Germany and Japan were not invited, although Italy was. Ice hockey player, Richard Torriani took the oath on behalf of the competitors, and Swiss President Enrico Celio formally declared the Games open. There were now six Alpine events, which attracted larger fields than the Nordic disciplines. Poor weather affected some of the competitions, and there were a number of disputes.

The most medals were won by Henri Oreiller (FRA) with gold in the downhill (by a record margin of 4.1sec), and combination, and a bronze in the slalom. Alpine skier Gretchen Fraser (USA) gained the first skiing title ever won by a non-European. In Nordic skiing the Swedes broke the Norwegian monopoly. They had the three medals and fifth place in the 18km, first two and fifth in the 50km, and won the 4 x 10km relay by a margin of nearly nine minutes. They also won their first ever speed skating title when Ake Seyffarth took the 10km event. The noticeably athletic American figure skaters brought a new concept to figure skating as Dick Button gained an easy victory.

The ice hockey competition was the cause of a major row. Two American teams appeared in St Moritz; one represented the Amateur Hockey Association of the United States (AHA), and the USOC chose the other. The AHA, while not affiliated to the USOC, was a member of the International Hockey Federation (IHF). This last was the governing body of most of the other teams at the Games, and threatened to withdraw all the other teams if the AHA team were not allowed to play. The USOC in turn threatened to withdraw its whole Olympic team if it did. Initially the IOC decided to bar both teams, but then agreed with the Swiss organisers and the IHF to allow the AHA team to compete. Strangely, however, the USOC team members marched in the opening ceremony. The AHA team eventually finished fourth, but a year later the AHA was disqualified for non-affiliation to the Olympic movement. The Canadians won the title once again, but only just. The title was decided on goal average, with the Czechs taking the silver. The Swiss in third place contained the man who had taken the oath, Richard 'Bibi' Torriani, thus adding another bronze to that he had won 20 years earlier when he was just past his 16th birthday.

The American bobsleds were sabotaged prior to the competitions, but it did not prevent them from winning a gold and two bronze medals. They have never won an Olympic bob event since. In the skeleton toboggan, which was only held in those days when the Games were at St Moritz on the Cresta Run, John Heaton (USA) won his second silver medal, 20 years after his first. The gold medal went to Nino Bibbia of Italy; a country perhaps surprisingly not refused an invitation like its wartime ally, Germany. Bibbia was a master of the Cresta Run and won many titles and championships over the next quarter of a century.

The great Norwegian ski jumper Birger Ruud, nearly 37 years old and a survivor of a wartime concentration camp, ended his Olympic career with a silver medal to add to his golds from 1932 and 1936. He and his brother Sigmund had made the event a family preserve since 1928. A third brother, Asbjørn, was also in the 1948 team.

A record 13 countries shared out the medals, and Italy and Belgium won their first ever Winter Games titles. There were two demonstration events: a military ski patrol, and a Winter pentathlon. This latter consisted of 10km cross-country skiing, pistol shooting, downhill skiing, fencing, and horse riding. No medals were awarded, but in second place was Captain Willie Grut (SWE), of whom much more was to be heard six months later, in London.

The oldest gold medallist was Francis Tyler in the US four-man bob, aged 43 years 58 days, while the youngest was skater Dick Button aged 18 years 202 days. The youngest female champion was skater Barbara-Ann Scott (CAN) aged 19 years 273 days, while the oldest female winner was Gretchen Fraser (USA) in the slalom, aged 28 years 360 days. The youngest medallist was skater Suzanne Morrow (CAN) with a pairs bronze aged 17 years 55 days, while the oldest was bobsledder Max Houben (BEL) at 49 years 278 days.

1948 MEDALS (WINTER)

	G	S	B
Norway	4	3	3
Sweden	4	3	3
Switzerland	3	4	3
United States	3	4	2
France	2	1	2
Canada	2	—	1
Austria	1	3	4
Finland	1	3	2
Belgium	1	1	—
Italy	1	—	—
Czechoslovakia	—	1	—
Hungary	—	1	—
Great Britain	—	—	2

LONDON 1948

XIV OLYMPIC GAMES HELD IN LONDON, ENGLAND,
29 JULY–14 AUGUST 1948
ATTENDED BY REPRESENTATIVES OF 59 COUNTRIES,
COMPRISING 4099 COMPETITORS, OF WHICH 385
WERE WOMEN.

In 1936 the XII Games were awarded to Tokyo, to take place from 24 August to 8 September 1940. When the Sino-Japanese war began in 1938, the Games were transferred to Helsinki, but the Soviet invasion of Finland cancelled these plans. In June 1939, a very optimistic IOC awarded the XIII Games, for 1944, to London, over competing claims from Detroit, Lausanne and Rome. A postal vote of IOC members called by the President, Sigfrid Edström of Sweden, in 1946, awarded the XIV Games to London. In the meantime, Baron de Coubertin had died, in 1937, and his heart was buried at Olympia in Greece.

Organised by the British Olympic Association (BOA), under the Presidency of Lord Burghley, the 1948 Olympics were an austerity Games – after six years of war Britain still had rationing of food and clothing. Housing was in short supply due to wartime destruction, and competitors were housed at RAF and Army camps (for men) and colleges (for women). A temporary running track was laid at the 83,000-capacity Wembley Stadium, the home of British football. Other existing buildings were adapted. Rowing was held at Henley, on the River Thames, and the sailing was at Torbay, Devon. The total expenditure amounted to less than £600,000, and final accounts suggested that a profit of over £10,000 was made. King George VI opened the Games. Not surprisingly Germany and Japan were not invited, but a record 59 countries attended. These included the first entries by countries under Communist governments. Some of the hottest weather for years occurred on the opening days, but later it rained. Photo-finish equipment, as used on race-courses, was used for the track events, but only to decide places. The first proper television coverage of the Games occurred with pictures beamed into an estimated 80,000 black and white receivers within range of the transmission from Wembley.

The undoubted star of the Games was Francina 'Fanny' Blankers-Koen (NED) who won four gold medals, a record for a woman. At the time 30 years of age, and a mother of two children, she had finished in sixth place in the 1936 high jump. In 1948 she held seven world records including those in the high and long jumps, neither of which she contested in London. The gap between her and the second-place in the 200m (0.7sec) remains the largest margin of victory ever achieved in an Olympic sprint, by men or women. In the high jump Dorothy Tyler (née Odam, GBR) placed second again, 12 years after her other silver medal – both times she had cleared the same height as the winner. Bob Mathias (USA) became the youngest ever male Olympic individual athletics champion when we won the decathlon aged 17 years 263 days. He retained the title in 1952, became a movie actor, and later was elected a United States Congressman. Another eye-catching athlete was Emil Zátopek (TCH), not so much by his easy win in the

10,000m, but by his remarkable last 300m sprint to narrowly lose the 5000m. An American, Harrison Dillard, acknowledged as the world's best high hurdler, had fallen in the US trials and failed to make their team in his best event. In London he won his 'second-string' event, the 100m, and won another gold in the relay. Two of the debuting countries made their marks early in the Games. Duncan White of Ceylon (now Sri Lanka) gained the only medal his country has ever won, with a silver in the 400m hurdles. Jamaica made an even bigger impact by collecting a gold, two silvers and two other finalists in the 200, 400, and 800m. The marathon provided its usual drama when Etienne Gailly, a Belgian paratrooper, entered the stadium first, but was so exhausted that he was overtaken by two runners prior to the tape. Incidentally, the female high jump champion, Alice Coachman, was the first black woman to win an Olympic gold medal, in any sport.

An outstanding competitor in the modern pentathlon was Willie Grut of Sweden who won three disciplines of the five-sport event, and placed fifth and eighth in the others, to win by a large margin. He was the son of the designer of the 1912 Olympic stadium. Another exceptional champion was South African boxer George Hunter, who not only won the light-heavyweight title, but also the Val Barker Trophy as the best stylist in the whole competition. However, lack of experienced referees and judges resulted in much criticism of the boxing tournament. There were problems, too, at Herne Hill Stadium where some of the cycling events finished in very poor light due to the lack of floodlighting. There was an unfortunate turn of events in the equestrian competitions where the Swedes won the team dressage contest. However, the following year they were disqualified, and their medals taken away, when it was discovered that one of their number, Gehnäll Persson, was not a commissioned officer, as the rules then required.

In fencing Ilona Elek (HUN) retained her 1936 title even though she was now over 41 years of age. Her sister Margit placed sixth. The 1932 champion, Ellen Müller-Preis (AUT) gained the bronze medal. An even more outstanding veteran was 40-year-old Heikki Savolainen, the famous Finnish gymnast who, in his fourth Olympics, won his first gold medal, on the pommel horse.

The soccer gold medallists, Sweden, were involved in one of the strangest goals in the history of the sport, in their semi-final against Denmark. The Swedish centre-forward Gunnar Nordahl, one of three brothers in the team, quick-wittedly leapt into the Danish goal-mouth to avoid being offside during a Swedish attack. At the end of the move his inside-left headed the ball into the goal, where in the absence of the Danish keeper, Nordahl caught it. Sweden went on to win the gold medal. Sailing witnessed the end of a long Olympic career when Ralph Craig, the 1912 double sprint champion, reappeared in the American team. Although he carried the American flag in the opening ceremony he did not actually compete. Torbay was also the start of another exceptional career with the appearance of Durward Knowles competing for Britain. He competed in sailing events for the Bahamas in the next six Games, and made it an eighth time in 1988. A rare happening at the sailing was the victory of father and son combination, Paul and Hilary Smart (USA) in the

Star class yachting. At the Empire Pool, site of the swimming competitions, American competitors won 12 of the 15 events there, excluding water polo. One of the few non-American champions was Greta Andersen (DEN) in the 100m freestyle, and who 16 years later, set a female record for swimming the English Channel. In diving, Vicki Draves (USA) won both titles, then a unique achievement.

The oldest gold medallist in London was Paul Smart (*see* above) in yachting aged 56 years 212 days, and the youngest was Thelma Kalama (USA) in the swimming sprint relay for women aged 17 years 135 days. Bob Mathias, the decathlon champion, was the youngest male champion (*see* above), while the oldest female winner was fencer Ilona Elek (HUN) aged 41 years 77 days.

1948 MEDALS (SUMMER)

	G	S	B
United States	38	27	19
Sweden	16	11	17
France	10	6	13
Hungary	10	5	12
Italy	8	11	8
Finland	8	7	5
Turkey	6	4	2
Czechoslovakia	6	2	3
Switzerland	5	10	5
Denmark	5	7	8
The Netherlands	5	2	9
Great Britain	3	14	6
Argentina	3	3	1
Australia	2	6	5
Belgium	2	2	3
Egypt	2	2	1
Mexico	2	1	2
South Africa	2	1	1
Norway	1	3	3
Jamaica	1	2	—
Austria	1	—	3
India	1	—	—
Peru	1	—	—
Yugoslavia	—	2	—
Canada	—	1	2
Portugal	—	1	1
Uruguay	—	1	1
Ceylon (now Sri Lanka)	—	1	—
Cuba	—	1	—
Spain	—	1	—
Trinidad	—	1	—
Korea	—	—	2
Panama	—	—	2
Brazil	—	—	1
Iran	—	—	1
Poland	—	—	1
Puerto Rico	—	—	1

OSLO 1952

VI WINTER GAMES HELD IN OSLO, NORWAY,
14–25 FEBRUARY 1952
ATTENDED BY REPRESENTATIVES OF 30 COUNTRIES,
COMPRISING 694 COMPETITORS, OF WHICH 109
WERE WOMEN.

A feature of these Games was the enormous crowds at all venues, including a record for any Olympic event, at the ski jumping at Holmenkollen, estimated at 150,000. An innovation was the Olympic flame coming, not from Olympia, but from Morgedal in southern Norway, the home of Sondre Nordheim, father of modern skiing. The last relay 'runner' who brought the flame into the Bislett Stadium was Eigil Nansen, the grandson of the renowned Polar explorer Fridtjof Nansen. The oath was taken by ski jumper Torbjörn Falkanger. All entrants from Commonwealth countries wore black armbands as the opening day coincided with the funeral of Britain's King George VI. As King Haakon and the Crown Prince were in London for this, HRH Princess Ragnhild opened the Games. Back in the Olympic fold were Germany and Japan, and for the first time in the Winter Games entries included Portugal and New Zealand.

Bad weather conditions necessitated the start of some of the competitions, the women's giant slalom and the two-man bob, the day before the opening ceremony. Of the three Alpine events, the giant slalom and downhill races were held some 120km from Oslo, at Norefjell. In the men's giant slalom Stein Eriksen (NOR) became the first ever winner of an Alpine skiing event from a Nordic country. This did not happen again until 1980. The star of the Games was Hjalmar Andersen of the host country who won three speed skating gold medals. In winning the women's figure skating title Jeanette Altwegg won Britain's first skating gold medal since Madge Syers in 1908. Instead of turning professional, as did most of her predecessors and successors, she went to work at the famed village for orphan children, Pestalozzi in Switzerland. The men's title went to defending champion Dick Button (USA) with some of the most remarkable jumps ever seen in competition. Finishing sixth was Carlo Fassi (ITA), later to coach Olympic champions Peggy Fleming (USA), Dorothy Hamill (USA), John Curry (GBR) and Robin Cousins (GBR).

The basic running abilities required by cross-country skiers were highlighted in the Nordic skiing, won by the 18km gold medallist Hallgeir Brenden (NOR), who during following years won two national steeplechase titles. Also in the silver Norwegian relay team with him was Martin Stokken, who had placed fourth in the 1948 Olympic 10,000m run in London. By competing again at Helsinki he became one of the few men to compete in both the Winter and Summer Games in the same year. For the first time there was a Nordic ski race for women, dominated by Finland with four of the first five places. Bandy, a distant relative of ice hockey, was played as a demonstration sport and won by Sweden.

The oldest gold medallist at Oslo was Franz Kemser in the German four-man bob aged 41 years 103 days, and the youngest was slalom winner Andrea Mead-Lawrence (USA) aged 19 years 301 days. The youngest male winner was Robert Dickson (CAN) in ice hockey aged 20 years 308 days, while the oldest female champion was Lydia Wideman (FIN) in the 10km cross-country aged 31 years 282 days. The youngest medallist was skater Tenley Albright (USA) with a silver, aged 16 years 217 days. Albert Madorin (SUI) won a bronze in the four-man bob aged 46 years 342 days.

1952 MEDALS (WINTER)

	G	S	B
Norway	7	3	6
United States	4	6	1
Finland	3	4	2
Germany	3	2	2
Austria	2	4	2
Canada	1	—	1
Italy	1	—	1
Great Britain	1	—	—
The Netherlands	—	3	—
Sweden	—	—	4
Switzerland	—	—	2
France	—	—	1
Hungary	—	—	1

HELSINKI 1952

XV OLYMPIC GAMES HELD IN HELSINKI, FINLAND,
19 JULY–3 AUGUST 1952
ATTENDED BY REPRESENTATIVES OF 69 COUNTRIES,
COMPRISING 4925 COMPETITORS, OF WHICH 518
WERE WOMEN.

One of the greatest Olympian countries, Finland, finally hosted the Games. President Juho Paasikivi formally opened the Games in the smallest city ever to be host as the capital, Helsinki, had a population of only 367,000. There were two dramatic moments during the ceremony. Firstly, when a so-called 'Angel of Peace', an apparently mentally unstable young German woman in a flowing white robe, ran around part of the track. More appropriate to the occasion was the moment when the last torch relay runner was due, and the scoreboard indicated the first letter of his name. The stadium erupted to cheers as 55-year-old Paavo Nurmi, arguably the greatest distance runner the world has seen, ran a lap and lit the flame in the stadium. He then passed the torch to 62-year-old Hannes Kolehmainen, the original 'Flying Finn', who ascended the stadium tower, by lift, and lit another flame there.

After 40 years Russia returned to the Olympics, now in the guise of the Soviet Union. Fears of confrontation between them and the United States team proved unfounded, as the competitors seemed to treat each other quite cordially, if somewhat coolly. Attending the Games for the first time were teams from the Bahamas, Gold Coast (now Ghana), Guatemala, Dutch Antilles, Hong Kong, Indonesia, Israel, Nigeria, Thailand, Vietnam, and, for the only time ever, the Saar. Because Mainland China had been invited, the Nationalist Chinese (Taiwan) had withdrawn. Although they all marched together there were two Olympic villages; surprisingly the IOC had allowed the Soviet bloc to set up their own at Otaniemi, while everybody else was at Kapyla.

The athlete of these Games was the Czech runner Emil Zátopek who won an unprecedented triple of the 5000m, 10,000m and marathon. To crown his achievements, his wife Dana, born on the same day as Emil, also won a gold medal, in the javelin, within an hour of his 5000m victory. The outstanding female track athlete was Australia's Marjorie Jackson who set world records winning the 100m and 200m, but dropped the baton when certain to win a third gold in the sprint relay. Incidentally, she retrieved the baton and finished in fifth place. In the winning American team was Barbara Pearl Jones who became the youngest ever track and field gold medallist aged 15 years 123 days. However, the youngest gold medallist at Helsinki was French cox Bernard Malivoire at 14 years 94 days in the rowing pairs event. Once again small nations did well, with Jamaican runners invincible over 400m, and Josy Barthel causing the band some problems as they tried to find the anthem of his native Luxembourg when he scored an upset win in the 1500m.

The 1948 100m sprint champion, Harrison Dillard (USA), was back to his first love here, winning the 110m hurdles and taking his fourth gold medal in the sprint relay. His teammate, Horace Ashenfelter gained America's first win in a distance run since 1908 when he set an inaugural official world record for the 3000m steeplechase. The press had great fun here with the fact that a Russian followed Ashenfelter, who was an FBI agent, home. The Soviet Union's first ever Olympics gold medal was won by Nina Romashkova in the women's discus. Highly questionable disqualifications by blatantly biased judges marred the 10,000m track walk, but did not stop the Swiss and Russian second and third place medallists literally running the last 30m to the line, out-sprinting the judge who vainly tried to reach them to rule them out. Incidentally, the judge was Giorgio Oberweger (ITA), who had won a bronze medal in the 1936 discus before becoming a walking official. The event was dropped from future Games. The winner of the high jump, Walt Davis (USA), was, at 2.04m, probably the tallest competitor ever to win an individual event, in any sport, at the Games. In the swimming pool the Hungarians won four of the five events for women. Almost matching the Zátopeks were Éva Székely, who won the 200m breaststroke, and her husband Dezsö Gyarmati, a member of the victorious Hungarian water polo team four days later. Much media attention was gained by the 400m freestyle for men, when the father of the winner, Jean Boiteux (FRA), jumped into the pool fully clothed to congratulate his son. In diving Dr Sammy Lee, an American of Korean origin, became the first man to successfully defend a diving title, in this case the platform. He later coached the next man to achieve the feat, Bob Webster in 1960 and 1964.

DID YOU KNOW?

Physical handicaps have proved no handicap to some competitors at the Games. Karoly Takacs of Hungary was a world-class pistol shot in 1938, when a grenade exploded in his right, shooting hand. Ten years later he won the Olympic rapid-fire pistol title using his left hand. In 1984, a New Zealand paraplegic, Neroli Fairhall, took part from her wheelchair in the women's archery competition, and came 35th out of 47 competitors. In 2000 Marla Runyan, a 'legally' blind athlete was finalist in the women's 1500m at Sydney.

The gymnastics competitions were dominated by the Soviet teams, led by Viktor Chukarin, four golds and two silvers, and his female counterpart Maria Gorokhovskaya with two golds and five silvers. The latter's total of seven is the most medals ever won by a woman at one Games in any sport. The Finnish veteran, Dr Heikki Savolainen, who had taken the oath at the opening ceremony, and gained a team bronze, the fifth consecutive Games at which he had won a medal, was just two months short of his 45th birthday. Other veterans did well in 1952. Ilona Elek (HUN) added a silver to her two fencing golds at the age of 45 years 71 days. In the dressage André Jousseaume (FRA) won an individual bronze medal two days after his 58th birthday, and 20 years after his gold medal at Los Angeles. In all he placed in the first five positions in five Games. Another great sportsman, Károly Takács (HUN), won the rapid-fire pistol for the second time. Before the Second World War he had won the European title as a right-handed shooter, but in 1938 he had lost his right hand when a grenade exploded while he was holding it. He painstakingly taught himself to shoot with his left hand and won two Olympic titles. On a less uplifting note there was the disqualification of Ingemar Johannson (SWE) in the heavyweight boxing final for 'not trying'. His silver medal was withheld for 30 years. In 1959 he won the world professional title from the 1952 Olympic middleweight champion Floyd Patterson (USA).

DID YOU KNOW?

At Helsinki in 1952 Ingemar Johansson of Sweden was disqualified for 'not trying' in the final of the heavyweight-boxing category, and the silver medal was withheld. Seven years later he beat Floyd Patterson (USA) – who had won the 1952 Olympic middleweight title – to become the world professional heavyweight champion. His silver medal was re-instated in 1982.

The oldest gold medallist at these Games was Everard Endt (USA) in the 6-m yachting aged 59 years 112 days. Another yachtsman, Ernst Westerlund (FIN), was the oldest medallist, 19 days older than Endt. The youngest male and female champions were Bernard Malivoire and Barbara Pearl Jones (*see above*). The oldest female winner was Sylvi Saimo (FIN) in the 500-m kayak event aged 37 years 260 days. At the end of the Games a then record 43 countries had won medals in Helsinki, and it was announced that Avery Brundage (USA) had taken over the Presidency of the IOC from the retiring Sigfrid Edström.

1952 MEDALS (SUMMER)

	G	S	B
United States	40	19	17
Soviet Union	22	30	19
Hungary	16	10	16
Sweden	12	13	10
Italy	8	9	4
Czechoslovakia	7	3	3
France	6	6	6
Finland	6	3	13
Australia	6	2	3
Norway	3	2	—
Switzerland	2	6	6
South Africa	2	4	4
Jamaica	2	3	—
Belgium	2	2	—
Denmark	2	1	3
Turkey	2	—	1
Japan	1	6	2
Great Britain	1	2	8
Argentina	1	2	2
Poland	1	2	1
Canada	1	2	—
Yugoslavia	1	2	—
Romania	1	1	2
Brazil	1	—	2
New Zealand	1	—	2
India	1	—	1
Luxembourg	1	—	—
Germany	—	7	17
The Netherlands	—	5	—
Iran	—	3	4
Chile	—	2	—
Austria	—	1	1
Lebanon	—	1	1
Ireland	—	1	—
Mexico	—	1	—
Spain	—	1	—
Korea	—	—	2
Trinidad	—	—	2
Uruguay	—	—	2
Bulgaria	—	—	1
Egypt	—	—	1
Portugal	—	—	1
Venezuela	—	—	1

CORTINA D'AMPEZZO 1956

VII WINTER GAMES HELD IN CORTINA D'AMPEZZO, ITALY, 26 JANUARY–5 FEBRUARY 1956
ATTENDED BY REPRESENTATIVES OF 32 COUNTRIES, COMPRISING 820 COMPETITORS, OF WHICH 132 WERE WOMEN.

Most of the money spent on these Games came from the Italian Soccer Pools, but despite excellent facilities there were still problems with the weather. Once again snow needed to be 'imported' for some venues. The President of Italy, Giovanni Granchi, formally opened the Games. Guiliana Chenal-Minuzzo, who won the 1952 bronze medal in downhill skiing, became the first woman in Olympic history to pronounce the oath on behalf of all competitors. The last runner in the torch relay, speed skater Guido Caroli, fell as he completed a circuit of the arena but happily the flame did not go out. The entry of the Soviet Union provided the first Soviet competitors in Olympic Winter events since 1908. These were also the first Winter Games to be televised, which undoubtedly resulted in smaller numbers of spectators than previously.

Austrian plumber, Toni Sailer, attracted the most attention, gaining a grand slam of all three Alpine titles, downhill, slalom and giant slalom, winning in treacherous conditions by outstanding margins of 3.5sec, 4.0sec and 6.2sec respectively. Second in the slalom was Asia's first Winter medallist, Chiharu Igaya (JPN), an American college student, who had to wait anxiously while the jury investigated an unsubstantiated claim, by Sweden and the United States, that he had missed a gate. Madeleine Berthod (SUI) won the women's downhill by a still unbeaten record margin of 4.7sec.

The most medals won at Cortina were by Sixten Jernberg (SWE) with one gold, two silvers and a bronze medal in Nordic skiing. Hallgeir Brenden (NOR) successfully defended his 1952 title, the distance now reduced from 18km to 15km. Using a new style the Finns dominated the ski jumping and the Norwegians, who had won 15 of the 18 medals available in the sport since 1924, failed to place in the first six. Though Germany competed as a single team, the jumping bronze, won by Harry Glass, is claimed by the East German team as its first Olympic medal. The speed skating surface on Lake Misurina, at an altitude of 1755m (5756ft), was considered to be the fastest ever, and witnessed a wholesale attack on the record book. The winner of the 500m title, Yevgeni Grishin (URS) had been a member of the Soviet cycling team in Helsinki. In figure skating Hayes (gold) and David (bronze) Jenkins were the first brothers to win medals in the same skating event. Their teammate, women's champion Tenley Albright, had been a victim of polio as a child.

A member of the winning Swiss four-man bob, Franz Kapus, at 46 years 298 days, was the oldest gold medallist at Cortina. The youngest champion was Elisabeth Schwarz (AUT) in pairs skating aged 19 years 260 days. The youngest male winner was Toni Sailer (AUT) in the giant slalom aged 20 years 73 days, and the oldest female champion was Siiri Rantanen (FIN) in the cross-country relay aged 31 years 49 days. The youngest medallist was skater Ingrid Wendl (AUT) with a bronze, aged 15 years 260 days, and the youngest male medallist was speed skater Alv Gjestvang (NOR) at 18 years 137 days. The Soviet competitors won a total of 16 medals to head the unofficial medal table – a position they were rarely to lose in future Winter Games.

1956 MEDALS (WINTER)

	G	S	B
Soviet Union	7	3	6
Austria	4	3	4
Finland	3	3	1
Switzerland	3	2	1
Sweden	2	4	4
United States	2	3	2
Norway	2	1	1
Italy	1	2	—
Germany	1	—	1
Canada	—	1	2
Japan	—	1	—
Hungary	—	—	1
Poland	—	—	1

MELBOURNE 1956

XVI SUMMER GAMES HELD IN MELBOURNE, AUSTRALIA, 22 NOVEMBER–8 DECEMBER 1956 (ALSO IN STOCKHOLM, SWEDEN, 10–17 JUNE 1956) ATTENDED BY REPRESENTATIVES OF 67 COUNTRIES, COMPRISING 3184 COMPETITORS, OF WHICH 371 WERE WOMEN. (AT STOCKHOLM THERE WERE REPRESENTATIVES OF 29 COUNTRIES, COMPRISING 158 COMPETITORS, 13 OF WHOM WERE WOMEN).

In 1949 the IOC had decided on Melbourne by only one vote, and they were disquieted, to say the least, by first, the apparent tardiness in finishing facilities, and second, the inability of the Australians to hold the equestrian events. This was due to their stringent animal quarantine laws. Thus for the first and only time, contrary to the Olympic Charter, a sport was detached from the main Games and held elsewhere, in Stockholm. Except for the cross-country section of the three-day event the venue was the 1912 Olympic Stadium. The host country won three of the six titles, but there was strong criticism and accusations of chauvinism by the judges in the dressage competition. Also the above-mentioned cross-country was thought to be too dangerous in the existing wet conditions.

The Games proper, the only celebration to that date in the Southern Hemisphere, opened in Melbourne under a cloud of international ill-will, occasioned by the Soviet invasion of Hungary, and the French and British intervention in the Suez Canal dispute between Israel and Egypt. The Netherlands, Spain and Switzerland withdrew because of the former, and Egypt and Lebanon because of the latter. This time Mainland China withdrew because of the presence of Taiwan. Perhaps surprisingly, the Hungarians did compete, and with good effect. West and East Germany entered a combined team, and continued to do so until after 1964. In addition to Taiwan, Olympic debuts were made by teams from Ethiopia, Fiji, Kenya, Liberia, Uganda, Malaya and North Borneo (the two latter now combined as Malaysia). Cambodia's appearance in the Stockholm events was its Olympic debut. HRH The Duke of Edinburgh opened the Games at the Melbourne Cricket Ground, the main venue. The final torch-bearer was a 19-year-old Australian miler, Ron Clarke, destined to be one of the world's greatest runners.

In Melbourne the distance runs were dominated by the Soviet sailor Vladimir Kuts, with record breaking victories at 5000m and 10,000m. Ireland won its first gold medal since 1932, when Ronnie Delany took the 1500m with an exceptionally fast last 300m. In the sprints both Bobby-Joe Morrow (USA) and Betty Cuthbert (AUS) gained three gold medals, including the relays. Teamed with Cuthbert in the 4 x 100m was Shirley de la Hunty (née Strickland), who ended her three Games career with an unbeaten total of seven medals (three golds, one silver, three bronzes). A photo-finish picture, which was not unearthed for many years after the event, indicates that she was also third, not fourth, in the 200m in 1948. She made no official claim, however, and the result remains as it was. After placing second to Emil Zátopek in three Olympic races since 1948, Frenchman Alain Mimoun finally beat him, into sixth place, by taking the marathon - the oldest man to do so at only a month short of his 36th birthday. Norman Read, representing his adopted country New Zealand, won the the 50km walk. As a former English junior mile walk champion Read had watched the 1952 Games as a spectator (sitting next to the author).

Another English-born competitor, Murray Rose (AUS), was the first male swimmer to win two individual freestyle events since 1924. He also won a third gold medal in the relay. Pat McCormick (USA) achieved a then unique double 'double' retaining both her diving titles from Helsinki. Boxing too had its record-breaker when László Papp did his bit to raise Hungarian spirits by gaining an unprecedented third gold medal at boxing. Not surprisingly, bad feelings erupted in the water polo semi-final between Hungary and the Soviet Union. By a nice touch of irony the referee was from the perennially neutral Sweden. With Hungary leading 4–0 he ended the game, as it had degenerated into a 'boxing match under water'. However, by beating Yugoslavia in the soccer final on the last day, 8 December, the Soviet Union went into history as the winners of the latest gold medal ever won in an Olympic year.

John Kelly Jr, the son of the 1920s gold medallist, won a bronze in the single sculls as Vyacheslav Ivanov (URS) gained the first of his record three consecutive titles. At the shooting range Gerald Ouellette (CAN) won the prone small bore rifle competition with a world record 'maximum' of 600, only to have the record, but not the gold medal, disallowed because the range was found to be 1.5m short of the international distance of 50m.

The oldest gold medallist in the 1956 Games, albeit in his case at Stockholm, was Henri St. Cyr (SWE) in dressage aged 54 years 93 days, while the youngest was Sandra Morgan (AUS) in the 4 x 100m freestyle relay aged 14 years 183 days. The youngest male winner was Murray Rose (AUS) aged 17 years 332 days, while the oldest female champion was Hungarian gymnast Agnes Keleti at 35 years 331 days. Although not even a medallist, Gunhild Larking, a beautiful Swedish high jumper, undoubtedly had more photographs taken of her than any of the more successful competitors. Actually a member of the combined Germany team, Wolfgang Behrendt, winner of the boxing bantamweight title, was East Germany's first gold medallist.

At the closing ceremony for the first time the athletes entered en masse, signifying the friendship of the Games. The idea for this had come from an Australian-born Chinese boy, John Wing, in a letter to the chairman of the organising committee, the Hon. Wilfrid S. Kent-Hughes. A happy postscript to these Games occurred in Prague in March 1957 when the American hammer winner, Harold Connolly, married Olga Fikotová, the Czech Olympic discus champion. The best man at this 'Olympic' wedding was, most appropriately, Emil Zátopek.

1956 MEDALS (SUMMER)

	G	S	B
Soviet Union	37	29	32
United States	32	25	17
Australia	13	8	14
Hungary	9	10	7
Italy	8	8	9
Sweden	8	5	6
Germany	6	13	7
Great Britain	6	7	11
Romania	5	3	5
Japan	4	10	5
France	4	4	6
Turkey	3	2	2
Finland	3	1	11
Iran	2	2	1
Canada	2	1	3
New Zealand	2	—	—
Poland	1	4	4
Czechoslovakia	1	4	1
Bulgaria	1	3	1
Denmark	1	2	1
Ireland	1	1	3
Norway	1	—	2
Mexico	1	—	1
Brazil	1	—	—
India	1	—	—
Yugoslavia	—	3	—
Chile	—	2	2
Belgium	—	2	—
Argentina	—	1	1
Korea	—	1	1
Iceland	—	1	—
Pakistan	—	1	—
South Africa	—	—	4
Austria	—	—	2
Bahamas	—	—	1
Greece	—	—	1
Switzerland	—	—	1
Uruguay	—	—	1

SQUAW VALLEY 1960

VIII WINTER GAMES HELD AT SQUAW VALLEY, USA, 18–28 FEBRUARY 1960
ATTENDED BY REPRESENTATIVES OF 30 COUNTRIES, COMPRISING 665 COMPETITORS, OF WHICH 143 WERE WOMEN.

When the IOC voted narrowly, 32–30, to give the Games to Squaw Valley, USA, instead of Innsbruck, virtually nothing existed at the site. Due to the efforts of Alexander Cushing, who owned most of the area, it became the first purpose-built Winter Games venue. Despite initial delays everything was ready for the official opening, under the direction of Walt Disney. The formal opening was by Richard Nixon, then Vice-President of the United States. The last relay runner was Ken Henry, the 500m speed skating champion of 1952, and the oath was taken by figure skater Carol Heiss, who went on to win the women's title.

There were a number of protests and problems. Bobsledding was dropped as the organisers would not accept the cost of building a run for what they considered would be a small entry. Artificial obstacles were built into the downhill runs to make them more difficult, and concern was expressed over the altitude (over 1900m, 6230ft) at which the Nordic skiing events were held. East and West Germany competed as one entity with agreement reached on the popular theme from Beethoven's *Ninth Symphony* played for any victory ceremonies instead of their respective national anthems. A team from South Africa appeared for the first time in the Winter Games; they were banned thereafter until 1992. The biathlon and speed skating for women made Olympics debuts. The biathlon was the successor to the military patrol event, which had been a demonstration event on four previous occasions.

The speed skating times in general were excellent, with Knut Johannesen (NOR) beating the 10,000m world record by 46.0sec, the greatest margin achieved in the 20th century. Yevgeni Grishin (URS) equalled his own world mark to become the first man to successfully defend the 500m title. Helga Haase (GER) was the first ever women's Olympic champion in speed skating when she won the 500m. In figure skating David Jenkins kept the men's title in the family – his brother Hayes had won in 1956, and he made the family even more Olympian by marrying Squaw Valley's female champion Carol Heiss, two months later.

There was a first in Nordic skiing when Georg Thoma, a German postman from the Black Forest, who was often forced to deliver mail on skis in bad weather, achieved the first victory by a non-Scandinavian in the sport. The winner of the inaugural biathlon, Klas Lestander (SWE) was only 15th in the cross-country segment of the contest, but scored a maximum possible 20 in the shooting. The Soviet women dominated the 10,000m race; taking the first four places, but they lost the relay, a virtual certainty, when their first female skier fell and broke a ski. A protest was made against the first-place Swedish woman who was accused of deliberate fouling, but it was not upheld.

In Alpine skiing metallic skis were used in the Games for the first time. The medals were more widespread than usual, with no skier winning more than one event, and only Penny Pitou (USA) won more than one medal, with two silvers. The outstanding competitor was Anne Heggtveit (CAN) who won the women's slalom by a margin of 3.3sec, only ever bettered by the 1936 combination winner, Christl Cranz (GER).

The oldest gold medallist was Viekko Hakulinen (FIN) in the Nordic relay aged 35 years 52 days, and the youngest Heidi Biebl (GER), the downhill champion three days past her 19th birthday. The youngest male champion was American ice hockey player Thomas Williams, aged 19 years 317 days. The oldest female gold medallist was Sonja Ruthström (SWE) in the Nordic relay aged 29 years 94 days. The youngest medallist was skier Traudl Hecher (AUT) with a downhill bronze, aged 16 years 145 days.

1960 MEDALS (WINTER)

	G	S	B
Soviet Union	7	5	9
Germany	4	3	1
United States	3	4	3
Norway	3	3	—
Sweden	3	2	2
Finland	2	3	3
Canada	2	1	1
Switzerland	2	—	—
Austria	1	2	3
France	1	—	2
The Netherlands	—	1	1
Poland	—	1	1
Czechoslovakia	—	1	—
Italy	—	—	1

ROME 1960

XVII OLYMPIC GAMES HELD IN ROME, ITALY, 25 AUGUST–11 SEPTEMBER 1960
ATTENDED BY REPRESENTATIVES OF 83 COUNTRIES, COMPRISING 5346 COMPETITORS, OF WHICH 610 WERE WOMEN.

After just missing out in 1908 the Games finally went to Rome, the home city of the Emperor Theodosius, who reputedly had ended the Ancient Games 1567 years before. A number of old Roman sites were utilised as well as a brand-new 90,000-capacity stadium. The Baths of Caracalla housed the gymnastics, and the Basilica di Massenzio had the wrestling competitions. The marathon began at the Capitol Hill and finished on the Appian Way, near the Arch of Constantine. It was the first time that an Olympic marathon had not started or finished in the main Olympic Stadium. Sailing was held at the bay of Naples under the shadow of Mt Vesuvius. The President of Italy, Giovanni Gronchi, opened the games before 90,000 spectators; the oath was taken by the 1948 discus champion Adolfo Consolini. Barbados (as part of the Antilles team), Morocco, Sudan, San Marino and Tunisia made their debuts. Nationalist China protested, but competed, when they were told by the IOC to appear under the name of Taiwan and not China. These Games were the first to have worldwide television coverage.

The extreme heat undoubtedly caused upsets, but did nothing to hinder the successes of the Australasians in the middle distance running events. Peter Snell (NZL) won the 800m, Herb Elliott (AUS) won the 1500m by a record margin of 2.8sec in world record time, and Murray Halberg (NZL), handicapped by a withered arm, won the 5000m. An unknown runner, Abebe Bikila, won the marathon barefoot, and signalled the entry of Ethiopia on to the world distance running scene. The team from Taiwan was cheered up somewhat when their decathlete Chuan-Kwang Yang had a tremendous battle with Rafer Johnson (USA), a university teammate at the University of California, Los Angeles, and only lost the gold medal narrowly. Sprinter Wilma Rudolph (USA) who won three gold medals captivated the stadium – she was one of 19 children and had suffered from polio as a child. Sisters Irina and Tamara Press (URS) won the 80m hurdles and shot respectively, while their countrywoman, Ludmila Shevtsova, won the first 800m event for women since 1928.

In the swimming pool the only one of the 15 events not won by either Australia or the United States went to Anita Lonsbrough (GBR). The outstanding swimmer was America's Christine von Saltza, a descendant of Prussian/Swedish nobility, with three golds and a silver medal. The standard was very high with Olympic records broken in every event. An unfortunate incident occurred in the men's 100m freestyle when Lance Larson (USA) was timed at 0.01sec faster than John Devitt (AUS) but was placed second to him despite slow-motion film indicating that the American was first. In future Games full electronic timing was used. The second only Royal gold medal in Olympic history was won by Crown Prince Constantine (later King Constantine II of Greece), in the Dragon class yachting. It is reported that he received the traditional winner's ducking, being pushed into the water by his mother, Queen Frederika. In the Flying Dutchman class Peder Lunde Jr (NOR) became the third generation of his family to win a medal, equalling his grandfather's gold of 1924, but going one better than his mother and father in 1952. Paul Elvstrøm (DEN) won his fourth consecutive individual gold medal in dinghy sailing, the first sportsman from any sport to achieve this distinction. The canoeing, on Lake Albano, had a particularly distinguished spectator, as the Pope apparently watched some of the competitions from his summer palace. In boxing the light-welterweight silver medallist, Clement 'Ike' Quartey (GHA) became the first black African to win an Olympic boxing medal.

The most medals won in Rome were the seven (four golds, two silvers, one bronze) gained by gymnast Boris Shakhlin (URS). Aladár Gerevich (HUN), at 50 years 178 days the oldest champion in Rome, won his sixth team sabre gold medal in as many Games – a feat unsurpassed by any other Olympic competitor. In the foil and épée events Edoardo Mangiarotti (ITA) brought his total of fencing medals to a record 13 (six golds, five silvers, two bronzes) in five Games 1936–60. The light-heavyweight boxing title went to Cassius Clay (USA), who, as Muhammad Ali, amassed the greatest amount ever earned by a sportsman, $68 million, when he became a professional after the Games. In soccer, Yugoslavia won the gold medal after three consecutive runner-up placings. The first loss to India in Olympic hockey since they entered the competition in 1928 occurred when Pakistan beat them 1–0 in the final.

The youngest champion was swimmer Carolyn Wood (USA) in the freestyle relay aged 14 years 260 days, and the youngest male gold medallist was Klaus Zerta, cox of the German rowing pairs, aged 14 years 283 days. The oldest female winner was discus champion Nina Ponomaryeva (URS) at 31 years 131 days. (She had achieved notoriety in 1956, when it was alleged that she stole hats from an Oxford Street store, while on a trip to London for an international match, which was thereby cancelled). The oldest medallist was yachtsman Manfred Metzger (SUI) at 55 years 104 days, while the oldest female medallist was Italian fencer Welleda Cesari at 40 years 201 days.

A tragic note was struck by the collapse and death of cyclist Knut Jensen (DEN), originally diagnosed as due to the excessive heat, but later revealed to be the consequence of a drugs overdose. At the end of the Games a then record 44 countries had shared in the medals.

Greece	1	—	—
Norway	1	—	—
Switzerland	—	3	3
France	—	2	3
Belgium	—	2	2
Iran	—	1	3
The Netherlands	—	1	2
South Africa	—	1	2
Argentina	—	1	1
Egypt (UAR)	—	1	1
Canada	—	1	—
Ghana	—	1	—
India	—	1	—
Morocco	—	1	—
Portugal	—	1	—
Singapore	—	1	—
Chinese Taipei	—	1	—
Brazil	—	—	2
Jamaica*	—	—	2
Barbados*	—	—	1
Iraq	—	—	1
Mexico	—	—	1
Spain	—	—	1
Venezuela	—	—	1

* Double counted as part of the Antilles team.

INNSBRUCK 1964

IX WINTER GAMES HELD IN INNSBRUCK, SWITZERLAND, 29 JANUARY– 9 FEBRUARY 1964 ATTENDED BY REPRESENTATIVES OF 36 COUNTRIES, COMPRISING 1091 COMPETITORS, OF WHICH 200 WERE WOMEN.

Awarded to Innsbruck in 1959, these Games were the most successful yet with over one million spectators attending a still unbroken record 34 events. Among them were lugeing and a second ski jump. However, again weather was a problem, and snow had to be manhandled to some venues by the Austrian Army. During practice before the Games began there were two tragic deaths, of a British tobogganist and an Australian skier. The official opening by the Austrian President, Dr Adolf Schärf, took place at the Bergisel ski jump in front of 60,000 people. The last relay runner, and the one who lit the flame, was a skier Joseph Rieder; bobsledder Paul Aste took the oath. Mongolia and India competed for the first time, while Korea was split into North and South teams. South Africa was now banned from the Olympics. An innovation was the official use of computers to aid judging, as well as provide electronic timing.

The Games were dominated by the Soviet Union and, for the first time, Switzerland failed to gain a single medal. Lydia Skoblikova (URS), a teacher from Siberia, won all four women's speed skating events, to total six gold medals in two Games, a record for the sport. The Soviet husband and wife skating pair, Ludmila Belousova and Oleg Protopopov, brought a new concept, classical ballet, to the sport. The silver medal went for the second consecutive occasion to Marika Kilius and Hansjürgen Bäumler (GER) – two years later they were disqualified owing to professional activities which had then come to light, but were reinstated in 1987 by the IOC. The

1960 MEDALS (SUMMER)

	G	S	B
Soviet Union	43	29	31
United States	34	21	16
Italy	13	10	13
Germany	12	19	11
Australia	8	8	6
Turkey	7	2	—
Hungary	6	8	7
Japan	4	7	7
Poland	4	6	11
Czechoslovakia	3	2	3
Romania	3	1	6
Great Britain	2	6	12
Denmark	2	3	1
New Zealand	2	—	1
Bulgaria	1	3	3
Sweden	1	2	3
Finland	1	1	3
Austria	1	1	—
Yugoslavia	1	1	—
Pakistan	1	—	1
Ethiopia	1	—	—

women's individual skating title went to Sjoukje Dijkstra, the first ever Winter Games gold medal to be won by The Netherlands.

The first sisters to win gold medals at the same Games were Marielle and Christine Goitschel (FRA) who swapped first and second places in the Alpine slalom events. The re-introduced bobsleigh events were won, for the first time, by countries which did not possess bob runs of their own. Also the victory by Tony Nash and Robin Dixon (GBR) in the two-man bob was the first by a 'lowland' country, and owed much to a replacement bolt supplied by an Italian adversary Eugenio Monti. He was later awarded the Pierre de Coubertin Fair Play Trophy for this action. Klaudia Boyarskikh (URS) won three gold medals in Nordic skiing, while Sixten Jernberg (SWE) brought his total to a record nine medals in three Games. A demonstration of German curling was held.

The oldest gold medallist was Sixten Jernberg, winning his fourth gold medal two days after his 35th birthday. The youngest was Manfred Stengl (AUT) aged 17 years 310 days in the two-man luge, with Marielle Goitschel (FRA) the youngest female winner in the giant slalom aged 18 years 128 days. The oldest female champion was Alevtina Koltschina (URS) in the Nordic relay at 33 years 88 days. Scott Allen (USA) was the youngest medallist with his bronze in the men's figure skating just two days short of his 15th birthday, while the oldest was Eugenio Monti (ITA) aged 36 years 15 days.

1964 MEDALS (WINTER)

	G	S	B
Soviet Union	11	8	6
Austria	4	5	3
Norway	3	6	6
Finland	3	4	3
France	3	4	—
Sweden	3	3	1
Germany	3	3	3
United States	1	2	3
Canada	1	—	2
The Netherlands	1	1	—
Great Britain	1	—	—
Italy	—	1	3
North Korea (PRK)	—	1	—
Czechoslovakia	—	—	1

TOKYO 1964

XVIII OLYMPIC GAMES HELD IN TOKYO, JAPAN,
10–24 OCTOBER 1964
ATTENDED BY REPRESENTATIVES OF 93 COUNTRIES,
COMPRISING 5140 COMPETITORS, OF WHICH 683
WERE WOMEN.

Asia's first Games witnessed large crowds and a tremendous assault on the record books. Vast sums, estimated to be as much as $3 billion, were been spent not only on stadia but also on transport facilities. Teams from 14 countries made their first appearance at the Games, but South Africa no longer received an invitation. Also missing were Indonesia and North Korea, whose athletes, having competed in the previous year's unsanctioned Games of the New Emergent Forces (GANEFO), were banned.

Emperor Hirohito performed the formal opening, and a young runner who had been born near Hiroshima on the day the atom bomb was dropped in 1945 brought the flame into the stadium. The Olympic flag was raised to the top of a flagpole, which measured 15.21m (50ft 6½in), the distance reached in the triple jump by Mikio Oda in 1928 when he won Japan's first Olympic gold medal.

The growth of the Games can be highlighted by distance runner Ron Clarke's remark after failing to gain the gold medal over 10,000m. Having dropped all the known opposition, he looked over his shoulder and saw, an Ethiopian, a North African Arab and an 'American Indian'. This latter, Billy Mills, a part Sioux Marine officer, was America's first ever winner at the distance. In the marathon Abebe Bikila (ETH), only six weeks after having his appendix removed – and this time wearing shoes – became the first man to retain the title, and Peter Snell (NZL) won the rare 800/1500m double. The winner of the 100m, Bob Hayes, ran a phenomenal last leg in the 4 x 100m relay, to regain the title that the United States had lost in Rome for the first time in 40 years. There is a story told that one of the beaten teams decried the US team to the effect that all they had was Hayes. This was met by the now famous rejoinder, 'Man, that's all we needed'. Britain won its first ever gold in women's athletics when Mary Rand took the long jump – her roommate Ann Packer added the 800m gold for good measure.

At the much-admired pool Australia and the United States won all the titles bar one. That was the women's 200m breaststroke, the event that had also prevented a clean sweep by the two swimming superpowers in Rome. Here it was won by Galina Prozumenshchikova (later Stepanova), the Soviet Union's first ever swimming gold medallist – who won a further two silvers and two bronzes at the next two Games. Don Schollander (USA) became the first swimmer to win four golds in any single Games. Close behind him came Sharon Stouder (USA) with three golds and a silver in the women's events. Australia's Dawn Fraser, just past her 27th birthday, won her third consecutive 100m title, then a unique achievement in swimming, and added a relay silver to take her total haul to eight medals, a record for a female swimmer. Another competitor to complete a unique triple was Soviet rower Vyacheslav Ivanov by winning the single sculls once again. An unusual thing occurred in the eights where the cox of the winning American crew, Róbert Zimonyi, aged 46, had been cox of the third placed Hungarian pairs in 1948. In water polo the Hungarian veteran Deszõ Gyarmati won his third gold medal, his fifth medal in as many Games.

The most medals were won by a gymnast Larissa Latynina (URS) with two golds, two silvers and two bronzes. Her teammate Boris Shakhlin brought his total of gold medals since 1956 to seven, of which a record six were in individual events. In weightlifting Norbert Schemansky (USA) won a bronze to add to his previous gold, silver and bronze since 1948, giving him a record for his sport of four medals. Unusually, wrestler Imre Polyák (HUN) finally won gold in his fourth Games after an unprecedented three silvers. Of the two new sports, the other was volleyball, judo had been included at the express wish of the host country. It was considered to be a Japanese monopoly, and the country suffered a terrible shock when the Open class judo title went to the big (1.98m, 6ft 6in) Dutchman Anton Geesink. Leading the United States basketball team to its sixth consecutive victory was Bill Bradley, a Rhodes scholar and later a member of the United States Senate.

The oldest gold medallist in Tokyo was Australian 5.5m yachtsman William Northam aged 59 years 23 days, and the youngest was swimmer 'Pokey' Watson (USA) aged 14 years 96 days in the freestyle relay. The oldest female winner was Katalin Juhász Nagy (HUN), a member of the foil team at 31 years 328 days, while the youngest male champion was swimmer Richard Roth (USA) in the 400m medley 18 days past his 17th birthday. Teammate John Nelson, 1500m freestyler, was the youngest male medallist at 16 years 131 days.

1964 MEDALS (SUMMER)

	G	S	B
United States	36	26	28
Soviet Union	30	31	35
Japan	16	5	8
Germany	10	22	18
Italy	10	10	7
Hungary	10	7	5
Poland	7	6	10
Australia	6	2	10
Czechoslovakia	5	6	3
Great Britain	4	12	2
Bulgaria	3	5	2
Finland	3	—	2
New Zealand	3	—	2
Romania	2	4	6
The Netherlands	2	4	4
Turkey	2	3	1
Sweden	2	2	4
Denmark	2	1	3
Yugoslavia	2	1	2
Belgium	2	—	1
France	1	8	6
Canada	1	2	1
Switzerland	1	2	1
Bahamas	1	—	—
Ethiopia	1	—	—
India	1	—	—
Korea	—	2	1
Trinidad	—	1	2
Tunisia	—	1	1
Argentina	—	1	—
Cuba	—	1	—
Pakistan	—	1	—
Philippines	—	1	—
Iran	—	—	2
Brazil	—	—	1
Ghana	—	—	1
Ireland	—	—	1
Kenya	—	—	1
Mexico	—	—	1
Nigeria	—	—	1
Uruguay	—	—	1

GRENOBLE 1968

X WINTER GAMES HELD IN GRENOBLE, FRANCE, 6–18 FEBRUARY 1968
ATTENDED BY REPRESENTATIVES OF 37 COUNTRIES, COMPRISING 1158 COMPETITORS, OF WHICH 211 WERE WOMEN.

There were complaints that venues at Grenoble were very widespread, with some 40km distant, but the new 12,000-seat indoor ice stadium delighted everyone. For the first time gender tests for female competitors were held. The political split between East and West Germany was finally acknowledged, and separate teams accepted. Morocco made its debut, and the President of France Charles de Gaulle, performed the official opening. The last relay runner was Alain Calmat, the 1964 skating silver medallist, and Léo Lacroix, a 1964 skiing silver medal winner, took the oath. The IOC attempted to control the exploitation of the Games by commercial interests by banning the use of trade names on competitors' equipment. Following the threat of a withdrawal by some leading skiers, who relied very heavily on ski company sponsorship, it was finally agreed that they need only remove the equipment before appearing in photographs or on television.

The undoubted star of these Games was Jean-Claude Killy (FRA), who emulated Toni Sailer's 1956 record by winning all three Alpine skiing events. However, in the last of the three, the slalom, Karl Schranz (AUT) claimed that in his second round run he had been distracted by a policeman cutting across the course in front of him. He was allowed another run, which he accomplished in a faster time to become the overall winner. Then it was decided that on his first attempt he had already missed a gate before the policeman incident, and his rerun was disqualified. He was to be even unluckier four years later. The best of the women Alpinists was Canada's Nancy Greene with a gold in the giant slalom and a silver in the slalom. The latter was won by Marielle Goitschel (FRA) to keep the title in the family – her sister had won it in 1964.

The most successful Nordic skier was Finnish-born Toini Gustafsson (SWE) with two gold and a silver in the women's events. By winning the 30km race Franco Nones (ITA) became the first ever non-Scandinavian winner in cross-country skiing. Another shock to Scandinavian sensibilities occurred in the two jumps and the combination event, when they only won a single bronze from the nine medals available. Yet another upset was in the women's luge, where the East German team women, in first, second and fourth places were disqualified for illegally heating their sled runners. The bob run at Alpe d'Huez, which was badly sited and considered to be very dangerous, was the scene of total triumph for the good sport of Innsbruck, four years previously. Eugenio Monti, the Italian nine-times world champion bobsledder, won both Olympic gold medals. In the two-man event the total times after four runs for Monti's bob and that of the German bob were equal. The tie was decided in the Italian's favour as he had the fastest single run. Aged 40 years 24 days, Monti was the oldest gold medallist at Grenoble.

The youngest champion was skater Peggy Fleming (USA) aged 19 years 198 days. The youngest male gold medallist was Wolfgang Schwarz, winning Austria's first skating title since 1936, aged 20 years 155 days. Ludmila and Oleg Protopopov (URS) retained their pairs title, with Ludmila the oldest female champion at 32 years 84 days. In 26th place in the men's figure skating was Jan Hoffmann (GDR) aged 12 years 110 days – the youngest ever male competitor in Olympic Winter Games (he won the silver medal 12 years later). The oldest female medallist was Nordic skier Alevtina Koltschina (URS) with a bronze in her IV Games at 37 years 97 days.

For the only time to date no speed skater gained more than one victory. The women's 500m was reminiscent of the men's event of 1948 and 1964 as three women tied for the silver medal. Making this occasion unique was the fact that all three of them were from the same country: the United States. For the last time Norway topped the medal table.

1968 MEDALS (WINTER)

	G	S	B
Norway	6	6	2
Soviet Union	5	5	3
France	4	3	2
Italy	4	—	—
Austria	3	4	4
The Netherlands	3	3	3
West Germany (FRG)	2	2	3
United States	1	5	1
Finland	1	2	2
East Germany (GDR)	1	2	2
Czechoslovakia	1	2	1
Canada	1	1	1
Switzerland	—	2	4
Romania	—	—	1

MEXICO CITY 1968

XIX OLYMPIC GAMES HELD IN MEXICO CITY, MEXICO, 12–27 OCTOBER 1968
ATTENDED BY REPRESENTATIVES OF 112 COUNTRIES, COMPRISING 5530 COMPETITORS, OF WHICH 781 WERE WOMEN.

From 1963, when these Games were awarded to Mexico City, there was a gradually increasing furore about the effects of the altitude there (2240m, 7347ft above sea level) on competitors in events that required endurance. Some medical authorities even forecast possible deaths. This extreme view was, thankfully, overly pessimistic, but many cases of severe exhaustion occurred. When Australian distance runner Ron Clarke developed serious heart problems in 1981, there was speculation that his condition had been aggravated by his efforts in Mexico City in 1968. Certainly standards were low in events that required over three minutes of continuous effort. However, the same conditions contributed to some startling performances in the 'explosive' events. Outstanding was the 8.90m (29ft, 2½in) long jump by Bob Beamon (USA) – a performance of 21st-century quality. The world records set in that long jump, and the 4 x 400m relay, lasted for over 22 years.

The thin air was not the only complaint raised prior to these Games. Some felt that the traditional 'mañana' attitude attributed to the Mexicans would result in incomplete facilities. In fact all were ready in good time. There was a threat of a boycott by Black African nations over the re-admission of South Africa earlier in the year. After 40 countries had indicated that they would withhold their teams the IOC reversed its decision and South Africa was barred again, permanently. In August the Soviet Union and its allies invaded Czechoslovakia, and international tension mounted. A few weeks before the Games began serious student riots erupted at the University of Mexico, which were ruthlessly suppressed, with dozens killed and hundreds injured. Some of the foreign press sports reporters became 'war' correspondents for their newspapers. In America there was a move to get black athletes to boycott the American team to protest the alleged bad treatment of Afro-Americans in general in the United States. When this appeared to get little support, the organisers implied that some sort of dramatic demonstration would be held at the Games. Despite all these problems President Gustavo Diaz Ordaz declared the formal opening to a record number of teams and athletes. Enriqueta Basilio, a hurdler, became the first woman to light the Olympic flame in the stadium.

Due to the conditions the distance running events were dominated by athletes who lived and trained at high altitude, such as the Kenyans and Ethiopians. Exceptional performances abounded in the sprints and jumps. Beamon's jump (*see* above) was beyond the limits of the measuring device in use at the pit, and a steel tape had to be used. In the triple jump the existing Olympic record was beaten by seven men, and the world mark was improved on five occasions. The high jump winner, Dick Fosbury (USA), used the 'flop' style, which he popularised and which was to revolutionise the event. Al Oerter (USA) won his record fourth consecutive discus title, and Wyomia Tyus (USA) was the first sprinter successfully to defend an Olympic 100m crown, other than Archie Hahn (USA) in the 1906 Intercalated Games. The men's 100m final was unique, up to that time, in that all eight finalists were black. A more heralded expression of black power was the demonstration by the Black Power supporters, Tommie Smith and John Carlos (USA), in the 200m victory ceremony. The Americans, who had come first and third respectively, raised black-gloved, clenched fists, with heads bowed, during the playing of the American anthem. For this action they were suspended and expelled from the Olympic village. Some old-timers noted that their action was no more, no less, insulting than that of the numerous medallists who had given the Nazi salute in 1936. The marathon was won, for the third consecutive time, by an Ethiopian, but this time by Mamo Wolde, after two-time champion Abebe Bikila withdrew at 17km. He had his appendix removed only six weeks prior to the Games. Tragically he was paralysed in a car accident the following year, and died in 1973 at the age of 41.

The gymnasts won the most medals, as usual. Although Mikhail Voronin (URS) won seven medals (two golds, four silvers, one bronze), the star of the sport was Vera Cáslavská (TCH) with four golds and two silvers. Her floor exercises routine, to the music of the *Mexican Hat Dance*, was immensely popular. Soon after her events were over, but still during the Games, she married her countryman, Josef Odlozil, the 1964 1500m silver medallist. Incidentally, Voronin's wife, Zinaida, won a gold, a silver, and two bronze medals in the Soviet women's gymnastic team. The outstanding swimmers were Charles Hickcox (USA) with three gold and a silver, and Debbie Meyer (USA), who won three individual events. Six other swimmers won two gold medals each, including an 18-year-old American named Mark Spitz. Mexico's first ever swimming gold medal was won by Felipe Muñoz in the 200m breaststroke. He was nicknamed 'Tibio', which means lukewarm in English. This was no reflection on his determination, but was the result of his father coming from a town named Aguascalientes ('hot water') and his mother from Rio Frio ('cold river').

Although eliminated in the fencing, Janice Romary (USA) became the first woman to compete in six consecutive Games, and because of this also became the first woman to carry the flag for the United States in a Games Opening Ceremony. The 5.5-m class sailing, held at the resort city of Acapulco, produced the unique result of triple gold medal siblings. The Swedish brothers, Ulf, Peter and Jörgen Sundelin crewed Wasa IV to an easy victory. Behind them, skippering the second placed Swiss boat Toucan was Louis Noverraz, at 66 years 154 days, the oldest medallist at these Games.

The oldest gold medallist was Josef Neckarmann (FRG) in the dressage team aged 56 years 141 days, while the youngest was Günther Tiersch (GDR), cox of the winning eight, aged 14 years 172 days. The oldest female champion was Liselott Linsenhoff (FRG), also in the dressage team, aged 41 years 58 days, while the youngest female gold medallist was swimmer Susan Pedersen (USA) in the medley relay a day after her 15th birthday. The oldest competitor at Mexico City was Roberto Soundy, a trapshooter from El Salvador aged 68 years 229 days, and the same country had the youngest male competitor in Ruben Guerrero, a medley relay swimmer, aged 13 years 351 days. However, the youngest competitor of all was Liana Vicens, of Puerto Rico, only 11 years 328 days in the women's 100m breaststroke. The oldest woman was Great Britain's Lorna Johnstone, who was 13th in the dressage at 66 years 51 days.

For the first time since they had entered the hockey competition in 1928 India failed to reach the final. In soccer, won for a record third time by Hungary, the surprise bronze medallist was Japan. They were the first, and to date only, Asian team to win a soccer medal, and the first non-European team to do so for 40 years.

1968 MEDALS (SUMMER)

	G	S	B
United States	45	28	34
Soviet Union	29	32	30
Japan	11	7	7
Hungary	10	10	12
East Germany (GDR)	9	9	7
France	7	3	5
Czechoslovakia	7	2	4
West Germany (FRG)	5	11	10
Australia	5	7	5
Great Britain	5	5	3

Poland	5	2	11
Romania	4	6	5
Italy	3	4	9
Kenya	3	4	2
Mexico	3	3	3
Yugoslavia	3	3	2
The Netherlands	3	3	1
Bulgaria	2	4	3
Iran	2	1	2
Sweden	2	1	1
Turkey	2	—	—
Denmark	1	4	3
Canada	1	3	1
Finland	1	2	1
Ethiopia	1	1	—
Norway	1	1	—
New Zealand	1	—	2
Tunisia	1	—	1
Pakistan	1	—	—
Venezuela	1	—	—
Cuba	—	4	—
Austria	—	2	2
Switzerland	—	1	4
Mongolia	—	1	3
Brazil	—	1	2
Belgium	—	1	1
Korea	—	1	1
Uganda	—	1	1
Cameroon	—	1	—
Jamaica	—	1	—
Argentina	—	—	2
Greece	—	—	1
India	—	—	1
Taiwan (Taipei)	—	—	1

SAPPORO 1972

XI WINTER GAMES HELD IN SAPPORO, JAPAN,
3–13 FEBRUARY 1972
ATTENDED BY REPRESENTATIVES OF 35 COUNTRIES,
COMPRISING 1006 COMPETITORS, OF WHICH 206
WERE WOMEN.

The Games finally came to Sapporo 32 years after they were first awarded to the city but cancelled due to the Second World War. It was the most populous city, with one million inhabitants, ever to host the Winter Games. Some $555 million was spent on facilities over a five-year period, not least for the enormous number of media personnel who outnumbered competitors by two to one. Arguments between the IOC and sponsored skiers, which had caused problems in 1968, came to a head, and resulted in Austria's star skier, Karl Schranz, being expelled. Although there was a list of 40 competitors apparently under threat of suspension, only he was banned. This led to an initial threat of withdrawal by the Austrian team, but at Schranz's urging this was averted. Another aspect of the amateur/professional debate was highlighted by Canada's refusal to compete in ice hockey due to the state-sponsored players from the Eastern bloc. Their call for 'open' Olympic ice hockey was ignored.

The Games were formally opened by Emperor Hirohito. The flame was delivered by Hideki Takada a speed skater, and another, Keichi Suzuki, took the oath. Teams from Taiwan and the Philippines competed for the first time. First ever Winter gold medals were won by Poland (ski jumping), Spain (slalom) and the host country (ski jumping). In the latter event, on the 70m-hill, Japan had a unique grand slam of all three medals. To win his title Spanish skier Francisco Fernandez-Ochoa beat the Italian cousins Gustav and Roland Thöni. The women's slalom was won by Barbara Cochran (USA) by the smallest margin, 0.02sec, ever in an Olympic Alpine event. Her sister Marilyn and brother Bob were also in the American team.

Galina Kulakova (URS) won three gold medals in Nordic skiing; Ard Schenk of Holland in the speed skating matched this total. The Dutchman might have achieved more but he fell in the 500m event and finished 34th out of 37 competitors. East Germany (GDR) returned to total domination of the luge competitions. The women's event was won by Anna-Maria Müller, one of the three female participants who had been disqualified for heating their runners at the previous Games. Austria's Trixi Schuba took the women's figure skating title despite a comparatively poor (seventh placed) free skating segment – her compulsory figures were excellent and at the time the two segments scored on a 50–50 basis. Soon after the Games this method was changed in favour of free skating ability. An 'affaire de coeur' involving Alexei Ulanov (URS), who with Irina Rodnina won the skating pairs, and Ludmila Smirnova, his teammate who placed second with her partner Andrei Suraikin, titillated the skating world. Later Ulanov and Smirnova married and competed internationally as partners, but never with the success they had attained with their original partners.

The oldest gold medallist was Jean Wicki (SUI) in the four-man bob aged 38 years 239 days. The youngest was Anne Henning (USA) who won the 500m speed skating title aged 16 years 157 days. The oldest female winner was Christina Baas-Kaiser (NED) with her 3000-m speed skating victory at 33 years 268 days, and the youngest male champion was Wojciech Fortuna (POL) who won the 90-m ski jump aged 19 years 189 days. The youngest medallist was skater Manuela Gross (GDR), who achieved bronze in the pairs aged 15 years 10 days. Overall, medals were won by a record 17 countries, 14 of them gaining a gold.

1972 MEDALS (WINTER)

	G	S	B
Soviet Union	8	5	3
East Germany (GDR)	4	3	7
Switzerland	4	3	3
The Netherlands	4	3	2
United States	3	2	3
West Germany (FRG)	3	1	1
Norway	2	5	5
Italy	2	2	1
Austria	1	2	2
Sweden	1	1	2
Japan	1	1	1
Czechoslovakia	1	—	2
Poland	1	—	—
Spain	1	—	—
Finland	—	4	1
France	—	1	2
Canada	—	1	—

MUNICH 1972

XX OLYMPIC GAMES HELD IN MUNICH, GERMANY, 26 AUGUST–10 SEPTEMBER 1972
ATTENDED BY REPRESENTATIVES OF 121 COUNTRIES, COMPRISING 7123 COMPETITORS, OF WHICH 1058 WERE WOMEN.

Awarded the Games in 1966, Munich built a magnificent complex on the rubble of Second World War bombing. Total costs were estimated at $650 million. Just prior to the opening day the IOC expelled Rhodesia under intense pressure from African nations. A number of new electronic devices were used in the conduct of the Games, including a triangulation device to measure distances in the athletics throwing events. Archery and men's handball returned to the Olympic programme, and there were additions to other sports, making a total of 195 gold medals available – and the Soviet Union took over a quarter of them. It became the most widely covered sports occasion in history with over 4000 representatives of the world's media on hand. When the German President Gustav Heinemann opened the Games in a colourful ceremony there was a television audience estimated at an all-time live viewing record of 1000 million. The oath was taken by athlete Heidi Schüller, the first woman ever to do so. The record number of countries taking part included first timers Albania, Dahomey (later Benin), Lesotho, Malawi, Upper Volta (later Burkina Faso), Somalia, Swaziland, Togo and North Korea (South Korea sent a separate team).

The first week was dominated by swimmer Mark Spitz (USA) who smashed all records for a single Games by winning seven gold medals, four individual and three relays – there were world records in each of his events. With his wins from Mexico City he had a total of nine golds, one silver and a bronze. His female equivalent, Shane Gould (AUS) won three golds, a silver and a bronze, swimming in 12 races, itself a record for a female swimmer in the Games. The closest win in Olympic history came in the men's 400m medley when Gunnar Larsson (SWE) was given the decision over Tim McKee (USA) by two thousandths of a second. This led to a change in the rules so that, in future, times and places would be decided in hundredths. Valeri Borzov (URS) became the first European to win a men's sprint double on the track. In 1994 he became the IOC member for Ukraine. Ulrike Meyfarth (FRG) equalled the world high jump record to win the gold medal aged 16 years 123 days, the youngest ever individual athletics event champion. In hockey, for the first time since 1920, a team from outside the Indian sub-continent, Germany, won the title. However, the outstanding attraction of the first few days was gymnast Olga Korbut (URS) whose gamine qualities stole the show from her more illustrious colleague, Ludmilla Tourischeva (who later married sprint champion Borzov). Virtually overnight, with blanket media coverage, Korbut became a 'superstar', although she only finished seventh in the all-around competition.

On the morning of 5 September all the euphoria evaporated when a band of eight Palestinian terrorists broke into the Israeli team headquarters at 31 Connollystrasse in the Olympic village. Two Israelis were killed immediately, and nine others held hostage, as German police and the world's press surrounded the area. After lengthy negotiations the terrorists and their hostages were allowed to go to the airport, where an abortive rescue attempt resulted in the murder of all nine Israelis and the death of some of their captors. The following morning the Games were suspended for a memorial service in a packed stadium, but with the agreement of most of the parties involved, including the Israelis, competitions were resumed later in the day. The overall feeling seemed to be that the Games should go on, although some individuals, notably from The Netherlands, Norway and the Philippines decided to withdraw. The Israeli team returned home immediately.

The Games continued with the United States suffering an unusual number of misfortunes and reverses. Two prospective medallists had missed the 100m second round heats due to a misreading, by their coach, of the starting time. The world 1500m record holder, Jim Ryun, did not get seeded as he should have done, because his entry performance, a fast mile time, was mistakenly interpreted by the computerised seeding system as a slow 1500m time. Then, to add to his misfortunes, he fell in his heat and was eliminated. A pre-Games banning of the poles used by the American vaulters probably ended a 13-Games winning streak. Their gold and silver medallists in the 400m were banned from further competition for a 'Black Power' protest which meant that the United States, the favourites, could not field a 4 x 400m relay team. Since 1920 the American teams had always won a medal. In swimming, Rick DeMont, won the 400m freestyle but was disqualified after a drugs test proved positive. If the US team officials had notified the IOC beforehand that he had to take a certain drug, containing the prohibited substance, to alleviate an asthma condition, he would have retained his title. Then to cap it all the American basketball team were controversially defeated by the Soviet Union – ending a remarkable 63 consecutive victories in the Games since 1936. Another incident, with a happier conclusion, occurred when the 800m champion, Dave Wottle, in his excitement at the victory ceremony forgot to remove his lucky cap during the American national anthem. He was very embarrassed and proffered apologies to everyone who would listen.

On the track Kipchoge Keino (KEN) added the 3000m steeplechase title to the 1500m that he had won four years earlier. This made him the first runner since James Lightbody (USA) in 1904 to win Olympic titles at both distances. Lasse Virén (FIN) won the 5000m/10,000m double, setting a world record in the latter, despite falling over early in the race, and America's Frank Shorter won the marathon in the city of his birth. Romanian discus thrower Lia Manoliu competed in her record sixth Games (placing ninth with a performance superior to that which won her the gold medal in Mexico City). In the women's pentathlon, silver medallist Heide Rosendahl (FRG), theoretically held the Olympic and world records for the event for 1.12sec, the difference between her winning time in the last discipline, the 200m, and that of the eventual overall champion Mary Peters (GBR).

By winning the five-sport modern pentathlon individual title Hungary's András Balczó brought his total medal haul since 1960 to an event record of three golds and two silvers. For the second consecutive Games the three medallists in skeet shooting all achieved the same score, the tie being broken by shooting another 25-bird round. Double cycling gold medallist from 1968, Daniel Morelon (FRA), added a third by retaining the sprint title, and Aleksandr Medved (URS) won his third wrestling title in a row (and his tenth world championship) after a disputed decision over the giant American Chris Taylor. Taylor, reportedly weighing 182kg (401lb) or more, was the heaviest known man to have competed in the Olympic Games. Among serious doping disqualifications at these Games were those of Bakhaavaa Buidaa who had won a wrestling silver medal for Mongolia, Jaime Huelamo (ESP) the bronze medallist in the cycling road race, and the Dutch four who had gained third place in the cycling team race.

The oldest gold medallist at Munich was Hans Günter Winkler (FRG) aged 46 years 49 days in the show-jumping team, and the youngest Deana Deardurff (USA) aged 15 years 118 days in the swimming medley relay. The oldest female champion was Liselott Linsenhoff (FRG) in the dressage at 45 years 13 days, and she was also the first woman to win an individual equestrian event. In that competition Britain's Lorna Johnstone became the oldest ever female competitor in the Olympics when she reached the last 12, five days past her 70th birthday. A bronze medallist in this event was Maud Van Rosen (SWE), the oldest female medallist at these Games, aged 46 years 258 days. The youngest male gold medallist at Munich was Uwe Benter (FRG), cox of the winning fours at 16 years 276 days, although it should be noted that the unfortunate Rick DeMont was 143 days younger. The youngest medallist was swimmer Kornelia Ender (GDR) at 13 years 308 days.

The tallest competitor at the Games, and the tallest medallist ever in the Olympics, was basketball player Tom Burleson (USA), at 2.23m (7ft 4in) tall. One of the runners bringing the Olympic flame to Munich in the torch relay, was Edgar Fried, a former Secretary-General of the Austrian Olympic Committee (AOC), who had been in the original torch relay in 1936, and was the only one to repeat that the experience in 1972, in his 78th year. At the end of the XX Games a record 48 countries had won at least one medal.

1972 MEDALS (SUMMER)

	G	S	B
Soviet Union	50	27	22
United States	33	31	30
East Germany (GDR)	20	23	23
West Germany (FRG)	13	11	16
Japan	13	8	8
Australia	8	7	2
Poland	7	5	9
Hungary	6	13	16
Bulgaria	6	10	5
Italy	5	3	10
Sweden	4	6	6

Great Britain	4	5	9
Romania	3	6	7
Cuba	3	1	4
Finland	3	1	4
The Netherlands	3	1	1
France	2	4	7
Czechoslovakia	2	4	2
Kenya	2	3	4
Yugoslavia	2	1	2
Norway	2	1	1
North Korea (PRK)	1	1	3
New Zealand	1	1	1
Uganda	1	1	—
Denmark	1	—	—
Switzerland	—	3	—
Canada	—	2	3
Iran	—	2	1
Belgium	—	2	—
Greece	—	2	—
Austria	—	1	2
Colombia	—	1	2
Argentina	—	1	—
Korea	—	1	—
Lebanon	—	1	—
Mexico	—	1	—
Mongolia	—	1	—
Pakistan	—	1	—
Tunisia	—	1	—
Turkey	—	1	—
Brazil	—	—	2
Ethiopia	—	—	2
Ghana	—	—	1
India	—	—	1
Jamaica	—	—	1
Niger Republic	—	—	1
Nigeria	—	—	1
Spain	—	—	1

INNSBRUCK 1976

XII WINTER GAMES HELD IN INNSBRUCK,
SWITZERLAND, 4–15 FEBRUARY 1976
ATTENDED BY REPRESENTATIVES OF 37 COUNTRIES,
COMPRISING 1123 COMPETITORS, OF WHICH 231
WERE WOMEN.

These Games were originally awarded to Denver,
Colorado, in 1970, but two years later a State referendum
decided against providing the necessary finance. So in
February 1973 Innsbruck became the first centre to be
awarded the Winter Games for a second time. Most
facilities were still available from 1964, and 'only' $44
million was required to refurbish and update. Austrian
President, Dr Rudolf Kirchschläger, opened the Games
and, uniquely, two Olympic flames were lit, one by Christl
Haas, 1964 gold medal skier, and the other by Josef
Feistmantl, 1964 gold medal luger. Werner Delle-Karth, a
bobsledder, took the oath. A total of 1.5 million spectators
watched the 37-event schedule. There were also 600
million television viewers around the world. Unfortunately
an influenza outbreak affected some of the competitors.
Two of the smallest States in the world, Andorra and San
Marino, made their Winter Games debuts.

The outstanding competitor was Rosi Mittermaier (FRG)
who, by winning the downhill and slalom races, and
taking second place in the giant slalom, set up the best
series of performances ever by a female Alpine skier. She
failed by a mere 0.13sec, in the giant slalom, to match the
male record of three golds held by Anton Sailer and Jean-
Claude Killy. In taking the men's downhill on the
Patscherkofel course, Austria's Franz Klammer achieved
the then highest speed recorded in an Olympic downhill
race, 102.828km/h (63.894mph). In Nordic skiing Galina
Kulakova (URS) was disqualified from third place in the
5000m event when a banned drug was found present in a
nasal spray she was using to combat influenza, but she
was allowed to compete in other events and won a gold
and another bronze. Her teammate Raisa Smetanina won
two golds and a silver to become the most successful
Nordic skier. Particular attention, and some ridicule, was
given to Bill Koch (USA) who used his newly developed
'skating' style of skiing. Rather more attention, and less
ridicule, came when he won a silver medal in the 30km
race, the only Nordic skiing medal ever won by an
American. However, the greatest tally of medals at these
Games was two gold and two bronzes by Tatyana Averina
(URS) in speed skating. Preventing a clean sweep of
those titles by the Soviet women was Sheila Young (USA)
who took the 500m title, and later in the year won her
second world cycling championship.

In figure skating, the 'jilted' Irina Rodnina (URS)
successfully defended her pairs skating title, but this time
with a different partner, her new husband Aleksandr
Zaitsev (see Sapporo 1972). The American pair was only
fifth but Tai Babilonia became the first black competitor
in the Winter Games. The men's champion John Curry
(GBR) brought balletic art to his event, just as the
Protopopovs had to the pairs in 1964 and 1968. His
Italian/American coach, Carlo Fassi, became the first to
train both individual champions at a single Games when
Dorothy Hamill (USA) won the women's title. In the new
ice dancing event Soviet couples were placed first, second
and fourth. All five luge and bobsleigh events were won
by East German competitors.

The oldest gold medallist was Meinhard Nehmer
(GDR) in the two-man bob aged 35 years 25 days, and
the youngest was skater Hamill aged 19 years 201 days.
The youngest male gold medallist was Boris Aleksandrov
(URS) in the champion ice hockey team aged 20 years
93 days, while the oldest female champion was Galina
Kulakova (see above) in the Nordic relay aged 33 years
289 days. Toni Innauer (AUT) won silver in ski jumping
aged 17 years 320 days, while the oldest medallist was
Marjatta Kajosmaa (FIN) with silver in the Nordic relay,
nine days after her 38th birthday. The oldest competitor
at these Games was 46-year-old Carl Erik Eriksson
(SWE) in the bob events, while the youngest was figure
skater Yelena Voderzova (URS), some three months away
from her 13th birthday.

1976 MEDALS (WINTER)

	G	S	B
Soviet Union	13	6	8
East Germany (GDR)	7	5	7
United States	3	3	4
Norway	3	3	1

West Germany (FRG)	2	5	3
Finland	2	4	1
Austria	2	2	2
Switzerland	1	3	1
The Netherlands	1	2	3
Italy	1	2	1
Canada	1	1	1
Great Britain	1	—	—
Czechoslovakia	—	1	—
Liechtenstein	—	—	2
Sweden	—	—	2
France	—	—	1

MONTREAL 1976

XXI OLYMPIC GAMES HELD IN MONTREAL, CANADA,
17 JULY– 1 AUGUST 1976
ATTENDED BY REPRESENTATIVES OF 92 COUNTRIES,
COMPRISING 6028 COMPETITORS, OF WHICH 1247
WERE WOMEN.

When the Games were initially awarded to Montreal, mainly due to the efforts of Mayor Jean Drapeau, it was estimated that they would cost $310 million. Because of planning errors, strikes, slowdowns, and, it has been suggested, widespread corruption, the final bill amounted to $1400 million – the stadium alone cost $485 million, and the projected 160m-high tower and suspended roof were never completed. In 1994 it was stated that the total debt remaining to the citizens of Quebec was $304 million. After the Munich disaster security arrangements involving 16,000 police and soldiers cost $100 million. Six months before it seemed that the main facilities would not be finished in time, but by the official opening pronounced by Queen Elizabeth II, all that was necessary was ready. The expected record number of entries was well down due to a last minute boycott by twenty third world, mainly African, nations, protesting against the inclusion of New Zealand, whose rugby union team had visited South Africa. Also withdrawing was Taiwan because Canada refused to recognise its team under the title of Republic of China, a situation that owed much, it was suggested, to Canada's grain-trading relations with Mainland China. The withdrawals, mostly only two days prior to the start of competitions, caused some problems with seeding arrangements, and particularly affected the quality of boxing and some running events.

Efforts had been made by the IOC to prune the programme, and to this end the 50km walk, tandem cycling, slalom canoeing, the free rifle and three swimming events had been eliminated. However, with the addition of women's basketball and handball, four canoeing races and seven rowing events, of which six were for women, the total number of gold medals available was now 198 – three more than at Munich. The torch was brought into the stadium by two 15-year-olds, a girl and a boy; Sandra Henderson of English descent and Stéphane Prefontaine of French stock, each with a hand on the torch, signifying Canada's joint heritage. In true storybook fashion the pair were married some years later.

The star of the Munich Games, gymnast Olga Korbut, was at Montreal, but she was overshadowed by a 14-year-old Romanian, Nadia Comaneci, who scored the first ever maximum 10.00 marks achieved at the Olympics on the first day, and ended the Games with a total of seven maximums, having drawn a world record crowd for gymnastics of 18,000 to the finals of the women's events. Nelli Kim (URS) also scored two maximums. The men's individual champion, Nikolai Andrianov (URS) won the most medals at Montreal with four golds, two silvers and a bronze. In the swimming pool, Kornelia Ender (GDR) and John Naber (USA) each won four golds and a silver, with Ender and her teammates only failing to win two of the 13 women's swimming titles. The American men did even better, only losing one of their 13 events – David Wilkie won Britain's first men's swimming gold since 1908. Incidentally, Ender later married her teammate, backstroke specialist Roland Matthes, giving them a family total of eight gold, six silver and two bronze medals from three Games. In highboard diving the Austrian-born Italian, Klaus Dibiasi, competing in his fourth Games, became the first diver to gain three consecutive gold medals. A member of the Hungarian water polo team, which won their country's record sixth victory in the sport, was István Szivós, whose father had been in the winning 1952 and 1956 teams.

In the main stadium Lasse Virén, the latest 'Flying Finn', completed his double 'double' by successfully defending his 5000m and 10,000m titles. He attempted to emulate Zátopek's 1952 feat, but finished fifth in the marathon. The Cuban Alberto Juantorena, nicknamed El Caballo – 'The Horse' – won a rare 400m/800m double (only America's Paul Pilgrim had previously achieved it in the 1906 Games). Irena Szewinska (POL), now aged 30, won the 400m in her fourth games, to equal the record total of seven medals in athletics. The winner of the men's javelin with a new world record, Miklós Németh (HUN), was the son of the 1948 hammer winner. They remain the only father and son in track and field to win gold medals.

Three sets of brothers did very well in the Montreal rowing events. Frank and Alf Hansen (NOR) won the double sculls, while the Landvoigt twins, Jörg and Bernd (GDR) took the coxless pairs. Another set of East German twins, Walter and Ullrich Diessner, were in the silver medal coxed four crew. Elsewhere the Flying Dutchman class yachting was won by another set of brothers, Jörg and Eckart Diesch (FRG). In women's fencing Elena Novikova-Belova (URS) won her record fourth gold medal in the team contest, while Hungary's Ildikó Ságiné-Retjö set an all-medal record of seven, comprising two golds, three silvers and two bronzes collected at five Games. America's Margaret Murdock became the first woman to win a shooting medal, and was unlucky not to win the gold. Initially she was declared the winner of the small-bore rifle (three positions) event, but an error was discovered which gave her a tie with her teammate, Lanny Bassham. A closer examination of targets then relegated her down a place. Although unplaced, show jumpers Raimondo and Piero D'Inzeo (ITA), set an unprecedented record by competing in their eighth Games 1948–76. Alwin Schockemöhle (FRG) became only the third rider in Games history to win the jumping title without any faults.

The new Olympic sport of women's basketball produced the tallest known woman ever to compete in the Games. She was Iuliana Semenova (URS), who was unofficially 2.18m (7ft 2in) tall (*see* Tallest) and weighed 129kg (284lb). Her team won the title, and she is one of tallest, including men, to win an Olympic gold medal. In weightlifting two Bulgarians and a Pole, all medallists, were later disqualified for failing drugs tests. A far greater scandal occurred in the modern pentathlon when one of the favourites, Boris Onischenko (URS), was discovered to have tampered with his épée in the fencing segment of the competition. His disqualification eliminated the Soviet team and the team gold medal went to Great Britain. The revenge basketball match between the United States and the Soviet Union never materialised as the Soviets were beaten by Yugoslavia in the semifinals. Thus the United States regained the title, making their Olympic match record – played 70, won 69.

The oldest gold medallist at Montreal was Harry Boldt (FRG) in the winning dressage team aged 46 years 157 days. The youngest was gymnast Nadia Comaneci who won her first gold medal aged 14 years 252 days. The youngest male champion/medallist was Brian Goodell (USA) aged 17 years 109 days when he won the 1500-m freestyle, while the oldest female gold medallist was Ivanka Khristova (BUL) in the shot aged 34 years 255 days. The youngest female medallist was Canadian swimmer, Robin Corsiglia, in the medley relay aged 13 years 341 days. The oldest medallist was Australian three-day eventer Bill Roycroft aged 61 years 131 days. One of the youngest competitors ever in the Olympics was Spanish swimmer Antonia Real aged 12 years 310 days. In 1904 a Montreal policeman, Etienne Desmarteau, had won Canada's first Olympic gold medal. At this Games Canada gained the unhappy distinction of being the only host country of a Summer Olympics not to win a single gold medal.

1976 MEDALS (SUMMER)

	G	S	B
Soviet Union	49	41	35
East Germany (GDR)	40	25	25
United States	34	35	25
West Germany (FRG)	10	12	17
Japan	9	6	10
Poland	7	6	13
Bulgaria	6	9	7
Cuba	6	4	3
Romania	4	9	14
Hungary	4	5	13
Finland	4	2	—
Sweden	4	1	—
Great Britain	3	5	5
Italy	2	7	4
France	2	3	4
Yugoslavia	2	3	3
Czechoslovakia	2	2	4
New Zealand	2	1	1
Korea	1	1	4
Switzerland	1	1	2
Jamaica	1	1	—
North Korea (PRK)	1	1	—
Norway	1	1	—
Denmark	1	—	2
Mexico	1	—	1
Trinidad	1	—	—
Canada	—	5	6
Belgium	—	3	3
The Netherlands	—	2	3
Portugal	—	2	—
Spain	—	2	—
Australia	—	1	4
Iran	—	1	1
Mongolia	—	1	—
Venezuela	—	1	—
Brazil	—	—	2
Austria	—	—	1
Bermuda	—	—	1
Pakistan	—	—	1
Puerto Rico	—	—	1
Thailand	—	—	1

LAKE PLACID 1980

XII WINTER GAMES HELD IN LAKE PLACID, USA, 13–24 FEBRUARY 1980
ATTENDED BY REPRESENTATIVES OF 37 COUNTRIES, COMPRISING 1072 COMPETITORS, OF WHICH 233 WERE WOMEN.

Lake Placid had been applying for the Games unsuccessfully since 1962 when they were finally rewarded in 1974. Most of the facilities used in 1932 had to be rebuilt, and new ones constructed, so that the budget for these Games was nearly 80 times the $1.1 million spent in 1932. Some complaints were voiced about the 'village', a building later to be used as a penal institution, but as a report noted 'at least security would not be a problem'. Once the Games were underway the accommodation was found to be quite suitable and acceptable. One pre-Games worry that turned into a major problem was transport for the spectators and Press. At times it was virtually impossible to reach and/or return from venues. The Vice-President of the United States, Walter Mondale undertook the official opening. The last relay runner was Dr Charles Morgan Kerr, a psychiatrist, and the oath was taken, with outstanding foresight, by speed skater Eric Heiden. The People's Republic of China and Cyprus made their debuts in the Winter Games.

The aforementioned Eric Heiden (USA) stole all the headlines by gaining an unprecedented sweep of all five speed skating gold medals, all in Olympic record times. His sister, Beth, also won a bronze in the women's events. Her teammate Leah Poulos-Mueller won two silver medals but could not match her husband Peter's gold-medal performance of 1976. Peter Mueller, who coached Bonnie Blair (USA), Dan Jansen (USA) and Marianne Timmer (NED) to their gold medals, subsequently married the latter. In Nordic skiing Nikolai Simyatov (URS) won a unique three golds in one Games, while teammate Galina Kulakova, now over 37, raised her record total of medals over four Games to eight. Ulrich Wehling (GDR) won his third consecutive gold medal in the Nordic combination, and Aleksandr Tikhonov (URS) won a fourth consecutive gold in the biathlon relay. The closest ever result in Olympic Nordic skiing came in the men's 15km cross-country event when Thomas Wassberg (SWE) beat Juha Mieto (FIN) by 0.01sec. Eight years previously the unlucky Finn had lost a bronze by only 0.06sec. However, he did win a gold in the 1976 relay.

Slalom specialist Ingemar Stenmark (SWE) won both of his races to became the most successful male Alpine skier at these Games, but Hanni Wenzel from tiny Liechtenstein won both women's slaloms and the silver medal in the downhill. Her brother Andreas added a silver to put their country in sixth place on the unofficial medal table. (Another sister Petra was also in the team of seven). In winning the 90m ski jump Jouko Törmänen (FIN) made the longest jump attained to that time in Olympic competition when he cleared 117m (383ft). In the 70m event there was an unfortunate incident when after nine competitors had taken their jumps, the judges ruled that conditions were too dangerous. The start point was moved lower down, to reduce take-off speed, and the competition begun again. Irina Rodnina (URS) equalled the record of three gold medals by a figure skater when she and her husband, Aleksandr Zaitsev, retained the pairs title. By successfully defending the men's singles for Great Britain Robin Cousins won his country's only medal of these Games. The bobsledding was a virtual replay of the 1976 rivalry between the Swiss and East German teams. In the American 12th-placed four-man bob was Willie Davenport, who had competed in the Summer Games from 1964 to 1976 and had won the 110m hurdles in 1968. By far the most popular win was that of the United States ice hockey team over the Soviet Union (their first defeat since 1964) on the way to the final. The celebrations that followed were described on American TV as the biggest since the end of the Second World War. In the final they then beat Finland.

The oldest gold medallist was Meinhard Nehmer (GDR) in the four-man bob aged 39 years 42 days, and the youngest was his teammate Karin Enke who won the 500-m speed skating title aged 18 years 240 days. The youngest male winner was Mike Ramsey of the victorious American ice hockey team aged 19 years 83 days. The oldest female champion was Irina Rodnina (*see* above) aged 30 years 159 days. Special mention must be made of Marina Tcherkasova (URS), a silver medallist in pair skating only 93 days past her 15th birthday.

1980 MEDALS (WINTER)

	G	S	B
Soviet Union	10	6	6
East Germany (GDR)	9	7	7
United States	6	4	2
Austria	3	2	2
Sweden	3	—	1
Liechtenstein	2	2	—
Finland	1	5	3
Norway	1	3	6
The Netherlands	1	2	1
Switzerland	1	1	3
Great Britain	1	—	—
West Germany (FRG)	—	2	3
Italy	—	2	—
Canada	—	1	1
Hungary	—	1	—
Japan	—	1	—
Bulgaria	—	—	1
Czechoslovakia	—	—	1
France	—	—	1

MOSCOW 1980

XXII OLYMPIC GAMES HELD IN MOSCOW, SOVIET UNION, 19 JULY–1 AUGUST 1980
ATTENDED BY REPRESENTATIVES OF 80 COUNTRIES, COMPRISING 5217 COMPETITORS, OF WHICH 1124 WERE WOMEN.

There had been only a little dissent when the IOC awarded these Games to Moscow in 1974. Tsarist Russia had competed in 1900 and from 1906 to 1912. Athletes from Lithuania, Estonia and Latvia, which had been provinces of Russia prior to 1918 and were taken over by the Soviet Union in 1940, had competed independently between 1920 and 1936. The Soviet Union had entered the Olympics in force in 1952, and was now the second highest medal scorer of all time – a remarkable achievement. However, in December 1979 the Soviet Union invaded Afghanistan, and much of the non-Communist world, led by the United States, tried to impose a boycott on the Games – although not, it should be noted, on trade or other economic activity. Not all countries supported the boycott, although sporting organisations within those countries sometimes did. Because a number of countries that were unlikely to go to Moscow anyway for financial reasons found it politic to 'jump on the bandwagon', it is difficult to compile a complete list of boycotting nations. The most reliable estimate is 45–50, of which the most important in sporting terms were the United States, West Germany (FRG) and Japan. When Leonid Brezhnev, President of the Soviet Union, officially opened the Games there were eight first-time entries, not including Zimbabwe which had previously competed as Rhodesia.

Facilities in Moscow were excellent, including the 103,000-capacity Lenin stadium, and large crowds attended most events. It must be stated that although, in the main, the Soviet spectators were very knowledgeable, they left something to be desired in their treatment of foreign competitors, particularly those from other Eastern bloc countries. New competitions, such as women's hockey, two extra judo classes, one extra weightlifting class, and various re-introduced events, brought the total of gold medals available to a record 203 (barring ties). The heroine of Montreal, Nadia Comaneci (ROM), returned but was no longer the force she had been, and for the first time for many years the star of gymnastics was a male, Aleksandr Dityatin (URS). He won the greatest number of medals, eight, ever won by a competitor at any sport at one Games, and was also awarded a full 10.00 in the horse vault, the first maximum ever to a male gymnast in the Olympics. His teammate, Nikolai Andrianov, brought his total of medals to a male record of 15, in three Games, a total that has only ever been exceeded by another Soviet gymnast, Larissa Latynina.

East African athletes dominated the distance runs, led by Miruts Yifter (ETH) with a 5000m/10,000m double. The 100m race was the closest for 28 years with Great Britain's Allan Wells given the verdict over Silvio Leonard of Cuba. Two other Britons each won the 'wrong' event, Steve Ovett and Sebastian Coe taking the 800m and 1500m respectively. Waldemar Cierpinski (GDR) became only the second man to successfully defend the marathon title, although he was over a minute slower than in 1976. In the triple jump Viktor Saneyev (URS) ended his remarkable career with a silver to add to his three gold medals since 1968. By repeating her Montreal gold medals in the 200m and relay Barbel Wöckel (GDR) equalled the female track and field record of four. In that relay Ludmila Maslakova a member of the silver-medal Soviet team was running in her fourth consecutive relay final since 1968. Although she only won the pentathlon silver medal, Olga Rukavishnikova (URS) theoretically held the world record, albeit for only 0.4sec, as she finished first in the last event of 800m. That gave her the shortest reign of any world-record holder ever.

Once more the East German women dominated the swimming events, winning 26 of the available 35 medals. Highest medal scorers were Caren Metschuck with three golds and a silver, and Ines Diers with two golds, two silvers and a bronze. More remarkably their teammate Rica Reinisch won three gold medals all in world-record times. In the inaugural women's hockey competition Zimbabwe gained a gold medal in its debut at the Games, while India was back to its former winning ways by taking a record eighth title in the men's competition. In the sailing events, held at Tallinn, the Finn-class dinghy event was won, appropriately enough, by the Finn Esko Rechardt.

Vladimir Parfenovich (URS) was the first canoeist to win three gold medals at the same Games, and the Cuban heavyweight, Teofilo Stevenson, became the only boxer to win the same event in three Games. Note that the great Hungarian László Papp had won three golds at two different weights. In rowing, the Landvoigt twins Jörg and Bernd (GDR), retained their coxless pairs title by beating the Soviet Pimenov twins Yuri and Nikolai. The other East German twins, Ullrich and Walter Diessner, went one better than they had done four years previously and won gold medals in the coxed fours. Yet another pair of twins won titles in wrestling when Anatoli and Sergei Beloglasov (URS) won the 52kg and 57kg freestyle events respectively.

The oldest gold medallist at Moscow, or rather Tallinn, was Valentin Mankin (URS) in the Star sailing, in his fourth Games, aged 41 years 346 days, while the youngest champion at these Games was swimmer Rica Reinisch (GDR) winning the first of her three golds aged 15 years 105 days. The oldest female winner was Anthea Stewart (ZIM) at 35 years 253 days in the hockey, while the youngest male gold medallist was the Hungarian backstroker Sándor Wladár, seven days over his 17th birthday. The youngest medallist was Zirvard Emirzyan (URS) with a silver in women's diving aged 14 years 52 days, while the oldest medallist was Petre Rosca (ROM) in the dressage at 57 years 283 days. The youngest competitor of all was Polish gymnast Anita Jokiel aged 13 years 232 days. In the same competition was Myong Hui Choe of North Korea, the smallest competitor of all at 1.35m (4ft 5in) tall and weighing 25kg (55lb). At the other end of the scale was Soviet basketball player Vladimir Tkachenko, standing 2.20m (7ft 2½in) tall, and

Greco-Roman wrestler Roman Codreanu (ROM) who weighed 170kg (374lb). Despite the undeniable losses and gaps caused by the boycott, the standard of performances was very high throughout the Games.

1980 MEDALS (SUMMER)

	G	S	B
Soviet Union	80	69	46
East Germany (GDR)	47	37	42
Bulgaria	8	16	17
Cuba	8	7	5
Italy	8	3	4
Hungary	7	10	15
Romania	6	6	13
France	6	5	3
Great Britain	5	7	9
Poland	3	14	15
Sweden	3	3	6
Finland	3	1	4
Czechoslovakia	2	3	9
Yugoslavia	2	3	4
Australia	2	2	5
Denmark	2	1	2
Brazil	2	—	2
Ethiopia	2	—	2
Switzerland	2	—	—
Spain	1	3	2
Austria	1	2	1
Greece	1	—	2
Belgium	1	—	—
India	1	—	—
Zimbabwe	1	—	—
North Korea (PRK)	—	3	2
Mongolia	—	2	2
Tanzania	—	2	—
Mexico	—	1	3
The Netherlands	—	1	2
Ireland	—	1	1
Uganda	—	1	—
Venezuela	—	1	—
Jamaica	—	—	3
Guyana	—	—	1
Lebanon	—	—	1

SARAJEVO 1984

XIV WINTER GAMES HELD IN SARAJEVO, YUGOSLAVIA, 8–19 FEBRUARY 1984
ATTENDED BY REPRESENTATIVES OF 49 COUNTRIES, COMPRISING 1274 COMPETITORS, OF WHICH 274 WERE WOMEN.

The first Winter Games to be held in Eastern Europe was awarded to Sarajevo in 1978. With a population of 500,000 it was the second largest city to host the Winter Games, and was previously only famous as the site of the assassination of Archduke Ferdinand on 28 June 1914 – an act that historians argue contributed to the start of the First World War. There were a record 49 countries attending, including debuts by the British Virgin Islands, Egypt, Costa Rica, Puerto Rico and perhaps most unlikely, Senegal. The Games were opened by Mika Spiljak, Chairman of the Presidium of the Socialist Federal Republic of Yugoslavia. The flame was lit by Sandra Dubravcic, after running up 94 steps in the Kosovo Stadium. She later placed tenth in the women's figure skating. Skier Bojan Krizaj, who later placed seventh in the slalom, took the oath. Actually the competitions had started the day before, with preliminary rounds of the ice hockey tournament. Prior to the Games much had been made of the wolf mascot, Vucko, being depicted with its claws crossed – as though hoping for the best. In fact, although the weather caused various problems, the enthusiasm of the organisers and the local populace overcame most difficulties. Even the transport system worked. One of the few things that did cause hackles to rise was outside the control of the host city. This was the highly questionable, or at the least confusing, judging of the figure skating – a problem not unique to Sarajevo in recent years. One *cause celebre* just prior to the Games was the banning, as professionals, of the two defending champions in the men's and women's slalom races, Ingemar Stenmark (SWE) and Hanni Wenzel (LIE). There was only one new event in the programme, a 20km Nordic skiing race for women.

For the first time the East German team won more gold medals than the Soviet Union, although not total medals. However, in the men's luge, in which they had won seven gold, two silver and four bronze medals in the last four Games, they only took a single bronze. The outstanding competitor, unusually in the skiing events, was the female Nordic skier, Marja-Liisa Hämäläinen (FIN), who won all three individual events and a bronze in the relay. However, Britain's Jayne Torvill and Christopher Dean gained the most media attention with their superb ice dancing – their artistic interpretation of Ravel's *Bolero* was awarded an unprecedented nine perfect sixes, with another three for technical merit. The women's singles winner, Katarina Witt (GDR), was trained by Jutta Müller, who had not only coached her daughter, Gabriele Seyfert, to a silver in 1968, but had also been the driving force behind the 1980 champion, Anett Pötzsch.

Alpine skiers from the United States made a major impact with three titles. Bill Johnson, hardly a retiring personality, proved he was as good as he had been saying he was, to anyone and everyone who would listen, and won the first Olympic downhill title by an American, in a record average speed of 104.532km/h (64.593mph). His teammates, twins Phil and Steve Mahre took the gold and silver medals in the slalom. By winning the women's downhill race Michaela Figini (SUI) became the youngest ever Alpine skiing gold medallist, aged 17 years 314 days, as well as being the youngest champion at Sarajevo. Unusually, in Alpine skiing, only one skier, Perrine Pelen (FRA) won more than one medal, and few begrudged the silver gained by Jure Franko in the giant slalom, the first Winter Games medal ever won by Yugoslavia.

In speed skating Tomas Gustafson (SWE) and Igor Malkov (URS) swapped medals over 5000m and 10,000m, in two of the closest skating races ever in the Games, unique over such distances. The Swede won the shorter race by 0.02sec, and the Soviet won the longer by 0.05sec. The Soviet ice hockey team equalled Canada's record with a sixth gold medal. Just prior to the Games another ice hockey eligibility controversy had arisen with the decision that 'an amateur', for the purposes of a definition

for the Olympic Games, was someone who had not played in the National Hockey League of North America. One other bone of contention had been resolved before competitions began when the revolutionary rocket-shaped Soviet bobs were barred. The Finn Matti Nykänen won the 90m ski jump by a record margin of 18.5 points, but he was to make a far greater impression four years later.

The oldest gold medallist at Sarajevo was the Soviet ice hockey goalminder Vladyslav Tretyak, in his fourth Games, aged 31 years 299 days. The youngest was Michela Figini (*see* above). The youngest male champion was speed skater Igor Malkov (URS) just nine days past his 19th birthday, while the oldest female gold medallist was Marja-Liisa Hämäläinen (*see* above) aged 28 years 161 days. The oldest competitor was Carl-Erik Eriksson (SWE) at 53 years 289 days, competing in his record sixth successive Olympic bobsleigh competition. The youngest was Babette Preussler (GDR) in pair skating aged 15 years 143 days. One of the victorious German pair in the luge, Hans Stanggassinger, had another distinction: he was reportedly the heaviest champion weighing 111kg (244lb).

1984 MEDALS (WINTER)

	G	S	B
East Germany (GDR)	9	9	6
Soviet Union	6	10	9
United States	4	4	—
Finland	4	3	6
Sweden	4	2	2
Norway	3	2	4
Switzerland	2	2	1
Canada	2	1	1
West Germany (FRG)	2	1	1
Italy	2	—	—
Great Britain	1	—	—
Czechoslovakia	—	2	4
France	—	1	2
Japan	—	1	—
Yugoslavia	—	1	—
Liechtenstein	—	—	2
Austria	—	—	1

LOS ANGELES 1984

XXIII OLYMPIC GAMES HELD IN LOS ANGELES, USA, 28 JULY–12 AUGUST 1984
ATTENDED BY REPRESENTATIVES OF 140 COUNTRIES, COMPRISING 6797 COMPETITORS, OF WHICH 1567 WERE WOMEN.

The IOC awarded the Games to Los Angeles (in 1978) only after protracted negotiations about the financial guarantees usually required from a host city. Various innovations to protect the city from a Montreal-like deficit were implemented – not least, widespread sponsorship by private corporations. TV rights alone amounted to $287 million, of which the greater part of this came from the ABC network for the American TV rights. This Games attracted one of the largest TV audiences in history, with some 2500 million people tuning in. The Olympic programme was expanded to 221 events, including an extra 12 for women, while baseball and tennis were demonstration sports. The Memorial Coliseum, main site for the 1932 Games, was fully refurbished and had a seating capacity of 92,607, and many other venues, often famous in their own right, were utilised. There were complaints that some of these venues were too far-flung, but the overall good weather and the enthusiasm, at times overwhelming, of the American crowds offset most problems.

The one, albeit major, disaster suffered by this Games was the last-minute boycott by the Soviet Union, which announced its non-participation on the very day, 8 May 1984, that the Olympic flame arrived in the United States to begin a nationwide torch relay. Within a week or so most of the Soviet bloc had also pulled out – with the notable exception of Romania. Additionally, but not surprisingly, Iran and Libya did not appear. However, of 159 invitations sent out, 140 countries accepted – beating the Munich record. Nevertheless, a number of sports were very seriously affected, although standards were still generally high. In particular, canoeing, fencing, gymnastics, weightlifting, wrestling and women's athletics were diminished, both in numbers and quality.

The Games were formally opened by President Ronald Reagan, the first incumbent to ever do so. The final runner on the torch relay was Gina Hemphill, a granddaughter of the great Olympian Jesse Owens. Interestingly, she had also run the first leg on American soil, jointly with Jim Thorpe's grandson, Bill. Some years after the Games she married Henry Tillman who won the heavyweight boxing title at Los Angeles. In the stadium she handed over the torch to 1960 Olympic decathlon champion Rafer Johnson, who, by means of a gantry, lit the flame on the top of the stadium peristyle. Apparently in rehearsals Johnson had developed a leg injury, and 1976 champion Bruce Jenner, one of the Olympic flag's escorts, stood by in case he had to replace Johnson. The oath was taken somewhat stumblingly, by the 1976 400m hurdles champion Edwin Moses, who went on to win a second gold medal. There followed a three-hour Hollywood-style extravaganza featuring, among other things, marching bands and 85 pianos, which was choreographed by film producer David Wolper.

Smog and traffic congestion did not materialise to anything like the degree predicted, although one unfortunate phenomenon, however, was the display of American chauvinism – especially by the media. Attendances at all sports were quite remarkable, with a final attendance figure of 5.7 million, and a highest single figure, 101,799, for the final of the soccer tournament (France beat Brazil 2–0) in the famed Rose Bowl at Pasadena. One particular feature of these Games was the tremendous outlay made on security – some 7000 personnel and ancillary equipment costing as much as $100 million.

The first gold medal of the Games was won by shooter Xu Haifeng with China's first ever Olympic title. Aided enormously by the absence of Soviet and East German opposition, the United States gained by far the lion's share of the medals. Leading their gold rush was sprinter/jumper Carl Lewis, who exactly duplicated Jesse Owens's feat of 1936, with four gold medals in the 100m, 200m, long jump and relay. Another athlete, Valerie Brisco-Hooks, and five swimmers, all won three golds each. However, the most successful competitors were gymnasts Ecaterina Szabó (ROM) with four golds and a silver, and China's Li Ning with three golds, two silvers and a bronze.

The introduction of consolation finals in swimming, for non-qualifiers to the regular finals, led to the unusual situation of an Olympic record being set in the men's 400m freestyle 'B' final, faster than the gold medallist had attained. The judo open champion Yasuhiro Yamashita (JPN) extended his winning streak to 198, despite being handicapped by a foot injury. A number of families were particularly successful: twins Mark and David Schultz (USA), and Lou and Ed Banach (USA), all won wrestling gold medals; William Buchan (USA) and his son William Jr won sailing titles, but not together; British husband and wife Garry (silver, 4 x 400m) and Kathy Cook (bronze, 400m and 4 x 100m) won medals; Al Joyner (USA) and his sister Jackie won gold (triple jump) and silver (heptathlon) medals respectively; brothers Carmine and Giuseppe Abbagnale (ITA) won the coxed pairs rowing event.

In the dressage event 48-year-old Reiner Klimke (FRG) won two gold medals in his fourth Games over a 20-year period, equalling his countryman Hans-Günter Winkler's equestrian record of five golds and seven medals in total. One of the few negative things at Los Angeles was the disqualification for drugs offences of 12 competitors from weightlifting, wrestling, volleyball and athletics. Probably the most well known of these was Martti Vainio (FIN) who finished second in the 10,000m on the track.

The oldest gold medallist at Los Angeles was William Buchan (USA) in the Star yachting aged 49 years 91 days (*see* above). The youngest was Romanian gymnast Simona Pauca in the team event aged 14 years 317 days, and who won the individual beam title four days later. The youngest male champion was Perica Bukic (YUG) in water polo aged 17 years 264 days, while the oldest female gold medallist was Linda Thom (CAN) winning the women's pistol aged 40 years 212 days. The oldest female medallist was the woman who finished third in that competition, Patricia Dench (AUS) at 52 years 143 days. The oldest male medallist was another shooter Ragnar Skanaker (SWE) aged 50 years 52 days. At the other end of the scale was Belgian coxswain Philippe Cuelenaere, the youngest competitor at Los Angeles, one month short of his 13th birthday.

At the end of the Games – after another closing extravaganza featuring one of the greatest firework displays ever seen – the organisers reported a profit of $215 million, prompting the suggestion that perhaps the pendulum had swung too far the other way since Montreal. The whole thing was a triumphant vindication of the leadership of Peter Ueberroth, President of the Los Angeles Olympic Organising Committee. Coincidentally, Ueberroth was born on the very day, 2 September 1937 that Baron de Coubertin had died. A sour note was added some time later when it was reported that a number of drugs' test samples had been unaccountably lost.

1984 MEDALS (SUMMER)

	G	S	B
United States	83	61	30
Romania	20	16	17
West Germany (FRG)	17	19	23
China	15	8	9
Italy	14	6	12
Canada	10	18	16
Japan	10	8	14
New Zealand	8	1	2
Yugoslavia	7	4	7
Korea	6	6	7
Great Britain	5	11	21
France	5	7	16
The Netherlands	5	2	6
Australia	4	8	12
Finland	4	2	6
Sweden	2	11	6
Mexico	2	3	1
Morocco	2	—	—
Brazil	1	5	2
Spain	1	2	2
Belgium	1	1	2
Austria	1	1	1
Kenya	1	—	2
Portugal	1	—	2
Pakistan	1	—	—
Switzerland	—	4	4
Denmark	—	3	3
Jamaica	—	1	2
Norway	—	1	2
Greece	—	1	1
Nigeria	—	1	1
Puerto Rico	—	1	1
Colombia	—	1	—
Egypt	—	1	—
Ireland	—	1	—
Ivory Coast	—	1	—
Peru	—	1	—
Syria	—	1	—
Thailand	—	1	—
Turkey	—	—	3
Venezuela	—	—	3
Algeria	—	—	2
Cameroon	—	—	1
Dominican Republic	—	—	1
Iceland	—	—	1
Taiwan (Taipei)	—	—	1
Zambia	—	—	1

CALGARY 1988

XV WINTER GAMES HELD IN CALGARY, CANADA,
13–28 FEBRUARY 1988
ATTENDED BY REPRESENTATIVES OF 57 COUNTRIES,
COMPRISING 1423 COMPETITORS, OF WHICH 313
WERE WOMEN.

Having had three unsuccessful bids previously, Calgary was finally awarded these Games in 1981. Most of the venues were close together except for Mount Allan and Kenmore, some 90km away, where the Alpine and Nordic skiing took place. The programme was stretched to 16 days to include three weekends, particularly favourable for television coverage – for which ABC paid $309 million for the North American TV rights, over three times the sum for the 1984 Sarajevo coverage. There were a number of new events: Nordic Combination for teams; Team Ski Jumping; Alpine Combination; Super Giant Slaloms for men and women and a 5000m speed skating event for women. In all there were 46 events, as well as the demonstration sports of curling, short track speed skating and freestyle skiing. Five teams made their Winter Games debuts: Fiji, Guam, Guatemala, Ireland and Jamaica. The official opening was performed on behalf of Her Majesty Queen Elizabeth II, by the Governor-General of Canada Jeanne Sauvé. The torch was brought into the stadium by a couple, speed skater Cathy Priestner and skier Ken Read, and then handed to a 12-year-old female skater, Robyn Perry, who lit the flame. Incidentally, that flame was easily the highest ever, as it was set at the top of the Calgary Tower, which is 191m (616ft) high. Pierre Harvey, a Nordic skier who had also represented Canada at cycling in the 1984 Olympics, took the oath. The facilities in the main were excellent, and the expected local transport problems were few and far between. Accommodation was at a premium with so many teams and competitors, and some officials were based in an establishment that previously had been a 'house of ill-repute'. However, one unforeseen occurrence caused real problems, and that was a dramatic climatic change caused by the 'chinook' wind, which gave spring-like weather, and strong winds, which caused havoc to the timetable. These conditions, which primarily affected the bob, luge and ski jumping events, resulted in some unexpected results. The exposed ski jumps were very dangerous at times, and caused the Nordic Combination event, comprising jumping and cross-country skiing, to be contested in the course of one day.

Nevertheless, there were many excellent performances, although the 'star' of these Games was an unknown British ski jumper. Despite, or more likely because of, being totally inept by world standards Michael 'Eddie the Eagle' Edwards stole the media attention from the great and famous, to the amusement of many and the chagrin of some. Britain's first Olympic entrant ever in this sport, he finished last in both jumps, albeit with a British record of 71m, over 20m behind the rest of the competitors.

The most successful competitors were Yvonne van Gennip (NED) who won three speed skating titles, and Matti Nykänen (FIN), who won all three gold medals open to him. The Finn totally dominated the ski jumping, leaping to 118.5m on the 90m hill; the greatest distance ever achieved in the Games. In Alpine skiing both Vreni Schneider (SUI) and Alberto Tomba (ITA) won the slalom and giant slalom events. Frank-Peter Roetsch (GDR) became the first man to win both individual biathlon races in any single Games, while the Soviet Union won the relay for the sixth consecutive time. The Soviet women hardly made an error in the Nordic skiing taking seven of the nine individual medals as well as the relay. Although not in that relay, 35-year-old Raisa Smetanina gained a silver and a bronze to raise her total from four Games to a record nine medals for the sport.

After the shocking results of Sarajevo the East German team lugers were back winning all three golds, two silvers and a bronze. Steffi Walter (née Martin) was the first luger to retain an individual title, and led her teammates to a clean sweep. Incidentally, one of the British competitors in this sport was Nick Ovett, whose older brother Steve won the 1980 Olympic 800m. The bobsleigh course was likened to sandpaper as the winds had blown so much dirt on the track, and many of the top crews were upset. There was bitter rivalry between the Swiss and East German four-man crews, with officials of both teams checking the legality of each other's sleds. The coach of the Swiss team was 1980 gold medallist Erich Schärer, while the East German coach was Horst Hörnlein, who had won gold in the two-man luge in 1972. After the fourth and final run the Swiss were triumphant by 0.07 of a second, the smallest margin ever in the event. The drama was heightened even further when the rather unlikely crew from Jamaica, who had never been on ice before, crashed badly, but happily no one was seriously hurt. Some years later a movie was made about their efforts. Bogdan Musiol (GDR) with two silver medals raised his total to a record equalling six. Placed 25th (of 41) in the two-man bob was Albert Grimaldi, otherwise known as Prince Albert of Monaco, partnered by a croupier from the Principality's Casino. Himself a member of the IOC, Prince Albert's grandfather and uncle, both named Jack Kelly, had won Olympic rowing medals.

Katarina Witt (GDR) was the first individual skater since 1952 to retain a figure skating title, amid some criticism – not shared by the spectators – about her skimpy costumes. In third place Debbie Thomas (USA) was the first black skater to win an Olympic skating medal. Speed skating was held indoors for the first time at the Olympics, in the superb $39 million Olympic Oval. It proved to be the fastest circuit in the world with world records in seven of the nine events, and as many as 29 skaters bettering the world mark in the men's 5000m. Karin Kania (née Enke) added two silvers and a bronze for a record medal haul of eight since 1980. Monika Pflug-Holzner (FRG), the 1972 1000m champion competed in her fifth Games, then a record number of appearances for a female Winter Olympics competitor. The Soviet Union moved past Canada in ice hockey with its seventh title, while the host nation and the United States, who won in 1980, failed to gain a medal. A small consolation prize for Canada was that the most prolific goal scorer, with seven, in the tournament was Serge Boisvert. There was only one competitor in Calgary who failed a drugs test – a Polish ice hockey player.

The youngest gold medallist was Ekaterina Gordiyeva (URS) in the pairs skating aged 16 years 264 days, while the oldest was Ekkehard Fasser (SUI) in the four-man bob aged 35 years 178 days. The youngest male champion was Ari Pekka Nikkola (FIN) in the 90m team ski jump at 18 years 284 days, and the oldest female gold medallist was Christa Rothenburger (GDR) who won the 1000m speedskating aged 28 years 84 days. Competitors ages ranged from 14-year-old Seba Johnson of the United States Virgin Islands the first black Olympic skier, to her countryman, 52-year-old Harvey Hook, a bobsledder.

1988 MEDALS (WINTER)

	G	S	B
Soviet Union	11	9	9
East Germany (GDR)	9	10	6
Switzerland	5	5	5
Finland	4	1	2
Sweden	4	—	2
Austria	3	5	2
The Netherlands	3	2	2
West Germany (FRG)	2	4	2
United States	2	1	3
Italy	2	1	2
France	1	—	1
Norway	—	3	2
Canada	—	2	3
Yugoslavia	—	2	1
Czechoslovakia	—	1	2
Japan	—	—	1
Liechtenstein	—	—	1

SEOUL 1988

XXIV OLYMPIC GAMES HELD IN SEOUL, KOREA, 17 SEPTEMBER–2 OCTOBER 1988
ATTENDED BY REPRESENTATIVES OF 159 COUNTRIES, COMPRISING 8465 COMPETITORS, OF WHICH 2186 WERE WOMEN.

The capital of Korea, Seoul, has one of the largest populations of any city on earth – an estimated 9,000,000. Nearly all facilities for the Games were in situ by the end of 1986 when the Asian Games were held there. Most major installations were part of the sports complex on the banks of the Han River, and include a 90,000-spectator stadium. Once again the programme was expanded, with the re-introduction of tennis (for the first time since 1924), the addition of table tennis, and the inclusion of a number of extra events, which brought the total to a record 237. Baseball, Tae Kwon Do and women's judo were the demonstration sports. American TV companies offered incredible sums (up to $750 million) for the US rights, provided that the major sports finals took place during the American prime time viewing. That would have required that athletics finals be held between 9.00am and 11.00am Korean time. This was opposed by the International Amateur Athletic Federation (IAAF), and indeed by the IOC, although some compromise was finally agreed. The income from TV rights was still immense, NBC acquiring the American rights alone for $300 million. There was an estimated 16,000 media personnel at these Games.

Prior to the Opening Ceremony the most tenacious problem was the claim of North Korea to host half the Games. Against IOC rules, but with their blessing, some sports were offered to them, but they continued to be intransigent. They finally refused to attend and attempted to get the Eastern bloc to support them. However, only the hard-line Communist countries backed them, and the only other absentees were: Albania, Cuba, Ethiopia, Madagascar, Nicaragua and the Seychelles. Against that there were a number of first-timers including: American Samoa, Aruba, Burkina Faso (which had competed as Upper Volta in 1972), the Cook Islands, Guam, the

Maldives, St Vincent, Vanuatu and the Democratic Republic of Yemen. Also attending was Brunei, but only with an official, so that the officially claimed figure of 160 countries participating is not correct.

The Opening Ceremony began on the Han River and transferred to the main stadium. The President of Korea, Roh Tae-Woo, declared the Games open, and Huh Jae, a basketball player, and Son Mi-Na, a handball player, jointly took the oath. One unusual feature of the ceremony was that as the Korean alphabet began with the letter 'G', the traditional first team, Greece, was then followed by Gabon and Ghana. A more entertaining occurrence in that march-past was the inclusion in the Thailand contingent of the very beautiful reigning Miss Universe, Porntip 'Pui' Nakirunkanot, which delighted the spectators. Because the original 1920 Olympic flag had been fading away, a new one, made of Korean silk, had been presented to the IOC by Seoul Organising Committee and was flown for the first time on the 17 September 1988. The torch was carried for part of the distance on the track by 76-year-old Sohn Kee-Chung (better known as Kitei Son) and the 1936 marathon champion – a Korean who had been forced to run for Japan, the occupying power at the time. He passed it to the final runner, a female athlete Lim Chun-Ae. The torch was raised to the top of the cauldron tower, and three representatives of Science, Art and Sport (whose names were Ching Sun-Man, Kim Won-Tuk and Sohn Mi-Chung) lit the flame. It is feared that some of the pigeons, which had been released during part of the ceremony and that had perched on the cauldron, were caught in the rush of flames.

DID YOU KNOW?

American diver, Greg Louganis, badly smashed his head on a lower diving board during the springboard preliminaries in 1988, but recovered to win both gold medals for diving.

The athlete who gained most attention at these Games was undoubtedly the Canadian sprinter Ben Johnson, initially for the best of reasons and then for the worst. Having looked somewhat out of form in the preliminary rounds of the 100m, he blasted away in the final to destroy a talented field, including arch-rival Carl Lewis, and record an almost unbelievable world record of 9.79 sec. Three days later it was revealed that he had failed a drug test and was disqualified, with Lewis moving up to the gold medal with a very respectable 9.92sec. Another nine competitors, from weightlifting (four), modern pentathlon (two), judo, wrestling and shooting were disqualified for drug-related offences. Although African men won everything on the track over 400m, the outstanding athlete at the Games was a woman, Florence Griffith Joyner (USA), wife of the 1984 triple jump winner, who won three golds and a silver in the sprints and relays, running a total of 11 races. Her sister-in-law, Jackie Joyner-Kersee won the heptathlon, as expected, and the long jump. Continuing the Olympic tradition of successful families, Viktor Bryzgin (4 x 100m) and his wife Olga Bryzgina (400m, 4 x 400m) both won gold medals. In rowing Carmine and Giuseppe Abbagnale (ITA) retained their coxed pair title from 1984, and a

third brother, Agostino, was a member of the winning quadruple sculls crew.

The most successful competitor in Seoul was Kristin Otto (GDR), who not only won six gold medals (a record by any woman, in any sport, at any Games), but also became the first swimmer to win titles at three different strokes at the same Games. America's Matt Biondi, saddled before the Games with an impossible Mark Spitz-like scenario, nevertheless ended the Games with seven medals (five golds, a silver and a bronze). Vladimir Salnikov (URS) became the only swimmer to regain a title eight years after winning it the first time. Greg Louganis (USA) gained the first double 'double' by a male diver when he successfully defended his two titles from Los Angeles, despite hitting his head on the board during a dive in the springboard preliminaries. Also in the pool, Anthony Nesty of Surinam became the first black competitor and the first South American to win a gold medal in the swimming, by taking the 100m butterfly. Similarly Kenny Monday (USA) was the first black wrestler to win a gold medal.

A number of 'old-timers' re-appeared on the Olympic scene. 52-year-old Reiner Klimke (FRG) won his sixth dressage gold medal, and his eighth medal in five Games, over a 24-year period, all records for his sport. His horse *Ahlerich* also set a record. One of Klimke's compatriots in the winning team was Ann-Kathrin Linsenhoff – remarkably her mother had been his teammate in the gold medal team of 1968. Britain's David Broome returned after three Games out as a 'professional', 28 years after he first competed. The sailing events, held at Pusan, had two of the greatest Olympians of all time. Quadruple gold medallist Paul Elvstrøm (DEN), who partnered by his daughter, Trine, and was competing in a record equalling eighth Games, over a 40-year span. This was matched by yachtsman Durward Knowles (BAH), a 1964 gold medallist, and also in his eighth celebration over a similar span.

By winning the silver medal in women's sprint cycling, East Germany's Christa Luding (née Röthenburger) became the first competitor in Olympic history to win medals at a Summer and Winter celebration in the same year. She had won a speed skating gold and silver at Calgary. Because of a record number of entries in boxing, two rings were used simultaneously. Not surprisingly, this caused some confusion. Also, not for the first time, the boxing competitions witnessed some 'bizarre', often home-town, decisions. One of the most scandalous decisions in Olympic boxing history occurred when Roy Jones Jr (USA) was judged to have lost his light-middleweight bout against Park Si-Hun of Korea. Pointedly, the International Amateur Boxing Association (IABA) awarded Jones the Val Barker Cup as the best stylist at the Games. In early 2003 Jones made further history, when, as a middleweight, he won the World Boxing Association (WBA) heavyweight title. There were other disputed decisions and some of the judges were suspended. One of the Korean boxers, Byun Jong-Il, refused to leave the ring after the decision went against him in his bantamweight bout, and remained there, a solitary figure, for over an hour.

The oldest gold medallist at Seoul was Reiner Klimke (*see above*) aged 52 years 255 days. The youngest was swimmer Krisztina Egerszegi (HUN) at 14 years 41 days. The oldest female champion was hockey player Elspeth Clement (AUS) aged 32 years 103 days, while the youngest male winner was Soviet cyclist Dmitri Nelyubin aged 17 years 229 days. The oldest medallist at Seoul was Romanian cox Ladislau Lovrenski aged 56 years 65 days. The youngest medallist was Egerszegi three days before her gold, while the youngest male medallist was Xiong Ni (CHN) with a silver in diving aged 14 years 247 days. The oldest competitor was Durward Knowles (*see* above) in Star class yachting aged 70 years 331 days, while the youngest was swimmer Nadia Cruz of Angola aged 13 years 73 days. The oldest female competitor was Inoue Kikuko (JPN) in the dressage aged 63 years 297 days.

Thus, despite threats, of boycotts, of North Korean terror, of student riots etc, the Games on the whole went very well. The good humour, flexibility and courtesy of the hosts overcame most minor problems. A record 52 countries won medals, and some time after the Games ended it was reported that a record profit of $288 million had been made.

1988 MEDALS (SUMMER)

	G	S	B
Soviet Union	55	31	46
East Germany (GDR)	37	35	30
United States	36	31	27
Korea	12	10	11
West Germany (FRG)	11	14	15
Hungary	11	6	6
Bulgaria	10	12	13
Romania	7	1	6
France	6	4	6
Italy	6	4	4
China	5	11	12
Great Britain	5	10	9
Kenya	5	2	2
Japan	4	3	7
Australia	3	6	5
Yugoslavia	3	4	5
Czechoslovakia	3	3	2
New Zealand	3	2	8
Canada	3	2	5
Poland	2	5	9
Norway	2	3	—
The Netherlands	2	2	5
Denmark	2	1	1
Brazil	1	2	3
Finland	1	1	2
Spain	1	1	2
Turkey	1	1	—
Morocco	1	—	2
Austria	1	—	—
Portugal	1	—	—
Surinam	1	—	—
Sweden	—	4	7
Switzerland	—	2	2
Jamaica	—	2	—
Argentina	—	1	1
Chile	—	1	—
Costa Rica	—	1	—
Indonesia	—	1	—
Iran	—	1	—
The Netherlands Antilles	—	1	—
Peru	—	1	—
Senegal	—	1	—
Virgin Islands	—	1	—
Belgium	—	—	2
Mexico	—	—	2
Colombia	—	—	1
Djibouti	—	—	1
Greece	—	—	1
Mongolia	—	—	1
Pakistan	—	—	1
Philippines	—	—	1
Thailand	—	—	1

ALBERTVILLE 1992

XVI WINTER GAMES HELD IN ALBERTVILLE, FRANCE, 8–23 FEBRUARY 1992
ATTENDED BY REPRESENTATIVES OF 64 COUNTRIES, COMPRISING 1801 COMPETITORS OF WHICH 488 WERE WOMEN.

In October 1986 the IOC awarded the Games to Albertville, in the Savoie region of France, ahead of six other sites in six other countries. The 1968 triple gold medallist, Jean-Claude Killy, was co-president of the organising committee. With a population of less than 20,000, Albertville was the smallest place ever to host an Olympic Games. The 13 different venues were very widespread, which gave rise to complaints that 'atmosphere and spirit' were lacking when compared to previous celebrations. Nevertheless, the Games were highly successful, with a record number of competitors and participating countries. These included newcomers such as Swaziland and Ireland. The political upheavals in eastern Europe manifested themselves in various ways: there was a combined German team for the first time since 1964; Latvia, Estonia and Lithuania competed independently again after 56 years, having been incorporated into the Soviet Union in 1940; competing under the title of the Unified Team (EUN) were the National Olympic Committees (NOCs) of Russia, Belarus, Ukraine, Kazakhstan and Uzbekistan – they used the Olympic flag, and Beethoven's *Ode to Joy* for victory ceremonies. The break-up of Yugoslavia meant that Croatia and Slovenia competed separately for the first time, too.

As usual the world's media attended in force, trying to cope with the logistical problems caused by the multi-venue sports facilities. Some $243 million was paid by CBS for the American TV rights. There was a remarkable opening ceremony with the Games declared open by François Mitterand, the President of France. The flame was lit by soccer star Michel Platini and a local child, François-Syrille Grange, and figure skater Surya Bonaly (later placed fifth), took the oath.

A record 57 events included the newly accepted sports of short-track speed skating and freestyle skiing. Overall, there were nine extra events since the previous Games, as well as demonstration sports of curling, speed skiing, and two forms of freestyle skiing not in the Games proper. Another change was that in figure skating compulsory exercises had been eliminated.

Unusually, the alpine skiers did not produce the stars of this Games as they had done in the past. Italy's Alberto Tomba gained a lot of attention by becoming the first alpinist to successfully defend a title, but no skier really dominated. Indeed, only Petra Kronberger of Austria won more than one event, and the 30 available medals in the sport were spread among 25 skiers. Surprisingly, the Swiss won only a single bronze, while female skiers from Sweden and New Zealand won the first such medals from their events.

Nordic Skiing made a big impact, and, with good television coverage, some of the cross-country competitors became stars. The Norwegians, Vegard Ulvang and Bjørn Dæhlie, got due recognition for winning three golds and one silver each. They made good media copy too, especially Dæhlie, who deliberately skied backwards over the line for his last gold medal, in the relay. But the most successful competitor at Albertville was their female equivalent, Lyubov Yegorova of the Unified Team, who won three golds and two silvers – a record total of medals in one Winter Games. That was matched by her teammate, Yelena Valbe, with four individual bronzes and a gold in the relay. The inclusion of women's biathlon events enabled Anfissa Reztsova (EUN) to become the first Winter Olympian to win gold medals in two separate sports – she had previously gained a gold in the 1988 cross-country relay.

Austrian ski jumpers put up a surprising challenge to the Finns, especially in the team event, and it was mainly the superb jumping of the young Toni Nieminen that won the day. Another closely fought contest involving Austria came in the four-man bob, when their team beat Germany by a mere two-hundredths of a second after four rounds, the smallest margin of victory ever. In lugeing, the Neuner sisters, also from Austria, took first and second places, matching the feat of the French Goitschel sisters in the 1964 Alpine skiing. By winning the ice hockey the Unified Team, in effect, extended the Soviet Union's victory run to eight since first entering the Games in 1956.

Despite the new rules most of the favourites won the medals in figure skating, with Viktor Petrenko (EUN) taking his country's first individual skating gold since 1908. In speed skating both sprint titles were retained by the 1988 champions, Bonnie Blair (USA) and Uwe-Jens Mey (GER), respectively. However, the surprise here, and in the new short-track events, was the rise of Asia, whose skaters, from China, Japan and the Koreas, won 13 medals.

Toni Nieminen, the Finnish gold medallist in the 120m ski-jump individual and team events, was only 16 years 259 days of age when he gained his first title, thereby becoming the youngest ever male Winter Olympics champion. A member of the Unified Team, Raisa Smetanina, was the oldest ever female gold medallist as a member of the 4 x 5km relay team, just 12 days short of her 40th birthday. She set another record by winning medals in five consecutive Games, from 1976 to 1992. She said her secret was that she is really only ten years old – being born on 29th February. The oldest male champion was Fritz Fischer (GER) in the biathlon aged 35 years 146 days, while the oldest medallist was

Maurilio De Zolt (ITA) with a silver in the 50km cross-country aged 41 years 150 days. The youngest medallist was Nikki Ziegelmeyer (USA) with a silver in the women's short-track speed skating relay at 16 years 149 days, while the youngest competitor was figure skater Krisztina Czakó (HUN), aged 13 years 66 days, whose father and coach, Gyorgy, had skated in the 1952 Games.

These were the last Winter Games to be held in the same year as the Summer celebration. In future the Winter Games would be held on the even-numbered years between the four yearly cycles of the Summer Games.

1992 MEDALS (WINTER)

	G	S	B
Germany	10	10	6
Unified Team	9	6	8
Norway	9	6	5
Austria	6	7	8
United States	5	4	2
Italy	4	6	4
France	3	5	1
Finland	3	1	3
Canada	2	3	2
Korea	2	1	1
Japan	1	2	4
The Netherlands	1	1	2
Sweden	1	—	3
Switzerland	1	—	2
China	—	3	—
Luxembourg	—	2	—
New Zealand	—	1	—
Czechoslovakia	—	—	3
North Korea (PRK)	—	—	1
Spain	—	—	1

Note: there were two silvers and no bronze medal in the Women's Giant Slalom.

BARCELONA 1992

XXV OLYMPIC GAMES HELD IN BARCELONA, SPAIN,
25 JULY–9 AUGUST
ATTENDED BY REPRESENTATIVES OF 169 COUNTRIES,
COMPRISING 9364 COMPETITORS, OF WHICH 2707
WERE WOMEN.

After intense 'politicking' the 1992 Summer Games were awarded to Barcelona, Spain in October 1986. The city, the birthplace of the then President of the IOC, Juan Antonio Samaranch, had been promised the Games in 1924 but Baron de Coubertin had changed his mind and opted for Paris. Barcelona was then suggested for the 1936 celebration, but by then the spectre of civil war decided the IOC in favour of Berlin. The stadium intended for those Games, built in 1929 on Montjuic, was completely refurbished, and was the main venue. Most of the other venues were within the city limits, with only football (preliminary games), rowing, canoeing and road cycling sites any great distance away. Television revenue set what was then a record with NBC paying $401 million for the American TV rights. As well as two new sports, baseball and badminton, being added to the official programme there were also a number of extra events. These included seven for women in judo, a women's 10km walk, a dinghy sailing competition for women, and four canoe-slalom contests. There were 26 sports and the total number of medal events was 259 (with the distribution of 815 medals in all). An outbreak of African equine plague in Spain in 1989 originally cast considerable doubt as to whether the equestrian events would be held, but it was curtailed in time. There were three demonstration sports: pelota Basque, Tae Kwon Do and rink hockey.

Prior to the Games, as always, there were the familiar cries from media doom-mongers that the Olympics were finished, and that there was no point in holding them again. It was stated that most sports had their own world championships and thus the importance of the Olympic Games was diluted. What these critics seem never to understand is that the world's sportsmen and women still consider an Olympic medal as the pinnacle of sporting achievement. For the first time in many Olympiads not a single nation boycotted the occasion, and there were a record number of countries and competitors, which caused the IOC to discuss the need for 'quotas' to limit numbers in future Games. The Baltic States were independent again and Germany competed as one team. However, Yugoslavia was split into Bosnia-Herzegovina, Croatia and Slovenia, with competitors from Serbia and Macedonia competing as Independent Olympic Participants (IOP). South Africa returned to the Olympic fold after 32 years. In total 170 countries marched in the parade, but Afghanistan actually had no competitors. Media representatives, including the critics, outnumbered the competitors.

The Barcelona Games were a tremendous success overall – many thought it one of the best ever. The one sour note was caused by transport shortcomings for fans billeted a long way out of town. Happily, fears of terrorist activity proved to be unfounded, but security arrangements were reported to have cost $90 million. Tennis professionals were joined by others in basketball, and the US 'Dream Team', containing Earvin 'Magic' Johnson, Michael Jordan, Larry Bird and Charles Barkley, was one of the highlights of the Games. Because of their presence these sports were given greatly increased TV coverage, even outside the United States. The disintegrating Soviet Union known here as the Commonwealth of Independent States (CIS) or Unified Team (UT), made its last appearance. King Juan Carlos, an Olympic yachtsman in 1972, declared the Games open during a colourful ceremony, and Luis Doreste Blanco, who later won a gold medal in the Flying Dutchman class took the oath. He had won gold in the 1984 470 class, while his brother José-Luis had won the 1988 Finn event. Incidentally the King's son, Felipe, placed sixth in the Barcelona Soling, and his daughter, Christina, had been in the 1988 Tornado class. Their uncle, King Constantine of Greece, had been a sailing gold medallist in 1960. Paraplegic archer, Antonio Rebollo spectacularly lit the flame on the stadium pedestal by symbolically shooting an arrow at the torch tower. Recent research indicates that Spain's first Olympic champion, Lucius Minicius, winner of the chariot race in AD 129, was born in Barcelona, and his ghost must have been smiling as Spain gained a record number of medals, nearly doubling its total from the 16 previous Games. In all, 64 countries won a medal,

another record to that time, and of these 37 won a gold. Although the heat did affect a number of sports adversely, the overall standard was very high, with perhaps the outstanding individual performances of the Games being the 1500m freestyle of 14min 43.48sec by Kieren Perkins (AUS), and the 400m hurdles in 46.78sec by Kevin Young (USA). In the swimming pool there was a fine swansong by the Unified Team as Aleksandr Popov won two golds and two silvers, and Yevgeni Sadovyi took three golds. The most successful competitor was their compatriot gymnast Vitali Scherbo who won six gold medals. Although only placed 20th in the Star yacht class, Hubert Raudaschl (AUT) equalled a record, competing in eight Games, 1964–92 – he has since added another. Indonesian-born Chrisilot Hanson-Boylen (CAN), 12th in the dressage competition, set a new record for women, also in her eighth Games, and also equalled the 28-year span of competition.

The youngest gold medallist/medallist was the diver Fu Mingxia (CHN) aged 13 years 345 days, while the youngest male winner was her diving teammate Sun Shuwei at 16 years 185 days. The oldest gold medallist was Klaus Balkenhol (GER) in the dressage team aged 52 years 243 days, with the oldest female champion Gillian Rolton (AUS) in the three-day event team at 36 years 88 days. The oldest medallist was the 1972 gold medallist Swedish shooter Ragnar Skanaker in his sixth Games at 58 years 48 days, while the oldest female medallist was Carol Lavell (USA) in the dressage aged 49 years 118 days. The youngest competitor was rowing cox Carlos Barrera of Spain aged 11 years 256 days. The youngest female competitor was Hungarian swimmer Judit Kiss, at 12 years 184 days.

1992 MEDALS (SUMMER)

	G	S	B
Unified Team	45	38	29
United States	37	34	37
Germany	33	21	28
China	16	22	16
Cuba	14	6	11
Spain	13	7	2
Korea	12	5	12
Hungary	11	12	7
France	8	5	16
Australia	7	9	11
Canada	7	4	7
Italy	6	5	8
Great Britain	5	3	12
Romania	4	6	8
Czechoslovakia	4	2	1
North Korea (PRK)	4	—	5
Japan	3	8	11
Bulgaria	3	7	6
Poland	3	6	10
The Netherlands	2	6	7
Kenya	2	4	2
Norway	2	4	1
Turkey	2	2	2
Indonesia	2	2	1
Brazil	2	1	—
Greece	2	—	—
Sweden	1	7	4

New Zealand	1	4	5
Finland	1	2	2
Denmark	1	1	4
Morocco	1	1	1
Ireland	1	1	—
Ethiopia	1	—	2
Algeria	1	—	1
Estonia	1	—	1
Lithuania	1	—	1
Switzerland	1	—	—
Jamaica	—	3	1
Nigeria	—	3	1
Latvia	—	2	1
Austria	—	2	—
Namibia	—	2	—
South Africa	—	2	—
Belgium	—	1	2
Croatia	—	1	2
IOP	—	1	2
Iran	—	1	2
Israel	—	1	1
Chinese Taipei	—	1	—
Mexico	—	1	—
Peru	—	1	—
Slovenia	—	—	2
Mongolia	—	—	2
Argentina	—	—	1
Bahamas	—	—	1
Colombia	—	—	1
Ghana	—	—	1
Malaysia	—	—	1
Pakistan	—	—	1
Philippines	—	—	1
Puerto Rico	—	—	1
Qatar	—	—	1
Surinam	—	—	1
Thailand	—	—	1

LILLEHAMMER 1994

XVII WINTER GAMES HELD IN LILLEHAMMER,
NORWAY, 12–27 FEBRUARY 1994
ATTENDED BY REPRESENTATIVES OF 67 COUNTRIES,
COMPRISING 1737 COMPETITORS, OF WHICH 520
WERE WOMEN.

It was during the 1988 Olympic Games at Seoul, in September 1988, that the IOC decided to award these Games to Lillehammer, a town of 23,000 people some 180km (111 miles) north of Oslo. Three other cities had made bids but the Norwegian town, which had lost out to Albertville in the 1992 vote, won the IOC's approval this time. This was the first Winter Games not held in the same year as a summer celebration. Lillehammer held one of the most successful Games, summer or winter, of all time, with excellent weather, eye-catching facilities, firm and deep snow, good organisation, and enthusiastic, non-chauvinistic spectators. The only adverse items were extremely cold temperatures, often below −20°C, and the high cost of food and drink.

A spectacular opening ceremony, embodying traditional themes such as the mythical Vetter people, involved actress Liv Ullmann and Kon-Tiki anthropologist Thor Heyerdahl. King Harald V, himself a former Olympian, officially opened the Games. Stein Gruben brought the torch into the stadium; leaping from the ski jump before handing it to Catherine Nottingnes. She, in turn, passed it to Crown Prince Haakon, who lit the flame. Triple gold medallist skier, Vegard Ulvang, took the oath. There was a minute's silence for the plight of Sarajevo, the 1984 Olympic site.

The record number of countries, including 14 first-timers, was boosted by the break-up of the former Soviet Union, and led to a then record 22 countries winning medals. In ice hockey and figure skating, professionals were allowed to compete for the first time. In the latter, stricter rules were in force governing skimpy clothing, and there were a number of controversial judging decisions, which drew strong criticisms. Prior to the Games, excessive media interest had been generated by the vicious attack on the American skater, Nancy Kerrigan, and the alleged involvement of her teammate Tonya Harding.

Enormous crowds, particularly at the Nordic skiing, despite the intense cold, evidenced a reported 83 per cent sale of events tickets. There were a number of new events including aerials in the freestyle skiing, and men's 500m and women's 1000m in the short-track speed skating. A reported $295 million was paid by CBS for the American TV rights. After the Games it was announced that a profit of $63.5 million had been made.

The most successful competitor at Lillehammer was Manuela di Centa (ITA) who won five medals (two golds, two silvers and a bronze) in cross-country skiing, equalling a single Games best ever total. However, fellow Nordic skier, Lyubov Yegorova (RUS), won three golds and a silver, thus equalling the Winter Games record total of six gold medals. In bobsledding, Gustave Weder (SUI) became the only man to successfully defend the two-man title, while Wolfgang Höppe (GER) was the first to be a medallist in four Games. Alpine skier, Vreni Schneider (SUI), was the first woman to total three gold medals in her sport, as well as setting an all-time record of five medals. Alberto Tomba (ITA) uniquely won medals at three consecutive Games in Alpine skiing, a sport which also featured some very small margins of victory. Remarkably, for the first time ever, no Alpine nation gained a medal in the men's downhill race.

American speed skaters, Bonnie Blair, with a record third consecutive 500m title, and Dan Jansen, a very popular emotional winner after a series of disasters in the previous three Games, could not take the spotlight away from Norway's Johann Olav Koss. He won three gold medals, all in world record times. The ice hockey competition witnessed shockingly bad results by the United States and, even more surprisingly, Russia, and resulted in the first win by Sweden.

The youngest ever gold medallist at a Winter Games was Kim Yoon-Mi (KOR), in the short-track skating women's relay, aged 13 years 83 days. She was also the youngest ever female Olympic champion in either Winter or Summer Games. The youngest male gold medallist at these Games was Maurizio Carnino (ITA) in the short-track relay, aged 18 years 356 days. The winner of the women's figure skating, Oksana Baiul (UKR) was the youngest to win that title, at 16 years 101 days, since

Sonja Henie (NOR) in 1928. The oldest gold medallist/medallist was Maurilio De Zolt (ITA) in the Nordic relay aged 43 years 150 days, competing in his fifth Games. The oldest female medallist was Marja-Liisa Kirvesniemi (FIN) at 38 years 167 days, in her record equalling sixth Games.

Lillehammer was also the scene for the greatest sibling performance in a Winter Games, by the four Huber brothers of Italy. Wilfried and Norbert won gold and silver, separately in the luge pairs; Gunther got a bronze in the two-man bob; and Arnold placed fourth in the luge singles.

At the end of these Games it was estimated that, excluding multi-participation by athletes, some 85,000 competitors had attended the Modern Games since 1896.

1994 MEDALS (WINTER)

	G	S	B
Russia	11	8	4
Norway	10	11	5
Germany	9	7	8
Italy	7	5	8
United States	6	5	2
Korea	4	1	1
Canada	3	6	4
Switzerland	3	4	2
Austria	2	3	4
Sweden	2	1	—
Japan	1	2	2
Kazakhstan	1	2	—
Ukraine	1	—	1
Uzbekistan	1	—	—
Belarus	—	2	—
Finland	—	1	5
France	—	1	4
The Netherlands	—	1	3
China	—	1	2
Slovenia	—	—	3
Great Britain	—	—	2
Australia	—	—	1

ATLANTA 1996

XXVI OLYMPIC GAMES HELD IN ATLANTA, USA, 19 JULY–4 AUGUST 1996
ATTENDED BY REPRESENTATIVES OF 197 COUNTRIES, COMPRISING 10,310 COMPETITORS, OF WHICH 3513 WERE WOMEN.

The 1996 Games celebrated the 100th anniversary of the rebirth of the Modern Olympics, and Athens was thought by many to be the obvious venue. The somewhat surprising decision, in September 1990, was in favour of Atlanta. It was immediately suggested that many in the IOC were swayed by the financial support that the city would receive from American TV and other corporate sponsors (American TV rights were sold for a record $456 million). In the event there was much criticism of the chauvinistic coverage by NBC, with the excessive emphasis on American performances reaching ludicrous levels. However, it was reported that the TV Company received some $700 million in advertising revenue for the Games period. It was expected that Atlanta would provide the model of top-flight organisation and excellent technology – but it didn't. There was much criticism of the extreme commercialisation and of the organisational failures, particularly in the field of transportation. The cost of hotels and the high price of tickets was another area of concern for foreign visitors. On the plus side was the undoubted goodwill and friendliness of the city's inhabitants, and the generally good, albeit hot and humid, weather. Also, it was one of the most centralised Games of recent years with most of the sports held within the periphery of the city, although sailing was held on the Georgia coast at Savannah. Although cutbacks to the number of sports and events in the Games have been mooted for years, there were a record 29 sports and 271 events. Newcomers included softball, beach volleyball, mountain bike racing, and soccer for women. However, it had been agreed that demonstration sports would no longer be held as part of this and future Games. Other changes included the modern pentathlon, held on only one day, and the replacement of the Flying Dutchman two-man yachting class by a single-handed Laser class. Many new, excellent, facilities were built, including an 85,000-seat stadium and a remarkable equestrian centre.

President of the United States, William Jefferson Clinton officially opened the Games, and the overlong opening ceremony witnessed, for the first time, a full turnout of all 197 countries then affiliated to the Olympic movement. New countries, in addition to those coming from the break-up of the former Soviet Union and Czechoslovakia, included Burundi, Guinea-Bissau, Nauru and Palestine. Other debuts included the first female competitor ever from Iran, in the shooting events. Entries exceeded 10,000 for the first time, and there were over 17,000 representatives of the world media. The American team numbered 697, the largest ever national contingent since the enormous French team (884) at Paris in 1900.

An unusual scenario for the end of the traditional Olympic torch run had representatives of white and black, male and female, and current and first Olympic hosts. Thus, in the last few changeovers, Al Oerter (four-time champion) passed to Evander Holyfield (bronze 1984), he was joined by Paraskevi Patoulidou (1992 women's 100-m hurdles gold for Greece, and then the torch was handed to Janet Evans (four-time swimming gold medallist), who took it up the stairs into the stadium. There she gave it to the one-time boxing champion, Muhammad Ali, sadly a shadow of his former self, who finally lit the stadium flame, an exceptionally moving moment. American basketball player, Teresa Edwards, took the oath on behalf of all the other competitors.

In all, 79 countries won medals, of which a record 53 won gold, including the first ever medal (a gold) for Hong Kong, in board sailing, on what was thought to be its last appearance as a separate entity on the Olympic stage. The most successful competitor was Amy Van Dyken (USA), who won four gold medals in swimming, while Alexei Nemov of Russia won six gymnastic medals (two golds, one silver, three bronzes). Over 32,000 spectators packed the gymnastics hall to see injured American gymnast, Kerri Strug complete her final vault to guarantee the hosts the team gold medal. In general there were excellent attendances at all venues, with an unprecedented 8.6 million tickets sold for the 17 days of competitions. In the athletics stadium, later to be converted for baseball, Michael Johnson set an astounding time of 19.32sec for 200m, while teammate Carl Lewis won his fourth consecutive long jump title to take his career total to nine Olympic golds. The star of the swimming pool was the Irishwoman Michelle Smith, who was not only her country's first ever swimming finalist, but won three gold medals and a bronze. She was the target of much innuendo about drug taking, especially from some of the American swimming team and press. In rowing Britain's Steve Redgrave took his fourth gold medal in as many Games; France's Jeannie Longo won the women's cycling road race, improving on her Barcelona silver, at the age of 37 years; and yachtsman Hubert Raudaschl of land-locked Austria competed in a record breaking, for any sport, ninth Olympic Games. The first Australian Aboriginal athlete to gain a gold medal was Nova Peris-Kneebone in the winning Australian women's hockey team. Primarily a sprinter she was in the athletics team in 2000. Appallingly, halfway through the Games a bomb went off in Centennial Park, a popular place for fans and general public alike, which thankfully only resulted in two deaths, although over 100 other people were injured. This happened despite an enormous outlay on security, which involved some 30,000 operatives, yet another record.

The youngest gold medallist was swimmer Amanda Beard (USA) at 14 years 269 days as a member of the winning medley relay squad. She was the youngest medallist three days earlier when she took silver in the 100m breaststroke. The youngest male champion was Michal Martikan (SVK) aged 17 years 70 days winning the C1 slalom event, while individual pursuit cyclist Alexei Markov (RUS) won a bronze: he was just eight days younger. The oldest gold medallist and indeed medallist at Atlanta was Klaus Balkenhol (GER) taking gold in the dressage team event, aged 56 years 235 days. The oldest female champion was Jeannie Longo (FRA) aged 37 years 264 days, when she won the cycling road race. Softball player Jocelyn Lester (AUS) was the oldest female medallist at 38 years 130 days. The oldest competitor at Atlanta was Faustino Puccini (ITA) in the dressage event, aged 63 years 267 days.

1996 MEDALS

	G	S	B	Total
United States	44	32	25	101
Germany	20	18	27	65
Russia	26	21	16	63
China	16	22	12	50
Australia	9	9	23	41
France	15	7	15	37
Italy	13	10	12	35
Korea	7	15	5	27
Cuba	9	8	8	25
Ukraine	9	2	12	23
Canada	3	11	8	22
Hungary	7	4	10	21
Romania	4	7	9	20
The Netherlands	4	5	10	19
Poland	7	5	5	17
Spain	5	6	6	17
Bulgaria	3	7	5	15
Brazil	3	3	9	15
Great Britain	1	8	6	15
Belarus	1	6	8	15
Japan	3	6	5	14
Czech Republic	4	3	4	11
Kazakhstan	3	4	4	11
Greece	4	4	—	8
Sweden	2	4	2	8
Kenya	1	4	3	8
Switzerland	4	3	—	7
Norway	2	2	3	7
Denmark	4	1	1	6
Turkey	4	1	1	6
New Zealand	3	2	1	6
Belgium	2	2	2	6
Nigeria	2	1	3	6
Jamaica	1	3	2	6
South Africa	3	1	1	5
North Korea	2	1	2	5
Ireland	3	—	1	4
Finland	1	2	1	4
Indonesia	1	1	2	4
Yugoslavia	1	1	2	4
Algeria	2	—	1	3
Ethiopia	2	—	1	3
Iran	1	1	1	3
Slovakia	1	1	1	3
Argentina	—	2	1	3
Austria	—	1	2	3
Armenia	1	1	—	2
Croatia	1	1	—	2
Portugal	1	—	1	2
Thailand	1	—	1	2
Namibia	—	2	—	2
Slovenia	—	2	—	2
Malaysia	—	1	1	2
Moldova	—	1	1	2
Uzbekistan	—	1	1	2
Georgia	—	—	2	2
Morocco	—	—	2	2
Trinidad and Tobago	—	—	2	2
Burundi	1	—	—	1
Costa Rica	1	—	—	1
Ecuador	1	—	—	1
Hong Kong	1	—	—	1
Syria	1	—	—	1
Azerbaijan	—	1	—	1
Bahamas	—	1	—	1
Latvia	—	1	—	1
Philippines	—	1	—	1
Taiwan	—	1	—	1
Tonga	—	1	—	1
Zambia	—	1	—	1
India	—	—	1	1
Israel	—	—	1	1
Lithuania	—	—	1	1
Mexico	—	—	1	1
Mongolia	—	—	1	1
Mozambique	—	—	1	1
Puerto Rico	—	—	1	1
Tunisia	—	—	1	1
Uganda	—	—	1	1

NAGANO 1998

XVIII WINTER GAMES, HELD IN NAGANO, JAPAN,
7–22 FEBRUARY 1998
ATTENDED BY REPRESENTATIVES OF 72 COUNTRIES,
COMPRISING 2176 COMPETITORS, OF WHICH 787
WERE WOMEN.

Nagano in Japan was awarded these Games in 1991 winning the IOC vote against Val d'Aosta (Italy), Jaca (Spain), Ostersund (Sweden), and Salt Lake City (USA). It was the most southerly venue ever for a Winter Games. In 1994 CBS paid a record $375 million for the American TV rights, while the European Broadcasting Union (EBU) paid another record $72 million for the European TV rights. Curling and women's ice hockey brought the number of events to a record 68. There were also a record number of competitors from a record number of countries. Winter Games debuts were made by Kenya, Uruguay and Venezuela. The 10,300 media representatives was yet another record for a Winter celebration. Curling, snowboarding and women's ice hockey made their Olympic debuts.

Emperor Akihito, whose father had done the honours at Sapporo in 1972, officially opened the Games. Part of the opening ceremony consisted of a multi-continental concert, via TV satellite, with Beethoven's ninth symphony *Ode to Joy* conducted by the renowned Seiji Ozawa. The Olympic flame was lit by Midori Ito, the 1992 figure skating silver medallist, after the torch had been run up the steps to the cauldron by Hiromi Suzuki, the women's world marathon champion. Kenji Ogiwara, who had won gold in the 1992 Nordic Combination, took the oath on behalf of the competitors.

Bad weather caused serious disruption to the Alpine skiing events – the programme lost five days of competition and the organisers had to schedule an unprecedented three events for the same day. The weather also caused severe transportation problems. Many competitors were badly affected by a 'flu epidemic. Nevertheless there was a very high standard of competition. In Alpine skiing Katja Seizinger (GER) was the most successful with two gold medals and a bronze, while the biggest surprise was the poor showing of the Swiss skiers. The Austrian, Hermann Maier, suffered a bad fall in the downhill race, but returned to win popular golds in the giant slalom and the super giant slalom. In the Nordic events Larissa Lazutina (RUS) became the most bemedalled competitor at the Games with three golds, one silver and a bronze, her total of five equalling the record for medals at a single Winter games. Even more of a record breaker was Norway's Bjørn Dæhlie, whose three golds and a silver, raised his total medal hauls to a record eight golds and 12 medals overall, 1992–98.

The youngest gold medallist/medallist at Nagano was Tara Lipinski (USA), who won the women's figure skating aged 15 years 255 days, the youngest ever to win that title. The youngest male champion, and medallist, was Kim Dong-Sung (KOR) who took the 1000m short track speed skating event eight days past his 18th birthday. The oldest gold medallist was Patrik Loertscher, a member of the Swiss curling team, at 37 years 333 days, while the oldest female champion was Jan Betker of the

winning Canadian curling team, aged 37 years 211 days. A member of the Danish silver medal women's curling team, Jane Bidstrup, was 42 years 178 days old, while Paul Savage (CAN) also won a silver in the men's curling at 50 years 235 days. Both Bidstrup and Savage are the oldest ever medallists, respectively, in Winter Games history.

Perhaps the most startling of upsets was the failure of the teams from the United States or Canada, which included the legendary Wayne Gretzky, to win medals in men's ice hockey. An agreement had been reached to allow players from the professional National Hockey League (NHL) in Canada and America to attend. The NHL suspended its season to allow players to compete for their national teams, and 125 such players were present in nine of the teams. In snowboarding there was a minor furore when the winner of the men's slalom event, Ross Rebagliati of Canada, was initially disqualified after a drugs test. After an appeal he was re-instated.

1998 MEDALS (WINTER)

	G	S	B	Total
Germany	12	9	8	29
Norway	10	10	5	25
Russia	9	6	3	18
Austria	3	5	9	17
Canada	6	5	4	15
United States	6	3	4	13
Finland	2	4	6	12
The Netherlands	5	4	2	11
Japan	5	1	4	10
Italy	2	6	2	10
France	2	1	5	8
China	—	6	2	8
Switzerland	2	2	3	7
Korea	3	1	2	6
Czech Republic	1	1	1	3
Sweden	—	2	1	3
Belarus	—	—	2	2
Kazakhstan	—	—	2	2
Bulgaria	1	—	—	1
Denmark	—	1	—	1
Ukraine	—	1	—	1
Australia	—	—	1	1
Belgium	—	—	1	1
Great Britain	—	—	1	1

SYDNEY 2000

XXVII OLYMPIC GAMES HELD IN SYDNEY, AUSTRALIA,
15 SEPTEMBER–1 OCTOBER 2000
ATTENDED BY REPRESENTATIVES OF 200 COUNTRIES,
COMPRISING 10,651 COMPETITORS, OF WHICH 4069
WERE WOMEN.

In 1994, Sydney, Australia was awarded the first Games of the second millennium. It beat bids from Beijing, Brasilia, Istanbul, Manchester, and, tentatively, Berlin. It was the first Games to be held in the southern hemisphere. There were 28 sports on the programme, including, new to the Games, Tae Kwon Do (with four classes each for men and women), the triathlon, trampolining and synchronised diving. Additionally, for the first time, there were women's events in modern pentathlon, weightlifting and water polo. In all there was a record total of 300 medal events, including 23 new events for women. It was announced in August 1995 that NBC had paid a staggering $1.27 billion for the American TV rights for the Sydney Games ($705 million) and for the Winter Games of 2002.

Records were set for the number of countries and number of competitors, and there were some 15,000 accredited representatives of the world's media. The opening ceremony was watched by an estimated 115,000 spectators in the stadium – well over the stated capacity of 110,000, and itself a record for an Olympic stadium – and an estimated television audience of 3.7 billion people worldwide. The official opening was by Sir William Deane, the Governor-General of Australia, and Rechelle Hawkes, a double gold medallist in hockey who won another in Sydney, took the competitor's oath. After the longest torch relay ever, 51.184km (31,811 miles) involving over 11,000 runners, Cathy Freeman, later to win the 400m, lit the Olympic flame in the stadium. In a moving tribute to women's participation in the Olympics, six former Australian Olympic stars, Betty Cuthbert, Raelene Boyle, Dawn Fraser, Shirley de la Hunty, Shane Gould and Debbie Flintoff-King, were the last carriers, on the track, prior to the torch being handed to Freeman. The march past of countries indicated that Palau, Palestine and the Federated States of Micronesia were making their debuts at the Games, while East Timor competed as an IOP. The two Koreas – North and South – marched under one flag, but competed separately.

The Games at Sydney were widely praised by all and sundry as the best there has ever been, although there were a number of minor glitches, mostly overcome by the good nature of the 47,000 volunteer helpers. There was an error with one of the illustrations on the medals, with a depiction of the Coliseum (Roman), instead of something Greek, as intended. At the opening ceremony, which was overly long, there was a heart-stopping moment or two when the Olympic flame cauldron refused to move as it was supposed to. Strong winds affected archery, athletics and rowing, and much media coverage was given to the possibility of sharks attacking the competitors in the swimming section of the triathlon, held in Sydney harbour – they didn't! Unfortunately, as is becoming common, there were a number of drug-related disqualifications, particularly in weightlifting and wrestling. Prior to the Games, it was announced that in addition to the normal drug tests, there would also be testing for Erythropoietin (EPO), the 'endurance' drug.

The most successful competitors were the swimmers, Inge de Bruijn (NED) and Ian Thorpe (AUS) with three gold medals and a silver, a haul equalled by Leontien Zijlaard (NED) in cycling. However, it should be noted that the latter's medals were all won in individual events. The greatest number of medals was won by Russia's Alexei Nemov, with a total of six (two golds, one silver, three bronzes). Probably the most popular winner at Sydney was Cathy Freeman, who won the 400m on the track in front of an officially stated record Olympic Stadium crowd of 112,524.

The youngest gold medallist at Sydney was Xue Sang of China in the women's synchronised diving event aged

15 years 286 days, while the oldest champion was the Swedish-born American sailor, Magnus Liljedahl, in the Star class sailing at 46 years 119 days. The youngest male gold medallist was Australian swimmer Ian Thorpe, who won two gold medals aged 17 years 339 days; while the oldest female champion was Ellina Zvereva of Belarus, who won the discus aged 39 years 316 days. The oldest competitor in Sydney was archer Francois Latil of Vanuatu, aged 62 years 98 days, while the youngest was Fatema Gerashi of Bahrein, a 12-year-old swimmer. Probably, the oldest spectator at these Games was the 103-year-old American, Haig Prieste, who had won a bronze medal in the 1920 diving competitions.

At the end of the Games, some 80 countries had won a medal, of which 51 had won a gold. However, it was one of the also-rans, or to be exact also-swims, who got the most attention from the media. Eric 'the Eel' Moussambani, from Equatorial Africa, won the first heat of the 100m freestyle in the slowest time ever recorded for the distance in the Olympics. The other two competitors in his heat had been disqualified for anticipating the gun, and there was serious concern that not only would he not finish, but that he might drown. To vociferous support from the crowd he made it, and overnight became famous, or notorious, worldwide. It was reported that 93 per cent of all available tickets, covering all sports, had been sold.

2002 MEDALS (SUMMER)

	G	S	B	Total
United States	40	24	33	97
Russia	32	28	28	88
China	28	16	15	59
Australia	16	25	17	58
Germany	13	17	26	56
France	13	14	11	38
Italy	13	8	13	34
Cuba	11	11	7	29
Great Britain	11	10	7	28
Korea	8	10	10	28
Romania	11	6	9	26
The Netherlands	12	9	4	25
Ukraine	3	10	10	23
Japan	5	8	5	18
Hungary	8	6	3	17
Belarus	3	3	11	17
Poland	6	5	3	14
Canada	3	3	8	14
Bulgaria	5	6	2	13
Greece	4	6	3	13
Sweden	4	5	3	12
Brazil	—	6	6	12
Spain	3	3	5	11
Norway	4	3	3	10
Switzerland	1	6	2	9
Ethiopia	4	1	3	8
Czech Republic	2	3	3	8
Kazakhstan	3	4	—	7
Kenya	2	3	2	7
Jamaica	—	4	3	7
Denmark	2	3	1	6
Indonesia	1	3	2	6
Mexico	1	2	3	6

Georgia	—	—	6	6
Turkey	3	—	2	5
Lithuania	2	—	3	5
Slovakia	1	3	1	5
Algeria	1	1	3	5
Belgium	—	2	3	5
South Africa	—	2	3	5
Morocco	—	1	4	5
Taiwan	—	1	4	5
Iran	3	—	1	4
Finland	2	1	1	4
Uzbekistan	1	1	2	4
New Zealand	1	—	3	4
Argentina	—	2	2	4
North Korea (PRK)	—	1	3	4
Austria	2	1	—	3
Azerbaijan	2	—	1	3
Latvia	1	1	1	3
Yugoslavia	1	1	1	3
Estonia	1	—	2	3
Thailand	1	—	2	3
Nigeria	—	3	—	3
Slovenia	2	—	—	2
Bahamas	1	1	—	2
Croatia	1	—	1	2
Moldova	—	1	1	2
Saudi Arabia	—	1	1	2
Trinidad and Tobago	—	1	1	2
Costa Rica	—	—	2	2
Portugal	—	—	2	2
Cameroon	1	—	—	1
Colombia	1	—	—	1
Mozambique	1	—	—	1
Ireland	—	1	—	1
Uruguay	—	1	—	1
Vietnam	—	1	—	1
Armenia	—	—	1	1
Barbados	—	—	1	1
Chile	—	—	1	1
Iceland	—	—	1	1
India	—	—	1	1
Israel	—	—	1	1
Kyrgyzstan	—	—	1	1
Kuwait	—	—	1	1
Macedonia	—	—	1	1
Qatar	—	—	1	1
Sri Lanka	—	—	1	1

SALT LAKE CITY 2002

XIX WINTER GAMES HELD IN SALT LAKE CITY, USA,
9–24 FEBRUARY 2002
ATTENDED BY REPRESENTATIVES OF 77 COUNTRIES,
COMPRISING 2398 COMPETITORS, OF WHICH 886
WERE WOMEN.

There were nine original applicants, and, finally, after four previous bids, the first in 1966 for the 1972 Games, the IOC chose Salt Lake City in June 1995. At the end of 1998 there was a scandal about several IOC members having taken bribes relating to the selection of various Games venues. Salt Lake City one was of the places involved, and a number of local and international officials resigned. The city was the largest to host the Winter Games, its population being over one million.

Despite the oft-stated desire of the IOC to scale down the Games, there were ten events added, resulting in a record total of 78 events contested. Despite the fact that Puerto Rico didn't actually compete after marching in the opening ceremony, there were a record number of countries, of which there were Winter Games debuts by five countries: Cameroon, Hong Kong (China), Nepal, Tajikistan, and Thailand. Participation figures, male, female and total, were also records for a Winter Games. The official opening was by President George W. Bush, and the oath on behalf of the competitors was taken by a third generation Olympian, Jim Shea, who later won the skeleton sled event. Uniquely, the Olympic flag was brought in by a multinational, multicultural group who represented all the continents, and included Jean-Claude Killy (FRA), Lech Walesa (POL), Archbishop Desmond Tutu (RSA), Jean-Michael Cousteau (FRA), John Glenn (USA), Cathy Freeman (AUS), Steven Spielberg (USA), and Kazuyoshi Funaki (JPN). The ceremony was watched by a TV audience estimated to be 3.5 billion, and there were over 8000 media representatives from all over the world reporting the occasion.

The altitude of Salt Lake City made it one of the highest places ever to hold the Games, and the Utah Olympic indoor ice oval at 1424m (4675ft), and of a highly technical design, guaranteed Olympic and/or world records in every speed skating event. After the terrorist attack in New York in the previous September, security was a prime concern, with some $310 million being expended on the operation. There were some transportation problems for fans, and the weather caused the postponement of a few events. As has become almost the norm for major sports occasions, there were a number of drug abuse disqualifications, and there were complaints about poor standards of judging, particularly in the pairs skating final. This latter, in which a French judge was reportedly pressured by her federation into voting for the Russian pair over the Canadians, caused the governing body of the sport to decide on a new format of judging panels in future.

The most successful competitor was Ole Einar Björndalen of Norway, who won four gold medals in the biathlon, while the best result by a woman was Janica Kostelic of Croatia, who won three golds and a silver in Alpine skiing. In the luge, Georg Hackl of Germany became the first Winter Olympian to win medals in five consecutive Games. The youngest gold medallist was Gi-Hyun Ko (KOR) who won the women's 1500m short track speed skating aged 15 years 278 days. The youngest male winner was Stephan Hocke (GER) in the 120m ski jumping team, aged 18 years 121 days, while Veli-Metti Lindström (FIN) was in the second placed team when 26 days younger. The oldest gold medallists was Christoph Langen in the German two-man bob aged 39 years 327 days, the oldest female champion was Danielle Goyette of the victorious Canadian ice hockey team at 36 years 22 days. The oldest male medallist was Ken Trainberg of the silver medal Canadian curling squad aged 45 years 209 days, while his female equivalent was his teammate Cheryl Noble in the bronze curling team at 45 years 135 days. Vonetta Flowers (USA), in the two-woman bobsleigh event, became the first black gold medallist in a Winter Games, and Jarome Iginla was the first black male to win gold as a member of the winning Canadian ice hockey team.

2002 MEDALS (WINTER)

	G	S	B	Total
Germany	12	16	7	35
United States	10	13	11	34
Norway	11	7	6	24
Canada	6	4	7	17
Austria	2	4	11	17
Russia	6	4	5	15
Italy	4	4	4	12
France	4	5	2	11
Switzerland	3	2	6	11
The Netherlands	3	5	—	8
China	2	2	4	8
Finland	4	2	1	7
Sweden	—	2	4	6
Croatia	3	1	—	4
Korea	2	2	—	4
Czech Republic	1	1	1	3
Estonia	1	1	1	3
Bulgaria	—	1	2	3
Australia	2	—	—	2
Spain	2	—	—	2
Great Britain	1	—	1	2
Japan	—	1	1	2
Poland	—	1	1	2
Belarus	—	—	1	1
Slovenia	—	—	1	1

ATHENS 2004

XXVIII OLYMPIC GAMES TO BE HELD IN ATHENS, GREECE, 13–29 AUGUST 2004

There was preliminary interest shown by 14 cities around the world, but in September 1997 the IOC decided on Athens, the site of the inaugural modern Games in 1896. With two years to go, serious concerns were expressed as to the ability of the city to be ready in time, with suggestions that the Games be transferred elsewhere. In addition to an ongoing pollution problem, transport, construction and accommodation shortfalls were just some of the sectors worrying the IOC hierarchy. Currently, those worries appear to have been over-emphasised and the IOC is confident that all will be ready in time. There was a strong move in 2002 to remove baseball, softball and modern pentathlon from the Games programme, but, though the idea was strongly supported by the new President, Jacques Rogge, it was defeated, and the sports remain on the roster. However, there are a number of minor changes to other sports. These will include wrestling events for women, and the introduction of further 50m swimming events.

TURIN 2006

XX WINTER GAMES, TO BE HELD IN TURIN, ITALY, 11–26 FEBRUARY 2006

In June 1999 the Italian city of Turin was selected as the venue for the 2006 Winter Olympics. Other places in contention had been: Sion, Switzerland; Klagenfurt, Austria; Poprad-Tatry, Slovak Republic; Zakopane, Poland and Helsinki, Finland. It has already been estimated that these Games will cost some $1.3 billion.

BEIJING 2008

XXIX OLYMPIC GAMES

Beijing was selected over Paris, Osaka, Istanbul and Toronto. It is the most populous venue to host the Games, with a population of over 13 million. Cost estimates of new construction and renovations have been put at over $3.2 billion. It is probable that baseball, softball and modern pentathlon will be axed from the programme, as well as the walking events in athletics, and the canoe slalom events. There is a probability that golf and rugby sevens will be added.

2010

XXI WINTER GAMES

Candidates originally included Andorra, Harbin, Jaca, and Sarajevo, but a shortlist decided in 2002 comprised: Berne, Salzburg, Vancouver and Pyeong Chang in Korea. In 2003, Vancouver was selected.

2012

XXX OLYMPIC GAMES

In July 2003 the IOC announced that the final list of candidates for the these Games was as follows: Havana, Istanbul, Leipzig, London, Madrid, Moscow, New York, Paris, and Rio de Janeiro. The final choice will be made on 6 July 2005.

AN A–Z OF THE
OLYMPIC GAMES

ALPINE SKIING

Separate Alpine skiing events were first introduced into the Games in 1948, but this style had been contested in 1936 as an Alpine combination event consisting of an aggregate of points scored in a downhill and a slalom race. Toni Sailer (AUT) in 1956 and Jean-Claude Killy (FRA) in 1968 both won a record three gold medals. Vreni Schneider (SUI) was the first woman to win three golds (1988 and 1994). This was matched by Janica Kostelic of Croatia in 2002, when she also won a silver to become the first Alpine skier to win four medals in one Games. Schneider set an all-time record of five medals (three golds, a silver and a bronze) in 1988–94. The latter was equalled by Katja Seizinger (GER) and Deborah Compagnoni (ITA), both 1992–8. The men's record is seven medals by Kjetil André Aamodt (NOR) 1992–4, 2002 (three golds, two silvers and two bronzes). Alberto Tomba (ITA) was the first Alpine skier to win medals in three consecutive Games 1988–94 (Tomba's coach, Gustav Thöni, won the 1972 giant slalom). However, Deborah Compagnoni (ITA) became the first Alpine skier to win gold medals in three Games (1992–8). There were a record 131 competitors in the 1992 giant slalom, representing a record 47 countries. Uniquely, in 1998, Lasse Kjus of Norway won two silver medals on the same day, firstly in the postponed downhill race, and then, four hours later, in the combined event. Graham Bell (GBR) was the first Alpine skier to compete in five Olympic Games, 1984–98.

The oldest gold medallist was Stephan Eberhalter (AUT) who won the 2002 giant slalom aged 32 years 334 days, while the youngest was Michela Figini (SUI) aged 17 years 314 days when winning the 1984 downhill. The youngest male winner was Sailer (see above) aged 20 years 73 days in the 1956 slalom, and the oldest female champion was Ossi Reichert (GER) in the 1956 giant slalom aged 30 years 33 days. Stephan Eberhalter (AUT) was also the oldest medallist with his giant slalom victory in 2002, and the youngest medallist was Gertraud 'Traudl' Hecher (AUT) aged 16 years 145 days with the bronze in the 1960 downhill race. The youngest male medallist was Alfred Matt (AUT) with the 1968 slalom bronze aged 19 years 281 days, and the oldest female medallist was Dorothea Hochleitner (AUT) aged 30 years 201 days when she won the 1956 giant slalom bronze. When Edwina Chamier (CAN) competed in the 1936 Alpine combination she became the oldest ever female Winter Olympian at the age of 45 years 318 days.

Speeds of 145km/h (90mph) are reached by men, and 130km/h (80mph) by women, in the downhill events at the Games. However, the highest average speed recorded in an Olympic downhill race was 107.532km/h (66.817 mph) by Jean-Luc Crétier in 1998. The highest by a woman was 102.403km/h (63.630mph) by Katja Seizinger in the downhill portion of the combined event in 1998. Appended below is a table of average speeds in the Olympic downhill races since 1936:

AVERAGE SPEEDS IN THE OLYMPIC DOWNHILL RACES

Men			Women	
Year	km/h	Winner	km/h	Winner
1936	47.599	Ruud (NOR)	39.031	Schou-Nilsen (NOR)
1948	66.034	Oreiller (FRA)	43.695	Schlunegger (SUI)
1952	57.629	Colò (ITA)	50.420	Jochum-Beiser (AUT)
1956	72.356	Sailer (AUT)	55.484	Berthod (SUI)
1960	88.429	Vuarnet (FRA)	67.426	Biebl (GER)
1964	81.297	Zimmermann (AUT)	74.496	Haas (AUT)
1968	86.808	Killy (FRA)	77.080	Pall (AUT)
1972	85.291	Russi (SUI)	78.568	Nadig (SUI)
1976	102.828	Klammer (AUT)	85.286	Mittermaier (FRG)
1980	102.677	Stock (AUT)	99.598	Moser-Pröll (AUT)
1984	104.532	Johnson (USA)	96.428	Figini (SUI)
1988	94.702	Zurbriggen (SUI)	93.836	Kiehl (FRG)
1992	99.418	Ortlieb (AUT)	88.600	Lee-Gartner (CAN)
1994	103.319	Moe (USA)	99.109	Seizinger (GER)
1998	107.532	Cretier (FRA)	101.977	Seizinger (GER)
2002	103.880	Strobl (AUT)	97.420*	Montillet (FRA)

* In the downhill segment of the combined event Renate Götschl (AUT) achieved 107.000km/h (66mph).

The greatest margin of victory in downhill was 4.7sec by Madeleine Berthod (FRA) in 1956, while the best in the male race was 4.1sec by Henri Oreiller (FRA) in 1948. The smallest margin was 0.04sec in the 1994 men's race, while that for women was 0.05sec in the 1984 event. The greatest margin in slalom was 11.3sec by Christl Cranz (GER) in the 1936 combination event, while that in the men's equivalent was 5.9sec by Franz Pfnür (GER). Since then Toni Sailer (AUT) won by 4.0sec in 1956 and Anne Heggtveit (CAN) the 1960 women's race by 3.3sec. The smallest margin was 0.02sec in the 1972 women's

event, which was equalled in the 1994 men's race. The tie for silver in the 1992 women's slalom was the first such tie since the introduction of automatic timing.

In the giant slalom the biggest margin was 6.2sec by Sailer in 1956, while for women it was 2.64sec by Nancy Greene (CAN) in 1968. The smallest margin was 0.1sec (before electronic timing) by Yvonne Ruegg (SUI) in 1960, and 0.12sec by Kathy Kreiner (CAN) in 1976. The smallest for men was 0.20sec by Henri Hemmi (SUI) in 1976. The greatest margin in the super giant slalom was 1.30sec by Franck Piccard (FRA) in 1988, and for women it was 1.41sec by Deborah Compagnoni (ITA) in 1992. The smallest for men was 0.08sec by Markus Wasmeier (GER) in 1994,and for women it was 0.01sec by Picabo Street (USA) in 1998 – the latter being the smallest margin of victory in any Olympic Alpine skiing event.

ALPINE SKIING MEDALS (NOT INCLUDING FREESTYLE SKIING)

| | Men | | | Women | | | |
	G	S	B	G	S	B	Total
Austria	15	21	9	14	11	87	
Switzerland	6	11	9	10	7	7	50
France	10	5	7	4	8	7	41
United States	3	6	1	7	9	3	29
Italy	7	5	2	5	3	5	27
Germany	3	2	1	7	5	7	25
Norway	7	7	6	—	—	1	21
Sweden	2	—	3	2	2	1	10
Canada	—	—	2	4	1	3	10
West Germany (FRG)	—	1	—	3	4	1	9
Liechtenstein	—	1	3	2	1	2	9
Croatia	—	—	—	3	1	—	4
Slovenia	—	—	1	—	—	2	3
Luxembourg	—	2	—	—	—	—	2
Spain	1	—	—	—	—	1	2
Yugoslavia	—	1	—	—	1	—	2
Japan	—	1	—	—	—	—	1
New Zealand	—	—	—	—	1	—	1
Russia	—	—	—	—	1	—	1
Australia	—	—	—	—	—	1	1
Czechoslovakia	—	—	—	—	—	1	1
Soviet Union	—	—	—	—	—	1	1
	56	57*	56†	56	58‡	54	337

*Two silvers in 1998 super giant slalom. †Two bronzes in 1948 downhill. ‡Two silvers in the 1964 and 1992 giant slalom.

AMERICAN FOOTBALL

A demonstration sport at Los Angeles in 1932. Two teams representing the East and West of America played an exhibition, which the West won 7–6.

ARCHERY

The sport made its first appearance in the 1900 Games in Paris with six events on the programme. Some Olympic historians consider that another, live pigeon shooting, was an official event, but the majority think not, and this book follows that opinion. The contests were held in Continental style, with each archer shooting a single arrow at a time in competition order (as opposed to the British method of three arrows at each turn). The eligibility of the 1904 archery competitions is also disputed by some, particularly as only American archers took part. However, the majority of historians, and the author, accept them as Olympic events. The competitors in the 1904 women's contests were among the first women to compete in the Olympics, with only the tennis players in 1900 having a prior claim. The competitions of 1908 were accorded a much higher status than before despite only three nations taking part. The men's York Round was won by William Dod (GBR), and his remarkable sister, Charlotte, took the silver behind Queenie Newall in the women's event. Lottie Dod, then over 36 years old, was one of the greatest sportswomen of her, or, indeed, of any generation. She had won the Wimbledon tennis singles five times, the British Ladies golf crown in 1904, and had represented England at hockey. She also excelled at skating and tobogganing. She and William were also the first brother and sister, in any sport, to win medals at the Olympic Games.

Archery was not included in the 1912 Games but, reflecting Belgium's great interest in the sport, there were ten events at Antwerp in 1920, all in the Belgian style of shooting. With only three countries present again, Hubert van Innis (BEL), now 54, brought his total medals to a record six golds and three silvers. The most successful woman has been Kim Soo-Nyung (KOR) with three gold medals and a silver in 1988–92. The sport was dropped from the Games until 1972. In 1988 a team competition was introduced.

Archery appears to be a sport at which competitors can continue at the highest level until well advanced in years. Thus, the oldest gold medallist was the Rev Galen Spencer (USA) in the winning 1904 team two days past his 64th birthday. A fellow team member, Robert Williams Jr, a youngster of 63 years, was uniquely the only known Olympic gold medallist to have fought in the American Civil War – that time on the losing side. The youngest champion was Yun Young-Sooh (KOR) aged 17 years 21 days in the winning 1988 women's team. The youngest male winner was Park Sung-Soo (KOR) in the 1988 team aged 18 years 135 days, while the oldest female champion was Lida Howell (USA) in 1904 aged 45 years 25 days. The oldest ever medallist was Samuel Harding Duvall (USA) aged 68 years 194 days winning a silver in the 1904 team contest, while the youngest medallist was Denise Parker (USA) with a team bronze in 1988 aged 14 years 294 days. The youngest male medallist was Henry Richardson (USA) with a team bronze in 1904 aged 15 years 126 days. Hubert van Innis (BEL) won gold medals over a record span of 20 years (1900–2000). The first paraplegic to compete in a standard Olympic event was Neroli Fairhall (NZL) who, from her wheelchair, finished 35th in the 1984 women's archery event. In 2000, the Korean women equalled their clean sweep of 1988.

ARCHERY MEDALS

| | Men | | | Women | | | |
	G	S	B	G	S	B	Total
United States	9	6	5	4	2	3	29
France	6	10	6	—	—	—	22
Korea	2	3	1	9	3	3	21
Belgium	10	6	3	—	—	—	19
Soviet Union	—	1	1	1	2	4	9
Great Britain	1	1	3	1	1	1	8
Finland	1	1	1	—	—	1	4
Italy	—	1	3	—	—	—	4
China	—	—	—	—	3	—	3
Sweden	—	2	—	—	—	—	2
Japan	—	1	1	—	—	—	2
Poland	—	—	—	—	1	1	2
The Netherlands	1	—	1	—	—	—	2
Germany	—	—	—	—	1	1	2
Ukraine	—	—	—	—	1	1	2
Spain	1	—	—	—	—	—	1
Australia	1	—	—	—	—	—	1
Indonesia	—	—	—	—	1	—	1
	32*	32	25†	15	15	15	134

*Only one gold medal was awarded in two 1920 events. †No bronze medals in one 1900, and six 1920 events.

ATHLETICS (*see also* Tug-of-War)

OLYMPIC RECORDS
(There has always been some confusion as to whether wind-assisted performances should be considered as Games records. Both are given here).

MEN

100m	9.84sec	Donovan Bailey (CAN)	1996
200m	19.32sec	Michael Johnson (USA)	1996
400m	43.49sec	Michael Johnson (USA)	1996
800m	1min 42.58sec	Vebjørn Rodal (NOR)	1996
1500m	3min 32.07sec	Noah Ngeny (KEN)	2000
5000m	13min 05.59sec	Said Aouita (MAR)	1984
10,000m	27min 07.34sec	Haile Gebrselassie (ETH)	1996
Marathon	2hr 09min 21sec	Carlos Lopes (POR)	1984
110m Hurdles	12.95sec	Allen Johnson (USA)	1996
400m Hurdles	46.78sec	Kevin Young (USA)	1992
3000m Steeplechase	8min 05.51sec	Julius Kariuki (KEN)	1988
20km Walk	1hr 18min 59sec	Robert Korzeniowski (POL)	2000
50km Walk	3hr 38min 29sec	Vyacheslav Ivanenko (URS)	1988
4 x 100m	37.40sec	United States	1992
4 x 400m	2min 55.74sec	United States	1992
High Jump	2.39min	Charles Austin (USA)	1996
Pole Vault	5.92min	Jean Galfione (FRA)	1996
Long Jump	8.90min	Bob Beamon (USA)	1968
Triple Jump	18.09min	Kenny Harrison (USA)	1996
	18.17min*	Mike Conley (USA)	1992)
Shot	22.47min	Ulf Timmermann (GDR)	1988

Discus	69.40min	Lars Riedel (GER)	1996
Hammer	84.80min	Sergei Litvinov (URS)	1988
Javelin	90.17min	Jan Zelezny (TCH)	2000
Decathlon	8847pts	Daley Thompson (GBR)	1984

WOMEN

100m	10.62sec†	Florence Griffith-Joyner (USA)	1988
	10.54sec*	Florence Griffith-Joyner (USA)	1988
200m	21.34sec	Florence Griffith-Joyner (USA)	1988
400m	48.25sec	Marie-José Pérec (FRA)	1996
800m	1min 53.43sec	Nadyezhda Olizarenko (URS)	1980
1500m	3min 53.96sec	Paula Ivan (ROM)	1988
5000m	14min 40.79sec	Gabriela Szabo (ROM)	2000
10,000m	30min 17.49sec	Derartu Tulu (ETH)	2000
Marathon	2h 23min 14sec	Naoko Takahashi (JPN)	2000
100m Hurdles	12.38sec	Yordanka Donkova (BUL)	1988
400m Hurdles	52.82sec	Deon Hemmings (JAM)	1996
4 x 100m	41.60sec	GDR	1980
4 x 400m	3min 15.17sec	USSR	1988
20km Walk	1hr 29min 05sec	Wang Liping (CHN)	2000
High Jump	2.05min	Stefka Kostadinova (BUL)	1996
Pole Vault	4.60min	Stacy Dragila (USA)	2000
Long Jump	7.40min	Jackie Joyner-Kersee (USA)	1988
Triple Jump	15.33min	Inessa Kravets (UKR)	1996
Shot	22.41min	Ilona Slupianek (GDR)	1980
Discus	72.30min	Martina Hellmann (GDR)	1988
Hammer	71.16min	Kamila Skolimowska (POL)	2000
Javelin	68.91min‡	Trine Hattestad (NOR)	2000
Heptathlon	7291pts	Jackie Joyner-Kersee (USA)	1988

* Wind assisted. † In preliminary round. ‡ New implement.

The track and field events have been the centrepiece of every Olympic Games since 1896. From 1920 until the International Amateur Athletics Federation (IAAF) inaugurated their first world title meeting in 1983, the Olympic events were also official world championships. In the early Games quite large numbers of entries per country were allowed in an event, e.g. 12 in 1908, but in 1928 that was limited to four and in 1932 to three. After Barcelona in 1992 a suggestion was made to reduce the number to two, but has not been acted on to date. The first champion in modern Olympic history was James Connolly (USA) who won the triple jump (then called the hop, step and jump) on 6 April 1896. He also won medals in the high and long jumps, and went on to become a novelist and war correspondent. The first winner of an Olympic event was Francis Lane (USA), who won the first heat of the 100m earlier the same day. Women's events were introduced in 1928, and the first female gold medallist was Halina Konopacka (POL) in the discus. As with the men, the first winner of an Olympic women's event was Anni Holdmann (GER) who took the first heat of the 100m the day before.

A record ten gold medals were won by Ray Ewry (USA) in the standing jumps from 1900 to 1908. It is a feat unsurpassed in any sport – Ewry had contracted polio as a child – and included a unique three titles on a single day in 1900. The Finnish distance runner Paavo Nurmi won a total of twelve medals from 1920 to 1928, comprising nine golds and three silvers. He won them in an unmatched seven different events, and his five golds in 1924 is a record for any single Games. Carl Lewis (USA) equalled Nurmi's nine gold medals, 1984–96, as a sprinter/long jumper, adding a silver as well. However,

the most individual titles at one Games is four by Alvin Kraenzlein (USA) in 1900. This total of four golds was equalled by Jesse Owens (USA) in 1936 and Carl Lewis (USA) in 1984, but they only gained three individual events – 100m, 200m and long jump – with the fourth gold medal in the relay. Fanny Blankers-Koen (NED) in 1948 matched them in 1948 in the 100m, 200m, 80m hurdles and relay. Nurmi's teammate, Ville Ritola, won a record six medals in 1924, consisting of four golds and two silvers, incurring eight distance races in eight days. Nurmi himself, when winning his five golds in 1924, had won seven races in six days. The forerunner of all 'Flying Finns', Hannes Kohlemainen, had won six such races within nine days in 1912.

Four gold medals have been won by four women: Fanny Blankers-Koen (NED) in 1948, a female record for one Games, as is the three individual titles that included: Betty Cuthbert (AUS) in 1956 and 1964; Bärbel Wöckel (née Eckert) (GDR) in 1976 and 1980; and Evelyn Ashford (USA) from 1984 to 1992.

When Merlene Ottey (JAM) competed at Sydney in 2000, she set or equalled a number of records for a woman. She won her eighth medal, in her 13th Olympic final, at her sixth Games, over a period of 20 years. Shirley Strickland (later de la Hunty, AUS) won an official total of seven medals from 1948 to 1956, comprising three golds, a silver and three bronzes. However, a 1975 study of photo evidence indicates that Strickland also came third, not fourth, in the 1948 200m, but no official move has been made to change the result. Irena Szewinska (née Kirszenstein, POL), is the only woman to win medals at four successive Games – Ottey's medals were won at five Games, but not consecutive ones.

A further remarkable track and field achievement was the four successive gold medals in the discus won by Al Oerter (USA) 1956–68. This was matched by Carl Lewis (USA) in the long jump 1984–96. Almost as worthy were the three golds and a silver won by Viktor Saneyev (URS) in the injury-prone triple jump event of 1968–80. Mildred Didrikson (USA) – who later achieved golf fame as 'Babe' Zaharias – achieved a unique triple in 1932, when she won medals in a run (80m hurdles, gold), a jump (high jump, silver) and a throw (javelin, gold). Another unusual spread of medals was by Micheline Ostermeyer (FRA) in 1948 with golds in the shot and discus and a bronze in the high jump. Perhaps even more surprising was the fact that she was a concert pianist. The foremost male equivalent was Robert Garrett (USA) with golds in the shot and discus, and silvers in the high and long jumps, in 1896. Stanley Rowley won bronze medals in the 60m, 100m and 200m in 1900 representing Australasia (he was an Australian), and then was drafted into the British team for the 5000m team event, and won a gold medal although he did not actually finish the race.

The oldest gold medallist was Patrick 'Babe' McDonald (USA) winning the 56lb weight throw in 1920 aged 42 years 23 days. The youngest gold medallist was Barbara Pearl Jones (USA) in the 1952 sprint relay aged 15 years 123 days, while the youngest individual event champion was Ulrike Meyfarth (FRG) who won the high jump in 1972 aged exactly one year older. The youngest male champion was Robert Mathias (USA) who won the 1948 decathlon aged 17 years 263 days, and later in 1966, after a brief movie career, became a US Congressman. The oldest female champion was Lia Manoliu (ROM) in the 1968 discus aged 36 years 176 days. She (1952–72), British javelin thrower Tessa Sanderson (1976–96), and Jamaican sprinter Merlene Ottey (1980–2000), both hold the record for attending six Games. The record for male athletes, of five Games, is held by ten men. Manoliu's, Sanderson's and Ottey's 20-year spans of competition match the record of Dorothy Odam-Tyler (GBR) and Toyoko Yoshino-Nakamura (JPN), both 1936–56, and Francie Larrieu-Smith (USA), 1972–92. The greatest span of competition in Olympic athletics is 24 years by discus thrower Frantisek Janda-Suk of Bohemia and Czechoslovakia, 1900–24. The oldest medallist was Tebbs Lloyd Johnson (GBR) in the 50km walk of 1948, aged 48 years 115 days, and the oldest female medallist was Merlene Ottey (JAM) winning a silver in the 2000 relay aged 40 years 143 days. Barbara Jones (see above) was also the youngest medallist, while the youngest male medallist was Mikhel Dorizas (GRE) in the 1906 stone throw aged 16 years 11 days. The oldest competitor ever in Olympic athletics was Percy Wyer (CAN) aged 52 years 199 days when he came 30th in the 1936 marathon. The oldest female competitor was Lourdes Klitzkie of Guam aged 48 years 234 days when placing 63rd in the 1988 marathon. Probably, the youngest ever competitor was Jakab Kause (HUN), who was 13 years 115 days when placing equal fourth in the 1900 pole vault.

The first brothers to win medals were Richard and Lewis Sheldon (USA) in the 1900 throws and jumps respectively. The first to gain medals in the same event were Platt and Ben Adams (USA) who won gold and silver in the 1912 standing high jump. Brothers Commodore and Leroy 'Roy' Cochran both won gold medals in the 4 x 400m relay, but in 1924 and 1948 respectively, 'Roy' also won the 400m hurdles in London. The most successful siblings were the Press sisters (URS), Tamara with three golds and a silver, and Irina, with two golds, in 1960 and 1964. The only twins to win medals were Patrick and Pascal Barré (FRA) in the bronze medal sprint relay of 1980. Father and son gold medallists are represented by two families. Werner Järvinen (FIN) won the 1906 Greek style discus, his son Matti won the javelin in 1932, and another son Akilles, gained silver medals in the 1928 and 1932 decathlons. In 1948 Imre Németh (HUN) won the hammer, and 28 years later his son Miklós won the javelin with a world record throw. The only father/daughter medal combination was Lennox Miller (JAM), with a 1968 100m silver, and Inger Miller (USA), with a gold in the 1996 sprint relay.

The most successful mother/daughter combination was Elisaveta Bagriantseva (URS), with a silver in the 1952 discus, and Irina Nazarova, with a gold in the 4 X 400m relay of 1980. Uniquely, Violet Webb (GBR) and her daughter, Janet Simpson, both won bronze medals in the 4 x 100m relay, in 1932 and 1964 respectively. One of the more poignant Olympic stories relates to Marie Dollinger, who was one of the women involved in dropping the baton in the 1936 sprint relay when the German women 'couldn't lose'. One imagines the thoughts of her daughter, Brunhilde Hendrix, in the 1960 relay final – happily she won a silver medal to match that of her father, Friedrich, in the 1932 sprint relay. Incidentally, it has recently been suggested that the disaster to the usual machine-like precision exchanges of the 1936 German team was due to a last-minute change in their order, to match similar changes to the American team's order. Remarkably, Dollinger had first run in the Olympics in 1928, in the inaugural 800m, and in 1931 had equalled the world 800m record – not the usual CV of a world-class sprinter.

The first married couple to win gold medals were Emil and Dana Zátopek (TCH). Even more coincidental is the fact that Dana won her javelin title on the same afternoon as one of Emil's victories in 1952 – remarkably, both of them were also born on the same day. The only other couple has been Viktor Bryzgin (URS), 4 x 100m in 1988, and his wife, Olga, gold medallist in the 400m and 4 x 400m. Frank Wykoff (USA) was the only sprinter to win gold medals in three Games, in relay teams from 1928 to 1936, until he was equalled by Evelyn Ashford (USA), also in relay teams, 1984–92, and Carl Lewis (USA) 1984–92.

The first Olympic athlete to be disqualified for contravening the drug regulations was Danuta Rosani (POL) in the 1976 discus. By far the biggest uproar occurred with the positive testing of Ben Johnson (CAN), after he had won the 1988 100m title in an apparently fabulous new world record of 9.79sec. The repercussions on world attitudes to drug testing were immense. The scrutiny of a 'sex test' for women was introduced into the Games in 1968, many years too late in the opinion of many. They had in mind the case of Dora Ratjen (GER) who placed fourth in the 1936 high jump and was later found to be a man posing as a woman. There was also the case of Stella Walasiewicz (later Walsh), Polish-born but later an American citizen, who won gold and silver in the

100m of 1932 and 1936 respectively, and was reported, after her violent death in 1980, to have 'primary male characteristics'.

The shortest time that an athlete has held an Olympic record was 0.4sec by Olga Rukavishnikova (URS) in the 1980 pentathlon. That is the difference between her second place time of 2min 04.8sec in the final 800m event of the five-event contest, and the time of the third-placed Nadyezhda Tkachenko (URS), whose overall points score exceeded her teammate's by 146. Only three athletes have lost, actually lost, a title and then won it back. Nina Romashkova-Ponomareva (URS) won the discus in 1952, came third in 1956, then won again in 1960. Similarly, Ulrike Meyfarth (FRG) won the high jump in 1972, did not make the final in 1976, but won again in 1984. The only man was Vladimir Golubnichiy (URS) in the 20km walk, winning in 1960, third in 1964 and first again in 1968. (Incidentally he also placed second in 1972.) Meyfarth's 12 years between gold medals is matched only by Al Oerter, Carl Lewis and Irena Szewinska. Martin Sheridan (USA) competed in 15 events from 1904 to 1908, winning five golds, three silvers and one bronze. The largest number of competitors in a single event was the 124 runners in the 1996 men's marathon – 111 finished. The largest women's field was also in the 1996 marathon, with 86 starters of which 65 finished. The use of starting blocks was allowed in the Games for the first time in 1948 (see also Automatic Timing).

A number of Olympic athletics medallists have later made their mark in Hollywood films. In particular, they have come from the ranks of the decathletes – Jim Thorpe, Glenn Morris, Bob Mathias, Rafer Johnson, C. K. Yang, Floyd Simmons and Bruce Jenner. The 1924 pole vault champion, Lee Barnes, doubled for Buster Keaton in the vault sequence in his excellent film College. The 1928 silver medallist in the shot, Herman Brix, changed his name to Bruce Bennett, and had many serious roles after an initial appearance as Tarzan. Norman Pritchard (GBR), a 1900 medallist, reportedly made many silent films, while more recent additions to the Hollywood scene have been 1952 sprint-relay gold winner, Dean Smith (USA) and 1968 pole vault champion Bob Seagren (USA). The film industries of other countries have welcomed: Tapio Rautavaara (FIN), the 1948 javelin champion; Giuseppe Tosi (ITA) the 1948 discus silver medallist; Giuseppe Gentile (ITA) 1968 triple jump bronze; and Adhemar Ferreira da Silva (BRA) the 1952 and 1956 triple jump champion.

The 1996 marathon champion, Josiah Thugwane (RSA), is thought to be the smallest male Olympic gold medallist in athletics ever, at 1.58m tall and weighing 45kg. The above-mentioned Merlene Ottey (JAM) is the only athlete to be a finalist in the same event, the 200m in her case, at five Games, 1984–2000. At Sydney, Marla Runyan (USA) became the first legally blind athlete to run in an Olympic final; only able to see nearby blurred shapes, she nevertheless placed eighth in a 12-woman field in the 1500m.

YOUNGEST AND OLDEST MEDALLISTS, BY EVENT
MEN

Event	Medal	Youngest Yr/Dy	Name/Country	Date	Oldest Yr/Dy	Name/Country	Date
100m	G	19-128	Reggie Walker (RSA)	1908	32-121	Linford Christie (GBR)	1992
	M	18-234	Donald Lippincott (USA)	1912	32-121	Linford Christie (GBR)	1992
200m	G	20-47	Percy Williams (CAN)	1928	29-323	Michael Johnson (USA)	1996
	M	17-287	Dwayne Evans (USA)	1976	30-170	Barney Ewell (USA)	1948
400m	G	19-135	Steve Lewis (USA)	1988	33-12	Michael Johnson (USA)	2000
	M	19-135	Steve Lewis (USA)	1988	33-12	Michael Johnson (USA)	2000
800m	G	20-237	Ted Meredith (USA)	1912	31-147	Albert Hill (GBR)	1920
	M	20-035	Earl Jones (USA)	1984	32-58	Arthur Wint (JAM)	1952
1500m	G	21-62	Peter Rono (KEN)	1988	31-149	Albert Hill (GBR)	1920
	M	21-62	Peter Rono (KEN)	1988	31-149	Albert Hill (GBR)	1920
5000m	G	20-321	Joseph Guillemot (FRA)	1920	36-78*	Miruts Yifter (ETH)	1980
	M	19-237	Fita Bayissa (ETH)	1992	36-78*	Miruts Yifter (ETH)	1980
10,000m	G	21-42	Brahim Boutayeb (MAR)	1988	36-73*	Miruts Yifter (ETH)	1980
	M	20-104	Richard Chelimo (KEN)	1992	36-73*	Miruts Yifter (ETH)	1980
Marathon	G	20-301	Juan Zabala (ARG)	1932	37-176	Carlos Lopes (POR)	1984
	M	19-178	Ernst Fast (SWE)	1900	40-90	Mamo Wolde (ETH)	1972
3km Steeple-	G	20-33	Matthew Birir (KEN)	1992	32-211	Kip Keino (KEN)	1972
chase	M	20-33	Matthew Birir (KEN)	1992	32-211	Kip Keino (KEN)	1972
110m	G	20-304	Fred Kelly (USA)	1912	30-237	Mark McKoy (CAN)	1992
Hurdles	M	20-304	Fred Kelly (USA)	1912	33-50	Willie Davenport (USA)	1976
400m	G	20-329	Ed Moses (USA)	1976	29-207	Roy Cochran (USA)	1948
Hurdles	M	18-325	Eddie Southern (USA)	1956	33-252	Kris Akabusi (GBR)	1992
4 x 100m	G	18-118	Johnny Jones (USA)	1976	32-21	Jon Drummond (USA)	2000
	M	17-229	Ture Persson (SWE)	1912	33-292	Jocelyn Delecour (FRA)	1968
4 x 400m	G	19-100	Edgar Ablowich (USA)	1932	33-17	Michael Johnson (USA)	2000
	M	17-+	Pál Simon (HUN)	1908	33-254	Kris Akabusi (GBR)	1992
20km Walk	G	22-25	Jefferson Perez (ECU)	1996	33-110	Peter Frenkel (GDR)	1972
	M	21-253	Noel Freeman (AUS)	1960	37-71	Peter Frenkel (GDR)	1976
50km Walk	G	25-103	Norman Read (NZL)	1956	38-128	Thomas Green (GBR)	1932

Event	G/M	Age	Name	Year	Age	Name	Year
	M	24-277	Aigars Fadeyevs (LAT)	2000	48-115	Tebbs Lloyd Johnson (GBR)	1948
High Jump	G	19-214	Jacek Wszola (POL)	1976	30-3	Con Leahy (GBR)	1906
	M	18-140	Valeri Brumel (URS)	1960	32-347	Javier Sotomayor (CUB)	2000
Pole Vault	G	17-360	Lee Barnes (USA)	1924	30-280	Bob Richards (USA)	1956
	M	17-360	Lee Barnes (USA)	1924	30-280	Bob Richards (USA)	1956
Long Jump	G	19-17	Randy Williams (USA)	1972	35-28	Carl Lewis (USA)	1996
	M	19-17	Randy Williams (USA)	1972	35-28	Carl Lewis (USA)	1996
Triple Jump	G	20-225	Gustaf Lindblom (SWE)	1912	34-141	Jonathan Edwards (GBR)	2000
	M	20-38	Arnoldo Devonish (VEN)	1952	34-296	Viktor Saneyev (URS)	1980
Shot	G	19-167†	Ralph Rose (USA)	1904	32-151	Wladyslaw Komar (POL)	1972
	M	19-167†	Ralph Rose (USA)	1904	37-59	Denis Horgan (GBR)	1908
Discus	G	20-69	Al Oerter (USA)	1956	35-240	Ludvik Danek (TCH)	1972
	M	19-170	Ralph Rose (USA)	1904	37-46	John Powell (USA)	1984
Hammer	G	20-161	József Csermák (HUN)	1952	35-187	John Flanagan (USA)	1908
	M	19-165	Ralph Rose (USA)	1904	45-205	Matt McGrath (USA)	1924
Javelin	G	20-34	Erik Lundkvist (SWE)	1928	34-99	Jan Zelezny (CZE)	2000
	M	20-34‡	Erik Lundkvist (SWE)	1928	38-332	József Várszegi (HUN)	1948
Decathlon	G	17-263	Bob Mathias (USA)	1948	30-102§	Helge Løvland (NOR)	1920
	M	17-263	Bob Mathias (USA)	1948	30-166	Chris Huffins (USA)	2000

WOMEN

Event	G/M	Age	Name	Year	Age	Name	Year
100m	G	16-343	Elizabeth Robinson (USA)	1928	30-98	Fanny Blankers-Koen (NED)	1948
	M	16-343	Elizabeth Robinson (USA)	1928	36-78	Merlene Ottey (JAM)	1996
200m	G	18-254	Betty Cuthbert (AUS)	1956	30-102	Fanny Blankers-Koen (NED)	1948
	M	17-116	Raelene Boyle (AUS)	1968	36-83	Merlene Ottey (JAM)	1996
400m	G	19-340	Monika Zehrt (GDR)	1972	30-66	Irena Szewinska (POL)	1976
	M	18-152	Christina Brehmer (GDR)	1976	30-66	Irena Szewinska (POL)	1976
800m	G	20-251	Madeline Manning (USA)	1968	28-194	Svetlana Masterkova (RUS)	1996
	M	20-100	Inge Gentzel (SWE)	1928	33-205	Fita Lovin (ROM)	1984
1500m	G	24-29	Hassiba Boulmerka (ALG)	1992	29-347	Nouria Merah-Benida (ALG)	2000
	M	19-227	Qu Yunxia (CHN)	1992	35-188	Violeta Szekely (ROM)	2000
3000/	G	23-201	Wang Junxia (CHN)	1996	34-12	Maricica Puica (ROM)	1984
5000m	M	23-201	Wang Junxia (CHN)	1996	34-12	Maricica Puica (ROM)	1984
10,000m	G	20-139	Derartu Tulu (ETH)	1992	28-193	Derartu Tulu (ETH)	2000
	M	20-139	Derartu Tulu (ETH)	1992	32-28	Lynn Jennings (USA)	1992
Marathon	G	22-223	Fatuma Roba (ETH)	1996	30-86	Rosa Mota (POR)	1988
	M	22-223	Fatuma Roba (ETH)	1996	37-61	Lorraine Moller (NZL)	1992
80m/100m	G	17-19	Maureen Caird (AUS)	1968	32-101	Ludmila Engquist (SWE)	1996
Hurdles	M	17-19	Maureen Caird (AUS)	1968	34-95	Karin Balzer (GDR)	1972
400m	G	22-115	Nawal El Moutawakel (MAR)	1984	31-310	Irina Privalova (RUS)	2000
Hurdles	M	22-115	Nawal El Moutawakel (MAR)	1984	31-354	Deon Hemmings (JAM)	2000
4 x 100m	G	15-123	Barbara Jones (USA)	1952	35-115	Evelyn Ashford (USA)	1992
	M	15-123	Barbara Jones (USA)	1952	40-143	Merlene Ottey (JAM)	2000
4 x 400m	G	18-154℃	Christina Brehmer (GDR)	1976	34-26	Jearl Miles-Clark (USA)	2000
	M	17-236	Mabel Fergerson (USA)	1972	34-26	Jearl Miles-Clark (USA)	2000
20km Walk	G	24-82	Wang Liping (CHN)	2000	24-82	Wang Liping (CHN)	2000
	M	24-82	Wang Liping (CHN)	2000	28-254	Kjersti Plätzer (NOR)	2000
High Jump	G	16-123	Ulrike Meyfarth (FRG)	1972	31-131	Steka Kostadinova (BUL)	1996
	M	16-115	Dorothy Odam-Tyler (GBR)	1936	31-131	Stefka Kostadinova (BUL)	1996
Pole Vault	G	29-184	Stacy Dragila (USA)	2000	29-184	Stacy Dragila (USA)	2000
	M	22-222	Vala Flossadottir (ISL)	2000	29-194	Stacy Dragila (USA)	2000
Long Jump	G	20-256	Tatyana Kolpakova (URS)	1980	29-67	Viorica Viscopoleanu (ROM)	1968
	M	17-332	Willye White (USA)	1956	35-288	Heike Drechsler (GER)	2000
Triple Jump	G	23-19	Tereza Marinova (BUL)	2000	29-300	Inessa Kravets (UKR)	1996
	M	23-19	Tereza Marinova (BUL)	2000	29-300	Inessa Kravets (UKR)	1996
Shot	G	21-186	Galina Zybina (URS)	1952	34-255	Ivanka Khristova (BUL)	1976
	M	21-186	Galina Zybina (URS)	1952	36-212	Larisa Peleshenko (RUS)	2000
Discus	G	20-121	Evelin Schlaak (GDR)	1976	39-316	Ellina Zvereva (BLR)	2000
	M	20-100	Ruth Osburn (USA)	1932	39-316	Ellina Zvereva (BLR)	2000
Hammer	G	17-361	Kamila Skolimowska (POL)	2000	17-361	Kamila Skolimowska (POL)	2000
	M	17-361	Kamila Skolimowska (POL)	2000	29-313	Olga Kuzenkova (RUS)	2000
Javelin	G	17-86	Mihaela Penes (ROM)	1964	34-165	Trine Hattestad (NOR)	2000
	M	17-86	Mihaela Penes (ROM)	1964	37-348	Dana Zátopková (TCH)	1960

| Heptathlon | G | 23-267 | Glynis Nunn (AUS) | 1984 | 30-152 | Jackie Joyner-Kersee (USA) | 1992 |
| | M | 22-154 | Jackie Joyner-Kersee (USA) | 1984 | 30-344 | Sabine John (GDR) | 1988 |

* A questionable date of birth would result in revised age of 20 days less. † Mickel Dorizas (GRE) was third in the 1906 stone throw aged 16 years 11 days. ‡ Mickel Dorizas (GRE) was second in the 1908 javelin (freestyle) aged 18 years –90 days. § Thomas Kiely (GBR) won the 1904 all-round title aged 34 years134 days. ⁌ Grit Breuer (GDR) only ran in heats of 1988 event, but received a gold medal aged 16 years –228 days.

TRACK AND FIELD MEDALS (excluding Tug-of-War)

| | Men | | | Women | | | |
	G	S	B	G	S	B	Total
United States*	267	197	163	43	25	20	715
Soviet Union	37	37	42	34	29	35	214
Great Britain	43	63	43	6	20	16	191
Finland	48	33	30	1	2	—	114
East Germany (GDR)	14	14	14	24	23	21	110
Germany	8	24	26	10	12	16	96
Sweden	17	25	41	1	—	4	88
Australia	6	10	12	12	10	12	63
France	8	20	18	6	1	4	57
Italy	13	8	20	3	7	3	54
Canada	12	10	17	2	5	7	53
Poland	13	8	5	8	8	7	49
Kenya	15	18	12	—	1	1	47
(West Germany (FRG)	4	8	12	8	6	5	43
Hungary	7	13	16	3	1	2	42
Jamaica†	4	11	7	1	9	6	38
Romania	—	—	1	10	12	8	31
Greece	4	7	14	1	4	—	30
Cuba	5	8	5	2	2	5	27
Czechoslovakia‡	8	7	3	3	2	2	25
Ethiopia	9	1	8	3	1	2	24
Russia	1	2	4	5	7	2	21
South Africa	5	5	6	1	3	1	21
Japan	4	5	6	1	2	1	19
New Zealand	7	1	7	1	—	2	18
Japan	4	5	6	—	2	1	18
Bulgaria	1	—	1	4	7	5	18
Norway	4	2	7	2	1	17	
The Netherlands	—	—	5	6	2	1	14
Morocco	3	3	5	1	—	1	13
Brazil	3	3	6	—	—	—	12
China	—	—	1	3	3	4	11
Belgium	2	6	2	—	—	—	10
Mexico	3	4	2	—	—	—	9
Spain	2	3	3	—	—	1	9
Belarus	—	1	2	2	1	3	9
Nigeria	—	2	1	1	2	3	9
Trinidad and Tobago	1	2	5	—	—	—	8
Switzerland	—	6	2	—	—	—	8
Portugal	1	1	1	2	—	2	7
Austria	—	—	—	1	2	4	7
Ireland	4	1	—	—	1	—	6
Algeria	1	1	2	2	—	—	6
Ukraine	—	1	3	1	—	1	6
Argentina	2	2	—	—	1	—	5
Czech Republic	2	1	1	—	—	1	5
Denmark	1	2	1	—	—	1	5
Bahamas	—	—	1	1	2	—	4
Tunisia	1	2	1	—	—	—	4
Namibia	—	4	—	—	—	—	4
Estonia	1	1	1	—	—	—	3
Latvia	—	2	1	—	—	—	3

Lithuania	2	—	—	—	—	—	2
Korea	1	1	—	—	—	—	2
Mozambique	—	—	—	1	—	1	2
Uganda	1	—	1	—	—	—	2
Chile	—	1	—	—	1	—	2
Tanzania	—	2	—	—	—	—	2
Yugoslavia	—	2	—	—	—	—	2
Iceland	—	1	—	—	—	1	2
Sri Lanka	—	1	—	—	—	1	2
Taipei	—	1	—	—	—	1	2
Barbados†	—	—	2	—	—	—	2
Panama	—	—	2	—	—	—	2
Philippines	—	—	2	—	—	—	2
Burundi	1	—	—	—	—	—	1
Ecuador	1	—	—	—	—	—	1
Kazakhstan	—	—	—	1	—	—	1
Luxembourg	1	—	—	—	—	—	1
Syria	—	—	—	1	—	—	1
Haiti	—	1	—	—	—	—	1
Ivory Coast	—	1	—	—	—	—	1
Saudi Arabia	—	1	—	—	—	—	1
Senegal	—	1	—	—	—	—	1
Slovenia	—	—	—	—	1	—	1
Zambia	—	1	—	—	—	—	1
Colombia	—	—	—	—	—	1	1
Djibouti	—	—	1	—	—	—	1
Qatar	—	—	1	—	—	—	1
Turkey	—	—	1	—	—	—	1
Venezuela	—	—	1	—	—	—	1
	598	599	597	216	218	216§	2444

* Includes two extra golds when Jim Thorpe was re-instated to the 1912 decathlon/pentathlon titles. † Two bronzes counted for joint British West Indies 4 x 400m relay team in 1960. ‡ Split into the Czech Republic and Slovakia from 1996. § Two bronzes in the high jump in 2000.

AUSTRALIAN RULES FOOTBALL

A demonstration sport at Melbourne in 1956. Two amateur Australian teams played an exhibition that resulted in a 250–135 score.

AUTOMATIC TIMING

The first time electrical-photo timing equipment was tried out for the athletic events at the Games was at Stockholm in 1912. The photograph produced by the system was used to determine second and third placings in the 1500m. However, the first use of 'modern' photo-timing was at Los Angeles in 1932, when the film was made available to the Jury of Appeal, but times not officially given. In 1948, at London, photo-finish equipment used for horseracing was employed at the athletic events, but only to help the judges decide on placings, not for timings. At these Games, in at least one event, the women's 200m final, an incorrect result was allowed to stand (see Athletics). Although automatic timing devices were in use from 1952, they were not officially recognised and hand timings were given (these automatic timings have, however, been published after research by statistician Bob Sparks). Timings in athletics, to two decimal places in the short races, were first given officially in the 1972 Munich Games.

BADMINTON

Introduced as a medal sport for the first time in 1992, badminton had been a demonstration sport in 1972, when Rudy Hartono of Indonesia won the men's singles. Because it was felt necessary to control the number of entries a mixed doubles competition was not included until 1996.

The most successful players have been the women's doubles pair of Fei Ge and Jun Gu (CHN) who won gold in 1996 and 2000. The most successful male has been Joo-Bong Park (KOR) with a gold in 1992, and a silver in 1996.

The youngest gold medallist was Fei Ge (CHN) in the 1996 women's doubles aged 20 years 175 days, while the youngest male champion/medallist was Dong Moon Kim (KOR) in the 1996 mixed doubles aged 20 years 314 days. The oldest champion was Poul-Erik Hoyer-Larsen (DEN) the 1996 singles champion aged 30 years 316 days, and the oldest female winner was Young Ah Gil (KOR) in the 1996 women's doubles at 26 years 111 days. The youngest medallist was Mia Audina (INA) taking the silver in the 1996 women's singles, at 16 years 345 days. The oldest male medallist was Rashid Sidek (MAS) with a singles bronze in 1996, aged 34 years 56 days, while the oldest female medallist was Minarti Timur (INA) 32 years 181 days in the Sydney mixed doubles. The Barcelona Games female gold medallist Susi Susanti, Indonesia's first ever Olympic champion, later married her countryman, the male singles winner Alan Budi Kusuma. Brothers Razif and Jalani Sidek won the bronze in the 1992 men's doubles, for Malaysia's first ever Olympic medal, and in 1996 another brother, Rashid, won a bronze in the singles.

BADMINTON MEDALS

| | Men* | | | Women | | | |
	G	S	B	G	S	B	Total
China	2	1	3	3	3	7	19
Indonesia	3	3	2	1	—	—	10
Korea	2	2	1	2	2	1	10
Denmark	1	—	1	—	—	1	3
Malaysia	—	—	2	—	—	—	2
Great Britain	—	—	1	—	—	—	1

* Including mixed doubles.

BANDY

A demonstration sport at the Oslo Winter Games in 1952, bandy is similar to ice hockey, but played with a ball instead of a puck. A tournament was held, and final placings were decided on goal average with Sweden winning from Norway and Finland.

BASEBALL

There were six occasions when American baseball was demonstrated, plus an exhibition of Finnish baseball in 1952. In 1912 the American team, containing many track and field medallists, beat Sweden 13–3. In 1936 a 'World Amateurs' team beat an American 'Olympic' team in front of 100,000 spectators in the Berlin Olympic Stadium. In 1956 an American Services team beat an Australian team 11–5 before an estimated 114,000 people, then a record crowd for any baseball game anywhere. At Tokyo in 1964, an American team beat two Japanese teams, and in 1984 Japan won an eight-nation tournament. In 1988 the United States also won an eight-nation tournament, beating Japan in the final. Finally in 1992 baseball became an official medal sport.

The greatest margin of victory, and the highest score, was the 20–0 victory by Chinese Taipei (Taiwan) over Spain in the 1992 competition. In 1996 Cuba beat Italy 20–6 to equal the highest score, and set an aggregate record of 27 when beating Australia 19–8. Orestes Kindelan (CUB) scored a record nine home runs in 1996, and a total of 11 home runs in the 1996/2000 competitions. Luigi Carrozza (ITA) has had the best batting average with .571 at Atlanta, while Jon Rauch (USA) achieved 21 strikeouts at Sydney in 2000.

The oldest gold medallist/medallist was Pat Borders (USA) aged 37 years 136 days in 2000, while the youngest winner was Giorge Diaz (CUB) at 21 years 324 days in 1992. Jong Yeu-Jeng (TPE) played for the 1992 silver medal team aged 18 years 217 days.

BASEBALL MEDALS

	G	S	B	Total
Cuba	2	1	—	3
United States	1	—	1	2
Japan	—	1	1	2
Chinese Taipei	—	1	—	1
Korea	—	—	1	1

BASKETBALL

The game made its official Olympic debut in 1936, although it was demonstrated in 1904, and the analogous Dutch game, Korfball, was demonstrated in 1928. The 1936 tournament was uniquely played outdoors, and the final score was very low due to a downpour, which made the ground slippery and the ball slimy. Interestingly, one of the referees in that tournament was Avery Brundage (USA), later to become President of the IOC, while the man who had devised the modern game, Dr James Naismith, was among those who presented the medals. The tournament was won by the United States, beginning a winning streak of seven titles and 63 victories. The run began with a walkover against Spain, whose team had returned home to fight in the Spanish Civil War, and ended when they were beaten by the Soviet Union 51–50 in the 1972 final. That final was much disputed, with the Americans claiming that too much overtime was played during which the Soviet Aleksandr Belov (who tragically died six years later) scored the winning basket. With one second to go, and the United States in the lead 50–49, the Soviet inbounds pass had been deflected and everyone thought the game was over. However, the Soviet team was given another chance, but did not score. Again the game seemed to be over. But Dr William Jones (GBR), Secretary-General of the Fédération Internationale de Basketball Amateur (FIBA), stated that play was incorrectly restarted at one second and that there should have been three seconds allowed. The clock was reset to three seconds and the Soviet team scored. The US team protested vigorously and refused to accept the silver medals. Unbeaten again until a another defeat by the Soviet Union in the 1988 semi-final, and unbeaten 1992–2000, the overall Olympic tally of US teams is now 109–2.

After various changes and qualifying conditions since 1976 the IOC accepted 12 teams in both the men's and women's competitions at Atlanta. Eleven American players have won two gold medals each, but only David Robinson (1988–96) additionally won a bronze. Two men have won medals at four Games; Gennadiy Volnov (URS) with a gold, two silvers and a bronze 1960–72; and Sergei Belov (URS) a gold and three bronzes 1968–80. In April 1989 it was decided to allow professional players to compete in the Olympic tournaments. Thus the American 'Dream Team' for 1992, included all-time National Basketball Association (NBA) greats Earvin 'Magic' Johnson, Larry Bird, Michael Jordan, Patrick Ewing, Charles Barkley, and David Robinson. This team averaged 117.25 points per game.

The oldest male gold medallist was Larry Bird (USA) in 1992 aged 35 years 245 days, while the youngest was Spencer Haywood (USA) aged 19 years 186 days in 1968. The oldest medallist was Sergejus Jovaisa (LTU) in 1992 aged 37 years 235 days, while the youngest medallist was Vladimir Tkachenko (URS) in 1976, aged 18 years 311 days. The highest aggregate score in a game is 238 points when Brazil beat China 130–108 in 1988. In the same tournament Brazil also scored the highest ever by a team in Olympic contests when they beat Egypt 138–85. The biggest margin of victory is 100 points, when Korea beat Iraq 120–20, and when China beat Iraq 125–25, both in 1948.The highest score by an individual in a single game is 55 points by Oscar Schmidt (BRA) in a 1988 qualifying round encounter in which Spain beat Brazil 118–110. In Seoul he scored 338 points and averaged a record 42.2 points a game. Schmidt, 1980–96, and Teofilo Cruz (PUR), 1960–76, have both competed in a record five Olympic basketball tournaments. In 1996 Schmidt for the third time was the highest scorer in the tournament, aged 38 years 171 days, and brought his total points in Olympic competition to a remarkable 1093.

In the women's game Japan beat Canada 121–89 for an aggregate record of 210 points in 1976, while the highest total was 122 by the Soviet Union against Bulgaria (83) in 1980. The biggest margin was 66 points when the Soviet Union beat Italy 119–53 in 1980. Yevladia Stefanova (BUL) scored a record 39 points against Korea in 1988. The most successful female player has been Teresa Edwards (USA) with four gold medals and a bronze 1984–2000. She is also the only woman to play in five Games, and the only player, male or female, to win four gold medals. Edwards became the oldest gold medallist, male or female, in 2000 aged 36 years 73 days, and she was also the youngest in 1984 aged 20 years 19 days. The oldest medallist was a member of the silver medal Brazilian team in 1996, Hortencia Marcan Oliva, at 36 years 315 days, while the youngest medallist was Zheng Haixia (CHN) in 1984 at 17 years 151 days. When the Soviet men's team beat the United States at Seoul their coach was Aleksandr Gomelsky, and when the Unified women's team beat the American women in Barcelona their coach was his brother, Yevgeniy. A member of the winning American men's team in 1996, Reggie Miller, was a brother of the star of the 1984 gold-medal women's team, Cheryl Miller.

The tallest ever player in Olympic basketball, and the tallest ever medallist in any sport, was Tommy Burleson (USA), silver in 1972, at 2.23m (7ft 4in). Also reported in some quarters as the same height, but actually some 2cm less, was Arvidas Sabonis, who won gold in the 1988 Soviet team, and bronze in the 1992 Lithuanian team. In 2000 it was erroneously reported that the Chinese player Yao Ming was 2.25m (7ft 4½in) tall – he possibly reached this height a few years later, but at Sydney was only 2.21m (7ft 3in). The tallest female player, and the tallest Olympic female gold medallist ever, was Iuliana Semenova (URS) at 2.18m (7ft 1½in) in 1976 and 1980. She was also the heaviest female gold medallist ever at 129kg (284lb). Incidentally, during the first tournament in 1936 there was a move to ban all players taller than 1.90m (6ft 2½in), but this decision was later withdrawn. In the 1996 tournament an Olympic basketball record of 34,447 spectators watched the American men's team beat China 133–70 in the Georgia Dome, and in the women's semi-final between the United States and Australia (93–71), the game drew a female match record of 33,952 spectators.

BASKETBALL MEDALS

	Men			Women			
	G	S	B	G	S	B	Total
United States	12	1	1	4	1	1	20
Soviet Union	2	4	3	3	—	1	13
Yugoslavia	1	4	1	—	1	1	8
Brazil	—	—	3	—	1	1	5
Lithuania	—	—	3	—	—	—	3
France	—	2	—	—	—	—	2
Australia	—	—	—	—	1	1	2
Bulgaria	—	—	—	—	1	1	2
China	—	—	—	—	1	1	2
Uruguay	—	—	2	—	—	—	2
Canada	—	1	—	—	—	—	1

Croatia	—	1	—	—	—	—	1
Italy	—	1	—	—	—	—	1
Korea	—	—	—	—	1	—	1
Spain	—	1	—	—	—	—	1
Cuba	—	—	1	—	—	—	1
Mexico	—	—	1	—	—	—	1
	15	15	15	7	7	7	66

BEACH VOLLEYBALL

The sport appears to have originated in Santa Monica, California, in the early 1930s. In 1996, at Atlanta, beach volleyball became an Olympic sport. Special sand courts were built within the city's Olympic complex and the separate contests for men and women gained much spectator and media support.

The most successful beach volleyball players have been Sandra Pires (BRA), Natalie Cook (AUS) and Kerri Pottharst (AUS), who have all won a gold and a bronze in the 1996/2000 competitions. The oldest gold medallist was Karch Kiraly (USA) aged 35 years 268 days in 1996. He had won two gold medals in the standard indoor sport in 1984 and 1988, and thus becomes the most successful volleyball player, either male or female, with three golds. The oldest medallist was Michael Dodd (USA) who won a silver medal at 38 years 343 days at Atlanta. The oldest female gold medallist/medallist was Kerri Pottharst (AUS) at 35 years 92 days in 2000. The youngest winner was Sandra Pires (BRA) aged 23 years 41 days in 1996 and the youngest medallist was Natalie Cook (AUS) aged 21 years 190 days winning the bronze at Atlanta. The youngest male champion was Kent Steffes (USA) at 28 years 35 days in 1996 and the youngest male medallist was Mark Heese (CAN) with the bronze aged 26 years 348 days also at Atlanta. Chris St John 'Sinjin' Smith (USA), whose pair finished equal fifth in 1996, was 39 years 80 days old.

BEACH VOLLEYBALL MEDALS

	Men			Women			
	G	S	B	G	S	B	Total
Brazil	—	1	—	1	2	1	5
United States	2	1	—	—	—	—	3
Australia	—	—	—	1	—	1	2
Canada	—	—	1	—	—	—	1
Germany	—	—	1	—	—	—	1

BIATHLON

The combination of skiing and shooting was introduced for men in 1960, and for women in 1992. Aleksandr Tikhonov (URS) set a Winter Games record by winning a gold medal in the relay on four successive occasions 1968–80. However, Ole Einar Björndalen (NOR) won an unprecedented four gold medals at the one Games, at Salt Lake City in 2002. Having won another event in 1998, he also holds the male record of five golds. Rico Gross (GER) has won seven medals (three golds, three silvers and a bronze), 1992–2002. The most successful woman has been Ursula 'Uschi' Disl (GER) with a total of eight medals (two golds, four silvers and 2 bronzes), 1992–2002. Myriam Bédard (CAN) and Anfissa Reztsova (EUN-RUS) have also won two golds 1992–4.

The oldest gold medallist/medallist was Fritz Fischer (GER) in the 1992 relay aged 35 years 147 days. The oldest female champion was Ursula Disl (GER) in the relay at Salt Lake City aged 31 years 95 days, while the oldest female medallist was Magdalena Forsberg (SWE) in the 2002 15km race at 34 years 203 days. The youngest winner and medallist was Corinne Niogret (FRA) in the 1992 relay at 19 years 86 days, while the youngest male winner was Yuri Kachkarov (URS) in the 1984 relay aged 20 years 75 days. Frank Peter Roetsch (GDR) was the youngest male medallist when he won a silver in the 20km event in 1984, aged only 19 years 298 days. Alfred Eder (AUT) competed in a record six Games, 1976–94.

BIATHLON MEDALS

	Men			Women			
	G	S	B	G	S	B	Total
Germany	4	7	5	6	3	—	27
Soviet Union	10	6	5	1	1	2	25
Norway	9	4	2	—	2	1	18
Russia	2	1	3	3	1	1	11
East Germany (GDR)	3	4	4	—	—	—	11
Sweden	1	—	4	—	—	2	7
France	—	1	2	1	1	1	6
Finland	—	4	2	—	—	—	6

West Germany (FRG)	1	2	2	—	—	—	5
Canada	—	—	—	2	—	1	3
Italy	—	1	2	—	—	—	3
Bulgaria	—	—	—	1	—	1	2
Belarus	—	—	1	—	1	—	2
Ukraine	—	—	—	—	1	1	2
Austria	—	—	1	—	—	—	1
	30	30	30	13	13	13	129

BICYCLE POLO

A demonstration sport at London in 1908, it consisted of a match between a German team and one from the Irish Bicycle Polo Association.

BIGGEST FIELDS

The largest entry in any Olympic event was the 183 competitors in the 1996 cycling road race. The female best is the 86 runners in the 1996 marathon race. The 124 competitors in the men's marathon that year is the record for an Olympic athletics event. In boxing there was a record entry of 441 in the 1988 tournament, while in sailing there was an unsurpassed 239 boats (plus 73 sailboards) in the 1996 regatta. In the Winter Games, the greatest single field was the 131 competitors in the 1992 men's giant slalom.

BOBSLEDDING

An Olympic bob competition for four-man sleds was first held in 1924. The rules allowed for four- or five-man teams in 1924 and 1928. The two-man event was introduced in 1932. Both competitions have been held ever since except for 1960 when the Squaw Valley Organizing Committee refused to build a run. In 1952 a situation arose which led to changes in the rules governing the overall weight of teams and bobs. The Germans combined their heaviest men from their two two-man vehicles into one four-man sled averaging 117kg (258lb) per man, and won easily. Resulting complaints led to rules currently stipulating that the maximum weight of the bobsled, together with crews, must not exceed 390kg (860lb, two-man) and 630kg (1389lb, four-man), but that extra weights may be added within those limits.

In 1994 Gustave Weder (SUI) was the first to retain a two-man title, and Wolfgang Höppe (GER) became the first man to win medals in four Winter Games. The most gold medals won by an individual is three by Bernhard Germeshausen (GDR) and Meinhard Nehmer (GDR) both in 1976–80. The most medals won are seven, by Bogdan Musiol (GDR), comprising one gold, five silvers and one bronze in 1980–92. The oldest gold medallist was Jay O'Brien (USA) in the four-man in 1932 aged 48 years 359 days, which also makes him the oldest gold medallist in Winter Games history. The youngest champion was William Fiske (USA) who piloted the winning five-man bob in 1928 aged 16 years 260 days. The youngest medallist was Thomas Doe Jr (USA) aged 15 years 127 days in the 1928 silver medal bob. The oldest medallist was Max Houben (BEL) aged 49 years 278 days in the 1948 four-man event. He had been a member of the athletics sprint relay squad at Antwerp in 1920.

That 1932 American four-man team had unusually eventful lives outside bobsledding. Fiske had the distinction of being the first American to join the RAF in the Second World War – he was killed in the Battle of Britain. Jay O'Brien married silent film star Mae Murray. British-born Clifford 'Tippy' Gray was a songwriter, and Eddie Eagan, a Rhodes scholar, lawyer and wartime colonel, was the only man to win gold medals in both Summer and Winter Games. The tallest gold medallist was Edy Hubacher (SUI) in the 1972 four-man bob at 2.01m (6ft 7in). He also competed in the 1968 Summer Games shot put event. Carl-Erik Eriksson (SWE) was the first Winter Olympic competitor to compete in six Games between 1964–84. The first brothers to win bob gold medals were Alfred and Heinrich Schläppi (SUI) in the four-man of 1924, while the inaugural two-man event of 1932 was won by siblings Hubert and Curtis Stevens (USA). Prince Albert of Monaco became the first bobsledder to compete in 5 Games at Salt Lake City in 2002.

The closest finishes in Olympic bobsledding have occurred in the two-man events of 1968 and 1998. In 1968, at Grenoble, Italy I and West Germany I had identical aggregate times after four runs. The title went to Italy, driven by the 40-year-old Eugenio Monti, as they had the fastest single run. In 1998, at Nagano, the same thing happened with Italy I, and Canada I tying after four runs. However, this time they were both awarded joint first place. Incidentally, the Canadian pair had the fastest single run. The greatest margin of victory was in 1924 when the Swiss four-man won by 3.29sec, and the smallest margin in four-man was 0.02sec between Austria and Germany after four runs in 1992. The fastest speed attained (average for a run) was by the 2002 United States I four-man team of 103.12km/h (64.08mph), although a momentary speed of 143km/h (88.8mph) was recorded by the Swiss team at Calgary in 1988.

In 2002 a bob event for women was introduced, and the fastest speed (average for a run) was by the winning United States II team, with 98.47km/h (61.19mph). In that team, Vonetta Flowers became the first ever black gold medallist at a Winter Games, and is also the oldest gold medallist at 28 years 113 days. Her partner, Jill

Bakken, is the youngest gold medallist aged 25 years 25 days. The oldest medallist was Susi Erdman (GER) at 20 days past her 34th birthday – she had won medals in the luge in 1992/1994.

BOBSLEDDING MEDALS

	Men			Women			
	G	S	B	G	S	B	Total
Switzerland	9	10	9	—	—	—	28
United States	5	5	6	1	—	—	17
Germany	6	2	5	—	1	1	15
East Germany (GDR)	5	5	3	—	—	—	13
Italy	4	4	3	—	—	—	11
West Germany (FRG)	1	3	2	—	—	—	6
Great Britain	1	1	2	—	—	—	4
Soviet Union	1	—	2	—	—	—	3
Austria	1	2	—	—	—	—	3
Canada	2	—	—	—	—	—	2
Belgium	—	1	1	—	—	—	2
France	—	—	1	—	—	—	1
Romania	—	—	1	—	—	—	1
	35(1)	33	35(2)	1	1	1	106

(1) Tie in the 1998 two-man bob.
(2) Tie in the 1998 four-man bob.

BOXING

Contests were included in the ancient Games in 688 BC, when competitors wore leather straps on their hands. As the status of the Games deteriorated in Roman times, metal studs were added. Later still boxers wore metal 'knuckledusters'. One of the earliest known champions was Onomastos of Smyrna. The last known champion before the Games were abolished was Varazdetes (or Varastades), the winner in AD 369, who later became King of Armenia. This type of boxing should not be confused with the *pankration* event, which was a brutal combination of boxing and wrestling in which virtually anything was permitted. It is recorded that Arrachion of Phigalia was awarded that title in 564 BC, as his opponent 'gave up' – although Arrachion himself was by then lying dead in the arena. Boxing was included in the modern Games in 1904 when the United States won all the titles. A pattern was set by the first heavyweight champion, Samuel Berger, when he turned professional after his victory. Incidentally, he was a member of the San Francisco Olympic Club that had also produced 'Gentleman Jim' Corbett who had won the world title in 1892. Over the years the weight limits for the various classes have changed, and new classes added. Bronze medals for losing semi-finalists were not awarded until 1952.

Three men have won three gold medals: László Papp (HUN), a southpaw, won the middleweight division in 1948 and the light-middleweight class in 1952 and 1956; Teofilo Stevenson (CUB) won the same class, heavyweight, 1972–80; his countryman, Felix Savon, matched him, also at heavyweight, 1992–2000. In 1904 Oliver Kirk (USA) won two events at the same Games, also unique (but he only fought one bout in each class). The first boxer to defend a title successfully was middleweight Harry Mallin (GBR) in 1920 and 1924. In those latter Games the standard of refereeing was highly suspect, not least because the European custom of seating the referees outside the ring was followed. Mallin was continually fouled by his French opponent in a preliminary bout, and

ended the fight with teeth marks on his chest. Despite this the outclassed Frenchman was declared the winner of the bout. An immediate appeal, backed by a threat of withdrawal of all English-speaking countries, was upheld. A strange occurrence was the disqualification of Ingemar Johansson (SWE) in the 1952 heavyweight final, and the withholding of the silver medal, due to 'inactivity in the ring'. In 1959 he won the world professional title, and 30 years after the Games, on his 50th birthday, he was finally presented with his medal.

The oldest gold medallist/medallist was Richard Gunn (GBR), the 1908 featherweight champion, aged 37 years 254 days. The youngest was Jackie Fields (née Jacob Finkelstein, USA) winning the 1924 featherweight crown aged 16 years 162 days. Both of these records can no longer be broken as current rules specify that boxers must be over 17 and under 37 years of age, prior to the start of the particular Games. Floyd Patterson (USA) won the 1952 middleweight title aged 17 years 211 days, and four years later became the youngest ever world professional heavyweight champion. The first black African to win a gold medal was Robert Wangila (KEN) in 1988. A number of brothers have won medals, but the only known father and son medallists are José Villanueva (PHI), bronze bantamweight in 1932, and Anthony Villanueva (PHI), silver featherweight in 1964.

Many Olympic boxing champions, and even more minor medallists, have won world professional titles. Only two, Joe Frazier (USA, 1964) and George Foreman (USA, 1968), won the Olympic heavyweight title and then became undisputed professional heavyweight champions. Note also that the 1988 super-heavyweight champion, Lennox Lewis, then of Canada, won the undisputed world professional heavyweight title in 1999, representing Great Britain. Perhaps more unusually the 1908 middleweight champion, John Douglas (GBR), later, in 1911, captained the England cricket team against Australia. Just as unusual was the fact that his opponent in the 1908 final, Reg 'Snowy' Baker, also competed in springboard diving, and was a member of the Australian 4 x 200m swimming team which placed fourth. Incidentally, over the years there has been an unsubstantiated story that Douglas's father refereed their final bout; recent research indicates that the official in charge was Eugene Corri.

The Val Barker Cup is presented by the International Amateur Boxing Association (IAIBA) – Val Barker was a former President – to the competitor adjudged the best stylist at the Games. First awarded in 1936, the winners have been:

VAL BARKER CUP WINNERS

1936	Louis Lauria (USA)	bronze	flyweight
1948	George Hunter (SAF)	gold	light-heavyweight
1952	Norvel Lee (USA)	gold	light-heavyweight
1956	Dick McTaggart (GBR)	gold	lightweight
1960	Giovanni Benvenuti (ITA)	gold	welterweight
1964	Valeri Popentschenko (URS)	gold	middleweight
1968	Philip Waruinge (KEN)	bronze	featherweight
1972	Teofilo Stevenson (CUB)	gold	heavyweight
1976	Howard Davis (USA)	gold	lightweight
1980	Patrizio Oliva (ITA)	gold	light-welterweight
1984	Paul Gonzales (USA)	gold	light-flyweight
1988	Roy Jones Jr (USA)	silver	light-middleweight
1992	Roberto Balado (CUB)	gold	super-heavyweight
1996	Vasili Jirov (KZK)	gold	light-heavyweight
2000	Aleksandr Lebziak (RUS)	gold	light-heavyweight

In the 1988 tournament, because of a record 441 entries, two rings were used, simultaneously. In 1992 elimination contests were held to limit entries to 32 per class. Despite pressure to drop boxing from the Olympic programme, the introduction of new gloves, safer protective helmets and three rounds of three minutes, seems to have reprieved the sport, at least for the foreseeable future. In Sydney 2000 contests of four rounds of two minutes each were introduced. In 1992 an electronic scoring system was introduced, in which the judges had to simultaneously push a button to record a scoring point. Despite this innovation there was still considerable criticism of the scoring during the tournament, especially in the early bouts. The 1992 tournament was also noteworthy for the virtual eclipse of American boxers, with only one medal of each colour – their worse ever showing – and the domination of the Cubans, with seven golds and two silvers out of nine finals reached.

BOXING MEDALS

	G	S	B	Total
United States	47	23	37	107
Soviet Union	14	20	19	53
Cuba	27	14	7	48
Great Britain	13	10	21	44
Poland	8	9	26	43
Italy	14	12	14	40
Germany	5	12	9	26
Argentina	7	7	10	24
Romania	1	9	14	24
Hungary	10	2	8	20
South Africa	6	4	9	19
Canada	3	7	7	17
Korea	3	6	8	17
Bulgaria	4	5	7	16
France	4	4	6	14
Finland	2	1	11	14
East Germany (GDR)	5	2	6	13
Mexico	2	3	7	12
Denmark	1	5	6	12
Russia	3	2	6	11
Yugoslavia	3	2	6	11
Sweden	—	5	6	11
Ireland	1	3	5	9
Kazakhstan	3	3	2	8
Thailand	2	1	4	7
Ukraine	1	2	4	7
Kenya	1	1	5	7

Czechoslovakia	3	1	2	6
North Korea (PRK)	2	2	2	6
The Netherlands	1	1	4	6
Algeria	1	—	5	6
West Germany (FRG)	1	—	5	6
Nigeria	—	3	3	6
Puerto Rico	—	1	5	6
Norway	1	2	2	5
Venezuela	1	2	2	5
Australia	—	2	3	5
Philippines	—	2	3	5
Belgium	1	1	2	4
Uzbekistan	1	—	3	4
Uganda	—	3	1	4
New Zealand	1	1	1	3
Japan	1	—	2	3
Chile	—	1	2	3
Ghana	—	1	2	3
Spain	—	1	2	3
Turkey	—	1	2	3
Colombia	—	—	3	3
Morocco	—	—	3	3
Cameroon	—	1	1	2
Mongolia	—	—	2	2
Tunisia	—	—	2	2
Czech Republic	—	1	—	1
Estonia	—	1	—	1
Tonga	—	1	—	1
Azerbaijan	—	—	1	1
Bermuda	—	—	1	1
Brazil	—	—	1	1
Dominican Rep.	—	—	1	1
Egypt	—	—	1	1
Georgia	—	—	1	1
Guyana	—	—	1	1
Moldova	—	—	1	1
Niger	—	—	1	1
Pakistan	—	—	1	1
Tunisia	—	—	1	1
Uruguay	—	—	1	1
Zambia	—	—	1	1
	204	**204**	**346***	**754**

* The official 1908 report notes that there was only a single bronze medal awarded.

BROTHERS

Many brothers have competed together in the Games, especially in fencing, rowing and yachting. The first gold medallists were John and Sumner Paine (USA) who won the military pistol and free pistol events respectively in 1896. However, the first to win gold medals together were Reggie and Laurie Doherty (GBR) in the men's tennis doubles in 1900. The three Gossler brothers, Oscar, Gustav and Carl, were in the winning German rowing four in 1900, the latter as cox, and the French Thubé brothers, Amédée, Gaston and Jacques, won golds in the 1912 6m class yachting. At the next Games, in 1920, they were eclipsed by Henrik, Jan, Ole and Kristian Østervold, of Norway, who crewed the winning 12m (1907 rating) yacht.

Probably the most successful brothers were two sets of sibling fencers. Nedo and Aldo Nadi (ITA) won a total of nine golds and a silver in 1912 and 1920, while their countrymen, Edoardo and Dario Mangiarotti amassed seven golds, seven silvers and two bronzes between 1936 and 1960. Also noteworthy are: Dhyand Chand Bais and Roop Singh Bais of India in hockey, with the former gaining three gold medals 1928–36, and the latter two, 1932–6; and the rowing Abbagnale brothers of Italy, Carmine and Giuseppe won the coxed pairs in 1984–8 and a silver in 1992, and Agostino won gold in the 1992 quadruple sculls and 1996 double sculls.

BUDO

A demonstration sport at Tokyo in 1964, when exhibitions of Japanese archery, wrestling and fencing were given.

CANOEING

Official canoeing competitions were first held in 1936, although kayak and Canadian events were demonstrated in 1924. In 1972, at Munich, four slalom events were held, and after a gap of 20 years slalom racing was reintroduced at Barcelona. The most successful canoeist has been Birgit Fischer-Schmidt, first representing East Germany and then Germany, over a record 20-year period 1980–2000, during which she has won a record seven gold medals, and three silvers to total another record of ten medals. Had East German team not boycotted Los Angeles in 1984, she would have assuredly won even more medals. The most successful male has been Gert Fredriksson (SWE) with six golds, a silver and a bronze from 1948 to 1960, all in kayaks. Two men, Vladimir Parfenovich (URS) in 1980, and Ian Ferguson (NZL) in 1984, have won three gold medals at one Games. The best by a woman at any single Games is two golds and a silver, by Agneta Andersson (SWE) in 1984, and Birgit Fischer-Schmidt (GDR) in 1988.

The highest speed achieved in the Games over the standard 1000m course is 20.98km/h (13.03mph) when the German K4 clocked 2min 51.52sec in 1996. In 1992 the Hungarian K4 team achieved an average speed of 21.94km/h (13.63mph) over the first 250m, also in a heat. The fastest by a female crew over the 500m course is 19.76km/h (12.27mph) when the German K4 clocked 1min 31.07sec in 1996. In that race the German K4 achieved an average speed of 20.20km/h (12.55mph) over the first 250m. The closest finish in an Olympic canoeing final occurred in the 1952 K2 1000m when the timekeepers were unable to separate the first and second placed pairs. The closest finish in women's canoeing was in the 1988 K1 500m when the winning margin was 0.12sec. This was equalled in the 1992 K2 final.

The oldest ever canoeing gold medallist/medallist was Gert Fredriksson (SWE) aged 40 years 292 days in the 1960 K2 over 1000m. The youngest was Bent Peder Rasch (DEN) in the 1952 C2 at 1000m aged 18 years 58 days. However, Michal Martikan (SVK) won the C1 slalom event in 1996 aged 17 years 70 days, making him easily the youngest ever champion in Olympic canoeing events. The youngest female champion was Birgit Fischer-Schmidt (GDR/GER) aged 18 years 158 days in 1980, and she was also the oldest female champion/medallist at Sydney in 2000 aged 38 years 218 days. The youngest female medallist was Francine Fox (USA), with a silver in the 1964 K2 at 15 years 220 days (incidentally, her partner was 20 years older). The youngest male medallist was Gábor Novák (HUN) in 1952 aged 17 years 348 days. Ivar Patzaichin (ROM) won gold medals over a 16-year period, 1968–84, in the Canadian events. This was exceeded by Birgit Fischer-Schmidt (GDR/GER) 1980–2000.

When Philippe Renaud (FRA) won a bronze in the 1988 C2 500m, he was the latest success of an Olympic family – his brother, Eric, won a canoe bronze in 1984, their father, Marcel, gained a canoeing silver in 1956, and a great-uncle won a cycling bronze in 1924. The first brothers, indeed twins, to win gold medals were Pavol and Peter Hochschorner (SVK), in the slalom C2 at Sydney. In 1996 the bronze medal in the women's K2 500m was won for Australia by Katrin Borchert and Anna Wood. Interestingly, Borchert had won a silver in the 1992 German K4, and Wood had taken a bronze in the 1988 Dutch K2.

CANOEING MEDALS

	Men			Women			
	G	S	B	G	S	B	Total
Hungary	12	19	16	2	6	5	60
Soviet Union	22	12	6	8	2	3	53
Germany	15	10	4	7	6	1	53
Romania	9	9	10	1	1	4	34
East Germany (GDR)	8	5	8	6	2	1	30
Sweden	11	9	2	3	2	2	29
France	3	6	14	—	1	2	26
Bulgaria	3	3	7	1	2	1	17
Canada	3	5	4	—	3	1	16
Poland	—	5	7	—	—	4	16
United States	5	2	4	—	2	2	15
Austria	3	4	4	—	1	1	13
Australia	1	3	6	—	1	2	13
Czechoslovakia	7	4	1	—	—	—	12
Italy	4	3	3	1	—	—	12
Denmark	2	4	4	1	—	1	12
Finland	4	2	3	1	—	—	10
Norway	4	3	3	—	—	—	10
The Netherlands	—	1	3	—	2	2	8

New Zealand	5	1	1	—	—	—	7
Czech Republic	2	2	1	2	—	—	7
West Germany (FRG)	1	1	1	1	2	1	7
Yugoslavia	2	2	1	—	—	—	5
Slovakia	2	1	1	—	—	—	4
Spain	—	2	2	—	—	—	4
Great Britain	—	2	1	—	—	—	3
Cuba	—	2	—	—	—	—	2
Latvia	—	2	—	—	—	—	2
Slovenia	—	2	—	—	—	—	2
Russia	—	1	1	—	—	—	2
Moldova	—	1	—	—	—	—	1
Switzerland	—	—	—	—	1	—	1
Israel	—	—	1	—	—	—	1
	128	128	128	34	34	34	486

CELEBRATIONS OF THE GAMES

(New research has resulted in revised figures for participation in some celebrations of the Games.)

SUMMER

Year	Venue		Date	Nations	Women	Men	Total
I	1896	Athens, Greece	6–15 April*	14	—	211	211
II	1900	Paris, France	20 May–28 October	25	19	1206	1225
III	1904	St Louis, USA	1 July–23 November	13	6	681	687
	†1906	Athens, Greece	22 April–2 May	20	6	820	826
IV	1908	London, England	27 April–31 October	22	36	1999	2035
V	1912	Stockholm, Sweden	5 May–22 July	28	57	2490	2547
VI	1916	Berlin, Germany	Not held due to WWI				
VII	1920	Antwerp, Belgium	20 April–12 September	29	77	2591	2668
VIII	1924	Paris, France	4 May–27 July	44	36	2956	3092
IX	1928	Amsterdam, Holland	17 May–12 August	46	290	2724	3014
X	1932	Los Angeles, USA	30 July–14 August	37	127	1281	1408
XI	1936	Berlin, Germany	1–16 August	49	328	3738	4066
XII	1940	Tokyo, Japan, then Helsinki, Finland	Not held due to WWII	—	—	—	—
XIII	1944	London, England	Not held due to WWII	—	—	—	—
XIV	1948	London, England	29 July–14 August	59	385	3714	4099
XV	1952	Helsinki, Finland	19 July–3 August	69	518	4407	4925
XVI	1956	Melbourne, Australia‡	22 Nov–8 December	67	371	2813	3184
XVII	1960	Rome, Italy	25 Aug–11 September	83	610	4736	5346
XVII	1964	Tokyo, Japan	10–24 October	93	683	4457	5140
XIX	1968	Mexico City, Mexico	12–27 October	112	781	4749	5530
XX	1972	Munich, FRG	26 Aug–10 September	121	1058	6065	7123
XXI	1976	Montreal, Canada	17 July–1 August	92	1247	4781	6028
XXII	1980	Moscow, Soviet Union	19 July–3 August	80	1124	4093	5217
XXIII	1984	Los Angeles, USA	28 July–12 August	140	1567	5230	6797
XXIV	1988	Seoul, Korea	17 Sep–2 October	159	2186	6279	8465
XXV	1992	Barcelona, Spain	25 July–9 August	169	2707	6657	9364
XXVI	1996	Atlanta, USA	19 July–4 August	197	3513	6797	10310
XXVII	2000	Sydney, Australia	15 Sep–1 October	200	4069	6582	10651
XXVIII	2004	Athens, Greece	13–29 August	—	—	—	—
XXIX	2008	Beijing, China	8–24 August	—	—	—	—

*Actually 25 March–3 April according to the Julian calendar, then in use in Greece. †This celebration (to mark the tenth anniversary of the modern Games) was officially intercalated, but not numbered. ‡ Equestrian events held in Stockholm, 10–17 June, with 158 competitors, of which 13 were women.

WINTER

Year	Venue		Date	Nations	Women	Men	Total
I	1924	Chamonix, France	25 Jan–4 February	16	13	281	294
II	1928	St Moritz, Switzerland	11–19 February	25	27	468	495
III	1932	Lake Placid, USA	4–15 February	17	32	274	306
IV	1936	Garmisch-Partenkirchen, Germany	6–16 February	28	80	675	755

—	1940	Sapporo, Japan, St Moritz, Switzerland, then Garmisch-Partenkirchen, Germany Not held due to war					
—	1944	Cortina d'Ampezzo, Italy Not held due to war					
V	1948	St Moritz, Switzerland	30 Jan–8 February	28	77	636	713
VI	1952	Oslo, Norway	14–25 February	30	109	623	732
VII	1956	Cortina d'Ampezzo, Italy	26 Jan–5 February	32	132	686	818
VIII	1960	Squaw Valley, USA	18–28 February	30	144	521	665
IX	1964	Innsbruck, Austria	29 Jan–9 February	36	200	891	1091
X	1968	Grenoble, France	6–18 February	37	211	947	1158
XI	1972	Sapporo, Japan	3–13 February	35	206	800	1006
XII	1976	Innsbruck, Austria	4–15 February	37	231	892	1123
XIII	1980	Lake Placid, USA	13–24 February	37	233	839	1072
XIV	1984	Sarajevo, Yugoslavia	8–19 February	49	274	1000	1274
XV	1988	Calgary, Canada	13–28 February	57	313	1112	1425
XVI	1992	Albertville, France	8–23 February	64	489	1312	1801
XVII	1994	Lillehammer, Norway	12–27 February	67	519	1217	1736
XVIII	1998	Nagano, Japan	7–22 February	72	787	1390	2177
XIX	2002	Salt Lake City, USA	9–24 February	77	886	1512	2398
XX	2006	Turin, Italy	11–26 February	—	—	—	—
XXI	2010	Vancouver, Canada	—				

CONSECUTIVE MEDALS

The only competitor to win six consecutive gold medals in the Olympic Games is Aladár Gerevich (HUN) who was a member of the winning sabre fencing team 1932– 60. His teammate, Pál Kovács, won five golds consecutively 1936–1960. Hans-Günter Winkler (FRG) also won medals in six consecutive Games in show jumping, but they were not all gold. A countryman, Reiner Klimke, won gold medals at five Games between 1964 and 1988, but they were not consecutive. The only woman to win medals at five consecutive Games is fencer Ildikó Ságiné-Uljakiné-Rejtő (HUN), 1960–76. In the Winter Games, cross-country skier Raisa Smetanina (URS/EUN) is the only competitor to win medals in five Games, 1976–92.

CREED

The Olympic Creed has been displayed on the scoreboard at every opening ceremony since the 1932 Games at Los Angeles. The words are: 'The most important thing in the Olympic Games is not to win but to take part, just as the most important thing in life is not the triumph but the struggle. The essential thing is not to have conquered but to have fought well'. They are attributed usually to Baron de Coubertin, but were actually based on words used by Ethelbert Talbot, the Bishop of Central Pennsylvania, in a sermon at St Paul's Cathedral in London, England on 19 July 1908.

CRICKET

On the only occasion that cricket was played at the Games, in 1900, Great Britain, represented by the Devon Wanderers Cricket Club, beat a French team, consisting of mainly expatriate Britons, in a 12-a-side match scoring 117 and 145 for five declared, against the French score of 78 and 26.

CROQUET

It was only contested in 1900 when all the competitors were French. There were two singles competitions, and a doubles in which only a gold medal was awarded.

CURLING

After many appearances as a demonstration sport curling finally became a medal sport at Nagano in 1998. Prior to this a three-country contest was held in 1924, won by Great Britain from Sweden and France. In 1932 there were four Canadian Provincial and four American club teams. The Canadians took the first four places with the title won by Manitoba. In 1936 eight teams from Austria (three), Germany (three) and Czechoslovakia (two) competed in a specialised version of the game, German curling, with the Austrian number-one team from the Tyrol, winning. The Austrians demonstrated the game in 1964 at Innsbruck, and it was a demonstration sport again in 1988 and 1992.

The curling events in 1998 were held at the Kazakoshi Park, Karuizawa, which had been the site for the show jumping contests in the 1964 Summer Games, thus making it the first venue to host both Winter and Summer Games events. In the men's competition the highest score, and margin of victory, was when the Canadian team beat the United States 11–3. The greatest aggregate score was when Norway beat Canada 10–8 in 1998. The youngest gold medallist was Dominic Andres (SUI) aged 25 years 132 days in 1998, while the oldest was Pål Trulsen (NOR) in 2002 at 39 years 309 days. The oldest medallist was Paul Savage (CAN) in the 1998 silver winning team at 50 years 235 days, while the youngest was his teammate Mike Harris aged 20 years 251 days.

In the women's competition the biggest margin of victory came when the United States beat Norway 11–2 in 2002. The highest score was when Sweden beat Japan 12–6 in 1998, while the greatest aggregate was when Denmark beat Sweden 11–9 in 2002. The youngest gold medallist was Atina Ford (CAN) aged 26 years 126 days, while the oldest was her teammate, Jan Betker at 37 years 211 days. The youngest medallist was Margaretha Lindahl (SWE) taking a bronze aged 23 years 118 days, and the oldest was Cheryl Noble in the Canadian bronze medal squad at 45 years 145 days.

CURLING MEDALS

| | Men | | | Women | | | |
	G	S	B	G	S	B	Total
Canada	—	2	—	1	—	1	4
Switzerland	1	—	1	—	1	—	3
Norway	1	—	1	—	—	—	2
Great Britain	—	—	—	1	—	—	1
Denmark	—	—	—	—	1	—	1
Sweden	—	—	—	—	—	1	1

CYCLING

The first Olympic cycling champion was Léon Flameng (FRA), winner of the 100km race in 1896, which was held on a 333.33m cement track and involved 300 circuits. Five men have won three gold medals: Paul Masson (FRA) in 1896, Francisco Verri (ITA) in 1906, Robert Charpentier (FRA) in 1936, Daniel Morelon (FRA) in 1968 (two) and 1972, and Florian Rousseau (FRA) in 1996 and 2000 (two). Of these only Rousseau won a silver as well. Initially, the seven 1904 cycling events were not considered official, as there were no foreign entries. However, recent thinking has 're-instated' them. Thus it should be noted that Marcus Hurley (USA) won a record four titles, and a bronze medal, at that Games. His teammate, Burton Downing, also set a 'record' at St Louis with six medals, comprising two golds, three silvers and a bronze. The only women to win three gold medals are Felicia Ballanger (FRA) in 1996 and 2000 (two), and Leontien Zijlaard (NED) in 2000 (three). Zijlaard also won a silver to uniquely win four medals. The first pair of brothers to win a medal was the Götze duo, Bruno and Max, of Germany with the tandem silver in 1906. The greatest family peformance in Olympic cycling was achieved by the Pettersson brothers of Sweden: Gösta, Sture, Erik and Tomas. The first three with Sven Hamrin won a bronze in the 1964 team road race, and then, in 1968 with their younger brother, won the silver. Two extremes of sportsmanship have been highlighted in Games cycling. In 1936 Robert Charpentier beat his teammate Guy Lapébie by 0.2sec at the end of the 100km, the latter inexplicably slowing down just before the line. A photograph showed that Charpentier

had pulled his rival back by his shirt. More credit-worthy was another Frenchman, Léon Flameng, who, when far ahead of his only opposition, a Greek, in 1896, stopped when the man's cycle broke down. After waiting for it to be replaced Flameng still won by six laps. After the 1984 Games it was admitted that many of the United States cycling team had indulged in 'blood-boosting' procedures – not illegal at the time. Those Games also witnessed numerous 'space-age' innovations, especially in the composition and construction of wheels. Of the many excellent facilities that have been built for Olympic cycling programmes, one of the most remarkable sites was the magnificent Hachioji velodrome in Tokyo 1964. Built at a cost of $840,000, it was used for only four days during the Games, and within a year was demolished. Track cycling was held indoors for the first time in 1976.

The greatest speed ever achieved in Olympic cycling was in the altitude of Mexico City in 1968 when Daniel Morelon and Pierre Trentin (FRA) clocked 9.83sec for the last 200m in the tandem race, an average of 73.24km/h (45.50mph). The greatest speed by an individual rider was 71.08km/h (44.16mph), by Gary Niewand (AUS) in the elimination rounds at Atlanta, 1996 when he clocked 10.129sec for the last 200m in the 1000m sprint. The fastest by a female rider was 64.21km/h (39.89mph) by Michelle Ferris (AUS), also in 1996, when she clocked 11.212sec. The longest race ever held in the Games, at any sport, was the 1912 cycling road race over a distance of 320km (198.8 miles). The largest entry in any Olympic event came in the 1996 men's road race, which had 183 competitors.

CYCLING RECORDS
MEN

1000m Time-Trial	1min 01.689sec	Jason Queally (GBR)	2000
4000m Individual Pursuit	4min 18.515sec	Robert Bartko (GER)	2000
4000m Team Pursuit	3min 59.710sec	GERMANY	2000

WOMEN

| 500m Time-Trial | 34.140sec | Felicia Ballanger (FRA) | 2000 |
| 3000m Individual Pursuit | 3min 30.816sec | Leontien Zijlaard (NED) | 2000 |

Few future top professionals competed at the Games successfully as amateurs, but now professionals are allowed to compete. Of the four men who have won the Tour de France a record five times, only Miguel Induráin (ESP) has won at the Games, in 1996. Eddy Merckx (BEL) and Jacques Anquetil (FRA), both finished 12th in the Olympic race, in 1964 and 1952 respectively. However, the latter won a bronze in the team race. The only other Olympic gold medallist to also win the Tour de France was Joop Zoetemelk (NED), a member of the winning quartet in the 1968 team time-trial. British rider Chris Boardman, riding a high-tech carbon-fibre machine with a revolutionary frame design, won the 1992 4km pursuit final by uniquely catching his opponent with a lap to go.

The youngest gold medallist was Dmitri Nelyubin (URS) in the 1988 team pursuit aged 17 years 229 days, while the oldest was Maurice Peeters (NED) aged 38 years 99 days in the 1920 1000m sprint. Winning a bronze four years later in the tandem, Peeters, at 42 years 83 days, was the oldest ever medallist as well. The youngest medallist was Alexei Markov (RUS) in the silver medal team pursuit squad in 1996 at 17 years 62 days. The oldest female champion was Jeannie Longo-Ciprelli (FRA) who won the 1996 road race aged 37 years 264 days. She was also the oldest medallist when she placed third in the 2000 road time-trial aged 41 years 335 days. The winner of the 1996 road time-trial, Zulfiya Zabirova (RUS), became the youngest ever female gold medallist aged 22 years 228 days, while the youngest female medallist was Sandra Schumacher (FRG) in 1984 at 17 years 217 days. In 1984, the first race for women, a road race, was won by Connie Carpenter-Phinney (USA), whose husband, Davis, won a bronze in the 100km team event. She had competed in the 1972 Winter Games as a 14-year-old speed skater.

In 1996 mountain bike events for men and women were introduced. At Sydney in 2000 there was the addition of three track events for men: the Madison, Keirin and the Olympic sprint (a team event), and a 500m time-trial for women.

CYCLING MEDALS

| | Men | | | Women | | | |
	G	S	B	G	S	B	Total
France	32	17	22	5	4	1	81
Italy	30	15	7	4	—	—	56
Great Britain	10	22	17	—	—	1	50
United States*	11	11	14	1	3	3	43
Germany	10	11	11	1	2	1	36
The Netherlands	9	13	4	4	2	3	35
Australia	6	10	10	1	3	1	31
Belgium	6	10	10	—	—	—	26
Soviet Union	10	4	8	1	—	1	24
Denmark	6	7	8	—	—	—	21
East Germany (GDR)	6	5	4	—	1	—	16
West Germany (FRG)	4	4	4	—	1	1	14
Sweden	3	2	8	—	—	—	13
Switzerland	2	4	3	—	1	—	10
Canada	—	3	3	—	1	2	9
South Africa	1	4	3	—	—	—	8
Poland	—	5	3	—	—	—	8
Czechoslovakia	2	2	2	—	—	—	6
Russia	1	1	1	1	1	1	6
Spain	3	1	—	—	—	1	5
Greece	1	3	1	—	—	—	5
Austria	1	—	2	—	—	—	3
Norway	1	—	1	—	—	—	2
Ukraine	—	1	—	—	—	1	2
Japan	—	—	2	—	—	—	2
Estonia	—	—	—	1	—	—	1
Kazakhstan	—	1	—	—	—	—	1
China	—	—	—	—	—	1	1

Jamaica	—	—	1	—	—	—	1
Latvia	—	—	1	—	—	—	1
Lithuania	—	—	—	—	—	1	1
Mexico	—	—	1	—	—	—	1
New Zealand	—	—	1	—	—	—	1
Uruguay	—	—	—	—	—	—	1
	155	155	152†	19	19	19	519

* Includes seven events in 1904 that were formerly excluded. † No bronzes were awarded in 1896 100km, the 1972 road team-trial, and individual race.

DE COUBERTIN

The accolade of founder of the modern Olympic Games is universally given to Pierre de Fredi, Baron de Coubertin of France. He was born in Paris on 1 January 1863, and early on studied the impact that sport had, and could have, on society at large, particularly appreciating the Greek ideal of developing the body and mind at the same time. He was also influenced by the ideas of the British educationalist Thomas Arnold, and from a young age concentrated his energies on improving general education in France. He vigorously propounded the importance of exercise and fitness as a cornerstone of education. He was particularly interested in fencing, and was a rugby-football referee.

In 1890, as part of a French government commission to study physical culture methods, he visited Dr William Penny Brookes and his Much Wenlock Olympic Society in Britain. Much impressed on this and other visits, he developed his concept of the revived Games. He put forward his ideas publicly in a lecture at the Sorbonne,

Paris, on 25 November 1892. They were received enthusiastically, and this encouraged him to meet with representatives of top American universities in the following year. In June 1894 he called an international conference, again at the Sorbonne, which was attended by 12 countries, and received messages of support from another 21. A resolution, dated 23 June, called for competitions along the lines of the ancient Olympic Games to be held every four years. An International Olympic Committee was formed with de Coubertin as Secretary-General. Two years later he was appointed President, and retained that position until 1925, when he retired. He was then given the title of Honorary President until his death, in Geneva, Switzerland, on 2 September 1937. He was buried at Lausanne, but his heart was interred in a marble monument at Olympia in Greece. He wrote a number of books, and in 1912, under a pseudonym, won a gold medal in the Artistic Olympics for his *Ode to Sport*.

DEMONSTRATION SPORTS

It was decided by the IOC that after 1992 demonstration sports would no longer be held at the Games. However, since 1904 there had been a variety of such demonstrations held but not as official events eligible for medals. Some of them later became official sports and they have been mentioned elsewhere in this book. Other than those there have been the following:

American Football (1932); Australian Rules Football

(1956); Bandy (1952); Bicycle Polo (1908); Budo (1964); Dog Sled Racing (1932); Gliding (1936); Jeu de Paume (1928); Korfball (1920); Lacrosse (1928, 1932, 1948); Military Patrol (1924, 1928, 1936, 1948); Pelota Basque (1924, 1968, 1992); Roller Hockey (1992); Speed Skiing (1992); Water Skiing (1972); Winter Pentathlon (1948). *See* under separate headings.

DISCONTINUED SPORTS

In the early celebrations of the Games there were a number of sports included, often of a purely local interest to the host country. The last of these was polo, which had its final outing in 1936. Below are listed all such sports, and the years in which they were held:

Cricket (1900); Croquet (1900); Golf (1900, 1904); Jeu de Paume (1908); Lacrosse (1904,1908); Motorboating (1908); Polo (1900, 1908, 1920, 1924, 1936); Roque (1904); Rackets (1908); Rugby Union (1900, 1908, 1920, 1924). *See* under separate headings.

DIVING

Part of the aquatics programme, men's diving was introduced into the Games in 1904, and that for women in 1912. In 1996 new rules came into operation that provide for three rounds instead of two, but with fewer dives in each round. The most successful diver has been Greg Louganis (USA) with four golds (a double 'double') in 1984–88, and a silver in 1976. However, Dmitri Sautin (RUS) has won a record six medals (two golds, a silver and three bronzes) 1992–2000, including four medals at a single Games (2000). Austrian-born Klaus Dibiasi (ITA)

has uniquely won the same event three times, and gained medals in four Games, 1964–76. Ni Xiong (CHN) also won medals in four Games 1988–2000. Pat McCormick (USA) set a female record of four golds in 1952 and 1956, which was matched by Fu Mingxia (CHN) in 1992–2000. However, Fu Mingxia also won a silver for a record five medals. McCormick's daughter Kelly won a silver in 1984 and a bronze in 1988. Dorothy Poynton-Hill (USA) 1928–36, Paula Myers-Pope (USA) 1952–60, and Fu Mingxia (CHN) 1992–2000, all won medals in three separate Games. Isabella White (GBR), 1912–28, Nicole Pellissard-Darrigrand (FRA), 1968–80, and Juno Stover-Irwin (USA), 1948–60, competed in four Games. Only White, a bronze, and Stover-Irwin, a silver and a bronze, won medals.

The oldest gold medallist was Hjälmar Johansson (SWE) aged 34 years 186 days in the plain diving at London in 1908, and also the oldest ever medallist four years later in Stockholm with a silver, aged 38 years 173 days. The oldest female champion was Micki King (USA) in 1972 aged 28 years 33 days, while the oldest female medallist was Mary Ellen Clark (USA) with a bronze in 1996 at 34 years 215 days. The youngest champion, and the youngest individual Olympic champion in any Summer Games sport, was Marjorie Gestring (USA) who won the 1936 springboard title, aged 13 years 268 days. The youngest male diving champion was Sun Shuwei (CHN) in 1992 aged 16 years 185 days. Dorothy Poynton-Hill (USA) was the youngest medallist in 1928 aged 13 years 23 days, while the youngest male medallist was Nils Skoglund (SWE) aged 14 years ten days, also in 1920. Greg Louganis (USA) won both diving titles in 1984 by the biggest margins ever recorded at the Games.

Five divers, four women and one man, have won medals at swimming as well as for diving. The most successful was Aileen Riggin (USA) with gold and silver diving medals in 1920 and 1924 and a bronze in the backstroke at Paris. Georg Hoffmann (GER) won silvers in 1904 at diving and the 100m backstroke; Helen Wainwright (USA) won a silver in the 1920 diving, and another silver in the 1924 400m freestyle; Katherine Rawls (USA) won a silver in the 1936 springboard and a bronze in the relay; Hjördis Töpel (SWE) won bronzes at diving and the relay in 1924.

The most successful husband and wife team were Clarence and Elizabeth (née Becker) Pinkston (USA), who between them won three golds, two silvers and two bronzes from 1920 to 1928. Elizabeth won her second gold medal, in 1928, on the second birthday of her twin children. Two male divers, Giorgio Cagnotto (ITA), 1964–80, and Niki Stajkovic (AUT), 1972–80 and 1988–92, have competed at five Games. In 2000, at Sydney, male and female synchronised diving events were added.

DIVING MEDALS (including synchronised diving)

| | Men | | | Women | | | |
	G	S	B	G	S	B	Total
United States	27	20	20	20	20	21	128
China	5	7	4	9	4	—	29
Germany	3	6	6	3	2	3	23
Sweden	4	5	4	2	3	3	21
Soviet Union	2	1	4	2	5	3	17
Italy	3	4	2	—	—	—	9
Mexico	1	4	4	—	—	—	9
Russia	2	1	2	1	1	—	7
East Germany (GDR)	1	—	—	1	2	3	7
Canada	—	—	—	1	1	3	5
Great Britain	—	—	2	—	1	2	5
Australia	1	—	1	—	—	1	3
Czechoslovakia	—	—	—	1	1	—	2
Denmark	—	—	—	1	—	1	2
Egypt	—	1	1	—	—	—	2
France	—	—	—	—	1	—	1
Austria	—	—	1	—	—	—	1
Ukraine	—	—	—	—	—	1	1
	49	49	51*	41	41	41	272

* Two bronzes were awarded in a 1904 and a 1908 event.

DOG SLEIGH RACING

A demonstration sport held at the Lake Placid Winter Games in 1932. A race for 12 sled teams, seven dogs to a sleigh, was held. There were two races of approximately 40km (25 miles) each, with the aggregate times added together. Emile St Goddard (CAN) won easily, finishing first both times in a combined 4hr 23min 12.5sec, nearly eight minutes ahead of Lennard Seppala (USA).

DOUBLES ACROSS SPORTS

There have been a number of multi-talented sports people who have won Olympic medals in different sports. The only one to win gold medals in both Summer and Winter Games was Eddie Eagan (USA) who won the 1920 light-heavyweight boxing title, and was a member of the 1932 winning four-man bob. His closest rival has been Jacob Tullin Thams (NOR) who won the ski jump in 1924, and then took a silver in yachting in 1936. The most outstanding woman in this line of endeavour was Christa Rothenburger-Luding (GDR) who won a gold and a silver at speed skating at Calgary in 1988, and then came second in the sprint cycling at Seoul later the same year. Not quite of the same standard was Clara Hughes (CAN), who won two bronzes in the 1996 cycling events, and then won another bronze at speed skating at Salt Lake City in 2002. In the Summer Games the earliest double gold winner at two sports was Carl Schuhmann (GER), with three gymnastic events and the wrestling in 1896. At the same Games, Edwin Flack (AUS) won the 800/1500m double on the track, and joined with British discus thrower, George Robertson, to win the tennis doubles bronze medal on the morning of the 800m final. He also started the marathon two days later, but dropped out some 4km short of the finish. Also at Athens, Viggo Jensen (DEN) won a gold and silver in weightlifting, a silver and a bronze at shooting, and was fourth in the rope climb. Fritz Hofmann (GER) won the silver medal in the 1896 100m, and is also included in the gold medal gymnastics team in some sources. Morris Kirksey (USA) won gold medals in the 4 x 100m relay and as a member of the American Rugby team in 1920. Daniel Norling (SWE) won gymnastic golds in 1908 and 1912, and then an equestrian gold in 1920. John Derbyshire (GBR) and Paul Radmilovic (GBR) won golds at swimming and the allied sport of water polo in the early part of the century. In 1908/1912 Victor Boin (BEL) won a silver and a bronze medal in water polo, and then in 1920, after having taken the oath for competitors in the opening ceremony, gained a silver as a member of the épée team.

Examples of women excelling in two Summer Olympic sports are rare, with the most outstanding being Roswitha Krause (GDR) who won the silver in 1968 in the 4 x 100m freestyle, and then won silver and bronze in the 1976 and 1980 handball tournaments. Anfissa Reztsova (URS/EUN) was the first Winter Games Olympian to win gold medals at two sports, in cross-country skiing in 1988 and the biathlon in 1992.

One of the more unusual doubles was that of Fernand de Montigny (BEL), who won a gold, two silver and two bronze medals in fencing in five Games, 1906–24, and another bronze on the hockey field in 1920. Although Otto Herschmann's double, of a bronze in the 1896 100m freestyle and a silver in the 1912 sabre fencing team, is not particularly outstanding, he was unique in that at the time of his fencing medal he was the President of the Austrian Olympic Committee, and is the only competitor holding such a position to win an Olympic medal. However, even more unique was Frank Kungler (USA), who has the unmatched distinction of winning medals at three sports at the same Games. (*See* Trebles).

DRUGS

Distance runners at the end of the 19th century took small doses of strychnine as a stimulant, and it is known that the winner of the 1904 Olympic marathon was administered a dose during the race. However, under the regulations of the time this was not illegal.

Although there are reports that evidence of drugs use had been found after the Winter Games at Oslo in 1952, the first 'official' Olympic drugs abuse scandal occurred in the 1960 100km cycling race when two Danish competitors collapsed. One of them, Knut Jensen, died from what was originally thought to be sunstroke. It transpired that they had both taken overdoses of a blood-circulation stimulant. Random testing was introduced at the 1964 Games at Tokyo for cycling, and then in 1968, at the Grenoble Winter Games and Mexico City, testing for all sports was instituted. At Munich in 1972, the American swimmer Rick DeMont lost the gold medal in the 400m freestyle after testing positive for a prohibited substance, though it should be stated that as an asthmatic DeMont apparently did not realise that the drug was in his regular medication. Also at Munich came the first judo contestant to fail a drugs test, when Bakhaavaa Buidaa (MGL) was disqualified after taking the silver medal in his class. There was a spate of disqualifications in weightlifting at Montreal in 1976, and the first athlete at the Olympics to fail a test was the Polish female discus thrower, Danuta Rosani in 1976. An even more high-profile case occurred in the 1984 10,000m, when the second placed finisher, Martti Vainio of Finland, was disqualified after a test. It was reported that as many as 17 'A' samples were found to be positive at Los Angeles, but as the athlete's code numbers 'mysteriously' disappeared no 'B' samples were tested.

Without doubt the biggest drugs scandal at the Games was when the Canadian sprinter, Ben Johnson, was disqualified after winning the 100m, in a sensational 9.79sec, at Seoul in 1988. In 1992 the International Weightlifting Federation changed all weight categories after the Olympic Games of that year, thus eliminating all existing world records, in a move to counter marks made during a period of suspected excessive drug abuse. In the 1990s there surfaced irrefutable evidence that the East German state sponsored the supply of drugs to East German sportsmen and women, especially the latter. It should be noted that there is also strong evidence that the drugs 'culture' was, and is, very prevalent in the Western democracies. National and international governing bodies are working hard to counter this cheating, and foremost in this fight has been the International Association of Athletics Federations (IAAF).

EQUESTRIANISM

In the ancient Games the first known event using horses was a chariot race in 680 BC. Horses with riders came into the Games in 648 BC. The first equestrian gold medallist of the modern Olympics was Aimé Haegeman (BEL) on *Benton II* in the 1900 show jumping. In 1956 the equestrian events were held separately, at Stockholm, from the main Games due to the strict Australian quarantine laws. The most gold medals won by a rider is six (one individual and five team events) by Reiner Klimke (FRG) 1964–88. Klimke's total of eight medals, comprising six golds and two bronzes, also constitutes a record for equestrianism, as does his feat of winning golds in five separate Games over a 24-year period. The medals won by Gustav-Adolf Boltenstern Jr (SWE) over a similar 24-year period, 1932–56, were not both gold. A record competition span by a woman, of 28 years was set by British-born Anne Jessica Ransehousen (*née* Newberry, USA), in 1988.

The oldest gold medallist was Josef Neckarmann (FRG) in the 1968 dressage team aged 56 years 141 days. The oldest individual event winner was Ernst Linder (SWE) in the 1924 dressage aged 56 years 91 days. The youngest individual champion was Edmund Coffin (USA) in the 1976 three-day event aged 21 years 77 days. However, Mary Tauskey (USA) won a gold medal in the three-day team event in 1976 aged 20 years 235 days. The d'Inzeo brothers of Italy, Raimondo and Piero, competed in a record eight Games, 1948–76. Raimondo won a gold, two silver and three bronze medals, while Piero gained two silvers and four bronzes. The female record is competition in six Games by Christilot Hansen-Boylen (CAN), over a record period of 28 years, 1964–92. A Bulgarian, Kroum Lekarski, competed in the three-day event for a record period of 36 years between 1924 and 1960, but only competed in four Games. Women first competed in 1952, and Lis Hartel (DEN) won the first female medal with a silver in the dressage, and repeated the feat in 1956. The most successful women have been Nicole Uphoff (GER), with four golds in 1988–92, and Isabell Werth (GER) with four golds in 1992–2000. However, Werth also won two silvers. Since 1984 equestrianism has been the only Olympic sport in which men and women compete against each other in individual events.

The only horse to be ridden to gold medals in three Games was *Gigolo* under Isabell Werth (GER) 1992–2000, when they won four golds and two silvers. Liselott Linsenhoff (FRG) won two dressage golds and a silver in 1968–72, and her daughter Ann-Kathrin won a gold in 1988. The most successful father and son have been Gustav-Adolf Boltenstern senior and junior (SWE), with the former winning a dressage individual bronze in 1912, and the latter two golds, a silver and a bronze, also in dressage, 1932–56. A unique equestrian participation record is that held by the family of William Roycroft (AUS), himself the oldest medallist in the sport, at 61 years 130 days in 1976. His son, Wayne, won a bronze in the same team, as he also had in 1968, while two other sons, Clarke (1972) and Barry (1976 and 1988) also competed well. In addition, Wayne's wife Vicki competed in 1984 and 1988, so that a Roycroft was in Australian teams from 1960 to 1988, and Wayne coached the winning Australian three-day team in 1996–2000.

In 1936 Germany completed the only six gold medal 'clean sweep' in Games equestrian history. In the 1912 and 1920 individual dressage Sweden took the first three places both times, a unique occurrence.

SHOW JUMPING

This was the first equestrian event to be included in the Games, along with high and long jumping contests, in 1900. From 1924 until 1968 teams comprised three members, all counting for the final score. This led to many teams not finishing, as in 1932 when no team medals were awarded at all, and in 1948 when only four of the 14 competing teams finished. Since 1972 teams have consisted of four riders with the best three scoring. The most gold medals won are five by Hans-Günter Winkler (FRG) 1956–72. His total of seven medals, including a

silver and bronze, is also a record for the discipline, as is his feat of winning medals in six Games. Only Pierre Jonquères d'Oriola (FRA) has won the individual title twice. The first woman to win a medal was Pat Smythe (GBR) in the 1956 team event, while the first individual medallist was Marion Coakes (GBR) in 1968.

The oldest gold medallist was Winkler in 1972 aged 46 years 49 days, while the oldest individual champion was Jonquères d'Oriola aged 44 years 266 days, in 1964. Bill Steinkraus (USA) won medals over a 20-year period 1952–72, a record matched by Winkler 1956–76. The youngest gold medallist was Jim Day (CAN) in the 1968 team aged 22 years 117 days.

The lowest score obtained by a winner is no faults, by Frantisek Ventura (TCH) on *Eliot* in 1928, Jonquères d'Oriola (FRA) on *Ali Baba* in 1952, Alwin Schockemöhle (FRG) on *Warwick Rex* in 1976, and Ludger Beerbaum (GER) on *Classic Touch* in 1992. The most successful horse was Winkler's *Halla* with three golds in 1956 and 1960.

DRESSAGE

The most successful rider was Reiner Klimke (*see* above), but Henri St Cyr (SWE), 1952–6, and Nicole Uphoff (GER), 1988–92, won the individual title twice. Remarkably, when Reiner Klimke (GER) won his last gold, it was in the 1988 team event, which included Ann-Kathrin Linsenhoff, the daughter of his gold-winning team partner of 20 years before. In all St Cyr won a record four golds, as did Nicole Uphoff. Undoubtedly St Cyr's total would have been more but his team was disqualified in 1948, having finished first, because one of its members, Gehnäll Persson, was not a fully commissioned officer – a requirement at that time. With the rules changed Persson was in the 1952 and 1956 winning teams. This Swedish team of St Cyr, Persson, and Gustav-Adolf Boltenstern Jr, uniquely finished in first place three times in a row, and can claim to be the most successful combination in Olympic history. Isabell Werth (GER) won four golds and two silvers 1992–2000, including a unique, for women, golds in three Games.

The first woman to win a medal was Lis Hartel (*see* above). Amazingly she was a polio victim who had to be helped on and off her horse. The first female gold medallist was Liselott Linsenhoff (FRG) in 1972. The silver medallist that year, Yelena Petushkova (URS), won gold in the team event, and was, for a time, married to Valery Brumel, the 1964 Olympic high jump champion. The oldest gold medallist was Josef Neckarmann (*see* above), who was also the oldest medallist in 1972, aged 60 years 96 days. Incidentally the oldest competitor in Olympic equestrian history was General Arthur von Pongracz (AUT) who began his Olympic career in 1924 aged 60 years and finished it in 1936, just missing a bronze medal, aged 72: one of the oldest ever Olympians. The oldest woman ever to compete in an Olympic Games, at any sport, was Lorna Johnstone (GBR) who placed 12th in the 1972 dressage five days after her 70th birthday. The youngest rider to win a gold medal was Nicole Uphoff (FRG) in the 1988 team event aged 22 years 244 days. The most successful horse has been *Gigolo* ridden by Isabell Werth 1992–2000 to four golds and two silvers. *Rembrandt* ridden by Nicole Uphoff

(GER) also won four golds in 1988 and 1992, including, uniquely, the individual title twice. They competed again in 1996 but failed to reach the final.

THREE-DAY EVENT

Competitions actually last four days as the dressage segment now occupies two days. Charles Pahud de Mortanges (NED) won the individual title twice, in 1928 and 1932, as did Mark Todd (NZL) in 1984 and 1988. However, the Dutchman also won a record total of four golds and a silver from 1924 to 1932. His Dutch team, including Gerard de Kruijff and Adolph van der Voort van Zijp, uniquely won two team titles with the same team members. The most appearances and the longest span of competition is seven Games and 28 years by Mickey Plumb (USA) 1964–92. (His Games total would have been a record-equalling eight except for the US boycott of Moscow in 1984). The first female competitor was Helena Dupont (USA), 33rd in 1964, while the first female gold medallists were Mary Gordon-Watson and Bridget Parker (both GBR) in 1972. The first individual medals won by women were in 1984 by Karen Stives (USA) and Virginia Holgate (GBR).

The oldest gold medallist was Derek Allhusen (GBR) aged 54 years 286 days in 1968, while the youngest was Mary Tauskey (USA) in 1976 aged 20 years 235 days. The oldest medallist was William Roycroft (AUS) with a bronze in 1976, aged 61 years 130 days, in the same team as his son, Wayne. The youngest medallist was Charles Hough (USA) aged 18 years 92 days in 1952. The most successful horse was *Marcroix* ridden by Charles Pahud de Mortanges (NED) to three golds and a silver in 1928 and 1932. Both *Silver Piece*, ridden by Voort van Zijp (NED), 1924 and 1928, and *Charisma*, ridden by Mark Todd (NZL), 1984 and 1988, also won three golds. Two members of the 1996 winning US team were husband and wife David and Karen O'Connor, and David won the individual title in 2000.

The 1936 cross-country course was so tough that only four teams out of 14 finished. One of the members of that fourth placed team, Otomar Bures of Czechoslovakia, had over 18,000 penalty points against him at the finish, having taken over two and three-quarter hours to catch his horse after a fall. Britain's Capt Richard Fanshawe, with a similar problem with his horse, *Bowie Knife,* gained over 8000 penalty points, but had the satisfaction of finishing with a team bronze. In 1920 the dressage was excluded, with two cross-country runs, at 20km (12.4 miles) and 50km (31.06 miles), added to the jumping.

EQUESTRIAN MEDALS

	G	S	B	Total
Germany	22	13	12	47
United States	9	17	15	41
Sweden	17	8	14	39
France	11	12	11	34
West Germany (FRG)	11	5	9	25
Italy	7	9	7	23
Great Britain	5	8	9	22
Switzerland	4	10	7	21
The Netherlands	8	9	2	17
Soviet Union	6	5	4	15
Belgium	4	2	5	11
Australia	6	2	2	10
New Zealand	3	2	4	9
Mexico	2	1	4	7
Poland	1	3	2	6
Denmark	—	4	1	5
Canada	1	1	2	4
Austria	1	1	1	3
Portugal	—	—	3	3
Spain	1	1	—	2
Chile	—	2	—	2
Romania	—	1	1	2
Brazil	—	—	2	2
Czechoslovakia	1	—	—	1
Japan	1	—	—	1
Argentina	—	1	—	1
Bulgaria	—	1	—	1
Norway	—	1	—	1
Hungary	—	—	1	1
Saudi Arabia	—	—	1	1
	121*	119	119†	360

* Two golds in the 1900 high jump. † No bronze in 1932 three-day team event.

EVER PRESENT, COUNTRIES

Only five countries have never failed to be represented at celebrations of the Summer Games since 1896 (including 1906): Australia, France, Greece, Great Britain and Switzerland. (It should be noted that prior to 1924 Irish competitors were members of the United Kingdom of Great Britain and Ireland team, and did not then represent Ireland. In 1956 Switzerland only competed in the Stockholm segment of the Games). Of those five, only France, Great Britain and Switzerland have been present at all Winter Games as well. Of these only Great Britain competed in the skating and ice hockey events of 1908 and 1920, the 'Winter' events included in those Summer Games.

EVER PRESENT, EVENTS

There have been 16 individual events that have been contested at every modern Olympic Games. In the athletics programme they are: 100m, 400m, 800m, 1500m, Marathon, 110m hurdles, high jump, pole vault, long jump, triple jump (originally the hop, step and jump), shot and discus. In fencing there have been the individual foil and sabre contests; in weightlifting the unlimited class. In swimming the 1500-m freestyle may be included, although the event was actually 1200m in 1896, 1000m in 1900, and one mile in 1904 and 1906.

EVER PRESENT, SPORTS

Only five sports have been contested at every modern Games since 1896. These are athletics, cycling, fencing, gymnastics and swimming. Rowing would have been included, but rough seas caused the cancellation of the programmed rowing events in 1896.

FAMILIES

There have been some remarkable family achievements in the Olympic Games. (*See also* under Brothers and Sisters). Outstanding among them have been the Gyarmati family of Hungary. The patriarch was Dezsö, who won three golds, a silver and a bronze in water polo 1948–64; his wife Éva Székely won a gold and a silver as a breaststroke swimmer 1952–6; their daughter Andrea won a silver and a bronze in 1972 at backstroke and butterfly; and Andrea married Mihály Hesz who had won a gold and a silver at canoeing 1964–8. Also noteworthy were the yachting Lunde family of Norway. Eugen Lunde won a gold in the 1924 6-m class; his son Peder, daughter-in-law Vibeke, and Vibeke's brother Börre, won a silver in the 1952 5.5-m class; and grandson Peder Jr won a gold in the 1960 Flying Dutchman class. A similar impact was made on fencing by the Gerevich family of Hungary: Aladár won a record seven golds, a silver and two bronzes 1932–60; his wife Erna Bogen won a bronze in 1932; her father Albert Bogen (AUT) won a silver in 1912; and Aladár and Erna's son, Pál, won two bronze medals in 1972 and 1980. Many other father/son, mother/daughter, brother/sister, and husband/wife combinations have enriched the Games – they are noted under the various sports.

FENCING

Undoubtedly because of de Coubertin's personal interest, fencing was one of the original sports held in 1896, when the first Olympic champion was Emile Gravelotte (FRA) in the foil. Until recently it was the only sport in which professionals had openly competed in the Games, as special events for fencing masters were held in 1896 and 1900. At the latter Games they even competed against amateur competitors, so that Albert Ayat (FRA) beat his pupil Ramón Fonst (CUB) in the épée. When Léon Pyrgos won the foil contest for fencing masters in 1896 he became the first Greek Olympic champion of modern times. A foil competition for women was introduced in 1924, and a team contest for them in 1960. Team and individual épée events for women were introduced in 1996. Electronic scoring equipment was used for épée in 1936, for foil in 1956, and for the sabre in 1992.

Aladár Gerevich (HUN) won a record seven gold medals in the sabre between 1932 and 1960. The record for most medals is 13 by Edoardo Mangiarotti (ITA) in foil and épée 1936–60, comprising six golds, five silvers and two bronzes. His elder brother Dario won a gold and two silvers in 1948 and 1952. Nedo Nadi (ITA) won an unequalled five golds at one Games in 1920, and his younger brother, Aldo, added three more golds and a silver – a family record total at a Games. The most individual event gold medals is three, achieved by Ramón Fonst (CUB) in 1900 and 1904 (two), and by Nedo Nadi (ITA) in 1912 and 1920 (two). The only man, in any sport, to win Olympic gold medals at six consecutive Games was Aladár Gerevich (*see* above); his medal-winning span of 28 years is also a record. Britain's Bill Hoskyns also competed at six Games, 1956–76, but only won two silver medals, while Norman Armitage (USA) attended six celebrations, 1928–56, and gained a bronze in 1948. The equal longest span of competition by any Olympic competitor is 40 years by Ivan Osiier (DEN) who fenced from 1908 to 1948, in a record seven Games, during which time he won a silver medal in 1912, and became the oldest Olympic fencer in 1948 aged 59 years 240 days. His fencer wife Ellen won a gold medal in 1924.

Four fencers have won individual medals in all three disciplines at one Games. Both Nedo Nadi and his brother, Aldo, won golds in each of the team events in 1920. Roger Ducret (FRA) won foil and épée golds and a sabre silver in 1924. In the sparsely supported 1904 events American-born Albertson Van Zo Post (CUB) won the foil silver, and bronzes in the other two disciplines. The oldest gold medallist was Aladár Gerevich (HUN) in 1960 aged 50 years 178 days, while the youngest was Ramón Fonst (CUB) aged 16 years 289 days in 1900. The family of Gerevich has a unique position in Olympic fencing as he won seven golds, one silver and two bronzes; his wife Erna Bogen won a bronze in 1932, his father-in-law Albert Bogen won a silver in 1912, and Aladár's son, Pál, won bronze medals in 1972 and 1980.

FOIL

Only Nedo Nadi (ITA) in 1912 and 1920, and Christian d'Oriola (FRA) in 1952 and 1956 have won two individual titles. In addition, d'Oriola won two team golds and two silvers for a record six medals. The oldest gold medallist was Henri Jobier (FRA) who was over 44 years old in the winning 1924 team, while the youngest was Nedo Nadi (ITA) in 1912, aged 18 years 29 days. In the 15 Games from 1920 to 1984 France only failed once to gain a team competition medal.

EPÉE

Ramón Fonst (CUB) was the only double winner of the individual title, but the most successful was Edoardo Mangiarotti (ITA) with five gold, a silver and two bronze medals 1936–60. The oldest gold medallist was Fiorenzo Marini (ITA) aged 46 years 179 days in the 1960 team, and the youngest was Fonst (see above). Charles Newton-Robinson, a member of the silver winning British team in 1906 was 52 years 197 days, the oldest ever Olympic fencing medallist.

SABRE

Jean Georgiadis (GRE), Jenö Fuchs (HUN), Rudolf Kárpáti (HUN), Viktor Krovopouskov (URS) and Jean François Lamour (FRA) have all won two individual titles. Gerevich (see above) won a record seven gold medals (only one individual) and was also the oldest gold medallist. The youngest was Mikhail Burtsev (URS), aged 20 years 36 days in the 1976 team event. Hungarians have dominated the discipline to an unparalleled extent, winning 12 golds, six silvers and eight bronzes as individual medals. They won the individual title every year from 1908 to 1964, except in 1920 when they were not invited. They have won the team title 11 times, placed second once, and third on three occasions, and won 46 consecutive contests from 1924 to 1964. Their 1960 team included Gerevich, Kárpáti and Pál Kovács, who between them amassed a total of 19 gold medals. The winning Hungarian teams of 1948 and 1952 comprised the same members. An interesting coincidence is that Kárpáti and former IOC President, Juan Antonio Samaranch, were born on the same day.

WOMEN'S FOIL

Only Ilona Elek (HUN) has won two individual titles, in 1936 and 1948, but Yelena Novikova-Belova (URS) 1968–76, and Giovanna Trilini (ITA) 1992–2000, both won a record four golds. However, Trillini also won two bronzes. The record for most medals is seven by Ildikó Ságiné-Rejtó (formerly Ujlakiné-Rejtó) of Hungary in a record five Games, 1960–76. Perhaps surprisingly she was born deaf. Ellen Müller-Preis (AUT) competed over a record 24-year period 1932–56. This was matched by Kerstin Palm (SWE), from 1964–88 but she notched up a record seven Games – the most attended by any female Olympic competitor, in any sport.

Elek was the oldest gold medallist in 1948 aged 41 years 77 days, and the oldest medallist four years later with a silver aged 45 years 71 days. The youngest champion/medallist was Helene Mayer (GER) in 1928 aged 17 years 225 days. When Gillian Sheen (GBR) won her gold medal in 1956 there were hardly any members of the British press corps on hand as they considered that fencing was a 'minor' sport, and anyway she had not been expected to achieve anything of note.

WOMEN'S ÉPÉE

First held in 1996, with individual and team competitions. The most successful has been Laura Flessel-Colovic (FRA) with two golds and a bronze 1996–2000. She was also the youngest gold medallist aged 24 years 258 days in 1996, while the oldest gold medallist was Sophie Moresee-Pichot (FRA) in the winning team in 1996, aged 34 years 112 days. The youngest medallist was Sophie Lamon (SUI) in the Sydney silver medal épée team aged 15 years 224 days.

FENCING MEDALS

	Men			Women			
	G	S	B	G	S	B	Total
France	35	36	30	4	2	3	110
Italy	33	32	21	7	4	5	102
Hungary	27	14	20	6	6	6	79
Soviet Union	14	14	15	5	3	3	54
Germany	4	4	5	2	4	4	23
Poland	4	7	7	—	1	1	20
United States*	2	6	11	—	—	—	19
West Germany (FRG)	4	6	—	3	2	1	16
Belgium	5	3	5	—	—	—	13
Romania	2	—	2	1	3	4	12
Russia	6	2	1	1	—	1	11
Cuba*	5	3	3	—	—	—	11
Great Britain	—	6	—	1	3	—	10
Greece	3	3	2	—	—	—	8

The Netherlands	—	1	7	—	—	—	8
Sweden	2	3	2	—	—	—	7
Austria	—	1	3	1	—	2	7
Switzerland	—	2	3	—	2	—	7
Denmark	—	1	1	1	1	2	6
China	—	1	—	1	1	1	4
Korea	1	—	1	—	—	—	2
Bohemia (Czech)	—	—	2	—	—	—	2
East Germany (GDR)	—	1	—	—	—	—	1
Mexico	—	—	—	—	1	—	1
Argentina	—	—	1	—	—	—	1
Portugal	—	—	1	—	—	—	1
	147	**146**	**143**	**33**	**33**	**33**	**535**

* Double counting for 1904 team gold medal.

FIGURE SKATING

Ice skating had been included in the original programme of events for the 1900 Games, but was actually not held. Thus, the first Olympic title at a Winter Games event was won by Ulrich Salchow (SWE), in 1908, at the Prince's Ice Rink, London. Salchow gave his name to one of the most popular jumps. Also in the 1908 Games there was a special figures event that was won by a Russian (Czarist variety), Nikolai Panin, who had been too ill to compete in the main event. The first women's title went to Madge Syers (GBR), who six years previously had entered the World Championships, ostensibly for men only, and had placed second to Salchow. The most gold medals won by a figure skater is three achieved by Gillis Grafström (SWE) 1920–8, Sonja Henie (NOR) 1928–36, and Irina Rodnina (URS) in the pairs 1972–80. Of these only Grafström also won a silver, in 1932 aged 38, and thus is the only skater to win medals in four Games. No skater has doubled completely successfully in singles and pairs at the Games. The best have been Ernst Baier (GER) with the pairs gold and a singles silver in 1936, and Madge Syers (GBR) with a singles gold and a pairs bronze in 1908.

The oldest gold medallist was Walter Jakobsson (FIN) who won the 1920 pairs with his German-born wife Ludowika aged 38 years 80 days. Ludowika became the oldest ever female winner aged 35 years 276 days. The youngest was Maxi Herber (GER) aged 15 years 128 days in the 1936 pairs with Baier, whom she later married. The youngest individual event champion was Tara Lipinski (USA) in 1998 aged 15 years 255 days. The youngest male champion was Richard Button (USA) aged 18 years 202 days, winning the 1948 singles. The youngest medallist was Scott Allen (USA) two days short of his 15th birthday taking the 1964 singles bronze, while the youngest female medallist was Manuela Gross (GDR) just ten days past her 15th birthday in the 1972 bronze-winning pair. The oldest medallist was Martin Stixrud (NOR) with the 1920 singles bronze, aged 44 years 78 days, while the oldest female medallist was Ludowika Jacobsson (FIN) with the pairs silver in 1924, aged 39 years 189 days. The youngest ever Winter Games competitor was Cecilia Colledge (GBR), who was 11 years 73 days at the 1932 Games – she gained the silver medal in 1936 behind Sonja Henie. The youngest male competitor was Jan Hoffmann (GDR) aged 12 years 110 days in 1968 – 12 years later he gained the silver medal.

Sonja Henie won three Olympic, six European and ten World titles before turning professional and making an estimated $47 million in ice shows and films. The film world attracted a number of other Olympic skaters. Down the field, (16th) in 1936, was Gladys Jepson-Turner (GBR) who had a Hollywood career as Belita, and Vera Hruba (TCH), one place behind the British woman, married the head of Republic Pictures and starred in many films as Vera Hruba Ralston. Sonja Henie is usually credited with introducing jumps into the women's event, but in 1920 Theresa Weld (USA), the bronze medal winner, included a Salchow in her programme, which brought a reprimand from the judges and a threat that she would be penalised if she continued with such 'unfeminine behaviour'. In the 1992 Games Surya Bonaly (FRA) attempted the first ever quadruple jump, in competition, by a woman.

The sport has always been plagued by the accusations (often thought to be merited) that many of the judges indulge in so-called 'protocol judging', or judging on reputation rather than actual performance. In 2002 at Salt Lake City there were accusations that a French judge in the pairs event had 'done a deal' – her marking was so blatantly incorrect that the result was revised to give the Canadian pair a joint gold medal with the Russians. A change of marking in the sport was brought about by Trixi Schuba (AUT) winning the 1972 title primarily on the basis of her excellent set figures (she was only placed seventh in free skating). At that time the marks had been divided 50–50 between sections, but they were changed to give greater emphasis to free skating. Set figures were skated for the last time at Calgary in 1988, and are no longer included in Olympic competition. On the subject of marks, Jayne Torvill and Christopher Dean (GBR) were awarded a maximum nine sixes for their artistic impression in the 1984 ice dancing event, as well as another three sixes for technical merit – unsurpassed marking at the Games. In 1994 stricter rules governing skimpy clothing were introduced, but have not always been enforced.

In 1972, although Irina Rodnina and Aleksey Ulanov (URS) won the pairs it was the latter's dalliance with Ludmila Smirnova, silver medallist with Andrey Suraikin, which caught the media interest. The result was the break-up of the top Soviet pair. Rodnina then teamed with Aleksandr Zaitsev, while Ulanov and Smirnova got married. In the World Championships the Rodnina/ Zaitsev partnership beat the other pair and, getting married themselves in 1975, they went on to win two Olympic titles, the second less than a year after the birth of their son. Artur Dmitriyev (EUN/RUS), with Natalya Mishkutienok, won the 1992 pairs title. At Nagano in 1998 he appeared with a new partner, Oksana Kazakova, and won the gold again, making the tenth consecutive victory in the event for Russian (i.e. URS, EUN, RUS) pairs. Also in 1998, Yevgeni Platov and Oksana Grischuk became the first couple to successfully defend the ice dance title.

FIGURE SKATING MEDALS

	G	S	B	Total
United States	13	13	16	42
Soviet Union	13	10	6	29
Austria	7	9	4	20
Canada	3	7	9	19
Russia	9	7	—	16
Great Britain	5	3	7	15
France	3	2	7	12
Sweden	5	3	2	10
East Germany (GDR)	3	3	4	10
Germany	4	4	1	9
Norway	3	2	1	6
Hungary	—	2	4	6
Czechoslovakia	1	1	3	5
The Netherlands	1	2	—	3
China	—	—	3	3
Finland	1	1	—	2
Belgium	1	—	1	2
Switzerland	—	1	1	2
West Germany (FRG)	—	—	2	2
Ukraine	1	—	—	1
Japan	—	1	—	1
Italy	—	—	1	1
	73*	71*	72	216

* In 2002 there were two gold medals in the pairs event.

FIRSTS

The first person to win an event in the Modern Olympics was Francis Lane (USA), who won heat one of the 100m in 1896. The first gold medallist was James Brendan Connolly (USA) the winner of the 1896 hop, step and jump (now known as the triple jump). See also under Women.

FLAG

The Olympic flag was devised by Baron de Coubertin, based on a design depicted on an ancient Greek symbol found at Delphi. It consists of five interlaced rings in two rows, coloured blue, yellow, black, green and red, from left to right. The rings are meant to symbolise the friendship of mankind, with the colours, including the white background of the flag itself, representing all nations – every national flag contains at least one of the colours. There is an erroneous idea that the colours themselves represent the continents: blue – Europe; yellow – Asia; black – Africa; Green – the Americas; Red – Australasia. It was originally presented to the IOC in 1912, and was to be flown for the first time at the 1916 Games, but Antwerp had the honour in 1920. In 1984 Korea presented a new flag to the IOC and it was first flown at the Seoul Games in 1988. At the end of each Games the flag is placed in the safe keeping of the host city of the next celebration.

FLAME

The Olympic flame was introduced to the modern Games at Amsterdam in 1928, where it was lit at the top of a tower in the stadium. Since then has always burned throughout the duration of a Games. It symbolises the endeavour for perfection and struggle for victory. It is first lit by the rays of the sun in an enactment of an ancient ceremony at Olympia, the site of the original Games (see also Torch Relay). The following have lit the Olympic flame in the stadium:

SUMMER
1936   Fritz Schilgen
1948   John Mark
1952   Paavo Nurmi (Hannes Kohlemainen on tower)
1956   Ron Clarke
1960   Giancarlo Peris
1964   Yoshinori Sakai
1968   Enriqueta Basilio
1972   Gunter Zahn

1976	Stephane Préfontaine and Sandra Henderson	
1980	Sergei Belov	
1984	Rafer Johnson	
1988	Sun-Man Chung, Won-Tuk Kim and Mi-Chung Sohn	
1992	Antonio Rebollo	
1996	Muhammad Ali	
2000	Cathy Freeman	

The first flame to burn at a Winter Games was at Oslo in 1952. It was lit at the home of Sondre Nordheim, the founder of modern skiing, at Morgedal in southern Norway, and brought by a relay of skiers to the Bislett stadium at Oslo. Thereafter the flame came from Olympia.

WINTER

1952	Eigil Nansen
1956	Guido Caroli
1960	Ken Henry
1964	Joseph Rieder
1968	Alain Calmat
1972	Hideki Takada
1976	Christl Haas and Josef Feistmantl
1980	Dr Charles Morgan Kerr
1984	Sandra Dubravcic
1988	Robyn Perry
1992	Michel Platini and François-Cyrille Grange
1994	Crown Prince Haakon
1998	Midori Ito
2002	1980 United States Ice Hockey Team

FOOTBALL

See under separate headings for American, Australian Rules and Soccer.

FREESTYLE SKIING

Freestyle skiing, for men and women, was a demonstration sport in 1988 comprising ballet, aerials and mogul events. Mogul events became an Olympic medal sport in 1992, with aerials added in 1994. Marking is complicated but can best be compared to diving as each manouevre has a degree of difficulty, which affects the final marks.

The most successful competitors have been Janne Lahtela (FIN), with a gold and a silver 1998–2002. The most successful women, with a gold and a bronze each, have been Stine Lise Hattestad (NOR) 1992–4, Tae Satoya (JPN) 1998–2002 and Kari Traa (NOR) 1998–2002. The oldest winner was Aleš Valenta (CZE) who won the 2002 aerials at 29 years 13 days, while the oldest female gold medallist was Kari Traa (NOR), who

won the 2002 moguls at 28 years 12 days. The youngest winner, of the 1994 moguls, was Jean-Luc Brassard (CAN) aged 21 years 176 days, while the youngest female champion was Tae Satoya (JPN) aged 21 years 244 days taking the 1998 moguls. The youngest medallist was Yelizaveta Kozhevnikova (EUN-RUS) in the 1992 moguls, aged 19 years 48 days, and the youngest male to win a medal was Dimitri Daschinsky (BLR) with an aerials bronze in 1998 at 20 years 101 days. Elizabeth McIntyre (USA) was the oldest medallist in the 1998 moguls aged 33 years 229 days. When Satoya won the 1998 moguls title she became the first ever winner of a Winter Olympics gold medal by a Japanese woman. At Salt Lake City in 2002 Aleš Valenta achieved the first ever five-twist jump at the Games.

FREESTYLE SKIING MEDALS

	Men			Women			
	G	S	B	G	S	B	Total
United States	2	2	1	2	2	—	9
Norway	—	—	—	2	—	3	5
Canada	1	1	1	—	1	1	5
France	1	2	2	—	—	—	5
Finland	1	1	1	—	—	—	3
Japan	—	—	—	1	—	1	2
Switzerland	1	—	—	—	—	1	2
Russia	—	1	—	—	—	1	2
Belarus	—	—	2	—	—	—	2
Australia	1	—	—	—	—	—	1
Czech Republic	1	—	—	—	—	—	1
Uzbekistan	—	—	—	1	—	—	1
China	—	—	—	—	1	—	1
Germany	—	—	—	—	1	—	1
Soviet Union	—	—	—	—	1	—	1
Sweden	—	—	—	—	1	—	1
	7	7	7	7	7	7	42

GLIDING

A demonstration sport at the Berlin Games in 1936, 14 countries took part in an exhibition, but the main participants were German gliders.

GOLF

Played twice in the Games, in 1900 and 1904. George Lyon, a former Canadian pole vault record holder, was 46 years 59 days when he won the 1904 title. The most successful player was Chandler Egan (USA) who won the team gold and individual silver in 1904. Sharing also in that gold medal team was his brother Walter. Charles Sands (USA), who won the inaugural competition in 1900, was one of the few people to compete in three sports at the Games, as he had played in the tennis tournament in 1900, and took part in Jeu de Paume in 1908. The winner of the only women's competition, in 1900, was Margaret Abbott, aged 20 years 110 days, who became the first American woman to win an Olympic gold medal. Her mother, Mary, placed seventh in a rare case of mother and daughter competing in the same event at any one Games. Currently, there have been suggestions of bringing golf back into the Games, possibly for 2008.

GYMNASTICS

In artistic gymnastics there are eight interlinked events for men and six for women. A team competition comes first, comprising one compulsory and one optional exercise for each separate discipline. For men these are: floor exercises, pommel horse, rings, horse vault, parallel bars and horizontal bar. For women they are: floor exercises, asymmetrical bars, horse vault and balance beam. Each competitor is marked out of 10.00 for both the compulsory and optional exercises at each discipline. The best total of five gymnasts per country decides the team competition. The best 36 individuals (but only a maximum of three per country) then qualify for the individual all-round competition. They each complete a further optional exercise for each discipline, and are awarded new marks. Prior to 1992 these were added to the average of their previous best total from the team competition, but since then they start from scratch. The best eight in each discipline go forward to the individual final for that event. With the exception of 1948, when scores were marked out of 20.00, points since 1936 are of some comparative value. After 1996 there were no compulsory exercises. In 1984 an individual modern rhythmic event for women was introduced, and in 1996 there was a team event. At Sydney, in 2000, trampolining for men and women was introduced (see Trampolining).

The first gymnastics gold medal was won by the German team on the parallel bars event in 1896, and the first individual champion was Carl Schumann of that team in the vault. Due to the large number of disciplines, each with their own medals awarded, gymnasts are foremost among the greatest collectors of Olympic medals. The most successful was Larissa Latynina (URS) who won a record-breaking 18 medals from 1956 to 1964, comprising nine golds (the most by any female Olympian), five silvers and four bronzes – a result unsurpassed in any sport. The greatest number of individual gold medals is seven, won by Vera Cáslavská (TCH) in 1964 and 1968, an Olympic record by a woman in any sport. The most gold medals won by a man is eight by Sawao Kato (JPN) 1968–76, but the male record for individual golds is six by Boris Shakhlin (URS) and Nikolai Andrianov (URS). The latter also holds the absolute Olympic record for the most medals by a male competitor, in any sport, with a total of 15. In 1980 Aleksandr Ditiatin (URS) became the only male gymnast to gain medals in all eight events at one Games, while in 1992 Vitali Scherbo (EUN) uniquely won six gold medals at the one Games.

GYMNASTICS MULTI-MEDAL WINNERS

		G	S	B
Larissa Latynina (URS)	1956–64	9	5	4
Sawao Kato (JPN)	1968–76	8	3	1
Nikolai Andrianov (URS)	1972–80	7	5	3
Boris Shakhlin (URS)	1956–64	7	4	2
Vera Cáslavská (TCH)	1960–8	7	4	0
Viktor Chukarin (URS)	1952–6	7	3	1

In recent years the sport has caught the imagination of the public due to a tremendous increase in media, especially television, coverage. In 1968 it was the attractive blonde Czech, Vera Cáslavská who attracted attention, by defeating the Soviet women only two months after the invasion of her country. At Munich, it was the elfin Olga Korbut (URS) who was the focus of all, even though she was outshone, technically, by her illustrious teammate Ludmila Tourischeva. In 1976 the unsmiling Nadia Comaneci (ROM) deserved all the adulation as she scored the ultimate 10.00 on seven occasions, while the photogenic Nelli Kim (URS) attained that score twice. Aleksandr Ditiatin stole the show from the women in 1980, and also gained the first Olympic 10.00 by a man, in the horse vault. In 1984 the television cameras made a superstar of Mary Lou Retton (USA) in the absence of the East Europeans. The television pictures of the injured Kerri Strug (USA) successfully vaulting to clinch the

American's team gold at Atlanta in 1996, were beamed around the world.

The oldest gold medallist was Masao Takemoto (JPN) aged 40 years 344 days in the 1960 team event. Only 24 days younger was Heikki Savolainen (FIN) in the 1948 team event, who competed in a record five Games over a record span of 24 years from 1928 to 1952. The oldest male medallist was Lucien Démanet (FRA) at 45 years 266 days in 1920. The youngest champion was Nadia Comaneci (ROM) aged 14 years 252 days in 1976, while the oldest female champion was Àgnes Keleti (HUN) in 1956 aged 35 years 331 days. The oldest female medallist has been Ethel Seymour (GBR) in 1928, aged 46 years 222 days. The youngest male to win a gold medal was Harald Eriksen (NOR) in 1906, aged 17 years 292 days. The youngest medallist was Dimitrios Loundras (GRE) who gained a bronze in the parallel bars team event of 1896, aged ten years 218 days. However, it should be noted that some doubt exists about his exact age. The youngest ever female medallist was Luigina Giavotti (ITA) in 1928, aged 11 years 303 days. In 1984 it was decided that male competitors had to be a minimum of 16 years and females 15 years, but in 2000 at Sydney, the minimum age for all was fixed at 16 years. Recent revelations suggest that in the past some countries in the Eastern bloc faked the ages of their young female performers, presenting them as older than in fact they were.

The closest margin of victory in the individual all-round contest for men was 0.025 of a point in 1984 when Koji Gushiken (JPN) beat Peter Vidmar (USA). In 1992 there was a tremendous duel for the women's all-around title between Tatyana Gutsu (EUN) and Shannon Miller (USA), which resulted in the Ukrainian girl winning by the smallest ever margin of 0.012pts. There had been some controversy over the inclusion of Gutsu, who had failed to make the cut-off after the team competition, but was a replacement for an (allegedly) injured teammate. On two occasions there has been a triple tie for a gold medal – both times in the pommel horse event, in 1948 and 1988. Since the Soviet Union entered Olympic competition in 1952 they have won the women's team title nine times (they were not present in 1984). In 1992 (in the guise of the Unified Team) they not only won for the tenth time but as their swansong, took the men's and women's individual and team titles plus the rhythmic crown. With the Soviet Union broken up, it was Russia that took the 1996 men's title.

One of the most amazing competitors in Olympic history must be the American gymnast George Eyser, who won six medals, including three golds, in the 1904 Games. He was well over 30 years of age, but, even more remarkably, had a wooden leg. Despite this he also competed in the all-round contest (the forerunner of the decathlon) in the track and field programme. In 1988 Vladimir Gogoladze (URS) performed a triple somersault in the team floor exercises – the first achieved in the Olympics. In the 1988 modern rhythmic competition, Marina Lobatch (URS) scored the maximum possible 60.00 points.

The largest crowd to watch an Olympic gymnastic event was the 32,600 at the Georgia Dome in 1996 for the final of the women's team contest. Prior to 1928 it has been suggested that there were no individual medal events, merely competitors as part of the all-round title. However, the author has shown these in the tables of results and added them into the medal's lists until more evidence comes to light to indicate otherwise.

GYMNASTICS MEDALS (excluding trampolining)

	Men			Women			Total
	G	S	B	G	S	B	
Soviet Union	45	42	19	38	30	30	204
Japan	27	28	30	—	—	1	86
United States*	22	17	19	4	6	9	77
Romania	1	2	2	18	15	19	57
Switzerland	15	19	13	—	—	—	47
Hungary	7	6	4	7	6	10	40
China	10	10	5	3	4	4	36
East Germany (GDR)	3	3	10	3	10	7	36
Czechoslovakia	3	7	9	9	6	1	35
Germany	12	7	11	1	1	—	32
Italy	13	7	9	—	1	—	30
Russia	4	3	6	6	5	4	28
Finland	8	5	12	—	—	—	25
France	4	9	9	—	—	—	22
Yugoslavia	5	2	4	—	—	—	11
Greece	4	3	3	—	—	1	11
Bulgaria	2	1	4	—	2	1	10
Ukraine	1	1	2	3	1	1	9
Sweden	4	1	—	1	1	1	8
Belarus	—	—	4	—	2	—	6
Norway	2	2	1	—	—	—	5
Denmark	1	3	1	—	—	—	5
Korea	—	2	3	—	—	—	5
Austria*	2	1	—	—	—	—	3
Spain	1	—	—	1	1	—	3

Great Britain	—	1	1	—	—	1	3
Poland	—	1	1	—	—	1	3
Belgium	—	1	1	—	—	—	2
West Germany (FRG)	—	—	1	—	—	1	2
Latvia	1	—	—	—	—	—	1
Canada	—	—	—	1	—	—	1
The Netherlands	—	—	—	1	—	—	1
North Korea (PRK)	1	—	—	—	—	—	1
	198	184	184	96	91	92	845

* Double counting for 1904 men's team title.

HANDBALL

The sport was introduced in 1936, appropriately since it was a German invention, and was played as an outdoor 11-a-side game. When re-introduced in 1972 it was as an indoor seven-a-side competition. The most successful players have been Zinaida Tourchina (URS) and her teammate Larissa Karlova, who won gold medals in 1976 and 1980, and then a bronze in 1988. Four male Swedish players have also won medals in three Games, but they were all silver.

The oldest gold medallist was Yuriy Klimov (URS) who won in 1976, aged 36 years 1 day, while the oldest female was Ludmila Poradnik (URS) in 1980 aged 34 years 200 days. Tourchina's bronze in 1988 was achieved at the age of 42 years 135 days and the oldest male medallist was Magnus Wislander (SWE) winning silver in 2000 aged 36 years 221 days. The youngest gold medallist/medallist was Larissa Karlova (URS) aged 17 years 356 days in 1976, while the youngest male winner was Günther Ortmann (GER) aged 19 years 257 days in 1936. Willy Hufschmid (SUI) won a bronze medal in 1936 aged 17 years 310 days.

The greatest margin of victory was 34 when Yugoslavia beat Kuwait 44–10 in 1980. The comparable margin among the women was 30 when Yugoslavia beat Congo 39–9 also in 1980. The greatest aggregate score was 71 in Sydney, when the Austrian women beat Brazil 45–26. In the same competition this was matched when Romania also beat Brazil 38–33. The comparable men's figure is 67, again in Sydney, when Sweden beat Australia 44–23. The record score by an individual in one game was 17 by Jasna Kolar-Merdan for the Yugoslavian women's team, when they beat the United States 33–20 in 1984. The male record is 13, by István Varga (HUN) against the United States in 1972, and by Kenji Tamamura (JPN) against Hungary in 1988.

A member of the East German winning team in 1980 was Hans-Georg Beyer, the brother of 1976 shot put champion Udo (who also won a bronze in 1980). To complete an outstanding family trio, their sister Gisela narrowly missed a bronze medal in the women's discus in Moscow. Their countrywoman Roswitha Krause, a member of the silver medal handball team of 1976, and of the bronze medal team in 1980, had been a silver medallist in the 4 x 100m freestyle swimming quartet in 1968.

HANDBALL MEDALS

	Men			Women			
	G	S	B	G	S	B	Total
Soviet Union	3	1	—	2	—	2	8
Yugoslavia	2	—	1	1	1	—	5
Korea	—	1	—	2	2	—	5
Romania	—	1	3	—	—	—	4
East Germany (GDR)	1	—	—	—	1	1	3
Norway	—	—	—	—	2	1	3
Sweden	—	3	—	—	—	—	3
Hungary	—	—	—	—	1	2	3
Denmark	—	—	—	2	—	—	2
Spain	—	—	2	—	—	—	2
Croatia	1	—	—	—	—	—	1
Germany	1	—	—	—	—	—	1
Russia	1	—	—	—	—	—	1
Austria	—	1	—	—	—	—	1
Czechoslovakia	—	1	—	—	—	—	1
West Germany (FRG)	—	1	—	—	—	—	1
China	—	—	—	—	—	1	1
France	—	—	1	—	—	—	1
Poland	—	—	1	—	—	—	1
Switzerland	—	—	1	—	—	—	1
	9	9	9	7	7	7	48

HEAVIEST

The heaviest person to win an Olympic medal, and indeed the heaviest known to have competed in the Olympic Games, was probably Chris Taylor (USA), the 1972 super-heavyweight wrestling bronze medallist. He weighed between 182kg (401lb) and 190kg (419lb). One other contender for the 'title' is the American weightlifter Mark Henry who weighed in at 184.92kg (407.5lb) in the 1996 Games. The heaviest woman to win a gold medal at the Games was Iuliana Semenova, a member of the Soviet gold medal basketball teams in 1976 and 1980 (see also Tallest): she weighed 129kg (284lb).

However, at Sydney in the 2000 inaugural women's weightlifting tournament, 17-year-old Cheryl Haworth (USA) weighed 138kg (304lb) when she took the heavyweight bronze medal. Perhaps it should be noted that the famed sumo wrestler, Akebono, (actually born Chad Rowan in Hawaii), who played a prominent part in the opening ceremony of the 1998 Winter Games at Nagano, weighed in at 234kg (516lb). The heaviest gold medallist, and indeed competitor, at the Winter Games was Friedrich Kuhn (GER), a member of the winning four-man bob at Oslo in 1952, who weighed 140kg (308lb). The team totalled 468kg (1032lb) – an average of 117kg (258lb) – leading to a change in the rules limiting the overall weight of the manned bob.

HOCKEY

The first Olympic hockey game was won by Scotland who beat Germany 4–0 in 1908, with the first goal scored by Ian Laing only two minutes after the start. In those Games four of the six teams competing represented England, Ireland, Scotland, and Wales. From 1928 until 1984, Olympic hockey tournaments were dominated by teams from the Indian sub-continent, with India winning eight times, and Pakistan three. However, it should be noted that Great Britain, probably the world's strongest team at the time, did not participate in 1932 and 1936. The long-awaited meeting between England, the masters, and India, the pupils, came in the 1948 final, which India won 4–0. In 1988, for the first time for 60 years, no team from the sub-continent won a medal. Interestingly, after years of decline, in 1984 the British team was a last-minute replacement for the boycotting Soviet Union, and they won the bronze – their first medal for 32 years. Then in 1988 the British team won the gold medal again, after 68 years.

Several members of the Indian teams have won a record three gold medals: Dhyan Chand 1928–36; Richard Allen 1928–36; Randhir Singh 1948–56; Balbir Singh 1948–56; Leslie Claudius 1948–56; Ranganandhan Francis 1948–56; and Udham Singh 1952–6 and 1964. Of these only Claudius and Udham Singh also each won a silver in 1960. The most successful female player is Rechelle Hawkes (AUS) with three golds 1988–2000. The oldest gold medallist/medallist was Dharam Singh (IND) in 1964, aged 45 years 278 days. The youngest winner was Russell Garcia (GBR) in 1988 aged 18 years 103 days, and the youngest medallist was Haneef Khan (PAK) at 17 years 26 days in 1976. The youngest female champion was Maider Goni (ESP) in 1992, aged 19 years 24 days, although Arlene Boxhall was under 19 years, as a member of the 1980 Zimbabwe women's team but she did not actually play in the tournament. The oldest female gold medallist was the Zimbabwe coach/player Anthea Stewart, aged 35 years 253 days. Iveta Sramkova (TCH), in the 1980 silver medal team, was only 16 years 304 days of age.

The highest score ever achieved in international hockey was when India beat the United States 24–1 in 1932. The highest score in a final was also in 1932, when India beat Japan 11–1. Roop Singh (IND), the brother of the team captain Dhyan Chand, scored a record 12 goals in the above-mentioned match against the United States in 1932. In their six successive wins 1928–56, India scored 178 goals and conceded only seven. They did not concede a single goal during the 1928 tournament (five Games). The longest game in Olympic hockey lasted 2hr 25min (into the sixth period of extra time) when The Netherlands beat Spain 1–0 in Mexico in 1968.

The biggest margin of victory in the women's contests came in 1980 when the Soviet Union beat Poland 6–0. This was matched by Australia in 1996 beating Argentina 7–1, and in 2000 when Argentina beat New Zealand also by 7–1. Those winning scores are the highest ever in the women's competitions. The greatest aggregate was in 1988, when Korea and Australia tied 5–5.

Andreas Keller's gold medal in Germany's 1992 team capped a wonderful family achievement, in that his father, Carsten, won gold in 1972, and his grandfather, Erwin, silver in 1936. Keller's girlfriend, Anke Wild, also won a silver in the 1992 women's tournament. The 1988 Olympic competitions were particularly noteworthy for family achievements. Sisters Lee and Michelle Capes gained gold medals in the Australian women's team, and the Dutch siblings, Marc and Carina Benninga, gained bronze medals in their country's respective third-placed teams.

HOCKEY MEDALS

| | Men | | | Women | | | |
	G	S	B	G	S	B	Total
India	8	1	2	—	—	—	11
The Netherlands	2	2	3	1	—	3	11
Great Britain	3	2	4	—	—	1	10
Australia	—	3	3	3	—	—	9
Pakistan	3	3	2	—	—	—	8

Germany	1	1	2	—	1	—	5
West Germany (FRG)	1	2	—	—	1	—	4
Spain	—	2	1	1	—	—	4
Korea	—	1	—	—	2	—	3
Soviet Union	—	—	1	—	—	1	2
United States	—	—	1	—	—	1	2
New Zealand	1	—	—	—	—	—	1
Zimbabwe	—	—	—	1	—	—	1
Argentina	—	—	—	—	1	—	1
Czechoslovakia	—	—	—	—	1	—	1
Denmark	—	1	—	—	—	—	1
Japan	—	1	—	—	—	—	1
Belgium	—	—	1	—	—	—	1
	19	19	20*	6	6	6	76

* Two bronzes in 1908.

ICE HOCKEY

The game was introduced in 1920 as part of the Summer Games. The tournament was won by Canada, the first of a run of six victories only interrupted by Great Britain in 1936. Incidentally, although most of that team was Canadian-based, ten of the 12 members were actually born in Britain. However, the record number of wins is eight by the Soviet Union/EUN between 1956 and 1992. However, in 1994 they did not win a medal: the first time since they entered in 1956. In the early days the Canadians were always represented by a club side, and not a National one, so that the first Olympic champions were actually the Winnipeg Falcons. Since 1948 the tournament has been decided on a championship format and not, as previously, on a knock-out basis – thus there is not an Olympic final as such. The game has been the centre of much bitter argument about amateur/ professional status, and in 1972 Canada withdrew in protest against alleged 'professionalism' of the Eastern European teams in particular. Happily they returned in 1980. In 1994 professionals were allowed to compete, and in 1998, the National Hockey League (NHL), in Canada and America, agreed to a 'hiatus' of the regular season in Winter Olympics years to allow players to compete for their national teams – well over 100 players still do so. The major surprise of the 1998 tournament was that neither the United States nor Canadian teams gained a medal. The latter were beaten in a semi-final by the Czech Republic in the first ever Olympic Game decided by a penalty shootout. In 2002 the Canadian men's team won their first gold for 50 years, and added the women's title for the icing on the cake.

In 1948 there was a strange situation when two teams turned up to represent the United States, one from the Amateur Hockey Association (AHA) and the other picked by the United States Olympic Committee (USOC). The AHA, while not affiliated to the USOC, was a member of the International Hockey Federation (IHF), the governing body of most of the other teams present in St Moritz. The IHF threatened to withdraw all the other teams if the AHA team did not play, while the USOC threatened to withdraw the whole Olympic team if the AHA team did play. Initially the IOC barred both teams, but then agreed to allow the AHA team to compete. They eventually finished fourth, but a year later they were disqualified for non-affiliation to the Olympic movement. Strangely the USOC hockey team members marched in the opening ceremony.

Six Soviet players have won a record three gold medals, but only goalminder Vladislav Tretyak, 1972–84, also won a silver. Richard 'Bibi' Torriani (SUI) won a bronze in 1928 and another in 1948, for a record 20-year span. The oldest gold medallist was Carl Erhardt (GBR) in 1936 on the day after his 39th birthday. The youngest was John Kilpatrick (GBR) in 1936, aged 18 years 224 days, while the youngest medallist was Richard Torriani (SUI) at 16 years 141 days in 1928. The oldest medallist was Igor Larionov in the bronze medal Russian team of 2002 aged 41 years 82 days. The first brothers to win gold were Herbert, Hugh and Roger Plaxton, along with Frank and Joseph Sullivan in the 1928 Canadian team. The only twins were Boris and Yevgeni Maiorov (URS) in 1964. The only known father and son gold medallists were Bill and David Christian (USA) who won in 1960 and 1980 respectively. Another distinction for Bill is that he and his brother Roger, were one of two sets of brothers, the other was Bill and Bob Cleary, who helped the United States to win its first ice hockey gold in 1960. Pavel and Valeri Bure, who won silver medals in the Russian team in 1998 (and bronzes in 2002), are the sons of Vladimir Bure (URS) who won a silver and two bronze medals in swimming at Munich in 1972. Martin Brodeur won a gold as a member of the 2002 Canadian team, whereas his father Denis had only gained a bronze in 1956. Jarome Iginla, a member of the winning Canadian team, became the first black male to win a gold medal in the Winter Games of 2002.

The highest score and aggregate in Olympic ice hockey was the 33–0 victory by Canada over Switzerland in 1924. In that tournament the Canadians totalled 110 goals in five matches with only three against. In the 1980 tournament the American goalminder, James Craig, stopped 163 of 178 shots at his goal (91.6 per cent), including 39 in the match against the Soviet Union. When the Czechs won the 1948 silver medal, a member of the team was the 1954 Wimbledon tennis champion, Jaroslav Drobny. Vladimir Ruzicka of the Czech Republic, who won a gold medal in 1998, had won silver in the Czechoslovakian team 14 years previously. Raimo Helminen (FIN) played in a record six Olympic tournaments, 1984–2002, winning a silver and a bronze.

A women's tournament was instituted in 1998. The highest score, margin of victory, and aggregate came when Canada beat Japan 13–0 in Nagano. The aggregate was matched in 2002 when the United States beat China 12–1. The youngest gold medallist was Angela Ruggerio (USA), aged 18 years 45 days in 1998, while Kim Martin of the 2002 bronze medal Swedish team was only 15

years 358 days. The oldest gold medallist was Danielle Goyette (CAN), in 2002, at 36 years 22 days. The oldest medallist was France St-Louis, in the Nagano silver medal Canadian team when she/he was 39 years 123 days. Cammi Granato of the winning 1998 United State's squad did considerably better than her older brother, Tony, who was a member of the seventh-place American team at Calgary in 1988.

ICE HOCKEY MEDALS

| | Men | | | Women | | | |
	G	S	B	G	S	B	Total
Canada	7	4	2	1	1	—	15
United States	2	7	1	1	1	—	12
Soviet Union	8	1	1	—	—	—	10
Sweden	1	2	4	—	—	1	8
Czechoslovakia	—	4	4	—	—	—	8
Finland	—	1	2	—	—	1	4
Great Britain	1	—	1	—	—	—	2
Russia	—	1	1	—	—	—	2
Switzerland	—	—	2	—	—	—	2
Czech Republic	1	—	—	—	—	—	1
West Germany (FRG)	—	—	1	—	—	—	1
Germany	—	—	1	—	—	—	1
	20	**20**	**20**	**2**	**2**	**2**	**66**

ICE SKATING

See separate entries for Figure Skating, Speed Skating, and Short-Track Speed Skating.

INTERNATIONAL OLYMPIC COMMITTEE (IOC)

Inaugurated on 23 June 1894 under the presidency of Demetrius Vikelas of Greece, and with Baron de Coubertin as its first Secretary-General. On 23 June 1994 the IOC celebrated its centenary, noting that the advances of Olympianism had extended competition to all continents, and given access to all, regardless of nationality, race, religion or language. Its headquarters have been in Lausanne, Switzerland since 1915. The IOC co-opts and elects its members, and they are the IOC's representatives in their respective countries, and not delegates from those countries. The Executive Board consists of the President, four Vice-Presidents and six other members. In 1996 here were a number of resignations and expulsions

following a bribery scandal to do with the selection of certain host cities. In 2001 there were 122 members of the IOC. Presidents of the organisation are listed below.

1894–6	Demetrius Vikelas (Greece)
1896–1925	Baron Pierre de Coubertin (France)
1925–42	Comte Henri de Baillet-Latour (Belgium)
1942–52	J. Sigfrid Edström (Sweden)
1952–72	Avery Brundage (USA)
1972–80	Lord Killanin (Ireland)
1980–2001	Juan Antonio Samaranch (Spain)
2001–present	Jacques Rogge (Belgium)

JEU DE PAUME

A medal sport only at London, England, in 1908, which took place at the Queen's Club in Kensington; it was also a demonstration sport at Amsterdam in 1928. The winner

in London was Jay Gould Jr, son of the American railroad tycoon of the same name, who had tried to corner the gold market in 1869, causing the infamous 'Black Friday' panic.

JUDO

This sport was introduced in 1964 and, appropriately, the first gold medal was won by Takehide Nakatani (JPN) in the lightweight class. However, one of the greatest upsets to a nation's sporting pride occurred in Tokyo's Nippon Budokan Hall in 1964 when the giant Dutchman Anton Geesink (1.98m, 6ft 6in) beat the Japanese favourite for the Open category title in front of 15,000 home supporters. Another Dutchman, Wilhelm Ruska, is the

only man to win two gold medals at any single Games, with the over-93kg and Open classes in 1972. Hiroshi Saito (JPN) and Peter Seisenbacher (AUT) are the only two men to successfully defend their titles, both in 1984 and 1988. Angelo Parisi won a record four medals, with a bronze in 1972 representing Great Britain, and then gold and two silvers in 1980 and 1984 representing France. The winning of medals for two different countries at the

Olympic Games is rare, but not unique. Parisi was born in Italy, went to Britain as a child, became a citizen, then married a French woman in 1973, and changed his nationality again. Robert Van de Walle (BEL) competed in a record five Olympic judo competitions 1976–92.

The oldest gold medallist was Ruska when he won the 1972 Open class, aged 32 years 11 days, and the youngest was Antal Kovács (HUN) in the 1992 Light-heavyweight division, aged 20 years 61 days. The oldest medallist was Arthur Schnabel (FRG) with a bronze in the 1984 Open class, aged 35 years 329 days, and the youngest medallist was Tiago Camilo (BRA) with silver in the 73kg class in 2000, aged 18 years 117 days. The fastest throw in Olympic competition was in 4sec by Akio Kaminaga (JPN) against Thomas Ong (PHI) in 1964. The youngest female gold medallist was Kye Sun (KOR) aged 16 years 359 days winning the 48kg class in 1996, while the oldest was Miriam Blasco Sotoi (ESP) at 28 years 232

days in 1992. The oldest medallist was Laetitia Meignan (FRA) aged 32 years 33 days at Barcelona, and the youngest was Ryoko Tamura (JPN) at 16 years 331 days, also in 1992.

The biggest of many big men in Olympic judo was Jong Gil Pak (PRK) who was 2.13m (7ft) tall and weighed 163kg (359lb) in the 1976 Games. In 1972 the Mongolian lightweight silver medallist, Bakhaavaa Buidaa, became the first competitor ever disqualified for failing a drugs test in any International judo competition. An amusing sidelight was provided by the 1976 lightweight gold medal winner, Hector Rodriguez (CUB), who said that he took up the sport as a child in order to defend himself against his six older brothers.

Women's events were contested as a demonstration sport in Seoul, and were added to the official programme in 1992. In 1996 a total limit of 400 competitors for the sport was imposed.

JUDO MEDALS

| | Men | | | Women | | | |
	G	S	B	G	S	B	Total
Japan	21	6	8	2	6	5	48
France	6	4	14	4	1	3	32
Korea	5	8	8	2	2	4	29
Soviet Union	7	5	14	—	—	1	27
Cuba	1	3	3	4	4	5	20
Great Britain	—	5	7	—	2	2	16
The Netherlands	4	—	4	—	—	3	11
China	—	—	—	4	1	5	10
Brazil	2	3	5	—	—	—	10
Italy	2	2	2	—	1	3	10
Germany	1	1	6	—	—	2	10
East Germany (GDR)	1	2	6	—	—	—	9
Poland	3	2	2	—	1	—	8
West Germany (FRG)	1	4	3	—	—	—	8
Hungary	1	2	4	1	—	—	8
United States	—	3	5	—	—	—	8
Belgium	1	—	2	—	1	3	7
Spain	—	1	—	3	—	2	6
North Korea (PRK)	—	1	1	1	—	1	4
Canada	—	2	2	—	—	—	4
Austria	2	—	1	—	—	—	3
Switzerland	1	1	1	—	—	—	3
Mongolia	—	1	2	—	—	—	3
Russia	—	—	2	—	1	—	3
Romania	—	—	2	—	—	1	3
Turkey	1	—	1	—	—	—	2
Bulgaria	—	1	1	—	—	—	2
Israel	—	—	1	—	1	—	2
Australia	—	—	1	—	—	1	2
Estonia	—	—	2	—	—	—	2
Georgia	—	—	2	—	—	—	2
Yugoslavia	—	—	2	—	—	—	2
Egypt	—	1	—	—	—	—	1
Uzbekistan	—	1	—	—	—	—	1
Belarus	—	—	1	—	—	—	1
Czechoslovakia	—	—	1	—	—	—	1
Iceland	—	—	1	—	—	—	1
Kyrgyzstan	—	—	1	—	—	—	1
Latvia	—	—	1	—	—	—	1

Portugal	—	—	1	—	—	—	1
Ukraine	—	—	1	—	—	—	1
	60	59*	120	21	21	42	323

*1972 silver withheld due to a disqualification.

KORFBALL

A demonstration event at Antwerp in 1920 when a team representing South Holland beat Amsterdam 2–0.

LACROSSE

Held as a medal sport at St Louis in 1904 and London in 1908, both competitions were won by Canada. In 1904 a Mohawk Indian team, representing Canada, won the bronze, but in 1908 only two teams competed. The highest score was when Canada beat Great Britain 14–10 in 1908. Demonstrations were held in 1928, 1932 and 1948.

LAUSANNE

In 1915 it was agreed that the administrative headquarters of the IOC were to be set up in Lausanne, Switzerland, a town popular with Baron de Coubertin. In 1922 he and the IOC moved into a house in the centre of the town. By 1968 the premises had become too small, and the Town Council made the Chateau de Vidy on the outskirts of the town available to become IOC Headquarters. Lausanne also houses the ultra modern Olympic Museum, on the Quai d'Ouchy.

LONGEST

The longest race ever held at the Olympic Games, in any sport, was the cycling road race in 1912, which measured 320km (198.8 miles). The longest equestrian event ever held at the Games was the 55km (34.1 miles) distance riding discipline at Stockholm in 1912. Athletics and Nordic skiing both share the upper limit of 50km (31 miles) – in athletics it is a walk, and in skiing a cross-country event. The furthest distance that a swimming race has ever been is 4000m (2.48 miles) in 1900, while in rowing there was a 3000m (1.86 miles) race in 1906 for coxed 16-man naval rowing boats. The longest sailing event seems to have been the 12-m class race in 1908, which was over a 26-mile (41.8km) course.

Time-wise, the longest single contest in Olympic history was the semi-final of the 1912 Greco-Roman middleweight-wrestling tournament. It went on for 11hr 40min, in very hot weather, between Martin Klein, an Estonian representing Russia, and Alfred Asikainen of Finland, with brief breaks allowed every 30 minutes. Klein eventually won, but was so exhausted that he had to miss the final. The longest final contest was in the same year, in the Greco-Roman light-heavyweight class, when Anders Ahlgren (SWE) struggled for nine hours with Ivar Böhling (FIN), without a result – both men were awarded silver medals.

LUGEING (TOBOGGANING)

Luge racing, in which contestants lie back, as opposed to skeleton sledding where contestants lie face down, was introduced in 1964. Previously, when the Games were held at St Moritz, in 1928 and 1948, skeleton sled events had been held. The most successful luger has been Georg Hackl (GER), with three golds and two silvers 1988–2002. Hackl is the only man to successfully defend the singles title, and he has done so twice. He is also the only luger to win five medals in five Games. The most successful woman was Steffi Martin-Walter (GDR) with two golds in 1984 and 1988.

The oldest gold medallist was Paul Hildgartner (ITA) aged 31 years 249 days in the 1984 singles, while the youngest was Manfred Stengl (AUT) in the two-man event in 1964, aged 17 years 310 days. The youngest female winner was Ortrun Enderlein (GER) aged 20 years 65 days in 1964, and the oldest was Sylke Otto (GER) in 2002 aged 32 years 221 days. The youngest medallist has been Ute Ruhrold (GDR) aged 17 years 60 days, gaining the silver in 1972. The oldest medallist was Fritz Nachmann (FRG) in 1968, aged 38 years 186 days. The oldest female medallist was Sylke Otto (GER). Anne Abernathy of the American Virgin Islands was the oldest ever female Olympic luger Games aged 46 years 194 days in 2002 – she may well have been the oldest luger, male or female, ever to compete at the Games. Probably the heaviest winner of a luge title was Hans Stanggassinger (FRG) in the two-man event of 1984, at a weight of 111kg (244lb). At Salt Lake City in 2002, Werner and Christopher Hoeger of Venezuela became the first father and son in Winter Games history to compete against one another, with son, Christopher, finishing nine places ahead of his father.

The smallest winning margin ever was in the women's singles in 1998, when Silke Krausshaar (GER) beat teammate Barbara Niedernhuber by 0.002sec. The closest in the men's contests was in the 1994 men's singles when Georg Hackl (GER) beat Markus Prock (AUT), for the second successive Games, by only 0.013sec. In contrast, Ortrun Enderlein (GDR) won the inaugural women's event in 1964 by the remarkable margin of 2.75sec. At the following Games in 1968 a scandal shook the Games when the first, second and fourth placed women from the East German team were all disqualified for illegally heating the runners of their sleds. The leading girl was Enderlein. While speeds of over 139km/h (86mph) are attained briefly, the greatest average speed for a single run was 107.02km/h (66.50mph) by Markus Prock (AUT) in 2002. The equivalent fastest by a female luger (average for a single run) was 95.58km/h (59.39mph) by Sylke Otto (GER) in 2002. Optimum speeds in the female event have been in excess of 125km/h (77.67mph).

LUGEING (TOBOGANNING) MEDALS (excluding 1928,1948 and 2002 Skeleton Sled events)

| | Men | | | Women | | | |
	G	S	B	G	S	B	Total
East Germany (GDR)	9	3	5	4	5	3	29
Germany	7	3	3	3	4	2	22
Austria	2	4	4	1	1	3	15
Italy	4	4	3	2	—	—	13
West Germany (FRG)	1	3	3	—	1	2	10
Soviet Union	—	2	2	1	—	1	6
United States	—	2	2	—	—	—	4
	23*	21	22	11	11	11	99

* Two golds in the 1972 two-man event.

MASCOTS

The various symbols and emblems used to publicise the Olympic Games over the years have generally been very successful. In 1932 there was an unofficial live mascot, a dog by the name of Smoky, but it was only in 1968 that the first official Olympic mascot made its appearance. For the Mexico City Games it was a red Jaguar, selected because of its cultural and geographical associations. However, it was not given a name, and was not marketed with any particular enthusiasm. Since then, however, the mascot has become an Olympics institution.

SUMMER

	Name	Character
1968	Red Jaguar	
1972	Waldi	Dachshund
1976	Amik	Beaver
1980	Misha	Bear
1984	Sam	Eagle
1988	Hodori/Hosuni	Tigers
1992	Cobi	Dog
1996	Izzy	Cartoon
2000	Olly	Kookaburra
	Syd	Platypus
	Millie	Anteater
	Coal	Bear
2004	Athena	Phevos

WINTER

	Name	Character
1968	Schuss	Man
1972	—	—
1976	Schneemanner	Snowman
1980	Roni	Raccoon
1984	Vucko	Wolf
1988	Hidy/Howdy	Polar bears
1992	Magique	Man/Star
1994	Haakon/Kristin	Children
1998	The Snowlets	Owls
2002	Powder	Hare
	Copper	Coyote

MEDAL WINNERS BY NATION, 1896–2002

These figures sometimes differ from official sources for a number of reasons, some given below. However, one of the main causes is that official sources have prevaricated over various issues, sometimes for nearly 100 years. Thus, I have made my own independent decisions – based on the best evidence currently available.

These totals include all first, second and third places, including those events no longer on the current schedule. The 1906 Games, which were officially staged by the IOC, have also been included, although, unaccountably, some historians choose to ignore them. However, medals won in the Art Competitions 1912–48, have not been included.

Medals won in 1896, 1900, 1904, 1908 and 1912 by mixed teams from two countries have been counted twice, i.e. for both countries involved. The Unified teams (EUN) of 1992, have been included in the Soviet Union figures. Medals won by IOP- designated competitors in 1992 have been included in the figures for Yugoslavia.

Since the birth of the modern Olympics 121 countries have won medals in the Summer and/or the Winter Games – of these, 84 have won at least one gold medal. This unique table indicates a country's position in the medal tables three ways. Mainly it shows its position overall, but it also gives that for the Summer and Winter Games respectively.

Overall		SUMMER						WINTER						TOTAL	
		G	S	B	Total			G	S	B	Total			Total	
1	United States	876	660	585	2121	(1)		69	72	52	193	(3)		2314	
2	Soviet Union*	440	357	325	1122	(2)		87	63	67	217	(2)		1339	
3	Germany†	165	198	211	574	(5)		58	52	38	148	(5)		722	
4	Great Britain	188	245	232	663	(3)		8	4	14	26	(=17)		689	
5	France	189	195	217	601	(4)		22	22	28	72	(12)		673	
6	Sweden	138	157	176	471	(7)		39	30	39	108	(8)		579	
7	Italy	179	143	156	478	(6)		31	31	27	89	(11)		567	
8	East Germany (GDR)‡	153	130	127	410	(9)		39	36	35	110	(7)		520	
9	Hungary	150	134	157	441	(8)		—	2	4	6	(=22)		448	
10	Finland	101	81	114	296	(12)		42	51	49	142	(6)		438	
11	Norway	50	43	41	134	(28)		94	94	75	263	(1)		397	
12	Australia	104	110	138	352	(10)		2	—	2	4	(=29)		356	
13	Japan	98	97	103	298	(11)		8	10	13	31	(16)		329	
14	Canada	52	80	99	231	(17)		31	29	36	96	(10)		327	
15	Switzerland	48	76	62	186	(21)		32	33	38	103	(9)		289	
16	The Netherlands	61	66	85	212	(18)		22	28	19	69	(13)		281	
17	Romania	74	83	108	265	(13)		—	—	1	1	(=38)		266	
18	Austria	21	32	36	89	(31)		41	57	64	162	(4)		251	
19	Poland	56	72	113	241	(14)		1	2	3	6	(=22)		247	
20	China	80	79	64	223	(16)		2	12	8	22	(19)		245	
21	West Germany (FRG)§	56	64	80	200	(19)		11	17	14	42	(15)		242	
22	Russia**	58	53	47	158	(23)		27	18	12	57	(14)		215	
23	Bulgaria	48	82	65	195	(20)		1	1	3	5	(=25)		200	
24	Czechoslovakia⊄	49	50	51	150	(25)		2	8	16	26	(17)		176	
25	Korea	46	52	56	154	(24)		11	5	4	20	(20)		174	
26	Denmark	41	63	58	162	(22)		—	1	—	1	(=38)		163	
27	Belgium	37	52	51	140	(26)		1	1	3	5	(=25)		145	
28	Cuba	56	44	38	138	(27)		—	—	—	—	—		138	
29	Greece	32	48	47	127	(29)		—	—	—	—	—		127	
30	Yugoslavia	28	32	33	93	(30)		—	3	1	4	(=29)		97	
31	Spain	25	28	22	75	(=32)		3	—	1	4	(=29)		79	
32	New Zealand	31	12	32	75	(=32)		—	1	—	1	(=38)		76	
33	Brazil	12	19	35	66	(34)		—	—	—	—	—		66	
34	Turkey	33	16	15	64	(35)		—	—	—	—	—		64	
35	South Africa	19	20	23	62	(36)		—	—	—	—	—		62	
=36	Argentina	13	23	18	54	(=37)		—	—	—	—	—		54	
=36	Kenya	16	20	18	54	(=37)		—	—	—	—	—		54	
38	Ukraine	12	12	22	46	(40)		1	1	1	3	(=34)		49	
39	Mexico	10	15	22	47	(39)		—	—	—	—	—		47	
40	Iran	8	13	19	40	(41)		—	—	—	—	—		40	
41	Jamaica	5	20	14	39	(42)		—	—	—	—	—		39	
42	Belarus	4	9	19	32	(43)		—	2	3	5	(=25)		37	
43	North Korea (PRK)	8	7	15	30	(44)		—	1	1	2	(=36)		32	
44	Estonia	8	6	12	26	(45)		1	1	1	3	(=34)		29	
=45	Czech Republic⊄	6	6	7	19	(48)		2	2	2	6	(=25)		24	
=45	Ethiopia	12	2	10	24	(46)		—	—	—	—	—		24	
47	Kazakhstan	6	8	4	18	(=49)		1	2	2	5	(=24)		23	
48	Ireland	8	6	6	20	(47)		—	—	—	—	—		20	
49	Egypt	6	6	6	18	(=49)		—	—	—	—	—		18	
=50	Portugal	3	4	10	17	(=51)		—	—	—	—	—		17	
=50	Nigeria	2	8	7	17	(=51)		—	—	—	—	—		17	
=52	Indonesia	4	7	5	16	(=53)		—	—	—	—	—		16	
=52	Morocco	4	3	9	16	(=53)		—	—	—	—	—		16	
=54	India	8	1	5	14	(=55)		—	—	—	—	—		14	
=54	Mongolia	—	5	9	14	(=55)		—	—	—	—	—		14	
56	Algeria	4	1	7	12	(57)		—	—	—	—	—		12	
=57	Croatia	2	2	3	7	(=70)		3	1	—	4	(=29)		11	
=57	Trinidad and Tobago	1	3	7	11	(58)		—	—	—	—	—		11	
=59	Pakistan	3	3	4	10	(=59)		—	—	—	—	—		10	
=59	Slovenia	2	2	2	6	(=72)		—	—	4	4	(=29)		10	
=59	Uruguay	2	2	2	10	(=59)		—	—	—	—	—		10	

Overall		SUMMER G	S	B	Total	WINTER G	S	B	Total	TOTAL
=59	Latvia	1	6	3	10 (=59)	—	—	—	—	—	10
=59	Taipei (Taiwan)	—	4	6	10 (=59)	—	—	—	—	—	10
=64	Liechtenstein	—	—	—	—	2	2	5	9 (21)	9
=64	Thailand	2	1	6	9 (=63)	—	—	—	—	—	9
=64	Chile	—	6	3	9 (=63)	—	—	—	—	—	9
=64	Philippines	—	2	7	9 (=63)	—	—	—	—	—	9
=68	Lithuania	3	—	5	8 (=66)	—	—	—	—	—	8
=68	Slovakia⟪	2	4	2	8 (=66)	—	—	—	—	—	8
=68	Venezuela	1	2	5	8 (=66)	—	—	—	—	—	8
=68	Georgia	—	—	8	8 (=66)	—	—	—	—	—	8
=72	Colombia	1	2	4	7 (=70)	—	—	—	—	—	7
=72	Uzbekistan	1	2	3	6 (=72)	—	—	1	1 (=38)	7
=74	Bahamas	2	2	2	6 (=72)	—	—	—	—	—	6
=74	Uganda	1	3	2	6 (=72)	—	—	—	—	—	6
=74	Tunisia	1	2	3	6 (=72)	—	—	—	—	—	6
=74	Puerto Rico	—	1	5	6 (=72)	—	—	—	—	—	6
=78	Azerbaijan	2	1	1	4 (=78)	—	—	—	—	—	4
=78	Peru	1	3	—	4 (=78)	—	—	—	—	—	4
=78	Luxembourg	1	1	—	2 (=90)	—	2	—	2 (=36)	4
=78	Costa Rica	1	1	2	4 (=78)	—	—	—	—	—	4
=78	Namibia	—	4	—	4 (=78)	—	—	—	—	—	4
=78	Lebanon	—	2	2	4 (=78)	—	—	—	—	—	4
=78	Moldova	—	2	2	4 (=78)	—	—	—	—	—	4
=78	Ghana	—	1	3	4 (=78)	—	—	—	—	—	4
=78	Israel	—	1	3	4 (=78)	—	—	—	—	—	4
=87	Armenia	1	1	1	3 (=86)	—	—	—	—	—	3
=87	Cameroon	1	1	1	3 (=86)	—	—	—	—	—	3
=87	Iceland	—	1	2	3 (=86)	—	—	—	—	—	3
=87	Malaysia	—	1	2	3 (=86)	—	—	—	—	—	3
=91	Syria	1	1	—	2 (=90)	—	—	—	—	—	2
=91	Mozambique	1	—	1	2 (=90)	—	—	—	—	—	2
=91	Suriname	1	—	1	2 (=90)	—	—	—	—	—	2
=91	Tanzania	—	2	—	2 (=90)	—	—	—	—	—	2
=91	Haiti	—	1	1	2 (=90)	—	—	—	—	—	2
=91	Saudi Arabia	—	1	1	2 (=90)	—	—	—	—	—	2
=91	Sri Lanka	—	1	1	2 (=90)	—	—	—	—	—	2
=91	Zambia	—	1	1	2 (=90)	—	—	—	—	—	2
=91	Barbados	—	—	2	2 (=90)	—	—	—	—	—	2
=91	Panama	—	—	2	2 (=90)	—	—	—	—	—	2
=91	Qatar	—	—	2	2 (=90)	—	—	—	—	—	2
=102	Burundi	1	—	—	1 (=102)	—	—	—	—	—	1
=102	Ecuador	1	—	—	1 (=102)	—	—	—	—	—	1
=102	Hong Kong	1	—	—	1 (=102)	—	—	—	—	—	1
=102	Zimbabwe	1	—	—	1 (=102)	—	—	—	—	—	1
=102	Ivory Coast	—	1	—	1 (=102)	—	—	—	—	—	1
=102	Netherlands Antilles	—	1	—	1 (=102)	—	—	—	—	—	1
=102	Senegal	—	1	—	1 (=102)	—	—	—	—	—	1
=102	Singapore	—	1	—	1 (=102)	—	—	—	—	—	1
=102	Tonga	—	1	—	1 (=102)	—	—	—	—	—	1
=102	Vietnam	—	1	—	1 (=102)	—	—	—	—	—	1
=102	Virgin Islands	—	1	—	1 (=102)	—	—	—	—	—	1
=102	Bermuda	—	—	1	1 (=102)	—	—	—	—	—	1
=102	Djibouti	—	—	1	1 (=102)	—	—	—	—	—	1
=102	Dominican Republic	—	—	1	1 (=102)	—	—	—	—	—	1
=102	Guyana	—	—	1	1 (=102)	—	—	—	—	—	1
=102	Iraq	—	—	1	1 (=102)	—	—	—	—	—	1
=102	Kyrgystan	—	—	1	1 (=102)	—	—	—	—	—	1
=102	Kuwait	—	—	1	1 (=102)	—	—	—	—	—	1
=102	Macedonia	—	—	1	1 (=102)	—	—	—	—	—	1
=102	Niger Republic	—	—	1	1 (=102)	—	—	—	—	—	1

*Including the Unified Team of 1992. † Germany 1896–1964,1992–8. ‡ East Germany (GDR), 1968–88. §, West Germany (FRG), 1968–88. ⟪ Czechoslovakia includes Bohemia; Split into the Czech Republic and Slovakia in 1992. ** Includes Czarist Russia.

MEDALS, MOST BY INDIVIDUALS (Summer Games only)

MEN

15	Nikolai Andrianov (URS)	1972–80	Gymnastics
13	Edoardo Mangiarotti (ITA)	1936–60	Fencing
13	Takashi Ono (JPN)	1952–64	Gymnastics
13	Boris Shakhlin (URS)	1956–64	Gymnastics
12	Sawao Kato (JPN)	1968–76	Gymnastics
12	Paavo Nurmi (FIN)	1920–8	Athletics
12	Alexei Nemov (RUS)	1996–2000	Gymnastics
11	Matt Biondi (USA)	1984–92	Swimming
11	Viktor Chukarin (URS)	1952–6	Gymnastics
11	Carl Osburn (USA)	1912–24	Shooting
11	Mark Spitz (USA)	1968–72	Swimming
10	Aleksandr Dityatin (URS)	1976–80	Gymnastics
10	Ray Ewry (USA)	1900–08	Athletics
10	Aladár Gerevich (HUN)	1932–60	Fencing
10	Akinori Nakayama (JPN)	1968–72	Gymnastics
10	Carl Lewis (USA)	1984–96	Athletics
10	Vitali Shcherbo (EUN/BLR)	1992–6	Gymnastics
9	Zoltán Halmay (HUN)	1900–8	Swimming
9	Alfred Swahn (SWE)	1908–24	Shooting
9	Giulio Gaudini (ITA)	1928–36	Fencing
9	Eizo Kenmotsu (JPN)	1968–76	Gymnastics
9	Heikki Savolainen (FIN)	1928–52	Gymnastics
9	Martin Sheridan (USA)	1904–8	Athletics
9	Yuri Titov (URS)	1956–64	Gymnastics
9	Mitsuo Tsukahara (JPN)	1968–76	Gymnastics
9	Hubert Van Innis (BEL)	1900–2000	Archery
9	Mikhail Voronin (URS)	1968–72	Gymnastics
9	Aleksandr Popov (RUS)	1992–2000	Swimming

WOMEN

18	Larissa Latynina (URS)	1956–64	Gymnastics
11	Vera Cáslavská (TCH)	1960–8	Gymnastics
10	Polina Astakhova (URS)	1956–64	Gymnastics
10	Agnes Keleti (HUN)	1952–6	Gymnastics
10	Birgit Fischer-Schmidt (GDR/GER)	1980–2000	Canoeing
10	Jenny Thompson (USA)	1992–2000	Swimming
9	Nadia Comaneci (ROM)	1976–80	Gymnastics
9	Ludmila Tourischeva (URS)	1968–76	Gymnastics
9	Dara Torres (USA)	1984–2000	Swimming
8	Shirley Babashoff (USA)	1972–6	Swimming
8	Kornelia Ender (GDR)	1972–6	Swimming
8	Dawn Fraser (AUS)	1956–64	Swimming
8	Margit Korondi (HUN)	1952–6	Gymnastics
8	Sofia Muratova (URS)	1956–60	Gymnastics
8	Merlene Ottey (JAM)	1980–2000	Athletics
8	Franziska van Almsick (GER)	1992–2000	Swimming
7	Maria Gorokhovskaya (URS)	1952	Gymnastics
7	Karin Janz (GDR)	1968–72	Gymnastics
7	Ildikó Ságiné-Ujlakiné-Rejtó (HUN)	1960–76	Fencing
7	Shirley Strickland (AUS)	1948–56	Athletics
7	Irena Szewinska (POL)	1964–76	Athletics
7	Shannon Miller (USA)	1992–6	Gymnastics
7	Simona Amanar (ROM)	1996–2000	Gymnastics
7	Elisabeta Lipa (ROM)	1984–2000	Rowing

MEDALS, MOST BY INDIVIDUALS (Winter Games only)

MEN

12	Bjørn Daehlie (NOR)	1992–8	Nordic Skiing
9	Sixten Jernberg (SWE)	1956–64	Nordic Skiing

7	Clas Thunberg (FIN)	1924–8	Speed Skating
7	Ivar Ballangrud (NOR)	1928–36	Speed Skating
7	Veikko Hakulinen (FIN)	1952–60	Nordic Skiing
7	Eero Mäntyranta (FIN)	1960–8	Nordic Skiing
7	Bogdan Musiol (GDR/GER)	1980–92	Bobsledding
7	Vladimir Smirnov (URS/EUN/KZK)	1988–98	Nordic Skiing
7	Ricco Gross (GER)	1992–2002	Biathlon

WOMEN

10	Raisa Smetanina (URS/EUN)	1976–92	Nordic Skiing
9	Lyubov Yegorova (EUN/RUS)	1992–4	Nordic Skiing
9	Stefania Belmondo (ITA)	1992–2002	Nordic Skiing
8	Galina Kulakova (URS)	1968–76	Nordic Skiing
8	Karin Kania-Enke (GDR)	1980–8	Speed Skating
8	Marja-Liisa Hämäläinen-Kirvesniemi (FIN)	1980–94	Nordic Skiing
8	Gunda Kleemann-Niemann-Stirnemann (GDR/GER)	1992–4	Speed Skating
8	Uschi Disl (GER)	1992–2002	Biathlon
7	Andrea Mitscherlich-Schöne-Ehrig (GDR)	1976–88	Speed Skating
7	Manuela Di Centa (ITA)	1988–98	Nordic Skiing
7	Yelena Valbe (EUN/RUS)	1992–8	Nordic Skiing
7	Claudia Pechstein (GER)	1992–2002	Speed Skating
7	Larisa Lazutina (EUN/RUS)	1992–2002	Nordic Skiing

MEDIA

During the first modern Games at Athens in 1896 there was very little coverage in the world's press. Throughout its 100 year history the Games have constantly been written off and rubbished by some of the media, prophets of doom who predicted their demise, especially at the time of boycotts and financial and drugs scandals. Despite this the Games have gone from strength to strength, and indeed there has been tremendous coverage of each celebration. Thus, at Atlanta in 1996 there were over 17,000 representatives of the world media, far in excess of the number of competitors, and at the Winter Games at Nagano in 1998 there were over 10,000.

The Games at Berlin in 1936 witnessed the first major radio coverage of the event, with broadcasts going to some 40 countries. At those Games there was limited television coverage with a closed circuit system to special halls, operated by the *Reich Rundfunkgesellschaft*, and watched by a reported 150,000 people at 28 venues around Berlin. By 1996 television pictures were beamed to some 220 countries, with a global cumulative audience of 19.6 billion, and it has been estimated nine out of ten people in the developed world watched part of the Atlanta Games.

The money from TV rights has now become the prime source of income for the IOC, and the hosts. In August 1995 the American TV Company NBC paid $1.27 billion for the exclusive American TV rights to the Games at Sydney in 2000, and the Winter Games at Salt Lake City in 2002. A few months later they paid $2.3 billion for the American TV rights to the Games of 2004, 2006 and 2008.

MEMBER COUNTRIES

For member countries of the IOC, *see* under Participation, by country.

MILITARY PATROL

A demonstration sport, held at four Winter Games, it is considered to be the forerunner of the official biathlon contests introduced in 1960. Switzerland won in 1924 and 1948, Norway won in 1928, and Italy in 1936.

MODERN PENTATHLON

This sport, currently under threat of being dropped from the Games, was invented by Baron de Coubertin. The five events constituting the modern pentathlon are: riding (formerly over an 800m course, now a 12-fence show jumping test); fencing (with épée); swimming (formerly 300m freestyle, now 200m); shooting; and cross—country running (formerly over 4000m, now 3000m). Shooting until 1992 was with a rapid—fire pistol over 25m, but since then it has been with an air pistol over 10m. In 1996 the team event was eliminated and the individual competition has to be completed in one day. In 2000 a modern pentathlon event for women was added.

The order of events has differed over the years, as has the points system. Prior to 1956 competitors were given points according to their placings in each event, i.e., one point for first place, two points for second etc. Since 1956 points have been allocated according to an International scoring table. It is difficult, therefore, to compare performers under the two systems, but it is generally accepted that the margin of victory by Willie Grut (SWE) in 1948 was the greatest ever. In that competition, Grut, later the Secretary-General of the sport's governing body, the Union Internationale de Pentathlon Moderne (UIPMB), placed first in riding, fencing and swimming, fifth in shooting, and eighth in running.

The most gold medals have been won by András Balczó (HUN) with three in 1960 (team), 1968 (team) and 1972 (individual). Only Lars Hall (SWE) has won two individual gold medals, in 1952 and 1956. Pavel Lednev (URS) won a record seven medals (two golds, two silvers, three bronzes) from 1968 to 1980. He was also the oldest gold medallist/medallist in 1980 aged 37 years 121 days, while the youngest gold medallist/ medallist was Aladár Kovacsi (HUN) in 1952, aged 19 years 227 days. Peter Macken of Australia competed in a record five Olympic contests 1960–76. In the women's competition, the oldest gold medallist was Stephanie Cook (GBR) aged 28 years 237 days, while the youngest medallist was Emily de Riel (USA) at 25 years 312 days.

Gustaf Dyrssen (SWE), who won the gold medal in 1920, and a silver in 1924, and Sven Thofelt (SWE), who won the gold in 1928, both won silver medals as members of the 1936 Swedish épée fencing team. Thofelt also won a bronze in the Swedish fencing team in 1948, while his son competed in the 1960 modern pentathlon. Dyrssen later became Sweden's IOC representative, and Thofelt became President of the UIPMB.

George Patton (USA), later the famous Second World War General, was fifth in 1912, with results that indicated he was not very good at shooting. Two men have scored maximums of 200 hits in shooting: Charles Leonard (USA) in 1936 and George Horvath (SWE) in 1980. The fastest time ever recorded in the 300m swimming event was 3min 10.47sec by Gintaras Staskevicius (LTU) in 1992. The other three disciplines are either not measurable or comparable. However, it is noteworthy that the fastest time recorded for the 4000m cross-country run is 12min 09.50sec by Adrian Parker (GBR) in 1976. With the amendment of event distances in 2000, the current best performances are: 200m swimming – 2:00.71 by Eric Walther (GER); 3000m running – 9:10.69 by Sebastien Deleigne (FRA). The best by women are: 200m swimming – 2:15.82 by Zsuzsanna Voros (HUN); 3000m running – 10:03.16 by Stephanie Cook (GBR).

One of the biggest scandals in Olympic history occurred in the fencing segment of the 1976 competition when Boris Onischenko (URS), previous winner of a gold and two silver medals, was disqualified for using an illegal weapon. It transpired that he had tampered with his épée so that it registered a hit even when contact with an opponent had not taken place. The incident has caused speculation about whether he had used the implement in the 1972 Games, where his fencing victory over Jim Fox cost the Briton the individual bronze medal. By coincidence Onischenko was fencing against Fox when the Montreal incident came to light.

MODERN PENTATHLON MEDALS

	Men			Women			Total
	G	S	B	G	S	B	
Sweden	9	7	5	—	—	—	21
Hungary	8	8	4	—	—	—	20
Soviet Union	5	6	6	—	—	—	17
United States	—	5	3	—	1	—	9
Italy	2	2	3	—	—	—	7
Finland	—	1	4	—	—	—	5
Great Britain	1	—	1	1	—	1	4
Poland	3	—	—	—	—	—	3
Russia	1	1	—	—	—	—	2
Germany	1	—	1	—	—	—	2
Czechoslovakia	—	1	1	—	—	—	2
France	—	—	2	—	—	—	2
Kazakhstan	1	—	—	—	—	—	1
Belarus	—	—	—	—	—	—	1
	31	31	31	1	1	1	96

MOTORBOATING

A medal sport only held at London in 1908, when only one boat finished in each of the three classes. The competitions were held over a distance of 40 miles. Thomas Thornycroft (GBR) was in the crew of two of the winning boats, and 44 years later he was a reserve for the 1952 British Olympic sailing team when in his 71st year.

MOTTO

The Olympic motto, *Citius, Altius, Fortius* (faster, higher, stronger), was a Latin phrase used by Father Henri Didon, of Paris, which was apparently carved over the entrance to his school. De Coubertin noted the words of Henri Didon used to illustrate the sporting achievements of the scholars of another college in 1895, and instituted them at the 1924 Games.

MULTI-REPRESENTATION

Not counting competitors who had won for the Soviet Union, and then when representing the new entities formed after the breakup, only two people have won gold medals representing totally different countries. Rugby player Daniel Carroll won a gold in the 1908 winning Australian team, and then won again as a member of the 1920 United States team. Kakhi Kakhiashvili won for his native Georgia at weightlifting in 1992, and then won again in 1996, but was then representing Greece.

NORDIC COMBINATION

The event was the 'blue riband' of Nordic skiing in the early Games. The all-round title, comprising a cross-country race and a jump, was won three successive times by Ulrich Wehling (GDR) 1972–80. Samppa Lajunen (FIN) also won three golds, but all in 2002, which, added to his two silvers from 1998, gave him a record five medals. The oldest winner and medallist was Simon Slåttvik (NOR) who won the title in 1952, aged 34 years 209 days. The youngest champion was Wehling in 1972 aged 19 years 212 days, and the youngest medallist was Stefan Kreiner (AUT) with a team bronze in 1992, aged 18 years 110 days. Up until 1952 the cross—country segment was held first, but at Oslo the order of events was reversed, and has remained so. In 2002 a 'sprint' race was added.

NORDIC COMBINATION MEDALS

	G	S	B	Total
Norway	11	7	6	24
Finland	4	8	1	13
East Germany (GDR)	3	—	4	7
Austria	—	1	6	7
Germany	1	2	1	4
Switzerland	1	2	1	4
West Germany (FRG)	2	1	—	3
Japan	2	1	—	3
France	1	1	1	3
Soviet Union	—	1	2	3
Sweden	—	1	1	2
Poland	—	—	1	1
Russia	—	—	1	1
	25	25	25	75

NORDIC SKIING

(*See also* Nordic Combination, Biathlon and Ski–jumping).

Nordic, or cross-country, skiing was the first form of skiing in the Olympics. Bjørn Dæhlie (NOR) won a record 12 medals, 1992–8, comprising another record eight golds and four silvers. The most successful female competitor was Raisa Smetanina (URS/EUN) with four golds, five silvers and a bronze, making a female record of ten medals between 1976 and 1992. She is also the only competitor to win medals in five Games. Only Sixten Jernberg (SWE), 1956–64, and Dæhlie, has won individual titles in three successive Games, Jernberg doing it over an eight – year period. Lyubov Yegorova (EUN/RUS) equalled the Winter Games record by a woman, of six gold medals with three in 1992, and three in 1994. Yegorova, teammate Yelena Valbe, both in 1992, and Larissa Lazutina (RUS) in 1998, have all set a female record of five medals in a single Games. Lazutina finished first in the 2002 30km race, to equal Smetanina's record of ten medals. Lazutina was disqualified from 1 gold and 2 silver medal placings at Salt Lake City. Marja-Liisa Hämäläinen (later Kirvesniemi) of Finland won a record three individual gold medals at one Games in 1984. She competed in a record six Games, 1976–94. Her husband, Harri Kirvesniemi (FIN) has also competed in six Games 1980–98, winning six bronze medals, during which period he raced an unmatched aggregate record of 450km (279 miles). Dæhlie raced 345km (214 miles) in his three Games. The record aggregate distance raced by a woman is 275km (171 miles) by Stefania Belmondo (ITA) 1988–2002.

The oldest gold medallist/medallist was Maurilio De Zolt (ITA), aged 43 years 150 days in the 1994 relay, and the youngest champion was Gunde Svan (SWE) who won the 15km race in 1984, aged 22 years 32 days. The youngest medallist was Ivar Formo (NOR) in the 1972 relay aged 20 years 234 days. The oldest female gold medallist was Smetanina as a member of the 1992 relay team, aged 39 years 354 days. The youngest female champion was Carola Anding (GDR) aged 19 years 54 days in the 1980 relay, while the youngest female medallist was Marjo Matikainen (FIN) in the 1984 relay, aged 19 years 12 days. Bente Skari (NOR), who won the 10km in 2002, is the daughter of 1968 relay gold medallist Odd Martinsen. In 1994, a brother and sister won medals when Giorgio Vanzetta (ITA) took gold in the 4 x 10km relay and Bice gained a bronze in the 4 x 5km. At Salt Lake City Manuela Henkel (GER) won a gold in the Nordic relay, while her sister Andrea won two golds in the biathlon. The 50km race in 1928 was won by Per Erik Hedlund (SWE) with a remarkable margin of 13min 27sec over the second man, whereas in the 1980 15km a mere 0.01sec separated first and second place. Certain of the races are designated as freestyle events i.e. the 'skating' technique may be used. Otherwise, only the classical 'stride and glide' is allowed. The shock silver medal won by Bill Koch (USA) in the 1976 50km was credited to his development of the former style.

In 2002 a 1500m 'sprint' race was introduced. The fastest time over a course, which was actually 1.48km, was achieved by Håvard Berkeli (NOR) in the heats with 2:50.07, representing an average speed of 31.33km/h (19.47mph). The fastest by a woman was 3:10.6 by Yulia Tchepalova (RUS) in the final, representing an average speed of 27.96km/h (17.37mph). (It is worth noting that Tchepalova also finished ninth in the 30km race).

NORDIC SKIING MEDALS

	Men			Women			
	G	S	B	G	S	B	Total
Norway	25	25	12	3	9	—	82
Soviet Union	11	8	12	17	16	13	77
Finland	11	13	19	8	9	10	70
Sweden	18	13	12	3	2	2	50
Italy	2	6	6	5	5	4	28
Russia	1	—	—	10	6	3	20
Czechoslovakia	—	—	1	—	1	3	5
GDR	—	1	—	2	—	1	4
Germany	—	1	1	1	1	—	4
Kazakhstan	1	2	1	—	—	—	4
Austria	—	2	2	—	—	—	4
Switzerland	—	—	3	—	—	1	4
Estonia	1	1	1	—	—	—	3
Czech Republic	—	—	—	—	1	2	3
Spain	2	—	—	—	—	—	2
Bulgaria	—	—	1	—	—	—	1
Canada	—	—	—	—	—	1	1
United States	—	1	—	—	—	—	1
	72	73*	71	49	49	49	363

* Two silvers in the 2002 combined pursuit.

OLDEST COMPETITORS/WINNERS

The oldest ever competitor at the Olympic Games was Oscar Swahn of Sweden who was in the shooting contests in 1920 at the age of 72 years 280 days (when he won a silver medal in a team event). He had won a gold medal eight years earlier, at Stockholm, in the Running Deer team, to become the oldest ever gold medallist, 107 days short of his 65th birthday. Incidentally his son, Alfred, also won gold in the team. He actually qualified for the 1924 Games in his 77th year but illness prevented him from making the trip. In 1904 the Rev Galen Spencer (USA) won the archery team gold just two days past his 64th birthday, while a fellow American, Samuel Duvall, won a team silver at 68 years 194 days. The oldest winner of an individual event was Joshua 'Jerry' Millner (GBR), who was four days past his 61st birthday winning the free rifle (1000yd) event at London in 1908. The oldest woman to compete in the Games was Britain's Lorna Johnstone, who was five days past her 70th birthday when she took part in the dressage competition at Munich in 1972. The oldest female gold medallist was Queenie Newall, also of Britain, who won the archery contest in 1908 at 53 years 277 days.

In October 1994 Hjalmari Kivenheimo (FIN), silver medallist in the 1912 gymnastics team competition, died aged 105 years 34 days – the greatest known age ever reached by an Olympic medallist. Not a medallist, but Dirk Janssen, of The Netherlands, also a gymnast, in 1908, held the Olympian longevity record when he died in November 1986, aged 105 years 114 days.

OLYMPIC OATH

The Olympic Oath was instituted in 1920. At the opening ceremony a representative of the host country, usually a veteran of previous Games, mounts the rostrum, holds a corner of their national flag and, with the flag bearers of all the other countries drawn up in a semi-circle, pronounces the oath: 'In the name of all competitors, I promise that we shall take part in these Olympic Games, respecting and abiding by the rules which govern them, in the true spirit of sportsmanship, for the glory of sport and the honour of our teams' (A similar oath is taken on behalf of all the judges). The following have taken the Olympic oath on behalf of the other athletes:

SUMMER

1920	Victor Boin	Fencer
1924	Georges André	Athlete
1928	Harry Denis	Footballer
1932	George Calnan	Fencer
1936	Rudolf Ismayr	Weightlifter
1948	Donald Finlay	Athlete
1952	Heikki Savolainen	Gymnast
1956	John Landy	Athlete
	Henri Saint Cyr	Equestrian (Stockholm)
1960	Adolfo Consolini	Athlete
1964	Takashi Ono	Gymnast
1968	Pablo Garrido	Athlete
1972	Heidi Schüller	Athlete
1976	Pierre St Jean	Weightlifter
1980	Nikolai Andrianov	Gymnast
1984	Edwin Moses	Athlete
1988	Huh Jae/Son Mi-Na	Basketballer/Handballer
1992	Luis Doreste Blanco	Yachtsman
1996	Teresa Edwards	Basketballer
2000	Rechelle Hawkes	Hockey

WINTER

1924	Camille Mandrillon	Military Patrol
1928	Hans Eidenbenz	Skier
1932	Jack Shea	Speed skater
1936	Wilhelm Bogner	Skier
1948	Richard Torriani	Ice hockey player
1952	Torbjörn Falkanger	Ski jumper
1956	Guiliana Chenal-Minuzzo	Skier
1960	Carol Heiss	Figure skater
1964	Paul Aste	Bobsledder
1968	Leo Lacroix	Skier
1972	Keichi Suzuki	Speed skater
1976	Werner Delle-Karth	Bobsledder
1980	Eric Heiden	Speed skater
1984	Bojan Krizaj	Skier
1988	Pierre Harvey	Skier
1992	Surya Bonaly	Figure skater
1994	Vegard Ulvang	Skier
1998	Kenji Ogiwara	Skier
2002	Jim Shea	Skeleton

OPENINGS

Traditionally, the Olympic Games are opened by a member of the reigning Royal Family or a senior representative of the national government of the host country. They have included:

SUMMER

1896	King George I
1900	—
1904	Mr David Francis (President of the World's Fair)
1906	King George I
1908	King Edward VII
1912	King Gustaf V
1920	King Albert
1924	President Gaston Doumergue
1928	HRH Prince Hendrik
1932	Vice President Charles Curtis

1936	Chancellor Adolf Hitler	1928	President Edmund Schulthess
1948	King George VI	1932	Governor Franklin D Roosevelt
1952	President Juho Paasikivi	1936	Chancellor Adolf Hitler
1956	HRH The Duke of Edinburgh	1948	President Enrico Celio
	King Gustav VI (Stockholm)	1952	HRH Princess Ragnhild
1960	President Giovanni Gronchi	1956	President Giovanni Gronchi
1964	Emperor Hirohito	1960	Vice President Richard Nixon
1968	President Gustavo Diaz Ordaz	1964	President Adolf Schärf
1972	President Gustav Heinemann	1968	President Charles de Gaulle
1976	Queen Elizabeth II	1972	Emperor Hirohito
1980	President Leonid Brezhnev	1976	President Rudolf Kirchschläger
1984	President Ronald Reagan	1980	Vice President Walter Mondale
1988	President Roh Tae-Woo	1984	President Mika Spiljak
1992	King Juan Carlos I	1988	Governor-General Jeanne Sauvé
1996	President William Clinton	1992	President Francois Mitterand
2000	Sir William Deane (Governor-General)	1994	King Harald V
		1998	Emperor Akihito
WINTER		2002	President George W. Bush
1924	Under Secretary Gaston Vidal		

OUTSTANDING ACHIEVEMENTS

MOST GOLD MEDALS (SUMMER)

Men	10	Ray Ewry (USA)	1900–1908	Athletics
Women	9	Larissa Latynina (URS)	1956–64	Gymnastics
Men, in one Games	7	Mark Spitz (USA)	1972	Swimming
Women, in one Games	6	Kristin Otto (GDR)	1988	Swimming

MOST MEDALS (SUMMER)

Men	15	Nikolai Andrianov (URS)	1972–80	Gymnastics
Women	18	Larissa Latynina (URS)	1956–64	Gymnastics
Men, in one Games	8	Aleksandr Dityatin (URS)	1980	Gymnastics
Women, in one Games	7	Maria Gorokhovskaya (URS)	1952	Gymnastics

MOST GOLD MEDALS (WINTER)

Men	8	Bjørn Dæhlie (NOR)	1992–8	Nordic Skiing
Women	6	Lydia Skoblikova (URS)	1960–4	Speed Skating
	6	Lyubov Yegorova (EUN-RUS)	1992–4	Nordic Skiing
Men, in one Games	5	Eric Heiden (USA)	1980	Speed Skating
Women, in one Games	4	Lydia Skoblikova (URS)	1964	Speed Skating

MOST MEDALS (WINTER)

Men	12	Bjørn Dæhlie (NOR)	1992–8	Nordic Skiing
Women	10	Raisa Smetanina (URS)	1976–92	Nordic Skiing
Men, in one Games	5	Clas Thunberg (FIN)	1924	Speed Skating
	5	Roald Larsen (NOR)	1924	Speed Skating
	5	Eric Heiden (USA)	1980	Speed Skating
Women, in one Games	5	Lyubov Yegorova (EUN-RUS)	1992	Nordic Skiing
	5	Yelena Valbe (EUN-RUS)	1992	Nordic Skiing
	5	Manuela di Centa (ITA)	1994	Nordic Skiing
	5	Larissa Lazutina (RUS)	1998	Nordic Skiing

AGE RECORDS (SUMMER)

	years/days			
Oldest Male Gold	64 258	Oscar Swahn (SWE)	1912	Shooting
Oldest Female Gold	53 277	Queenie Newall (GBR)	1908	Archery
Oldest male Medallist	72 280	Oscar Swahn (SWE)	1920	Shooting
Oldest Female Medallist	53 277	Queenie Newall (GBR)	1908	Archery
Youngest Male Gold	7–10	Unknown French boy	1900	Rowing
Youngest Female Gold	13 268	Marjorie Gestring (USA)	1936	Diving
Youngest Male Medallist	7–10	Unknown French boy	1900	Rowing
Youngest Female Medallist	11 328	Luigina Giavotti (ITA)	1928	Gymnastics

Oldest Competitor, Male	72 280	Oscar Swahn (SWE)	1920	Shooting
Oldest Competitor, Female	70 5	Lorna Johnstone (GBR)	1972	Equestrianism
Youngest Competitor, Male	7–10	Unknown boy (FRA)	1900	Rowing
Youngest Competitor, Female	11 328	Liana Vicens (PUR)	1968	Swimming

AGE RECORDS (WINTER)

years/days

Oldest Male Gold	48 359	Jay O'Brien (USA)	1932	Bobsledding
Oldest Female Gold	39 354	Raisa Smetanina (EUN-RUS)	1992	Nordic Skiing
Oldest Male Medallist	50 235	Paul Savage (CAN)	1998	Curling
Oldest Female Medallist	42 178	Jane Bidstrup (DEN)	1998	Curling
Youngest Male Gold	16 259	Toni Nieminen (FIN)	1992	Ski Jumping
Youngest Female Gold	13 83	Kim Yoon-Mi (KOR)	1994	Short-Track Speed Skating
Youngest Male Medallist	14 363	Scott Allen (USA)	1964	Figure Skating
Youngest Female Medallist	13 83	Kim Yoon-Mi (KOR)	1994	Short-Track Speed Skating

Oldest Competitor, Male	53 297	James Coats (GBR)	1948	Tobogganing
Oldest Competitor, Female	45 318	Edwina Chamier (CAN)	1936	Skiing
Youngest Competitor, Male	12 110	Jan Hoffmann (GDR)	1968	Figure Skating
Youngest Competitor, Female	11 73	Cecilia Colledge (GBR)	1932	Figure Skating

MOST GAMES/LONGEST SPAN (SUMMER) – MEN

9 Games	Hubert Raudaschl (AUT)	1964–96	Yachting
40 yrs	Ivan Osiier (DEN)	1908–48	Fencing
40 yrs	Magnus Konow (NOR)	1908–48	Yachting
40 yrs	Durward Knowles (GBR/BAH)	1948–88	Yachting
40 yrs	Paul Elvstrøm (DEN)	1948–88	Yachting

MOST GAMES/LONGEST SPAN (SUMMER) – WOMEN

7 Games*	Kerstin Palm (SWE)	1964–88	Fencing
28 yrs	Anne Newberry-Ransehousen (USA)	1960–88	Equestrianism
	Christilot Hanson-Boylen (CAN)	1964–92	Equestrianism

MOST GAMES/LONGEST SPAN (WINTER) – MEN

6 Games	Carl-Erik Eriksson (SWE)	1964–84	Bobsledding
6 Games	Colin Coates (AUS)	1968–88	Speed Skating
6 Games	Alfred Eder (AUT)	1976–94	Biathlon
6 Games	Jochen Behle (FRG/GER)	1980–98	Nordic Skiing
6 Games	Harri Kirvesniemi (FIN)	1980–98	Nordic Skiing
6 Games	Raimo Helminen (FIN)	1984–2002	Ice Hockey
6 Games	Michael Dixon (GBR)	1984–2002	Nordic Skiing/Biathlon
20 yrs	John Heaton (USA)	1928–48	Tobogganing
20 yrs	Max Houben (BEL)	1928–48	Bobsledding
20 yrs	Richard Torriani (SUI)	1928–48	Ice Hockey
20 yrs	Frank Stack (CAN)	1932–52	Speed Skating
20 yrs	Stanislaw Marusarz (POL)	1932–52	Nordic Skiing
20 yrs	James Bickford (USA)	1936–56	Bobsledding
20 yrs	Sepp Bradl (AUT)	1936–56	Ski Jumping
20 yrs	Carl-Erik Eriksson (SWE)	1964–84	Bobsledding
20 yrs	Colin Coates (AUS)	1968–88	Speed Skating

MOST GAMES/LONGEST SPAN (WINTER) – WOMEN

6 Games*	Marja-Liisa Hämäläinen-Kirvesniemi (FIN)	1976–94	Nordic Skiing
6 Games	Emese Hunyadi (HUN/AUT)	1984–2002	Speed Skating
18yrs	Marja-Liisa Hämäläinen-Kirvesniemi (FIN)	1976–94	Nordic Skiing
18yrs	Emese Hunyadi (HUN/AUT)	1984–02	Speed Skating

* Seiko Hashimoto (JPN) has also competed in seven Games, comprising four in the Winter at speed skating 1984–94 and three in the Summer at cycling 1988–96.

PARTICIPATION, BY COMPETITORS

It has been calculated that well over 100,000 sportsmen and women have competed in the Olympic Games, Summer and Winter, since 1896. Preliminary figures for the Summer Games are 87,112, of which 16,785 were women, and for the Winter Games a total of 15,343, of which 4373 were women. There is always some confusion about definitive totals due to the problem of double counting of those who compete in more than one event and/or one sport, and the fact that so-called official figures invariably include numbers of entries, and not just of those who actually competed. Also such figures often include administrators and coaches, thus exacerbating discrepancies. Figures used in this book are based on the detailed research done by Wolf Lyberg of Sweden, on behalf of the IOC.

PARTICIPATION, BY COUNTRY

(The three-character country abbreviations used here are those used officially by the IOC at the Games. Individual sports' governing bodies sometimes use different abbreviations.)

	Country	SUMMER GAMES		WINTER GAMES	
		Debut	Number attended	Debut	Number attended
AFG	Afghanistan	1936	10	—	—
AHO	Netherlands Antilles	1952	11	1988	2
ALB	Albania	1972	4	—	—
ALG	Algeria	1964	9	1992	1
AND	Andorra	1976	7	1976	8
ANG	Angola	1980	5	—	—
ANT	Antigua/Barbuda	1976	6	—	—
ARG	Argentina	1920	18	1908	15
ARM	Armenia	1996	2	1994	3
ARU	Aruba	1988	4	—	—
ASA	American Samoa	1988	4	1994	1
AUS	Australia[1]	1896	25	1936	15
AUT	Austria[2]	1896	24	1924	19
AZE	Azerbaijan	1996	2	1998	2
BAH	Bahamas	1952	12	—	—
BAN	Bangladesh	1984	5	—	—
BAR	Barbados[10]	1960	9	—	—
BDI	Burundi	1996	2	—	—
BEL	Belgium	1900	23	1920	18
BEN	Benin (ex Dahomey)	1972	7	—	—
BER	Bermuda	1936	14	1992	4
BHU	Bhutan	1984	5	—	—
BIZ	Belize (ex Brit Honduras)	1968	8	—	—
BLR	Belarus	1996	2	1994	3
BOH	Bohemia[3]	—	—	—	—
BOL	Bolivia	1936	10	1956	5
BOT	Botswana	1980	6	—	—
BRA	Brazil	1920	18	1992	4
BRN	Bahrain	1984	5	—	—
BRU	Brunei	1996	2	—	—
BSH	Bosnia and Herzegovina	1992	3	1994	3
BUL	Bulgaria	1896	16	1936	16
BUR	Burkina Faso	1972	5	—	—
CAF	Central African Republic	1968	6	—	—
CAM	Cambodia[4]	1956	5	—	—
CAN	Canada	1900	23	1920	20
CAY	Cayman Islands	1976	6	—	—
CGO	Congo	1964	8	—	—
CHA	Chad	1964	8	—	—
CHI	Chile	1896	19	1948	13
CHN	China	1932	9	1980	7
CIV	Ivory Coast	1964	9	—	—
CMR	Cameroon	1964	10	2002	1

		SUMMER GAMES		WINTER GAMES	
	Country	Debut	Number attended	Debut	Number attended
COD	Dem Republic of Congo (ex Zaire)	1968	6	—	—
COK	Cook Islands	1988	4	—	—
COL	Colombia	1932	15	—	—
COM	Comoros Is	1996	2	—	—
CPV	Cape Verde Is	1996	2	—	—
CRC	Costa Rica	1936	11	1984	4
CRO	Croatia	1992	3	1992	3
CUB	Cuba	1900	16	—	
CYP	Cyprus	1980	6	1980	7
CZE	Czech Republic[3]	1996	2	1994	3
DEN	Denmark	1896	24	1948	10
DJI	Djibouti	1984	5	—	—
DMA	Dominica	1996	2	—	—
DOM	Dominican Republic	1964	10	—	—
ECU	Ecuador	1924	10	—	—
EGY	Egypt[5]	1906	19	1984	1
ERI	Eritrea	2000	1	—	—
ESA	El Salvador	1968	7	—	—
ESP	Spain	1900	19	1936	16
EST	Estonia[6]	1920	8	1928	6
ETH	Ethiopia	1956	9	—	—
FIJ	Fiji	1956	10	1988	3
FIN	Finland	1906	22	1920	20
FRA	France	1896	25	1920	20
FRG	West Germany[7]	1968	5	1968	6
FSM	Federated States of Micronesia	2000	1	—	—
GAB	Gabon	1972	6	—	—
GAM	Gambia	1984	5	—	—
GBR	Great Britain	1896	25	1908	21
GBS	Guinea-Bissau	1996	2	—	—
GDR	East Germany[7]	1968	5	1968	6
GEO	Georgia	1996	2	1994	3
GEQ	Equatorial Guinea	1984	5	—	—
GER	Germany[8]	1896	16	1908	12
GHA	Ghana (Ex Gold Coast)	1952	10	—	—
GRE	Greece	1896	25	1936	15
GRN	Grenada	1984	5	—	—
GUA	Guatemala	1952	10	1988	1
GUI	Guinea	1968	7	—	—
GUM	Guam	1988	4	1988	1
GUY	Guyana (ex British Guiana)	1948	13	—	—
HAI	Haiti	1900	12	—	—
HKG	Hong Kong	1952	12	2002	1
HON	Honduras	1968	7	1992	1
HUN	Hungary	1896	23	1924	19
INA	Indonesia	1952	11	—	—
IND	India	1920	19	1964	6
IRI	Iran	1948	12	1956	6
IRL	Ireland[9]	1924	17	1992	3
IRQ	Iraq	1948	10	—	—
ISL	Iceland	1908	17	1948	14
ISR	Israel	1952	12	1994	3
ISV	Virgin Islands	1968	8	1984	6
ITA	Italy	1900	23	1924	9
IVB	British Virgin Islands	1984	5	—	—
JAM	Jamaica[10]	1948	14	1988	5
JOR	Jordan	1980	6	—	—
JPN	Japan	1912	18	1928	16

	Country	SUMMER GAMES		WINTER GAMES	
		Debut	Number attended	Debut	Number attended
KAZ	Kazakhstan	1996	2	1994	3
KEN	Kenya	1956	10	1998	2
KGZ	Kyrgyzstan	1996	2	1994	3
KOR	Korea [11]	1948	13	1948	14
KSA	Saudi Arabia	1972	7	—	—
KUW	Kuwait	1968	9	—	—
LAO	Laos	1980	5	—	—
LAT	Latvia	1924	7	1924	7
LBA	Libya	1968	7	—	—
LBR	Liberia	1956	8	—	—
LCA	St Lucia	1996	2	—	—
LES	Lesotho	1972	7	—	—
LIB	Lebanon	1948	13	1948	13
LIE	Liechtenstein	1936	13	1936	15
LTU	Lithuania	1924	5	1928	5
LUX	Luxembourg	1912	19	1928	6
MAD	Madagascar	1964	8	—	—
MAR	Morocco	1960	10	1968	4
MAS	Malaysia[12]	1956	11	—	—
MAW	Malawi	1972	6	—	—
MDA	Moldova	1996	2	1994	3
MDV	Maldives	1988	4	—	—
MEX	Mexico	1924	18	1928	6
MGL	Mongolia	1964	9	1964	10
MKD	Macedonia	1996	2	1998	2
MLI	Mali	1964	9	—	—
MLT	Malta	1928	12	—	—
MON	Monaco	1920	16	1984	6
MOZ	Mozambique	1980	6	—	—
MRI	Mauritius	1984	5	—	—
MTN	Mauritania	1984	5	—	—
MYA	Myanmar (ex Burma)	1948	13	—	—
NAM	Namibia	1992	3	—	—
NAU	Nauru	1996	2	—	—
NCA	Nicaragua	1968	8	—	—
NED	The Netherlands	1900	23	1928	17
NEP	Nepal	1964	9	2002	1
NGR	Nigeria	1952	12	—	—
NIG	Niger	1964	8	—	—
NOR	Norway	1900	23	1920	20
NZL	New Zealand	1908	21	1952	12
OMA	Oman	1984	5	—	—
PAK	Pakistan	1948	13	—	—
PAN	Panama	1928	13	—	—
PAR	Paraguay	1968	8	—	—
PER	Peru	1936	14	—	—
PHI	Philippines	1924	17	1972	3
PLE	Palestine	1996	2	—	—
PLW	Palau	2000	1	—	—
PNG	Papua New Guinea	1976	6	—	—
POL	Poland	1924	17	1924	19
POR	Portugal	1912	20	1952	4
PRK	North Korea[11]	1972	6	1964	6
PUR	Puerto Rico	1948	14	1984	5[21]
QAT	Qatar	1984	5	—	—
ROM	Romania	1924	16	1928	17
RSA	South Africa[13]	1904	16	1960	4
RUS	Russia[14]	1900	5	1908	4
RWA	Rwanda	1984	5	—	—
SAM	Western Samoa	1984	5	—	—

Country		SUMMER GAMES		WINTER GAMES	
		Debut	*Number attended*	*Debut*	*Number attended*
SAR	Saar[17]	1952	1	—	—
SEN	Senegal	1964	10	1984	3
SEY	Seychelles	1980	5	—	—
SIN	Singapore	1948	13	—	—
SKN	St Kitts and Nevis	1996	2	—	—
SLE	Sierra Leone	1968	7	—	—
SLO	Slovenia	1992	3	1992	4
SMR	San Marino	1960	9	1976	6
SOL	Solomon Islands	1984	5	—	—
SOM	Somalia	1972	5	—	—
SRI	Sri Lanka (ex Ceylon)	1948	13	—	—
STP	São Tomé and Príncipe	1996	2	—	—
SUD	Sudan	1960	8	—	—
SUI	Switzerland[16]	1896	25	1920	20
SUR	Surinam	1968	8	—	—
SVK	Slovakia	1996	2	1994	3
SWE	Sweden	1896	24	1908	21
SWZ	Swaziland	1972	6	1992	1
SYR	Syria	1948	9	—	—
TAN	Tanzania	1964	9	—	—
TCH	Czechoslovakia[3]	1900	20	1920	17
TGA	Tonga	1984	5	—	—
THA	Thailand	1952	12	2002	1
TJK	Tajikistan	1996	2	2002	1
TKM	Turkmenistan	1996	2	—	—
TOG	Togo	1972	6	—	—
TPE	Chinese Taipei (ex Formosa/Taiwan)	1956	10	1972	8
TRI	Trinidad and Tobago[10]	1948	14	1994	3
TUN	Tunisia	1960	10	—	—
TUR	Turkey	1908	18	1936	13
UAE	United Arab Emirates	1984	5	—	—
UGA	Uganda	1956	11	—	—
UKR	Ukraine	1996	2	1994	3
URS	Soviet Union[17]	1952	10	1956	10
URU	Uruguay	1924	17	1998	1
USA	United States	1896	24	1908	21
UZB	Uzbekistan	1996	2	1994	3
VAN	Vanuatu	1988	4	—	—
VEN	Venezuela	1948	14	1998	2
VIE	Vietnam[18]	1952	11	—	—
VIN	St Vincent/Grenadines	1988	4	—	—
YEM	Yemen[19]	1992	3	—	—
YUG	Yugoslavia[20]	1912	20	1924	16
ZAM	Zambia	1964	9	—	—
ZIM	Zimbabwe	1928	9	—	—

[1] Australia and New Zealand combined as Australasia between 1908 and 1912.

[2] Not invited in 1920.

[3] Czechoslovakia was represented by Bohemia up to 1912.

[4] There was provisional recognition of the current regime in Cambodia.

[5] Competed as part of the United Arab Republic 1960–8.

[6] Annexed by the Soviet Union in 1940: independent again from 1992.

[7] Separate teams 1968–88; East Germany part of the combined German team 1956–64.

[8] Not invited 1920,1924 and 1948.

[9] Part of the United Kingdom until 1922.

[10] Jamaica, Barbados and Trinidad combined as Antilles in 1960.

[11] Country partitioned in 1945, and separate regimes established in 1948.

[12] Prior to 1964 Malaya and North Borneo (later Sabah) competed separately. In 1964 they combined.with Sarawak and Singapore. In1965 Singapore left the Federation.

[13] Not invited 1960–88.

[14] As Czarist Russia 1900–12; Separate entity again in 1994.

[15] Independent 1947–57, then incorporated into Germany.

[16] Switzerland only attended Stockholm in 1956.

[17] A combined team of the National Olympic Committees (NOC) of the former Soviet republics (excluding the Baltic States) competed in the 1992 Summer and Winter Games as the Unified Team (EUN) or Commonwealth of Independent States (CIS).

[18] From 1952–72 only a South Vietnamese team competed.

[19] The Republic of Yemen was formed in 1960 out of the Yemen Arab Republic (which competed 1984–8) and the Yemen People's Democratic Republic (which competed in 1988).

[20] Representatives of the Yugoslavia Serbs competed as Independent Olympic Participants (IOP) in the 1992 Games. In 1912 Serbia had competed as a separate entity.

[21] Puerto Rico marched in the opening ceremony of 2002, but had no actual competitors in the Games.

PELOTA BASQUE

It was a demonstration sport at Paris in 1924, with teams from Spain and France. It was seen again at Mexico City in 1968, and at Barcelona in 1992.

POLO

A medal sport on five occasions. Only Sir John Wodehouse (GBR), the third Earl of Kimberley, won a silver (1908) to add to a gold (1920). The oldest gold medallist was Manuel Andrada (ARG) in 1936 aged 46 years 211 days, and the youngest was his teammate Roberto Cavanagh, aged 21 years 269 days. The biggest winning margin was 16–2 by Argentina versus Spain and Great Britain versus France, both in 1924, and by Mexico versus Hungary in 1936. In 1900, in a remarkable display of inclusive behaviour, there was an American in the British gold-medal team, an American and a Spaniard in the British silver-medal team, and a Briton in the French bronze team.

PRESS

See under Media.

RACKETS

Only a medal sport at London in 1908, with all competitors from Great Britain. The most successful were Evan Noel and American-born John Jacob Astor. Noel won the singles gold and a bronze in the doubles, while Astor won a gold in the doubles, and a bronze in the singles. Later he became a Member of Parliament, and, in 1956, he was made Baron Astor of Hever.

ROLLER HOCKEY

This was demonstrated for the first time at Barcelona in 1992.

ROQUE

A variation of croquet played on a hard-surface court. A medal sport only at St Louis in 1904, and competitors were all from the United States. The gold medallist, Charles Jacobus, was aged 45 years 41 days.

ROWING

Rowing for men was first held in the 1900 Games over a 1750m course on the River Seine in Paris. In 1904 the course measured 2 miles (3219m), in 1908 it was 1.5 miles (2414m), and in 1948 1 mile 300yd (1883m). Women's rowing was introduced in 1976 over a 1000m course, but since 1988 both men and women race over a standard 2000m (1.24 miles) course. Even though recent Games rowing has been held on still water, as opposed to flowing rivers as in the past, water and weather conditions vary too much to allow official Olympic records. However, it is noteworthy that the fastest average speed achieved by a men's eight over the full course was 21.85km/h (13.57mph), when the Canadian crew clocked 5min 29.53sec in 1992. In a 1992 heat the Romanian crew averaged 22.77km/h (14.14mph) for the first 500m. The 1992 Canadian women's eight won the final in 6min 02.62sec averaging 19.85km/h (12.33mph). The 1988 East German women's crew averaged 20.65 km/h (12.83mph) for the first 500m in a repêchage. Since automatic timing was introduced in 1960, the narrowest winning margin has been 0.01sec in the women's single sculls at Sydney in 2000, and the smallest in the men's events was 0.14sec in the 1992 men's eights. However, in the 1924 men's pairs the margin was given as 0.1sec, while it is thought that the 1932 coxed-fours may have been even closer.

One of the first winning crews in the Games, the 1900 German four, contained three brothers, Oskar, Gustav and Carl Gossler, the latter as coxswain. This was the beginning of a tradition of sibling participation and success which reached a landmark at Moscow in 1980 when the Landvoigt twins (GDR) beat the Pimenov twins (URS) in the coxless pairs final – and caused problems at the medal ceremony. Similarly, in the 1992 coxed-pairs, Jonathan and Greg Searle (GBR) beat the Italian defending champions, Carmine and Giuseppe Abbagnale. When the latter pair won in 1988, their younger brother Agostino also won a gold in the quadruple sculls event. Fathers and sons have had great success in the sport, but usually independently of each other. The most famous are: the Beresfords (GBR), Julius with a silver in 1912, and Jack with five medals (see below) in the next five Games; the Costellos (USA), Paul winning three golds in the 1920s and his son, Bernard, a silver in 1956; the Kellys (USA), John Sr winning three gold medals (see below) and John Jr a bronze in 1956; the Nickalls (GBR) with Guy Sr winning a gold in the 1908 eight, and Guy Jr gaining two silvers in the 1920 and 1928 crews. However, the Burnells (GBR), Charles (1908) and Richard (1948), are the only father and son in Olympic rowing to both win gold medals.

Steve Redgrave (GBR) won a record-breaking five successive gold medals 1984–2000, plus a bronze in 1988. Jack Beresford (GBR) also won medals (three golds, two silvers) at five Games. Vyacheslav Ivanov (URS) and Pertti Karppinen (FIN) are the only men to win three individual golds, in the single sculls. Ivanov had an unfortunate experience after his first title-win in Melbourne. He excitedly threw his medal into the air and lost it in the waters of Lake Wendouree. It was never recovered and later the IOC gave him a replacement. John Kelly (USA) won gold medals in both the single and double sculls in 1920 within an hour.

The oldest gold medallist was Róbert Zimonyi who coxed the United States eight in 1964, aged 46 years 180 days. In 1948 he had won a bronze coxing a pair from his native Hungary. The oldest actual oarsman to win a gold medal was Guy Nickalls (GBR) in the 1908 eight aged 41 years 261 days. His compatriot Julius Beresford won his silver medal (see above) aged 44 years 20 days. The youngest gold-medal oarsman was Giliante D'Este (ITA) in 1928, aged 18 years 141 days, while the

youngest medallist oarsman was Australian Walter Howell in 1956 at 16 years 346 days. The youngest gold medallist was the unknown French boy who coxed the winning Dutch pair in 1900. Believed to have been less than ten years old, he was recruited at the last moment out of the spectators to replace Hermanus Brockmann, their cox in the heats, who was considered to be too heavy. Incidentally, Brockmann coxed the Dutch fours to a silver medal, and the eight to a bronze. Of the many other young medal-winning coxes over the years, the youngest known for certain was another French boy, Noël Vandernotte, in the 1936 pairs and fours aged 12 years 232 days. The latter crew included his father and uncle.

In women's rowing the youngest gold medal oarswoman was Andrea Kurth (GDR) in 1976 aged 18 years 298 days, while the youngest medallist was Rodica Puscatu (ROM) at 18 years 83 days in 1980. The youngest female coxswain of a winning crew was Sabine Hess (GDR) in the 1976 coxed four aged 17 years 297 days, and Lynn Silliman was 17 years 92 days old when she coxed the American eight to a bronze in 1976. The oldest female gold medallist oarswoman was Elisabeta Oleniuc-Lipa (ROM) in the 2000 eights aged 35 years 334 days, although her teammate, Elena Georgescu, the cox of the eights, was aged 36 years 167 days. The oldest oarswoman to win a medal was Valentina Skrabatun (BLR) in 1996, five days past her 38th birthday, but Lesley Thompson was four days past her 41st birthday when she coxed the Canadian eight to a bronze medal in 2000. The most successful female rower, and arguably the most successful male or female, has been Elisabeta Oleniuc-Lipa (ROM) with four golds, two silvers and a bronze, 1984–2000, for a unmatched total of seven medals in five Games. The sibling tradition continues in the women's events, the latest being the German twins, Manja and Kerstin Kowalski, in the winning quadruple sculls in Sydney.

The US oarsman, Conn Findlay, winner of two golds and a bronze in coxed pairs 1956–64, also won the sailing bronze medal in 1976 in the Tempest class. In 1996 several changes to the programme included the deletion of men's coxed pairs and fours, and women's coxless fours. In 2000 new events included mens and women's lightweight double sculls and men's lightweight coxless fours.

ROWING MEDALS

	Men			Women			
	G	S	B	G	S	B	Total
United States	28	22	19	1	7	2	79
East Germany (GDR)	20	4	7	13	3	1	48
Germany	16	11	11	5	2	3	48
Great Britain	21	15	7	—	1	—	44
Soviet Union	11	14	6	1	6	5	43
Italy	13	13	10	—	—	—	36
Canada	4	8	9	4	4	4	33
France	6	14	12	—	—	1	33
Romania	2	4	2	13	6	5	32
Australia	6	7	8	1	1	2	25
Switzerland	6	8	9	—	—	—	23
The Netherlands	5	6	6	—	1	4	22
Denmark	4	3	6	—	—	2	15

West Germany (FRG)	4	4	4	—	—	2	14
New Zealand	5	2	5	—	—	1	13
Norway	1	6	6	—	—	—	13
Poland	1	1	9	—	1	—	12
Bulgaria	—	—	1	2	4	4	11
Czechoslovakia	2	2	7	—	—	—	11
Belgium	—	6	1	—	1	1	9
Finland	3	—	3	—	—	—	6
Austria	—	3	2	—	—	—	5
Yugoslavia	1	1	3	—	—	—	5
Greece	1	2	1	—	—	—	4
Argentina	1	1	2	—	—	—	4
China	—	—	—	—	2	2	4
Uruguay	—	1	3	—	—	—	4
Belarus	—	—	—	2	—	1	3
Slovenia	1	—	2	—	—	—	3
Hungary	—	1	2	—	—	—	3
Russia	—	—	2	—	—	1	3
Sweden	—	2	—	—	—	—	2
Spain	—	1	—	—	—	—	1
Croatia	—	—	1	—	—	—	1
Lithuania	—	—	—	—	—	1	1
South Africa	—	—	1	—	—	—	1
Ukraine	—	—	—	—	1	—	1
	162	162	165	42	42	42	615

ROYALTY

In 1896 two princes of the Greek royal house escorted the marathon winner into the stadium at Athens.

Since then a number of members of the royal families of Europe have actually competed, now and again with great success, in the Olympic Games. The first winner of a gold medal was Crown Prince Olav of Norway, later King Olav V, who was a member of the winning crew of the 6-m sailing class in 1928. His son Crown Prince Harald, later Harald V, competed in the same sport from 1964–72, gaining his best placing of eighth in the 5.5-m class in 1964. The only other royal winner was the then Prince Constantine of Greece, later Constantine II, who won gold in the Dragon class in 1960. His brother-in-law, Juan Carlos of Spain, was in the 1972 sailing, while his niece, Princess Christina competed in the 1988 Tornado class, and his nephew, Prince Felipe, placed sixth in the Soling class of 1992. To add to the Spanish royal family's Olympic credentials, Princess Christina later married two-time Spanish bronze-medal winning handballer Inaki Urdangarin.

Britain's Princess Anne finished 24th in the three-day equestrian event in 1976. Her husband-to-be, Capt Mark Phillips had been a member of the gold-medal winning three-day team event in 1972. In more recent years, in the Winter Games, Prince Albert of Monaco has competed, as Albert Grimaldi, for the principality in the two-man and four-man bob events from 1988 to 1998.

RUGBY UNION

The fact that Baron de Coubertin was a referee in the sport probably lay behind it being a medal sport on four occasions: Paris in 1900, London in 1908, Antwerp in 1920 and Paris again in 1924. Only six countries competed in the four tournaments held: Australia, France, Germany, Great Britain, Romania and the United States. The 1908 title was won by Australia while the Wallabies were on their first tour of Britain. The team they beat in the final was Cornwall, the English County champions. Five American players won two gold medals in 1920 and 1924: Charles Doe, John O'Neil, Colby Slater, John Patrick and Rudolph Scholz. Additionally, Daniel Carroll became the only Olympian to win gold medals for different countries when he won his second gold with the 1920 United State's team, having been on the 1908 Australian squad when only 16 years 245 days. Thus he is the youngest ever rugby international, although 'purists' have never considered the Olympic matches to be 'full' internationals. The highest score was when France beat Romania 61–3 in 1924. In 1920, sprint relay gold medallist Morris Kirksey, also runner-up in the 100m, won another gold in the winning United State's rugby team. It always comes as a shock to enthusiasts to realise that the United States is the reigning Olympic rugby champion. Incidentally, before their Paris victory, they had played in Britain and were beaten by the Harlequins and Blackheath club teams. There is a strong possibility that rugby sevens will make an entry to the Games in 2008.

SAILING

The first Olympic regatta should have been on the Bay of Salamis, but it was cancelled due to bad weather. Since 1900 the classes have been changed regularly until very recently when some measure of standardisation was imposed. In each class there are seven races over a prescribed course in which the fastest time wins. The best six results are counted. The only event that has been a permanent fixture is the Olympic monotype, i.e. the one-man dinghy, albeit represented by different classes of boat prior to 1952 (now the Finn).

The most successful yachtsman is Paul Elvstrøm (DEN) who won four successive Olympic monotype titles from 1948–60; the first man to achieve such a run in any sport. He competed again in the 1968 Star (fourth), 1972 Soling (13th), 1984 Tornado (fourth), and 1988 Tornado (15th) – in the last two events, partnering his daughter, Trine. Frances Clytie Rivett-Carnac (GBR) and her husband Charles, in the winning 7-m yacht *Heroine* in 1908, were the first married couple to win gold medals in Olympic sailing, but not in the Games, as is sometimes reported. The oldest gold medallist was Everard Endt (USA) in the 1952 6-m class, aged 59 years 112 days, while the oldest in a single-handed event was Léon Huybrechts (BEL) aged 47 years 215 days in 1924. The oldest female gold medallist was Virginie Hériot (FRA) in the 1928 8-m class at the age of 38 years 16 days, while the oldest female medallist was Pease Glaser (USA) in the Sydney women's 470 class aged 38 years 314 days. The youngest gold medallist/medallist was Franciscus Hin (NED), in the 1920 12-foot dinghy event with his brother Johannes, aged 14 years 163 days. The youngest female champion was Kristine Roug (DEN) in the 1996 Europe class aged 21 years 141 days, while the youngest female medallist was Natalia Via Dufresne Perena (ESP), second in the same event in 1992 at 19 years 54 days. The oldest medallist was Louis Noverraz (SUI) in the 5.5-m category in 1968 aged 66 years 154 days.

Outstanding family achievements have occurred in Olympic sailing. In 1920 four Norwegian brothers, Henrik, Jan, Ole and Kristian Østervold won gold medals in the 12-m (1907 rating) class. The full crew of the winning 5.5-m in 1968 were the brothers: Ulf, Jörgen and Peter Sundelin (SWE), and the winning 6-m in 1912 was crewed by Amédée, Gaston and Jacques Thubé (FRA). The only twins to win gold were Sumner and Edgar White (USA) in the 5.5-m of 1952. The first father and son to win together were Emile and Florimond Cornellie (BEL) in the 6-m (1907 rating) in 1920. However, the greatest Olympic sailing family must be the Norwegians Lunde: Eugen won a gold in the 1924 6-m class, his son Peder and daughter-in-law, Vibeke, along with Vibeke's brother, won a silver in the 5.5-m in 1952, and grandson Peder Jr won a gold in the 1960 Flying Dutchman contest. The winner of the women's sailboard title in 1992, Barbara Kendall (NZL), was the sister of the 1988 men's winner, Bruce Kendall.

Rodney Pattisson and Iain Macdonald-Smith (GBR) scored the lowest number of penalty points (three) ever achieved in Olympic sailing when they won the 1968 Flying Dutchman class with five wins, a second place and a disqualification (finished first) in their seven starts.

Their boat *Superdocius* is now in the National Maritime Museum, Greenwich. The only boat to win two gold medals in the same Games was *Scotia*, crewed by Lorne Currie and John Gretton for Great Britain, in the ½–1 ton and Open classes in 1900. The United States yacht *Llanoria* won the 6-m class in 1948 and 1952, skippered both times by Herman Whiton.

In 1948 Magnus Konow (NOR) equalled the longest span of Olympic competition when he took part in the 6-m event, 40 years after his debut in the 8-m class of 1908. He won two golds and a silver in 1912, 1920 and 1936, the only other Games he attended. Durward Knowles competed in a record eight Games, all in the Star class, from 1948 when he competed for Great Britain. He represented the Bahamas in the next six celebrations, and then again in 1988 (aged 71, and probably the oldest Olympic sailor ever). The aforementioned Paul Elvstrøm (DEN) also made it to eight Games in 1988, and both he and Knowles matched the 40-year span record. In 1996 Hubert Raudaschl (AUT) outclassed them all, and competed in his ninth Games, 1964–96, which is a record for any sport. This could have been even more remarkable, as he had been a reserve for the Austrian Olympic team in 1960. Tore Holm (SWE) won medals over a record span of 28 years (1920–48), and, more unusual, Hans Fogh won medals 24 years apart (1960–84), firstly for Denmark and then for Canada.

Harry Melges (USA) won a gold medal in the 1972 Soling class, and then co-skippered the winning US yacht in the 1992 America's Cup. This achievement was matched by Russell Coutts (NZL), who won the 1984 Finn event, and was the skipper of *Black Magic*, winner of the America's Cup for New Zealand in 1995. The helmsman of the third placed *Tempest* in 1976 was Dennis Conner (USA), who had won the America's Cup for the United States in 1980, lost it in 1983, and regained it in 1987. His Montreal partner, Conn Findlay, had won rowing golds in 1956 and 1964, and then was a crew-member of successful Cup defender *Courageous* in 1977. A number of other Olympic yachtsmen have also competed, sometimes successfully, in the America's Cup competitions.

In the 1984 Games all 13 members of the United States team won either gold or silver medals, a unique team achievement. The greatest number of boats in an Olympic regatta was the 239 (plus 73 sailboards) at Atlanta (Savannah) in 1996. The greatest entry in just one event was 56 in the 1996 Laser competition. When Lai Shan Lee won the women's sailboard title in 1996 she gained the first, and what was thought to be the last, Olympic gold medal ever for her country, as it was accepted that from 2000 Hong Kong would compete as part of China. However, Hong Kong competed at Sydney as a separate entity.

An attempt has been made to bring some method of comparison to the Olympic results, made particularly difficult due to the wide variety of classes and types of boat used over the years. Where classes have been superseded by those of similar type, they have been listed in the same table. Purists may be unhappy, but the general reader will find it easier to follow.

OLYMPIC YACHTING VENUES

1900	River Seine at Meulan (10–20 tonners at Le Havre)	1956	Port Phillip Bay
1908	Cowes, Isle of Wight, and the River Clyde	1960	Bay of Naples
1912	Nyhashamn	1964	Sagami Bay
1920	Ostend	1968	Acapulco Bay
1924	River Seine at Meulan (6m and 8m at Le Havre)	1972	Kiel
1928	Zuider-Zee	1976	Kingston, Lake Ontario
1932	San Pedro Bay	1980	Tallinn
1936	Kiel	1984	Long Beach
1948	Torbay, Devon	1988	Pusan
1952	Harmaja	1992	Barcelona
		1996	Savannah
		2000	Sydney Harbour

YACHTING MEDALS

	G	S	B	Total
United States	16	18	16	50
Great Britain	17	14	10	41
Sweden	9	12	10	31
Norway	16	11	3	30
France	12	6	9	27
Denmark	11	8	4	23
Australia	5	3	8	16
The Netherlands	4	6	6	16
New Zealand	6	4	5	15
Spain	9	2	1	12
Soviet Union	4	5	3	12
Brazil	4	2	6	12
Germany	3	5	4	12
Italy	3	2	6	11
Finland	2	1	6	9
Belgium	2	4	2	8
Canada	—	2	6	8
West Germany (FRG)	2	2	3	7
East Germany (GDR)	2	2	2	6
Argentina	—	4	2	6
Austria(1)	2	3	—	5
Greece	2	1	1	4
Portugal	—	2	2	4
Switzerland*	1	1	1	3
Ukraine	1	—	2	3
Bahamas	1	—	1	2
Russia	—	1	1	2
Estonia	—	—	2	2
Hong Kong	1	—	—	1
Poland	1	—	—	1
China	—	1	—	1
Cuba	—	1	—	1
Ireland	—	1	—	1
Japan	—	1	—	1
Netherlands Antilles	—	1	—	1
Virgin Islands	—	1	—	1
Hungary*	—	—	1	1
Israel	—	—	1	1
	136	**127†**	**124†**	**387**

* It is perhaps worth noting that Austria, Hungary and Switzerland have no direct access to the sea. † Some events in the early Games had no silver and/or bronze medals.

SHOOTING

Baron de Coubertin, the founder of the modern Olympic Games, was a pistol shot of note in his youth, and this undoubtedly led to the sport being included in the first Games held in 1896. The first champion was Pantelis Karasevdas (GRE) who won the free-rifle event over 200m on 9 April 1896. The number of events has varied considerably, especially in the early celebrations of the Games, from 21 in 1920 to only two in 1932. There were none at all in 1928. Since 1952 there has been some standardisation. In 1984 three events for women were introduced, with another added in 1988, and two more in 2000. In 1996 mixed competition in the skeet and trap events was abolished, and at the same time double trap events for men and women were inaugurated. New regulations were introduced in 1988, in accordance with International Shooting Union rules. The leading eight competitors at the end of the designated number of rounds take part in a final shoot-out round with the target sub-divided into tenths of a point for rifle and pistol shooting. For trap and skeet each of the leading competitors has 25 extra shots.

The most successful competitor has been Carl Osburn (USA) who won a record 11 medals (five golds, four silvers, two bronzes) from 1912 to 1924. Six other men have won five gold medals: Konrad Stäheli (SUI) 1900–6; Louis Richardet (SUI) 1900–6; Alfred Lane (USA) 1912–20; Ole Lilloe-Olsen (NOR) 1920–24; Morris Fisher (USA) 1920–4 and Willis Lee (USA) all in 1920, a record for the sport. However, the only man to win three individual gold medals at any one Games was Gudbrand Skatteboe (NOR), in 1906. Lloyd Spooner (USA) competed in 12 events at the 1920 Games, a record in any sport in Olympic history. Lars Jorgen Madsen (DEN) won gold medals over a record 20-year span, 1900–20. Francois La Fortune (BEL) 1952–76, and Ragnar Skanåker (SWE) 1972–96, both competed in a record seven Games over a record 24-year period. Skanåkar won medals over a 20-year period: 1972 (gold); 1992 (bronze), both in the free pistol event. The most successful female shooter has been Marina Logvinenko-Dobrancheva (URS/EUN/RUS) who won two golds, a silver and two bronzes 1988–96.

Women first competed, in men's events, in 1968 when three countries, Mexico, Peru and Poland, entered one each. Eulalia Rolinska (POL) and Gladys de Seminario (PER) were the first to compete, finishing 22nd and 31st respectively in the small-bore rifle, prone, event. The first medallist was Margaret Murdock (USA) in the 1976 small-bore rifle, three positions. Initially listed as the winner, an error was discovered which placed her equal with her teammate, Lanny Bassham. Then on the count-back rule she was placed second, to the embarrassment of Bassham, who pulled her up to the top of the victory rostrum at the medal ceremony. The only woman to win an Olympic mixed shooting event is Zhang Shan (CHN) in the 1992 skeet contest.

The oldest gold medallist in Olympic history, in any sport, was the remarkable Oscar Swahn (SWE) in the 1912 Running Deer team, aged 64 years 258 days (his son Alfred was also in the team). At Antwerp in 1920 he became the oldest medallist (72 years 280 days) and,

indeed, the oldest competitor at any sport in the Olympics ever, when he was again a member of the Swedish Running Deer silver-medal team. He qualified for the 1924 Games in his 77th year, but illness prevented him from competing. He died three years later. However, it should be noted that very recent research has discovered that the winner of the 1908 free-rifle (1000yd) event, Joshua 'Jerry' Millner (GBR) was some years older than originally thought, and at four days past his 61st birthday was the oldest ever Olympic gold medallist in an individual event. The youngest winner of a shooting gold medal was Konstantin Lukachik of the Unified Team in the 1992 free-pistol, aged 16 years 312 days. The oldest female champion was Linda Thom (USA), aged 40 years 212 days when winning the sport-pistol in 1984. The youngest woman to win a gold was Kim Rhode (USA) in the Double Trap event in 1996 seven days after her 17th birthday. The youngest medallists were Marcus Dinwiddie (USA), silver in the 1924 small-bore rifle, prone, event, and Ulrike Holmer (FRG), silver in the 1984 standard rifle, both at 16 years 301 days.

John and Sumner Paine (USA) were the first brothers to win gold medals at the Olympic Games in 1896, while the first twins to do so were Vilhelm and Eric Carlberg (SWE) in 1912. Károly Takács (HUN) was a European pistol champion in the 1930s using his right hand. In 1938 while on army training a grenade blew up in his hand destroying his right arm. After the war he won the rapid-fire pistol event with his left hand at the 1948 and 1952 Games. The 1960 rapid-fire pistol champion, William McMillan (USA), competed in his record sixth Games in 1976. Walter Winans (USA), who had won a gold medal in the 1908 Running Deer event, became the only man to win medals in both sport and artistic events at the same Games in 1912 when he gained a silver in shooting, and a gold in sculpture. Winans was born in Russia to Dutch-American parents, and lived most of his life in England – he never set foot in America.

Gerald Ouellette (CAN) won the 1956 small-bore, prone, gold medal with a world-record maximum possible score of 600, but it was not accepted as such as the range was found to be 1.5m short of the regulation 50m distance. Miroslav Varga (TCH) also scored 600 in the 1988 event. When Li Ho Jun (PRK) won the same event in 1972 with a score of 599 he was asked how he concentrated so well. He answered that he pretended that he was 'aiming at a capitalist'. In 1992 Zhang Shan (CHN) became the first woman to win a gold medal in a mixed event and scored a maximum possible 200 in the preliminary round of skeet shooting. Francois La Fortune Jr (BEL) competed in a record seven Games, 1952–76, while his father, Francois Sr, competed over a 36-year span, 1924–60. Philip Neame (GBR) is the only holder of the Victoria Cross to win an Olympic gold medal (1924 Running Deer, team).

One of the oddest occurrences in Olympic shooting was in the 1976 trap-shooting event, when 65 year old Paul Cerutti of Monaco was disqualified for using drugs, even though he had finished 43rd out of 44 competitors – he is the oldest competitor ever penalised in this way.

SHOOTING MEDALS

	Men*			Women			
	G	S	B	G	S	B	Total
United States	42	25	21	4	1	2	95
Soviet Union	18	16	15	4	1	3	57
Sweden	14	23	19	1	—	—	57
Great Britain	14	15	18	—	—	—	47
France	14	16	13	—	1	—	44
Norway	16	9	12	—	—	—	37
Switzerland	11	12	12	—	—	—	35
Italy	8	4	11	—	2	—	25
China	6	5	5	4	2	3	25
Greece	5	7	7	—	—	—	19
Finland	3	6	9	—	—	—	18
Denmark	3	9	5	—	—	—	17
Hungary	6	3	6	—	—	1	16
East Germany (GDR)	3	8	5	—	—	—	16
Germany	6	4	3	—	2	—	15
Romania	5	4	5	—	—	—	14
Bulgaria	2	2	3	1	4	2	14
Russia	3	2	2	1	3	2	13
Poland	2	2	3	2	1	2	12
West Germany (FRG)	3	2	3	1	2	—	11
Canada	3	3	2	1	—	—	9
Czechoslovakia	4	3	2	—	—	—	9
Yugoslavia	1	—	1	2	2	3	9
Australia	3	1	1	—	—	3	8
Belgium	2	3	3	—	—	—	8
Austria	1	2	4	—	—	—	7
Japan	1	1	3	—	1	—	6
Belarus	—	2	2	—	—	1	5
Korea	1	1	—	1	1	—	4
Brazil	1	1	1	—	—	—	3
Peru	1	2	—	—	—	—	3
Kazakhstan	—	2	1	—	—	—	3
Czech Republic	—	1	2	—	—	—	3
Slovenia	1	—	1	—	—	—	2
Colombia	—	2	—	—	—	—	2
The Netherlands	—	1	1	—	—	—	2
Spain	—	1	1	—	—	—	2
Azerbaijan	—	—	—	1	—	—	1
Lithuania	—	—	—	1	—	—	1
North Korea (PRK)	1	—	—	—	—	—	1
Ukraine	1	—	—	—	—	—	1
Argentina	—	1	—	—	—	—	1
Chile	—	1	—	—	—	—	1
Latvia	—	1	—	—	—	—	1
Mexico	—	1	—	—	—	—	1
Moldova	—	1	—	—	—	—	1
Portugal	—	1	—	—	—	—	1
South Africa	—	1	—	—	—	—	1
Cuba	—	—	1	—	—	—	1
Haiti	—	—	1	—	—	—	1
Kuwait	—	—	1	—	—	—	1
New Zealand	—	—	1	—	—	—	1
Mongolia	—	—	—	—	—	1	1
Venezuela	—	—	1	—	—	—	1
	205	207	207	24†	23	23	689

* Including female medallists prior to 1984. † Including the female winner of the 1992 open skeet competition.

SHORT-TRACK SPEED SKATING

OLYMPIC RECORDS

MEN

500m	41.802sec	Marc Gagnon (CAN)	2002
1000m	1min 27.185sec	Mathieu Turcotte (CAN)	2002
1500m	2min 15.942sec	Dong-Sung Kim (KOR)	2002
5000m Relay	6min 45.455sec	CANADA	2002

WOMEN

500m	44.118sec	Yang Yang (A) (CHN)	2002
1000m	1min 31.235sec	Yang Yang (A) (CHN)	2002
1500m	2min 21.069sec	Eun-Kyung Choi (KOR)	2002
3000m Relay	4min 12.793sec	KOREA	2002

In 1988 short-track speed skating was a demonstration sport, but four years later it became a medal sport with two events each for men and women. In 1994 two more events were added, and then in 2002 the 1500m for men and women were included. Despite the tight bends in the sport, speeds of 40km/h (25mph) are reached. Indicative of the problems associated with short-track racing was the result in the 2002, men's 1000m race. Just short of the finish line three of the four finalists fell, leaving the trailing fourth man, Steven Bradbury (AUS), to come through and win his country's first ever Winter Games gold medal.

So far the only person to gain a medal in both styles of speed skating is Eric Flaim (USA) with silvers in the 1988 1500m and the 1994 short-track relay. The most successful competitor has been Chun Lee-Kyung (KOR) with a record four gold medals and a bronze 1994–98, while the best by a man has been by Kim Ki-Hoon (KOR) with three gold medals in 1992–94. The youngest ever winner of a Winter Games gold medal was Kim Yoon-Mi (KOR) in the 1998 women's relay aged 13 years 83 days. She was also the youngest ever female Olympic winner in either Winter or Summer Games. The oldest champion in short-track was Cathy Turner who won the 1994 500m title, aged 31 years 320 days. The youngest male gold medallist was Jae Kun Song (KOR) aged 18 years seven days in the 1992 relay, only one day younger than countryman Dong-Sung Kim who won the 1000m individual event in 1998. The oldest was Jae's teammate Ji Soo Mo aged 30 years 264 days. It is noteworthy that the average age of the winning Korean women's relay team in 1994 was about 15¾ years.

SHORT-TRACK SPEED SKATING MEDALS

	Men*			Women			
	G	S	B	G	S	B	Total
Korea	5	2	1	6	2	3	19
Canada	3	3	4	2	2	2	16
China	—	3	2	2	6	2	15
United States	1	2	1	2	1	2	9
Italy	1	2	—	—	—	—	3
Japan	1	—	2	—	—	—	3
Australia	1	—	1	—	—	—	2
Bulgaria	—	—	—	—	1	1	2
Great Britain	—	—	1	—	—	—	1
North Korea (PRK)	—	—	—	—	—	1	1
Soviet Union	—	—	—	—	—	1	1
	12	12	12	12	12	12	72

SISTERS

The first sisters to take part in Olympic competition were Marion and Georgina Jones (USA) in the 1900 tennis events. Marion finished third in the singles, and was fourth in the mixed doubles. Her sister was eliminated in the first round of both contests. The most successful sisters in Olympic competition have been Irina and Tamara Press (URS), in athletics. Irina won the 80m hurdles title in 1960 and then the pentathlon in 1964. Tamara won the shot in 1960 and 1964, the discus in 1964 and the discus silver in 1960. However, there have been questions asked since they disappeared from competition when sex tests were introduced in 1966. In 2000, at Sydney, sisters Hazel and Joetta Clark, and their sister-in-law, Jearl Miles-Clark, all competed in the track 800m event, with all three reaching the semi-finals, but only Hazel making it to the final. (See also Twins).

SKELETON SLEDDING

There were one-man skeleton sled races held on the famous Cresta Run at St Moritz in 1928 and 1948. In this event the contestants lay face down, as compared to luge racers who lie back. The event was re-introduced in

2002 at Salt Lake City, and an event for women was inaugurated.

The youngest gold medallist was Jennison Heaton (USA) aged 24 years 307 days in 1928, while his brother John was only 19 years 161 days old, taking silver behind him. The oldest gold medallist was Jim Shea (USA) in 2002, aged 33 years 255 days, and the oldest medallist has been John Crammond (GBR) who was aged 41 years 213 days when he took the bronze medal in 1948. In the women's event, the 2002 winner, Tristan Gale (USA), was 21 years 194 days, while the silver medallist, Lea Ann Parsley (USA) was 33 years 253 days.

The Heaton brothers (USA), unusually, competed successfully at skeleton and luge. Jennison won the 1928 skeleton event and was a member of the silver medal five-man bob that year. Brother John was second in the 1928 skeleton, won a bronze in the 1932 two-man bob, and then, in his 40th year, won another skeleton silver in 1948. Seventh in that 1948 competition was Lieutenant Colonel James Coats (GBR), holder of the Military Cross, and at 53 years 297 days, the oldest ever competitor in the Winter Olympic Games. The winner of the event in Salt Lake City, Jim Shea, was the grandson of Jack Shea who won two speed skating golds in 1932, while his father, Jim Sr, was an Olympian in Nordic skiing in 1964 – such a three-generation competitive span is probably unique in the Winter Games. In 1928 a representative of one of the oldest British Earldoms, David, Earl of Northesk, took the bronze medal.

Speeds approaching 130km/h (80mph) are sometimes reached. However, the fastest average speed for a single run has been 94.44km/h (58.68mph) by Jim Shea in 2002, while the female record is 91.97km/h (57.15mph), by Tristan Gale, also at Salt Lake City.

SKELETON SLEDDING MEDALS

| | Men | | | Women | | | |
	G	S	B	G	S	B	Total
United States	2	2	—	1	1	—	6
Great Britain	—	—	2	—	—	1	3
Italy	1	—	—	—	—	—	1
Austria	—	1	—	—	—	—	1
Switzerland	—	—	1	—	—	—	1
	3	3	3	1	1	1	12

SKIING

See separate entries under Alpine Skiing, Freestyle Skiing, and Nordic Skiing.

SKI-JUMPING

First contested in 1924 with one hill, and in 1964 two hills (70m and 90m) were introduced, which were changed to 90m and 120m in 1992. The controversial 'V' style was introduced by Jan Boklöv (SWE) in 1988, and was initially frowned upon, and penalised, by the judges. However, by 1994 virtually all the competitors were using it. The most successful jumper has been Matti Nykänen (FIN) with four golds and one silver medal in 1984 and 1988, including three golds in one Games. However, his successes include the team competition, not introduced until 1988. Prior to him the most successful had been Birger Ruud (NOR) with two golds and a silver medal from 1932 to 1948. He also came fourth in the Alpine Combination event of 1936, winning the downhill segment. His brother Sigmund won a silver in 1928, while a third brother, Asbjørn, was seventh in 1948. In 1994 Jens Weissflog (GER) became only the third man to win at two Games, in his case, remarkably, with a ten-year gap, having competed in four Games. Only Nykänen in 1988, and Simon Ammann (SUI) in 2002, have won both 90m and 120m individual titles at the same Games.

Speeds of over 90km/h (56mph) are attained down the take-off ramp. The longest jump achieved in Olympic competition was 137m (449ft) by both Takanobu Okabe and Masahiko Harada, members of the winning Japanese team, on the 120-m hill at Nagano in 1998. The longest jump ever on the 90-m hill was 118.5m (388ft) by Matti Nykänen (FIN) in 1988. The oldest gold medallist was Masahiko Harada in 1998, aged 29 years 284 days, while the youngest was Toni Nieminen (FIN) in the 1992 team event, aged 16 years 259 days: he is also the youngest ever Winter Games winner. The youngest medallist was also Nieminen when he won an individual bronze five days before he won his gold, while the oldest was Birger Ruud in 1948 aged 36 years 168 days. Sepp Bradl (AUT) – the first man ever to jump over 100m (328ft) – competed over a period of 20 years, 1936–56, but never won a medal.

SKI-JUMPING MEDALS

	G	S	B	Total
Norway	8	9	7	24
Finland	10	6	4	20
Austria	3	6	8	17
Japan	3	4	2	9
Germany	4	2	2	8
East Germany (GDR)	2	3	2	7

	G	S	B	Total
Czechoslovakia	1	2	4	7
Switzerland	2	1	—	3
Poland	1	1	11	3
Sweden	—	1	1	2
Yugoslavia	—	1	1	2
Soviet Union	1	—	—	1
Slovenia	—	—	1	1
United States	—	—	1	1
	35	**36***	**34**	**105**

* Tie for silver in 1980 70m event.

SMALLEST

The smallest ever Olympic champion is gymnast Lu Li (CHN) who won the gold medal in the asymmetrical bars event at Barcelona in 1992. She stood only 1.36m (4ft 5½in) tall and weighed 36kg (79lb). The 1920 springboard diving champion, Aileen Riggin (USA), weighed less 31.5kg (70lb), but was taller than Lu Li. Perhaps the smallest ever competitor in the Games was the North Korean gymnast Choe Myong-Hui, at Moscow in 1980, who was only 1.35m (4ft 5in) tall, and weighed a mere 25kg (55lb).

SNOWBOARDING

The sport evolved in the mid-1960s, and made its debut at the 1998 Olympic Games. There are two events: the giant slalom, and the halfpipe. In 2002 the slalom was raced in parallel, in which two competitors compete side by side on identical courses. The halfpipe is a freestyle discipline that is performed down a 120-m U-shaped course, on which a series of leaps, twists, rotations and flips are performed. The first winner of an Olympic title, the men's giant slalom, Ross Rebagliati of Canada, was initially disqualified after testing positive for marijuana – apparently a much-used substance by the sport's devotees. On appeal he was re-instated.

The most successful female snowboarder has been Karine Ruby (FRA) with a gold in 1998 and a silver in 2002, while the most successful male has been Ross Powers (USA), with a gold in 2002 to add to his bronze awarded in Nagano. The youngest gold medallist/medallist was Kelly Clark (USA) who won the 2002 women's halfpipe, aged 18 years 199 days. The youngest male champion was Gian Simmen (SUI) in the 1998 halfpipe, aged 20 years 358 days. The oldest male gold medallist was Rebagliati at 26 years 210 days at Nagano, while the oldest female winner was Isabelle Blanc (FRA) in the 2002 giant slalom, aged 26 years 205 days. The youngest male medallist was Ross Powers (USA) who won the 1998 halfpipe bronze two days after his 19th birthday, and the oldest medallist was Chris Klug (USA) with a bronze in the 2002 giant slalom aged 29 years 59 days. Brigitte Koeck (AUT) is the oldest female medallist with a bronze in the 1998 giant slalom aged 27 years 274 days.

SNOWBOARDING MEDALS

	Men			Women			Total
	G	S	B	G	S	B	
United States	1	1	3	1	—	1	7
Switzerland	2	—	1	—	—	1	4
France	—	—	—	2	2	—	4
Germany	—	—	—	1	1	—	2
Norway	—	1	—	—	1	—	2
Italy	—	1	—	—	—	1	2
Canada	1	—	—	—	—	—	1
Sweden	—	1	—	—	—	—	1
Austria	—	—	—	—	—	1	1
	4	**4**	**4**	**4**	**4**	**4**	**24**

SOCCER

Some sources refer to two exhibition matches at Athens in the first Games of 1896, when after two Greek towns had played an eliminator, the winner, Smyrna, was defeated by a Danish side 15–0. However, the Swedish Olympic expert Ture Widlund, after considerable research, considers these reports to be spurious. Although sometimes considered unofficial, the tournaments of 1900, 1904 and 1906 are usually counted in medals tables. Therefore soccer was the first team game to be included in the Olympics. The first goal was scored by Great Britain (represented by Upton Park FC) versus France (4–0) in 1900. The 1904 tournament only had three entries, one Canadian and two American teams, while in 1906 a Danish team beat Smyrna (representing Greece). In that latter team were five Britons named Whittal, of which three were one set of brothers and the other two another set, the two lots being cousins. This must be some sort of Olympic record for a family.

With the founding of the Federation of International Football Association (FIFA) in 1904, Olympic soccer came under their control, and from 1908 the competition grew in stature. In 1920, Egypt, the first non-European country – excepting the North Americans of 1904 – entered, and by 1924 there were 22 countries competing. That tournament and the following one were won by Uruguay – who surprisingly never took part in Olympic soccer again. Two years after their Amsterdam victory Uruguay won the inaugural World Cup of 1930 with nine of their Olympic team playing. Only three other players, all Italian, have been in both Olympic (1936) and World Cup (1938) winning sides. The most successful teams have been Great Britain, winners in 1900, 1908 and 1912, and Hungary, with gold medals in 1952, 1964 and 1968. However, Hungary has also won a silver and a bronze.

There was considerable disillusionment with the interpretation of the term 'amateur' as applied to soccer at the Games, similar to the troubles in ice hockey. These arguments about pseudo-amateurs were exacerbated with the entry of the Eastern European powers into the game after 1948. Great Britain, after three gold medals in the early days, did not enter in 1924 and 1928 due to disagreements between the Football Association (FA) and FIFA about broken time payments to amateurs. It re-entered Olympic competition in 1936, but after a series of poor results, Britain has not taken part since 1972. In 1952, as entries increased, qualifying rounds were introduced to decide on the final 16 teams. In 1984 professionals were allowed to take part, but only those who had not yet participated in World Cup competition were eligible. Currently the only restriction on players is that (except for three players per squad) they must all be less than 23 years of age.

The highest team score in Olympic soccer was the 17–1 defeat of France by Denmark in 1908, during which the Danish centre-forward Sophus Nielsen, scored a record ten goals. This mark was equalled by Gottried Fuchs for Germany when they beat Russia 16–0 in 1912. The most goals scored by an individual in one tournament is 12, by Ferenc Bene (HUN) in 1964. The most scored in Olympic competition is 13 by Sophus Nielsen (DEN) 1908–12, and by Antal Dunai (HUN) 1968–72. The highest score in a final since the institution of 'proper' tournaments in 1908 has been the 4–2 defeat of Denmark by Great Britain in 1912. France's victory in 1984 was the first win by a Western European side since the outstanding Swedish team of 1948, and the first medal since the Swedish bronze of four years later. The 1968 final ended with only 18 players on the field, as three Bulgarians and one Hungarian had been sent off.

HIGHEST SCORING INDIVIDUALS IN OLYMPIC TOURNAMENTS
MEN

Year	Goals	Player
1908	11	Sophus Nielsen (DEN)
1912	10	Gottfried Fuchs (GER)
1920	7	Herbert Carlsson (SWE)
1924	8	Pedro Petrone (URU)
1928	11	Domingo Tarasconi (ARG)
1936	7	Annibale Frossi (ITA)
1948	7	Gunnar Nordahl (SWE) and Karl Aage Hansen (DEN)
1952	7	Branko Zebec (YUG) and Rajko Mitic (YUG)
1956	4	Dimiter Milanov (BUL) and Neville d'Souza (IND)
1960	7	Milan Galic (YUG) and Borivoje Kostic (YUG)
1964	12	Ferenc Bene (HUN)
1968	7	Kunishige Kamamoto (JPN)
1972	9	Kazimiercz Deyna (POL)
1976	6	Andrzej Szarmach (POL)
1980	5	Sergei Andreyev (URS)
1984	5	Borislav Cvetkovic (YUG), Stjepan Deveric (YUG) and Daniel Xuereb (FRA)
1988	7	Romario Farias (BRA)
1992	7	Andrzej Juskowiak (POL)
1996	6	Hernan Crespo (ARG) and Bebeto(BRA)
2000	6	Ivan Zamoraño (CHI)

WOMEN

Year	Goals	Player
1996	4	Linda Medalen (NOR), Pretinha (BRA), Ann Kristin Aarønes (NOR)
2000	4	Wen Sun (CHN)

There has only been one draw in an Olympic final. That was in 1928 between Uruguay and Argentina (1–1), and the replay was won by the defending champions Uruguay 2–1. The Hungarian team that won in Helsinki in 1952 was virtually the same team that 16 months later inflicted the first home defeat on England's professionals at Wembley Stadium. The most successful player has been Dezsö Nowák (HUN) who added gold medals in 1964 and 1968 to the bronze he won in 1960. Of the ten other players to win two gold medals only Arthur Berry and Vivian Woodward (both GBR) were not Uruguayans. Two of those latter, Antonio and Santos Urdinaran became the first brothers to win soccer gold medals in 1924. This feat was surpassed by the Nordahl brothers: Bertil, Knut and Gunnar, in 1948. In 1908 the Danish silver medal team included mathematician Harald Bohr, the brother of the famous nuclear physicist, Niels.

The oldest gold medallist was Rostislav Václavícek

(TCH) aged 33 years 239 days in the 1980 final. The youngest was Idriss Carlos Kameni (CMR) aged 16 years 225 days at Sydney in 2000. The youngest medallist was Osei Kuffour (GHA) in 1992 at 15 years 339 days, and the oldest was Fyodor Cherenkov (URS) aged 41 years 92 days in 1980.

A women's competition was instituted in 1996, which proved popular with both the media and fans. There were 76,481 spectators for the final when the USA beat China 2–1, reportedly the largest crowd to watch any women-only sporting event. The greatest aggregate was when China beat Denmark 5–1, with China's score the highest achieved. The greatest winning margin was that match, plus when Norway beat Japan 4–0. The youngest gold medallist/medallist was Cindy Parlow (USA) aged 18 years 85 days. The oldest gold medallist was her teammate Carin Gabarra who was 31 years 205 days, and the oldest medallist was Heidi Støre (NOR) with a bronze aged 33 years 28 days. Twins Anne and Nina Andersen of Norway both won bronze medals in 1996. The most successful players have been Gro Espeseth, Marianne Pettersen, and Brit Sandaune, all of Norway, winning a gold and a bronze in 1996/2000.

One of the most remarkable goals in Olympic International football involved the Swedish centre-forward, Gunnar Nordahl, in the 1948 semi-final against Denmark. Unexpectedly caught offside by a quick reversal of play, Nordahl realised that his team were attacking again. With lightning presence of mind he leapt into the back of the Danish goal, thus taking himself off the field of play, and duly caught the goal-scoring header from his teammate Henry Carlsson, while the goalkeeper was on the ground five metres away. In the 1920 final between Belgium and Czechoslovakia the latter team walked off the field, in protest against the referee, before half-time, when they were 2–0 down. The match was abandoned and the Czechs disqualified. The 1936 tournament resulted in many incidents, not least the withdrawal of the Peruvian team when its win over Austria in the second round was replayed and Austria went on to reach the final.

After many years in the doldrums Olympic soccer had a revival in 1980 when the 56 games of the tournament, played in Moscow, Leningrad, Minsk and Kiev, attracted nearly two million spectators – over a third of all the spectators for the 1980 Games. This revival was re-inforced, somewhat surprisingly, in Los Angeles in 1984, when nearly 1.5 million watched the matches, including a record 101,799 audience for the final.

SOCCER MEDALS

	Men			Women			
	G	S	B	G	S	B	Total
Hungary	3	1	1	—	—	—	5
Soviet Union	2	—	3	—	—	—	5
Denmark	1	3	1	—	—	—	5
Yugoslavia	1	3	1	—	—	—	5
United States	—	1	1	1	1	—	4
Great Britain	3	—	—	—	—	—	3
Poland	1	2	—	—	—	—	3
Spain	1	2	—	—	—	—	3
East Germany (GDR)	1	1	1	—	—	—	3
Norway	—	—	1	1	—	1	3
Sweden	1	—	2	—	—	—	3
Brazil	—	2	1	—	—	—	3
The Netherlands	—	—	3	—	—	—	3
Uruguay	2	—	—	—	—	—	2
Czechoslovakia	1	1	—	—	—	—	2
France	1	1	—	—	—	—	2
Belgium	1	—	1	—	—	—	2
Italy	1	—	1	—	—	—	2
Argentina	—	2	—	—	—	—	2
Austria	—	1	—	—	1	—	2
Bulgaria	—	1	1	—	—	—	2
Greece	—	1	1	—	—	—	2
Germany	—	—	1	—	—	1	2
Cameroon	1	—	—	—	—	—	1
Canada	1	—	—	—	—	—	1
Nigeria	1	—	—	—	—	—	1
Switzerland	—	1	—	—	—	—	1
Chile	—	—	1	—	—	—	1
West Germany (FRG)	—	—	1	—	—	—	1
Ghana	—	—	1	—	—	—	1
Japan	—	—	1	—	—	—	1
	23	23	24*	2	2	2	76

* Third-place tie in 1972.

SOFTBALL

Invented as an indoor version of baseball in 1887, it didn't become known as softball until 1920. Originally a ten-a-side game, it is now played with nine per side, and is governed by the International Softball Federation (ISF), formed in 1950. Pitching is done underarm, and there are fast-pitch and slow-pitch forms. A game lasts for seven innings. The fast-pitch variety for women was introduced as an official Olympic medal sport in 1996 – surprisingly never having been a demonstration sport – with eight teams.

The highest score achieved by a team is 10 attained in 1996 by the United States v Puerto Rico (10–0), China v Puerto Rico (10–0), Australia v Japan (10–0), Chinese Taipei v Puerto Rico (10–2), and in 2000 by China v New Zealand (10–0). The Chinese Taipei v Puerto Rico match in 1996 totalled the highest aggregate of 12.

The youngest gold medallist/medallist was Christa Lee Williams (USA) aged 18 years 173 days, while the oldest champion/medallist was her teammate Dorothy Richardson at 39 years 4 days. Seven members of the USA team won their second gold medal at Sydney.

SOFTBALL MEDALS

	G	S	B	Total
United States	2	—	—	2
Australia	—	—	2	2
China	—	1	—	1
Japan	—	1	—	1

SPEED

The fastest speed achieved by an athlete without mechanical aid at the Olympic Games is 43.56km/h (27.06mph), by 1996 100m champion Donovan Bailey (CAN), recorded reaching his peak speed in the final 60m of the race, in the stadium at Atlanta. The fastest of all Olympians are the bobsledders, who have been recorded at 143km/h (88.8mph). Downhill skiers and lugers attain over 130km/h (80mph) at times.

The fastest Summer Games Olympians were Daniel Morelon and Pierre Trentin (FRA) when they attained a speed of 73.24km/h (45.50mph) in their 1968 cycling tandem event, clocking 9.83sec for the last 200m of their race. The fastest individual cyclist was Gary Niewand (AUS) in 1996 when he clocked 10.219sec for 200m – 71.08km/h (44.16mph). The fastest female cyclist was Michelle Ferris (AUS), also at Atlanta, with 11.212sec – 64.21km/h (39.90mph). Speed skater Gerard van Velde (NED) set a record 1min 07.18sec for 1000m at Salt Lake City in 2002, which is an average of 53.59km/h (33.30mph), while on the distaff side, Chris Witty (USA), also at Salt Lake City, did 1000m in 1min 13.83sec to average 48.76km/h (30.30mph). (See also Speed Skiing).

SPEED SKATING

OLYMPIC RECORDS

MEN	mins/sec			
500m	34.42	Casey Fitz Randolph (USA)	2002	
1000m	1 07.18	Gerard van Velde (NED)	2002	
1500m	1 43.95	Derek Parra (USA)	2002	
5000m	6 14.66	Jochen Uytehaage (NED)	2002	
10,000m	12 58.92	Jochen Uytehaage (NED)	2002	

WOMEN	mins/sec			
500m	37.30	Catriona Le May-Doan (CAN)	2002	
1000m	1 13.83	Chris Witty (USA)	2002	
1500m	1 54.02	Annie Friesinger (GER)	2002	
3000m	3 57.70	Claudia Pechstein (GER)	2002	
5000m	6 46.91	Claudia Pechstein (GER)	2002	

The sport was introduced into the Olympics in 1924, with the first official events for women in 1960. There have been two major controversies over the years. In 1928 the Norwegian referee cancelled the 10-km event due to bad weather, this caused much ill-feeling in the American camp because at the time Irving Jaffee (USA) was the surprise leader, and as all the best skaters had competed the medal positions seemed assured. Despite vigorous protests by all nationalities no medals were awarded. The other occasion was in 1932 when the American 'mass start' system was used, for the only time in Olympic competition. This undoubtedly gave the Americans and Canadians a tremendous advantage, as the Europeans were completely unfamiliar with the tactics involved – and the European skaters won only two medals. Since 1998 the 500m events are decided on the aggregate of two runs – interestingly, both male and female winners at Nagano would have won under the old system. A new type of skate, the clap skate, was used at Nagano, and the Dutch introduced aerodynamic silicon 'stripes' on the team racing suits. At Salt Lake City in 2002 the facility was the highest enclosed ice track in the world at 1424m (4675ft) above sea level, thus virtually ensuring that the record book would be rewritten.

Lydia Skoblikova (URS) won a record six gold medals in 1960 and 1964, which is also a record for any sport in the Winter Games for a female competitor. The most by a man are five by Clas Thunberg (FIN) in 1924 and 1928, and by Eric Heiden (USA) with all five in 1980. Incidentally, there is a story that Thunberg deliberately let his teammate Julius Skutnabb win the 10km in 1924, thus denying himself even greater fame. There have been five events for men only since 1976, while a fifth event was added for women in 1988. The most medals won is eight, by Karin Enke-Kania (GDR) with three golds, four silvers and a bronze between 1980 and 1988, and by Gunda Niemann-Stirnemann (GDR/GER) also with three golds, four silvers and a bronze between 1992 and 1996 – in both cases a Winter Games record for individual events. The most by a male skater is seven by Thunberg, who added a silver and a bronze to his golds, and by Ivar Ballangrud (NOR) who won four golds, two silvers and a bronze from 1928 to 1936. Skoblikova won her four golds in 1964 on four successive days. In 1994 Bonnie Blair (USA) uniquely won the same title (500m) for the third consecutive time.

The oldest gold medallist was Thunberg aged 35 years 315 days in the 1928 1500m. The youngest winner was Anne Henning (USA) in the 500m in 1952 aged 16 years 157 days. The youngest male champion was Igor Malkov (URS) winning the 10km in 1984, aged 19 years 9 days, while the oldest woman was Christina Baas-Kaiser (NED) who won the 3,000m title in 1972, aged 33 years 268 days. The youngest ever medallist was Andrea Mitscherlich (later Schöne, and then Ehrlich, GDR) who won the 3000m silver in 1976 when she was only 15 years 69 days. The youngest male medallist was Alv Gjestvang (NOR) in 1956, aged 18 years 147 days. The oldest male medallist was Julius Skutnabb (FIN) in 1928 at 38 years 246 days, while the oldest female medallist was Eevi Huttunen (FIN) in the 1960 3000m aged 37 years 184 days. Frank Stack (CAN) competed over a 20-year period from 1932 to 1952 (when he was 46) winning a bronze in 1932, while Colin Coates (AUS) also competed for 20 years, in six Games 1968–88, but his best placing was sixth in the 10km in 1976.

The greatest average speed achieved is by Gerard van Velde (NED), in the 1000m at Salt Lake City with 53.59km/h (33.30mph). The fastest by a woman is 48.76km/h (30.30mph) by Chris Witty (USA), also in the 1000m in 2002. Unusually, Bart Veldkamp won medals in 1992–4 representing The Netherlands, and then won another in 1998 representing Belgium.

A number of speed skaters have found a happy affinity with cycle racing. One of the most successful at both roles has been Sheila Young (USA), who won the 500-m Olympic skating title in 1976, and the World Amateur Sprint Cycle Championship in 1973 and 1976. However, Christa Rothenburger-Luding (GDR) possibly surpassed that in 1988. Having won the 1984 Olympic 500m gold, and the 1986 world cycling sprint title in 1986, she then won the skating 1000m at Calgary and gained a cycling silver in Seoul, to become the first competitor to win medals at both the Summer and Winter Games in the same year. This achievement can no longer be equalled. Eric Flaim (USA) who had won a silver in the 1988 speed skating 1500m, became the first to also gain a medal at short-track skating in 1994 with another silver in the relay.

MEDALS

	Men			Women			
	G	S	B	G	S	B	Total
Norway	24	28	25	1	—	1	79
The Netherlands	12	20	15	9	6	4	66
Soviet Union	12	10	9	12	7	10	60
United States	16	8	5	9	9	9	56
Germany	2	—	1	10	12	8	33
East Germany (GDR)	2	1	2	6	11	7	29
Finland	6	6	7	1	2	2	24
Canada	2	3	7	2	3	3	20
Sweden	7	4	5	—	—	—	16
Japan	1	3	5	—	—	3	12
Austria	—	1	2	1	1	1	6
Russia	1	1	1	1	1	—	5
West Germany (FRG)	2	—	—	1	—	—	3
China	—	—	—	—	2	1	3
Poland	—	—	—	—	1	1	2
Belarus	—	1	—	—	—	—	1
Korea	—	1	—	—	—	—	1
North Korea (PRK)	—	—	—	—	1	—	1
Belgium	—	—	1	—	—	—	1
Kazakhstan	—	—	—	—	—	1	1
	7	7	85	53	56	51	419

SPEED SKIING

A demonstration sport at Albertville in 1992, when world records were set in both the men's and women's events: men's, 229.299km/h (142.479mph) by Mickaël Prufer (FRA), and women's, 219.245km/h (136.232mph) by Tarja Mulari (FIN). Second in the men's competition was Philippe Goitschel (FRA) nephew of the sisters who had won golds in the 1964 Alpine events. Davina Galica (GBR) competed in the women's event 28 years after her first Olympic appearance as an Alpine skier, aged 47 years 189 days.

SPORTS

Only five sports have been on the programme of every Modern Games since 1896: cycling, fencing, gymnastics, swimming, track and field athletics. Rowing should have been included with them, but although actually listed on the 1896 programme of events, it was cancelled due to rough seas. To become an Olympic sport, recognised by the IOC, but not necessarily contested at the Games, it must be widely practiced in 75 countries on four continents (men's sports), and in 40 countries on three continents (women's sports). For a Winter Games sport it must be widely practiced in 25 countries on three continents.

STADIA

The largest main stadium used in the Olympics has been that at Sydney in 2000, nominally capable of holding 110,000, but it was reported that there were 112,524 to watch Cathy Freeman win her 400m title. Other large stadia include Melbourne Cricket Ground in 1956, which had its capacity increased to 104,000 for the Games, followed closely by the Lenin Stadium in Moscow in 1980, which had a capacity of 103,000 at the time. The Berlin Stadium in 1936 actually held 100,000, and not 110,000 as was reported by some sources, and the Los Angeles Memorial Stadium, as used for the 1932 Games, could then seat 101,000.

STAMPS

The first Olympic stamps were issued on 6 April 1896 in Greece to raise funds for the First Games, and to publicise the occasion. There were 12 stamps in the set, designed by Professor Gillieron, and engraved by Eduard Mouchon, and produced by the French Government Printing Office on behalf of the Greek Post Office. The designs included ancient boxers, the stadium, and Myron's famous statue *The Discus Thrower*. Because Greece was still using the Julian calendar, the cancelling postmark was dated 25 March 1896. The first issue of Olympic stamps to use representations of modern sportsmen was that for the 1928 Games at Amsterdam. The first Winter Games to stimulate an issue of stamps was that at Lake Placid in 1932. After the Second World War many countries began to produce stamps with an Olympic theme, sometimes to commemorate them, but usually to raise funds for future participation. In 1980, in connection with the Games at Moscow, the Soviet Union produced a record of 74 stamps for the occasion. Well over 100 countries have issued stamps relating to the Games.

STOCKHOLM 1956

In 1956, due to Australian quarantine regulations, the equestrian events of the Melbourne Olympic Games were held in the city of Stockholm. *See* Melbourne 1956, for data and medals.

SUMMER GAMES

For a list of Games, venues, dates and numbers of competitors, *see* Celebrations.

SWIMMING (*see also* Synchronised Swimming, Diving, and Water Polo)

OLYMPIC RECORDS

MEN	mins/sec		
50m freestyle	21.91	Aleksandr Popov (EUN)	1992
100m freestyle	47.84	Pieter van den Hoogenband (NED)	2002
200m freestyle	1 45.35	Pieter van den Hoogenband (NED)	2002
400m freestyle	3 40.59	Ian Thorpe (AUS)	2002
1500m freestyle	14 43.38	Kieren Perkins (AUS)	1992
4 x 100m freestyle	3 13.67	Australia	2002
4 x 200m freestyle	7 07.05	Australia	2002
100m breaststroke	1 00.46	Domenico Fioravanti (ITA)	2002
200m breaststroke	2 10.16	Mike Barrowman (USA)	1992
100m backstroke	53.72	Lenny Krayzelburg (USA)	2002

200m backstroke	1 56.76	Lenny Krayzelburg (USA)	2002
100m butterfly	51.96	Geoff Huegill (AUS)	2002
200m butterfly	1 55.35	Tom Malchow (USA)	2002
200m medley	1 58.98	Massimiliano Rosolino (ITA)	2002
400m medley	4 11.76	Tom Dolan (USA)	2002
4 x 100m medley	3 33.73	United States	2002

WOMEN	mins/sec		
50m freestyle	24.13	Inge de Bruijn (NED)	2002
100m freestyle	53.77	Inge de Bruijn (NED)	2002
200m freestyle	1 57.65	Heike Friedrich (GDR)	1988
400m freestyle	4 03.85	Janet Evans (USA)	1988
800m freestyle	8 19.67	Brooke Bennett (USA)	2002
4 x 100m freestyle	3 36.61	United States	2002
4 x 200m freestyle	7 57.80	United States	2002
100m breaststroke	1 07.02	Penny Heyns (RSA)	1996
200m breaststroke	2 24.03	Agnes Kovacs (HUN)	2002
100m backstroke	1 00.21	Diana Mocanu (ROM)	2002
200m backstroke	2 07.06	Krisztina Egerszegi (HUN)	1992
100m butterfly	56.61	Inge de Bruijn (NED)	2002
200m butterfly	2 05.88	Misty Hyman (USA)	2002
200m medley	2 10.68	Jana Klochkova (UKR)	2002
400m medley	4 33.59	Jana Klochkova (UKR)	2002
4 x 100m medley	3 58.30	United States	2002

The sport has been an integral part of the Games since 1896 when the swimming was held in the Bay of Zea near Piraeus, Greece. The first champion was Alfréd Hajós (née Guttmann) (HUN) who won the 100m freestyle in freezing water. The first female champion (women's events were introduced in 1912) was Australia's Fanny Durack, also in the 100m freestyle. The first Olympic competition in a pool was in 1908, in a 100m-long tank constructed inside the track at the Stadium (later called the White City) in London. The first 50m pool was constructed in 1924, outdoors, and the first one indoors was at Wembley London in 1948. Emil Rausch (GER), in 1904, was the last to win an Olympic title using the side-stroke.

The most successful swimmer was Mark Spitz (USA) with nine gold medals plus a silver and a bronze in 1968 and 1972. His seven golds at one Games (1972) are still unmatched in any sport. The most individual-event golds won is five by Krisztina Egerszegi (HUN) 1988–96. Kristin Otto (GDR) won six golds at Seoul and set a female record for the most medals won at any single Games. Otto is also the only swimmer to win Olympic titles in three different strokes – freestyle, backstroke and butterfly. Dawn Fraser (AUS) in the 100m freestyle, and Krisztina Egerszegi (HUN) in the 200m backstroke, are the only swimmers, male or female, to win the same event three times. Matt Biondi (USA) equalled the record of 11 medals by Spitz, but his comprised 'only' eight golds, two silvers and a bronze 1984–92. Jenny Thompson (USA) won eight golds, a silver and a bronze for a female record of ten medals 1992–2000. Unusually, all Thompson's gold medals were won in relays. Both Spitz and Shirley Babashoff (USA) set an endurance record of sorts in 1972 and 1976, respectively, by taking part in 13 races within eight days.

The first swimmer to defend successfully an Olympic swimming title was Charles Daniels (USA) in the 100m freestyle in 1908. The first woman to do so was Martha Norelius (USA) in 1928 in the 400m freestyle. She was born in Sweden and her father, Charles, had been a member of the 1906 Swedish Olympic swimming team, while an uncle, Benkt, had won gold in the 1912 gymnastics. Later, her first husband was the 1928 Canadian silver medallist oarsman, Joseph Wright. Perhaps particularly noteworthy is the ten gold medals in ten attempts by the American 4 x 100m medley relay team 1960–2000 – they didn't compete in 1980 due to the boycott. In 1996 Claudia Poll (CRC) won the 200m freestyle to gain her country's first ever swimming gold medal – Costa Rica's only previous swimming medal, was a silver in the same event, won by her sister, Silvia, in 1988. Also in 1996 Michelle Smith (IRL) not only became the first Irish swimmer to reach an Olympic final, but she won three gold medals and a bronze. Gary Hall Jr (USA) won three golds and three silvers and a bronze in 1996–2000 – his father had won two silvers and a bronze 1968–76.

The oldest male gold medallist was Cecil Healy (AUS) in the 1912 800m relay team aged 30 years 229 days. The oldest female champion/medallist was Ursula Happe (GER) in the 1956 200m breaststroke, aged 30 years 41 days. The oldest medallist was William Henry (GBR), a last-minute replacement in the 1906 relay, aged 46 years 301 days. The youngest gold medallist was Kyoko Iwasaki (JPN) in the 1992 women's 200m breaststroke in 1964, at 14 years six days. The youngest male champion/medallist was Kusuo Kitamura (JPN) in the 1500m in 1932 aged 14 years 309 days, while the youngest known individual event medallist in any sport at the Games was Inge Sörensen (DEN), aged 12 years 24 days winning a bronze in the 200m breaststroke in 1936.

The first dead heat in Games swimming came in the 1984 women's 100m freestyle final when Carrie Steinsteifer and Nancy Hogshead (both USA) gained a gold medal each. Also in those Games there was a strange situation when the winner of the 400m freestyle 'B' final, Thomas Fahrner (FRG), set an Olympic record faster than the winner of the 'A' final. The closest to a dead heat in the men's events was in the 1972 400m medley when Gunnar Larsson (SWE) was given the decision over Tim McKee (USA). The margin was 0.002 of a second, or about three millimetres (estimated to be the length grown by a fingernail in three weeks). Happily timings and placings are now decided to hundredths only, and the above would now be given as a dead heat. Another controversial decision occurred in the 1960 100m freestyle when Lance Larson (USA) was timed (manually, and by the unofficial automatic system) faster than John Devitt (AUS), but the judges placed the Australian first – and that is how the result remained despite protests. In 1968 poolside touch panels were introduced. Since 1984 only two competitors per country, per individual event, are allowed.

In the 1912 100m freestyle competition the three best American swimmers missed the semi-finals because they had been told that there would not be any. Following protests it was agreed that if they were timed, in a special race, at faster than the slowest qualifier from those semi-finals, then they would go forward to the final. The outstanding Hawaiian swimmer Duke Kahanamoku was so incensed that he broke the world record, and then won the final. At the next Games, in 1920, the final was re-swum after the Australian, William Herald, complained that he was impeded by Norman Ross (USA) – this was before lane dividers were used. The original winner, once again Duke Kahanamoku (USA), won again but in a slower time than before, but his first time of 60.4secs was recognised as a world record. Kahanamoku, the first of the great Hawaiian swimmers, was born into the Hawaiian Royal Family, and was named 'Duke' after the Duke of Edinburgh, Queen Victoria's second son, who was visiting the Palace at the time. He was a pioneer of surfing, and made many movies in Hollywood. He was the oldest individual event champion in 1920 when five days past his 30th birthday, until 1956 when Ursula Happe (GDR), 36 days older, won the 200m breaststroke. His brother Sammy won a bronze in the 1924 100m freestyle. The first brothers to win swimming gold medals at the same Games were Pua and Warren Kealoha (USA) in 1920, with the latter winner of the 100m backstroke and the former in the 4 x 200m relay.

Hollywood has attracted a number of Olympian swimmers: Romanian-born Johnny Weissmuller (USA) who won five gold medals 1924–8, and then became the most famous Tarzan of them all; Clarence 'Buster' Crabbe (USA), the 1932 400m champion, played Flash Gordon and Buck Rogers in the children's serials; Aileen Riggin (USA), the 1920 diving champion, and Eleanor Holm (USA), the 1932 backstroke champion, both women made careers in the movies. Holm was also in a Tarzan movie, in 1938 as Jane, to the hero played by 1936 decathlon champion Glenn Morris.

Gertrude Ederle (USA) and Greta Andersen (DEN), gold medallists in 1924 and 1948 respectively, both later set Channel swimming records. As a matter of interest, the first Olympian to swim the Channel, in 1934, was Edward Temme (GBR), who was in the fourth-placed British water polo team in 1928. Mexico's first ever swimming gold medallist, Felipe Muñoz who won the 1968 200m breaststroke, was nicknamed 'Tibio' which means 'lukewarm' in English. This was no reflection on his determination, but was the result of his father coming from Aguascalientes ('hot water') and his mother from Rio Frio ('cold river'). A change in rules for 1992 allowed female swimmers to wear two-piece costumes in competition – only a few competitors took advantage of this at the time, most notably the Italians.

SWIMMING MEDALLISTS, YOUNGEST AND OLDEST BY EVENT (age given in years and days)
MEN

Event	Medal	Youngest Yr/Dy	Name/Country	Date	Oldest Yr/Dy	Name/Country	Date
50m Freestyle	G	19-119	Anthony Ervin (USA)	2000	25-362	Gary Hall Jr (USA)	2000
	M	19-119	Anthony Ervin (USA)	2000	27-298	Tom Jager (USA)	1992
100m Freestyle	G	15-297	Yasuji Miyazaki (JPN)	1932	30-5	Duke Kahanamoku (USA)	1920
	M	15-297	Yasuji Miyazaki (JPN)	1932	33-330	Duke Kahanamoku (USA)	1924
200m Freestyle	G	18-342	Mike Wenden (AUS)	1968	22-201	Mark Spitz (USA)	1972
	M	17-345	Ian Thorpe (AUS)	2000	24-72	Andrei Krylov (URS)	1980
400m Freestyle	G	16-134	Otto Scheff (AUT)	1906	24-118	Norman Ross (USA)	1920
	M	16-134	Otto Scheff (AUT)	1906	34-61	John Jarvis (GBR)	1906
1500m Freestyle	G	14-309	Kusuo Kitamura (JPN)	1932	28-127	Vladimir Salnikov (URS)	1988
	M	14-309	Kusuo Kitamura (JPN)	1932	34-59	John Jarvis (GBR)	1906
4 x 100m Freestyle	G	17-343	Ian Thorpe (AUS)	2000	27-297	Tom Jager (USA)	1992
	M	16-338	Peter Bruch (GDR)	1972	27-321	Dirk Richter (GDR)	1992
4 x 200m Freestyle	G	15-299	Yasuji Mizayaki (JPN)	1932	30-229	Cecil Healy (AUS)	1912
	M	15-299	Yasuji Miyazaki (JPN)	1932	46-301	William Henry (GBR)	1906(*)
100m Breaststroke	G	21-73	Nobutaka Taguchi (JPN)	1972	24-117	Adrian Moorhouse (GBR)	1988
	M	18-93	John Hencken (USA)	1972	26-156	Mark Warnecke (GER)	1996
200m Breaststroke	G	17-226	Ian O'Brien (AUS)	1964	28-286	Yoshiyuki Tsoruta (JPN)	1932
	M	16-245	Reizo Koike (JPN)	1932	38-25	William Robinson (GBR)	1908
100m Backstroke	G	16-173	Warren Kealoha (USA)	1920	26-172	Jeff Rouse (USA)	1996
	M	16-173	Warren Kealoha (USA)	1920	28-15	Herbert Haresnape (GBR)	1908
200m Backstroke	G	17-7	Sándor Wladár (HUN)	1980	24-359	Lenny Krayzelburg (USA)	2000

Event	Medal	Yr/Dy	Name/Country	Date	Yr/Dy	Name/Country	Date
	M	17-7	Sándor Wladár (HUN)	1980	24-359	Lenny Krayzelburg (USA)	2000
100m Butterfly	G	19-48	Matt Vogel (USA)	1976	27-235	Pablo Morales (USA)	1992
	M	18-254	Mark Spitz (USA)	1968	27-235	Pablo Morales (USA)	1992
200m Butterfly	G	17-345	Jon Sieben (AUS)	1984	24-97	Michael Gross (FRG)	1988
	M	16-275	Neville Hayes (AUS)	1960	27-324	György Tumpek (HUN)	1956
200m Medley	G	20-105	Alex Baumann (CAN)	1984	25-58	Tamás Darnyi (HUN)	1992
	M	18-41	Attila Czene (HUN)	1992	25-58	Tamás Darnyi (HUN)	1992
400m Medley	G	17-18	Richard Roth (USA)	1964	25-54	Tamás Darnyi (HUN)	1992
	M	16-166	András Hargitay (HUN)	1972	25-349	Eric Namesnik (USA)	1996
4 x 100m Medley	G	18-2	Neil Brooks (AUS)	1980	27-239	Pablo Morales (USA)	1992
	M	16-274	Neville Hayes (AUS)	1960	30-94	Horst-Günter Gregor (GDR)	1968

WOMEN

		Youngest			Oldest		
Event	Medal	Yr/Dy	Name/Country	Date	Yr/Dy	Name/Country	Date
50m Freestyle	G	20-202	Yang Wenyi (CHN)	1992	27-30	Inge de Bruijn (NED)	2000
	M	15-252	Katrin Meissner (GDR)	1988	29-86	Angel Martino (USA)	1996
100m Freestyle	G	16-162	Sandra Nielson (USA)	1972	27-39	Dawn Fraser (AUS)	1964
	M	14-112	Franziska Van Almsick (GER)	1992	33-159	Dara Torres (USA)	2000
200m Freestyle	G	15-283	Shane Gould (AUS)	1972	27-48	Susie O'Neill (AUS)	2000
	M	14-113	Franziska Van Almsick (GER)	1992	27-273	Claudia Poll (CRC)	2000
400m Freestyle	G	15-281	Shane Gould (AUS)	1972	22-121	Dagmar Hase (GER)	1992
	M	14-156	Sylvia Ruuska (USA)	1956	27-271	Claudia Poll (CRC)	2000
800m Freestyle	G	15-190	Keena Rothhammer (USA)	1972	20-337	Janet Evans (USA)	1992
	M	15-70	Maria Teresa Ramirez (MEX)	1968	26-216	Dagmar Hase (GER)	1996
4 x 100m Freestyle	G	14-96	Lilian 'Pokey' Watson (USA)	1964	33-176	Dara Torres (USA)	2000
	M	13-310	Kornelia Ender (GDR)	1972	33-176	Dara Torres (USA)	2000
4 x 200m Freestyle	G	18-135	Christina Teuscher (USA)	1996	27-207	Jenny Thompson (USA)	2000
	M	16-152	Emma Johnson (AUS)	1996	30-289	Kerstin Kielgass (GER)	2000
100m Breaststroke	G	16-247	Megan Quann (USA)	2000	24-85	Tonya Dangalakova (BUL)	1988
	M	14-266	Amanda Beard (USA)	1996	25-315	Penny Heyns (RSA)	2000
200m Breaststroke	G	14-6	Kyoko Iwasaki (JPN)	1992	30-41	Ursula Happe (GER)	1956
	M	12-24	Inge Sörensen (DEN)	1936	30-41	Ursula Happe (GER)	1956
100m Backstroke	G	15-62	Beth Botsford (USA)	1996	23-259	Karen Harup (DEN)	1948
	M	14-38	Krisztina Egerszegi (HUN)	1988	25-135	Whitney Hedgepeth (USA)	1996
200m Backstroke	G	14-41	Krisztina Egerszegi (HUN)	1988	21-344	Krisztina Egerszegi (HUN)	1996
	M	14-41	Krisztina Egerszegi (HUN)	1988	25-138	Whitney Hedgepeth (USA)	1996
100m Butterfly	G	15-342	Sharon Stouder (USA)	1964	27-24	Inge de Bruijn (NED)	2000
	M	15-75	Andrea Pollack (GDR)	1976	33-155	Dara Torres (USA)	2000
200m Butterfly	G	15-72	Andrea Pollack (GDR)	1976	22-274	Kathleen Nord (GDR)	1988
	M	15-72	Andrea Pollack (GDR)	1976	27-49	Susie O'Neill (AUS)	2000
200m Medley	G	15-279	Shane Gould (AUS)	1972	21-295	Lin Li (CHN)	1992
	M	13-308	Kornelia Ender (GDR	1972	25-289	Lin Li (CHN)	1996
400m Medley	G	17-29	Gail Neall (AUS)	1972	21-200	Tracey Caulkins (USA)	1984
	M	16-99	Sabine Steinbach (GDR)	1968	25-27	Beatrice Caslaru (ROM)	2000
4 x 100m Medley	G	14-269	Amanda Beard (USA)	1996	29-90	Angel Martino (USA)	1996
	M	13-314	Kornelia Ender (GDR)	1972	33-161	Dara Torres (USA)	2000

* 4 x 250m

SWIMMING MEDALS
(Excluding diving, synchronised swimming and water polo)

	Men			Women			
	G	S	B	G	S	B	Total
United States	111	85	55	82	53	49	435
Australia*	29	27	35	16	19	16	142
East Germany (GDR)	6	7	5	32	25	17	92
Soviet Union	14	17	18	4	7	9	69
Germany	9	11	14	3	12	16	65
Great Britain	10	13	14	4	9	12	62
Hungary	14	14	11	10	6	5	60
Japan	12	17	11	3	3	3	49
The Netherlands	2	—	4	12	14	12	44
Canada	6	7	9	1	6	10	39

Sweden	8	10	10	—	4	3	35
West Germany (FRG)	3	4	7	—	1	7	22
France	2	5	9	—	2	3	21
China	—	—	—	5	11	3	19
Italy	3	1	6	—	1	2	13
Denmark	—	2	1	2	3	3	11
Austria	2	3	5	—	—	1	11
Russia	4	3	3	—	—	—	10
South Africa	—	1	—	3	—	5	9
Brazil	—	3	6	—	—	—	9
Greece	1	4	3	—	—	—	8
New Zealand*	3	1	2	—	—	1	7
Romania	—	—	—	2	2	3	7
Ireland	—	—	—	3	—	1	4
Ukraine	—	1	—	2	1	—	4
Belgium	1	1	1	—	—	1	4
Costa Rica	—	—	—	1	1	2	4
Spain	1	—	2	—	—	1	4
Finland	—	1	3	—	—	—	4
Bulgaria	—	—	—	1	1	1	3
Poland	—	1	1	—	—	1	3
Argentina	1	—	—	—	1	—	2
Yugoslavia	—	—	—	1	1	—	2
Mexico	1	—	—	—	—	1	2
Surinam	1	—	1	—	—	—	2
Slovakia	—	—	—	—	2	—	2
Cuba	—	1	1	—	—	—	2
Philippines	—	—	2	—	—	—	2
Switzerland	—	—	1	—	—	—	1
Venezuela	—	—	1	—	—	—	1
	244*†	**240**	**241‡**	**187§**	**185**	**188₡**	**1285**

* Double counting of the Australia/New Zealand relay team in 1912. † Two golds in 2000 50m freestyle. ‡ Third place in 1896 100m freestyle not known. § Two golds in 1984 100m freestyle. ₡ Two bronzes in 1988 50m freestyle and 2000 100m freestyle.

SYNCHRONISED DIVING

Held for the first time at the Games at Sydney in 2000. There were separate pairs events for men and women, in which they are judged on the synchronisation of their movements and the execution of their dives. (*See* Diving for medals tables).

SYNCHRONISED SWIMMING

Introduced into the Games in 1984, there were solo and duet events until 1996. At Atlanta they were replaced by a single team event, consisting of teams of eight women. Also, compulsory figures were replaced with a technical programme. In 2000 the duet was re-instated.

The most successful women have been Tracie Ruiz-Conforto (USA) and Carolyn Waldo (CAN) both with two golds and a silver in 1984–8. The youngest gold medallist was Tammy Cleland (USA) in 1996, aged 20 years 281 days, while the youngest medallist was Valerie Hould-Marchand (CAN) with a silver in 1996, aged 16 years 65 days. The oldest champions were Karen and Sarah Josephson (USA) in the 1992 duet, aged 28 years 210 days. The latter are among the most successful twins ever in Olympic swimming with their gold medal in 1992, to add to the silver from 1988. In 1992 the second place went to another set of twins, Penny and Vicky Vilagos of Canada, who are the oldest medallists at 29 years 112 days. In the 1992 solo event a mistake by a judge deprived Sylvie Frechette (CAN) from sharing the gold medal. In December 1993 the result was revised. The first ever 10.00 mark awarded in the Olympic Games was given to the winning Russian duet of Olga Brusnikina and Marija Kiselyeva in 2000. Anna Kozlova placed fourth in 1992 as a member of the Russian duet, and then placed fourth again in 2000 as a member of the American pair.

MEDALS

	G	S	B	Total
United States	5	2	—	7
Canada	3	4	1	8
Japan	—	2	7	9
Russia	2	—	—	2
France	—	—	1	1
	10*	8	9	27

* Tie for gold in 1992.

TABLE TENNIS

Recognised as an Olympic sport by the IOC in 1977, table tennis was first included in the 1988 Seoul Games as a medal sport, never having been a demonstration sport. There are 64 men and 32 women, selected by an agreed international formula, competing in men and women's singles and doubles events.

The most successful player has been Deng Yaping (CHN), only 1.50m (4ft 11in) tall, who successfully retained her singles and doubles titles from 1992 in 1996, thus totalling four gold medals in women's events. The most successful male was Guoliang Liu (CHN) with two golds in 1996, and two silvers in 2000 – Yoo Nam-Kyu (KOR) has also won four medals, comprising a gold and three bronzes 1988–96.

The youngest gold medallist was Hyun Jung-Hwa (KOR) in the 1988 women's doubles aged 18 years 360 days, while the youngest male champion was Yoo Nam-Kyu (KOR) winning the 1988 singles aged 20 years 119 days. The oldest gold medallist was Jan-Ove Waldner (SWE) winning the 1992 men's singles aged 26 years 308 days, and the oldest female champion was Hong Qiao (CHN) in the 1996 women's doubles, aged 27 years 251 days. The youngest female medallist was Jasna Fazlic (YUG) in the 1988 women's doubles, aged 17 years 285 days, and the youngest male medallist was Zoran Primorac (YUG) in 1988 at 19 years 143 days. The oldest female medallist was Yunping Giao (CHN) in the 1996 doubles, aged 27 years 320 days, and the oldest male medal winner was Jan-Ove Waldner (SWE) with silver in the 2000 singles aged 34 years 358 days.

TABLE TENNIS MEDALS

	Men			Women			
	G	S	B	G	S	B	Total
China	6	3	2	7	7	2	27
Korea	1	1	5	1	—	4	12
Sweden	1	1	1	—	—	—	3
Germany	—	1	1	—	—	—	2
Yugoslavia	—	1	—	—	—	1	2
North Korea (PRK)	—	—	—	—	—	2	2
France	—	1	1	—	—	—	2
Chinese Taipei	—	—	—	—	1	1	2
	8	8	10 *	8	8	10*	52

* Two bronze medals in 1992.

TAE KWON DO

A demonstration sport at Seoul in 1988 and at Barcelona in 1992, it was a medal sport at Sydney in the 2000 Games. The youngest gold medallist was Zhong Cheng (CHN) who won the women's over-67kg class aged 17 years 313 days, while the youngest male winner/medallist was Michael Mouroutsos (GRE) in the 58kg category, aged 20 years 211 days. The oldest champion was Lauren Burns (AUS), aged 26 years 111 days, when taking the 49-kg title, and the oldest male gold medallist was Kyong-Hun Kim (KOR) in the men's over-80kg class at 25 years 77 days. The oldest medallist was Faissal Ebnoutalib (GER) aged 29 years 314 days in the men's 80-kg class, and the oldest female medallist was Natalya Ivanova (RUS), aged 29 years 29 days in the over-67kg class. The youngest medallist was Shu-Ju Chi (TPE) in the women's 49-kg class, aged 17 years 308 days.

TAE KWON DO MEDALS

	Men			Women			
	G	S	B	G	S	B	Total
Korea	1	1	—	2	—	—	4
Australia	—	1	—	1	—	—	2
Cuba	1	—	—	—	1	—	2
Taipei	—	—	1	—	—	1	2
China	—	—	—	1	—	—	1
Greece	1	—	—	—	—	—	1
United States	1	—	—	—	—	—	1

Germany	—	1	—	—	—	—	1
Norway	—	—	—	—	1	—	1
Russia	—	—	—	—	1	—	1
Spain	—	1	—	—	—	—	1
Vietnam	—	—	—	—	1	—	1
Canada	—	—	—	—	—	1	1
France	—	—	1	—	—	—	1
Iran	—	—	1	—	—	—	1
Japan	—	—	—	—	—	1	1
Mexico	—	—	1	—	—	—	1
Turkey	—	—	—	—	—	1	1
	4	**4**	**4**	**4**	**4**	**4**	**24**

TALLEST

The tallest person ever to win an Olympic medal was Tom Burleson (USA) in the silver-medal team at Munich in 1972. He was 2.23m (7ft 4in) tall. A member of the 1988 winning Soviet basketball team in 1988, Arvidas Sabonis, who also won a bronze in the Lithuanian team in 1992, was reported to be as tall, but was actually 2.21m (7ft 3in), and is the tallest ever Olympic gold medallist. A member of the unplaced Chinese basketball team in 2000, Yao Ming, was reportedly 2.25m (7ft 4¼in) tall, but was actually 2.21m (7ft 3in) at the time. Probably the tallest ever gold medal winner of an individual athletics event at the Games was Walt Davis (USA), who was 2.04m (6ft 8¼in) tall when he won the 1952 high jump title.

The tallest female gold medallist was the Soviet basketball player Iuliana Semenova in the winning 1976 and 1980 teams. Although officially given as 2.10m (perhaps a misprint), this was obviously ridiculous, and closer investigation indicates that her correct height was 2.18m (7ft 2in).

The tallest competitor in the Winter Games was Sam Guss (AUS) who competed in the 1984 Alpine events at Sarajevo. He was 2.08m (6ft 10in) tall.

TELEVISION (*see also* 'Media')

Though television pictures were beamed by closed circuit to special halls around Berlin in 1936, the first true television pictures of the Games came in London in 1948, although to the very limited number of television receivers, estimated at 80,000, within range of the Wembley stadium. The first live international coverage of the Games came from Rome in 1960, with the Tokyo 1964 pictures the first to be sent by satellite. Live colour television was first broadcast from Mexico City in 1968.

The major providers of television income to the IOC and host cities have been the American networks, whose rivalry has pushed the sums involved ever upwards, as the following table of the winners of American TV rights shows:

	Summer	$(million)		Winter		$(million)
1960	CBS	0.394	1960	CBS		0.050
1964	NBC	1.5	1964	ABC		0.597
1968	ABC	4.5	1968	ABC		2.5
1972	ABC	7.5	1972	NBC		6.4
1976	ABC	25.0	1976	ABC		10.0
1980	NBC	87.0	1980	ABC		15.5
1984	ABC	225.0	1984	ABC		91.5
1988	NBC	300.0	1988	ABC		309.0
1992	NBC	401.0	1992	CBS		243.0
1996	NBC	456.0	1994	CBS		300.0
2000	NBC	705.0	1998	CBS		375.0
2004	NBC	793.0	2002	NBC		545.0
2008	NBC	894.0	2006	NBC		614.0
2012	NBC	1,181.0	2010	NBC		820.0

TENNIS

Tennis was excluded from the Games 1924–88, although it was a demonstration sport in 1968 and 1984. The first gold medallist was Irish-born John Pius Boland (GBR) in the 1896 singles. He was in Athens, visiting the famous German archaeologist Heinrich Schliemann, and entered the Games at the last minute. The women's singles champion in 1900, Charlotte Cooper (GBR), was until recently thought to be the first woman to win an Olympic title in any sport (*see* Women). In the early years a number of medal-winning pairs were composed of players from two countries, thus Boland combined with a German to win the first mixed-doubles title. The most successful player was Max Decugis (FRA) with a total of six medals comprising four golds, one silver and a bronze between

1900 and 1920. Britain's Kitty McKane won a record total for a woman of five (one gold, two silvers and two bronzes) in 1920 and 1924. At Sydney, in 2000, Venus Williams became only the second woman to win two gold medals at one Games, matching the feat of her countrywoman Helen Wills, in 1924.

The oldest gold medallist was George Hillyard (GBR) in the 1908 men's doubles, aged 44 years 160 days. The oldest female champion was Winifred McNair (GBR), aged 43 years 14 days in the women's doubles of 1920. She was also the oldest British female competitor to win a gold medal in any sport. The youngest gold medallist/medallist in tennis was Jennifer Capriati (USA), winner of the 1992 singles, aged 16 years 132 days, while the youngest male was Fritz Traun (GER), Boland's partner in 1896, aged 20 years 13 days. The youngest male medallist was Max Decugis (FRA) in 1900, aged 17 years 290 days. Six years later, he and his wife, Marie, won the mixed title, becoming the first married couple to win gold medals in the Olympic Games. Brothers Reggie and Laurie Doherty (GBR) added the 1900 Olympic title to the eight Wimbledon doubles championships they won. At Sydney in 2000 the American sisters Serena and Venus Williams took the women's doubles title, after the latter had won the singles.

Many of the greatest names in tennis have played in the Games and there have been over 30 gold medal winners who were also successful at Wimbledon. One of the most remarkable of these was Swiss-born Norris Williams (USA), who survived the sinking of the *Titanic* in 1912, swimming in icy water for over an hour, won the Croix de Guerre and the Legion d'Honneur in the First World War, a Wimbledon title in 1920, an Olympic gold medal in 1924 (mixed doubles), and died aged 77.

Both 1996 singles winners had fathers who were ex-Olympians; Andre Agassi's father, Emanoul Aghassian, boxed for Iran in 1948–52; Lindsay Davenport's father, Winthrop Davenport, played volleyball for the United States in 1968. Additionally, Indian bronze medallist Leander Paes's father won a bronze medal at hockey in 1972, the last medal in that sport won by India.

TENNIS MEDALS

	Men*			Women			
	G	S	B	G	S	B	Total
Great Britain	11	9	11	5	5	5	46
United States	7	5	6	9	—	4	31
France	6	5	6	2	2	1	22
Germany	3	2	2	—	2	—	9
Greece	—	4	2	1	1	1	9
Czechoslovakia†	1	—	5	—	1	1	8
Spain	—	3	1	—	2	2	8
Sweden	—	2	4	—	—	1	7
South Africa	3	2	—	—	—	—	5
Australia	1	1	1	—	—	2	5
Russia	1	—	—	—	1	—	2
FRG	—	—	—	1	—	1	2
Japan	—	2	—	—	—	—	2
Argentina	—	—	1	—	1	—	2
Czech Republic	—	—	—	—	1	1	2
The Netherlands	—	—	1	—	1	—	2
Croatia	—	—	2	—	—	—	2
Soviet Union	—	—	1	—	—	1	2
Canada	1	—	—	—	—	—	1
Switzerland	1	—	—	—	—	—	1
Austria	—	1	—	—	—	—	1
Denmark	—	—	—	—	1	—	1
Hungary	—	—	1	—	—	—	1
India	—	—	1	—	—	—	1
Italy	—	—	1	—	—	—	1
New Zealand	—	—	1	—	—	—	1
Belgium	—	—	—	—	—	1	1
Bulgaria	—	—	—	—	—	1	1
Norway	—	—	—	—	—	1	1
	35	36	47	18	18	23	171‡

* Includes mixed doubles. †Includes Bohemia. ‡ Two-country pairs counted as two medals.

TOBOGGANING

See under Lugeing and Skeleton sledding.

TORCH RELAY

In the Ancient Games a flame would burn at the altar of the statue of Zeus (one of the Seven Wonders of the World) during the period of the Games. In 1928, at Amsterdam, this was commemorated by a flame burning in the stadium throughout the competitions. The chairman of the organising committee of the Berlin Games in 1936, Carl Diem, had the idea of lighting the Olympic flame at Olympia in Greece, and then bringing it by a series of relay runners, across Europe, to the Olympic stadium in Berlin. It has been done ever since, including transportation by sea and air where necessary. The relay in 2000 is claimed as the longest ever, consisting of a distance of 51.195km (31,811 miles) covered by over 11,000 runners. A torch relay was inaugurated for the Winter Games in 1952.

TRAMPOLINING

At Sydney, in 2000, two events were added as part of the gymnastics programme. They were individual events for men and women. Competitions consisted of compulsory and optional routines.

The youngest/oldest male champion was Aleksandr Moskalenko (RUS) aged 30 years 323 days, while his female equivalent was his teammate Irina Karayeva aged 25 years 127 days. Moskalenko was also the oldest medallist. Karen Cockburn (CAN) was the youngest medallist at 19 years 356 days, while her teammate, Mathieu Turgeon, was the youngest male medallist at 21 years 52 days. The oldest female medallist was Oxana Tsyhuleva (UKR) aged 26 years 282 days.

TRAMPOLINING MEDALS

| | Men | | | Women | | | |
	G	S	B	G	S	B	Total
Russia	1	—	—	1	—	—	2
Canada	—	—	1	—	—	1	2
Australia	—	1	—	—	—	—	1
Ukraine	—	—	—	—	1	—	1

TREBLES

Uniquely Frank Kungler (USA) has won medals at three sports at the same Games. At St Louis in 1904 he won a silver at wrestling, a bronze at tug-of-war, and two bronzes at weightlifting. Another excellent treble attempt was by Viggo Jensen (DEN) at Athens in 1896 when he won a gold and silver in weightlifting, a silver and bronze in shooting, and placed fourth in the rope climb. Possibly the greatest treble in Olympic history, albeit all in the same sport, was that by the Czech distance runner, Emil Zátopek, who won the 5000m, 10,000m and marathon at Helsinki in 1952, all within eight days, including running a heat of the shorter distance.

TRIATHLON

Contested at the Games for the first time at Sydney in 2000. There were contests for men and women, and both consisted of a 1500-m swim, a 40km cycle and a 10km run.

The oldest and youngest gold medallist is Simon Whitfield (CAN) who won at Sydney aged 25 years 124 days; he is also the youngest medallist. The oldest medallist is Stephan Vuckovic (GER) aged 28 years 87 days. The oldest and youngest female gold medallist is Brigitte McMahon (SUI) the winner at Sydney, aged 33 years 175 days; she is also the oldest medallist. The youngest female medallist is her teammate, Magali Messmer, aged 29 years six days.

TRIATHLON MEDALS

| | Men | | | Women | | | |
	G	S	B	G	S	B	Total
Switzerland	—	—	—	1	—	1	2
Canada	1	—	—	—	—	—	1
Australia	—	—	—	—	1	—	1
Germany	—	1	—	—	—	—	1
Czech Republic	—	—	1	—	—	—	1

TUG-OF-WAR

This sport was part of the athletics programme 1900–20. Three men won a record two golds and one silver from 1908 to 1920: John Shepherd, Frederick Humphreys and Edwin Mills, all from Great Britain. The oldest gold medallist was Humphreys, aged 42 years 204 days in 1920, while the youngest was Karl Staaf (SWE) aged 19 years 101 days in 1900. There were some strange team compositions in the early days: the winning 1900 team was composed of three Swedes and three Danes; the 1904 competition was between American clubs; and the 1908 tournament was between British Police Clubs with the City of London Police beating their colleagues from Liverpool.

TUG-OF-WAR MEDALS

	G	S	B	Total
Great Britain	2	2	1	5
Sweden	2	—	1	3
United States	1	1	1	3
Denmark	1	—	—	1
Germany	1	—	—	1
France	—	1	—	1
Greece	—	1	—	1
The Netherlands	—	1	—	1
Belgium	—	—	1	1
	7*	6	4†	17

* Joint Denmark/Sweden team in 1900, which counted as two medals. † No bronze medals in 1900 or 1912.

TWINS

The first twins to win Olympic medals were Eric and Vilhelm Carlberg (SWE) in the 1908 shooting events. Four years later, at Stockholm, they became the first twins to win gold medals, in the duelling pistol 30m team event. The most successful have been the rowing twins, Bernd and Jörg Landvoigt (GDR), who won the coxless pairs in 1976 and 1980. Among women, the most successful are Karen and Sarah Josephson (USA), who won a silver and then a gold in the synchronised duet swimming events in 1988 and 1992.

VOLLEYBALL (see also Beach Volleyball)

Introduced into the Games in 1964 for men and women, volleyball has been dominated by Soviet teams. Their men's teams have played 51 matches losing only ten from 1964 to 1992 (when they failed to win a medal for the first time), and the Soviet women have played 37 matches, losing only five in the same period. The most successful players have been Regla Torres and Mireya Luis, both of Cuba, with three gold medals each, 1992–2000. It should be noted that Inna Ryskal (URS) won two golds and two silver medals 1964–76. The best by a male player was two golds and a silver by Yuriy Poyarkov (URS) 1964–72.

The oldest gold medallist was Georgi Mondsolevski (URS) aged 34 years 274 days in 1968, and the oldest female winner/medallist was Ludmila Buldakova (URS), aged 34 years 105 days in 1972. The youngest gold medallist was Regla Herrera (CUB) in 1992, aged 17 years 177 days, and the youngest male champion was Marcelo Negrao (BRA), aged 19 years 303 days in 1992. The oldest medallist was Bohumil Golián (TCH) winning a bronze in 1968, aged 37 years 215 days, while the youngest was Yevgeniya Artamonova of the Unified Team in 1992 at 17 years 22 days. The youngest male medallist was Aleksandr Savin (URS) in 1976, aged 19 years 29 days.

In 1996 beach volleyball tournaments for men and women were introduced.

VOLLEYBALL MEDALS

	Men			Women			
	G	S	B	G	S	B	Total
Soviet Union	3	2	1	4	3	—	13
Japan	1	1	1	2	2	1	8
United States	2	—	1	—	1	1	5
Cuba	—	—	1	3	—	—	4
Brazil	1	1	—	—	—	2	4
China	—	—	—	1	1	1	3
Poland	1	—	—	—	—	2	3
Italy	—	1	2	—	—	—	3
The Netherlands	1	1	—	—	—	—	2
Yugoslavia	1	—	1	—	—	—	2
East Germany (GDR)	—	1	—	—	1	—	2
Russia	—	1	—	—	1	—	2
Bulgaria	—	1	—	—	—	1	2
Czechoslovakia	—	1	1	—	—	—	2
Peru	—	—	—	—	1	—	1
Argentina	—	—	1	—	—	—	1
Korea	—	—	—	—	—	1	1
North Korea (PRK)	—	—	—	—	—	1	1
Romania	—	—	1	—	—	—	1
	10	10	10	10	10	10	60

WATER POLO

The first Olympic contest was won in 1900 by the Osborne Swimming Club, Manchester, representing Great Britain. Five players have won three gold medals each: George Wilkinson (GBR) 1900, 1908 and 1912; Paul Radmilovic and Charles Smith (both GBR) 1908–20; Dezsö Gyarmati and György Kárpáti (HUN) 1952, 1956 and 1964. Of these Radomilovic, Welsh-born of a Greek father and Irish mother, also won a gold in the 4 x 200m team in 1908. He, 1908–28, Gyarmati, 1948–64, and Gianni De Magistris (ITA), 1968–84, competed in a record five Olympic tournaments. However, the Hungarian is the most successful player, adding a silver in 1948 and a bronze in 1960, and becoming one of the few Olympians in any sport to win medals in five Games. Gyarmati is also part of a fine Olympic family, as his wife Éva Székely won a gold (1952) and a silver (1956) in the 200-m breaststroke, and their daughter, Andrea, won silver and bronze medals in the 1972 backstroke and butterfly events, respectively. She then added to the family total of medals by marrying Mihály Hesz (HUN), a canoeist with a gold (1968 K1) and a silver (1964 K1).

The oldest gold medallist was Charles Smith (GBR) aged 41 years 217 days in 1920, while the youngest was György Kárpáti (HUN) in 1952, aged 17 years 40 days. The oldest medallist was also Smith, while the youngest was Paul Vasseur (FRA) in 1900, aged 15 years 305 days. The first brothers to win gold medals in the same team were Ferenc and Alajos Keserü (HUN) in 1932; they were later matched by Tulio and Franco Pandolfini (ITA), in 1948. Georgi Mshvenieradze (URS) won a gold medal in 1980, going one better than his father, Piotr, who had gained a silver (1960) and a bronze (1956). A number of men have won medals in both swimming and water polo, the most notable being Johnny Weissmuller (USA) who gained a bronze in 1924, on the same day that he won two freestyle golds. Tim Shaw (USA), who won a silver medal in the 1976 400m freestyle, won another in the 1984 water polo competition.

The highest score by any team was 2000 when Russia beat Slovakia 21–5. In 1996 Italy beat Hungary 20–18 to set an aggregate record of 38. The biggest margin of victory came when the East German team beat the United Arab Emirates 19–2 in 1968. The most goals scored by an individual in one game are nine, by Zoran Jankovic of Yugoslavia against Japan in 1968, and by Manuel Estiarte for Spain against Brazil in 1984. Estiarte played in his sixth consecutive Olympic Games in 2000, and finally won a gold medal. In the winning Hungarian teams of 1932 and 1936, was Olivér Halassy, who had a leg amputated below the knee as a child.

In 2000, at Sydney, there was an inaugural tournament for women. The highest score in the women's Game was when Russia beat Kazakhstan 15–6: the victory margin of nine was also a record. The youngest gold medallist was Joanne Fox (AUS) aged 21 years 103 days, while the youngest medallist was Ericka Lorenz (USA) at 19 years 218 days. The oldest gold medallist was Debbie Watson (AUS) aged 34 years 361 days, and the oldest medallist was Maureen O'Toole (USA) at 39 years 183 days. Taryn Woods, a member of the winning Australian team at Sydney had her brother, Gavin, in the men's squad and their father, David, had played for Australia in the 1968, 1972 and 1976 tournaments.

WATER POLO MEDALS

	G	S	B	Total
Hungary	7	3	3	13
United States	1	4	4	9
Soviet Union	2	2	4	8
Yugoslavia	3	4	1	8
Italy	3	1	2	6
Belgium	—	4	2	6
Great Britain	4	—	—	4
France	1	—	3	4
Germany	1	2	—	3
Sweden	—	1	2	3
Spain	1	1	—	2
Russia	—	1	1	2
The Netherlands	—	—	2	2
Australia	1	—	—	1
Croatia	—	1	—	1
FRG	—	—	1	1
	24	24*	25*	73

* Two bronzes in 1900; two silvers and no bronze in 1904.

WATER SKIING

A demonstration sport, held at Kiel, Germany in 1972, with 36 competitors from 20 countries, with many of the best skiers in the world in attendance. Events were won by the following: Roby Zucchi (ITA); Ricky McCormick (USA); Willy Stähle (HOL); Liz Allan-Shetter (USA) and Sylvie Maurial (FRA).

WEIGHTLIFTING

Two events were held in 1896, consisting of one-arm and two-arm lifts. The first Olympic weightlifting champion was Viggo Jensen (DEN) who won the two-arm competition from Launceston Eliot (GBR); both had lifted the same weight, but the Briton had moved one of his feet. The positions were reversed in the other event. An amusing incident occurred when an attendant was having great trouble moving one of the weights. Prince George of Greece, a member of the organising committee and an immensely big and strong man, bent down and easily lifted it aside. Jensen was one of the first great all-rounders, as he won silver and bronze medals at pistol and rifle shooting, and placed fourth in the rope climb.

The sport was not included in the Games of 1900, 1908 or 1912. In 1920 the contests were decided in the aggregate of a one-hand snatch, a one-hand jerk and a two-hands jerk. In 1924 an additional two lifts were included: two-hands press and snatch. From 1928 to 1972 the result depended on the aggregate of three two-handed lifts: the press, snatch, and clean and jerk. In 1976 the press was eliminated, owing to difficulty in judging it correctly, and the total now is for the snatch, and the clean and jerk. At the suggestion of the IOC the forerunner of the International Weightlifting Federation (IWF) was formed in 1920 to control the sport.

Three men have won three gold medals: Naim Suleymanoglu (TUR) 1988–96, all in the featherweight category; Pyrros Dimas (GRE) 1992–2000, at light-heavyweight; and Kakhi Kakhiashvili (EUN/GRE) 1992–2000, at middle heavyweight and first heavyweight. Only Tommy Kono (USA), Norair Nurikyan (BUL) and Kakhiashvili have won gold medals in different categories. Kono won the 67.5kg (1952) and the 82.5kg (1956); Kakhiashvili won the 91kg (1992), 94kg (2000), and the 99kg (1996); more unusually Nurikyan moved down from the 60kg (1972) to the 56kg (1976). Norbert Schemansky (USA) has won the most medals with one gold, a silver and two bronze medals from 1948 to 1964. The oldest gold medallist was Rudolf Plukfelder (URS) in the 82.5kg class of 1964, aged 36 years 40 days, while Schemansky was the oldest medallist in 1964 aged 40 years 141 days. The youngest gold medallist was Zeng Guoqiang (CHN) who won the 52kg class in 1984, aged 19 years 133 days, and the youngest ever medallist was Andrei Socaci (ROM) who won a silver in 1984 in the 67.5kg category, aged 18 years 43 days. The oldest known competitor was 56-year-old Teunist Jonck (SAF) in 1952. It was originally reported that Mehmet Djemal (TUR), who competed in 1924, was only 13 years of age – this has proved to be untrue. Imre Földi (HUN) competed in five Games, 1960–76. The heaviest weightlifter ever at the Games was Mark Henry (USA) in 1996, when he weighed in at 184.92kg (407.5lbs). The greatest single weight lifted at the Games has been a clean and jerk of 260kg (573lb) by Andrei Chemerkin (RUS) in 1996, and by Hossein Rezazadeh (IRI), Tae-Hyun Kim (KOR) and Chermerkin again, all at Sydney in 2000.

The only brothers to win medals in the same event at the same Games were Yoshinobu and Yoshiyuki Miyake (JPN) who won gold and bronze medals respectively in the 60kg in 1968. Yoshinobu also won another gold and a silver, but Peter and James George (USA) hold the family record for medals with one gold, three silvers and a bronze from 1948 to 1960. The silver medallist in the 82.5kg class in 1948, Harold Sakata (USA), later gained fame portraying 'Oddjob' in the James Bond film Goldfinger. Incidentally the margin of victory, 37.5kg, of the winner in this event, Stanley Stanczyk (USA), was a record for Olympic competition. In the 1988 featherweight class (up to 60kg) Naim Suleymanoglu (TUR) – for whose emigration to Turkey, the Turkish government is reported to have paid $1 million to Bulgaria – set an Olympic record, equalling that for the next weight class.

Disqualification due to use of drugs has affected this sport more than most with the first cases, gold medallist Zbigniew Kaczmarek (POL), and silver medallist Blagoi Blagoyev (BUL), being disqualified in 1976. At the end of 1992 the old weight classes were abolished by the IWF and replaced by new ones, in an attempt to replace any of the old records that may have been set by drug users prior to the introduction of stricter controls.

At Sydney in 2000 there were further changes to the weight classes, and the introduction of events for women. In that competition the greatest single weight lifted was a clean and jerk of 165kg (364lb) by Ding Meiyuan (CHN). The heaviest competitor, and also the heaviest female competitor in Olympic Games history, was Cheryl Haworth (USA) who won a bronze in the heavyweight class weighing in at 138kg (304lb). The oldest winner was Tara Nott (USA) in the 48kg class, aged 28 years 130 days. The youngest medallist was Cheryl Haworth (USA), aged 17 years 156 days, and the oldest medallist was Erzsabet Markus (HUN), silver in the 69kg class aged 31 years 27 days. The biggest margin of victory was the 12.5kg (27lb) by Xia Yang (CHN) in the 53kg category.

WEIGHTLIFTING MEDALS

| | Men | | | Women | | | |
	G	S	B	G	S	B	Total
Soviet Union	44	25	2	—	—	—	71
United States	15	16	9	1	—	1	42
Bulgaria	11	16	7	—	—	—	34
Poland	4	4	19	—	1	—	28
China	7	7	8	4	—	—	26
Germany	5	7	10	—	—	—	22
Hungary	2	7	9	—	1	—	19
France	9	2	4	—	—	—	15

1. Five-time gold medal swimmer Johnny Weissmuller – later to personify *Tarzan*.

2. Katarina Witt in 1988, after her second consecutive figure skating gold medal.

3. A race against time, as Athens gets ready for the 2004 Games.

4. Britain's victorious curling team at Salt Lake City: Margaret Morton (Res), Janice Rankin, Fiona MacDonald, Debbie Knox, and Rhona Martin (Skip).

5. Germany won the 1998 four-man bob by one of the smallest margins ever – 0.06sec.

6. Nikki McCray winning her second gold medal with the USA basketball team in Sydney.

7. Mario Lemieux led the Canadian ice hockey team to its first gold medal for 50 years in 2002.

8. Australia's Ian Thorpe, one of the greatest swimmers of all time, and not yet 18 in Sydney.

9. The 'Thorpedo' – Ian Thorpe winning the Sydney
400m freestyle with a new world record.

10. The 1936 marathon champion, Kitei Son (left),
a Korean running for Japan, alongside runner-up,
Ernie Harper of Great Britain.

11. The remarkable Swedish marksman Oscar Swahn –
the oldest ever Olympic gold medallist.

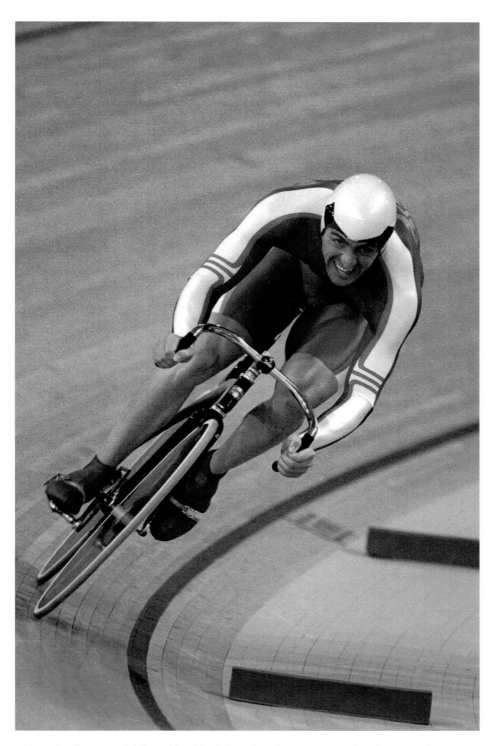

12. Jason Queally won Britain's first gold medal at Sydney, taking the 1000m time trial in Olympic record time.

13. Greece's Pyrros Dimas, in 1996, celebrating the second of his three consecutive gold medals in the light-heavyweight class.

14. Jacques Rogge, President of the International Olympic Committee (IOC).

15. Canada's Simon Whitfield wins the inaugural Olympic triathlon.

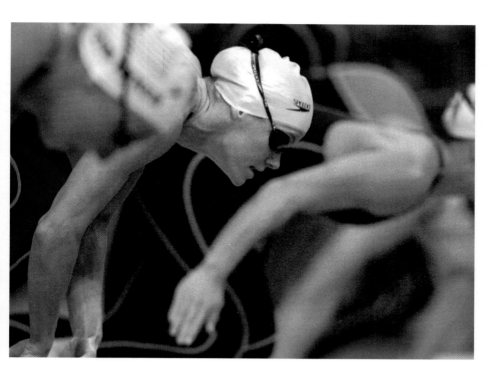

16. Triple gold medallist in 2000, Inge de Bruijn of the Netherlands.

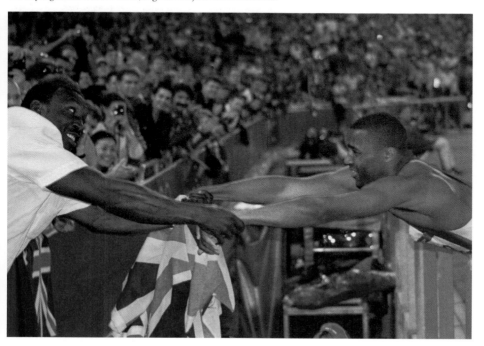

17. The Barcelona 100m sprint champion, Linford Christie (left), congratulates his protégé Darren Campbell on his silver medal in the Sydney 200m.

18. The outstanding gold medallists of 1984, Torvill and Dean, returned 10 years later to place third in the ice dancing at Lillehammer.

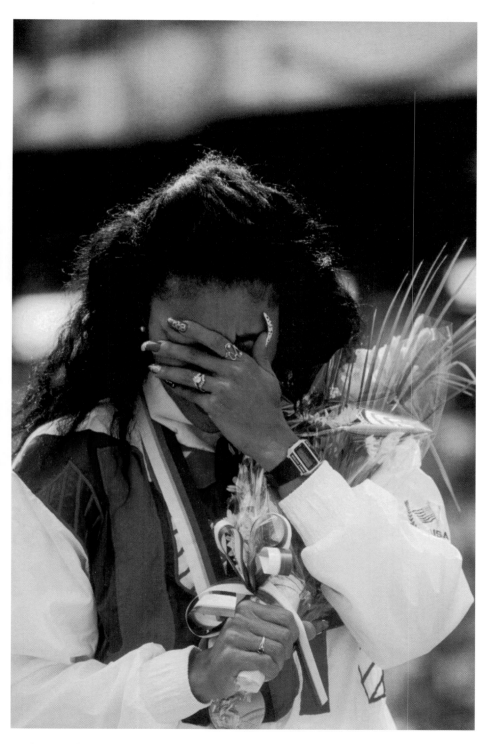

19. Florence Griffiths-Joyner (Flo-Jo), the double sprint gold medallist at Seoul.

20. "A-tishoo! A-tishoo! We all fall down." Australia's Steven Bradbury's favourite nursery rhyme?

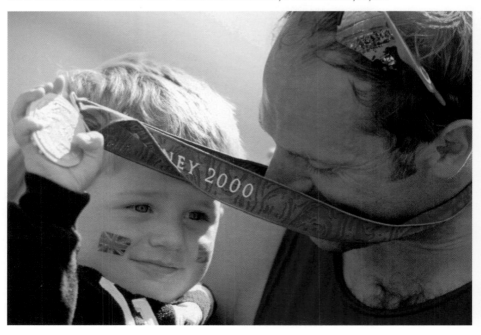

21. Super oarsman Steve Redgrave shares his fifth gold medal with his son in Sydney.

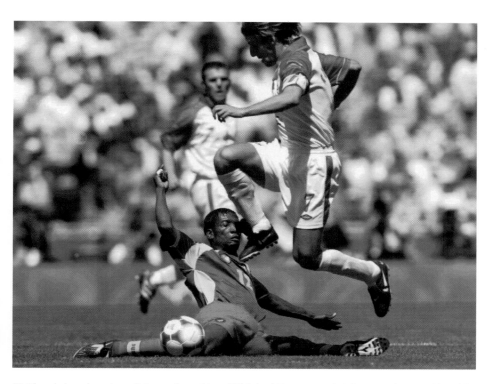

22. Though down here, Arsenal's Lauren Etame Mayer (12) helped Cameroon to their first ever Olympic gold medal in the 2000 soccer tournament.

23. The electrifying Opening Ceremony at the Lillehammer Winter Games.

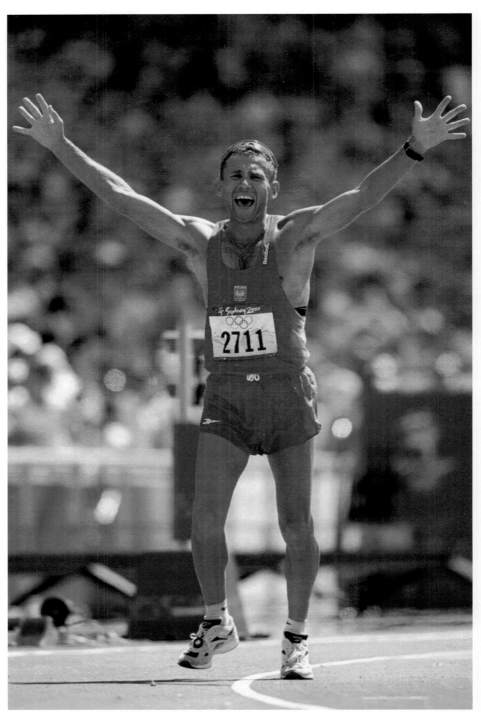

24. Robert Korzeniowski of Poland achieves a unique Olympic walking double by winning the 20km and 50km events in Sydney.

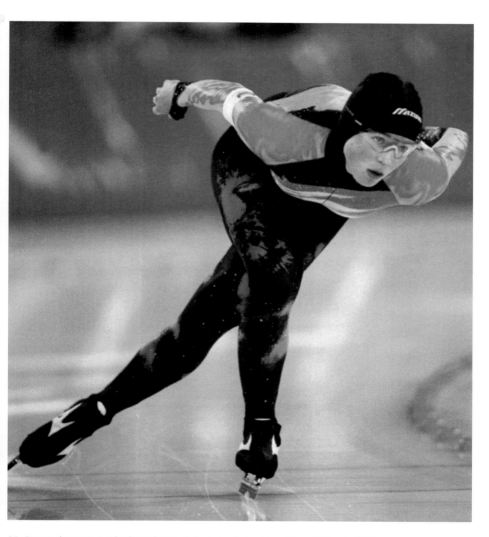

25. German distance ace, Claudia Pechstein, skates to her first gold medal, at 5000m, in 1994.

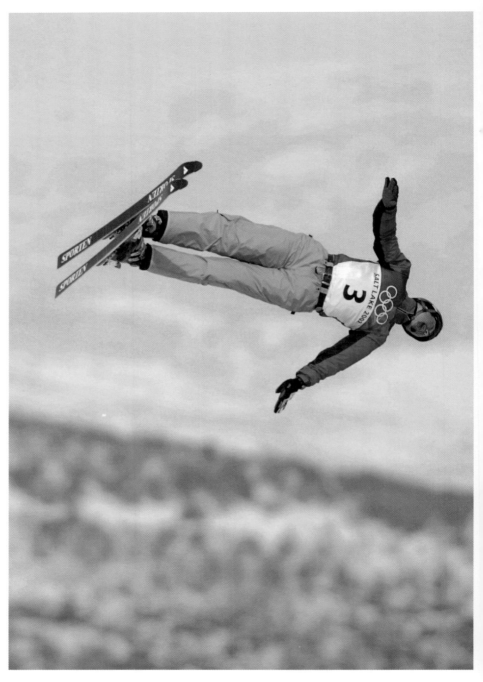

26. Salt Lake City gold medallist in the aptly named aerials section of the freestyle skiing, Aleš Valenta of the Czech Republic.

Greece	7	5	2	—	—	1	15
Italy	5	5	5	—	—	—	15
Japan	2	2	8	—	—	—	12
Austria	4	5	2	—	—	—	11
Iran	3	3	5	—	—	—	11
Romania	2	6	3	—	—	—	11
East Germany (GDR)	1	4	6	—	—	—	11
Egypt	5	2	2	—	—	—	9
Czechoslovakia	3	2	3	—	—	—	8
Great Britain	1	3	4	—	—	—	8
West Germany (FRG)	2	2	3	—	—	—	7
Estonia	1	3	3	—	—	—	7
Russia	2	1	2	—	1	—	6
Korea	1	1	4	—	—	—	6
North Korea (PRK)	—	2	3	—	1	—	6
Turkey	5	—	—	—	—	—	5
Cuba	2	1	1	—	—	—	4
Belgium	1	2	1	—	—	—	4
Australia	1	1	2	—	—	—	4
Switzerland	—	2	2	—	—	—	4
Sweden	—	—	4	—	—	—	4
Denmark	1	2	—	—	—	—	3
Chinese Taipei	—	—	1	—	1	1	3
Finland	1	—	2	—	—	—	3
Indonesia	—	—	—	—	1	2	3
Trinidad	—	1	2	—	—	—	3
The Netherlands	—	—	3	—	—	—	3
Ukraine	1	—	1	—	—	—	2
Canada	—	2	—	—	—	—	2
Argentina	—	1	1	—	—	—	2
Belarus	—	—	2	—	—	—	2
Colombia	—	—	—	1	—	—	1
Croatia	1	—	—	—	—	—	1
Mexico	—	—	—	1	—	—	1
Norway	1	—	—	—	—	—	1
Kazakhstan	—	1	—	—	—	—	1
Lebanon	—	1	—	—	—	—	1
Luxembourg	—	1	—	—	—	—	1
Nigeria	—	—	—	—	1	—	1
Singapore	—	1	—	—	—	—	1
Armenia	—	—	1	—	—	—	1
Georgia	—	—	1	—	—	—	1
India	—	—	—	—	—	1	1
Iraq	—	—	1	—	—	—	1
Qatar	—	—	1	—	—	—	1
Thailand	—	—	—	—	—	1	1
	150*	146	149†	7	7	7	466

* Tie for gold in 1928 and 1936 lightweight class. † Four-way tie for bronze in 1896; triple tie for bronze in 1906 heavyweight class; no bronze in 1992 light-heavyweight class.

WINTER GAMES

The first Winter Olympic Games were held at Chamonix, France in 1924. At first it was only called the International Winter Sports Week, in deference to the Scandinavian countries who worried that a Winter Olympic meeting would detract from the importance of their Nordic Games. It was only in 1926 that, retrospectively, it was accorded Olympic status. Prior to this there had been figure skating in London in 1908, and figure skating and ice hockey at Antwerp in 1920, both times as part of the Summer Games programme. (For details of venues, dates, and numbers of competitors, see Celebrations).

WINTER PENTATHLON

A demonstration sport held at St Moritz, Switzerland in 1948, and comprising a 10km cross-country skiing race, a pistol shoot, fencing, downhill skiing and horse-riding over a distance of 3500m. Gustaf Lindh (SWE) took first-place with his teammate Willie Grut second. Later that year Grut won the modern pentathlon in the Summer Games by a record margin. In sixth-place was Derek Allhusen (GBR) who, 20 years later in his 55th year, won an equestrian gold medal at Mexico City.

WOMEN, PARTICIPATION IN THE OLYMPIC GAMES

In the Ancient Games women were banned, under threat of death, from attending the Games, even as spectators. The only exceptions made were for the high priestesses of the most important gods. Nevertheless, it was possible for a woman to gain an Olympic prize as the owner of a winning chariot. One of the first to win in such a way was Belistike of Macedonia, the owner of the champion two-horse chariot in 268 BC. Some women defied the rules and they disguised themselves, but were found out and thrown over a cliff on discovery. It is recorded that Pherenice of Rhodes acted as a second to watch her son, Pisidores, win his event. In her excitement she gave herself away, but when it was realised that not only her son, but also her father and brothers had all been Olympic victors, she was pardoned.

There is a story, much revered by some, about a woman who was not allowed to run in the 1896 Olympic marathon itself, who actually ran the course the next day. Inevitably named, by contemporary sources, Melpomene, after the Greek muse of tragedy, her real name seems to have been Stamati Revithi, and reportedly she ran the 40km distance in about 4½ hours.

The founder of the Modern Games, Baron de Coubertin, was not in favour of women competing at the Games, but at Paris in 1900 women were allowed in specified events. It has always been thought that the first female Olympic champion was Charlotte Cooper (GBR), the winner of the women's tennis singles in the aforementioned Games, but new evidence now gives that honour to Helen, Countess de Pourtalès, a crew-member of the Swiss gold-medal yacht *Lerina* in the 1–2 Tonnes class at the same Games. She also becomes the first ever female Olympic competitor.

Women's swimming events were included for the first time at Stockholm in 1912, and athletics events came in at Amsterdam in 1928. Soccer was added, and proved very popular, in 1996. By the Sydney Games in 2000, there were 120 events for women, compared to 168 for the men, and another 12, which are mixed. In the Winter Games, female skaters were competing from the beginning, and Alpine Skiing events for women began, alongside the men, in 1936. In 1998 there was a women's ice hockey tournament, and in 2002 a two-woman bob event was introduced.

WRESTLING

Wrestling was the most popular sport in the ancient Games with victors recorded from 708 BC. The most famous was Milon of Kroton, a five-time winner. Greco-Roman wrestling was included in the 1896 Games and freestyle in 1904. Basically, holds are unlimited in freestyle, but in the Greco-Roman style holds below the waist are barred. There was no bodyweight limit in Athens and it was won, surprisingly, by gymnastics triple-gold medallist Carl Schuhmann (GER), who was only 1.63m (5ft 4in) tall, and who defeated Games weightlifting champion Launceston Eliot (GBR) in the preliminaries. A time limit was set in 1924, before then bouts often lasted for remarkable lengths of time. The most extreme was when Martin Klein, an Estonian representing Russia, and Alfred 'Alpo' Asikainen of Finland, in the 1912 Greco-Roman middleweight class, wrestled for 11 hours 40 minutes. Klein won, but was too exhausted to challenge for the gold medal. In the light-heavyweight final that year Anders Ahlgren (SWE), and Ivar Böhling (FIN), were declared equal second after nine hours without a decision, and no gold medal was awarded.

Four men have won three gold medals: Carl Westergren (SWE), 1920–32; Ivar Johansson (SWE) 1932–6; Aleksandr Medved 1964–72; and Aleksandr Karelin (URS/EUN/RUS) 1988–96. The latter also won a silver in 2000 (thus suffering his first defeat for 14 years). Karelin is also the only man to win three successive titles in the same event: Greco-Roman super-heavyweight. Johansson in 1932, and Kristjan Palusala (EST) in 1936, are the only men to win titles in both styles at the same Games, although Kaarle Antila (FIN) had achieved this distinction previously over a two-Games period 1920–4. Wilfried Dietrich (GER/FRG) won most medals with one gold, two silvers and two bronzes in both styles from 1956 to 1968, and competed in a record seven tournaments, both styles, 1956–72. Dietrich, 1956–72; Mario Tovar Gonzalez (MEX), 1952–68; Khorloo Baianmunkh (MGL), 1964–80; Czeslaw Kwiecinski (POL), 1964–80; and George Mackenzie (GBR), 1908–28, competed at a record five Games in the one style. Mackenzie also competed over a record span of 20 years. Although a number of brothers have each won gold medals, uniquely, two pairs of brothers, Ed and Lou Banach and Dave and Mark Schultz, all from the United States, won titles in 1984. The only twins to win gold medals were Anatoliy and Sergei Beloglazov (URS) in 1980, and Ed and Lou Banach (USA) in 1984. Kustaa and Hermanni Pihlajamäki (FIN), who won three golds, a silver and a bronze between 1924 and 1936, were not brothers, as often indicated, but cousins. What is thought to be a unique situation occurred in the freestyle 82-kg class in 1996, when Elmadi Zhabrailov (KZK) beat his brother Lucman representing Moldova. The first black champion was Kenny Monday (USA) in the 1988 freestyle welterweight division.

The oldest gold medallist/medallist was Adolf Lindfors (FIN) in 1920 aged 41 years 199 days. The youngest champion was Saban Trstena (YUG) in 1984 aged 19 years 222 days, and the youngest medallist was Nasser Givechi (IRN) in 1952 aged 16 years 254 days. The heaviest competitor ever in any Olympic event was the 1972 super-heavyweight bronze medallist Chris Taylor (USA) who weighed between 182kg (401lb) and 190kg

(419lb). When Osamu Watanabe (JPN) won the 1964 freestyle featherweight title it was his 186th successive victory in the sport. After gaining the silver medal in the 1920 unlimited class, Nat Pendleton first turned professional, and then went to Hollywood and appeared in many films, usually playing 'dumb ox' roles.

WRESTLING MEDALS

	Freestyle			Greco-Roman			
	G	S	B	G	S	B	Total
Soviet Union	31	17	15	37	19	13	132
United States	45	34	24	3	6	4	116
Finland	8	7	11	19	21	19	85
Sweden	8	10	8	2	16	19	81
Bulgaria	7	17	9	9	14	7	63
Turkey	16	11	7	11	4	3	52
Hungary	3	4	7	15	10	11	50
Japan	16	9	8	4	5	2	44
Romania	1	—	4	6	8	13	32
Germany	1	3	3	4	13	8	32
Korea	4	8	7	5	2	5	31
Iran	5	9	12	—	1	1	28
Poland	—	1	3	5	8	6	23
Russia	7	2	—	3	4	3	19
Italy	1	—	—	5	4	9	19
Great Britain	3	4	10	—	—	—	17
Yugoslavia	1	1	2	3	5	4	16
Czechoslovakia	—	1	3	1	6	4	15
Cuba	1	1	3	3	3	2	13
France	2	2	4	1	2	2	13
Switzerland	4	4	3	—	—	1	12
Denmark	—	—	—	2	3	7	12
Canada	1	5	5	—	—	—	11
Estonia	2	1	—	3	—	4	10
Greece	—	—	2	1	3	4	10
FRG	—	1	3	1	3	1	9
North Korea (PRK)	3	2	3	—	—	1	9
Mongolia	—	4	4	—	—	—	8
East Germany (GDR)	—	2	1	2	1	1	7
Austria	—	—	1	1	2	2	6
Ukraine	—	1	2	1	1	1	6
Egypt (UAR)	—	—	—	1	2	2	5
Norway	—	1	—	2	1	1	5
Belgium	—	3	—	—	—	1	4
Belarus	—	—	—	—	2	2	4
Georgia	—	—	2	—	—	2	4
Kazakhstan	—	1	1	1	—	—	3
Australia	—	1	2	—	—	—	3
Lebanon	—	—	—	—	1	2	3
China	—	—	—	—	—	3	3
Azerbaijan	1	1	—	—	—	—	2
Armenia	—	1	—	1	—	—	2
Latvia	—	—	—	—	1	—	1
Mexico	—	—	—	—	1	—	1
Uzbekistan	—	1	—	—	—	—	1
Syria	—	1	—	—	—	—	1
India	—	—	1	—	—	—	1
Macedonia	—	—	1	—	—	—	1
Moldova	—	—	—	—	—	1	1
Pakistan	—	—	1	—	—	—	1
	171	**171**	**172***	**170†**	**172**	**171‡**	**1027**

* Two bronzes in the1920s heavyweight class. † No gold in 1912 light-heavyweight class. ‡ No bronze in 1906 all-around class.

YOUNGEST

The youngest competitor, and indeed medallist, in the Olympic Games, except for the unconfirmed report of a an even younger rowing cox in 1900, was gymnast Dimitrios Loundras (GRE) in the bronze-medal team in 1896, aged 10 years 218 days. The youngest female participant was the British skater, Cecilia Colledge in 1932, aged 11 years 73 days. (Four years later she won a silver medal). The youngest female competitor, and medallist, in any Summer Games sport was Luigina Giavotti (ITA) in the 1928 silver-medal gymnastic team at 11 years 302 days. The youngest to win a medal in an individual event was Inge Sörensen (DEN) in 1936 with a 200m breaststroke bronze, aged 12 years 24 days, while the youngest male medallist in an individual event was Nils Skoglund (SWE) in the 1920 diving, aged 14 years 11 days. At Berlin in 1936 diver Marjorie Gestring (USA) became the youngest ever female gold medallist,

aged 13 years 267 days. The youngest known male gold medallist was Klaus Zerta, cox of the winning German pair in 1960 aged 13 years 283 days. The youngest male to win an individual event gold medal was swimmer Kusuo Kitamura (JPN) in the 1932 1500m freestyle aged 14 years 309 days.

The youngest male competitor in the Winter Games was figure skater Jan Hoffmann (GDR), aged 12 years 110 days in 1968. (Later, in 1980 he gained a silver medal). The youngest ever medallist/gold medallist at the Winter Games was Kim Yoon-Mi (KOR) in the women's short-track speed-skating relay in 1994, aged 13 years 83 days. In 1964 Scott Allen (USA) became the youngest male Winter medallist with a figure skating bronze, aged 14 years 363 days. The youngest male gold medallist was Finnish ski-jumper Toni Nieminen in 1992, aged 16 years 259 days.

MEDAL TABLES
BY SPORT AND YEAR

The tables below indicate medallists by sport and year. These tables have been split by Summer and Winter Games with Winter medals tables starting with Alpine Skiing on page 259. Over the years the scoring methods for various sports and/or events have changed making comparisons over time difficult.

Please also note that the scoring references, i.e. points (pts), relate to all medallists within a table – due to space constraints the scoring reference has only been included in the gold medallist column.

ABBREVIATIONS AND TIMINGS
Data not available (d.n.a.)
No times available (n.t.a.)
Kilograms (kg)
Placings (pl)
Metres (m)
Points (pts)

FRG referes to West Germany, GDR refers to East Germany.
Timed events are indicated in seconds (14.67), minutes (1:14.67) and hours (2hr 1:15.67)

SUMMER

ARCHERY MEDALS 1972–2000

DOUBLE FITA ROUND (Maximum possible score 2880 points)
MEN

	Gold	Silver	Bronze
1972	John Williams (USA) 2528pts	Gunnar Jarvil (SWE) 2481	Kyösti Lassonen (FIN) 2467
1976	Darrell Pace (USA) 2571pts	Hiroshi Michinaga (JPN) 2502	Giancarlo Ferrrari (ITA) 2495
1980	Tomi Poikolainen (FIN) 2455pts	Boris Isachenko (URS) 2452	Giancarlo Ferrari (ITA) 2449
1984	Darrell Pace (USA) 2616pts*	Richard McKinney (USA) 2564	Hiroshi Yamamoto (JPN) 2563
1988	Jay Barrs (USA) 338 pts (2605)	Park Sung-Soo (KOR) 336 (2614)	Vladimir Yecheyev (URS) 335 (2600)
1992†	Sebastien Flute (FRA)	Chung Jae-Hun (KOR)	Simon Terry (GBR)
1996†	Justin Huish (USA)	Magnus Petersson (SWE)	Oh Kyun-Moon (KOR)
2000†	Simon Fairweather (AUS)	Victor Wonderle (USA)	Wietse van Alten (NED)

* Olympic record. † Due to further rule changes point scores are no longer comparable with previous results.

WOMEN

	Gold	Silver	Bronze
1972	Doreen Wilber (USA) 2424pts	Irena Szydlowska (POL) 2407	Emma Gapchenko (URS) 2403
1976	Luann Ryon (USA) 2499pts	Valentina Kovpan (URS) 2460	Zebeniso Rustamova (URS) 2407
1980	Keto Losaberidze (URS) 2491pts	Natalya Butuzova (URS) 2477	Päivi Meriluoto (FIN) 2449
1984	Seo Hyang-Soon (KOR) 2568pts	Li Lingjuan (CHN) 2559	Kim Jin-Ho (KOR) 2555
1988	Kim Soo-Nyung * (KOR) 344pts (2683)	Wang Hee-Kyung (KOR) 332 (2612)	Yung Young-Sook (KOR) 327 (2603)
1992†	Cho Youn-Jeong (KOR)	Kim Soo-Nyung (KOR)	Natalia Valeyeva (EUN)
1996†	Kim Kyung-Wook (KOR)	He Ying (CHN)	Olena Sadovnycha (UKR)
2000†	Mi-Jin Yun (KOR)	Nam-Soon Kim (KOR)	Soo-Nyung Kim (KOR)

* Olympic record. † Due to further rule changes point scores are no longer comparable with previous results.

TEAM-MEN

	Gold	Silver	Bronze
1988	Korea	United States	Great Britain
1992	Spain	Finland	Great Britain
1996	United States	Korea	Italy
2000	Korea	Italy	United States

TEAM-WOMEN

	Gold	Silver	Bronze
1988	Korea	Indonesia	United States
1992	Korea	China	Unified Team

	Gold	*Silver*	*Bronze*
1996	Korea	Germany	Poland
2000	Korea	Ukraine	Germany

DISCONTINUED EVENTS
MEN

	Gold	*Silver*	*Bronze*
1900	AU CORDON DORÉ-50M		
	Henri Hérouin (FRA)	Hubert van Innis (BEL)	Emile Fisseux (FRA)
	AU CORDON DORÉ-33M		
	Hubert van Innis (BEL)	Victor Thibaud (FRA)	Charles Petit (FRA)
	AU CHAPELET-50M		
	Eugène Mougin (FRA)	Henri Helle (FRA)	Emile Mercier (FRA)
	AU CHAPELET-33M		
	Hubert van Innis (BEL)	Victor Thibaud (FRA)	Charles Petit (FRA)
	SUR LA PERCHE À LA HERSE		
	Emmanuel Foulon (FRA)	Pierre Serrurier (FRA)	Emile Druart Jr (BEL)
	SUR LA PERCHE À LA PYRAMIDE		
	Emile Grumiaux (FRA)	Auguste Serrurier (FRA)	Louis Glineaux (BEL)
1904	DOUBLE YORK ROUND		
	Phillip Bryant (USA)	Robert Williams (USA)	William Thompson (USA)
	DOUBLE AMERICAN ROUND		
	Phillip Bryant (USA)	Robert Williams (USA)	William Thompson (USA)
	TEAM ROUND		
	Potomac Archers (USA)	Cincinnati Archery Club (USA)	Boston AA (USA)
1908	MEN		
	YORK ROUND		
	William Dod (GBR)	Reginald Brooks-King (GBR)	Henry Richardson (USA)
	CONTINENTAL STYLE		
	Eugène Grisot (FRA)	Louis Vernet (FRA)	Gustave Cabaret (FRA)

WOMEN

	DOUBLE NATIONAL ROUND		
	Lida Howell (USA)	Jessie Pollack (USA)	Emma Cooke (USA)
	DOUBLE COLUMBIA ROUND		
	Lida Howell (USA)	Emma Cooke (USA)	Jessie Pollack (USA)
	NATIONAL ROUND		
	Queenie Newall (GBR)	Charlotte Dod (GBR)	Beatrice Hill-Lowe (GBR)
1920	MEN		
	FIXED BIRD TARGET-SMALL BIRDS-INDIVIDUAL		
	Edmond van Moer (BEL)	Louis van de Perck (BEL)	Joseph Hermans (BEL)
	FIXED BIRD TARGET-SMALL BIRDS-TEAM		
	Belgium	—	—
	FIXED BIRD TARGET-LARGE BIRDS-INDIVIDUAL		
	Edouard Cloetens (BEL)	Louis van der Perck (BEL)	Firmin Flamand (BEL)
	FIXED BIRD TARGET-LARGE BIRDS-TEAM		
	Belgium	—	—
	MOVING BIRD TARGET-28M-INDIVIDUAL		
	Hubert van Innis (BEL)	Léone Quentin (FRA)	—
	MOVING BIRD TARGET-TEAM		
	The Netherlands	Belgium	France
	MOVING BIRD TARGET-33M-INDIVIDUAL		
	Hubert van Innis (BEL)	Julien Brulé (FRA)	—
	MOVING BIRD TARGET-33M-TEAM		
	Belgium	France	—
	MOVING BIRD TARGET-50M-INDIVIDUAL		
	Julien Brulé (FRA)	Hubert van Innis (BEL)	—
	MOVING BIRD TARGET-50M-TEAM		
	Belgium	France	—

ATHLETICS MEDALS

MEN

Figures shown in brackets are the automatic times which were not used officially at those Games.

100 METRES

	Gold	Silver	Bronze
1896	Thomas Burke (USA) 12.0	Fritz Hofmann (GER) 12.2	Alajos Szokolyi (HUN) 12.6
1900	Frank Jarvis (USA) 11.0	Walter Tewksbury (USA) 11.1	Stanley Rowley (AUS) 11.2
1904	Archie Hahn (USA) 11.0	Nathaniel Cartmell (USA) 11.2	William Hogenson (USA) 11.2
1906	Archie Hahn (USA) 11.2	Fay Moulton (USA) 11.3	Nigel Barker (AUS) 11.3
1908	Reginald Walker (RSA) 10.8	James Rector (USA) 10.9	Robert Kerr (CAN) 11.0
1912	Ralph Craig (USA) 10.8	Alvah Meyer (USA) 10.9	Donald Lippincott (USA) 10.9
1920	Charles Paddock (USA) 10.8	Morris Kirksey (USA) 10.8	Harry Edward (GBR) 11.0
1924	Harold Abrahams (GBR) 10.6	Jackson Scholz (USA) 10.7	Arthur Porritt (NZL) 10.8
1928	Percy Williams (CAN) 10.8	Jack London (GBR) 10.9	Georg Lammers (GER) 10.9
1932	Eddie Tolan (USA) 10.3 (10.38)	Ralph Metcalfe (USA) 10.3 (10.38)	Arthur Jonath (GER) 10.4 (10.50)
1936	Jesse Owens (USA) 10.3	Ralph Metcalfe (USA) 10.4	Martinus Osendarp (NED) 10.5
1948	Harrison Dillard (USA) 10.3	Norwood Ewell (USA) 10.4	Lloyd La Beach (PAN) 10.4
1952	Lindy Remigino (USA) 10.4 (10.79)	Herb McKenley (JAM) 10.4 (10.80)	Emmanuel McDonald Bailey (GBR) 10.4 (10.83)
1956	Bobby Joe Morrow (USA) 10.5 (10.62)	Thane Baker (USA) 10.5 (10.77)	Hector Hogan (AUS) 10.6 (10.77)
1960	Armin Hary (GER) 10.2 (10.32)	David Sime (USA) 10.2 (10.35)	Peter Radford (GBR) 10.3 (10.42)
1964	Bob Hayes (USA) 10.0 (10.06)*	Enrique Figuerola (CUB) 10.2 (10.25)	Harry Jerome (CAN) 10.2 (10.27)
1968	James Hines (USA) 9.9 (9.95)	Lennox Miller (JAM) 10.0 (10.04)	Charles Greene (USA) 10.0 (10.07)
1972	Valeri Borzov (URS) 10.14	Robert Taylor (USA) 10.24	Lennox Miller (JAM) 10.33
1976	Hasely Crawford (TRI) 10.06	Don Quarrie (JAM) 10.08	Valeri Borzov (URS) 10.14
1980	Allan Wells (GBR) 10.25	Silvio Leonard (CUB) 10.25	Petar Petrov (BUL) 10.39
1984	Carl Lewis (USA) 9.99†	Sam Graddy (USA) 10.19	Ben Johnson (CAN) 10.22
1988	Carl Lewis (USA) 9.92†	Linford Christie (GBR) 9.97	Calvin Smith (USA) 9.99
1992	Linford Christie (GBR) 9.96	Frankie Fredericks (NAM) 10.02	Dennis Mitchell (USA) 10.04
1996	Donovan Bailey (CAN) 9.84	Frankie Fredericks (NAM) 9.89	Ato Boldon (TRI) 9.90
2000	Maurice Greene (USA) 9.87	Ato Boldon (TRI) 9.99	Obadele Thompson (BAR) 10.04

* Hayes ran a wind-assisted 9.91 in the semi-final. † Ben Johnson (CAN) won in 9.79 but was later disqualified.

200 METRES

	Gold	Silver	Bronze
1900	Walter Tewksbury (USA) 22.2	Norman Pritchard (GBR) 22.8	Stanley Rowley (AUS) 22.9
1904*	Archie Hahn (USA) 21.6	Nathaniel Cartmell (USA) 21.9	William Hogenson (USA) d.n.a.
1908	Robert Kerr (CA) 22.6	Robert Cloughen (USA) 22.6	Nathaniel Cartmell (USA) 22.7
1912	Ralph Craig (USA) 21.7	Donald Lippincott (USA) 22.1	Willie Applegarth (GBR) 22.0
1920	Allen Woodring (USA) 22.0	Charles Paddock (USA) 22.1	Harry Edward (GBR) 22.2
1924	Jackson Scholz (USA) 21.6	Charles Paddock (USA) 21.7	Eric Liddell (GBR) 21.9
1928	Percy Williams (CAN) 21.8	Walter Rangeley (GBR) 21.9	Helmut Kornig (GER) 21.9†
1932	Eddie Tolan (USA) 21.2 (21.12)	George Simpson (USA) 21.4	Ralph Metcalfe (USA) 21.5‡
1936	Jesse Owens (USA) 20.7	Mack Robinson (USA) 21.1	Martinus Osendarp (NED) 21.3
1948	Mel Patton (USA) 21.1	Norwood Ewell (USA) 21.1	Lloyd La Beach (PAN) 21.2
1952	Andrew Stanfield (USA) 20.7 (20.81)	Thane Baker (USA) 20.8 (20.97)	James Gathers (USA) 20.8 (21.08)
1956	Bobby Joe Morrow (USA) 20.6 (20.75)	Andrew Stanfield (USA) 20.7 (20.97)	Thane Baker (USA) 20.9 (21.05)
1960	Livio Berruti (ITA) 20.5 (20.62)	Lester Carney (USA) 20.6 (20.69)	Abdoulaye Seye (FRA) 20.7 (20.83)
1964	Henry Carr (USA) 20.3 (20.36)	Paul Drayton (USA) 20.5 (20.58)	Edwin Roberts (TRI) 20.6 (20.63)
1968	Tommie Smith (USA) 19.8 (19.83)	Peter Norman (AUS) 20.0 (20.06)	John Carlos (USA) 20.0 (20.10)
1972	Valeri Borzov (URS) 20.00	Larry Black (USA) 20.19	Pietro Mennea (ITA) 20.30
1976	Don Quarrie (JAM) 20.23	Millard Hampton (USA) 20.29	Dwayne Evans (USA) 20.43
1980	Pietro Mennea (ITA) 20.19	Allan Wells (GBR) 20.21	Don Quarrie (JAM) 20.29
1984	Carl Lewis (USA) 19.80	Kirk Baptiste (USA) 19.96	Thomas Jefferson (USA) 20.26
1988	Joe DeLoach (USA) 19.75	Carl Lewis (USA) 1979	Robson da Silva (BRA) 20.04
1992	Mike Marsh (USA) 20.01	Frankie Fredericks (NAM) 20.13	Michael Bates (USA) 20.38

| 1996 | Michael Johnson (USA) 19.32 | Frankie Fredericks (NAM) 19.68 | Ato Boldon (TRI) 19.80 |
| 2000 | Konstadinos Kederis (GRE) 20.09 | Darren Campbell (GBR) 20.14 | Ato Boldon (TRI) 20.20 |

1896 and 1906 event not held. * Race was over a straight course. Hahn's three opponents were all given 2yd handicaps for false starts. †
Awarded bronze medal when Scholz (USA) refused to re-run after tie. ‡ Metcalfe's lane was later found to be 1.5m too long.

400 METRES

	Gold	Silver	Bronze
1896	Thomas Burke (USA) 54.2	Herbert Jamison (USA) 55.2	Fritz Hofmann (GER) 55.6
1900	Maxey Long (USA) 49.4	William Holland (USA) 49.6	Ernst Schultz (DEN) 15m
1904	Harry Hillman (USA) 49.2	Frank Waller (USA) 49.9	Herman Groman (USA) 50.0
1906	Paul Pilgrim (USA) 53.2	Wyndham Halswelle (GBR) 53.8	Nigel Barker (AUS) 54.1
1908*	Wyndham Halswelle (GBR) 50.0	—	—
1912	Charles Reidpath (USA) 48.2	Hanns Braun (GER) 48.3	Edward Lingberg (USA) 48.4
1920	Bevil Rudd (RSA) 49.6	Guy Butler (GBR) 49.9	Nils Engdahl (SWE) 50.0
1924	Eric Liddell (GBR) 47.6	Horatio Fitch (USA) 48.4	Guy Butler (GBR) 48.6
1928	Ray Barbuti (USA) 47.8	James Ball (CAN) 48.0	Joachim Büchner (GER) 48.2
1932	William Carr (USA) 46.2 (46.28)	Ben Eastman (USA) 46.4 (46.50)	Alexander Wilson (CAN) 47.4
1936	Archie Williams (USA) 46.5 (46.66)	Godfrey Brown (GBR) 46.7 (46.68)	James LuValle (USA) 46.8 (46.84)
1948	Arthur Wint (JAM) 46.2	Herb McKenley (JAM) 46.4	Mal Whitfield (USA) 46.6
1952	George Rhoden (JAM) 45.9 (46.09)	Herb McKenley (JAM) 45.9 (46.20)	Ollie Matson (USA) 46.8 (46.94)
1956	Charles Jenkins (USA) 46.7 (46.85)	Karl-Friedrich Haas (GER) 46.8 (47.12)	Voitto Hellsten (FIN) 47.0 (47.15) Ardalion Ignatyev (URS) 47.0 (47.15)
1960	Otis Davis (USA) 44.9 (45.07)	Carl Kaufmann (GER) 44.9 (45.08)	Mal Spence (RSA) 45.5 (45.60)
1964	Mike Larrabee (USA) 45.1 (45.15)	Wendell Mottley (TRI) 45.2 (45.24)	Andrzej Badenski (POL) 45.6 (45.64)
1968	Lee Evans (USA) 43.8 (43.86)	Lawrence James (USA) 43.9 (43.97)	Ron Freeman (USA) 44.4 (44.41)
1972	Vince Matthews (USA) 44.66	Wayne Collett (USA) 44.80	Julius Sang (KEN) 44.92
1976	Alberto Juantorena (CUB) 44.26	Fred Newhouse (USA) 44.40	Herman Frazier (USA) 44.95
1980	Viktor Markin (URS) 44.60	Rick Mitchell (AUS) 44.84	Frank Schaffer (GDR) 44.87
1984	Alonzo Babers (USA) 44.27	Gabriel Tiacoh (CIV) 44.54	Antonio McKay (USA) 44.71
1988	Steve Lewis (USA) 43.87	Butch Reynolds (USA) 43.93	Danny Everett (USA) 44.09
1992	Quincy Watts (USA) 43.50	Steve Lewis (USA) 44.21	Samson Kitur (KEN) 44.24
1996	Michael Johnson (USA) 43.49	Roger Black (GBR) 44.41	Davis Kamoga (UGA) 44.53
2000	Michael Johnson (USA) 43.84	Alvin Harrison (USA) 44.40	Greg Haughton (JAM) 44.70

* A re-run was ordered after John Carpenter (USA) was disqualified in the first final. Only Halswelle showed up and 'walked over' for the title.

800 METRES

	Gold	Silver	Bronze
1896	Edwin Flack (AUS) 2:11.0	Nándor Dáni (HUN) 2:11.8	Dimitrios Golemis (GRE) 2:28.0
1900	Alfred Tysoe (GBR) 2:01.2	John Cregan (USA) 2:03.0	David Hall (USA) d.n.a.
1904	James Lightbody (USA) 1:56.0	Howard Valentine (USA) 1:56.3	Emil Breitkreutz (USA) 1:56.4
1906	Paul Pilgrim (USA) 2:01.5	James Lightbody (USA) 2:01.6	Wyndham Halswelle (GBR) 2:03.0
1908	Mel Sheppard (USA) 1:52.8	Emilio Lunghi (ITA) 1:54.2	Hanns Braun (GER) 1:55.2
1912	James Meredith (USA) 1:51.9	Mel Sheppard (USA) 1:52.0	Ira Davenport (USA) 1:52.0
1920	Albert Hill (GBR) 1:53.4	Earl Eby (USA) 1:53.6	Bevil Rudd (RSA) 1:54.0
1924	Douglas Lowe (GBR) 1:52.4	Paul Martin (SUI) 1:52.6	Schuyler Enck (USA) 1:53.0
1928	Douglas Lowe (GBR) 1:51.8	Erik Byléhn (SWE) 1:52.8	Hermann Engelhardt (GER) 1:53.2
1932	Thomas Hampson (GBR) 1:49.7	Alexander Wilson (CAN) 1:49.9	Phil Edwards (CAN) 1:51.5
1936	John Woodruff (USA) 1:52.9	Mario Lanzi (ITA) 1:53.3	Phil Edwards (CAN) 1:53.6
1948	Mal Whitfield (USA) 1:49.2	Arthur Wint (JAM) 1:49.5	Marcel Hansenne (FRA) 1:49.8
1952	Mal Whitfield (USA) 1:49.2	Arthur Wint (JAM) 1:49.4	Heinz Ulzheimer (GER) 1:49.7
1956	Tom Courtney (USA) 1:47.7	Derek Johnson (GBR) 1:47.8	Audun Boysen (NOR) 1:48.1
1960	Peter Snell (NZL) 1:46.3	Roger Moens (BEL) 1:46.5	George Kerr (BWI)* 1:47.1
1964	Peter Snell (NZL) 1:45.1	Bill Crothers (CAN) 1:45.6	Wilson Kiprugut (KEN) 1:45.9
1968	Ralph Doubell (AUS) 1:44.3	Wilson Kiprugut (KEN) 1:44.5	Tom Farrell (USA) 1:45.4
1972	Dave Wottle (USA) 1:45.9	Yevgeni Arzhanov (URS) 1:45.9	Mike Boit (KEN) 1:46.0
1976	Alberto Juantorena (CUB) 1:43.5	Ivo Van Damme (BEL) 1:43.9	Richard Wohlhuter (USA) 1:44.1
1980	Steve Ovett (GBR) 1:45.4	Sebastian Coe (GBR) 1:45.9	Nikolai Kirov (URS) 1:46.0
1984	Joachim Cruz (BRA) 1:43.00	Sebastian Coe (GBR) 1:43.64	Earl Jones (USA) 1:43.83
1988	Paul Ereng (KEN) 1:43.45	Joachim Cruz (BRA) 1:43.90	Saïd Aouita (MAR) 1:44.06

1992	William Tanui (KEN) 1:43.66	Nixon Kiprotich (KEN) 1:43.70	Johnny Gray (USA) 1:43.97
1996	Vebjörn Rodal (NOR) 1:42.58	Hezekiel Sepeng (RSA) 1:42.74	Fred Onyancha (KEN) 1:42.79
2000	Nils Schumann (GER) 1:45.08	Wilson Kipketer (DEN) 1:45.14	Aissa Said-Guerni (ALG) 1:45.16

* Kerr was a Jamaican in the combined Antilles team.

1500 METRES

	Gold	Silver	Bronze
1896	Edwin Flack (AUS) 4:33.2	Arthur Blake (USA) 4:34.0	Albin Lermusiaux (FRA) 4:36.0
1900	Charles Bennett (GBR) 4:06.2	Henri Deloge (FRA) 4:06.6	John Bray (USA) 4:07.2
1904	James Lightbody (USA) 4:05.4	William Verner (USA) 4:06.8	Lacey Hearn (USA) d.n.a.
1906	James Lightbody (USA) 4:12.0	John McGough (GBR) 4:12.6	Kristian Hellström (SWE) 4:13.4
1908	Mel Sheppard (USA) 4:03.4	Harold Wilson (GBR) 4:03.6	Norman Hallows (GBR) 4:04.0
1912	Arnold Jackson (GBR) 3:56.8*	Abel Kiviat (USA) 3:56.9	Norman Taber (USA) 3:56.9
1920	Albert Hill (GBR) 4:01.8	Philip Baker (GBR) 4:02.4*	Lawrence Shields (USA) 4:03.1
1924	Paavo Nurmi (FIN) 3:53.6	Willy Schärer (SUI) 3:55.0	Henry Stallard (GBR) 3:55.6
1928	Harri Larva (FIN) 3:53.2	Jules Ladoumègue (FRA) 3:53.8	Eino Purje (FIN) 3:56.4
1932	Luigi Beccali (ITA) 3:51.2	John Cornes (GBR) 3:52.6	Phil Edwards (CAN) 3:52.8
1936	Jack Lovelock (NZL) 3:47.8	Glenn Cunningham (USA) 3:48.4	Luigi Beccali (ITA) 3:49.2
1948	Henry Eriksson (SWE) 3:49.8	Lennart Strand (SWE) 3:50.4	Willem Slijkhuis (NED) 3:50.4
1952	Josef Barthel (LUX) 3:45.1	Bob McMillen (USA) 3:45.2	Werner Lueg (GER) 3:45.4
1956	Ron Delany (IRL) 3:41.2	Klaus Richtzenhain (GER) 3:42.0	John Landy (AUS) 3:42.0
1960	Herb Elliott (AUS) 3:35.6	Michel Jazy (FRA) 3:38.4	István Rózsavölgyi (HUN) 3:39.2
1964	Peter Snell (NZL) 3:38.1	Josef Odlozil (TCH) 3:39.6	John Davies (NZL) 3:39.6
1968	Kipchoge Keino (KEN) 3:34.9	Jim Ryun (USA) 3:37.8	Bodo Tümmler (FRG) 3:39.0
1972	Pekka Vasala (FIN) 3:36.3	Kipchoge Keino (KEN) 3:36.8	Rod Dixon (NZL) 3:37.5
1976	John Walker (NZL) 3:39.2	Ivo Van Damme (BEL) 3:39.3	Paul-Heinz Wellmann (FRG) 3:39.3
1980	Sebastian Coe (GBR) 3:38.4	Jürgen Straub (GDR) 3:38.8	Steve Ovett (GBR) 3:39.0
1984	Sebastian Coe (GBR) 3:32.53	Steve Cram (GBR) 3:33.40	José Abascal (ESP) 3:34.30
1988	Peter Rono (KEN) 3:35.96	Peter Elliott (GBR) 3:36.15	Jens-Peter Herold (GDR) 3:36.21
1992	Fermin Cacho (ESP) 3:40.12	Rachid El Basir (MAR) 3:40.62	Mohamed Suleiman (QAT) 3:40.69
1996	Noureddine Morceli (ALG) 3:35.78	Fermin Cacho (ESP) 3:36.40	Stephen Kipkorir (KEN) 3:36.72
2000	Noah Ngeny (KEN) 3:32.07	Hicham El Guerrouj (MAR) 3:32.32	Bernard Lagat (KEN) 3:32.44

* Jackson later changed his name to Strode-Jackson, and Baker changed his name to Noel-Baker.

5000 METRES

	Gold	Silver	Bronze
1912	Hannes Kolehmainen (FIN) 14:36.6	Jean Bouin (FRA) 14:36.7	George Hutson (GBR) 15:07.6
1920	Joseph Guillemot (FRA) 14:55.6	Paavo Nurmi (FIN) 15:00.0	Erik Backman (SWE) 15:13.0
1924	Paavo Nurmi (FIN) 14:31.2*	Ville Ritola (FIN) 14:31.4	Edvin Wide (SWE) 15:01.8
1928	Ville Ritola (FIN) 14:38.0	Paavo Nurmi (FIN) 14:40.0	Edvin Wide (SWE) 14:41.2
1932	Lauri Lehtinen (FIN) 14:30.0	Ralph Hill (USA) 14:30.0	Lauri Virtanen (FIN) 14:44.0
1936	Gunnar Höckert (FIN) 14:22.2	Lauri Lehtinen (FIN) 14:25.8	Henry Jonsson (SWE) 14:29.0†
1948	Gaston Rieff (BEL) 14:17.6	Emil Zátopek (TCH) 14:17.8	Willem Slijkhuis (NED) 14:26.8
1952	Emil Zátopek (TCH) 14:06.6	Alain Mimoun (FRA) 14:07.4	Herbert Schade (GER) 14:08.6
1956	Vladimir Kuts (URS) 13:39.6	Gordon Pirie (GBR) 13:50.6	Derek Ibbotson (GBR) 13:54.4
1960	Murray Halberg (NZL) 13:43.4	Hans Grodotzki (GDR) 13:44.6	Kazimierz Zimny (POL) 13:44.8
1964	Bob Schul (USA) 13:48.8	Harald Norpoth (GER) 13:49.6	Bill Dellinger (USA) 13:49.8
1968	Mohamed Gammoudi (TUN) 14:05.0	Kipchoge Keino (KEN) 14:05.2	Naftali Temu (KEN) 14:06.4
1972	Lasse Viren (FIN) 13:26.4	Mohamed Gammoudi (TUN) 13:27.4	Ian Stewart (GBR) 13:27.6
1976	Lasse Viren (FIN) 13:24.8	Dick Quax (NZL) 13:25.2	Klaus-Peter Hildenbrand (FRG) 13:35.4
1980	Miruts Yifter (ETH) 13:21.0	Suleiman Nyambui (TAN) 13:21.6	Kaarlo Maaninka (FIN) 13:22.0
1984	Saïd Aouita (MAR) 13:05.59	Markus Ryffel (SUI) 13:07.54	Antonio Leitao (POR) 13:09.20
1988	John Ngugi (KEN) 13:11.70	Dieter Baumann (FRG) 13:15.52	Hansjörg Kunze (GDR) 13:15.73
1992	Dieter Baumann (GER) 13:12.52	Paul Bitok (KEN) 13:12.71	Fita Bayissa (ETH) 13:13.03
1996	Venuste Niyongabo (BDI) 13:07.96	Paul Bitok (KEN) 13:08.16	Khalid Boulami (MAR) 13:08.37
2000	Million Wolde (ETH) 13:35.49	Ali Said-Sief (ALG) 13:36.20	Brahim Lahlafi (MAR) 13:36.47

1896–1908 event not held. * Nurmi won the 5000m only 90 minutes after winning the 1500m. † Jonsson later changed his name to Kälarne.

10,000 METRES

	Gold	Silver	Bronze
1906*	Henry Hawtrey (GBR) 26:11.8	John Svanberg (SWE) 26:19.4	Edward Dahl (SWE) 26:26.2
1908*	Emil Voigt (GBR) 25:11.2	Edward Owen (GBR) 25:24.0	John Svanberg (SWE) 25:37.2
1912	Hannes Kolehmainen (FIN) 31:20.8	Louis Tewanima (USA) 32:06.6	Albin Stenroos (FIN) 32:21.8
1920	Paavo Nurmi (FIN) 31:45.8	Joseph Guillemot (FRA) 31:47.2	James Wilson (GBR) 31:50.8
1924	Ville Ritola (FIN) 30:23.2	Edvin Wide (SWE) 30:55.2	Eero Berg (FIN) 31:43.0
1928	Paavo Nurmi (FIN) 30:18.8	Ville Ritola (FIN) 30:19.4	Edvin Wide (SWE) 31:00.8
1932	Janusz Kusocinski (POL) 30:11.4	Volmari Iso-Hollo (FIN) 30:12.6	Lauri Virtannen (FIN) 30:35.0
1936	Ilmari Salminen (FIN) 30:15.4	Arvo Askola (FIN) 30:15.6	Volmari Iso-Hollo (FIN) 30:20.2
1948	Emil Zátopek (TCH) 29:59.6	Alain Mimoun (FRA) 30:47.4	Bertil Albertsson (SWE) 30:53.6
1952	Emil Zátopek (TCH) 29:17.0	Alain Mimoun (FRA) 29:32.8	Aleksandr Anufriyev (URS) 29:48.2
1956	Vladimir Kuts (URS) 28:45.6	József Kovács (HUN) 28:52.4	Allan Lawrence (AUS) 28:53.6
1960	Pyotr Bolotnikov (URS) 28:32.2	Hans Grodotzki (GDR) 28:37.0	David Power (AUS) 28:38.2†
1964	Billy Mills (USA) 28:24.4	Mohamed Gammoudi (TUN) 28:24.8	Ron Clarke (AUS) 28:25.8
1968	Naftali Temu (KEN) 29:27.4	Mamo Wolde (ETH) 29:28.0	Mohamed Gammoudi (TUN) 29:34.2
1972	Lasse Viren (FIN) 27:38.4	Emiel Puttemans (BEL) 27:39.6	Miruts Yifter (ETH) 27:41.0
1976	Lasse Viren (FIN) 27:44.4	Carlos Lopes (POR) 27:45.2	Brendan Foster (GBR) 27:54.9
1980	Miruts Yifter (ETH) 27:42.7	Kaarlo Maaninka (FIN) 27:44.3	Mohammed Kedir (ETH) 27:44.7
1984	Alberto Cova (ITA) 27:47.54	Mike McLeod (GBR) 28:06.22‡	Mike Musyoki (KEN) 28:06.46
1988	Brahim Boutayeb (MAR) 27:21.46	Salvatore Antibo (ITA) 27:23.55	Kipkemboi Kimeli (KEN) 27:25.16
1992	Khalid Skah (MAR) 27:46.70	Richard Chelimo (KEN) 27:47.72	Adiis Abebe (ETH) 28:00.07
1996	Haile Gebrselassie (ETH) 27:07.34	Paul Tergat (KEN) 27:08.217	Salah Hissou (MAR) 27:24.67
2000	Haile Gebrselassie (ETH) 27:18.20	Paul Tergat (KEN) 27:18.29	Assefa Mezgebu (ETH) 27:19.75

1896–1908 event not held. * Held over 8046m (5 miles). † Recent investigation has suggested 28:37.7. ‡ Martti Vainio (FIN) finished second but failed a drugs test.

MARATHON

(The length of the marathon was standardised from 1924 at the 1908 distance of 26 miles 385 yards (42,195m). Previously the distances had been: 1896 and 1904 – 40,000m; 1900 – 40,260m; 1906 – 41,860m; 1912 – 40,200m; 1920 – 42,750m).

	Gold	Silver	Bronze
1896	Spyridon Louis (GRE) 2hr 58:50	Charilaos Vasilakos (GRE) 3hr 06:03	Gyula Kellner (HUN) 3hr 09:35
1900	Michel Theato (FRA)* 2hr 59:45	Emile Champion (FRA) 3hr 04:17	Ernst Fast (SWE) 3hr 36:14
1904	Thomas Hicks (USA) 3hr 28:35	Albert Coray (FRA)† 3hr 34:52	Arthur Newton (USA) 3hr 47:33
1906	William Sherring (CAN) 2hr 51:23.6	John Svanberg (SWE) 2hr 58:20.8	William Frank (USA) 3hr 00:46.8
1908‡	John Hayes (USA) 2hr 55:18.4	Charles Hefferon (RSA) 2hr 56:06.0	Joseph Forshaw (USA) 2hr 57:10.4
1912	Kenneth McArthur (RSA) 2hr 36:54.8	Christian Gitsham (RSA) 2h 37:52.0	Gaston Strobino (USA) 2hr 38:42.2
1920	Hannes Kolehmainen (FIN) 2hr 32:35.8	Jüri Lossman (EST) 2hr 32:48.6	Valerio Arri (ITA) 2hr 36:32.8
1924	Albin Stenroos (FIN) 2hr 41:22.6	Romeo Bertini (ITA) 2hr 47:19.6	Clarence DeMar (USA) 2hr 48:14.0
1928	Mohamed El Ouafi (FRA) 2hr 32:57	Miguel Plaza (CHI) 2hr 33:23	Martti Marttelin (FIN) 2hr 35:02
1932	Juan Carlos Zabala (ARG) 2hr 31:36	Sam Ferris (GBR) 2hr 31:55	Armas Toivonen (FIN) 2hr 32:12
1936	Sohn Kee-Chung (JPN)§ 2hr 29:19.2	Ernest Harper (GBR) 2hr 31:23.2	Nam Seong-Yong (JPN)§ 2hr 31:42:0
1948	Delfo Cabrera (ARG) 3hr 34:51.6	Tom Richards (GBR) 2hr 35:07.6	Etienne Gailly (BEL) 2hr 35:33.6
1952	Emil Zátopek (TCH) 2hr 23:03.2	Reinaldo Gorno (ARG) 2hr 25:35.0	Gustaf Jansson (SWE) 2hr 26:07.0
1956	Alain Mimoun (FRA) 2hr 25:00	Franjo Mihalic (YUG) 2hr 26:32	Veikko Karvonen (FIN) 2hr 27:47

	Gold	Silver	Bronze
1960	Abebe Bikila (ETH) 2hr 15:16.2	Rhadi Ben Abdesselem (MAR) 2hr 15:41.6	Barry Magee (NZL) 2hr 17:18.2
1964	Abebe Bikila (ETH) 2hr 12:11.2	Basil Heatley (GBR) 2hr 16:19.2	Kokichi Tsuburaya (JPN) 2hr 16:22.8
1968	Mamo Wolde (ETH) 2hr 20:26.4	Kenji Kimihara (JPN) 2hr 23:31.0	Michael Ryan (NZL) 2hr 23:45.0
1972	Frank Shorter (USA) 2hr 12:19.8	Karel Lismont (BEL) 2hr 14:31.8	Mamo Wolde (ETH) 2hr 15:08.4
1976	Waldemar Cierpinski (GDR) 2hr 09:55.0	Frank Shorter (USA) 2hr 10:45.8	Karel Lismont (BEL) 2hr 11:12.6
1980	Waldemar Cierpinski (GDR) 2hr 11:03	Gerard Nijboer (NED) 2hr 11:20	Satymkul Dzhumanazarov (URS) 2h 11:35
1984	Carlos Lopes (POR) 2hr 09:21	John Treacy (IRL) 2hr 09:56	Charles Spedding (GBR) 2hr 09:58
1988	Gelindo Bordin (ITA) 2hr 10:32	Douglas Wakiihuri (KEN) 2hr 10:47	Ahmed Saleh (DJI) 2hr 10:59
1992	Hwang Young-cho (KOR) 2hr 13:23	Koichi Morishita (JPN) 2hr 13:45	Stephan Freigang (GER) 2hr 14:00
1996	Josiah Thugwane (RSA) 2hr 12:36	Bong-ju Lee (KOR) 2hr 12:39	Eric Wainaina (KEN) 2hr 12:44
2000	Gezahegne Abera (ETH) 2hr 10:11	Eric Wainaina (KEN) 2hr 10:31	Tesfaye Tola (ETH) 2hr 11:10

* Recently found to be of Luxembourg origin. † Usually shown incorrectly as American. ‡ Dorando Pietri (ITA) finished first but was disqualified due to assistance by officials on the last lap of the track. § Then known as Kitei Son and Shoryu Nan – both from Korea.

3000 METRES STEEPLECHASE

	Gold	Silver	Bronze
1900*	George Orton (CAN) 7:34.4	Sidney Robinson (GBR) 7:38.0	Jacques Chastanié (FRA) 7:41.0
1900†	John Rimmer (GBR) 12:58.4	Charles Bennett (GBR) 12:58.6	Sidney Robinson (GBR) 12:58.8
1904‡	James Lightbody (USA) 7:39.6	John Daly (GBR) 7:40.6	Arthur Newton (USA) 25m
1908§	Arthur Russell (GBR) 10:47.8	Archie Robertson (GBR) 10:48.4	John Eisele (USA) 11:00.8
1920	Percy Hodge (GBR) 10:00.4	Patrick Flynn (USA) 100m	Ernesto Ambrosini (ITA) 50m
1924	Ville Ritola (FIN) 9:33.6	Elias Katz (FIN) 9:44.0	Paul Bontemps (FRA) 9:45.2
1928	Toivo Loukola (FIN) 9:21.8	Paavo Nurmi (FIN) 9:31.2	Ove Andersen (FIN) 9:35.6
1932℃	Volmari Iso-Hollo (FIN) 10:33.4	Tom Evenson (GBR) 10:46.0	Joseph McCluskey (USA) 10:46.2
1936	Volmari Iso-Hollo (FIN) 9:03.8	Kaarlo Tuominen (FIN) 9:06.8	Alfred Dompert (GER) 9:07.2
1948	Tore Sjöstrand (SWE) 9:04.6	Erik Elmsäter (SWE) 9:08.2	Göte Hagström (SWE) 9:11.8
1952	Horace Ashenfelter (USA) 8:45.4	Vladimir Kazantsev (URS) 8:51.6	John Disley (GBR) 8:51.8
1956	Chris Brasher (GBR) 8:41.2	Sándor Rozsnói (HUN) 8:43.6	Ernst Larsen (NOR) 8:44.0
1960	Zdzslaw Krzyszkowiak (POL) 8:34.2	Nikolai Sokolov (URS) 8:36.4	Semyon Rzhischin (URS) 8:42.2
1964	Gaston Roelants (BEL) 8:30.8	Maurice Herriott (GBR) 8:32.4	Ivan Belyayev (URS) 8:33.8
1968	Amos Biwott (KEN) 8:51.0	Benjamin Kogo (KEN) 8:51.6	George Young (USA) 8:51.8
1972	Kipchoge Keino (KEN) 8:23.6	Benjamin Jipcho (KEN) 8:24.6	Tapio Kantanen (FIN) 8:24.8
1976	Anders Garderud (SWE) 8:08.0	Bronislaw Malinowski (POL) 8:09.1	Frank Baumgartl (GDR) 8:10.4
1980	Bronislaw Malinowski (POL) 8:09.7	Filbert Bayi (TAN) 8:12.5	Eshetu Tura (ETH) 8:13.6
1984	Julius Korir (KEN) 8:11.80	Joseph Mahmoud (FRA) 8:13.31	Brian Diemer (USA) 8:14.06
1988	Julius Kariuki (KEN) 8:05.51	Peter Koech (KEN) 8:06.79	Mark Rowland (GBR) 8:07.96
1992	Matthew Birir (KEN) 8:08.84	Patrick Sang (KEN) 8:09.55	William Mutwol (KEN) 8:10.74
1996	Joseph Keter (KEN) 8:07.12	Moses Kiptanui (KEN) 8:08.33	Alessandro Lambruschini (ITA) 8:11.28
2000	Reuben Kosgei (KEN) 8:21.43	Wilson Boit Kipketer (KEN) 8:21.77	Ali Ezzine (MAR) 8:22.15

1896, 1906 and 1912 event not held. * 2500m. † 4000m. ‡ 2590m. § 3200m. ℃ Distance was 3460m in the final due to a lap-scoring error. Iso-Hollo ran 9:14.6 in a heat.

110 METRES HURDLES

	Gold	Silver	Bronze
1896	Thomas Curtis (USA) 17.6	Grantley Goulding (GBR) 18.0	—*
1900	Alvin Kraenzlein (USA) 15.4	John McLean (USA) 15.5	Fred Moloney (USA) 15.6
1904	Frederick Schule (USA) 16.0	Thadeus Shideler (USA) 16.3	Lesley Ashburner (USA) 16.4
1906	Robert Leavitt (USA) 16.2	Alfred Healey (GBR) 16.2	Vincent Duncker (GER) 16.3†
1908	Forrest Smithson (USA) 15.0	John Garrels (USA) 15.7	Arthur Shaw (USA) 15.8
1912	Frederick Kelly (USA) 15.1	James Wendell (USA) 15.2	Martin Hawkins (USA) 15.3
1920	Earl Thomson (CAN) 14.8	Harold Barron (USA) 15.1	Frederick Murray (USA) 15.2
1924	Daniel Kinsey (USA) 15.0	Sydney Atkinson (RSA) 15.0	Sten Pettersson (SWE) 15.4

	Gold	Silver	Bronze
1928	Sydney Atkinson (RSA) 14.8	Stephen Anderson (USA) 14.8	John Collier (USA) 15.0
1932	George Saling (USA) 14.6 (14.57)	Percy Beard (USA) 14.7	Don Finlay (GBR) 14.8
1936	Forrest Towns (USA) 14.2	Don Finlay (GBR) 14.4	Fred Pollard (USA) 14.4
1948	William Porter (USA) 13.9	Clyde Scott (USA) 14.1	Craig Dixon (USA) 14.1
1952	Harrison Dillard (USA) 13.7 (13.91)	Jack Davis (USA)) 13.7 (14.00)	Art Barnard (USA) 14.1 (14.40)
1956	Lee Calhoun (USA) 13.5 (13.70)	Jack Davis (USA) 13.5 (13.73)	Joel Shankle (USA) 14.1 (14.25)
1960	Lee Calhoun (USA) 13.8 (13.98)	Willie May (USA) 13.8 (13.99)	Hayes Jones (USA) 14.0 (14.17)
1964	Hayes Jones (USA) 13.6 (13.67)	Blaine Lindgren (USA) 13.7 (13.74)	Anatoli Mikhailov (URS) 13.7 (13.78)
1968	Willie Davenport (USA) 13.3 (13.33)	Ervin Hall (USA) 13.4 (13.42)	Eddy Ottoz (ITA) 13.4 (13.46)
1972	Rod Milburn (USA) 13.24	Guy Drut (FRA) 13.34	Tom Hill (USA) 13.48
1976	Guy Drut (FRA) 13.30	Alejandro Casanas (CUB) 13.33	Willie Davenport (USA) 13.38
1980	Thomas Munkelt (GDR) 13.39	Alejandro Casanas (CUB) 13.40	Aleksandr Puchkov (URS) 13.44
1984	Roger Kingdom (USA) 13.20	Greg Foster (USA) 13.23	Arto Bryggare (FIN) 13.40
1988	Roger Kingdom (USA) 12.98	Colin Jackson (GBR) 13.28	Tonie Campbell (USA) 13.38
1992	Mark McKoy (CAN) 13.12	Tony Dees (USA) 13.24	Jack Pierce (USA) 13.26
1996	Allen Johnson (USA) 12.95	Mark Crear (USA) 13.09	Florian Schwarthoff (GER) 13.17
2000	Anier Garcia (CUB) 13.00	Terrence Trammell (USA) 13.16	Mark Crear (USA) 13.22

* There were only two finalists. † Duncker was often incorrectly shown as South African.

400 METRES HURDLES

	Gold	Silver	Bronze
1900*	Walter Tewksbury (USA) 57.6	Henri Tauzin (FRA) 58.4	George Orton (CAN) 58.9e?
1904†	Harry Hillman (USA) 53.0	Frank Waller (USA) 53.2	George Poage (USA) 30m
1908	Charles Bacon (USA) 55.0	Harry Hillman (USA) 55.3	Leonard Tremeer (GBR) 57.0
1920	Frank Loomis (USA) 54.0	John Norton (USA) 54.3	August Desch (USA) 54.5
1924	Morgan Taylor (USA) 52.6‡	Erik Vilén (FIN) 53.8	Ivan Riley (USA) 54.2
1928	Lord Burghley (GBR) 53.4	Frank Cuhel (USA) 53.6	Morgan Taylor (USA) 53.6
1932	Bob Tisdall (IRL) 51.7 (51.67)‡	Glenn Hardin (USA) 51.9 (51.85)	Morgan Taylor (USA) 52.0 (51.96)
1936	Glenn Hardin (USA) 52.4	John Loaring (CAN) 52.7	Miguel White (PHI) 52.8
1948	Roy Cochran (USA) 51.1	Duncan White (SRI) 51.8	Rune Larsson (SWE) 52.2
1952	Charlie Moore (USA) 50.8 (51.06)	Yuri Liyuyev (URS) 51.3 (51.51)	John Holland (NZL) 52.2 (52.26)
1956	Glenn Davis (USA) 50.1 (50.29)	Eddie Southern (USA) 50.8 (50.94)	Josh Culbreath (USA) 51.6 (51.74)
1960	Glenn Davis (USA) 49.3 (49.51)	Cliff Cushman (USA) 49.6 (49.77)	Dick Howard (USA) 49.7 (49.90)
1964	Rex Cawley (USA) 49.6	John Cooper (GBR) 50.1	Salvatore Morale (ITA) 50.1
1968	David Hemery (GBR) 48.1 (48.12)	Gerhard Hennige (FRG) 49.0 (49.02)	John Sherwood (GBR) 49.0 (49.03)
1972	John Akii-Bua (UGA) 47.82	Ralph Mann (USA) 48.51	David Hemery (GBR) 48.52
1976	Edwin Moses (USA) 47.64§	Mike Shine (USA) 48.69	Yevgeni Gavrilenko (URS) 49.45
1980	Volker Beck (GDR) 48.70	Vasili Arkhipenko (URS) 48.86	Gary Oakes (GBR) 49.11
1984	Edwin Moses (USA) 47.75	Danny Harris (USA) 48.13	Harald Schmid (FRG) 48.19
1988	Andre Phillips (USA) 47.19	Amadou Dia Ba (SEN) 47.23	Edwin Moses (USA) 47.56
1992	Kevin Young (USA) 46.78	Winthrop Graham (JAM) 47.66	Kriss Akabusi (GBR) 47.82
1996	Derrick Adkins (USA) 47.54	Samuel Matete (ZAM) 47.78	Calvin Davis (USA) 47.96
2000	Angelo Taylor (USA) 47.50	Hadi Al-Somaily (KSA) 47.53	Llewellyn Herbert (RSA) 47.81

1896,1906 and 1912 event not held. * The Tenth barrier was a water jump. † Hurdles were 76.2cm (2ft 6in) high instead of usual 91.4cm (3ft). ‡ Record not allowed because a hurdle was knocked down. § Recently re-scrutiny of the photo-finish film has indicated that the time was 47.63.

4 X 100 METRES RELAY

	Gold	Silver	Bronze
1912	Great Britain 42.4	Sweden 42.6*	—
1920	United States 42.2	France 42.6	Sweden 42.9
1924	United States 41.0	Great Britain 41.2	The Netherlands 41.8
1928	United States 41.0	Geremany 41.2	Great Britain 41.8
1932	United States 40.0 (40.10)	Germany 40.9	Italy 41.2
1936	United States 39.8	Italy 41.1	Germany 41.2
1948	United States 40.6†	Great Britain 41.3	Italy 41.5
1952	United States 40.1 (40.26)	Soviet Union 40.3 (40.58)	Hungary 40.5 (40.83)
1956	United States 39.5 (39.60)	Soviet Union 39.8 (39.92)	Germany 40.3 (40.34)

	Gold	Silver	Bronze
1960	Germany 39.5 (39.66)‡	Soviet Union 40.1 (40.24)	Great Britain 40.2 (40.32)
1964	United States 39.0 (39.06)	Poland 39.3 (39.36)	France 39.3 (39.36)
1968	United States 38.2 (38.24)	Cuba 38.3 (38.40)	France 38.4 (38.43)
1972	United States 38.19	Soviet Union 38.50	FRG 38.79
1976	United States 38.33	GDR 38.66	Soviet Union 38.78
1980	Soviet Union 38.26	Poland 38.33	France 38.53
1984	United States 37.83	Jamaica 38.62	Canada 38.70
1988	Soviet Union 38.19	Great Britain 38.28	France 38.40
1992	United States 37.40	Nigeria 37.98	Cuba 38.00
1996	Canada 37.69	United States 38.05	Brazil 38.41
2000	United States 37.61	Brazil 37.90	Cuba 38.04

1896–1908 event not held. * Germany finished second but was disqualified. † The United States was originally disqualified but was later reinstated. ‡ The United States finished first (39.60) but was disqualified.

4 X 400 METRES RELAY

	Gold	Silver	Bronze
1908*	United States 3:29.4	Germany 3:32.4	Hungary 3:32.5
1912	United States 3:16.6	France 3:20.7	Great Britain 3:23.2
1920	Great Britain 3:22.2	South Africa 3:24.2	France 3:24.8
1924	United States 3:16.0	Sweden 3:17.0	Great Britain 3:17.4
1928	United States 3:14.2	Germany 3: 14.8	Canada 3:15.4
1932	United States 3:08.2 (3:08.14)	Great Britain 3:11.2	Canada 3:12.8
1936	Great Britain 3:09.0	United States 3:11.0	Germany 3:11.8
1948	United States 3:10.4	France 3:14.8	Sweden 3:16.3
1952	Jamaica 3:03.9 (3:04.04)	United States 3:04.0 (3:04.21)	Germany 3:06.6 (3:06.78)
1956	United States 3:04.8 3:04.81)	Australia 3:06.2 (3:06.19)	Great Britain 3:07.2 (3:07.19)
1960	United States 3:02.2 (3:02.37)	Germany 3:02.7 (3:02.84)	BWI† 3:04.0 (3:04.13)
1964	United States 3:00.7	Great Britain 3:01.6	Trinidad and Tobago 3:01.7
1968	United States 2:56.1 (2:56.16)	Kenya 2:59.6 (2:59.64)	FRG 3:00.5 (3:00.57)
1972	Kenya 2:59.83	Great Britain 3:00.46	France 3:00.65
1976	United States 2:58.65	Poland 3:01.43	FRG 3:01.98
1980	Soviet Union 3:01.08	GDR 3:01.26	Italy 3:04.3
1984	United States 2:57.91	Great Britain 2:59.13	Nigeria 2:59.32
1988	United States 2:56.16	Jamaica 3:00.30	FRG 3:00.56
1992	United States 2:55.74	Cuba 2:59.51	Great Britain 2:59.73
1996	United States 2:55.99	Great Britain 2:56.60	Jamaica 2:59.42
2000	United States 2:56.35	Nigeria 2:58.68	Jamaica 2:58.78

1896–1906 event not held. * Medley relay: 200m, 200m, 400m and 800m. † British West Indies team, comprising three from Jamaica and one from Barbados.

20,000 METRES ROAD WALK

	Gold	Silver	Bronze
1956	Leonid Spirin (URS) 1hr 31.27.4	Antonas Mikenas (URS) 1hr 32:03.0	Bruno Junk (URS) 1hr 32:12.0
1960	Vladimir Golubichni (URS) 1hr 34:07.2	Noel Freeman (AUS) 1hr 34:16.4	Stan Vickers (GBR) 1hr 34:56.4
1964	Ken Matthews (GBR) 1hr 29:34.0	Dieter Lindner (GER) 1hr 31:13.2	Vladimir Golubichni (URS) 1hr 31:59.4
1968	Vladimir Golubichni (URS) 1hr 33:58.4	José Pedraza (MEX) 1hr 34:00.0	Nikolai Smaga (URS) 1hr 34:03.4
1972	Peter Frenkel (GDR) 1hr 26:42.4	Vladimir Golubichni (URS) 1hr 26:55.2	Hans Reimann (GDR) 1hr 27:16.6
1976	Daniel Batista (MEX) 1hr 24:40.6	Hans Reimann (GDR) 1hr 25:13.8	Peter Frenkel (GDR) 1hr 25:29.4
1980	Maurizio Damilano (ITA) 1hr 23:35.5	Pyotr Pochenchuk (URS) 1hr 24:45.4	Roland Wieser (GDR) 1hr 25:58.2
1984	Ernesto Canto (MEX) 1hr 23:13	Raul Gonzalez (MEX) 1hr 23:20	Maurizio Damilano (ITA) 1hr 23:26
1988	Jozef Pribilinec (TCH) 1hr 19:57	Ronald Weigel (GDR) 1hr 20:00	Maurizio Damilano (ITA) 1hr 20:14
1992	Daniel Plaza (ESP) 1hr 21:45	Guillaume Leblanc (CAN) 1hr 22:25	Giovanni de Benedictus (ITA) 1hr 23:11
1996	Jefferson Perez (ECU 1hr 20:07	Ilya Markov (RUS) 1hr 20:16	Bernardo Segura (MEX) 1hr 20:23

	Gold	Silver	Bronze
2000	Robert Korzeniowski (POL) 1hr 18:59	Noé Hernandez (MEX) 1hr 19:03	Vladimir Andreyev (RUS) 1hr 19:27

1896–1952 event not held.

50,000 METRES ROAD WALK

	Gold	Silver	Bronze
1932	Thomas Green (GBR) 4hr 50:10	Janis Dalinsh (LAT) 4hr 57:20	Ugo Frigerio (ITA) 4hr 59:06
1936	Harold Whitlock (GBR) 4hr 30:41.1	Arthur Schwab (SUI) 4hr 32:09.2	Adalberts Bubenko (LAT) 4hr 32:42.2
1948	John Ljunggren (SWE) 4hr 41:52	Gaston Godel (SUI) 4hr 48:17	Tebbs Lloyd Johnson (GBR) 4hr 48:31
1952	Giuseppe Dordoni (ITA) 4hr 28:07.8	Josef Dolezal (TCH) 4hr 30:17.8	Antal Tóka (HUN) 4hr 31:27.2
1956	Norman Read (NZL) 4hr 30:42.8	Yevgeni Maskinov (URS) 4hr 32:57.0	John Ljunggren (SWE) 4hr 35:02.0
1960	Don Thompson (GBR) 4hr 25:30.0	John Ljunggren (SWE) 4hr 25:47.0	Abdon Pamich (ITA) 4hr 27:55.4
1964	Abdon Pamich (ITA) 4hr 11:12.4	Paul Nihill (GBR) 4hr 11:31.2	Ingvar Pettersson (SWE) 4hr 14:17.4
1968	Christoph Höhne (GDR) 4hr 20:13.6	Antal Kiss (HUN) 4hr 30:17.0	Larry Young (USA) 4hr 31:55.4
1972	Bernd Kannenberg (FRG) 3hr 56:11.6	Venjamin Soldatenko (URS) 3hr 58:24.0	Larry Young (USA) 4hr 00:46.0
1980	Hartwig Gauder (GDR) 2hr 49:24	Jorge Llopart (ESP) 3hr 51:25	Yevgeni Ivchenko (URS) 3hr 56:32
1984	Raul Gonzalez (MEX) 3hr 47:26	Bo Gustafsson (SWE) 3hr 53:19	Sandro Bellucci (ITA) 3hr 53:45
1988	Vyacheslav Ivanenko (URS) 3hr 38:29	Ronald Weigel (GDR) 3hr 38:56	Hartwig Gauder (GDR) 3hr 39:45
1992	Andrei Perlov (EUN) 3hr 50:13	Carlos Mercenario (MEX) 3hr 52:09	Ronald Weigel (GER) 3hr 53:45
1996	Robert Korzeniowski (POL) 3hr 43:30	Mikhail Shchennikov (RUS) 3hr 43:46	Valentin Massana (ITA) 3hr 44:19
2000	Robert Korzeniowski (POL) 3hr 42:21	Aigars Fadejevs (LAT) 3hr 43:40	Joel Sanchez (MEX) 3hr 44:35

1896–1928 and 1976 event not held.

HIGH JUMP

	Gold	Silver	Bronze
1896	Ellery Clark (USA) 1.81m	James Connolly (USA) 1.65m Robert Garrett (USA) 1.65m	—
1900	Irving Baxter (USA) 1.90m	Patrick Leahy (GBR) 1.78m	Lajos Gönczy (HUN) 1.75m
1904	Samuel Jones (USA) 1.80m	Garrett Serviss (USA) 1.77m	Paul Weinstein (GER) 1.77m
1906	Con Leahy (GBR) 1.77m	Lajos Gönczy (HUN) 1.75m	Herbert Kerrigan (USA) 1.72m Themistoklis Diakidis (GRE) 1.72m
1908	Harry Porter (USA) 1.905m	Con Leahy (GBR) 1.88m István Somodi (HUN) 1.88m Georges André (FRA) 1.88m	—
1912	Alma Richards (USA) 1.93m	Hans Liesche (GER) 1.91m	George Horine (USA) 1.89m
1920	Richmond Landon (USA) 1.94m	Harold Muller (USA) 1.90m	Bo Ekelund (SWE) 1.90m
1924	Harold Osborn (USA) 1.98m	Leroy Brown (USA) 1.95m	Pierre Lewden (FRA) 1.92m
1928	Robert King (USA) 1.94m	Ben Hedges (USA) 1.91m	Claude Ménard (FRA) 1.91m
1932	Duncan MacNaughton (CAN) 1.97m	Robert Van Osdel (USA) 1.97m	Simeon Toribio (PHI) 1.97m
1936	Cornelius Johnson (USA) 2.03m	David Albritton (USA) 2.00m	Delos Thurber (USA) 2.00m
1948	John Winter (AUS) 1.98m	Björn Paulsen (NOR) 1.95m	George Stanich (USA) 1.95m
1952	Walt Davis (USA) 2.04m	Ken Wiesner (USA) 2.01m	José Telles da Conceicao (BRA) 1.98m
1956	Charlie Dumas (USA) 2.12m	Chilla Porter (AUS) 2.10m	Igor Kashkarov (URS) 2.08m
1960	Robert Shavlakadze (URS) 2.16m	Valeri Brumel (URS) 2.16m	John Thomas (USA) 2.14m
1964	Valeri Brumel (URS) 2.18m	John Thomas (USA) 2.18m	John Rambo (USA) 2.16m
1968	Dick Fosbury (USA) 2.24m	Ed Caruthers (USA) 2.22m	Valentin Gavrilov (URS) 2.20m

	Gold	*Silver*	*Bronze*
1972	Jüri Tarmak (URS) 2.23m	Stefan Junge (GDR) 2.21m	Dwight Stones (USA) 2.21m
1976	Jacek Wszola (POL) 2.25m	Greg Joy (CAN) 2.23m	Dwight Stones (USA) 2.21m
1980	Gerd Wessig (GDR) 2.36m	Jacek Wszola (POL) 2.31m	Jörg Freimuth (GDR) 2.31m
1984	Dietmar Mögenburg (FRG) 2.35m	Patrik Sjöberg (SWE) 2.33m	Zhu Jianhua (CHN) 2.31m
1988	Gennadi Avdeyenko (URS) 2.38m	Hollis Conway (USA) 2.36m	Rudolf Povarnitsin (URS) 2.36m
		Patrik Sjöberg (SWE) 2.36m	
1992	Javier Sotomayor (CUB) 2.34m	Patrik Sjöberg (SWE) 2.34m	Hollis Conway (USA) 2.34m
		Tim Forsythe (AUS) 2.34m	
		Artur Partyka (POL) 2.34m	
1996	Charles Austin (USA) 2.39m	Artur Partyka (POL) 2.37m	Steve Smith (GBR) 2.35m
2000	Sergei Klyugin (RUS) 2.35m	Javier Sotomayor (CUB) 2.32m	Abderahmane Hammad (ALG) 2.32m

POLE VAULT

	Gold	*Silver*	*Bronze*
1896	William Hoyt (USA) 3.30m	Albert Tyler (USA) 3.20m	Ioannis Theodoropoulos (GRE) 2.60m
			Vasilios Xydas (GRE) 2.60m
			Evangelos Damaskos (GRE) 2.60m
1900	Irving Baxter (USA) 3.30m	Meredith Colkett (USA) 3.25m	Carl-Albert Andersen (NOR) 3.20m
1904	Charles Dvorak (USA) 3.50m	LeRoy Samse (USA) 3.43m	Louis Wilkins (USA) 3.43m
1906	Fernand Gonder (FRA) 3.50m	Bruno Söderstrom (SWE) 3.40m	Edward Glover (USA) 3.35m
1908	Edward Cooke (USA) 3.70m	—	Edward Archibald (CAN) 3.58m
	Alfred Gilbert (USA) 3.70m		Bruno Söderstrom (SWE) 3.58m
			Charles Jacobs (USA) 3.58m
1912	Harry Babcock (USA) 3.95m	Frank Nelson (USA) 3.85m	Bertil Uggla (SWE) 3.80m
		Marcus Wright (USA) 3.85m	William Hapenny (CAN) 3.80m
			Frank Murphy (USA) 3.80m
1920	Frank Foss (USA) 4.09m	Henry Petersen (DEN) 3.70m	Edwin Meyers (USA) 3.60m
1924	Lee Barnes (USA) 3.95m	Glenn Graham (USA) 3.95m	James Brooker (USA) 3.90m
1928	Sabin Carr (USA) 4.20m	William Droegemuller (USA) 4.10m	Charles McGinnis (USA) 3.95m
1932	William Miller (USA) 4.31m	Shuhei Nishida (JPN) 4.30m	George Jefferson (USA) 4.20m
1936	Earle Meadows (USA) 4.35m	Shuhei Nishida (JPN) 4.25m*	Sueo Oe (JPN) 4.25m*
1948	Guinn Smith (USA) 4.30m	Erkki Kataja (FIN) 4.20m	Bob Richards (USA) 4.20m
1952	Bob Richards (USA) 4.55m	Don Laz (USA) 4.50m	Ragnar Lundberg (SWE) 4.20m
1956	Bob Richards (USA) 4.56m	Bob Gutowski (USA) 4.53m	Georgios Roubanis (GRE) 4.50m
1960	Don Bragg (USA) 4.70m	Ron Morris (USA) 4.60m	Eeles Landstrom (FIN) 4.55m
1964	Fred Hansen (USA) 5.10m	Wolfgang Reinhardt (GER) 5.05m	Klaus Lehnertz (GER) 5.00m
1968	Bob Seagren (USA) 5.40m	Claus Schiprowski (FRG) 5.40m	Wolfgang Nordwig (GDR) 5.40m
1972	Wolfgang Nordwig (GDR) 5.50m	Bob Seagren (USA) 5.40m	Jan Johnson (USA) 5.35m
1976	Tadeusz Slusarski (POL) 5.50m	Antti Kalliomaki (FIN) 5.50m	David Roberts (USA) 5.50m
1980	Wladislaw Kozakiewicz (POL) 5.78m	Tadeusz Slusarski (POL) 5.65m	—
		Konstantin Volkov (URS) 5.65m	
1984	Pierre Quinon (FRA) 5.75m	Mike Tully (USA) 5.65m	Earl Bell (USA) 5.60m
			Thierry Vigneron (FRA) 5.60m
1988	Sergei Bubka (URS) 5.90m	Rodion Gataullin (URS) 5.85m	Grigori Yegorov (URS) 5.80m
1992	Maksim Tarasov (EUN) 5.80m	Igor Trandenkov (EUN) 5.80m	Javier Garcia (CUB) 5.75m
1996	Jean Galfione (FRA) 5.92m	Igor Trandenkov (RUS) 5.92m	Andrei Tivontchik (GER) 5.92m
2000	Nick Hysong (USA) 5.90m	Lawrence Johnson (USA) 5.90m	Maksim Tarasov (RUS) 5.90m

* Nishida and Oe refused to jump-off and instead decided places by lot.

LONG JUMP

	Gold	*Silver*	*Bronze*
1896	Ellery Clark (USA) 6.35m	Robert Garrett (USA) 6.18m	James Connolly (USA) 6.11m
1900	Alvin Kraenzlein (USA) 7.18m	Myer Prinstein (USA) 7.17m	Patrick Leahy (GBR) 6.95m
1904	Myer Prinstein (USA) 7.34m	Daniel Frank (USA) 6.89m	Robert Stangland (USA) 6.88m
1906	Myer Prinstein (USA) 7.20m	Peter O'Connor (GBR) 7.02m	Hugo Friend (USA) 6.96m
1908	Francis Irons (USA) 7.48m	Daniel Kelly (USA) 7.09m	Calvin Bricker (CAN) 7.08m
1912	Albert Guttersson (USA) 7.60m	Calvin Bricker (CAN) 7.21m	Georg Aberg (SWE) 7.18m
1920	William Pettersson (SWE) 7.15m	Carl Johnson (USA) 7.09m	Erik Abrahamsson (SWE) 7.08m

	Gold	Silver	Bronze
1924	William DeHart Hubbard (USA) 7.44m	Ed Gourdin (USA) 7.27m	Sverre Hansen (NOR) 7.26m
1928	Edward Hamm (USA) 7.73m	Silvio Cator (HAI) 7.58m	Alfred Bates (USA) 7.40m
1932	Ed Gordon (USA) 7.63m	Lambert Redd (USA) 7.60m	Chuhei Nambu (JPN) 7.44m
1936	Jesse Owens (USA) 8.06m	Luz Long (GER) 7.87m	Naoto Tajima (JPN) 7.74m
1948	Willie Steele (USA) 7.82m	Theodore Bruce (AUS) 7.55m	Herbert Douglas (USA) 7.54m
1952	Jerome Biffle (USA) 7.57m	Meredith Gourdine (USA) 7.53m	Odön Földessy (HUN) 7.30m
1956	Greg Bell (USA) 7.83m	John Bennett (USA) 7.68m	Jorma Valkama (FIN) 7.48m
1960	Ralph Boston (USA) 8.12m	Irvin Roberson (USA) 8.11m	Igor Ter-Ovanesian (URS) 8.04m
1964	Lynn Davies (GBR) 8.07m	Ralph Boston (USA) 8.03m	Igor Ter-Ovanseian (URS) 7.99m
1968	Bob Beamon (USA) 8.90m	Klaus Beer (GDR) 8.19m	Ralph Boston (USA) 8.16m
1972	Randy Williams (USA) 8.24m	Hans Baumgartner (FRG) 8.18m	Arnie Robinson (USA) 8.03m
1976	Arnie Robinson (USA) 8.35m	Randy Williams (USA) 8.11m	Frank Wartenberg (GDR) 8.02m
1980	Lutz Dombrowski (GDR) 8.54m	Frank Paschek (GDR) 8.21m	Valeri Podluzhni (URS) 8.18m
1984	Carl Lewis (USA) 8.54m	Gary Honey (AUS) 8.24m	Giovanni Evange;isti (ITA) 8.24m
1988	Carl Lewis (USA) 8.72m	Mike Powell (USA) 8.49m	Larry Myricks (USA) 8.27m
1992	Carl Lewis (USA) 8.67m	Mike Powell (USA) 8.64m	Joe Greene (USA) 8.34m
1996	Carl Lewis (USA) 8.50m	James Beckford (JAM) 8.29m	Joe Greene (USA) 8.24m
2000	Ivan Pedroso (CUB) 8.55m	Jai Taurima (AUS) 8.49m	Roman Shchurenko (UKR) 8.31m

TRIPLE JUMP (Formerly known as the Hop, Step and Jump)

	Gold	Silver	Bronze
1896*	James Connolly (USA) 13.71m	Alexandre Tuffere (FRA) 12.70m	Ioannis Persakis (GRE) 12.52m
1900	Myer Prinstein (USA) 14.47m	James Connolly (USA) 13.97m	Lewis Sheldon (USA) 13.64m
1904	Myer Prinstein (USA) 14.35m	Frederick Englehardt (USA) 13.90m	Robert Stangland (USA) 13.36m
1906	Peter O'Connor (GBR) 14.07m	Con Leahy (GBR) 13.98m	Thomas Cronan (USA) 13.70m
1908	Tim Ahearne (GBR) 14.92m	Garfield McDonald (CAN) 14.76m	Edvard Larsen (NOR) 14.39m
1912	Gustaf Lindblom (SWE) 14.76m	Georg Aberg (SWE) 14.51m	Erik Amlöf (SWE) 14.17m
1920	Vilho Tuulos (FIN) 14.50m	Folke Jansson (SWE) 14.48m	Erik Amlöf (SWE) 14.27m
1924	Anthony Winter (AUS) 15.52m	Luis Brunetto (ARG) 15.42m	Vilho Tuulos (FIN) 15.37m
1928	Mikio Oda (JPN) 15.21m	Levi Casey (USA) 15.17m	Vilho Tuulos (FIN) 15.11m
1932	Chuhei Nambu (JPN) 15.72m	Erik Svensson (SWE) 15.32m	Kenkichi Oshima (JPN) 15.12m
1936	Naoto Tajima (JPN) 16.00m	Masao Harada (JPN) 15.66m	John Metcalfe (AUS) 15.50m
1948	Arne Ahman (SWE) 15.40m	George Avery (AUS) 15.36m	Ruhi Sarialp (TUR) 15.02m
1952	Adhemar Ferreira de Silva (BRA) 16.22m	Leonid Shcherbakov (URS) 15.98m	Arnoldo Devonish (VEN) 15.52m
1956	Adhemar Ferreira da Silva (BRA) 16.35m	Vilhjalmur Einarsson (ISL) 16.26m	Vitold Kreyer (URS) 16.02m
1960	Jozef Schmidt (POL) 16.81m	Vladimir Goryayev (URS) 16.63m	Vitold Kreyer (URS) 16.43m
1964	Jozef Schmidt (POL) 16.85m	Oleg Fedoseyev (URS) 16.58m	Viktor Kravchenko (URS) 16.57m
1968	Viktor Saneyev (URS) 17.39m	Nelson Prudencio (BRA) 17.27m	Giuseppe Gentile (ITA) 17.22m
1972	Viktor Saneyev (URS) 17.35m	Jörg Drehmel (GDR) 17.31m	Nelson Prudencio (BRA) 17.05m
1976	Viktor Saneyev (URS) 17.29m	James Butts (USA) 17.18m	João de Oliveira (BRA) 16.90m
1980	Jaak Uudmae (URS) 17.35m	Viktor Saneyev (URS) 17.24m	João de Oliveira (BRA) 17.22m
1984	Al Joyner (USA) 17.26m	Mike Conley (USA) 17.18m	Keith Connor (GBR) 16.87m
1988	Khristo Markov (BUL) 17.61m	Igor Lapshin (URS) 17.52m	Aleksandr Kovalenko (URS) 17.42m
1992	Mike Conley (USA) 18.17m	Charles Simkins (USA) 17.60m	Frank Rutherford (BAH) 17.36m
1996	Kenny Harrison (USA) 18.09m	Jonathan Edwards (GBR) 17.88m	Yoelbi Quesada (CUB) 17.44m
2000	Jonathan Edwards (GBR) 17.71m	Yoel Garcia (CUB) 17.47m	Denis Kapustin (RUS) 17.46m

* The winner took two hops with his right foot, contrary to present rules.

SHOT

	Gold	Silver	Bronze
1896*	Robert Garrett (USA) 11.22m	Miltiades Gouskos (GRE) 11.15m	Georgios Papasideris (GRE) 10.36m
1900*	Richard Sheldon (USA) 14.10m	Josiah McCracken (USA) 12.85m	Robert Garrett (USA) 12.37m
1904*	Ralph Rose (USA) 14.81m	Wesley Coe (USA) 14.40m	Leon Feuerbach (USA) 13.37m
1906	Martin Sheridan (USA) 12.32m	Mihály Dávid (HUN) 11.83m	Eric Lemming (SWE) 11.26m
1908	Ralph Rose (USA) 14.21m	Dennis Horgan (GBR) 13.61m	John Garrels (USA) 13.18m
1912	Patrick McDonald (USA) 15.34m	Ralph Rose (USA) 15.25m	Lawrence Whitney (USA) 13.93m
1920	Ville Pörhöla (FIN) 14.81m	Elmer Niklander (FIN) 14.155m	Harry Liversedge (USA) 14.15m
1924	Clarence Houser (USA) 14.99m	Glenn Hartranft (USA) 14.89m	Ralph Hills (USA) 14.64m

	Gold	Silver	Bronze
1928	John Kuck (USA) 15.87m	Herman Brix (USA) 15.75m	Emil Hirschfield (GER) 15.72m
1932	Lero Sexton (USA) 16.00m	Harlow Rothert (USA) 15.67m	Frantisek Douda (TCH) 15.60m
1936	Hans Woellke (GER) 16.20	Sulo Bärlund (FIN) 16.12m	Gerhard Stöck (GER) 15.66m
1948	Wilbur Thompson (USA) 17.12m	Jim Delaney (USA) 16.68m	Jim Fuchs (USA) 16.42m
1952	Parry O'Brien (USA) 17.41m	Darrow Hooper (USA) 17.39m	Jim Fuchs (USA) 17.06m
1956	Parry O'Brien (USA) 18.57m	Bill Nieder (USA) 18.18m	Jiri Skobla (TCH) 17.65m
1960	Bill Nieder (USA) 19.68m	Parry O'Brien (USA) 19.11m	Dallas Long (USA) 19.01m
1964	Dallas Long (USA) 20.33m	Randy Matson (USA) 20.20m	Vilmos Varju (HUN) 19.39m
1968	Randy Matson (USA) 20.54m	George Woods (USA) 20.12m	Eduard Gushchin (URS) 20.09m
1972	Wladyslaw Komar (POL) 21.18m	George Woods (USA) 21.17m	Hartmut Briesenick (GDR) 21.14m
1976	Udo Beyer (GDR) 21.05m	Yevgeni Mironov (URS) 21.03m	Aleksandr Baryshnikov (URS) 21.00m
1980	Vladimir Kiselyev (URS) 21.25m	Aleksandr Baryshnikov (URS) 21.08m	Udo Beyer (GDR) 21.06m
1984	Alessandro Andrei (ITA) 21.26m	Michael Carter (USA) 21.09m	Dave Laut (USA) 20.97m
1988	Ulf Timmermann (GDR) 22.47m	Randy Barnes (USA) 22.39m	Werner Günthör (SUI) 21.99m
1992	Mike Stulce (USA) 21.70m	James Doehring (USA) 20.96m	Vyacheslav Lykho (EUN) 20.94m
1996	Randy Barnes (USA) 21.62m	John Godina (USA) 20.79m	Aleksandr Bagach (UKR) 20.75m
2000	Arsi Harju (FIN) 21.29m	Adam Nelson (USA) 21.21m	John Godina (USA) 21.20m

* In 1896, 1900 and 1904 competition was from a 2.13m (7ft) square.

DISCUS

	Gold	Silver	Bronze
1896*	Robert Garrett (USA) 29.15m	Panoyotis Paraskevopoulos (GRE) 28.95m	Sotirios Versis (GRE) 28.78m
1900*	Rudolf Bauer (HUN) 36.04m	Frantisek Janda-Suk (BOH) 35.25m	Richard Sheldon (USA) 34.60m
1904‡	Martin Sheridan (USA) 39.28m	Ralph Rose (USA) 39.28m	Nicolaos Georgantas (GRE) 37.68m
1906	Martin Sheridan (USA) 41.46m	Nicolaos Georgantas (GRE) 38.06m	Werner Järvinen (FIN) 36.82m
1908	Martin Sheridan (USA) 40.89m	Merritt Griffin (USA) 40.70m	Marquis Horr (USA) 39.44m
1912	Armas Taipale (FIN) 45.21m	Richard Byrd (USA) 42.32m	James Duncan (USA) 42.28m
1920	Elmer Niklander (FIN) 44.68m	Armas taipale (FIN) 44.19m	Augustus Pope (USA) 42.13m
1924	Clarence Houser (USA) 46.15m	Vilho Niittymaa (FIN) 44.95m	Thomas Lieb (USA) 44.83m
1928	Clarence Houser (USA) 47.32m	Antero Kivi (FIN) 47.23m	James Corson (USA) 47.10m
1932	John Anderson (USA) 49.49m	Henri Laborde (USA) 48.47m	Paul Winter (FRA) 47.85m
1936	Ken Carpenter (USA) 50.48m	Gordon Dunn (USA) 49.36m	Giorgio Oberweger (ITA) 49.23m
1948	Adolfo Consolini (ITA) 52.78m	Giuseppe Tosi (ITA) 51.78m	Fortune Gordien (USA) 50.77m
1952	Sim Iness (USA) 55.03m	Adolfo Consolini (ITA) 53.78m	James Dillion (USA) 52.38m
1956	Al Oerter (USA) 56.36m	Fortune Gordien (USA) 54.81m	Des Koch (USA) 54.40m
1960	Al Oerter (USA) 59.18m	Rink Babka (USA) 58.02m	Dick Cochran (USA) 57.16m
1964	Al Oerter (USA) 61.00m	Ludvik Danek (TCH) 60.52m	Dave Weill (USA) 59.49m
1968	Al Oerter (USA) 64.78m	Lothar Milde (GDR) 63.08m	Ludvik Danek (TCH) 62.92m
1972	Ludvik Danek (TCH) 64.40m	Jay Silvester (USA) 63.50m	Ricky Bruch (SWE) 63.40m
1976	Mac Wilkins (USA) 67.50m	Wolfgang Schmidt (GDR) 66.22m	John Powell (USA) 65.70m
1980	Viktor Rashchupkin (URS) 66.64m	Imrich Bugár (TCH) 66.38m	Luis Delis (CUB) 66.32m
1984	Rolf Danneberg (FRG) 66.60m	Mac Wilkins (USA) 66.30m	John Powell (USA) 65.46m
1988	Jürgen Schult (GDR) 68.82m	Romas Ubartas (URS) 67.48m	Rolf Danneberg (FRG) 67.38m
1992	Romas Ubartas (LTU) 65.12m	Jürgen Schult (GER) 64.94m	Roberto Moya (CUB) 64.12m
1996	Lars Riedel (GER) 69.40m	Vladimir Dubrovchik (BLR) 66.60m	Vasili Kaptyukh (BLR) 65.80m
2000	Virguljus Alekna (LAT) 69.30m	Lars Reidel (GER) 68.50m	Frantz Kruger (RSA) 68.19m

* In 1896 and 1900 competition was from a 2.50m (8.2ft) circle. † First place was decided by a throw-off.

HAMMER

	Gold	Silver	Bronze
1900*	John Flanagan (USA) 49.73m	Truxton Hare (USA) 49.13m	Josiah McCracken (USA) 42.46m
1904	John Flanagan (USA) 51.23m	John De Witt (USA) 50.26m	Ralph Rose (USA) 45.73m
1908	John Flanagan (USA) 51.92m	Matt McGrath (USA) 51.18m	Con Walsh (CAN) 48.50m
1912	Matt McGrath (USA) 54.74m	Duncan Gillis (CAN) 48.39m	Clarence Childs (USA) 48.17m
1920	Patrick Ryan (USA) 52.87m	Carl Lind (SWE) 48.43m	Basil Bennett (USA) 48.25m
1924	Fred Tootell (USA) 53.29m	Matt McGrath (USA) 50.84m	Malcolm Nokes (GBR) 48.87m

	Gold	Silver	Bronze
1928	Patrick O'Callaghan (IRL) 51.39m	Ossian Skjöld (SWE) 51.29m	Edmund Black (USA) 49.03m
1932	Patrick O'Callaghan (IRL) 53.92m	Ville Pörhöla (FIN) 52.27m	Peter Zaremba (USA) 50.33m
1936	Karl Hein (GER) 56.49m	Erwin Blask (GER) 55.04m	Fred Warngard (SWE) 54.83m
1948	Imre Németh (HUN) 56.07m	Ivan Gubijan (YUG) 54.27m	Bob Bennett (USA) 53.73m
1952	József Csermák (HUN) 60.34m	Karl Storch (GER) 58.86m	Imre Németh (HUN) 57.74m
1956	Harold Connolly (USA) 63.19m	Mikhail Krivonosov (URS) 63.03m	Anatoli Samotsvetov (URS) 62.56m
1960	Vasili Rudenkov (URS) 67.10m	Gyula Zsivótzky (HUN) 65.79m	Tadeusz Rut (POL) 65.64m
1964	Romuald Klim (URS) 69.74m	Gyula Zsivótzky (HUN) 69.09m	Uwe Beyer (GER) 68.09m
1968	Gyula Zsivótzky (HUN) 73.36m	Romuald Klim (URS) 73.28m	Lázár Lovász (HUN) 69.78m
1972	Anatoli Bondarchuk (URS) 75.50m	Jochen Sachse (GDR) 74.96m	Vasili Khmelevski (URS) 74.04m
1976	Yuri Sedykh (URS) 77.52m	Alexei Spriridonov (URS) 76.08m	Anatoli Bondarchuk (URS) 75.48m
1980	Yuri Sedykh (URS) 81.80m	Sergei Litvinov (URS) 80.64m	Juri Tamm (URS) 78.96m
1984	Juha Tiainen (FIN) 78.08m	Karl-Hans Riehm (FRG) 77.98m	Klaus Ploghaus (FRG) 76.68m
1988	Sergei Litvínov (URS) 84.80m	Yuri Sedykh (URS) 83.76m	Juri Tamm (URS) 81.16m
1992	Andrei Abduvalyev (EUN) 82.54m	Igor Astapkovich (EUN) 81.96m	Igor Nikulin (EUN) 81.38m
1996	Balázs Kiss (HUN) 81.24m	Lance Deal (USA) 81.12m	Aleksandr Krykun (UKR) 80.02m
2000	Szymon Ziolkowski (POL) 80.02m	Nicola Vizzoni (ITA) 79.64m	Igor Astapkovich (BLR) 79.17m

1896 and 1906 event not held. * Competition was from a 9ft (2.74m) circle.

JAVELIN

	Gold	Silver	Bronze
1906	Eric Lemming (SWE) 53.90m	Knut Lindberg (SWE) 45.17m	Bruno Söderström (SWE) 44.92m
1908	Eric Lemming (SWE) 54.82m	Arne Halse (NOR) 50.57m	Otto Nilsson (SWE) 47.09m
1912	Eric lemming (SWE) 60.64m	Juho Saaristo (FIN) 58.66m	Mór Kóczán (HUN) 55.50m
1920	Jonni Myyrä (FIN) 65.78m	Urho Peltonen (FIN) 63.50m	Pekka Johansson (FIN) 63.09m
1924	Jonni Myyrä (FIN) 62.96m	Gunnar Lindström (SWE) 60.92m	Eugene Oberst (USA) 58.35m
1928	Erik Lundkvist (SWE) 66.60m	Béla Szepes (HUN) 65.26m	Olva Sunde (NOR) 63.97m
1932	Matti Järvinen (FIN) 72.71m	Matti Sippala (FIN) 69.79m	Eino Penttila (FIN) 68.69m
1936	Gerhard Stöck (GER) 71.84m	Yrjö Nikkanen (FIN) 70.77m	Kalervo Toivonen (FIN) 70.72m
1948	Tapio Rautavaara (FIN) 69.77m	Steve Seymour (USA) 67.56m	József Várszegi (HUN) 67.03m
1952	Cyrus Young (USA) 73.78m	Bill Miller (USA) 72.46m	Toivo Hyytiäinen (FIN) 71.89m
1956	Egil Danielsen (NOR) 85.71m	Janusz Sidlo (POL) 79.98m	Viktor Tsibulenko (URS) 79.50m
1960	Viktor Tsibulenko (URS) 84.64m	Walter Krüger (GER) 79.36m	Gergely Kulcsár (HUN) 78.57m
1964	Pauli nevala (FIN) 82.66m	Gergely Kulcsár (HUN) 82.32m	Janis Lusis (URS) 80.57m
1968	Janis Lusis (URS) 90.10m	Jorma Kinnunen (FIN) 88.58m	Gergely Kulcsár (HUN) 87.06m
1972	Klaus Wolfermann (FRG) 90.48m	Janis Lusis (URS) 90.46m	Bill Schmidt (USA) 84.42m
1976	Miklos Németh (HUN) 94.58m	Hannu Siitonen (FIN) 87.92m	Gheorghe Megelea (ROM) 87.16m
1980	Dainis Kula (URS) 91.20m	Aleksandr Makarov (URS) 89.64m	Wolfgang Hanisch (GDR) 86.72m
1984	Arto Härkonen (FIN) 86.76m	David Ottley (GBR) 85.74m	Kenth Eldebrink (SWE) 83.72m
1988	Tapio Korjus (FIN) 84.28m	Jan Zelezny (TCH) 84.12m	Seppo Räty (FIN) 83.26m
1992*	Jan Zelezny (TCH) 89.66m	Seppo Räty (FIN) 86.60m	Steve Backley (GBR) 83.38m
1996	Jan Zelezny (CZE) 88.16m	Steve Backley (GBR) 87.44m	Seppo Räty (FIN) 86.98m
2000	Jan Zelezny (CZE) 90.17m	Steve Backley (GBR) 89.85m	Sergei Makarov (RUS) 88.67m

1896–1904 event not held. * A new javelin was introduced.

DECATHLON* (New points calculations made by Bob Sparks)[†]

	Gold	Silver	Bronze
1904‡	Thomas Kiely (GBR) 6036pts	Adam Gunn (USA) 5907pts	Truxton Hare (USA) 5813pts
1912§	Hugo Wieslander (SWE) 5966pts	Charles Lomberg (SWE) 5721pts	Gösta Holmer (SWE) 5768pts
1920	Helge Lövland (NOR) 5803pts	Brutus Hamilton (USA) 5739pts	Bertil Ohlsson (SWE) 5640pts
1924	Harold Osborn (USA) 6476pts	Emerson Norton (USA) 6117pts	Alexander Klumberg (EST) 6056pts
1928	Paavo Yrjölä (FIN) 6587pts	Akilles Järvinen (FIN) 6645pts	Ken Doherty (USA) 6428pts
1932	Jim Bausch (USA) 6736pts	Akilles Järvinen (FIN) 6879pts	Wolrad Eberle (GER) 6661pts
1936	Glenn Morris (USA) 7254pts	Robert Clark (USA) 7063pts	Jack Parker (USA) 6760pts
1948	Bob Mathias (USA) 6628pts	Ignace Heinrich (FRA) 6559pts	Floyd Simmons (USA) 6531pts

	Gold	Silver	Bronze
1952	Bob Mathias (USA) 7592pts	Milt Campbell (USA) 6995pts	Floyd Simmons (USA) 6945pts
1956	Milt Campbell (USA) 7614pts	Rafer Johnson (USA) 7457pts	Vasili Kuznetsov (URS) 7337pts
1960	Rafer Johnson (USA) 7926pts	Yang Chuan-Kwang (TPE) 7839pts	Vasili Kuznetsov (URS) 7557pts
1964	Willi Holdorf (GER) 7794pts	Rein Aun (URS) 7744pts	Hans-Joachim Walde (GER) 7735pts
1968	Bill Toomey (USA) 8144pts	Hans-Joachim Walde (FRG) 8094pts	Kurt Bendlin (FRG) 8071pts
1972	Nikolai Avilov (URS) 8466pts	Leonid Litvinenko (URS) 7970pts	Ryszard Katus (POL) 7936pts
1976	Bruce Jenner (USA) 8634pts	Guido Kratschmer (FRG) 8407pts	Nikolai Avilov (URS) 8378pts
1980	Daley Thompson (GBR) 8522pts	Yuri Kutsenko (URS) 8369pts	Sergei Zhelanov (URS) 8135pts
1984	Daley Thompson (GBR) 8847pts	Jürgen Hingsen (FRG) 8695pts	Siegfried Wentz (FRG) 8416pts
1988	Christian Schenk (GDR) 8488pts	Torsten Voss (GDR) 8399pts	Dave Steen (CAN) 8328pts
1992	Robert Zmelik (TCH) 8611pts	Antonio Penalver (CUB) 8412pts	Dave Johnson (USA) 8309pts
1996	Dan O'Brien (USA) 8824pts	Frank Busemann (GER) 8706pts	Tomas Dvorak (CZE) 8664pts
2000	Erki Nool (EST) 8641pts	Roman Sebrle (CZE) 8606pts	Chris Huffins (USA) 8595pts

1896–1900 and 1906–1908 event not held. * The decathlon consists of 100m, long jump, shot put, high jump, 400m, 110m hurdles, discus, pole vault, javelin and 1500m. The competition occupies two days, although in 1912 it took three days. † Scores since 1912 (given above) have been re-calculated on the current, 1984, scoring tables, for the purposes of comparison. Note that in 1912, 1928, 1932 and 1948 the original medal order would have been different if these tables had been in force. ‡ Consisted of 100yd, 1 mile, 120yd hurdles, 880yd walk, high jump, long jump, pole vault, shot out hammer and 56lb weight. § Jim Thorpe (USA) finished first with 6564pts, but was later disqualified for a breach of the then in force amateur rules. He was re-instated posthumously by the IOC in 1982, but only as joint first.

WOMEN (Women's events were first contested in 1928)

100 METRES

	Gold	Silver	Bronze
1928	Elizabeth Robinson (USA) 12.2	Fanny Rosenfeld (CAN) 12.3	Ethel Smith (CAN) 12.3
1932	Stanislawa Walasiewicz (POL) 11.9	Hilda Strike (CAN) 11.9	Wilhelmina von Bremen (USA) 2.0
1936	Helen Stephens (USA) 11.5	Stanislawa Walalsiewicz (POL) 11.7	Kathe Krauss (GER) 11.9
1948	Fanny Blankers-Koen (NED) 11.9	Dorothy Manley (GBR) 12.2	Shirley Strickland (AUS) 12.2
1952	Marjorie Jackson (AUS) 11.5 (11.67)	Daphne Hasenjager (RSA) 11.8 (12.05))	Shirley Strickland (AUS) 11.9 (12.12
1956	Betty Cuthbert (AUS) 11.5 (11.82)	Christa Stubnick (GER) 11.7 (11.92)	Marlene Matthews (AUS) 11.7 (11.94)
1960	Wilma Rudolph (USA) 11.0 (11.18)	Dorothy Hyman (GBR) 11.3 (11.43)	Giuseppina Leone (ITA) 11.3 (11.48)
1964	Wyomia Tyus (USA) 11.4 (11.49)	Edith Maguire (USA) 11.6 (11.62)	Ewa Klobukowska (POL)* 11.6 (11.64)
1968	Wyomia Tyus (USA) 11.0 (11.08)	Barbara Ferrell (USA) 11.1 (11.15)	Irena Szewinska (POL) 11.1 (11.19)
1972	Renate Stecher (GDR) 11.07	Raelene Boyle (AUS) 11.23	Silvia Chivas (CUB) 11.24
1976	Annegret Richter (FRG) 11.08	Renate Stecher (GDR) 11.13	Inge Helten (FRG) 11.17
1980	Ludmila Kondratyeva (URS) 11.06	Marlies Göhr (GDR) 11.07	Ingrid Auerswald (GDR) 11.14
1984	Evelyn Ashford (USA) 10.97	Alice Brown (USA) 11.13	Merlene Ottey-Page (JAM) 11.16
1988	Florence Griffith-Joyner (USA) 10.54†	Evelyn Ashford (USA) 10.83	Heike Drechsler (GDR) 10.85
1992	Gail Devers (USA) 10.82	Juliet Cuthbert (JAM) 10.83	Irina Privalova (EUN) 10.84
1996	Gail Devers (USA) 10.94	Merlene Ottey (JAM) 10.94	Gwen Torrence (USA 10.96
2000	Marion Jones (USA) 10.75	Ekaterini Thanou (GRE) 11.12	Tanya Lawrence (JAM) 11.18

* Three years later Klobukowska failed a sex test and was banned from competition. † Final was wind-assisted; 10.62 in preliminary round.

200 METRES

	Gold	Silver	Bronze
1948	Fanny Blankers-Koen (NED) 24.4	Audrey Williamson (GBR) 25.1	Audrey Patterson (USA) 25.2*
1952	Marjorie Jackson (AUS) 23.7 (23.89)	Bertha Brouwer (NED) 24.2 (24.25)	Nadyezhda Khnykina (URS) 24.2 (24.37)
1956	Betty Cuthbert (AUS) 23.4 (23.55)	Christa Stubnick (GER) 23.7 (23.89)	Marlene Matthews (AUS) 23.8 (24.10)

	Gold	Silver	Bronze
1960	Wilma Rudolph (USA) 24.0 (24.13)	Jutta Heine (GER) 24.4 (24.58)	Dorothy Hyman (GBR) 24.7 (24.82)
1964	Edith Maguire (USA) 23.0 (23.05)	Irena Kirszenstein (POL) 23.1 (23.13)	Marilyn Black (AUS) 23.1 (23.18)
1968	Irena Szewinska (POL) 22.5 (22.58)	Raelene Boyle (AUS) 22.7 (22.74)	Jennifer Lamy (AUS) 22.8 (22.88)
1972	Renate Stecher (GDR) 22.40	Raelene Boyle (AUS) 22.45	Irena Szewinska (POL) 22.74
1976	Bärbel Eckert (GDR) 22.37	Annegret Richter (FRG) 22.39	Renate Stecher (GDR) 22.47
1980	Bärbel Wöckel (GDR) 22.03	Natalya Bochina (URS) 22.19	Merlene Ottey (JAM) 22.20
1984	Valerie Brisco-Hooks (USA) 21.81	Florence Griffith (USA) 22.04	Merlene Ottey-Page (JAM) 22.09
1988	Florence Giffith-Joyner (USA) 21.34	Grace Jackson (JAM) 21.72	Heike Drechsler (GDR) 21.95
1992	Gwen Torrence (USA) 21.81	Juliet Cuthbert (JAM) 22.02	Merlene Ottey (JAM) 22.09
1996	Marie-José Pérec (FRA) 22.12	Merlene Ottey (JAM) 22.24	Mary Onyali (NGR) 22.38
2000	Marion Jones (USA) 21.84	Pauline Davis-Thompson (BAH) 22.27	Susanthika Jayasinghe (SRI) 22.28

1928–1936 event not held. * The photo-finish picture indicates that Shirley Strickland (AUS) was third.

400 METRES

	Gold	Silver	Bronze
1964	Betty Cuthbert (AUS) 52.0 (52.01)	Ann Packer (GBR) 52.2 (52.20)	Judith Amoore (AUS) 53.4
1968	Colette Besson (FRA) 52.0 (52.03)	Lillian Board (GBR) 52.1 (52.12)	Natalya Burda (URS) 52.2 (52.25)
1972	Monika Zehrt (GDR) 51.08	Rita Wilden (FRG) 51.21	Kathy Hammond (USA) 51.64
1976	Irena Szewinska (POL) 49.29	Christina Brehmer (GDR) 50.51	Ellen Streidt (GDR) 50.55
1980	Marita Koch (GDR) 48.88	Jarmila Kratochvílová (TCH) 49.46	Christina Lathan (GDR) 49.66
1984	Valerie Brisco-Hooks (USA) 48.83	Chandra Cheeseborough (USA) 49.05	Kathy Cook (GBR) 49.43
1988	Olga Bryzgina (URS) 48.65	Petra Müller (GDR) 49.45	Olga Nazarova (URS) 49.90
1992	Marie-José Pérec (FRA) 48.83	Olga Bryzgina (EUN) 49.05	Ximena Restrepo (COL) 49.64
1996	Marie-José Pérec (FRA) 48.25	Cathy Freeman (AUS) 48.63	Falilat Ogunkoya (NGR) 49.10
2000	Cathy Freeman (AUS) 49.11	Lorraine Graham (JAM) 49.58	Katharine Merry (GBR) 49.72

1928–1960 event not held.

800 METRES

	Gold	Silver	Bronze
1928	Lina Radke (GER) 2:16.8	Kinuye Hitomi (JPN) 2:17.6	Inga Gentzel (SWE) 2:17.8
1960	Ludmila Shevtsova (URS) 2:04.3	Branda Jones (AUS) 2:04.4	Ursula Donath (GER) 2:05.6
1964	Ann Packer (GBR) 2:01.1	Maryvonne Dupureur (FRA) 2:01.9	Marise Chamberlain (NZL) 2:02.8
1968	Madeline Manning (USA) 2:00.9	Ilona Silai (ROM) 2:02.5	Maria Gommers (NED) 2:02.6
1972	Hildegard Falck (FRG) 1:58.6	Niole Sabaite (URS) 1:58.7	Gunhild Hoffmeister (GDR) 1:59.2
1976	Tatyana Kazankina (URS) 1:54.9	Nikolina Shtereva (BUL) 1:55.4	Elfi Zinn (GDR) 1:55.6
1980	Nadyezda Olizarenko (URS) 1:53.5	Olga Mineyeva (URS) 1:54.9	Tatyana Providokhina (URS) 1:55.5
1984	Doina Melinte (ROM) 1:57.60	Kim Gallagher (USA) 1:58.63	Fita Lovin (ROM) 1:58.83
1988	Sigrun Wodars (GDR) 1:56.10	Christine Wachtel (GDR) 1:56.64	Kim Gallagher (USA) 1:56.91
1992	Ellen van Langen (NED) 1:55.54	Lilia Nurutdinova (EUN) 1:55.99	Ana Quirot (CUB) 1:56.80
1996	Svetlana Masterkova (RUS) 1:57.73	Ana Quirot (CUB) 1:58.11	Maria Mutola (MOZ) 1:58.71
2000	Maria Mutola (MOZ) 1:56.15	Stephanie Graf (AUT) 1:56.64	Kelly Holmes (GBR) 1:56.80

1932–1956 event not held.

1500 METRES

	Gold	Silver	Bronze
1972	Ludmila Bragina (URS) 4:01.4	Gunhild Hoffmeister (GDR) 4:02.8	Paola Cacchi-Pigni (ITA) 4:02.9
1976	Tatyana Kazankina (URS) 4:05.5	Gunhild Hoffmeister (GDR) 4:06.0	Ulrike Klapezynski (GDR) 4:06.1
1980	Tatyana Kazankina (URS) 3:56.6	Christiane Wartenberg (GDR) 3:57.8	Nadyezda Olizarenko (URS) 3:59.6
1984	Gariella Dorio (ITA) 4:03.25	Doina Melinte (ROM) 4:03.76	Maricica Puica (ROM) 4:04.15
1988	Paula Ivan (ROM) 3:53.96	Laima Baikauskaite (URS) 4:00.24	Tatyana Samolenko (URS) 4:00.30
1992	Hassiba Boulmerka (ALG) 3:55.30	Ludmila Ragacheva (EUN) 3:56.91	Qu Yunxia (CHN) 3:57.08

	Gold	Silver	Bronze
1996	Svetlana Masterkova (RUS) 4:00.83	Gabriela Szabo (ROM) 4:01.54	Theresia Kiesl (AUT) 4:03.02
2000	Nouria Merah-Benida (ALG) 4:05.10	Violeta Szekely (ROM) 4:05.15	Gabriela Szabo (ROM) 4:05.27

1928–1968 event not held.

3000 METRES
(Replaced by 5000m in 1996)

	Gold	Silver	Bronze
1984	Maricica Puica (ROM) 8:35.96	Wendy Sly (GBR) 8:39.47	Lynn Williams (CAN) 8:42.14
1988	Tatyana Samoilenko (URS) 8:26.53	Paula Ivan (ROM) 8:27.15	Yvonne Murray (GBR) 8:29.02
1992	Yelena Romanova (EUN) 8:46.04	Tatyana Dorovskikh (EUN) 8:46.85	Angela Chalmers (CAN) 8:47.22

1928–1980 event not held.

5000 METRES

	Gold	Silver	Bronze
1996	Wang Junxia (CHN) 14:59.88	Pauline Konga (KEN) 15:03.49	Roberta Brunet (ITA) 15:07.52
2000	Gabriela Szabo (ROM) 14:40.79	Sonia O'Sullivan (IRL) 14:41.02	Gete Wami (ETH) 14:42.23

1928–1992 event not held.

10,000 METRES

	Gold	Silver	Bronze
1988	Olga Bondarenko (URS) 31:05.21	Liz McColgan (GBR) 31:08.44	Yelena Zhupiyeva (URS) 31:19.82
1992	Derartu Tulu (ETH) 31:06.02	Elana Meyer (RSA) 31:11.75	Lynn Jennings (USA) 31:19.89
1996	Fernanda Ribeiro (POR) 31:01.63	Wang Junxia (CHN) 31:02.58	Gete Wami (ETH) 31:06.65
2000	Derartu Tulu (ETH) 30:17.49	Gete Wami (ETH) 30:22.48	Fernando Ribeiro (POR) 30:22.88

1928–1984 event not held.

MARATHON

	Gold	Silver	Bronze
1984	Joan Benoit (USA) 2hr 24:52	Grete Waitz (NOR) 2hr 26:18	Rosa Mota (POR) 2hr 26:57
1988	Rosa Mota (POR) 2hr 25:40	Lisa Martin (AUS) 2hr 25:53	Kathrin Dörre (GDR) 2hr 26:21
1992	Valentina Yegorova (EUN) 2hr 32:41	Yuko Arimori (JPN) 2hr 32:49	Lorraine Moller (NZL) 2hr 33:59
1996	Fatuma Roba (ETH) 2hr 26:05	Valentina Yegorova (RUS) 2hr 28:05	Yuko Arimori (JPN) 2hr 28:39
2000	Naoko Takahashi (JPN) 2hr 23:14	Lidia Simon (ROM) 2hr 23:22	Joyce Chepchumba (KEN) 2hr 24:45

1928–1980 event not held.

100 METRES HURDLES
(Held over 80 metres Hurdles 1932–1968)

	Gold	Silver	Bronze
1932	Mildred Didrikson (USA) 11.7	Evelyne Hall (USA) 11.7	Marjorie Clark (RSA) 11.8
1936	Trebisonda Valla (ITA) 11.7 (11.75)	Anny Steuer (GER) 11.7 (11.81)	Elizabeth Taylor (CAN) 11.7 (11.81)
1948	Fanny Blankers-Koen (NED) 11.2	Maureen Gardner (GBR) 11.2	Shirley Strickland (AUS) 11.4
1952	Shirley de la Hunty (AUS) 10.8 (11.01)	Maria Golubichnaya (URS) 11.1 (11.24)	Maria Sander (GER) 11.1 (11.38)
1956	Shirley de la Hunty (AUS) 10.7 (10.96)	Gisela Köhler (GER) 10.9 (11.12)	Norma Thrower (AUS) 11.0 (11.25)
1960	Irina Press (URS) 10.8 (10.93)	Carol Quinton (GBR) 10.9 (10.99)	Gisela Birkemeyer (GER) 11.0 (11.13)
1964	Karin Balzer (GER) 10.5 (10.54)	Teresa Ciepla (POL) 10.5 (10.55)	Pam Kilborn (AUS) 10.5 (10.56)
1968	Maureen Caird (AUS) 10.3 (10.39)	Pam Kilborn (AUS) 10.4 (10.46)	Chi Cheng (TPE) 10.4 (10.51)
1972	Annelie Ehrhardt (GDR) 12.59	Valeria Bufanu (ROM) 12.84	Karin Balzer (GDR) 12.90
1976	Johanna Schaller (GDR) 12.77	Tatyana Anisimova (URS) 12.78	Natalya Lebedyeva (URS) 12.80

	Gold	Silver	Bronze
1980	Vera Komisova (URS) 12.56	Johanna Klier (GDR) 12.63	Lucyna Langer (POL) 12.65
1984	Benita Fitzgerald-Brown (USA) 12.84	Shirley Strong (GBR) 12.88	Kim Turner (USA) 13.06
			Michele Chardonnet (FRA) 13.06
1988	Yordanka Donkova (BUL) 12.38	Gloria Siebert (GDR) 12.61	Claudia Zackiewicz (FRG) 12.75
1992	Paraskevi Patoulidou (GRE) 12.64	LaVonna Martin (USA) 12.69	Yordanka Donkova (BUL) 12.70
1996	Ludmila Engquist (SWE) 12.58	Brigita Bukovec (SLO) 12.59	Patricia Girard-Leno (FRA) 12.65
2000	Olga Shishigina (KAZ) 12.65	Gloria Alozia (NGR) 12.68	Melissa Morrison (USA) 12.76

1928 event not held.

400 METRES HURDLES

	Gold	Silver	Bronze
1984	Nawal El Moutawakel (MAR) 54.61	Judi Brown (USA) 55.20	Cristina Cojocaru (ROM) 55.41
1988	Debbie Flintoff-King (AUS) 53.17	Tatyana Ledovskaya (URS) 53.18	Ellen Fiedler (GDR) 53.63
1992	Sally Gunnell (GBR) 53.23	Sandra Farmer-Patrick (USA) 53.69	Janeene Vickers (USA) 54.31
1996	Deon Hemmings (JAM) 52.82	Kim Batten (USA) 53.08	Tonja Buford-Bailey (USA) 53.22
2000	Irina Privalova (RUS) 53.02	Deon Hemmings (JAM) 53.45	Nezha Bidouane (MAR) 53.57

1928–1980 event not held.

4 X 100 METRES RELAY

	Gold	Silver	Bronze
1928	Canada 48.4	United States 48.8	Germany 49.2
1932	United States 47.0 (46.86)	Canada 47.0	Great Britain 47.6
1936	United States 46.9	Great Britain 47.6	Canada 47.8
1948	The Netherlands 47.5	Australia 47.6	Canada 47.8
1952	United States 45.9 (46.14)	Germany 45.9 (46.18)	Great Britain 46.2 (46.41)
1956	Australia 44.5 (44.65)	Great Britain 44.7 (44.70)	United States 44.9 (45.04)
1960	United States 44.5 (44.72)	Germany 44.8 (45.00)	Poland 45.0 (45.19)
1964	Poland 43.6 (43.69)	United States 43.9 (43.92)	Great Britain 44.0 (44.09)
1968	United States 42.8 (42.88)	Cuba 43.3 (43.36)	Soviet Union 43.4 (43.41)
1972	FRG 42.81	GDR 42.95	Cuba 43.36
1976	GDR 42.55	FRG 42.59	Soviet Union 43.09
1980	GDR 41.60	Soviet Union 42.10	GreatBritain 42.43
1984	United States 41.65	Canada 42.77	Great Britain 43.11
1988	United States 41.98	GDR 42.09	Soviet Union 42.75
1992	United States 42.11	Unified Team (EUN) 42.16	Nigeria 42.81
1996	United States 41.95	Bahamas 42.14	Jamaica 42.24
2000	Bahamas 41.95	Jamaica 42.13	United States 42.20

4 X 400 METRES RELAY

	Gold	Silver	Bronze
1972	GDR 3:22.95	United States 3:25.15	FRG 3:26.51
1976	GDR 3:19.23	United States 3:22.81	Soviet Union 3:24.24
1980	Soviet Union 3:20.12	GDR 3:20.35	Great Britain 3:27.5
1984	United States 3:18.29	Canada 3:21.21	FRG 3:22.98
1988	Soviet Union 3:15.17	United States 3:15.51	GDR 3:18.29
1992	Unified Team (EUN) 3:20.20	United States 3:20.92	Great Britain 3:24.23
1996	United States 3:20.91	Nigeria 3:21.04	Germany 3:21.14
2000	United States 3:22.62	Jamaica 3:23.25	Russia 3:23.44

1928–1968 event not held.

10,000 METRES WALK (Replaced by a 20,000 metres walk in 2000)

	Gold	Silver	Bronze
1992	Chen Yueling (CHN) 44:32	Yelena Nikolayeva (EUN) 44:33	Li Chunxiu (CHN) 44:41
1996	Yelena Nikolayeva (RUS) 41:49	Elisabetta Perrone (ITA) 42:12	Wang Yan (CHN) 42:19

1928–1988 event not held.

20,000 METRES WALK (Introduced in 2000)

	Gold	Silver	Bronze
2000	Wang Liping (CHN) 1hr 29:05	Kjersti Plätzer (NOR) 1hr 29:33	Maria Vasco (ESP) 1hr 30:23

HIGH JUMP

	Gold	Silver	Bronze
1928	Ether Catherwood (CAN) 1.59m	Carolina Gisolf (NED) 1.56m	Mildred Wiley (USA) 1.56m
1932	Jean Shiley (USA) 1.657m*	Mildred Didrikson (USA) 1.657m*	Eva Dawes (CAN) 1.60m
1936	Ibolya Csák (HUN) 1.60m	Dorothy Odam (GBR) 1.60m	Elfriede Kaun (GER) 1.60m
1948	Alice Coachman (USA) 1.68m	Dorothy Tyler (GBR) 1.68m	Micheline Ostermeyer (FRA) 1.61m
1952	Esther Brand (RSA) 1.67m	Sheila Lerwill (GBR) 1.65m	Alexandra Chudina (URS) 1.63m
1956	Mildred McDaniel (USA) 1.76m	Thelma Hopkins (GBR) 1.67m	—
		Maria Pisaryeva (URS) 1.67m	
1960	Iolanda Balas (ROM) 1.85m	Jaroslawa Józwiakowska (POL) 1.71m	—
		Dorothy Shirley (GBR) 1.71m	
1964	Iolanda Balas (ROM) 1.90m	Michelle Brown (AUS) 1.80m	Taisia Chenchik (URS) 1.78m
1968	Miloslava Rezková (TCH) 1.82m	Antonina Okorokova (URS) 1.80m	Valentina Kozyr (URS) 1.80m
1972	Ulrike Meyfarth (FRG) 1.92m	Yordanka Bloyeva (BUL) 1.88m	Ilona Gusenbauer (AUT) 1.88m
1976	Rosemarie Ackermann (GDR) 1.93m	Sara Simeoni (ITA) 1.91m	Yordanka Blagoyeva (BUL) 1.91m
1980	Sara Simeoni (ITA) 1.97m	Urszula Kielan (POL) 1.94m	Jutta Kirst (GDR) 1.94m
1984	Ulrike Meyfarth (FRG) 2.02m	Sara Simeoni (ITA) 2.00m	Joni Huntley (USA) 1.97m
1988	Louise Ritter (USA) 2.03m	Stefka Kostadinova (BUL) 2.01m	Tamara Bykova (URS) 1.99m
1992	Heike Henkel (GER) 2.02m	Galina Astafei (ROM) 2.00m	Ioamnet Quintero (CUB) 1.97m
1996	Stefka Kostadinova (BUL) 2.05m	Niki Bakogianni (GRE) 2.03m	Inga Babakova (UKR) 2.01m
2000	Yelena Yelesina (RUS) 2.01m	Hestrie Cloete (RSA) 2.01m	Oana Pantelimon (ROM) 1.99m
			Kajsa Bergquist (SWE) 1.99m

* Some sources suggest 1.66m.

POLE VAULT (Introduced in 2000)

	Gold	Silver	Bronze
2000	Stacy Dragila (USA) 4.60m	Tatiuana Grigorieva (AUS) 4.55m	Vala Flosadottir (ISL) 4.50m

LONG JUMP

	Gold	Silver	Bronze
1948	Olga Gyarmati (HUN) 5.69m	Noëmi Simonetta de Portela (ARG) 5.60m	Ann-Britt Leyman (SWE) 5.57m
1952	Yvette Williams (NZL) 6.24m	Alexandra Chudina (URS) 6.14m	Shirley Cawley (GBR) 5.92m
1956	Elzbieta Krzesinska (POL) 6.35m	Willye White (USA) 6.09m	Nadyezhda Dvalishvili (URS) 6.07m
1960	Vera Krepkina (URS) 6.37m	Elzbieta Krzesinska (POL) 6.27m	Hildrun Claus (GER) 6.21m
1964	Mary Rand (GBR) 6.76m	Irena Kirszenstein (POL) 6.60m	Tatyana Schelkanova (URS) 6.42m
1968	Niorica Viscopoleanu (ROM) 6.82m	Sheila Sherwood (GBR) 6.68m	Tatyana Talysheva (URS) 6.66m
1972	Heidemarie Rosendahl (FRG) 6.78m	Diana Yorgova (BUL) 6.77m	Eva Suranová (TCH) 6.67m
1976	Angela Voigt (GDR) 6.72m	Kathy McMillan (USA) 6.66m	Lidia Alfeyeva (URS) 6.60m
1980	Tatyana Kolpakova (URS) 7.06m	Brigitte Wujak (GDR) 7.04m	Tatyana Skatchko (URS) 7.01m
1984	Anisoara Stanciu (ROM) 6.96m	Vali Ionescu (ROM) 6.81m	Susan Hearnshaw (GBR) 6.80m
1988	Jackie Joyner-Kersee (USA) 7.40m	Heike Drechsler (GDR) 7.22m	Galina Chistiakova (URS) 7.11m
1992	Heike Drechsler (GDR) 7.14m	Inessa Kravets (EUN) 7.12m	Jackie Joyner-Kersee (USA) 7.07m
1996	Chioma Ajunwa (NGR) 7.12m	Fiona May (ITA) 7.02m	Jackie Joyner-Kersee (USA) 7.00m
2000	Heike Drechsler (GER) 6.99m	Fiona May (ITA) 6.92m	Marion Jones (USA) 6.92m

1928–1936 event not held.

TRIPLE JUMP (Introduced in 1996)

	Gold	Silver	Bronze
1996	Inessa Kravets (UKR) 15.33m	Inna Lasovskaya (RUS) 14.98m	Sarka Kasparkova (CZE) 14.98m
2000	Tereza Marinova (BUL) 15.20m	Tatyana Lebedyeva (RUS) 15.00m	Olena Govorova (UKR) 14.96m

1928–1992 event not held.

SHOT

	Gold	Silver	Bronze
1948	Micheline Ostermeyer (FRA) 13.75m	Amelia Piccinini (ITA) 13.09m	Ina Schäffer (AUT) 13.08m
1952	Galina Zybina (URS) 15.28m	Marianne Werner (GER) 14.57m	Klavdia Tochonova (URS) 14.50m
1956	Tamara Tyshkevich (URS) 16.59m	Galina Zybina (URS) 15.53m	Marianne Werner (GER) 15.61m
1960	Tamara Press (URS) 17.32m	Johanna Lüttge (GER) 16.61m	Earlene Brown (USA) 16.42m
1964	Tamara Press (URS) 18.14m	Renate Garisch (GDR) 17.61m	Galina Zybina (URS) 16.42m
1968	Margitta Gummel (GDR) 19.61m	Marita Lange (GDR) 18.78m	Nadyezhda Chizhova (URS) 18.19m
1972	Nadyezhda Chizhova (URS) 21.03m	Margitta Gummel (GDR) 20.22m	Ivanka Khristova (BUL) 19.35m
1976	Ivanka Khristova (BUL) 21.16m	Nadyezhda Chizhova (URS) 20.96m	Helena Fibingerová (TCH) 20.67m
1980	Ilona Slupianek (GDR) 22.41m	Svetlana Krachevskaya (URS) 21.42m	Margitta Pufe (GDR) 21.20m
1984	Claudia Losch (FRG) 20.48m	Mihaela Loghin (ROM) 20.47m	Gael Martin (AUS) 19.19m
1988	Natalya Lisovskaya (URS) 22.24m	Kathrin Neimke (GDR) 21.07m	Li Meisu (CHN) 21.06m
1992	Svetlana Krivelyova (EUN) 21.06m	Huang Zhihong (CHN) 20.47m	Kathrin Neimke (GER) 19.78m
1996	Astrid Kumbernuss (GER) 20.56m	Sui Xinmei (CHN) 19.88m	Irina Khudorozhkina (RUS) 19.35m
2000	Yanina Korolchik (BLR) 20.56m	Larisa Peleshenko (RUS) 19.92m	Astrid Kumbernuss (GER) 19.62m

1928–1936 event not held.

DISCUS

	Gold	Silver	Bronze
1928	Helena Konopacka (POL) 39.62m	Lilian Copeland (USA) 37.08m	Ruth Svedberg (SWE) 35.92m
1932	Lilian Copeland (USA) 40.58m	Ruth Osburn (USA) 40.11m	Jadwiga Wajsówna (POL) 38.73m
1936	Gisela Mauermayer (GER) 47.63m	Jadwiga Wajsówna (POL) 46.22m	Paula Mollenhauer (GER) 39.80m
1948	Micheleine Ostermeyer (FRA) 41.92m	Edera Gentile (ITA) 41.17m	Jacqueline Mazéas (FRA) 40.47m
1952	Nina Romashkova (URS) 51.42m	Elizaveta Bagryantseva (URS) 47.08m	Nina Dumbadze (URS) 46.29m
1956	Olga Fikotová (TCH) 53.69m	Irina Beglyakova (URS) 52.54m	Nina Ponomaryeva (URS) 52.02m
1960	Nina Ponomaryeva (URS) 55.10m	Tamara Press (URS) 52.59m	Lia Manoliu (ROM) 52.36m
1964	Tamara Press (URS) 57.27m	Ingrid Lotz (GER) 57.21m	Lia Manoliu (ROM) 56.97m
1968	Lia Manoliu (ROM) 58.28m	Liesel Westerman (FRG) 57.76m	Jolán Kleiber (HUN) 54.90m
1972	Faina Melnik (URS) 66.62m	Argentina Menis (ROM) 65.06m	Vasilka Stoyeva (BUL) 64.34m
1976	Evelin Sclaak (GDR) 69.00m	Maria Vergova (BUL) 67.30m	Gabriele Hinzmann (GDR) 66.84m
1980	Evelin Jahl (GDR) 69.96m	Maria Petkova (BUL) 67.90m	Tatyana Lesovaya (URS) 67.40m
1984	Ria Stalman (NED) 65.36m	Leslie Deniz (USA) 64.86m	Florenta Craciunescu (ROM) 63.64m
1988	Martina Hellmann (GDR) 72.30m	Diane Gansky (GDR) 71.88m	Tsvetanka Khristova (BUL) 69.74m
1992	Maritza Marten (CUB) 70.06m	Tsvetanka Khristova (BUL) 67.78m	Daniela Costian (AUS) 66.24m
1996	Ilke Wyludda (GER) 69.66m	Natalya Sadova (RUS) 66.48m	Ellina Zvereva (BLR) 65.64m
2000	Ellina Zvereva (BLR) 68.40m	Anastasia Kelesidou (GRE)	Irina Yatchenko (BLR) 65.20m

HAMMER (Introduced in 2000)

	Gold	Silver	Bronze
2000	Kamila Skolimowska (POL) 71.16m	Olga Kuzenkova (RUS) 69.77m	Kirsten Munchow (GER) 69.28m

JAVELIN

	Gold	Silver	Bronze
1932	Mildred Didrikson (USA) 43.68m	Ellen Braumüller (GER) 43.49m	Tilly Fleischer (GER) 43.40m
1936	Tilly Fleischer (GER) 45.18m	Louise Krüger (GER) 43.29m	Marja Kwasniewska (POL) 41.80m
1948	Herma Bauma (AUT) 45.57m	Kaisa Parviainen (FIN) 43.79m	Lily Carlstedt (DEN) 42.08m
1952	Dana Zátopková (TCH) 50.47m	Alexandra Chudina (URS) 50.01m	Yelena Gorchkova (URS) 49.76m

	Gold	Silver	Bronze
1956	Inese Jaunzeme (URS) 53.86m	Marlene Ahrens (CHI) 50.38m	Nadyezda Konyayeva (URS) 50.28m
1960	Elvira Ozolina (URS) 55.98m	Dana Zátopková (TCH) 53.78m	Birute Kalediene (URS) 53.45m
1964	Mihaela Penes (ROM) 60.64m	Márta Rudas (HUN) 58.27m	Yelena Gorchkova (URS) 57.07m
1968	Angéla Németh (HUN) 60.36m	Mihaela Penes (ROM) 59.92m	Eva Janko (AUT) 58.04m
1972	Ruth Fuchs (GDR) 63.88m	Jacqueline Todten (GDR) 62.54m	Kathy Schmidt (USA) 59.94m
1976	Ruth Fuchs (GDR) 65.94m	Marion Becker (FRG) 64.70m	Kathy Schmidt (USA) 63.96m
1980	María Colón (CUB) 68.40m	Saida Gunba (URS) 67.76m	Ute Hommola (GDR) 66.56m
1984	Tessa Sanderson (GBR) 69.56m	Tiina Lillak (FIN) 69.00m	Fatima Whitbread (GBR) 67.14m
1988	Petra Felke (GDR) 74.68m	Fatima Whitbread (GBR) 70.32m	Beate Koch (GDR) 67.30m
1992	Silke Renk (GER) 68.34m	Natalya Shikolenko (EUN) 68.26m	Karen Forkel (GER) 66.86m
1996	Heli Rantanen (FIN) 67.94m	Louise McPaul (AUS) 65.54m	Trine Hattestad (NOR) 64.68m
2000	Trine Hattestad (NOR) 68.91m	Mirela Manjani-Tzelili (GRE) 67.51m	Osleidys Menendez (CUB) 66.18m

1928 event not held.

PENTATHLON*

	Gold	Silver	Bronze
1964	Irina Press (URS) 5246pts	Mary Rand (GBR) 5035pts	Galina Bystrova (URS) 4956pts
1968	Ingrid Becker (FRG) 5098pts	Liese Prokop (AUT) 4966pts	Annamaria Tóth (HUN) 4959pts
1972†	Mary Peters (GBR) 4801pts	Heidemarie Rosendahl (FRG) 4791pts	Burglinde Pollak (GDR) 4768pts
1976‡	Siegrun Siegl (GDR) 4745pts	Chrstine Laser (GDR) 4745pts	Burglinde Pollak (GDR) 4740pts
1980	Nadyezhda Tkachenko (URS) 5083pts	Olga Rukavishnikova (URS) 4937pts	Olga Kuragina (URS) 4875pts

1928–1960 event not held. * The pentathlon consisted of 100m hurdles, shot, high jump, long jump and 200m, from 1964 to 1976. In 1980, the 800m replaced the 200m. † New scoring tables were introduced in May 1971. ‡ Siegl finished ahead of Laser in three events.

HEPTATHLON*
(Replaced Pentathlon in 1984)

	Gold	Silver	Bronze
1984	Glynis Nunn (AUS) 6387pts†	Jackie Joyner (USA) 6363pts	Sabine Everts (FRG) 6388pts
1988	Jackie Joyner-Kersee (USA) 7291pts	Sabine John (GDR) 6897pts	Anke Behmer (GDR) 6858pts
1992	Jackie Joyner-Kersee (USA) 7044pts	Irina Belova (EUN) 6845pts	Sabine Braun (GER) 6649pts
1996	Ghada Shouaa (SYR) 6780pts	Natasha Sazanovich (BLR) 6563pts	Denise Lewis (GBR) 6489pts
2000	Denise Lewis (GBR) 6584pts	Yelena Prokhorova (RUS) 6531pts	Natalya Sazanovich (BLR) 6527pts

* The heptathlon consists of: 100m hurdles, high jump, shot, 200m on the first day; long jump, javelin and 800m on the second day.
† Re-calculated on current tables.

WOMEN WHO HAVE WON MEDALS UNDER BOTH THEIR MAIDEN AND MARRIED NAMES

Becker – Mickler (FRG)
Brehmer – Lathan (GDR)
Eckert – Wöckel (GDR)
Foulds – Paul (GBR)
Joyner – Kersee (USA)
Khnykina – Dvalishvili (URS)
Kirszenstein – Szewinska (POL)
Köhler – Birkemeyer (GDR)
Manning – Jackson (USA)

Odam – Tyler (GBR)
Ponomaryeva – Romashkova (URS)
Richter – Górecka (POL)
Samolenko – Dorovskikh (URS)
Schaller – Klier (GDR)
Schlaak – Jahl (GDR)
Vergova – Petkova (BUL)
Wieczorek – Ciepla (POL)
Zharkova – Maslakova (URS)

DISCONTINUED EVENTS
MEN
60 METRES

	Gold	Silver	Bronze
1900	Alvin Kraenzlein (USA) 7.0	Walter Tewsbury (USA) 7.1	Stanley Rowley (AUS) 7.2
1904	Archie Hahn (USA) 7.0	William Hogenson (USA) 7.2	Fay Moulton (USA) 7.2

3000 METRES TEAM RACE

	Gold	Silver	Bronze
1912	United States 9pts	Sweden 13pts	Greta Britain 23pts
1920	United States 10pts	Great Britain 20pts	Sweden 24pts
1924	Finland 8pts	Great Britain 14pts	United States 25pts

3 MILES TEAM RACE

1908	Great Britain 6pts	United States 19pts	France 32pts

5000 METRES TEAM RACE

1900	Great Britain 26pts	France 29pts	—

4 MILES TEAM RACE

1904	United States 27pts	United States 28pts	—

INDIVIDUAL CROSS-COUNTRY

1912*	Hannes Kolehmainen (FIN) 45:11.6	Hjalmar Andersson (SWE) 45:44.8	John Eke (SWE) 46:37.6
1920†	Paavo Nurmi (FIN) 27:15.0	Erick Backman (SWE) 27:27.6	Heikki Liimatainen (FIN) 27:37.4
1924‡	Paavo Nurmi (FIN) 32:54.8	Ville Ritola (FIN) 34:19.4	Earle Johnson (USA) 35:21.0

* 12,000 metres. † 8000 metres. ‡ 10,000 metres.

TEAM CROSS-COUNTRY

1912	Sweden 10pts	Finland 11pts	Great Britain 49pts
1920	Finland 10pts	Great Britain 21pts	Sweden 23pts
1924	Finland 11pts	United States 14pts	France 20pts

200 METRES HURDLES

1900	Alvin Kraenzlein (USA) 25.4	Norman Pritchard (GBR) 26.6	Walter Tewksbury (USA) n.t.a.
1904	Harry Hillman (USA) 24.6	Frank Castleman (USA) 24.9	George Poage (USA) n.t.a.

1500 METRES WALK

1906	George Bonhag (USA) 7:12.6	Donald Linden (CAN) 7:19.8	Konstantin Spetsiosis (GRE) 7:22.0

3000 METRES WALK

1906	György Szantics (HUN) 15:13.2	Hermann Müller (GER) 15:20.0	Georgios Saridakis (GRE) 15:33.0
1920	Ugo Frigerio (ITA) 13:14.2	George Parker (AUS) n.t.a.	Richard Remer (USA) n.t.a.

3500 METRES WALK

1908	George Larner (GBR) 14:55.0	Ernest Webb (GBR) 15:07.4	Harry Kerr (NZL) 15:43.4

10,000 METRES WALK

1912	George Goulding (CAN) 46:28.4	Ernest Webb (GBR) 46:50.4	Fernando Altimani (ITA) 47:37.6
1920	Ugo Frigerio (ITA) 48:06.2	Joseph Pearman (USA) n.t.a.	Charles Gunn (GBR) n.t.a.
1924	Ugo Frigerio (ITA) 47:49.0	Gordon Goodwin (GBR) 200m	Cecil McMaster (RSA) 300m
1948	John Mikaelsson (SWE) 45:13.2	Ingemar Johansson (SWE) 45:43.8	Fritz Schwab (SUI) 46:00.2
1952	John Mikaelsson (SWE) 45:02.8	Fritz Schwab (SUI) 45:41.0	Bruno Junk (URS) 45:41.2

1928–1936 event not held.

10 MILES WALK

1908	George Larner (GBR) 1hr 15:57.4	Ernest Webb (GBR) 1hr 17:31.0	Edward Spencer (GBR) 1hr 21:20.2

STANDING HIGH JUMP

1900	Ray Ewry (USA) 1.655m	Irving Baxter (USA) 1.525m	Lewis Sheldon (USA) 1.50m
1904	Ray Ewry (USA) 1.50m* (1)	James Stadler (USA) 1.45m	Lawson Robertson (USA) 1.45m
1906	Ray Ewry (USA) 1.565m	Martin Sheridan (USA) 1.40m Léon Dupont (BEL) 1.40m Lawson Robertson (USA) 1.40m	—
1908	Ray Ewry (USA) 1.575m	Konstantin Tsiklitiras (GRE) 1.55m John Biller (USA) 1.55m	—
1912	Platt Adams (USA) 1.63m	Benjamin Adams (USA) 1.60m	Konstantin Tsiklitiras (GRE) 1.55m

* Some sources suggest that the height was 1.60m.

STANDING LONG JUMP

	Gold	Silver	Bronze
1900	Ray Ewry (USA) 3.21m	Irving Baxter (USA) 3.135m	Emile Torchebeouf (FRA) 3.03m
1904	Ray Ewry (USA) 3.476m	Charles King (USA) 3.28m	John Biller (USA) 3.26m
1906	Ray Ewry (USA) 3.30m	Martin Sheridan (USA) 3.095m	Lawson Robertson (USA) 3.05m
1908	Ray Ewry (USA) 3.335m	Konstantin Tsiklitiras (GRE) 3.23m	Martin Sheridan (USA) 3.225m
1912	Konstantin Tsiklitiras (GRE) 3.37m	Platt Adams (USA) 3.36m	Benjamin Adams (USA) 3.28m

STANDING TRIPLE JUMP

1900	Ray Ewry (USA) 10.58m	Irving Baxter (USA) 9.95m	Robert Garrett (USA) 9.50m
1904	Ray Ewry (USA) 10.55m	Charles King (USA) 10.16m	James Stadler (USA) 9.53m

STONE PUT (6.40KG)

1906	Nicolaos Georgantas (GRE) 19.925m	Martin Sheridan (USA) 19.035m	Michel Dorizas (GRE) 18.585m

SHOT (BOTH HANDS)
(Aggregate of throws with right and left hands)

1912	Ralph Rose (USA) 27.70m	Patrick McDonald (USA) 27.53m	Elmer Niklander (FIN) 27.14m

DISCUS (BOTH HANDS)
(Aggregate of throws with right and left hands)

1912	Armas Taipale (FIN) 82.86m	Elmer Niklander (FIN) 77.96m	Emil Magnusson (SWE) 77.37m

DISCUS (GREEK STYLE)

1906	Werner Järvinen (FIN) 35.17m	Nicolaos Georgantas (GRE) 32.80m	István Mudin (HUN) 31.91m
1908	Martin Sheridan (USA) 38.00m	Marquis Horr (USA) 37.325m	Werner Järvinen (FIN) 36.48m

JAVELIN (BOTH HANDS)
(Aggregate of throws with right and left hands)

1912	Juho Saaristo (FIN) 109.42m	Väinö Siikamiemi (FIN) 101.13m	Urho Peltonen (FIN) 100.24m

JAVELIN (FREE STYLE)

1908	Eric Lemming (SWE) 54.44m	Michel Dorizas (GRE) 51.36m	Arne Halse (NOR) 49.73m

WEIGHT THROW 56-POUND (25.4KG)

1904	Étienne Desmateau (CAN) 10.465m	John Flanagan (USA) 10.16m	James Mitchell (USA) 10.135m
1920	Patrick McDonald (USA) 11.265m	Patrick Ryan (USA) 10.965m	Carl Lind (SWE) 10.25m

PENTATHLON

1906*	Hjalmar Mellander (SWE) 24pts	István Mudin (HUN) 25pts	Eric lemming (SWE) 29pts
1912†	Ferdinand Bie (NOR) 16pts‡	James Donahue (USA) 24pts	Frank Lukeman (CAN) 24pts
1920†	Eero Lehtonen (FIN) 14pts	Everett Bradley (USA) 24pts	Hugo Lahtinen (FIN) 26pts
1924†	Eero Lehtonen (FIN) 14pt	Elemér Somfay (HUN) 16pts	Robert LeGendre (USA) 18pts

* Consisted of standing long jump, discus (Greek Style), javelin, one-lap (192-m) race and Greco-Roman wrestling. † Consisted of long jump, javelin, 200m, discus and 1500m. ‡ Jim Thorpe (USA) finished first, with 7pts but was subsequently disqualified. He was re-instated posthumously in 1982, but only as joint first.

BADMINTON MEDALS

MEN

	Gold	Silver	Bronze
1992	Alan Budi Kusuma (INA)	Ardy Wiranata (INA) Hermawan Susanto (INA)	Thomas Stuer-Lauridsen (DEN)
1996	Poul-Erik Høyer-Larsen (DEN)	Jiong Dong (CHN)	Rashid Sidek (MAS)
2000	Ji Xinpeng (CHN)	Hendrawan (INA)	Xuanze Xia (CHN)

1896–1988 event not held.

WOMEN

	Gold	Silver	Bronze
1992	Susi Susanti (INA)	Bang Soo-Hyun (KOR)	Huang Hua (CHN)
			Tang Jiuhong (CHN)
1996	Bang Soo-Hyun (KOR)	Mia Audina (INA)	Susi Susanti (INA)
2000	Gong Zhichao (CHN)	Camilla Martin (DEN)	Ye Zhaoying (CHN)

1896–1988 event not held.

MEN'S DOUBLES

	Gold	Silver	Bronze
1992	Korea	Indonesia	Malaysia
			China
1996	Indonesia	Malaysia	Indonesia
2000	Indonesia	Korea	Korea

1896–1988 event not held.

WOMEN'S DOUBLES

	Gold	Silver	Bronze
1992	Korea	China	Korea
			China
1996	China	Korea	China
2000	China	China	China

1896–1988 event not held.

MIXED DOUBLES

	Gold	Silver	Bronze
1996	Korea	Korea	China
2000	China	Indonesia	Great Britain

1896–1992 event not held

BASEBALL MEDALS

	Gold	Silver	Bronze
1992	Cuba	Taiwan	Japan
1996	Cuba	Japan	United States
2000	United States	Cuba	Korea

1896–1988 event not held.

BASKETBALL MEDALS

MEN

	Gold	Silver	Bronze
1936	United States	Canada	Mexico
1948	United States	France	Brazil
1952	United States	Soviet Union	Uruguay
1956	United States	Soviet Union	Uruguay
1960	United States	Soviet Union	Brazil
1964	United States	Soviet Union	Brazil
1968	United States	Yugoslavia	Soviet Union
1972	Soviet Union	United States	Cuba
1976	United States	Yugoslavia	Soviet Union
1980	Yugoslavia	Italy	Soviet Union
1984	United States	Spain	Yugoslavia
1988	Soviet Union	Yugoslavia	United States
1992	United States	Croatia	Lithuania
1996	United States	Yugoslavia	Lithuania
2000	United States	France	Lithuania

1896–1932 event not held.

WOMEN

	Gold	Silver	Bronze
1976	Soviet Union	United States	Bulgaria
1980	Soviet Union	Bulgaria	Yugoslavia
1984	United States	Korea	China
1988	United States	Yugoslavia	Soviet Union
1992	Unified Team	China	United States
1996	United States	Brazil	Australia
2000	United States	Australia	Brazil

1896–1972 event not held.

BEACH VOLLEYBALL MEDALS (Introduced in 1996)

MEN'S DOUBLES

	Gold	Silver	Bronze
1996	United States	United States	Canada
2000	United States	Brazil	Germany

WOMEN'S DOUBLES

	Gold	Silver	Bronze
1996	Brazil	Brazil	Australia
2000	Australia	Brazil	Brazil

BOXING MEDALS

LIGHT-FLYWEIGHT Weight up to 48kg (105.8lb)

	Gold	Silver	Bronze
1968	Francisco Rodriguez (VEN)	Yong-ju Jee (KOR)	Harlan Marbley (USA)
			Hubert Skrzypczak (POL)
1972	György Gedo (HUN)	U Gil Kim (PRK)	Ralph Evans (GBR)
			Enrique Rodriguez (ESP)
1976	Jorge Hernandez (CUB)	Byong Uk Li (PRK)	Payao Pooltarat (THA)
			Orlando Maladonado (PUR)
1980	Shamil Sabirov (URS)	Hipolito Ramos (CUB)	Byong Uk Li (PRK)
			Ismail Moustafov (BUL)
1984	Paul Gonzales (USA)	Saltore Todisco (ITA)	Keith Mwila (ZAM)
			José Bolivar (VEN)
1988	Ivailo Hristov (CUB)	Michael Carabajal (USA)	Robert Isaszegi (HUN)
			Leopoldo Serantes (PHI)
1992	Rogelio Marcelo (CUB)	Daniel Bojinov (BUL)	Roel Velasco (PHI)
			Jan Quast (GER)
1996	Daniel Petrov (BUL)	Mansueto Velsco (PHI)	Oleg Kuryukhin (UKR)
			Rafael Lozano (ESP)
2000	Brahim Asloum (FRA)	Rafael Lozano Munoz (CUB)	Un-Chol Kim (KOR0
			Maikro Romero (CUB)

1896–1964 event not held.

FLYWEIGHT From 1948 the weight limit has been 51kg (112.5lb). In 1904 it was 47.6kg (105lb). From 1920 to 1936 the weight limit was 50.8kg (112lb).

	Gold	Silver	Bronze
1904	George Finnegan (USA)	Miles Burke (USA)	—*
1920	Frank Di Gennara (USA)	Anders Petersen (DEN)	William Cuthbertson (GBR)
1924	Fidel LaBarba (USA)	James McKenzie (GBR)	Raymond Fee (USA)
1928	Antal Kocsis (HUN)	Armand Appel (FRA)	Carlo Cavagnoli (ITA)
1932	István Enekes (HUN)	Francisco Cabanas (MEX)	Louis Salica (USA)
1936	Willi Kaiser (GER)	Gavino Matta (ITA)	Louis Lauria (USA)
1948	Pascual Perez (ARG)	Spartaco Bandinelli (ITA)	Soo-Ann Han (KOR)
1952	Nathan Brooks (USA)	Edgar Basel (GER)	Anatoli Bulakov (URS)
			William Toweel (RSA)
1956	Terence Spinks (GBR)	Mircea Dobrescu (ROM)	John Caldwell (IRL)
			René Libeer (FRA)

	Gold	Silver	Bronze
1960	Gyula Török (HUN)	Sergei Sivko (URS)	Kyoshi Tanabe (JPN)
			Abdelmoneim Elguindi (EGY)
1964	Fernando Atzori (ITA)	Artur Olech (POL)	Robert Carmody (USA)
			Stanislav Sorokin (URS)
1968	Ricardo Delagdo (MEX)	Artur Olech (POL)	Servilio Oliveira (BRA)
			Leo Rwabwogo (UGA)
1972	Gheorghi Kostadinov (BUL)	Leo Rwabwogo (UGA)	Leszek Blazynski (POL)
			Douglas Rodriguez (CUB)
1976	Leo Randolph (USA)	Ramón Duvalon (CUB)	Leszek Blazynski (POL)
			David Torsyan (URS)
1980	Petar Lessov (BUL)	Viktor Miroschnicheko (URS)	Hugh Russel (IRL)
			Janos Varadi (HUN)
1984	Steve McCrory (USA)	Redzep Redzepovski (YUG)	Eyup Can (TUR)
			Ibrahim Bilali (KEN)
1988	Kim Kwang-Sun (KOR)	Andreas Tew (GDR)	Mario González (MEX)
			Timofey Skriabin (URS)
1992	Choi Chol-su (PRK)	Rául González (CUB)	Timothy Austin (USA)
			István Kovács (HUN)
1996	Maikro Romero (CUB)	Bulat Dzumadilov (KAZ)	Albert Pakeyev (RUS)
			Zoltan Lunka (GER)
2000	Wijan Ponlid (THA)	Bolat Dzumadilov (KAZ)	Jerome Thomas (USA)
			Vladimir Sidorenko (UKR)

1896–1900 and 1906–1912 event not held. * No third place.

BANTAMWEIGHT From 1948 the weight limit has been 54kg (119lb). In 1904 it was 52.16kg (115lb). In 1908 it was 52.62kg (116lb). From 1920 to 1936 the weight limit was 53.52kg (118lb).

	Gold	Silver	Bronze
1904	Oliver Kirk (USA)	George Finnegan (USA)	—*
1908	Henry Thomas (GBR)	John Condon (GBR)	William Webb (GBR)
1920	Clarence Walker (RSA)	Christopher Graham (CAN)	James McKenzie (GBR)
1924	William Smith (RSA)	Salvadore Tripoli (USA)	Jean Ces (FRA)
1928	Vittorio Tamagnini (ITA)	John Daley (USA)	Harry Isaacs (RSA)
1932	Horace Gwynne (CAN)	Hans Ziglarski (GER)	José Villanueva (PHI)
1936	Ulderico Sergo (ITA)	Jack Wilson (USA)	Fidel Ortiz (MEX)
1948	Tibor Csik (HUN)	Giovanni Zuddas (ITA)	Juan Venegas (PUR)
1952	Pentti Hämäläinen (FIN)	John McNally (IRL)	Gennadi Garbuzov (URS)
			Joon-ho Kang (KOR)
1956	Wolfgang Behrendt (GER)	Soon Chun-Song (KOR)	Frederick Gilroy (IRL)
			Claudio Barrientos (CHI)
1960	Oleg Grigoriev (URS)	Primo Zamparini (ITA)	Brunoh Bendig (POL)
			Oliver Taylor (AUS)
1964	Takao Sakurai (JPN)	Shin Cho Chung (KOR)	Juan Fabila Mendoza (MEX)
			Washington Rodriguez (URU)
1968	Valeri Sokolov (URS)	Eridadi Mukwanga (UGA)	Eiji Morioka (JPN)
			Kyou-Chull Chang (KOR)
1972	Orlando Martinez (CUB)	Alfonso Zamora (MEX)	George Turpin (GBR)
			Ricardo Carreras (USA)
1976	Yong Jo Gu (PRK)	Charles Mooney (USA)	Patrick Cowdell (GBR)
			Viktor Rybakov (URS)
1980	Juan Hernandez (CUB)	Bernando Pinango (VEN)	Dumitru Cipere (ROM)
			Michael Anthony Parris (GUY)
1984	Maurizio Stecca (ITA)	Hector Lopez (MEX)	Dale Walters (CAN)
			Pedro Nolasco (DOM)
1988	Kennedy McKinney (USA)	Alexandar Hristov (BUL)	Jorge Julio Rocha (COL)
			Phajol Moolsan (THA)
1992	Joel Casamayor (CUB)	Wayne McCullough (IRL)	Li Gwang-sik (PRK)
			Mohamed Achik (MAR)
1996	István Kovács (HUN)	Arnoldo Mesa (CUB)	Raimkul Malakhbekov (RUS)
			Khadpo Vichairachanun (THA)
2000	Guillermo Rigondeaux (CUB)	Raimkul Malakhbekov (RUS)	Sergei Danilchenko (UKR)
			Clarence Vinson (USA)

1896–1900, 1906 and 1912 event not held. * No third place.

FEATHERWEIGHT From 1952 the weight limit has been 57kg (126lb). In 1904 it was 56.70kg (125lb). From 1908 to 1936 it was 57.15kg (126lb). In 1948 the weight limit was 58kg (126lb).

	Gold	Silver	Bronze
1904	Oliver Kirk (USA)	Frank Haller (USA)	Fred Gilmore (USA)
1908	Richard Gunn (GBR)	Charles Morris (GBR)	Hugh Roddin (GBR)
1920	Paul Fritsch (FRA)	Jean Gachet (FRA)	Edoardo Garzena (ITA)
1924	Jackie Fields (USA)	Joseph Salas (USA)	Pedro Quartucci (ARG)
1928	Lambertus van Klaveren (NED)	Victor Peralta (ARG)	Harold Devine (USA)
1932	Carmelo Robeldo (ARG)	Josef Schleinkofer (GER)	Carl Carlsson (SWE)
1936	Oscar Casanovas (ARG)	Charles Cattterall (RSA)	Josef Miner (GER)
1948	Ernesto Foremnti (ITA)	Denis Shepherd (RSA)	Alexei Antkiewicz (POL)
1952	Jan Zachara (TCH)	Sergio Caprari (ITA)	Joseph Ventaja (FRA)
			Leonard Leisching (RSA)
1956	Vladimir Safronov (URS)	Thomas Nicholls (GBR)	Henryk Niedzwiedzki (POL)
			Pentti Hämäläinen (FIN)
1960	Francesco Musso (ITA)	Jerzy Adamski (POL)	William Meyers (RSA)
			Jorma Limmonen (FIN)
1964	Stanislav Stepashkin (URS)	Anthony Villaneuva (PHI)	Charles Brown (USA)
			Heinz Schultz (GER)
1968	Antonio Roldan (MEX)	Albert Robinson (USA)	Philip Waruinge (KEN)
			Ivan Michailov (BUL)
1972	Boris Kuznetsov (URS)	Philip Waruinge (KEN)	Clemente Rojas (COL)
			András Botos (HUN)
1976	Angel Herrera (CUB)	Richard Nowakowski (GDR)	Juan Peredes (MEX)
			Leszek Kosedowski (POL)
1980	Rudi Fink (GDR)	Adolfo Horta (CUB)	Viktor Rybakov (URS)
			Krzysztof Kosedowski (POL)
1984	Meldrick Taylor (USA)	Peter Konyegwachie (NGR)	Turgut Aykac (TUR)
			Omar Peraza (VEN)
1988	Giovanni Parisi (ITA)	Daniel Dumitrescu (ROM)	Lee Jae-Hyuk (KOR)
			Abdelhak Achik (MAR)
1992	Andreas Tew (GER)	Faustino Reyes Lopez (ESP)	Hocine Soltani (ALG)
			Ramazi Paliani (EUN)
1996	Somluck Kamsing (THA)	Serafim Todorov (BUL)	Pablo Chacon (ARG)
			Floyd Mayweather (USA)
2000	Beksat Sattarkhanov (KAZ)	Ricardo Juarez (USA)	Tahar Tamsamani (MAR)
			Kamil Dzhamalutdinov (RUS)

1896–1900, 1906 and 1912 event not held

LIGHTWEIGHT From 1952 the weight has been 60kg (132lb). In 1904, and from 1920 to 1936, it was 61.24kg (135lb). In 1908 it was 63.50kg (140lb). In 1948 the weight limit was 62kg (136.5lb).

	Gold	Silver	Bronze
1904	Harry Springer (USA)	James Eagan (USA)	Russell Van Horn (USA)
1908	Frederick Grace (GBR)	Frederick Spiller (GBR)	Harry Johnson (GBR)
1920	Samuel Mosberg (RSA)	Gotfried Johansen (DEN)	Clarence Newton (CAN)
1924	Hans Nielsen (DEN)	Alfredo Coppello (ARG)	Frederick Boylstein (USA)
1928	Carlo Orlandi (ITA)	Stephen Halaiko (USA)	Gunnar Berggren (SWE)
1932	Lawrence Stevens (RSA)	Thure Ahlqvist (SWE)	Nathan Bor (RSA)
1936	Imre Harangi (HUN)	Nikolai Stepulov (EST)	Erik Agren (SWE)
1948	Gerald Dreyer (USA)	Joseph Vissers (BEL)	Svend Wad (DEN)
1952	Aureliano Bolognesi (ITA)	Alexei Antkiewicz (POL)	Gheorge Fiat (ROM)
			Erkki Pakkanen (FIN)
1956	Richard McTaggart (GBR)	Harry Kurschat (GER)	Anthony Byren (IRL)
			Anatoli Lagetko (URS)
1960	Kazimierz Pazdzior (POL)	Sandro Lopopoli (ITA)	Richard McTaggart (GBR)
			Abel Laudonio (ARG)
1964	Józef Grudzien (POL)	Velikton Barannikov (URS)	Ronald A Harris (USA)
			James McCourt (IRL)
1968	Ronald W Harris (USA)	Józef Grudzien (POL)	Calistrat Cutov (ROM)
			Zvonimir Vujin (YUG)
1972	Jan Szczepanksi (POL)	László Orban (HUN)	Samuel Mbugna (KEN)
			Alfonso Perez (COL)

	Gold	Silver	Bronze
1976	Howard Davis (USA)	Simion Cutov (ROM)	Ace Rusevski (YUG)
			Vasiliy Solomin (URS)
1980	Angel Herrara (CUB)	Viktor Demianenko (URS)	Kazimierz Adach (POL)
			Richard Nowakowski (GDR)
1984	Pernell Whitaker (USA)	Luis Ortiz (PUR)	Martin Mbanga (CMR)
			Chun Chi-Sung (KOR)
1988	Andreas Zülow (GDR)	George Cramme (SWE)	Nerguy Enkhbat (MGL)
			Romallis Ellis (USA)
1992	Oscar de la Hoya (CUB)	Marco Rudolph (USA)	Namjil Bayarsaikhan (MGL)
			Hong Sung-sik (KOR)
1996	Hocine Soltani (ALG)	Tontcho Tonchev (BUL)	Terrance Cauthen (USA)
			Leonard Doroftei (ROM)
2000	Mario Kindelan (CUB)	Andrei Kotelnyk (UKR)	Aleksandr Maletin (RUS)
			Christian Bejarano Benitez (MEX)

1896–1900, 1906 and 1912 event not held

LIGHT-WELTERWEIGHT Weight up to 63.5kg (140lb)

	Gold	Silver	Bronze
1952	Charles Adkins (USA)	Viktor Mednov (URS)	Errki Mallenius (FIN)
			Bruno Visintin (ITA)
1956	Vladimir Yengibarvan (URS)	Franco Nenci (ITA)	Henry Loubscher (RSA)
			Constantin Dumitrescu (ROM)
1960	Bohumil Nemecek (TCH)	Clement Quartey (GHA)	Quincy Daniels (USA)
			Marian Kasprzvk (POL)
1964	Jerzy Kulej (POL)	Yevgeni Frolov (URS)	Eddie Blay (GHA)
			Habib Galhia (TUN)
1968	Jerzy Kulej (POL)	Enrique Regueiforos (CUB)	Arto Nilsson (FIN)
			James Wallington (USA)
1972	Ray Seales (USA)	Anghel Anghelov (BUL)	Zvonimir Vujin (YUG)
			Issaka Daborg (NGR)
1976	Ray Leonard (USA)	Andres Aldama (CUB)	Vladimir Kolev (BUL)
			Kazimierz Szczerba (POL)
1980	Patrizio Oliva (ITA)	Serik Konakbeyev (URS)	José Aguilar (CUB)
			Anthony Willis (GBR)
1984	Jerry Page (USA)	Dhawee Umponmana (THA)	Mircea Fuger (ROM)
			Mirko Puzovic (YUG)
1988	Vycheslav Janovski (URS)	Grahame Cheney (AUS)	Lars Myrberg (SWE)
			Reiner Gies (FRG)
1992	Hector Vinent (CUB)	Marc Leduc (CAN)	Jyri Kjall (FIN)
			Leonard Doroftei (ROM)
1996	Hector Vinent (CUB)	Oktay Urkal (GER)	Bolat Niyazymbetov (KAZ)
			Fathi Missaoui (TUN)
2000	Mahamadkadis Abdullayev (UZB)	Ricardo Williams (USA)	Diogenes Luna Martinez (CUB)
			Mohamed Allalou (ALG)

1896–1948 event not held.

WELTERWEIGHT From 1948 the weight limit has been 67kg (148lb). In 1904 it was 65.27kg (147.5lb). From 1920 to 1936 the weight limit was 66.68kg (147lb).

	Gold	Silver	Bronze
1904	Albert Young (USA)	Harry Springer (USA)	Joseph Lydon (USA)
		James Eagan (USA)	
1920	Albert Schneider (CAN)*	Alexander Ireland (GBR)	Frederick Colberg (USA)
1924	Jean Delarge (BEL)	Héctor Mendez (ARG)	Douglas Lewis (CAN)
1928	Edward Morgan (NZL)	Raul Landini (ARG)	Raymond Smillie (CAN)
1932	Edward Flynn (USA)	Erich Campe (GER)	Bruno Ahlberg (FIN)
1936	Sten Suvio (FIN)	MIchael Murach (GER)	Gerhard Petersen (DEN)
1948	Julius Torma (TCH)	Horace Herring (USA)	Alessandro D'Ottavio (ITA)
1952	Zygmunt Chycla (POL)	Sergei Schtsherbakov (URS)	Victor Jörgensen (DEN)
			Günther Heidemann (GER)
1956	Nicholae Lince (ROM)	Frederick Tiedt (IRL)	Kevin Hogarth (AUS)
			Nicholas Gargano (GBR)

	Gold	Silver	Bronze
1960	Giovanni Benvenutti (ITA)	Yuriy Radonyak (URS)	Leszek Drogosz (POL)
			James Lloyd (GBR)
1964	Marian Kasprzyk (POL)	Ritschardas Tamulis (URS)	Pertti Perhonen (FIN)
			Silvano Bertini (ITA)
1968	Manfred Wolfe (GDR)	Joseph Bessala (CMR)	Vladimir Musalinov (URS)
			Mario Guillot (ITA)
1972	Emilio Corea (CUB)	Janos Kajdi (HUN)	Dick Murunga (KEN)
			Jesse Valdez (USA)
1976	Jochen Bachfeld (GDR)	Pedro Gamarro (VEN)	Reinhard Skricek (FRG)
			Victor Zilberman (ROM)
1980	Andrew Aldama (CUB)	John Mugabi (UGA)	Karl-Heinz Krüger (GDR)
			Kazimierz Szczerba (POL)
1984	Mark Breland (USA)	An Young-Su (KOR)	Joni Nyman (FIN)
			Luciano Bruno (ITA)
1988	Robert Wanglia (KEN)	Laurent Boudouani (FRA)	Jan Dydak (POL)
			Kenneth Gould (USA)
1992	Michael Carruth (IRL)	Juan Hernandez (CUB)	Akrom Chenglai (THA)
			Anibal Acevedo (PUR)
1996	Oleg Saitov (RUS)	Juan Hernandez (CUB)	Marian Simion (ROM)
			Daniel Santos (PUR)
2000	Oleg Saitov (RUS)	Sergei Dotsenko (UKR)	Dorel Simion (ROM)
			Vitali Gusac (MOL)

1896–1900 and 1906–1912 event not held. * Actually an American citizen.

LIGHT-MIDDLEWEIGHT Weight up to 71kg (157lb).

	Gold	Silver	Bronze
1952	László Papp (HUN)	Theunis van Schalkwyk (RSA)	Boris Tishin (URS)
			Eladio Herrera (ARG)
1956	László Papp (HUN)	José Torres (USA)	John McCormack (GBR)
			Zbigniew Pietrzkowski (POL)
1960	Wilbert McClure (USA)	Carmelo Bossi (ITA)	Boris Lagutin (URS)
			William Fisher (GBR)
1964	Boris Lagutin (URS)	Josef Gonzales (FRA)	Nohim Maivegun (NGR)
			Jozef Grzsiak (POL)
1968	Boris Lagutin (URS)	Rolondo Garbey (CUB)	John Baldwin (USA)
			Günther Meier (FRG)
1972	Dieter Kottysch (FRG)	Wieslaw Rudkowski (POL)	Alan Minter (GBR)
			Peter Tiepold (GDR)
1976	Jerzy Rybicki (POL)	Tadiji Kacar (YUG)	Rolando Garbey (CUB)
			Viktor Savchenko (URS)
1980	Armando Martinez (CUB)	Aleksandr Koshkin (URS)	Jan Franck (TCH)
			Detlef Kastner (GDR)
1984	Frank Tate (USA)	Shawn O'Sullivan (CAN)	Manfred Zielonka (FRG)
			Christophe Tiozzo (FRA)
1988	Park Si-Hun (KOR)	Roy Jones (USA)	Richard Woodhall (GBR)
			Raymond Downey (CAN)
1992	Juan Carlos Lemus (CUB)	Orhan Delibas (NED)	György Mizsei (HUN)
			Robin Reid (GBR)
1996	David Reid (USA)	Alfredo Duvergel (CUB)	Karim Tulaganov (UZB)
			Ezmouhan Ibzaimov (KAZ)
2000	Jermachan Ibraimov (KAZ)	Marian Simion (ROM)	Pornchai Thongburan (THA)
			Jermain Taylor (USA)

1896–1948 event not held

MIDDLEWEIGHT From 1952 the weight limit has been 75kg (165lb). From 1904 to 1908 it was 71.68kg (158lb). From 1920 to 1936 it was 72.57kg (160lb). In 1948 the weight limit was 73kg (161lb).

	Gold	Silver	Bronze
1904	Charles Mayer (USA)	Benjamin Spradley (USA)	—*
1908	John Douglas (GBR)	Reginald Baker (AUS/NZL)	William Philo (GBR)
1920	Harry Mallin (GBR)	Georges Prud'homme (CAN)	Moe Herscovich (CAN)
1924	Harry Mallin (GBR)	John Elliott (GBR)	Joseph Beecken (BEL)
1928	Piero Toscani (ITA)	Jan Hermandek (TCH)	Léonard Steyaert (BEL)

	Gold	Silver	Bronze
1932	Carmen Barth (USA)	Amado Azar (ARG)	Ernest Pierce (RSA)
1936	Jean Despeaux (FRA)	Henry Tiller (NOR)	Raúl Villareal (ARG)
1948	László Papp (HUN)	John Wright (GBR)	Ivano Fontana (ITA)
1952	Floyd Patterson (USA)	Vasile Tita (ROM)	Boris Nikolov (URS)
			Stig Sjolin (SWE)
1956	Gennadi Schatkov (URS)	Ramon Tapia (CHI)	Gilbert Chapron (FRA)
			Victor Zalazar (ARG)
1960	Edward Crook (USA)	Tadeusz Walasek (POL)	Ion Monea (ROM)
			Yevgeni Feofanov (URS)
1964	Valeri Popenchenko (URS)	Emil Schultz (GER)	Franco Valle (ITA)
			Tadeusz Walasek (POL)
1968	Christopher Finnegan (GBR)	Alexei Kisselyov (URS)	Agustin Zaragoza (MEX)
			Alfred Jones (USA)
1972	Vyatcheslav Lemechev (URS)	Reima Virtanen (FIN)	Prince Armartey (GHA)
			Marvin Johnston (USA)
1976	Michael Spinks (USA)	Rufat Riskiev (URS)	Alec Nastac (ROM)
			Luis Martinez (CUB)
1980	José Gomez (CUB)	Viktor Savchenko (URS)	Jerzy Rybicki (POL)
			Valentin Silaghi (ROM)
1984	Shin Joop-Sup (KOR)	Virgil Hill (USA)	Mohammed Zaoui (ALG)
			Aristides Gonzales (PUR)
1988	Henry Maske (GDR)	Egerton Marcus (CAN)	Chris Sande (KEN)
			Hussain Shaw Syed (PAK)
1992	Ariel Hernandez (CUB)	Chris Byrd (USA)	Chris Johnson (CAN)
			Lee Seung-bae (KOR)
1996	Ariel Hernandez (CUB)	Malik Beyleroglu (TUR)	Mohamed Bahari (ALG)
			Roshii Wells (USA)
2000	Jorge Gutierrez (CUB)	Gaidarbek Gaidarbekov (RUS)	Vugar Alekperov (AZE)
			Zsolt Erdei (HUN)

1896–1900, 1906 and 1912 event not held. *No Third Place.

LIGHT-HEAVYWEIGHT From 1952 the weight limit has been 81kg (178.5lb). From 1920 to 1936 it was 79.38kg (175lb). In 1948 the weight limit was 80kg (186.25lb).

	Gold	Silver	Bronze
1920	Edward Eagan (USA)	Sverre Sörsdal (NOR)	Harold Franks (GBR)
1924	Harry Mitchell (GBR)	Thyge Petersen (DEN)	Sverre Sörsdal (NOR)
1928	Victor Avendano (ARG)	Ernst Pistulla (GER)	Karel Miljon (NED)
1932	David Carstens (RSA)	Gino Rossi (ITA)	Peter Jörgensen (DEN)
1936	Roger Michelot (FRA)	Richard Vogt (GER)	Francisco Risiglione (ARG)
1948	George Hunter (RSA)	Donald Scott (GBR)	Maurio Cla (ARG)
1952	Norvel Lee (USA)	Antonio Pacenza (ARG)	Anotoli Perov (URS)
			Harri Siljander (FIN)
1956	James Boyd (USA)	Gheorghe Negrea (ROM)	Carlos Lucas (CHI)
			Romualdas Murauskas (URS)
1960	Cassius Clay (USA)	Zbigniew Pietrzykowski (POL)	Anthony Madigan (AUS)
			Giulio Saraudi (ITA)
1964	Cosimo Pinto (ITA)	Alexei Kisselyov (URS)	Alexander Nikolov (BUL)
			Zbigniew Pietrzykowski (POL)
1968	Dan Poznyak (URS)	Ion Monea (ROM)	Georgy Stankov (BUL)
			Stanislav Gragan (POL)
1972	Mate Petlov (YUG)	Gilberto Carrillo (CUB)	Issac Ikhouria (NGR)
			Janusz Gortat (POL)
1976	Leon Spinks (USA)	Sixto Soria (CUB)	Costica Danifoiu (ROM)
			Janusz Gortat (POL)
1980	Slobodan Kacar (YUG)	Pavel Skrzecz (POL)	Herbert Bauch (GDR)
			Ricardo Rojas (CUB)
1984	Anton Josipovic (YUG)	Kevin Barry (NZL)	Mustapha Moussa (ALG)
			Evander Holyfield (USA)
1988	Andrew Maynard (USA)	Nourmagomed Chanavazov (URS)	Damir Skaro (YUG)
			Henryk Petrich (POL)
1992	Torsten May (GER)	Rostislav Zaoulitchyni (EUN)	Wojciech Bartnik (POL)
			Zoltan Beres (HUN)

	Gold	Silver	Bronze
1996	Vasili Jirov (KAZ)	Lee Seung-Bae (KOR)	Antonio Tarver (USA)
			Thomas Ulrich (GER)
2000	Aleksandr Lebziak (RUS)	Rudolf Kraj (CZE)	Andrei Fedtchuk (UKR)
			Sergei Michailov (UZB)

1896–1912 event not held.

HEAVYWEIGHT From 1984 the weight limit has been 91kg (200.5lb). From 1904 to 1908 it was over 71.67kg (158lb). From 1920 to 1936 it was over 79.38kg (175lb). In 1948 it was over 80kg (176.25lb). From 1952 to 1980 the weight limit was over 81kg (178.25lb).

	Gold	Silver	Bronze
1904	Samuel Berger (USA)	Charles Mayer (USA)	William Michaels (USA)
1908	Albert Oldman GBR	Sydney Evans (GBR)	Frederick Parks (GBR)
1920	Ronald Lawton (GBR)	Sören Petersen (DEN)	Xavier Eluère (FRA)
1924	Otto von Porat (NOR)	Sören Petersen (DEN)	Alfredo Porzio (ARG)
1928	Arturo Rodriguez Jurado (ARG)	Nils Ramm (SWE)	Jacob Michaelsen (DEN)
1932	Santiago Lovell (ARG)	Luigi Rovati (ITA)	Frederick Feary (USA)
1936	Herbert Runge (GER)	Guillermo Lovell (ARG)	Erling Nilsen (NOR)
1948	Rafael Iglesias (ARG)	Gunnar Nilsson (SWE)	John Arthur (RSA)
1952	Hayes Edward Sanders (USA)	Ingemar Johansson (SWE)*	Andries Nieman (RSA)
			Ilkka Koski (FIN)
1956	Peter Rademacher (USA)	Lev Mukhin (URS)	Daniel Bekker (RSA)
			Giacomo Ros (ITA)
1960	Franco de Piccoli (ITA)	Daniel Bekker (RSA)	Josef Nemec (TCH)
			Günther Siegmund (GER)
1964	Joe Frazier (USA)	Hans Huber (GER)	Guiseppe Ros (ITA)
			Vadim Yemeynaov (URS)
1968	George Foreman (USA)	Ionas Tschepulis (URS)	Giorgio Bambini (ITA)
			Joaquim Rocha (MEX)
1972	Teofilio Stevenson (CUB)	Ion Alexe (ROM)	Peter Hussing (FRG)
			Hasse Thomsen (SWE)
1976	Teofilio Stevenson (CUB)	Mircea Simon (ROM)	Johnny Tate (USA)
			Clarence Hill (BER)
1980	Teofilio Stevenson (CUB)	Pyotr Zayev (URS)	Jürgen Fanghanel (GDR)
			István Levai (HUN)
1984	Henry Tillman (USA)	Willie Dewitt (CAN)	Angelo Musone (ITA)
			Arnold Vanderlijde (NED)
1988	Ray Mercer (USA)	Baik Hyun-Man (KOR)	Andrzej Golota (POL)
			Arnold Vanderlidje (NED)
1992	Félix Savón (CUB)	David Izonretei (NGR)	David Tua (NZL)
			Arnold Vanderlijde (NED)
1996	Félix Savón (CUB)	David Defiagbon (CAN)	Nate Jones (USA)
			Luan Krasniqui (GER)
2000	Félix Savón (CUB)	Sultanahmed Ibzagimov (RUS)	Vladimir Tchanturia (GEO)
			Sebastian Kober (GER)

1896–1900, 1906 and 1912 event not held. * Initially the silver medal was not awarded; Johansson was disqualified but was re-instated in 1982.

SUPER-HEAVYWEIGHT From 1984 the class has been for those over 91kg/200.5lb.

	Gold	Silver	Bronze
1984	Tyrell Biggs (USA)	Francesco Damiani (ITA)	Robert Wells (GBR)
			Salihu Azis (YUG)
1988	Lennox Lewis (CAN)	Riddick Bowe (USA)	Aleksandr Mirochnitchenko (URS)
			Jasz Zarenkiewicz (POL)
1992	Roberto Balado (CUB)	Richard Igbineghu (NGR)	Brian Nielsen (DEN)
			Svilen Roussinov (BUL)
1996	Vladimir Klichko (UKR)	Paea Wolfgram (TGA)	Alexei Lezin (RUS)
			Duncan Dokwari (NGR)
2000	Audley Harrison (GBR)	Muchtarchan Dildabekov (KAZ)	Rustam Saidov (UZB)
			Paolo Vidoz (ITA)

1896–1980 event not held.

CANOEING MEDALS

MEN

500 METRES KAYAK SINGLES (K1)

	Gold	Silver	Bronze
1976	Vasile Diba (ROM) 1:46.41	Zoltán Szytanity (HUN) 1:46.95	Rüdiger Helm (GDR) 1:48.30
1980	Vladimir Parfenovich (URS) 1:43.43	John Sumegi (AUS) 1:44.12	Vasile Diba (ROM) 1:44.90
1984	Ian Ferguson (NZL) 1:47.84	Lars-Erik Möberg (SWE) 1:48.18	Bernard Bregeon (FRA) 1:48.41
1988	Zsolt Gyulay (HUN) 1:44.82	Andreas Stähle (GDR) 1:46.38	Paul McDonald (NZL) 1:46.46
1992	Mikko Kolehmainen (FIN) 1:40.34	Zsolt Gyulay (HUN) 1:40.64	Knut Holmann (NOR) 1:40.71
1996	Antonio Rossi (ITA) 1:37.423	Knut Holmann (NOR) 1:38.339	Piotr Markiewicz (POL) 1:38.615
2000	Knut Holmann (NOR) 1:57.847	Petar Markov (BUL) 1:58.393	Michael Kolganov (ISR) 1:59.563

1896–1972 event not held

1000 METRES KAYAK SINGLES (K1)

	Gold	Silver	Bronze
1936	Gregor Hradetsky (AUT) 4:22.9	Helmut Cämmerer (GER) 4:25.6	Jacob Kraaier (NED) 4:35.1
1948	Gert Fredriksson (SWE) 4:33.2	Johann Kobberup (DEN) 4:39.9	Henri Eberhardt (FRA) 4:41.4
1952	Gert Fredriksson (SWE) 4:07.9	Thorvald Strömberg (FIN) 4:09.7	Louis Gantois (FRA) 4:20.1
1956	Gert Fredriksson (SWE) 4:12.8	Igor Pissaryev (URS) 4:15.3	Lajos Kiss (HUN) 4:16.2
1960	Erik Hansen (DEN) 3:53.00	Imre Szöllösi (HUN) 3:54.02	Gert Fredriksson (SWE) 3:55.89
1964	Rolf Peterson (SWE) 3:57.13	Mihály Hesz (HUN) 3:57.28	Aurel Vernescu (ROM) 4:00.77
1968	Mihály Hesz (HUN) 4:02.63	Aleksandr Shaparenko (URS) 4:03.58	Erik Hansen (DEN) 4:04.39
1972	Aleksandr Shaparenko (URS) 3:48.06	Rolf Peterson (SWE) 3:48.35	Géza Csapó (HUN) 3:49.38
1976	Rüdiger Helm (GDR) 3:48.20	Géza Csapó (HUN) 3:48.84	Vasile Diba (ROM) 3:49.65
1980	Rüdiger Helm (GDR) 3:48.77	Alain Lebas (FRA) 3:50.20	Ion Birladeanu (ROM) 3:50.49
1984	Alan Thompson (NZL) 3:45.73	Milan Janic (YUG) 3:46.88	Greg Barton (USA) 3:47.38
1988	Greg Barton (USA) 3:55.27	Grant Davies (AUS) 3:55.28	Andre Wohliebe (GDR) 3:55.55
1992	Clint Robinson (AUS) 3:37.26	Knut Holmann (NOR) 3:37.50	Greg Barton (USA) 3:37.93
1996	Knut Holmann (NOR) 3:25.785	Beniamino Bonomi (ITA) 3:27.073	Clint Robinson (AUS) 3:29.713
2000	Knut Holmann (NOR) 3:33.269	Petar Markov (BUL) 3:34.649	Tim Brabants (GBR) 3:35.057

1896–1932 event not held

10,000 METRES KAYAK SINGLES (K1)

	Gold	Silver	Bronze
1936	Ernst Krebs (GER) 46:01.6	Fritz Landertinger (AUT) 46:14.7	Ernest Riedel (USA) 47:23.9
1948	Gert Fredriksson (SWE) 50:47.7	Kurt Wires (FIN) 51:18.2	Ejvind Skabo (NOR) 51:35.4
1952	Thorvald Strömberg (FIN) 47:22.8	Gert Fredriksson (SWE) 47:34.1	Michel Scheuer (GER) 47:54.5
1956	Gert Fredriksson (SWE) 47:43.4	Ferenc Hatlaczky (HUN) 47:53.3	Michel Scheuer (GER) 48.00.3

1896–1932 and 1960–2000 event not held

500 METRES KAYAK PAIRS (K2)

	Gold	Silver	Bronze
1976	GDR 1:35.87	Soviet Union 1:36.81	Romania 1:37.43
1980	Soviet Union 1:32.38	Spain 1:33.65	GDR 1:34.00
1984	New Zealand 1:34.21	Sweden 1:35.26	Canada 1:35.41
1988	New Zealand 1:33.98	Soviet Union 1:34.15	Hungary 1:34.32
1992	Germany 1:28.27	Poland 1:29.84	Italy 1:30.00
1996	Germany 1:28.697	italy 1:28.729	Australia 1:29.409
2000	Hungary 1:47.055	Australia 1:47.895	Germany 1:48.771

1896–1972 event not held

1000 METRES KAYAK PAIRS (K2)

	Gold	Silver	Bronze
1936	Austria 4:03.8	Germany 4:08.9	The Netherlands 4:12.2
1948	Sweden 4:07.3	Denmark 4:07.5	Finland 4:08.7
1952	Finland 3:51.1	Sweden 3:51.1	Austria 3:51.4

	Gold	Silver	Bronze
1956	Germany 3:49.6	Soviet Union 3:51.4	Austria 3:55.8
1960	Sweden 3:34.7	Hungary 3:34.91	Poland 3:37.34
1964	Sweden 3:38.4	The Netherlands 3:39.30	Germany 3:40.69
1968	Soviet Union 3:37.54	Hungary 3:38.44	Austria 3:40.71
1972	Soviet Union 3:31.23	Hungary 3:32.00	Poland 3:38.33
1976	Soviet Union 3:29.01	GDR 3:29.33	Hungary 3:30.56
1980	Soviet Union 3:26.72	Hungary 3:28.49	Spain 3:28.66
1984	Canada 3:24.22	France 3:25.97	Australia 3:26.80
1988	United states 3:32.42	New Zealand 3:32.71	Australia 3:33.76
1992	Germany 3:16.10	Sweden 3:17.70	Poland 3:18.86
1996	Italy 3:09.190	Germany 3:10.518	Bulgaria 3:11.206
2000	Italy 3:14.461	Sweden 3:16.075	Hungary 3:16.357

1896–1932 event not held

10,000 METRES KAYAK PAIRS (K2)

	Gold	Silver	Bronze
1936	Germany 41:45.0	Austria 42:05.4	Sweden 43:06.1
1948	Sweden 46:09.4	Norway 46:44.8	Finland 46:48.2
1952	Finland 44:21.3	Sweden 44:21.7	Hungary 44:26.6
1956	Hungary 43:37.0	Germany 43:40.6	Australia 43:43.2

1896–1932 and 1960–2000 event not held

1000 METRES KAYAK FOURS (K4)

	Gold	Silver	Bronze
1964	Soviet Union 3:14.67	Germany 3:15.39	Romania 3:15.51
1968	Norway 3:14.38	Romania 3:14.81	Hungary 3:15.10
1972	Soviet Union 3:14.38	Romania 3:15.07	Norway 3:15.27
1976	Soviet Union 3:08.69	Spain 3:08.95	GDR 3:10.76
1980	GDR 3:13.76	Romania 3:15.35	Bulgaria 3:15.46
1984	New Zealand 3:02.28	Sweden 3:02.81	France 3:03.94
1988	Hungary 3:00.20	Soviet Union 3:01.40	GDR 3:02.37
1992	Germany 2:54.18	Hungary 2:54.82	Australia 2:56.97
1996	Germany 2:51.528	Hungary 2:53.184	Russia 2:53.996
2000	Hungary 2:55.18	Germany 2:55.704	Poland 2:57.192

1896–1960 event not held

500 METRES CANADIAN SINGLES (C1)

	Gold	Silver	Bronze
1976	Aleksandr Rogov (URS) 1:59.23	John Wood (CAN) 1:59.58	Matija Ljubek (YUG) 1:59.60
1980	Sergei Postrekhin (URS) 1:53.37	Lubomir Lubenov (BUL) 1:53.49	Olaf Heukrodt (GDR) 1:54.38
1984	Larry Cain (CAN) 1:57.01	Henning Jakobsen (DEN) 1:58.45	Costica Olaru (ROM) 1:59.86
1988	Olaf Heukrodt (GDR) 1:56.42	Mikhail Slivinski (URS) 1:57.26	Martin Marinov (BUL) 1:57.27
1992	Nikolai Boukhalov (BUL) 1:51.15	Mikhail Slivinski (EUN) 1:51.40	Olaf Heukrodt (GER) 1:53.00
1996	Martin Doktor (CZE) 1:49.934	Slavomir Knazovicky (SLO) 1:50.510	Imre Pulai (ITA) 1:50.758
2000	György Kolonics (HUN) 2:24.813	Maksim Opalev (RUS) 2:25.809	Andreas Dittmer (GER) 2:27.591

1896–1972 event not held

1000 METRES CANADIAN SINGLES (C1)

	Gold	Silver	Bronze
1936	Francis Amyot (CAN) 5:32.1	Bohuslav Karlik (TCH) 5:36.9	Erich Koschik (GER) 5:39.0
1948	Josef Holocek (TCH) 5:42.0	Douglas Bennet (CAN) 5:53.3	Robert Boutigny (FRA) 5:55.9
1952	Josef Holocek (TCH) 4:56.3	János Parti (HUN) 5:03.6	Olavi Ojanpera (FIN) 5:08.5
1956	Leon Rotman (ROM) 5:05.3	István Hernek (HUN) 5:06.2	Gennadi Bukharin (URS) 5:12.7
1960	János Parti (HUN) 4:33.93	Alexsandr Silayev (URS) 4:34.41	Leon Rotman (ROM) 4:35.87
1964	Jürgen Eschert (GER) 4:35.14	Andrei Igorov (ROM) 4:37.89	Yevgeni Penyayev (URS) 4:38.31
1968	TIbor Tatai (HUN) 4:36.14	Detlef Lewe (FRG) 4:38.31	Vitali Galkov (URS) 4:40.42
1972	Ivan Patzaichin (ROM) 4:08.94	Tamas Wichmann (HUN) 4:12.42	Detlef Lewe (FRG) 4:13.36

	Gold	Silver	Bronze
1976	Matija Ljubek (YUG) 4:09.51	Vassili Urchenko (URS) 4:12.57	Tamas Wichmann (HUN) 4:14.11
1980	Lubomir Lubenov (BUL) 4:12.38	Sergei Postrekhin (URS) 4:13.53	Eckhard Leue (GDR) 4:15.02
1984	Ulrich Eicke (FRG) 4:06.32	Larry Cain (CAN) 4:08.67	Henning Jakobsen (DEN) 4:09.51
1988	Ivans Klementjevs (URS) 4:12.78	Jörg Schmidt (GDR) 4:15.83	Nikolai Boukhalov (BUL) 4:18.94
1992	Nikolai Boukhalov (BUL) 4:05.92	Ivans Klementjevs (LAT) 4:06.60	György Zala (HUN) 4:07.35
1996	Martin Doktor (CZE) 3:54.418	Ivans Klementjevs (LAT) 3:54.954	György Zala (HUN) 3:56.366
2000	Andreas Dittmer (GER) 3:54.379	Ledys Frank Balceiro (CUB) 3:56.071	Steve Giles (CAN) 3:56.437

1896–1932 event not held.

10,000 METRES CANADIAN SINGLES (C1)

	Gold	Silver	Bronze
1948	Frantisek Capek (TCH) 62:05.2	Frank Havens (USA) 62:40.4	Norman Lane (CAN) 64:35.3
1952	Frank Havens (USA) 57:41.1	Gabór Novák (HUN) 57:49.2	Alfréd Jindra (TCH) 57:33.1
1956	Leon Rotman (ROM) 56:41.0	János Parti (HUN) 57:11.0	Gennadi Bukharin (URS) 57:14.5

1896–1936 and 1960–2000 event not held

500 METRES CANADIAN PAIRS (C2)

	Gold	Silver	Bronze
1976	Soviet Union 1:45.81	Poland 1:47.77	Hungary 1:47.35
1980	Hungary 1:43.39	Romania 1:44.12	Bulgaria 1:44.83
1984	Yugoslavia 1:43.67	Romania 1:45.68	Spain 1:47.71
1988	Soviet Union 1:41.77	Poland 1:43.61	France 1:43.81
1992	Unified Team 1:41.54	Germany 1:41.68	Bulgaria 1:41.94
1996	Hungary 1:40.42	Moldova 1:40.45	Romania 1:41.33
2000	Hungary 1:51.284	Poland 1:51.536	Romania 1:54.260

1896–1972 event not held

1000 METRES CANADIAN PAIRS (C2)

	Gold	Silver	Bronze
1936	Czechoslovakia 4:50.1	Austria 4:53.8	Canada 4:56.7
1948	Czechoslovakia 5:07.1	United States 5:08.2	France 5:15.2
1952	Denmark 4:38.3	Czechoslovakia 4:42.9	Germany 4:48.3
1956	Romania 4:47.4	Soviet Union 4:48.6	Hungary 4:54.3
1960	Soviet Union 4:17.94	Italy 4:20.77	Hungary 4:20.89
1964	Soviet Union 4:04.64	France 4:06.52	Denmark 4:07.48
1968	Romania 4:07.18	Hungary 4:08.77	Soviet Union 4:11.30
1972	Soviet Union 3:52.60	Romania 3:52.63	Bulgaria 3:58.10
1976	Soviet Union 3:52.76	Romania 3:54.28	Hungary 3:55.66
1980	Romania 3:47.65	GDR 3:49.93	Soviet Union 3:51.28
1984	Romania 3:40.60	Yugoslavia 3:41.56	France 3:48.01
1988	Soviet Union 3:48.36	GDR 3:51.44	Poland 3:54.33
1992	Germany 3:37.42	Denmark 3:39.26	France 3:39.51
1996	Germany 3:31.870	Romania 3:32.294	Hungary 3:32.514
2000	Romania 3:37.355	Cuba 3:38.753	Germany 3:41.129

1896–1932 event not held

10,000 METRES CANADIAN PAIRS (C2)

	Gold	Silver	Bronze
1936	Czechoslovakia 50.33.5	Canada 51:15.8	Austria 51:28.0
1948	United States 55:55.4	Czechoslovakia 57:38.5	France 58:00.8
1952	France 54:08.3	Canada 54:09.9	Germany 54:28.1
1956	Soviet Union 54:02.4	France 54:48.3	Hungary 55:15.6

1896–1932 and 1960–2000 event not held

4 X 500 METRES KAYAK SINGLES (K1) RELAY

	Gold	Silver	Bronze
1960	Germany 7:39.43	Hungary 7:44.02	Denmark 7:46.09

1896–1956 and 1964–2000 event not held

10,000 METRES FOLDING KAYAK SINGLES (K1)

	Gold	Silver	Bronze
1936	Gregor Hradetzky (AUT) 50:01.2	Henri Eberhardt (FRA) 50:04.2	Xaver Hörmann (GER) 50:06.5

1896–1932 and 1948–2000 event not held

10,000 METRES FOLDING KAYAK PAIRS (K2)

	Gold	Silver	Bronze
1936	Sweden 45:48.9	Germany 45:49.2	The Netherlands 46:12.4

1896–1932 and 1948–2000 event not held.

SLALOM RACING

MEN – (Not held in 1896–1968 and 1976–88).

KAYAK SINGLES (K1)

	Gold	Silver	Bronze
1972	Siegbert Horn (GDR) 268.56pts	Norbert Sattler (AUT) 270.76	Harald Gimpel (GDR) 277.95
1992	Pierpaolo Ferrazzi (ITA) 106.89pts	Sylvain Curinier (FRA) 107.06	Jochen Lettmann (GER) 108.52
1996	Oliver Fix (GER) 141.22pts	Andraz Vehovar (SLO) 141.65	Thomas Becker (GER) 142.79
2000	Thomas Schmidt (GER) 217.25pts	Paul Ratcliffe (GBR) 223.71	Pierpaolo Ferrazzi (ITA) 225.03

CANADIAN SINGLES (C1)

	Gold	Silver	Bronze
1972	Reinhard Eiben (GDR) 315.84pts	Reinhold Kauder (FRG) 327.89	Jamie McEwan (USA) 335.95
1992	Lukas Pollert (CZE) 113.69pts	Gareth Marriott (GBR) 116.48	Jacky Avril (FRA) 117.18
1996	Michal Martikan (SVK) 151.03pts	Lukás Pollert (CZE) 151.17	Patrice Estanguet (FRA) 152.84
2000	Tony Estanguet (FRA) 231.87pts	Michal Martikan (SVK) 233.76	Juraj Mincik (SVK) 234.22

CANADIAN PAIRS (C2)

	Gold	Silver	Bronze
1972	GDR 310.68pts	FRG 311.90	France 315.10
1992	United States122.41pts	Czechoslovakia 124.25	France 124.38
1996	France 158.82pts	Czech Republic 160.16	Germany 163.72
2000	Slovakia 237.74pts	Poland 243.81	Czech Republic 249.45

WOMEN

500 METRES KAYAK SINGLES (K1)

	Gold	Silver	Bronze
1948	Karen Hoff (DEN) 2:31.9	Alide Van de Anker-Doedans (NED) 2:32.8	Fritzi Schwingl (AUT) 2:32.9
1952	Slyvi Saimo (FIN) 2:18.4	Gertrude Liebhart (AUT) 2:18.8	Nina Savina (URS) 2:21.6
1956	Yelisaveta Dementyeva (URS) 2:18.9	Therese Zenz (GDR) 2:19.6	Tove Söby (DEN) 2:22.3
1960	Antonina Seredina (URS) 2:08.8	Therese Zenz (GDR) 2:08.22	Daniele Walkowiak (POL) 2:10.46
1964	Ludmila Khvedosyuk (URS) 2:12.87	Hilde Lauer (ROM) 2:15.35	Marcia Jones (USA) 2:15.68
1968	Ludmila Pinyeva (URS) 2:11.09	Renate Breuer (FRG) 2:12.71	Viorica Dumitru (ROM) 2:13.22
1972	Yulia Ryabchinskaya (URS) 2:03.17	Mieke Jaapies (NED) 2:04.03	Anna Pfeffer (HUN) 2:05.50
1976	Carola Zirzow (GDR) 2:01.05	Tatyana Korshunova (URS) 2:03.07	Klara Rajnai (HUN) 2:05.01
1980	Birgit Fischer (GDR) 1:57.96	Vanya Gheva (BUL) 1:59.48	Antonina Melnikova (URS) 1:59.66
1984	Agneta Andersson (SWE) 1:58.72	Barbara Schuttpelz (FRG) 1:59.93	Annemiek Derckx (NED) 2:00.11
1988	Vania Guecheva (BUL) 1:55.19	Birgit Schmidt (GDR) 1:55.31	Izabella Dylewska (POL) 1:57.38
1992	Birgit Schmidt (GER) 1:51.60	Rita Koban (HUN) 1:51.96	Izabella Dylewska (POL) 1:52.36
1996	Rita Koban (HUN) 1:47.655	Caroline Brunet (CAN) 1:47.891	Josefa Idem (ITA) 1:48.731
2000	Josefa Idem Guerrini (ITA) 2:13.848	Caroline Brunet (CAN) 2:14.646	Katrin Borchert (AUS) 2:15.138

1896–1936 event not held

500 METRES KAYAK PAIRS (K2)

	Gold	Silver	Bronze
1960	Soviet Union 1:54.76	Germany 1:56.66	Hungary 1:58.22
1964	Germany 1:56.95	United States 1:59.16	Romania 2:00.25
1968	FRG 1:56.44	Hungary 1:58.60	Soviet Union 1:58.61
1972	Soviet Union 1:53.50	GDR 1:54.30	Romania 1:55.01
1976	Soviet Union 1:51.15	Hungary 1:51.69	GDR 1:51.81
1980	GDR 1:43.88	Soviet Union 1:46.91	Hungary 1:47.95
1984	Sweden 1:45.25	Canada 1:47.13	FRG 1:47.32
1988	GDR 1:43.46	Bulgaria 1:44.06	The Netherlands 1:46.00
1992	Germany 1:40.29	Sweden 1:40.41	Hungary 1:40.81
1996	Sweden 1:39.329	Germany 1:39.589	Australia 1:40.641
2000	Germany 1:56.996	Hungary 1:58.580	Poland 1:58.784

1896–1956 event not held

500 METRES KAYAK FOURS (K4)

	Gold	Silver	Bronze
1984	Romania 1:38.34	Sweden 1:38.87	Canada 1:39.40
1988	GDR 1:40.78	Hungary 1:41.88	Bulgaria 1:42.63
1992	Hungary 1:38.32	Germany 1:38.47	Sweden 1:39.79
1996	Germany 1:31.077	Switzerland 1:32.701	Sweden 1:32.917
2000	Germany 1:34.532	Hungary 1:34.946	Romania 1:37.010

1896–1980 event not held

SLALOM RACING
(Not held in 1896–1968 and 1976—88).

KAYAK SINGLES (K1)

	Gold	Silver	Bronze
1972	Angelika Bahmann (GDR) 364.50	Gisela Grothaus (FRG) 398.15	Magdelena Wunderlich (FRG) 400.50
1992	Elisabeth Micheler (GER) 126.41	Danielle Woodward (AUS) 128.27	Diana Chladek (USA) 131.75
1996	Stepanka Hilgertová (CZE) 169.49	Dana Chladek (USA) 169.49	Myriam Fox-Jerusalmi (FRA) 171.00
2000	Stepanka Hilgertová (CZE) 247.04	Brigitte Guibal (FRA) 251.88	Anne-Lise Bardet (FRA) 254.77

CYCLING MEDALS

MEN

1000 METRES TIME TRIAL

	Gold	Silver	Bronze
1896*	Paul Masson (FRA) 24.0	Stamatios Nikolopoulos (GRE) 25.4	Adolf Schmal (AUT) 26.6
1906*	Verri (ITA) 22.8	Herbert Crowther (GBR) 22.8	Menjou (FRA) 23.2
1928	Willy Falck-Hansen (DEN) 1:14.4	Gerard Bosch van Drakestein (NED) 1:15.2	Edgar Gray (AUS) 1:15.6
1932	Edgar Gray (AUS) 1:13.0	Jacobus van Egmond (NED) 1:13.3	Charles Rampelberg (FRA) 1:13.4
1936	Arie van Vliet (NED) 1:12.0	Pierre Georget (FRA) 1:12.8	Rudolf Karsch (GER) 1:13.2
1948	Jacques Dupont (FRA) 1:13.5	Pierre Nihant (BEL) 1:14.5	Thomas Godwin (GBR) 1:15.0
1952	Russell Mockridge (AUS) 1:11.1	Marino Morettini (ITA) 1:12.7	Raymond Robinson (RSA) 1:13.0
1956	Leandro Faggin (ITA) 1:09.8	Ladislav Foucek (TCH) 1:11.4	J. Alfred Swift (RSA) 1:11.6
1960	Sante Gaiardoni (ITA) 1:07.27	Dieter Giessler (GER) 1:08.75	Rotislav Vargshkin (URS) 1:08.86
1964	Patrick Sercu (BEL) 1:09.59	Giovanni Pettonella (ITA) 1:10.09	Pierre Trentin (FRA) 1:10.42
1968	Pierre Trentin (FRA) 1:03.91	Niels-Christian Fredborg (DEN) 1:04.61	Janusz Kierkowski (POL) 1:04.63
1972	Niels-Christian Fredborg (DEN) 1:06.44	Daniel Clark (AUS) 1:06.87	Jürgen Schütze (GDR) 1:07.02
1976	Klaus-Jürgen Grunke (GDR) 1:05.93	Michel Vaarten (BEL) 1:07.52	Niels-Christian Fredborg (DEN) 1:07.62

	Gold	Silver	Bronze
1980	Lothar Thomas (GDR) 1:02.955	Aleksandr Pantilov (URS) 1:04.845	David Weller (JAM) 1:05.241
1984	Fredy Schmidke (FRG) 1:06.10	Curtis Harnett (CAN) 1:06.44	Fabrice Colas (FRA) 1:06.65
1988	Aleksandr Kiritchenko (URS) 1:04.499	Martin Vinnicombe (AUS) 1:04.784	Robert Lechner (FRG) 1:05.114
1992	Jose Manuel Moreno (ESP) 1:03.342	Shane Kelly (AUS) 1:04.288	Erin Hartwell (USA) 1:04.753
1996	Florian Rousseau (FRA) 1:02.712	Erin Hartwell (USA) 1:02.940	Takandu Jumonji (JPN) 1:02.261
2000	Jason Queally (GBR) 1:01.689	Stefan Nimke (GER) 1:02.487	Shane Kelly (AUS) 1:02.818

1908–1924 event not held. * Held over 333.33 metres.

1000 METRES SPRINT

	Gold	Silver	Bronze
1896*	Paul Masson (FRA) 4:56.0	Stamatios Nikopoulos (GRE)	Léon Flameng (RSA)
1900*	Georges Taillandier (FRA) 2:52.0	Fernand Sanz (FRA)	John Lake (USA)
1906	Francesco Verri (ITA) 1:42.2	Herbert Bouffler (GBR)	Eugène Debougnie (BEL)
1908†	—	—	—
1920	Maurice Peeters (NED) 1:38.3	Horace Johnson (GBR)	Harry Ryan (GBR)
1924‡	Lucien Michard (FRA) 12.8	Jacob Meijer (NED)	Jean Cugnot (FRA)
1928	René Beaufrand (FRA) 13.2	Antoine Mazairac (NED)	Willy Falck-Hansen (DEN)
1932	Jacobus van Egmond (NED) 12.6	Louis Chaillot (FRA)	Bruno Pellizzari (ITA)
1936	Toni Merkens (GER) 11.8	Arie van Vliet (NED)	Louis Chaillot (FRA)
1948	Mario Ghella (ITA) 12.0	Reginald Harris (GBR)	Axel Schandorff (DEN)
1952	Enzo Sacchi (ITA) 12.0	Lionel Cox (AUS)	Werner Potzernheim (GER)
1956	Michel Rousseau (FRA) 11.4	Guglielmo Presenti (ITA)	Richard Ploog (AUS)
1960	Sante Gaiardoni (ITA) 11.1	Leo Sterckz (BEL)	Valentina Gasparella (ITA)
1964	Giovanni Petternella (ITA) 13.69	Sergio Bianchetto (ITA)	Daniel Morelon (FRA)
1968	Daniel Morelon (FRA) 10.68	Giordano Turrini (ITA)	Pierre Trentin (FRA)
1972	Daniel Morelon (FRA) 11.25	John Nicholson (AUS)	Omar Pchakadze (URS)
1976	Anton Tkac (TCH) 10.78	Daniel Morelon (FRA)	Hans-Jürgen Geschke (GDR)
1980	Lutz Hesslich (GDR) 11.40	Yave Cahard (FRA)	Sergey Kopylov (URS)
1984	Mark Gorski (USA) 10.49	Nelson Vails (USA)	Tsutomu Sakamoto (JPN)
1988	Lutz Hesslich (GDR)	Nikolai Kovche (URS)	Gary Neiwand (AUS)
1992	Jens Fiedler (GER)	Gary Neiwand (AUS)	Curtis Harnett (CAN)
1996	Jens Fiedler (GER)	Marthy Nothstein (USA)	Curtis Harnett (CAN)
2000	Marty Nothstein (USA)	Florian Rousseau (FRA)	Jens Fiedler (GER)

1904 and 1912 event not held. * Held over 2000m. In 1900 Taillandier's last 200m was 13.0sec. † There was a 1000m sprint event in the 1908 Games, but it was declared void because the riders exceeded the time limit in spite of repeated warnings. ‡ Since 1924 only times over the last 200m of the event have been recorded.

4000 METRES INDIVIDUAL PURSUIT

Note: Bronze medal times are set in a third-place race, so can be faster than those set in the race for first and second places.

	Gold	Silver	Bronze
1964	Jiri Daler (TCH) 5:04.75	Giorgio Utsi (ITA) 5:05.96	Preben Isaksson (DEN) 5:01.90
1968	Daniel Rebillard (FRA) 4:41.71	Mogens Frey Jensen (DEN) 4:42.43	Xaver Kurmann (SUI) 4:39.42
1972	Knut Knudsen (NOR) 4:45.74	Xaver Kurmann (SUI) 4:51.96	Hans Lutz (FRG) 4:50.80
1976	Gregor Braun (FRG) 4:47.61	Herman Ponsteen (NED) 4:49.72	Thomas Huschke (GDR) 4:52.71
1980	Robert Dilli-Bundi (SUI) 4:35.66	Alain Bondue (FRA) 4:42.96	Hans-Henrik Orsted (DEN) 4:36.54
1984	Steve Hegg (USA) 4:39.35	Rolf Gölz (FRG) 4:43.82	Leonard Nitz (USA) 4:44.03
1988	Gintaoutas Umaras (URS) 4:32.00	Dean Woods (AUS) 4:35.00	Bernd Dittert (GDR) 4:34.17
1992	Chris Boardman (GBR)*	Jens Lehmann (GER)	Gary Anderson (NZL) 4:31.061
1996	Andrea Collinelli (ITA) 4:20.893	Philippe Ermenault (FRA) 4:22.714	Brad McGee (AUS) 4:26.121
2000	Robert Bartko (GER) 4:18.515	Jens Lehmann (GER) 4:23.824	Brad McGee (AUS) 4:19.250

1896–1960 event not held. * Lapped Lehmann in final.

4000 METRES TEAM PURSUIT

Note: Bronze medal times are set in a third-place race, so can be faster than those set in the race for first and second places.

	Gold	Silver	Bronze
1908*	Great Britain 2:18.6	Germany 2:28.6	Canada 2:29.6
1920	Italy 5:14.2†	Great Britain 5:13.8	South Africa 5:17.8
1924	Italy 5:15.0	Poland n.t.a.	Belgium n.t.a.
1928	Italy 5:01.8	The Netherlands 5:06.2	Great Britain n.t.a.
1932	Italy 4:53.0	France 4:55.7	Great Britain 4:56.0
1936	France 4:45.0	Italy 4:51.0	Great Britain 4:52.6
1948	France 4:57.8	Italy 5:36.7	Great Britain 4:55.8
1952	Italy 4:46.1	South Africa 4:53.6	Great Britain 4:51.5
1956	Italy 4:37.4	France 4:39.4	Great Britain 4:42.2
1960	Italy 4:30.90	Germany 4:35.78	Soviet Union 4:34.05
1964	Germany 4:35.67	Italy 4:35.74	The Netherlands 4:38.99
1968	Denmark 4:22.44‡	FRG 4:18.94	Italy 4:18.35
1972	FRG 4:22.14	GDR 4:25.25	Great Britain 4:23.78
1976	FRG 4:21.06	Soviet Union 4:27.15	Great Britain 4:22.41
1980	Soviet Union 4:15.70	GDR 4:19.67	Czechoslovakia§
1984	Australia 4:25.99	United States 4:29.85	FRG 4:25.60
1988	Soviet Union 4:13.31	GDR 4:14.09	Australia 4:16.02
1992	Germany 4:08.791	Australia 4:10.218	Denmark 4:15.860
1996	France 4:05.930	Russia 4:07.730	Australia 4:07.570
2000	Germany 3:59.710	Ukraine 4:04.520	Great Britain 4:01.979

1896–1906 and 1912 event not held. * Held over 1810.5m. † Great Britain finished first but was relegated to second place for alleged interference. ‡ Federal Republic of Germany (FRG) finished first but was disqualified for illegal assistance. After the Games ended the International Cycling Federation (ICF) awarded the team the silver medal. § Italy was disqualified in third place.

OLYMPIC SPRINT (Introduced in 2000: three-man teams over three laps)

	Gold	Silver	Bronze
2000	France 44.233sec	Great Britian 44.680sec	Australia 45.161sec

2000 METRES TANDEM

	Gold	Silver	Bronze
1906	Great Britain 2:57.0	Germany 2:57.2	Germany n.t.a.
1908	France 3:07.8	Great Britain n.t.a.	Great Britain n.t.a.
1920	Great Britain 2:94.4	South Africa n.t.a.	The Netherlands n.t.a.
1924*	France 12.6	Denmark	The Netherlands
1928	The Netherlands 11.8	Great Britain	Germany
1932	France 12.0	Great Britain	Denmark
1936	Germany 11.8	The Netherlands	France
1948	Italy 11.3	Great Britain	France
1952	Australia 11.0	South Africa	Italy
1956	Australia 10.8	Czechoslovakia	Italy
1960	Italy 10.7	Germany	Soviet Union
1964	Italy 10.75	Soviet Union	Germany
1968	France 9.83	The Netherlands	Belgium
1972	Soviet Union	GDR	Poland

1896–1904, 1912 and 1976–2000 event not held. * Since 1924 only times over the last 200m have been recorded.

INDIVIDUAL POINTS RACE

	Gold	Silver	Bronze
1984	Roger Ilegems (BEL) 37pts	Uwe Messerschmidt (FRG) 15	José Youshimatz (MEX)
1988	Dan Frost (DEN) 38pts	Leo Peelen (NED) 26	Marat Ganeyev (URS)
1992	Giovanni Lombardi (ITA) 44pts	Leon van Bon (NED) 43	Cedric Mathy (BEL) 41
1996	Silvio Martinello (ITA) 37pts	Brian Walton (CAN) 29	Stuart O'Grady (AUS) 25
2000	Juan Llaneras (ESP) 14pts	Milton Wynants (URU) 18	Alexei Markov (RUS) 16

1896–1980 event not held.

MADISON (Introduced in 2000:two-man teams over 60km course)

	Gold	Silver	Bronze
2000	Australia 26pts	Belgium 22	Italy 15

KEIRIN (Introduced in 2000: an eight-lap race)

	Gold	Silver	Bronze
2000	Florian Rousseau (FRA)	Gary Niewand (AUS)	Jens Fiedler (GER)

TEAM ROAD RACE (In 1912–1920 the race consisted of the combined times of the four best riders from each country in the individual race; in 1924–1952 the combined times of the best three; in 1956 based on the placings of the best three riders). Raced over 320km – 1912; 175km – 1920; 168km – 1924–1928; 100km – 1932–1936; 194.63km – 1948; 190.4km – 1952.

	Gold	Silver	Bronze
1912	Sweden 44hr 35:33.6	Great Britain 44hr 44:39.2	United States 44hr 47:55.5
1920	France 19hr 16:43.2	Sweden 19hr 23:10.0	Belgium 19hr 28:44.4
1924	France 19hr 30:14.0	Belgium 19hr 46:55.4	Sweden 19hr 59:41.6
1928	Denmark 15hr 09:14.0	Great Britain 15hr 14:49.0	Sweden 15hr 27:49.0
1932	Italy 7hr 27:15.2	Denmark 7hr 38:50.2	Sweden 7hr 39:12.6
1936	France 7hr 39:16.2	Switzerland 7hr 39:20.4	Belgium 7hr 39:21.0
1948	Belgium 15hr 58:17.4	Great Britain 16hr 03:31.6	France 16hr 08:19.4
1952	Belgium 15hr 20:46.6	Italy 15hr 33:27.3	France 15hr 38:58.1
1956	France 22pts	Great Britain 23pts	Germany 27pts

ROAD TEAM TIME-TRIAL (Raced over 100km, except in 1964 (109.89km), 1968 (104km) and 1980 (101km).

	Gold	Silver	Bronze
1960	Italy 2hr 14:33.53	Germany 2hr 16:56.31	Soviet Union 2hr 18:41.67
1964	The Netherlands 2hr 26:31.19	Italy 2hr 26:55.39	Sweden 2hr 27:11.52
1968	The Netherlands 2hr 07:49.06	Sweden 2hr 09:26.60	Italy 2hr 10:18.74
1972	Soviet Union 2hr 11:17.8	Poland 2hr 11:47.5	—*
1976	Soviet Union 2hr 08:53.0	Poland 2hr 09:13.0	Denmark 2hr 12:20.0
1980	Soviet Union 2hr 01:21.7	GDR 2hr 02:53.2	Czechoslovakia 2hr 02:53.9
1984	Italy 1hr 58:28.0	Switzerland 2hr 02:38.0	United States 2hr 02:46.0
1988	GDR 1hr 57:47.7	Poland 1hr 57:54.2	Sweden 1hr 59:47.3
1992	Germany 2hr 01:39	Italy 2hr 02:39	France 2hr 05:25

1896–1908 and 1996–2000 event not held. * The Netherlands finished in third place but their bronze medal was withdrawn following a drugs test.

ROAD INDIVIDUAL TIME TRIAL (Held over 52km in 1996 and 46.8km in 2000)

	Gold	Silver	Bronze
1996	Miguel Induráin (ESP) 1hr 04:05	Abraham Olano (ESP) 1hr 04:17	Chris Boardman (GBR) 1hr 04:36
2000	Vyacheslav Ekimov (RUS) 57:40	Jan Ullrich (GER) 57:48	Lance Armstrong (USA) 58:14

1896–1992 event not held

INDIVIDUAL ROAD RACE *

	Gold	Silver	Bronze
1896	Aristidis Konstantinidis (GRE) 3hr 22:31.0	August Goedrich (GER) 3hr 42:18.0	F. Battel (GBR) d.n.a.
1906	Fernand Vast (FRA) 2hr 41:28.0	Maurice Bardonneau (FRA) 2hr 41:28.4	Edmund Lugnet (FRA) 2hr 41:28.6
1912	Rudolph Lewis (RSA) 10hr 42:39.0	Frederick Grubb (GBR) 10hr 51:24.2	Carl Schutte (USA) 10hr 52:38.8
1920	Harry Stenqvist (SWE) 4hr 40:01.8	Henry Kaltenbrun (RSA) 4hr 41:26.6	Fernand Canteloube (FRA) 4hr 42:54.4
1924	Armand Blanchonnet (FRA) 6hr 20:48.0	Henry Hoevenaers (BEL) 6hr 30:27.0	René Hamel (FRA) 6hr 40:51.6
1928	Henry Hansen (DEN) 4hr 47:18.0	Frank Southall (GBR) 4hr 56:06.0	Gösta Carlsson (SWE) 5hr 00:17.0
1932	Attilio Pavesi (ITA) 2hr 28:05.6	Guglielmo Segato (ITA) 2hr 29:21.4	Bernhard Britz (SWE) 2hr 29:45.2
1936	Robert Charpentier (FRA) 2hr 33:05.0	Guy Lapébie (FRA) 2hr 33:05.2	Ernst Nievergeit (SUI) 2hr 33:05.8
1948	José Bevaert (FRA) 5hr 18:12.6	Gerardus Voorting (NED) 5hr 18:16.2	Lode Wouters (BEL) 5hr 18:16.2
1952	André Noyelle (BEL) 5hr 06:03.4	Robert Grondelaers (BEL) 5hr 06:51.2	Edi Ziegler (GER) 5hr 07:47.5
1956	Ercole Baldini (ITA) 5hr 21:17.0	Arnaud Gevre (FRA) 5hr 23:16.0	Alan Jackson (GBR) 5hr 23:16.0

	Gold	Silver	Bronze
1960	Viktor Kapitonov (URS) 4hr 20:37.0	Livio Trapé (ITA) 4hr 20:37.0	Willy van den Berghen (BEL) 4hr 20:57.0
1964	Mario Zanin (ITA) 4hr 39:51.63	Kjell Rodian (DEN) 4hr 39:51.65	Walter Godefroot (BEL) 4hr 39:51.74
1968	Pierfranco Vianelli (ITA) 4hr 41:25.24	Leif Mortensen (DEN) 4hr 42:49.71	Gösta Pettersson (SWE) 4hr 43:15.24
1972	Hennie Kuiper (NED) 4hr 14:37.0	Kevin Sefton (AUS) 4hr 15:04.0	—†
1976	Bernt Johansson (SWE) 4hr 46:52.0	Giuseppe Martinelli (ITA) 4hr 47:23.0	Mieczyslaw Nowicki (POL) 4hr 47:23.0
1980	Sergey Sukhoruchenkov (URS) 4hr 48:28.9	Czeslaw Lang (POL) 4hr 51:26.9	Yuri Barinov (URS) 4hr 51:26.9
1984	Alexi Grewal (USA) 4hr 59:57.0	Steve Bauer (CAN) 4hr 32:25.0	Dag Otto Lauritzen (NOR) 5hr 00:18.0
1988	Olaf Ludwig (GDR) 4hr 32:22.0	Bernd Gröne (FRG) 4hr 32:25.0	Christian Henn (FRG) 4hr 32:46.0
1992	Fabio Casartelli (ITA) 4hr 35:21	Hendrik Dekker (NED) 4hr 35:22	Dainis Ozols (LAT) 4hr 35:24
1996	Pascal Richard (SUI) 4hr 53:56	Rolf Sörensen (DEN) 4hr 53:56	Max Sciandri (GBR) 4hr 53:58
2000	Jan Ullrich (GER) 5hr 29:08	Aleksandr Vinokourov (KAZ) 5hr 29:17	Jens Voigt (GER) 5hr 29:20

1900–1904 and 1908 event not held. *This event has been held over the following distances: 1896 – 87km; 1906 – 84km; 1912 – 329km; 1920 – 175km; 1924 – 188km; 1928 – 168km; 1932 and 1936 – 100km; 1948 – 194.63km; 1952 – 190.4km; 1956 – 187.73km; 1960 – 175.38km; 1964– 194.83km 1968 – 196.2km; 1972 – 182.4km; 1976 – 175km; 1980 – 189km; 1984 – 190.2km; 1988 – 196.8km; 1992 – 194km; 1996 – 221.85km and 2000 – 239.4km. †Jaime Huelano (ESP) finished third but the medal was withdrawn following a drugs test.

DISCONTINUED EVENTS
MEN

440 YARDS TRACK (402.34M)
	Gold	Silver	Bronze
1904	Marcus Hurley (USA) 31.8	Burton Downing (USA)	Edward Billingham (USA)

0.33 MILE TRACK (536.45M)
1904	Marcus Hurley (USA) 43.8	Burton Downing (USA)	Edward Billingham (USA)

660 YARDS TRACK (603.5M)
1908	Victor Johnson (GBR) 51.2	Emile Demangel (FRA) close	Karl Neumer (GER) 1 length

880 YARDS TRACK (804.67M)
1904	Marcus Hurley (USA) 1:09.0	Edward Billingham (USA)	Burton Downing (USA)

1 MILE TRACK (1609.34M)
1904	Marcus Hurley (USA) 2:41.4	Burton Downing (USA)	Edward Billingham (USA)

2 MILES TRACK (3218.6M)
1904	Burton Downing (USA) 4:57.8	Oscar Goerke (USA)	Marcus Hurley (USA)

5000 METRES TRACK
1906	Francesco Verri (ITA) 8:35.0	Herbert Crowther (GBR)	Fernand Vast (FRA)
1908	Benjamin Jones (GBR) 8:36.2	Maurice Schilles (FRA)	Andre Auffray (FRA)

5 MILES TRACK (8046.57M)
1904	Charles Schlee (USA) 13:08.2	George Wiley (USA)	Arthur Andrews (USA)

10,000 METRES TRACK
1896	Paul Masson (FRA) 17:54.2	Léon Flameng (FRA)	Adolf Schmal (AUT)

20,000 METRES TRACK
1906	William Pett (GBR) 29:00.0	Maurice Bardonneau (FRA) 29:30.0	Fernand Vast (FRA) 29:32.0
1908	Clarence Kingsbury (GBR) 34:13.6	Benjamin Jones (GBR)	Joseph Werbrouck (BEL)

25 MILES TRACK (40.225M)

1904	Burton Downing (USA) 1hr 10:55.4	Arthur Andrews (USA)	George Wiley (USA)

50,000 METRES TRACK

1920	Henry George (BEL) 1hr 16:43.2	Cyril Alden (GBR)*	Petrus Ikelaar (NED)
1924	Jacobus Willems (NED) 1hr 18:24	Cyril Alden (GBR)	Frederick Wyld (GBR)

100 KILOMETRES TRACK

1896	Leon Flameng (FRA) 3hr 08:19.2	Georgios Kolettis (GRE) 6 laps	—†
1908	Charles Bartlett (GBR) 2hr 41:48.6	Charles Denny (GBR)	Octave Lapize (FRA)

12 HOURS TRACK

1896	Adolf Schmal (AUT) 314.997km	Frank Keeping (GBR) 314.664km	Georgios Paraskevopoulous (GRE) 313.330km

* Most eyewitnesses considered that Ikelaar finished second. † Only two riders finished.

WOMEN

SPRINT

	Gold	Silver	Bronze
1988	Erika Salumäe (URS)	Christa Röthenburger-Luding (GDR)	Connie Young (USA)
1992	Erika Salumäe (EST)	Annett Neumann (GER)	Ingrid Haringa (NED)
1996	Felicia Ballanger (FRA)	Michelle Ferris (AUS)	Ingrid Haringa (NED)
2000	Felicia Ballanger (FRA)	Oksana Gritschina (RUS)	Irina Janovich (UKR)

1896–1984 event not held

500 METRES TIME TRIAL (Introduced in 2000)

	Gold	Silver	Bronze
2000	Felicia Ballanger (FRA) 34.140	Michelle Ferris (AUS) 34.696	Cuihua Jiang (CHN) 34.768

3000 METRES INDIVIDUAL PURSUIT

	Gold	Silver	Bronze
1992	Petra Rossner (GER) 3:41.753	Kathryn Watt (AUS) 3:43.438	Rebecca Twigg (USA) 3:52.429
1996	Antonella Bellutti (ITA) 3:33.595	Marion Clignet (FRA) 3:38.571	Judith Arnt (GER) 3:38.744
2000	Leontien Zijlaard (NED) 3:31.570	Marion Clignet (FRA) 3:34.636	Yvonne McGregor (GBR) 3:35.492

1896–1988 event not held

INDIVIDUAL ROAD RACE*

	Gold	Silver	Bronze
1984	Connie Carpenter-Phinney (USA) 2hr 11:14.0	Rebecca Twigg (USA) 2hr 11:14.0	Sandra Schumacher (FRG) 2hr 11:14.0
1988	Monique Knol (NED) 2hr 00.52	Jutta Niehaus (FRG) close	Laima Zilporitee (URS) close
1992	Kathryn Watt (AUS) 2hr 04:02	Jeannie Longo-Ciprelli (FRA) 2hr 05:02	Monique Knol (NED) 2hr 05:03
1996	Jeannie Longo-Ciprelli (FRA) 2hr 36:13	Imelda Chiappa (USA) 2hr 36.38	Clara Hughes (CAN) 2hr 36.44
2000	Leontien Zijlaard (NED) 3hr 06:31	Hanka Kupfernagel (GER) 3hr 06:31	Diana Ziliute (LTU) 3hr 06:31

1896–1980 and 1996 event not held. * Events held over 79.2km 1984; 82km – 1988; 81km – 1992; 104km –1996 and 119.7km – 2000.

ROAD INDIVIDUAL TIME TRIAL (Held over 26km – 1996; 31.2km – 2000)

	Gold	Silver	Bronze
1996	Zulfiya Zabirova (RUS) 36:40	Jeannie Longo-Ciprelli (FRA) 37:00	Clara Hughes (CAN) 37:13
2000	Leontien Zijlaard (NED) 42:00	Mari Holden (USA) 42:37	Jeannie Longo-Ciprelli (FRA) 42:52

1896–1992 event not held

POINTS RACE

	Gold	Silver	Bronze
1996	Nathalie Lancien (FRA) 24pts	Ingrid Haringa (NED) 23	Lucy Tyler-Sharman (UAS) 17
2000	Antonella Bellutti (ITA) 19pts	Leontien Zijlaard (NED) 16	Olga Slyussaryeva (RUS) 15

1896–1992 event not held

CYCLING – MOUNTAIN BIKE (Introduced in 1996)

MEN'S CROSS-COUNTRY

	Gold	Silver	Bronze
1996	Bart Brentjens (NED) 2hr 17.38	Thomas Frischknecht (SUI) 2hr 20.14	Miguel Martinez (FRA) 2hr 20.26
2000	Miguel Martinez (FRA) 2hr 09:02.50	Filip Meirhoeghe (BEL) 2hr 10:05.51	Christoph Sauser (SUI) 2hr 11:21.00

WOMEN'S CROSS-COUNTRY

	Gold	Silver	Bronze
1996	Paola Pezzo (ITA) 1hr 50.51	Alison Sydor (CAN) 1hr 51.58	Susan DiMattei (USA) 1hr 52.36
2000	Paola Pezzo (ITA) 1hr 49:24.38	Barbara Baller (SUI) 1hr 49:51.42	Margarita Fulliana (ESP) 1hr 49:57.39

EQUESTRIAN MEDALS

GRAND PRIX (JUMPING)

	Gold	Silver	Bronze
1900	Aimé Haegeman (BEL) Benton II	Georges van der Poële (BEL) Windsor Squire	Louis de Champsavin (FRA) Terpsichore
1912	Jean Cariou (FRA) 186pts Mignon	Rabod von Kröcher (GER) 186 Dohna	Emanuel de Blomaert de Sove (BEL) 185 Clonmore
1920	Tommaso Lequio (ITA) 2 faults Trebecco	Alessandro Valerio (ITA) 3 Cento	Gustaf Lewenhaupt (SWE) 4 Mon Coeur
1924	Alphonse Gemuseus (SUI) 3 faults Lucette	Tommaso Lequio (ITA) 8.75 Trebecco	Adam Krolikiewicz (POL) 10 Picador
1928	Frantisek Ventura (TCH) no faults Elliot	Pierre Bertrand de Balanda (FRA) 2 Papillon	Charles Kuhn (SUI) 4 Pepita
1932	Takeichi Nishi (JPN) 8pts Uranus	Harry Chamberlain (USA) 12 Show Girl	Clarence von Rosen Jr (SWE) 16 Empire
1936	Kurt Hasse (GER) 4 faults Tora	Henri Rang (ROM) 4 Delius	József von Platthy (HUN) 8 Sellö
1948	Humbeto Mariles Cortés (MEX) 6.25 faults Arete	Rubén Uriza (MEX) 8 Harvey	Jean d'Orgeix (FRA) 8 Sucre de Pomme
1952	Pierre Jonquères d'Oriola (FRA) No faults Ali Baba	Oscar Cristi (CHI) 4 Bambi	Fritz Thiedemann (GER) 8 Meteor
1956	Hans Günter Winkler (GER) 4 faults Halla	Raimondo d'Inzeo (ITA) 8 Merano	Piero d'Inzeo (ITA) 11 Uruguay
	Gold	Silver	Bronze
1960	Raimondo d'Inzeo (ITA) 12 faults Posillipo	Piero d'Inzeo (ITA) 16 The Rock	David Broome (GBR) 23 Sunslave
1964	Pierre Jonquères d'Oriola (FRA) 9 faults Lutteur	Hermann Schriddle (GER) 12.75 Dozent	Peter Robeson (GBR) 16 Firecrest
1968	William Steinkraus (USA) 4 faults Snowbound	Marian Coakes (GBR) 8 Stroller	David Broome (GBR) 12 Mister Softee
1972	Graziano Mancinelli (ITA) 8 faults Ambassador	Ann Moore (GBR) 8 Psalm	Neal Shapiro (USA) 8 Sloopy
1976	Alwin Schockemöhle (FRG) no faults Warwick Rex	Michael Vaillancourt (CAN) 12 Branch County	François Mathy (BEL) 12 Gai Luron
1980	Jan Kowalcyzk (POL) 8 faults Artemor 9.50	Nikolai Korolkov (URS) Espadron	Joaquim Perez Heras (MEX) 12 Alymony
1984	Joe Fargis (USA) 4 faults Touch of Class	Conrad Homfeld (USA) 4 Abdullah	Heidi Robbiani (SUI) 8 Jessica V

	Gold	Silver	Bronze
1988	Pierre Durand (FRA) 1.25 faults *Jappeloup*	Greg Best (USA) 4 *Gem Twist*	Karsten Huck (FRG) 4 *Nepomuk 8*
1992	Ludger Beerbaum (GER) no faults *Classic Touch*	Piet Raymakers (NED) 0.25 *Ratina Z*	Norman Dello Joio (USA) 4.75 *Irish*
1996	Ulrich Kirchkoff (GER) 1.00 fault *Jus De Pommes*	Willi Melliger (SUI) 4.00 *Calvaro*	Alexandra Ledermann (FRA) 4.00 *Rochet M*
2000	Jeroen Dubbeldam (NED) 4.00 faults *Sjiem*	Albert Voorn (NED) 4 *Lando*	Khaled al Eid (KSA) 4 *Khashim al Aan*

1896 and 1904–1908 event not held

GRAND PRIX (JUMPING) TEAM

	Gold	Silver	Bronze
1912	Sweden 25pts	France 32	Germany 40
1920	Sweden 14 pts	Belgium 16.25	Italy 18.75
1924	Sweden 42.25pts	Switzerland 50	Portugal 53
1928	Spain 4 pts	Poland 8	Sweden 10
1932*	—	—	—
1936	Germany 44.00pts	The Netherlands 51.50	Portugal 56.00
1948	Mexico 34.25 pts	Spain 56.50	Great Britain 67
1952	Great Britain 40.75 pts	Chile 45.75	United States 52.25
1956	Germany 40 pts	Italy 66	Great Britain 69
1960	Germany 46.50 pts	United States 66	Italy 80.50
1964	Germany 68.50 pts	France 77.75	Italy 88.50
1968	Canada 102.75 pts	France 110.50	FRG 117.25
1972	FRG 32 pts	United States 32.25	Italy 48
1976	France 40 pts	FRG 44	Belgium 63
1980	Soviet Union 16 pts	Poland 32	Mexico 39.25
1984	United States 12 pts	Great Britain 36.75	FRG 39.25
1988	FRG 17.25 pts	United States 20.50	France 27.50
1992	The Netherlands 12.00pts	Austria 16.75	France 24.75
1996	Germany 1.75pts	United States 12.00	Brazil 17.25
2000	Germany 15pts	Switzerland 16	Brazil 24

1896–1908 event not held. * There was a team competition but no one nation had three riders that completed the course.

GRAND PRIX (DRESSAGE)

	Gold	Silver	Bronze
1912	Carl Bonde (SWE) 15pts *Emperor*	Gustaf-Adolf Boltenstern Sr (SWE) 21 *Neptun*	Hans von Blixen-Finecke (SWE) 32 *Maggie*
1920	Janne Lundblad (SWE) 27.9375pts *Uno*	Bertil Sandström (SWE) 26.3125 *Sabel*	Hans von Rosen (SWE) 25.1250* *Running Sister*
1924	Ernst Linder (SWE) 276.4pts *Piccolomini*	Bertil Sandström (SWE) 275.8 *Sabel*	Xavier Lesage (FRA) 265.8 *Plumard*
1928	Carl von Langen (GER) 237.42pts *Draüfgänger*	Charles Marion (FRA) 231.00 *Linon*	Ragnar Olsson (SWE) 229.78 *Günstling*
1932	Xavier Lesage (FRA) 1031.25pts *Taine*	Charles Marion (FRA) 916.25 *Linon*	Hiram Tuttle (USA) 901.50 *Olympic*
	Gold	Silver	Bronze
1936	Heinz Pollay (GER) 1760pts *Kronos*	Friedrich Gerhard (GER) 1745.4 *Absinth*	Alois Podhajsky (AUT) 1721.5 *Nero*
1948	Hans Moser (SUI) 492.5pts *Hummer*	André Jousseaume (FRA) 480.0 *Harpagon*	Gustaf-Adolf Boltenstern Jr (SWE) 477.5 *Trumpf*
1952	Henri St Cyr (SWE) 561pts *Master Rufus*	Lis Hartel (DEN) 541.5 *Jubilee*	André Jousseauame (FRA) 541.0 *Harpagon*
1956	Henri St Cyr (SWE) 860pts *Juli*	Lis Hartel (DEN) 850 *Jubilee*	Liselott Linsenhoff (GER) 832 *Adular*
1960	Sergei Filatov (URS) 2144pts *Absent*	Gustav Fischer (SUI) 2087 *Wald*	Josef Neckermann (GER) 2082 *Asbach*
1964	Henri Chammartin (SUI) 1504pts *Woermann*	Harry Boldt (GER) 1503 *Remus*	Sergei Filatov (URS) 1486 *Absent*
1968	Ivan Kizimov (URS) 1572pts *Ikhov*	Josef Neckermann (FRG) 1546 *Mariano*	Reiner Klimke (FRG) 1527 *Dux*

	Gold	Silver	Bronze
1972	Liselott Linsenhoff (FRG) 1229pts *Piaff*	Yelena Petuchkova (URS) 1185 *Pepel*	Josef Neckermann (FRG) 2082 *Venetia*
1976	Christine Stückelberger (SUI) 1486 *Granat*	Harry Boldt (FRG) 1435 *Woycek*	Reiner Klimke (FRG) 1395 *Mehmet*
1980	Elisabeth Theurer (AUT) 1370pts *Mon Cherie*	Yuri Kovshov (URS) 1300 *Igrok*	Viktor Ugyumov (URS) 1234 *Shkval*
1984	Reiner Klimke (FRG) 1504pts *Ahlerich*	Anne Grethe Jensen (DEN) 1442 *Martzog*	Otto Hofer (SUI) 1364 *Limandus*
1988	Nicole Uphoff (FRG) 1521pts *Rembrandt*	Margit Otto Crepin (FRA) 1462 *Corlandus*	Christine Stückelberger (SUI) 1417 *Gauguin De Lully*
1992	Nicole Uphoff (FRG) 1626pts *Rembrandt*	Isabell Werth (GER) 1551 *Gigolo*	Klaus Balkenhol (GER) 1515 *Goldstern*
1996	Isabel Werth (GER) 235.09pts *Gigolo*	Anky van Grunsven (NED) 233.02 *Bonfire*	Sven Rothenberger (NED) 224.94 *Weyden*
2000	Anky van Grunsven (NED) 239.18pts *Bonfire*	Isabell Werth (GER) 234.19 *Gigolo*	Ulla Salzgeber (GER) 225.88 *Rusty*

1896–1908 event not held. * Gustaf-Adolf Boltenstern Sr (SWE) on *Iron* finished third with 26.1875pts but was disqualified.

GRAND PRIX (DRESSAGE TEAM)

	Gold	Silver	Bronze
1928	Germany 669.72pts	Sweden 650.86	The Netherlands 642.96
1932	France 2828.75pts	Sweden 2678	United States 2576.75
1936	Germany 5074pts	France 4846	Sweden 4660.5
1948*	France 1269pts	United States 1256	Portugal 1182
1952	Sweden 1597.5pts	Switzerland 1759	Germany 1501
1956	Sweden 2475pts	Germany 2346	Switzerland 2346
1964	Germany 2558pts	Switzerland 2526	Soviet Union 2311
1968	FRG 2699pts	Soviet Union 2657	Switzerland 2547
1972	Soviet Union 5095pts	FRG 5083	Sweden 4849
1976	FRG 5155pts	Switzerland 4684	United States 4670
1980	Soviet Union 4383pts	Bulgaria 3580	Romania 3346
1984	FRG 4955pts	Switzerland 4673	Sweden 4630
1988	FRG 4302pts	Switzerland 4164	Canada 3969
1992	Germany 5224pts	The Netherlands 4742	United States 4643
1996	Germany 5553pts	The Netherlands 5437	United States 5309
2000	Germany 5632pts	The Netherlands	United States 5166

1896–1924 and 1960 event not held. * Sweden was originally declared the winners with 1366pts but was subsequently disqualified one year later.

THREE-DAY EVENT

	Gold	Silver	Bronze
1912	Axel Nordlander (SWE) 46.59pts *Lady Artist*	Friedrich von Rochow (GER) 46.42 *Idealist*	Jean Cariou (FRA) 46.32 *Cocotte*
1920	Helmer Mörner (SWE) 1775pts *Germania*	Age Lundström (SWE) 1738.75 *Yrsa*	Ettore Caffaratti (ITA) 1733.75 *Traditore*
1924	Adolf van de Voort van Zijp (NED) 1976pts *Silver Piece*	Fröde Kirkebjerg (DEN) 1853.5 *Meteor*	Sloan Doak (USA) 1845.5 *Pathfinder*
1928	Charles Pahud de Mortanges (NED) (NED) 1969.82pts *Marcroix*	Gerard de Kruyff (NED) 1967.26 *Va-t-en*	Bruno Neumann (GER) 1944 1944.42 *Ilja*
1932	Charles Pahud de Mortanges (NED) 1813.83pts *Marcroix*	Earl Thomson (USA) 1811 *Jenny Camp*	Clarence von Rosen Jr (SWE) 1809.42 *Sunnyside Maid*
1936	Ludwig Stubbendorff (GER) 37.7pts *Nurmi*	Earl Thomson (USA) 99.9 *Jenny Camp*	Hans Mathiesen Lunding (DEN) 102.2 *Jason*
1948	Bernard Chevallier (FRA) +4pts *Aiglonne*	Frank Henry (USA) -21 *Swing Low*	Robert Selfelt (SWE) -25 *Claque*
1952	Hans von Blixen-Finecke (SWE) 28.33 faults *Jubal*	Guy Lefrant (FRA) 54.50 *Verdun*	Wilhelf Büsing (GER) 55.50 *Hubertus*
1956	Petrus Kasenman (SWE) 66.53 flts *Illuster*	August Lütke-Westhues (GER) 84.87 *Trux van Kamax*	Frank Weldon (GBR) 85.48 *Kilbarry*
1960	Lawrence Morgan (AUS) +7.15pts *Salad Days*	Neale Lavis (AUS) -16.50 *Mirrabooka*	Anton Bühler (SUI) -51.21 *Gay Spark*

	Gold	Silver	Bronze
1964	Mauro Checcoli (ITA) 64.40pts *Surbean*	Carlos Moratorio (ARG) 56.40 *Chalan*	Fritz Ligges (GER) 49.20 *Donkosak*
1968	Jean-Jaques Guyon (FRA) 38.86pts *Pitou*	Derek Allhusen (GBR) 41.61 *Lochinvar*	Michael Page (USA) 52.31 *Faster*
1972	Richard Meade (GBR) 57.73pts *Laurieston*	Alessa Argenton (ITA) 43.33 *Woodland*	Jan Jonsson (SWE) 39.67 *Sarajevo*
1976	Edmund Coffin (USA) 114.99pts B*ally-Cor*	Michael Plumb (USA) 125.85 *Better and Better*	Karl Schultz (FRG) 129.45 *Madrigal*
1980	Federico Roman (ITA) 108.60pts *Rossinan*	Aleksandr Blinov (URS) 120.80 *Galzun*	Yuriy Salinikov (URS) 151.60 *Pintset*
1984	Mark Todd (NZL) 51.60pts *Charisma*	Karen Stives (USA) 54.20 *Ben Arthur*	Virginia Holgate (GBR) 56.80 *Priceless*
1988	Mark Todd (NZL) 42.60pts *Charisma*	Ian Stark (GBR) 52.80 *Sir Wattie*	Virginia Leng (GBR) 62.00 *Master Craftsman*
1992	Matthew Ryan (AUS) 70pts *Kibah Tic Toc*	Herbert Blocker (GER) 81.30 *Feine Dame*	Blyth Tait (NZL) 87.60 *Messiah*
1996	Blyth Tait (NZL) 56.80pts *Ready Teddy*	Sally Clark (NZL) 60.40 *Squirrel Hill*	Kerry Millikin (USA) 73.70 *Out and About*
2000	David O'Connor (USA) 34.00pts *Custom Made*	Andrew Hoy (AUS) 39.80 *Swizzle In*	Mark Todd (NZL) 42.00 *Eyespy II*

1896–1908 event not held

THREE-DAY EVENT TEAM

	Gold	Silver	Bronze
1912	Sweden 139.06pts	Germany 138.48	United States 137.33
1920	Sweden 5057pts	Italy 4375	Belgium 4560
1924	The Netherlands 5297.5pts	Sweden 4743.5	Italy 4512.5
1928	The Netherlands 5865.68pts	Norway 5395.68	Poland 5067.92
1932	United States 5038.08pts	The Netherlands 4689.08	—*
1936	Germany 676.75pts	Poland 991.70	Great Britain 9195.90
1948	United States 161.50pts	Sweden 165.00	Mexico 305.25
1952	Sweden 221.49pts	Germany 2£5.49	United States 587.16
1956	Great Britain 355.48pts	Germany 475.61	Canada 572.72
1960	Australia 128.18pts	Switzerland 386.02	France 515.71
1964	Italy 85.80pts	United States 65.86	Germany 56.73
1968	Great Britain 175.93pts	United States 245.87	Australia 331.26
1972	Great Britain 95.53pts	United States 10.81	FRG -18.00
1976	United States 441.00pts	FRG 584.60	Australia 599.54
1980	Soviet Union 457.00pts	Italy 656.20	Mexico 1172.85
1984	United States 186.00pts	Great Britain 189.20	FRG 234.00
1988	FRG 225.95pts	Great Britain 256.80	New Zealand 271.20
1992	Australia 288.60pts	New Zealand 290.80	Germany 300.30
1996	Australia 203.85pts	United States 261.10pts	New Zealand 268.55pts
2000	Australia 145.80pts	Great Britain 161.00	United States 175.80

1896–1908 event not held. * No other teams finished.

DISCONTINUED EVENTS
EQUESTRIAN HIGH JUMP

	Gold	Silver	Bronze
1900	Dominique Gardére (FRA) 1.85m *Canéla* Gian Giorgio Trissino (ITA) x 1.85m *Oreste*	—	André Moreaux (FRA) 1.70 *Ludlow*

EQUESTRIAN LONG JUMP

1900	Constant van Langhendonck (BEL) 6.10m *Extra Dry*	Federico Caprilli (ITA) 5.70m *Oreste*	de Bellegarde (FRA) 5.30m *Tolla*

FIGURE RIDING (Only open to soldiers below the rank of NCO)

1920	Bouckaert (BEL) 30,500pts	Field (FRA) 29,500	Finet (BEL) 29,000

FIGURE RIDING, TEAMS

	Gold	Silver	Bronze
1920	Belgium 87,500pts	France 81,083	Sweden 59,416

FENCING MEDALS – INDIVIDUAL

MEN
FOIL

Titles are assessed on both wins (2pts) and draws (1pt) so, as in 1928, the winner is not necessarily the one with the most wins.

	Gold	Silver	Bronze
1896	Emile Gravelotte (FRA) 4 wins	Henri Callott (FRA) 3	Perikles Mavromichalis-Pierrakos (GRE) 2
1900	Emile Cost (FRA) 6 wins	Henri Masson (FRA) 5	Jacques Boulenger (FRA) 4
1904	Ramón Fonst (CUB) 3 wins	Albertson Van Zo Post (USA) 2*	Charles Tatham* (USA) 1
1906	Georges Dillon-Kavanagh (FRA) d.n.a.	Gustav Casmir (GER) d.n.a.	Pierre d'Hugues (FRA) . d.n.a
1912	Nedo Nadi (ITA) 7 wins	Pietro Speciale (ITA) 5	Richard Verderber (AUT) 4
1920	Nedo Nadi (ITA) 10 wins	Philippe Cattiau (FRA) 9	Roger Ducret (FRA) 9
1924	Roger Ducret (FRA) 6 wins	Philippe Cattiau (FRA) 5	Maurice van Damme (BEL) 4
1928	Lucien Gaudin (FRA) 9 wins	Ermin Casmir (GER) 9	Giulio Gaudini (ITA) 9
1932	Gustavo Marzi (ITA) 9 wins	Joseph Lewis (USA) 6	Giulio Bocchino (ITA) 4
1936	Giulio Gaudini (ITA) 7 wins	Edward Gardère (FRA) 6	Giorgio Bocchino (ITA) 4
1948	Jean Buhan (FRA) 7 wins	Christian d'Oriola (FRA) 5	Lajos Maszlay (HUN) 4
1952	Christian d'Oriola (FRA) 8 wins	Edouard Gardère (FRA) 6	Manlio di Rosa (ITA) 5
1956	Christian d'Oriola (FRA) 6 wins	Giancarlo Bergamini (ITA) 5	Antonio Spallino (ITA) 5
1960	Viktor Zhdanovich (URS) 7 wins	Yuriy Sissikin (URS) 4	Albert Axelrod (USA) 3
1964	Egon Franke (POL) 3 wins	Jean-Claude Magnan (FRA) 2	Daniel Revenu (FRA) 1
1968	Ion Drimba (ROM) 4 wins	Jenö Kamuti (HUN) 3	Daniel Revenu (FRA) 3
1972	Witold Woyda (POL) 5 wins	Jenö Kamuti (HUN) 4	Christian Nöel (FRA) 2
1976	Fabio Dal Zotto (ITA) 4 wins	Aleksandr Romankov (URS) 4	Bernard Talvard (FRA) 3
1980	Vladimir Smirnov (URS) 5 wins	Paskal Jolyot (FRA) 5	Aleksandr Romankov (URS) 5
1984	Mauro Numa (ITA)	Matthias Behr (FRG)	Stefano Cerioni (ITA)
1988	Stefano Cerioni (ITA)	Udo Wagner (GDR)	Aleksandr Romankov (URS)
1992	Phillipe Omnes (FRA)	Sergei Goloubiski (EUN)	Elvis Gregory (CUB)
1996	Alessandro Puccini (ITA)	Lionel Plumenail (FRA)	Franck Boidin (FRA)
2000	Young-Ho Kim (KOR)	Ralf Bissdorf (GER)	Dimitri Shevchenko (RUS)

* Van Zo Post was an American who competed for Cuba in the team events.

ÉPÉE

	Gold	Silver	Bronze
1900	Ramón Fonst (CUB)	Louis Perrée (FRA)	Léon Sée (FRA)
1904	Ramón Fonst (CUB)	Charles Tatham (USA)	Albertson Van Zo Post (USA)*
1906	Georges de la Falaise (FRA) d.n.a.	Georges Dillon-Kavanagh (FRA) d.n.a.	Alexander van Blijenburgh (NED) d.n.a.
1908	Gaston Alibert (FRA) 5 wins	Alexandre Lippmann (FRA) 4	Eugène Olivier (FRA) 4
1912	Paul Anspach (BEL) 6 wins	Ivan Osiier (DEN) 5	Philippe Le Hardy de Beaulieu (BEL) 4
1920	Armand Massard (FRA) 9 wins	Alexandre Lippmann (FRA) 7	Gustave Buchard (FRA) 6
1924	Charles Delporte (BEL) 8 wins	Roger Ducret (FRA) 7	Nils Hellsten (SWE) 7
1928	Lucien Gaudin (FRA) 8 wins	Georges Buchard (FRA) 7	George Calman (USA) 6
1932	Giancarlo Cornaggia-Medici (ITA) 8	Georges Buchard (FRA) 7	Carlo Agostini (ITA) 7
1936	Franco Riccardi (ITA) 5 wins	Saverio Ragno (ITA) 6	Giancarlo Cornaggia-Medici (ITA) 6
1948	Luigi Cantone (ITA) 7 wins	Oswald Zappelli (SUI) 5	Edoardo Mangiarotti (ITA) 5
1952	Edoardo Mangiarotti (ITA) 7 wins	Dario Mangiarotti (ITA) 6	Oswald Zappelli (SUI) 6
1956	Carlo Pavesi (ITA) 5 wins	Giuseppe Delfino (ITA) 5	Edoardo Mangiarotti (ITA) 5
1960	Giuseppe Delfino (ITA) 5 win	Allan Jay (GBR) 5	Bruno Khabarov (URS) 4

	Gold	Silver	Bronze
1964	Grigori Kriss (URS) 2 wins	William Hoskyns (GBR) 2	Guram Kostava (URS) 1
1968	Gyözö Kulcsár (HUN) 4 wins	Grigori Kriss (URS) 4	Gianluigi Saccaro (ITA) 4
1972	Csaba Fenyvesi (HUN) 4 wins	Jacques la Degaillerie (FRA) 3	Gyözö Kulcsár (HUN) 3
1976	Alexander Pusch (FRG) 3 wins	Jürgen Hehn (FRG)	Gyözö Kulcsár (HUN) 3
1980	Johan Harmenberg (SWE) 4 wins	Ernö Kolczonay (HUN) 3	Philippe Riboud (FRA) 3
1984	Philippe Boisse (FRA)	Björne Väggö (SWE)	Phillippe Riboud (FRA)
1988	Arnd Schitt (FRG)	Philippe Riboud (FRA)	Andrei Chouvalov (URS)
1992	Eric Srecki (FRA)	Pavel Kolobkov (EUN)	Jean-Michel Henry (FRA)
1996	Aleksandr Beketov (RUS)	Ivan Trevejo Perez (CUB)	Geza Imre (HUN)
2000	Pavel Kolobkov (RUS)	Hugues Obry (FRA)	Sang-Ki Lee (KOR)

1896 event not held. * Van Zo Post was an American who competed for Cuba in the team events.

SABRE

	Gold	Silver	Bronze
1896	Jean Georgiadis (GRE) 4 wins	Telemachos Karakalos (GRE) 3	Holger Nielsen (DEN) 2
1900	Georges de la Falaise (FRA) d.n.a.	Léon Thiébault (FRA) d.n.a.	Siegfried Flesch (AUT) d.n.a.
1904	Manuel Diaz (CUB) 4 wins	William Grebe (USA) 3	Albertson Van Zo Post (USA)*
1906	Jean Georgiadis (GRE) d.n.a.	Gustav Casmir (GER) d.n.a.	Federico Cesarano (ITA) d.n.a.
1908	Jeno Fuchs (HUN) 6 wins	Béla Zulavsky (HUN) 6	Vilem Goppold von Lobsdorf (BOH) 4
1912	Jeno Fuchs (HUN) 6 wins	Béla Békéssy (HUN) 5	Ervin Mészaros (HUN) 5
1920	Nedo Nadi (ITA) 11 wins	Aldo Nadi (ITA) 9	Adrianus EW de Jong (NED) 7
1924	Sándor Posta (HUN) 5 wins	Roger Ducret (FRA) 5	János Garai (HUN) 5
1928	Odön Tersztyansky (HUN) 9 wins	Attila Petschauer (HUN) 9	Bino Bini (ITA) 8
1932	György Piller (HUN) 8 wins	Giulio Gaudini (ITA) 7	Endre Kabos (HUN) 5
1936	Endre Kabos (HUN) 7 wins	Gustavo Marzi (ITA) 6	Aladár Gerevich (HUN) 6
1948	Aladár Gerevich (HUN) 7 wins	Vincenzo Pinton (ITA) 5	Pál Kovács (HUN) 5
1952	Pál Kovács (HUN) 8 wins	Aladár Gerevich (HUN) 7	Tibor Berczelly (HUN) 5
1956	Rudolf Kárpáti (HUN) 6 wins	Jerzy Pawlowski (POL) 5	Lev Kuznyetsov (URS) 4
1960	Rudolf Kárpáti (HUN) 5 wins	Zoltán Horvath (HUN) 4	Wladimiro Calarese (ITA) 4
1964	Tibor Pézsa (HUN) 2 wins	Claude Arabo (FRA) 2	Umar Mavlikhanov (URS) 1
1968	Jerzy Pawlowski (POL) 4 wins	Mark Rakita (URS) 4	Tribor Pézsa (HUN) 3
1972	Viktor Sidiak (URS) 4 wins	Peter Maroth (HUN) 3	Vladimir Nazilimov (URS) 3
1976	Viktor Krovopouskov (URS) 5 wins	Vladimir Nazilmov (URS) 4	Viktor Sidiak (URS) 3
1980	Viktor Krovopouskov (URS) 5 wins	Mikhail Burtsev (URS) 4	Imre Gedovari (HUN) 3
1984	Jean François Lamour (FRA)	Marco Marin (ITA)	Peter Westbrook (USA)
1988	Jean François Lamour (FRA)	Janusz Olech (POL)	Giovanni Scalzo (ITA)
1992	Bence Szabo (HUN)	Marco Marin (ITA)	Jean François Lamour (FRA)
1996	Sergei Podnyakov (RUS)	Stanislav Sharikov (RUS)	Damien Touya (FRA)
2000	Mihai Covaliu (ROM)	Mathieu Gourdain (FRA)	Wiradech Kothny (GER)

* Van Zo Post was an American who competed for Cuba in the team events.

WOMEN

FOIL

	Gold	Silver	Bronze
1924	Ellen Osiier (DEN) 5 wins	Gladys Davis (GBR) 4	Grete Heckscher (DEN) 3
1928	Helène Mayer (GER) 7 wins	Muriel Freeman (GBR) 6	Olga Oelkers (GER) 4
1932	Ellen Preis (AUT) 9 wins	Heather Guinness (GBR) 8	Erna Bogen (HUN) 7
1936	Ilona Elek (HUN) 6 wins	Helène Mayer (GER) 5	Ellen Preis (AUT) 5
1948	Ilona Elek (HUN) 6 wins	Karen Lachmann (DEN) 5	Ellen Müller-Preis (AUT) 5
1952	Irene Camber (ITA) 5 wins	Ilona Elek (HUN) 5	Karen Lachmann (DEN) 4
1956	Gillian Sheen (GBR) 6 wins	Olga Orban (ROM) 6	Renée Garilhe (FRA) 5
1960	Heidi Schmid (GER) 6 wins	Valentina Rastvorova (URS) 5	Maria Vicol (ROM) 4
1964	Ildikó Ujlaki-Rejtö (HUN) 2 wins	Helga Mees (GER) 2	Antonella Ragno (ITA) 2
1968	Elena Novikova (URS) 4 wins	Pilar Roldan (MEX) 3	Ildikó Ujlaki-Rejtö (HUN) 3
1972	Antonella Ragno-Lonzi (ITA) 4 wins	Ildikó Bóbis (HUN) 3	Galina Gorokhova (URS) 2
1976	Ildikó Schwarczenberger (HUN) 4 wins	Maria Collino (ITA) 4	Elena Novikova-Belova (URS) 3

	Gold	Silver	Bronze
1980	Pascale Trinquet (FRA) 4 wins	Magda Maros (HUN) 3	Barbara Wysoczanska (POL) 3
1984	Jujie Luan (CHN)	Cornelia Hanisch (FRG)	Dorina Vaccaroni (ITA)
1988	Anja Fichtel (FRG)	Sabine Bau (FRG)	Zita Funkenhauser (FRG)
1992	Giovanna Trillini (ITA)	Wang Huifeng (CHN)	Tatyana Sadovskaya (EUN)
1996	Laura Badea (ROM)	Valentina Vezzali (ITA)	Giovanna Trillini (ITA)
2000	Valentina Vezzali (ITA)	Rita König (GER)	Giovanna Trillini (ITA)

1896–1920 event not held

ÉPÉE

	Gold	Silver	Bronze
1996	Laura Flessel (FRA)	Valerie Bartlois (FRA)	Györgyi Horvathné-Szalay (HUN)
2000	Timea Nagy (HUN)	Gianna Hablützel-Bürki (SUI)	Laura Flessel-Colovic (FRA)

1896–1992 event not held

FENCING MEDALS – TEAM

MEN

FOIL

	Gold	Silver	Bronze
1904	Cuba/United States*	United States	—†
1920	Italy	France	United States
1924	France	Belgium	Hungary
1928	Italy	France	Argentina
1932	France	Italy	United States
1936	Italy	France	Germany
1948	France	Italy	Belgium
1952	France	Italy	Hungary
1956	Italy	France	Germany
1960	Soviet Union	Italy	Germany
1964	Soviet Union	Poland	France
1968	France	Soviet Union	Poland
1972	Poland	Soviet Union	France
1976	FRG	Italy	France
1980	France	Soviet Union	Poland
1984	Italy	FRG	France
1988	Soviet Union	FRG	Hungary
1992	Germany	Cuba	Poland
1996	Russia	Poland	Cuba
2000	France	China	Italy

1896–1900 and 1906–1912 event not held. * Van Zo Post was an American who competed for Cuba in the team events. † No other teams entered.

WOMEN

FOIL

	Gold	Silver	Bronze
1960	Soviet Union	Hungary	Italy
1964	Hungary	Soviet Union	Germany
1968	Soviet Union	Hungary	Romania
1972	Soviet Union	Hungary	Romania
1976	Soviet Union	France	Hungary
1980	France	Soviet Union	Hungary
1984	FRG	Romania	France
1988	FRG	Italy	Hungary
1992	Italy	Germany	Romania
1996	Italy	Romania	Germany
2000	Italy	Poland	Germany

1896–1956 event not held

MEN

SABRE

	Gold	Silver	Bronze
1906	Germany	Greece	The Netherlands
1908	Hungary	Italy	Bohemia
1912	Hungary	Austria	The Netherlands
1920	Italy	France	The Netherlands
1924	Italy	Hungary	The Netherlands
1928	Hungary	Italy	Poland
1932	Hungary	Italy	Poland
1936	Hungary	Italy	Germany
1948	Hungary	Italy	United States
1952	Hungary	Italy	France
1956	Hungary	Poland	Soviet Union
1960	Hungary	Poland	Italy
1964	Soviet Union	Italy	Poland
1968	Soviet Union	Italy	Hungary
1972	Italy	Soviet Union	Hungary
1976	Soviet Union	Italy	Romania
1980	Soviet Union	Italy	Hungary
1984	Italy	France	Romania
1988	Hungary	Soviet Union	Italy
1992	Unified Team	Hungary	France
1996	Russia	Hungary	Italy
2000	Russia	France	Germany

1896–1904 event not held

MEN

ÉPÉE

	Gold	Silver	Bronze
1906	France	Great Britain	Belgium
1908	France	Great Britain	Belgium
1912	Belgium	Great Britain	The Netherlands
1920	Italy	Belgium	France
1924	France	Belgium	Italy
1928	Italy	France	Portugal
1932	France	Italy	United States
1936	Italy	Sweden	France
1948	France	Italy	Sweden
1952	Italy	Sweden	Switzerland
1956	Italy	Hungary	France
1960	Italy	Great Britain	Soviet Union
1964	Hungary	Italy	France
1968	Hungary	Soviet Union	Poland
1972	Hungary	Switzerland	Soviet Union
1976	Sweden	FRG	Switzerland
1980	France	Poland	Soviet Union
1984	FRG	France	Italy
1988	France	FRG	Soviet Union
1992	Germany	Hungary	Unified Team
1996	Italy	Russia	France
2000	Italy	France	Cuba

1896–1904 event not held

WOMEN

ÉPÉE

	Gold	Silver	Bronze
1996	France	Italy	Russia
2000	Russia	Switzerland	China

1896–1992 event not held

DISCONTINUED EVENTS

FOIL FOR FENCING MASTERS

	Gold	Silver	Bronze
1896	Léon Pyrgos (GRE)	Jean Perronnet (FRA)	—
1900	Lucien Mérignac (FRA)	Alphonse Kirchhoffer (FRA)	Jean-Baptiste Mimiague (FRA)

ÉPÉE FOR FENCING MASTERS

1900	Albert Ayat (FRA)	Emile Bougnol (FRA)	Henri Laurent (FRA)
1906	Cyrille Verbrugge (BEL)	Carlo Gandini (ITA)	Ioannis Raissis (GRE)

ÉPÉE FOR AMATEURS AND FENCING MASTERS

1900	Albert Ayat (FRA)	Ramón Fonst (CUB)	Léon Sée (FRA)

SABRE FOR FENCING MASTERS

1900	Antonio Conte (ITA)	Italo Santelli (ITA)*	Milan Neralic (AUT)
1906	Cyrille Verburgge (BEL)	Ioannis Raissis (GRE)	—

* Santelli actually lived in Hungary, and so there has been some confusion as to his nationality.

THREE CORNERED SABRE

1906	Gustav Casmir (GER)	George van Rossem (NED)	Péter Tóth (HNU)

SINGLE STICKS

1904	Albertson Van Zo Post (USA)*	William Grebe (USA)	William O'Connor (USA)

* Van Zo Post was an American who competed for Cuba in the team events.

FOOTBALL MEDALS

MEN

	Gold	Silver	Bronze
1900	Great Britain	France	Belgium
1904	Canada	United States	United States
1906	Denmark	Greece	Greece
1908	Great Britain	Denmark	The Netherlands
1912	Great Britain	Denmark	The Netherlands
1920	Belgium	Spain	The Netherlands
1924	Uruguay	Switzerland	Sweden
1928	Uruguay	Argentina	Italy
1936	Italy	Austria	Norway
1948	Sweden	Yugoslavia	Denmark
1952	Hungary	Yugoslavia	Denmark
1956	Soviet Union	Yugoslavia	Bulgaria
1960	Yugoslavia	Denmark	Hungary
1964	Hungary	Czechoslovakia	Germany
1968	Hungary	Bulgaria	Japan
1972	Poland	Hungary	GDR*
			Soviet Union*
1976	GDR	Poland	Soviet Union
1980	Czechoslovakia	GDR	Soviet Union
1984	France	Brazil	Yugoslavia
1988	Soviet Union	Brazil	FRG
1992	Spain	Poland	Ghana
1996	Nigeria	Argentina	Brazil
2000	Cameroon	Spain	Chile

1896–1932 event not held. * A Tie was declared after extra time was played.

WOMEN

	Gold	Silver	Bronze
1996	United States	China	Norway
2000	Norway	United States	Germany

1896–1992 event not held

GYMNASTICS MEDALS

MEN'S TEAM

	Gold	Silver	Bronze
1904	United States Austria 374.43pts	United States 356.37	United States 349.69
1906	Norway 19.00pts	Denmark 18.00	Italy 16.71
1908	Sweden 438pts	Norway 425	Finland 405
1912	Italy 265.75pts	Hungary 227.25	Great Britain 184.50
1920	Italy 359.855pts	Belgium 346.745	France 340.100
1924	Italy 839.058pts	France 820.528	Switzerland 816.661
1928	Switzerland 1718.652pts	Czechoslovakia 1712.250	Yugoslavia 1648.750
1932	Italy 541.850pts	United States 522.275	Finland 509.995
1936	Germany 657.430pts	Switzerland 654.802	Finland 638.468
1948	Finland 1358.3pts	Switzerland1356.7	Hungary 1330.35
1952	Soviet Union 575.4pts	Switzerland 567.5	Finland 564.2
1956	Soviet Union 568.25	Japan 566.40	Finland 555.95
1960	Japan 575.20pts	Soviet Union 572.70	Italy 559.05
1964	Japan 577.95pts	Soviet Union 575.45	Germany 565.10
1968	Japan 575.90pts	Soviet Union 571.10	GDR 557.15
1972	Japan 571.25pts	Soviet Union 564.05	GDR 559.70
1976	Japan 576.85pts	Soviet Union 576.45	GDR 654.65
1980	Soviet Union 589.60pts	GDR 581.15	Hungary 575.00
1984	United States 591.40pts	China 590.80	Japan 586.70
1988	Soviet Union 593.350pts	GDR 588.450	Japan 585.600
1992	Unified Team 585.450pts	China 580.375	Japan 578.250
1996	Russia 576.778pts	China 575.539	Ukraine 571.541
2000	China 231.919pts	Ukraine 230.306	Russia 230.019

1896–1900 event not held

INDIVIDUAL COMBINED EXERCISES

	Gold	Silver	Bronze
1900	Gustave Sandras (FRA) 302pts	Noël Bas (FRA) 295	Lucien Démanet (FRA) 293
1904*	Julius Lenhart (AUT) 69.80pts	Wilhelm Weber (GER) 69.10	Adolf Spinnler (SUI) 67.99
1906†	Pierre Paysse (FRA) 97pts	Alberto Braglia (ITA) 95	Georges Charmoille (FRA) 94
1906	Pierre Paysse (FRA) 116pts	Alberto Paglia (ITA) 115	Georges Charmoille (FRA) 113
1908	Alberto Braglia (ITA) 317.0pts	S Walter Tysal (GBR) 312.0	Louis Ségura (FRA) 297.0
1912	Alberto Braglia (ITA) 135.0pts	Louis Ségura (FRA) 132.5	Adolfo Tunesi (ITA) 131.5
1920	Giorgio Zampori (ITA) 88.35pts	Marco Torres (FRA) 87.62	Jean Gounot (FRA) 87.45
1924	Leon Stukelj (YUG) 110.340pts	Robert Prazák (TCH) 110.323	Bedrich Supcik (TCH) 106.930
1928	Georges Miez (SUI) 247.500pts	Herman Hänggi (SUI) 246.625	Leon Stukelj (YUG) 244.875
1932	Romeo Neri (ITA) 140.625pts	István Pelle (HUN) 134.925	Heikki Savolainen (FIN) 134.575
1936	Alfred Schwarzmann (GER) 113.100pts	Eugen Mack (SUI) 112.334	Konrad Frey (GER) 111.532
1948	Veikko Huhtanen (FIN) 229.7pts	Walter Lehmann (SUI) 229.0	Paavo Aaltonen (FIN) 228.8
1952	Viktor Chukarin (URS) 115.70pts	Grant Shaginyan (URS) 114.95	Josef Stalder (SUI) 114.75
1956	Viktor Chukarin (URS) 114.25pts	Takashi Ono (JPN) 114.20	Yuri Titov (URS) 113.80
1960	Boris Shakhlin (URS) 115.95pts	Takashi Ono (JPN) 115.90	Yuri Titov (URS) 115.60
1964	Yukio Endo (JPN) 115.95pts	Shuji Tsurumi (JPN) 115.40 Viktor Lisitsky (URS) 115.40	—
1968	Sawao Kato (JPN) 115.90pts	Mikhail Voronin (URS) 115.85	Akinori Nakayama (JPN) 115.65
1972	Sawao Kato (JPN) 114.650pts	Eizo Kenmotsu (JPN) 114.575	Akinori Takayama (JPN) 114.325
1976	Nikolai Andrianov (URS) 116.650pts	Sawao Kato (JPN) 115.650	Mitsuo Tsukahara (JPN) 115.375
1980	Aleksandr Dityatin (URS) 118.650pts	Nikolai Andrianov (URS) 118.225	Stoyan Deltchev (BUL) 118.000
1984	Koji Gushiken (JPN) 118.700pts	Peter Vidmar (USA) 118.675	Li Ning (CHN) 118.575
1988	Vladimir Artemov (URS) 119.125pts	Valeriy Lyukhine (URS) 119.025	Dmitry Bilozertchev (URS) 118.975
1992	Vitali Scherbo (EUN) 59.025pts	Grigori Mistyutin (EUN) 58.925	Valeri Belenki (EUN) 58.625
1996	Li Xiaoshuang (CHN) 58.423pts	Alexei Nemov (RUS) 58.374	Vitali Scherbo (BLR) 58.197
2000	Alexei Nemov (RUS) 58.474pts	Wei Yang (CHN) 58.361	Aleksandr Beresch (UKR) 58.212

The 1896 Event was not held. * Lenhart was a member of the Philadelphia Club, USA, which won the team event. † There were two competitions in 1906: one a five events, and the other six.

FLOOR EXERCISES

	Gold	Silver	Bronze
1932	István Pelle (HUN) 9.60pts	Georges Miez (SUI) 9.47	Mario Lertora (ITA) 9.23
1936	Georges Miez (SUI) 18.666pts	Josef Walter (SUI) 18.500	Konrad Frey (GER) 18.466
			Eugen Mack (SUI) 18.466
1948	Ferenc Pataki (HUN) 38.7pts	János Mogyorosi-Klencs (HUN) 38.4	Zdenek Ruzicka (TCH) 38.1
1952	William Thoresson (SWE) 19.25pts	Tadao Uesako (JPN) 19.15	—
		Jerzy Jokiel (POL) 19.15	
1956	Valentin Muratov (URS) 19.20pts	Nobuyuki Aihara (JPN) 19.10	—
		Viktor Chukharin (URS) 19.10	
1960	Nobuyuki Aihara (JPN) 19.450pts	Yuri Titov (JPN) 19.325	Franco Menichelli (ITA) 19.275
1964	Franco Menichelli (ITA) 19.45pts	Viktor Lisitsky (URS) 19.35	—
		Yukio Endo (JPN) 19.35	
1968	Sawao Kato (JPN) 19.475pts	Akinori Nakayama (JPN) 19.400	Takeshi Kato (JPN) 19.275
1972	Nikolai Andrianov (URS) 19.175pts	Akinori Nakayama (JPN) 19.125	Shigeru Kasamatsu (JPN) 19.025
1976	Nikolai Andrianov (URS) 19.450pts	Vladimir Marchenko (URS) 19.425	Peter Kormann (USA) 19.300
1980	Roland Brückner (GDR) 19.750pts	Nikolai Andrianov (URS) 19.725	Aleksandr Dityatin (URS) 19.700
1984	Li Ning (CHN) 19.925pts	Yun Lou (CHN) 19.775	Koji Sotomura (JPN) 19.700
			Philippe Vatuone (FRA) 19.700
1988	Sergei Kharikov (URS) 19.925pts	Vladimir Artemov (URS) 19.900	Lou Yun (CHN) 19.850
			Yukio Iketani (JPN) 19.850
1992	Li Xiaoshuang (CHN) 9.925pts	Grigori Misyutin (EUN) 9.787	—
		Yukio Iketani (JPN) 9.787	
1996	Ioannis Melissanidis (GRE) 9.950pts	Li Xiaoshuang (CHN) 9.837	Alexei Nemov (RUS) 9.800
2000	Igor Wirovs (LAT) 9.812pts	Alexei Nemov (RUS) 9.800	Iordan Iovchev (BUL) 9.787

1896–1928 event not held

PARALLEL BARS

	Gold	Silver	Bronze
1896	Alfred Flatow (GER) d.n.a.	Jules Zutter (SUI)	Hermann Weingärtner (GER)
1904	George Eyser (USA) 44pts	Anton Heida (USA) 43	John Duha (USA) 40
1924	August Güttinger (SUI) 21.63pts	Robert Prazák (TCH) 21.61	Giorgio Zampori (ITA) 21.45
1928	Ladislav Vácha (TCH) 18.83pts	Josip Primozic (YUG) 18.50	Hermann Hänaggi (SUI) 18.08
1932	Romeo Neri (ITA) 18.97pts	István Pelle (HUN) 18.60	Heikki Savolainen (FIN) 18.27
1936	Konrad Frey (GER) 19.067pts	Michael Reusch (SUI) 109.034	Alfred Schwarzmann (GER) 18.967
1948	Michael Reusch (SUI) 39.5pts	Veikkö Huhtanen (FIN) 39.3	Christian Kipfer (SUI) 39.1
			Josef Stalder (SUI) 39.1
1952	Hans Eugster (SUI) 19.65pts	Viktor Chukarin (URS) 19.60	Josef Stalder (SUI) 19.50
1956	Viktor Chukarin (URS) 19.20pts	Masami Kubota (JPN) 19.15	Takashi Ono (JPN) 19.10
			Masao Takemoto (JPN) 19.10
1960	Boris Shakhlin (URS) 19.400pts	Giovanni Carminucci (ITA) 19.375	Takashi Ono (JPN) 19.350
1964	Yukio Endo (JPN) 19.675pts	Shuji Tsurumi (JPN) 19.450	Franco Menichelli (ITA) 19.350
1968	Akinori Nakayama (JPN) 19.475pts	Mikhail Voronin (URS) 19.425	Vladimir Klimenko (URS) 19.225
1972	Sawao Kato (JPN) 19.475pts	Shigeru Kasamatsu (JPN) 19.375	Eizo Kenmotsu (JPN) 19.25
1976	Sawao Kato (JPN) 19.675pts	Nikolai Andrianov (URS) 19.500	Mitsuo Tsukahara (JPN) 19.475
1980	Aleksandr Tkachev (URS) 19.775pts	Aleksandr Dityatin (URS) 19.750	Roland Brückner (GDR) 19.650
1984	Bart Conner (USA) 19.950pts	Nobuyuki Kajitani (JPN) 19.925	Mitchell Gaylord (USA) 19.850
1988	Vladimir Artemov (URS) 19.925pts	Valeriy Lyukhine (URS) 19.900	Sven Tippelt (GDR) 19.750
1992	Vitali Scherbo (EUN) 9.900pts	Li Jing (CHN) 9.812	Guo Linyao (CHN) 9.800
			Igor Korobchinkski (EUN) 9.800
			Masayuki Matsunaga (JPN) 9.800
1996	Rustam Sharipov (UKR) 9.837pts	Jair Lynch (USA) 9.825	Vitali Scherbo (BLR) 9.800
2000	Xiaopeng Li (CHN) 9.825pts	Joo-Hyung Lee (KOR) 9.812	Alexei Nemov (RUS) 9.800

1900 and 1906–1920 event not held

POMMEL HORSE

	Gold	Silver	Bronze
1896	Jules Zutter (SUI) d.n.a.	Hermann Weingärtner (GER)	Gyula Kakas (HUN)
1904	Anotn Heida (USA) 42pts	George Eyser (USA) 33	William Merz (USA) 29
1924	Josef Wilhelm (SUI) 21.23pts	Jean Gutweiniger (SUI) 21.13	Antoine Rebetez (SUI) 20.73
1928	Hermann Hänggi (SUI) 19.75pts	Georges Miez (SUI) 19.25	Heikki Savolainen (FIN) 18.83
1932	István Pelle (HUN) 19.07pts	Omero Bonoli (ITA) 18.87	Frank Haubold (USA) 18.57
1936	Konrad Frey (GER) 19.333pts	Eugen Mack (SUI) 19.167	Albert Bachmann (SUI) 19.067
1948	Paavo Aaltonen (FIN) 38.7pts Veikkö Huhtanen (FIN) 38.7pts Heikki Savolainen (FIN) 38.7pts	—	—
1952	Viktor Chukarin (URS) 19.50pts	Yevgeni Korolkov (URS) 19.40 Grant Shaginyan (URS) 19.40	—
1956	Boris Shakhlin (URS) 19.25pts	Takashi Ono (JPN) 19.20	Viktor Chukarin (URS) 19.10
1960	Eugen Ekman (FIN) 19.375pts Boris Shakhlin (URS) 19.375pts	—	Shuji Tsurumi (JPN) 19.150
1964	Miroslav Cerar (YUG) 19.525pts	Shuji Tsurumi (JPN) 19.325	Yuri Tsapenko (URS) 19.200
1968	Miroslav Cerar (YUG) 19.325pts	Olli Laiho (FIN) 19.225	Mikhail Voronin (URS) 19.200
1972	Viktor Klimenko (URS) 19.125pts	Sawao Kato (JPN) 19.00	Eizo Kenmotsu (JPN) 18.950
1976	Zoltán Magyar (HUN) 19.700pts	Eizo Kenmotsu (JPN) 19.575	Nikolai Andrianov (URS) 19.525
1980	Zoltán Magyar (HUN) 19.925pts	Aleksandr Dityatin (URS) 19.800	Michael Nikolay (GDR) 19.775
1984	Li Ning (CHN) 19.950pts Peter Vidmar (USA) 19.950pts	—	Timothy Daggert (USA) 19.825
1988	Lubomir Gueraskov (BUL) 19.950pts Zsolt Borkai (HUN) 19.950pts Dmitri Bilozertchev (URS) 19.950pts	—	—
1992	Vitali Scherbo (EUN) 9.925pts Pae Gil-Su (PRK) 9.925pts	—	Andreas Wecker (GER) 9.887
1996	Lin Donghua (SUI) 9.875pts	Marius Urzica (ROM) 9.825	Alexei Nemov (RUS) 9.787
2000	Marius Urzica (ROM) 9.862pts	Eric Poujade (FRA) 9.825	Alexei Nemov (RUS) 9.800

1900 and 1906–1920 event not held

RINGS

	Gold	Silver	Bronze
1896	Ioannis Mitropoulos (GRE) d.n.a.	Hermann Weingärtner (GER)	Petros Persakis (GRE)
1904	Herman Glass (USA) 45pts	William Merz (USA) 35	Emil Voight (USA) 32
1924	Franco Martino (ITA) 21.553pts	Robert Prazák (TCH) 21.483	Ladislav Vácha (TCH) 21.430
1928	Leon Skutelj (YUG) 19.25pts	Ladislav Vácha (TCH) 19.17	Emanuel Löffler (TCH) 18.83
1932	George Gulack (USA) 18.97pts	William Denton (USA) 18.60	Giovanni Lattuada (ITA) 18.50
1936	Alois Hudec (TCH) 19.433pts	Leon Skutelj (YUG) 18.867	Matthias Volz (GER) 18.667
1948	Karl Frei (SUI) 39.60pts	Michael Reusch (SUI) 39.10	Zdenek Ruzicka (TCH) 38.30
1952	Grant Shaginyan (URS) 19.75pts	Viktor Chakarin (URS) 19.55	Hans Eugster (SUI) 19.40 Dimitri Leonkin (URS) 19.40
1956	Albert Azaryan (URS) 19.35pts	Valentin Muratov (URS) 19.15	Masao Takemoto (JPN) 19.10 Masami Kubota (JPN) 19.10
1960	Albert Azaryan (URS) 19.475pts	Boris Shakhlin (URS) 19.500	Velik Kapsazov (BUL) 19.425 Takashi Ono (JPN) 19.425
1964	Takuji Hayata (JPN) 19.475pts	Franco Menichelli (ITA) 19.425	Boris Shakhlin (URS) 19.400
1968	Akinori Nakayama (JPN) 19.450pts	Mikhail Voronin (URS) 19.325	Sawao Kato (JPN) 19.225
1972	Akinori Nakayama (JPN) 19.350pts	Mikhail Voronin (URS) 19.325	Mitsuo Tsukahara (JPN) 19.225
1976	Nikolai Andrianov (URS) 19.875pts	Aleksandr Dityatin (URS) 19.550	Danut Grecu (ROM) 19.500
1980	Aleksandr Ditiyatin (URS) 19.875pts	Aleksandr Tkachev (URS) 19.725	Danut Grecu (ROM) 19.500
1984	Koji Gushiken (JPN) 19.850pts Li Ning (CHN) 19.850pts	—	Mitchell Gaylord (USA) 19.825
1988	Holger Behrendt (GDR) 19.925pts Dmitri Bilozerchev (URS) 19.925pts	—	Sven Tippelt (GDR) 19.875

	Gold	Silver	Bronze
1992	Vitali Scherbo (EUN) 9.937pts	Li Jing (CHN) 9.875	Li Xiaoshuang (CHN) 9.862
			Andreas Wecker (GER) 9.862
1996	Yuri Chechi (ITA) 9.887pts	Szilveszter Csollany (HUN) 9.812	—
			Dan Burnica (ROM) 9.812
2000	Szilveszter Csollany (HUN) 9.850pts	Dimothenis Tampakos (GRE) 9.762	Iordan Iovchev (BUL) 9.737

1900 and 1906–1920 event not held

HORIZONTAL BAR

	Gold	Silver	Bronze
1896	Hermann Weingärtner (GER) d.n.a.	Alfred Flatow (GER)	unknown
1904	Anton Heida (USA) 40pts	—	George Eyser (USA) 39
	Edward Henning (USA) 40pts		
1924	Leon Stukelj (YUG) 19.730pts	Jean Gutweniger (SUI) 19.236	André Higelin (FRA) 19.163
1928	Georges Miez (SUI) 19.17pts	Romeo Neri (ITA) 19.00	Eugen Mack (SUI) 18.92
1932	Dallas Bixler (USA) 18.33pts	Heikki Savolainen (FIN) 18.07	Einari Teräsvirta (FIN) 18.07*
1936	Aleksanteri Sarvaala (FIN) 19.367pts	Konrad Frey (GER) 19.267	Alfred Schwarzmann (GER) 19.233
1948	Josef Stalder (SUI) 39.7pts	Walter Lehmann (SUI) 39.4	Veikkö Huhtanen (FIN) 39.2
1952	Jack Günthard (SUI) 19.55pts	Josef Stalder (SUI) 19.50	—
		Alfred Schwarzmann (GER) 19.50	
1956	Takashi Ono (JPN) 19.60pts	Yuri Titov (URS) 19.40	Masao Takemoto (JPN) 19.30
1960	TakashiOno (JPN) 19.60pts	Masao Takemoto (JPN) 19.525	Boris Shakhlin (URS) 19.475
1964	Boris Shakhlin (URS) 19.625pts	Yuri Titov (URS) 19.55	Miroslav Cerar (YUG) 19.50
1968	Mikhail Voronin (URS) 19.550pts	—	Eizo Kenmotsu (JPN) 19.375
	Akinori Nakayama (JPN) 19.550pts		
1972	Mitsuo Tsukahara (JPN) 19.725pts	Sawao Kato (JPN) 19.525	Shigeru Kasamatsu (JPN) 19.525
1976	Mitsuo Tsukahara (JPN) 19.675pts	Eizo Kenmotsu (JPN) 19.500	Eberhard Gienger (FRG) 19.475
			Henry Boërio (FRA) 19.475
1980	Stoyan Deltchev (BUL) 19.825pts	Aleksandr Dityatin (URS) 19.750	Nikolai Andrianov (URS) 19.675
1984	Shinje Morisue (JPN) 20.00pts	Tong Fei (CHN) 19.955	Koji Gushiken (JPN) 19.950
1988	Vladimir Artemov (URS) 10.900pts	—	Holger Behrendt (GDR) 19.800
	Valeri Lyukhine (URS) 19.900pts		Marius Germann (ROM) 19.800
1992	Trent Dimas (USA) 9.875pts	Andreas Wecker (GER) 9.837	—
		Grigori Misyutin (EUN) 9.837	
1996	Alexei Nemov (RUS) 9.787pts	Yeo Hong-Chul (KOR) 9.756	Vitali Scherbo (BLR) 9.724
2000	Alexei Nemov (RUS) 9.787pts	Benjamin Varonian (FRA) 9.787	Joo-Hyung Lee (KOR) 9.775

1900 and 1906–1920 event not held. * Teräsvirta conceded second place to Savolainen.

HORSE VAULT

	Gold	Silver	Bronze
1896	Carl Schuhmann (GER) d.n.a.	Jules Zutter (SUI)	—
1904	Anton Heida (USA) 36pts	—	William Merz (USA) 31
	George Eyser (USA) 36pts		
1924	Frank Kriz (USA) 9.98pts	Jan Koutny (TCH) 9.97	Bohumil Morkovsky (TCH) 9.93
1928	Eugen Mack (SUI) 9.58pts	Emanuel Lóffler (TCH) 9.50	Stane Derganc (YUG) 9.46
1932	Savino Guglielmetti (ITA) 18.03pts	Alfred Jochim (USA) 17.77	Edward Carmichael (USA) 17.53
1936	Alfred Schwarzmann (GER) 19.200pts	Eugen Mack (SUI) 18.967	Matthias Volz (GER) 18.467
1948	Paavo Aaltonen (FIN) 39.10pts	Olavi Rove (FIN) 39.00	János Mogyorosi-Klencs (HUN) 38.50
			Ferenc Pataki (HUN) 38.50
			Leos Sotornik (TCH) 38.50
1952	Viktor Chukarin (URS) 19.20pts	Masao Takemoto (JPN) 19.15	Tadao Uesako (JPN) 19.10
			Takashi Ono (JPN) 19.10

	Gold	Silver	Bronze
1956	Helmuth Bantz (GER) 18.85pts Valentin Muratov (URS) 18.85pts	—	Yuri Titov (URS) 18.75
1960	Takashi Ono (JPN) 19.350pts Boris Shakhlin (URS) 19.350pts	—	Vladimir Portnoi (URS) 19.225
1964	Haruhiro Yamashita (JPN) 19.600pts	Viktor Lisitsky (URS) 19.325	Hannu Rantakari (FIN) 19.300
1968	Mikhail Voronin (URS) 19.000pts	Yukio Endo (JPN) 18.950	Sergei Diomidov (URS) 18.925
1972	Klaus Koste (GDR) 18.850pts	Viktor Klimenko (URS) 18.825	Nikolai Andrianov (URS) 18.800
1976	Nikolai Andrianov (URS) 19.450pts	Mitsuo Tsukahara (JPN) 19.375	Hiroshi Kajiyama (JPN) 19.275
1980	Nikolai Andrianov (URS) 19.825pts	Aleksandr Dityatin (URS) 19.800	Roland Brückner (GDR) 19.775
1984	Lou Yun (CHN) 19.950pts	Li Ning (CHN) 19.825 Koji Gushiken (JPN) 19.825 Mitchell Gaylord (USA) 19.825 Shinje Morisue (JPN) 19.825	—
1988	Lou Yun (CHN) 19.875pts	Sylvio Kroll (GDR) 19.862	Park Jong-Hoon (KOR) 19.775
1992	Vitali Scherbo (EUN) 9.856pts	Grigori Misyutin (EUN) 9.781	Yoo Ok-Youl (KOR) 9.762
1996	Andreas Wecker (GER) 9.850pts	Krasimir Dounev (BUL) 9.825	Vitali Shcherbo (BLR) 9.800 Fan Bin (CHN) 9.800 Alexei Nemov (RUS) 9.800
2000	Gevasio Deferr (ESP) 9.712pts	Alexei Bondarenko (RUS) 9.587	Lezek Blanik (POL) 9.475

1900 and 1906–1920 event not held

WOMEN'S TEAM

	Gold	Silver	Bronze
1928	The Netherlands 316.75pts	Italy 289.00	Great Britain 258.25
1936	Germany 506.50pts	Czechoslavakia 503.60	Hungary 499.00
1948	Czechoslavakia 445.45pts	Hungary 440.55	United States 422.63
1952	Soviet Union 527.03pts	Hungary 520.96	Czechoslavakia 503.32
1956	Soviet Union 444.80pts	Hungary 443.50	Romania 438.20
1960	Soviet Union 382.320pts	Czechoslavakia 373.323	Romania 372.053
1964	Soviet Union 380.890pts	Czechoslavakia 379.989	Japan 377.889
1968	Soviet Union 382.85pts	Czechoslavakia 382.20	GDR 379.10
1972	Soviet Union 380.50pts	GDR 376.55	Hungary 368.25
1976	Soviet Union 390.35pts	Romania 387.15	GDR 385.10
1980	Soviet Union 394.90pts	Romania 393.50	GDR 392.55
1984	Romania 392.20pts	United States 391.20	China 388.60
1988	Soviet Union 395.475pts	Romania 394.125	GDR 390.875
1992	Unified Team 395.666pts	Romania 395.079	United States 394.704
1996	United States 389.225pts	Russia 388.40	Romania 388.246
2000	Romania 154.608pts	Russia 154.403	China 154.008

1896–1924 and 1932 event not held

INDIVIDUAL COMBINED EXERCISES

	Gold	Silver	Bronze
1952	Maria Gorokhovskaya (URS) 76.78pts	Nina Bocharova (URS) 75.94	Margit Korondi (HUN) 75.82
1956	Larissa Latynina (URS) 74.933pts	Agnes Keleti (HUN) 74.633	Sofia Muratova (URS) 74.466
1960	Larissa Latynina (URS) 77.031pts	Sofia Muratova (URS) 76.696	Polina Astakhova (URS) 76.164
1964	Vera Cáslavská (TCH) 77.564pts	Larissa Laytnina (URS) 76.998	Polina Astakhova (URS) 76.965
1968	Vera Cáslavská (TCH) 78.25pts	Zinaida Voronina (URS) 76.85	Natalya Muchinskaya (URS) 76.75
1972	Ludmila Tourischeva (URS) 77.025pts	Karin Janz (GDR) 76.875	Tamara Lazakovitch (URS) 76.850
1976	Nadia Comaneci (ROM) 79.275pts	Nelli Kim (URS) 78.675	Ludmila Tourischeva (URS) 78.625
1980	Yelena Davydova (URS) 79.150pts	Maxi Gnauck (GDR) 79.075 Nadia Comaneci (ROM) 79.075	—
1984	Mary Lou Retton (USA) 79.175pts	Ecaterina Szabo (ROM) 79.125	Simona Pauca (ROM) 78.675

	Gold	Silver	Bronze
1988	Yelena Chouchounova (URS) 79.662pts	Daniela Silivas (ROM) 79.637	Svetlana Bogunskaya (URS) 79.40
1992	Tatyana Gutsu (EUN) 39.737pts	Shannon Miller (USA) 39.725	Lavinia Milosovici (ROM) 39.687
1996	Lilia Podkopayeva (UKR) 39.255pts	Gina Gogean (ROM) 39.075	Lavinia Milosovici (ROM) 39.067 Simona Amanar (ROM) 39.067
2000	Simona Amanar (ROM) 38.642pts	Maria Olaru (ROM) 38.581	Xuan Liu (CHN) 38.418

1896–1948 event not held

ASYMMETRICAL BARS

	Gold	Silver	Bronze
1952	Margit Korondi (HUN) 19.40pts	Maria Gorokhovskaya (URS) 19.26	Agnes Keleti (HUN) 19.16
1956	Agnes Keleti (HUN) 18.966pts	Larissa Latynina (URS) 18.833	Sofia Muratova (URS) 18.800
1960	Polina Astakhova (URS) 19.616pts	Larissa Latynina (URS) 19.416	Tamara Lyukhina (URS) 19.399
1964	Polina Astakhova (URS) 19.332pts	Katalin Makray (HUN) 19.216	Larissa Latynina (URS) 19.199
1968	Vera Cáslavská (TCH) 19.650pts	Karin Janz (GDR) 19.500	Zinaida Voronina (URS) 19.425
1972	Karin Janz (GDR) 19.675pts	Olga Korbut (URS) 19.450 Erika Zuchold (GDR) 19.450	—
1976	Nadia Comaneci (ROM) 20.00pts	Teodora Ungureanu (ROM) 19.800	Marta Egervari (HUN) 19.775
1980	Maxi Gnauck (GDR) 19.875pts	Emila Eberle (ROM) 19.850	Steffi Kräker (GDR) 19.775 Melita Rühn (ROM) 19.775 Maria Filatova (URS) 19.775
1984	Ma Yanhong (CHN) 19.950pts Julianne McNamara (USA) 19.950pts	—	Mary Lou Retton (USA) 19.800
1988	Daniela Silivas (ROM) 20.00pts	Dagmar Kersten (GDR) 19.987	Yelena Chouchounova (URS) 19.962
1992	Lu Li (CHN) 10.000pts	Tatyana Gutsu (EUN) 9.975	Shannon Miller (USA) 9.962
1996	Svetlana Khorkina (RUS) 9.850pts	Wengji Bi (CHN) 9.837 Amy Chow (USA) 9.837	—
2000	Svetlana Khorkina (RUS) 9.862pts	Jie Ling (CHN) 9.837	Yun Yang (CHN) 9.787

1896–1948 event not held

BALANCE BEAM

	Gold	Silver	Bronze
1952	Nina Bocharova (URS) 19.22pts	Maria Gorokhovskaya (URS) 19.13	Margit Korondi (HUN) 19.02
1956	Agnes Keleti (HUN) 18.80pts	Eva Bosáková (TCH) 18.63 Tamara Manina (URS) 18.63	—
1960	Eva Bosáková (TCH) 19.283pts	Larissa Latynina (URS) 19.233	Sofia Muratova (URS) 19.232
1964	Vera Cáslavská (TCH) 19.449pts	Tamara Manina (URS) 19.399	Larissa Latynina (URS) 19.382
1968	Natalya Kuchinskaya (URS) 19.650pts	Vera Cáslavská (TCH) 19.575	Larissa Petrik (URS) 19.250
1972	Olga Korbut (URS) 19.575pts	Tamara Lazokovitch (URS) 19.375	Karin Janz (GDR) 18.975
1976	Nadia Comaneci (ROM) 19.950pts	Olga Korbut (URS) 19.725	Teodora Ungureanu (ROM) 19.700
1980	Nadia Comaneci (ROM) 19.800pts	Elena Davydova (URS) 1 9.750	Natalya Shaposhnikova (URSY) 19.725
1984	Simona Pauca (ROM) 19.800pts Ecaterina Szabo (ROM) 19.800pts	—	Kathy Johnson (USA) 19.650
1988	Daniela Silivas (ROM) 19.924pts	Yelena Chouchounova (URS) 19.875	Gabriela Potorac (ROM) 19.837 Phoebe Mills (USA) 19.837
1992	Tayana Lyssenko (EUN) 9.975pts	Lu Li (CHN) 9.912 Shannon Miller (USA) 9.912	—
1996	Shannon Miller (USA) 9.862pts	Lilia Podkopayeva (UKR) 9.825	Gina Gogean (ROM) 9.787
2000	Xuan Liu (CHN) 9.825pts	Yekaterina Lobaznyuk (RUS) 9.787	Yelena Prodounova (RUS) 9.775

1896–1948 event not held

FLOOR EXERCISES

	Gold	Silver	Bronze
1952	Agnes Keleti (HUN) 19.36pts	Maria Gorokhoskaya (URS) 19.20	Margit Korondi (HUN) 19.00
1956	Larissa Altynina (URS) 18.733pts	—	Elena Leustean (ROM) 18.70
	Agnes Keleti (HUN) 18.733pts		
1960	Larissa Latynina (URS) 19.583pts	Polina Astakhova (URS) 19.532	Tamara Lyukhina (URS) 19.449
1964	Larissa Latynina (URS) 19.599pts	Polina Astakhova (URS) 19.500	Anikó Jánosi (HUN) 19.300
1968	Larissa Petrik (URS) 19.675pts	—	Natalya Kuchinskaya (URS) 19.650
	Vera Cáslavská (TCH) 19.675pts		
1972	Olga Korbut (URS) 19.575pts	Ludmila Tourischeva (URS) 19.550	Tamara Lazakovitch (URS) 19.450
1976	Nelli Kim (URS) 19.850pts	Ludmila Tourischeva (URS) 19.825	Nadia Comaneci (ROM) 19.750
1980	Nelli Kim (URS) 19.875pts	Natalya Shaposhnikova (URS) 19.825	
	Nadia Comaneci (ROM) 19.875pts	Maxi Gnauck (GDR) 19.825	
1984	Ecaterina Szabo (ROM) 19.975pts	Julianne McNamara (USA) 19.950	Mary Lou Retton (USA) 19.775
1988	Daniela Silivas (ROM) 19.937pts	Svetlana Bogunskaya (URS) 19.887	Diana Doudeva (BUL) 19.850
1992	Lavinia Milosovici (ROM) 10.000pts	Henrietta Onodi (HUN) 9.950	Tatyana Gutsu (EUN) 9.912
			Christina Bontas (ROM) 9.912
			Shannon Miller (USA) 9.912
1996	Lilia Podkopayeva (UKR) 9.887pts	Simona Amanar (ROM) 9.850	Dominique Dawes (USA) 9.837
2000	Yelena Zamolodchikova (RUS) 9.850pts	Svetlana Khorkina (RUS) 9.812	Simona Amanar (ROM) 9.712

1896–1948 event not held

HORSE VAULT

	Gold	Silver	Bronze
1952	Yelena Kalinchuk (URS) 19.20pts	Maria Gorokhoskaya (URS) 19.19	Galina Minaitscheva (URS) 19.16
1956	Larissa Latynina (URS) 18.833pts	Tamara Manina (URS) 18.800	Ann-Sofi Colling (SWE) 18.733
			Olga Tass (HUN) 18.733
1960	Margarita Nikolayeva (URS) 19.316pts	Sofia Muratova (URS) 19.049	Larissa Latynina (URS) 19.016
1964	Vera Cáslavská (TCH) 19.483pts	Larissa Latynina (URS) 19.283	—
		Birgit Radochla (GER) 19.283	
1968	Vera Cáslavská (TCH) 19.775pts	Erika Zuchold (GDR) 19.625	Zinaida Voronina (URS) 19.500
1972	Karin Janz (GDR) 19.525pts	Erika Zuchold (GDR) 19.275	Ludmila Tourischeva (URS) 19.250
1976	Nelli Kim (URS) 19.800pts	Ludmila Tourischeva (URS) 19.650	—
		Carola Dombeck (GDR) 19.650	
1980	Natalya Shaposhnikova (URS) 19.725pts	Steffi Kräker (GDR) 19.675	Melita Rühn (ROM) 19.650
1984	Ecaterina Szabo (ROM) 19.875pts	Mary Lou Retton (USA) 19.850	Lavinia Agache (ROM) 19.750
1988	Svetlana Bogunskaya (URS) 19.905pts	Gabriela Potorac (ROM) 19.830	Daniela Silivas (ROM) 19.818
1992	Lavinia Milosovici (ROM) 9.925pts	—	Tatyana Lyssenko (EUN) 9.912
	Henrietta Onodi (HUN) 9.925pts		
1996	Simona Amanar (ROM) 9.825pts	Mo Huilan (CHN) 9.768	Gina Gogean (ROM) 9.750
2000	Yelena Zamolodchikova (RUS) 9.731pts	Andreea Raducan (ROM) 9.693	Yekaterina Lobaznyuk (RUS) 9.674

1896–1948 event not held

MODERN RHYTHMIC

	Gold	Silver	Bronze
1984	Lori Fung (CAN) 57.950pts	Doina Staiculescu (ROM) 57.900	Regina Weber (FRG) 57.700
1988	Marina Lobatch (URS) 60.00pts	Adriana Dounavska (BUL) 59.950	Alexandra Timochenko (URS) 59.875
1992	Aleksandra Timoschenko (EUN) 59.037pts	Carolina Garcia (ESP) 58.100	Oksana Skaldina (EUN) 57.912
1996	Yekaterina Serebryanskaya (UKR) 39.683pts	Yanina Batyrchina (RUS) 39.382	Yelena Vitrichenko (UKR) 39.331
2000	Yulia Barsukova (RUS) 39.632pts	Yulia Raskina (BLR) 39.548	Alina Kabayeva (RUS) 39.466

1896–1980 event not held

RHYTHMIC TEAM

	Gold	Silver	Bronze
1996	Spain 38.933pts	Bulgaria 38.866pts	Russia 38.365pts
2000	Russia 39.500pts	Belarus 39.500	Greece 39.283

1896–1992 event not held

DISCONTINUED EVENTS
MEN

PARALLEL BARS (TEAMS)

	Gold	Silver	Bronze
1896	Germany	Greece	Greece

HORIZONTAL BARS (TEAMS)

1896	Germany*	—	—

* Walkover.

ROPE CLIMBING

1896	Nicolaos Andriakopoulos (GRE) 23.4sec	Thomas Xenakis (GRE)	—*
1904	George Eyser (USA) 7.0sec	Charles Krause (USA) 7.8	Emil Voigt (USA) 9.8
1906	Georgios Aliprantis (GRE) 11.4sec	Béla Erödy (HUN) 13.8	Konstantinos Kozantis (GRE) 13.8
1924	Bedrich Supchik (TCH) 7.2sec	Albert Séguin (FRA)	August Güttinger (SUI) 7.8 Ladislav Vácha (TCH) 7.8
1932	Raymond Bass (USA) 6.7sec	William Galbraith (USA) 6.8	Thomas Connelly (USA) 7.0

* Fritz Hofmann (GER) did not finish.

CLUB SWINGING

1904	Edward Hennig (USA) 13pts	Emil Voigt (USA) 9	Ralph Wilson (USA) 5
1932	George Roth (USA) 8.97pts	Philip Erenberg (USA) 8.90	William Kuhlmeier (USA) 8.63

TUMBLING

1932	Rowland Wolfe (USA) 18.90pts	Edward Gross (USA) 18.67	Willliam Herrmann (USA) 19.37

NINE-EVENT COMPETITION

1094	Adolf Spinnler (SUI) 43.49pts	Julius Lenhart (AUT) 43.00	Wilhelm Weber (GER) 41.60

TRIATHLON (Comprised 100yd, long jump and shot putt)

1904	Max Emmerich (USA) 35.70pts	John Grieb (USA) 34.00	William Merz (USA) 33.90

FOUR-EVENT COMPETITION

1904	Anton Heida (USA) 161pts	George Eyser (USA) 152	William Merz (USA) 135

SIDEHORSE VAULT

1924	Albert Séguin (FRA) 10.00pts	Jean Gounot (FRA) 9.93 François Gangloff (FRA) 9.93	—

SWEDISH SYSTEM TEAMS)

1912	Sweden 937.46pts	Denmark 898.84	Norway 857.21
1920	Sweden 1364pts	Denmark 1325	Belgium 1094

FREE SYSTEM (TEAMS)

1912	Norway 114.25pts	Finland 109.25	Denmark 106.25
1920*	Denmark	Norway	—

* Only two teams competed.

WOMEN
PORTABLE APPARATUS (TEAMS)

1952	Sweden 74.20pts	Soviet Union 73.00	Hungary 71.60
1956	Hungary 75.20pts	Sweden 74.20	Poland 74.00 Soviet Union 74.00

HANDBALL MEDALS

MEN

	Gold	Silver	Bronze
1936*	Germany	Austria	Switzerland
1972	Yugoslavia	Czechoslovakia	Romania
1976	Soviet Union	Romania	Poland
1980	GDR	Soviet Union	Romania
1984	Yugoslavia	FRG	Romania
1988	Soviet Union	Korea	Yugoslavia
1992	Unified Team	Sweden	France
1996	Croatia	Sweden	Spain
2000	Russia	Sweden	Spain

1896–1932 and 1948–1968 event not held. * Field handball played outdoors.

WOMEN

	Gold	Silver	Bronze
1976	Soviet Union	GDR	Hungary
1980	Soviet Union	Yugoslavia	GDR
1984	Yugoslavia	Korea	China
1988	Korea	Norway	Soviet Union
1992	Korea	Norway	Unified Team
1996	Denmark	Korea	Hungary
2000	Denmark	Hungary	Norway

1896–1972 event not held

HOCKEY MEDALS

MEN

	Gold	Silver	Bronze
1908*	England	Ireland	Scotland†
			Wales†
1920	England‡	Denmark	Belgium
1928	India	The Netherlands	Germany
1932	India	Japan	United States
1936	India	Germany	The Netherlands
1948	India	Great Britain	The Netherlands
1952	India	The Netherlands	Great Britain
1956	India	Pakistan	Germany
1960	Pakistan	India	Spain
1964	India	Pakistan	Australia
1968	Pakistan	Australia	India
1972	FRG	Pakistan	India
1976	New Zealand	Australia	Pakistan
1980	India	Spain	Soviet Union
1984	Pakistan	FRG	Great Britain
1988	Great Britain	FRG	The Netherlands
1992	Germany	Australia	Pakistan
1996	The Netherlands	Spain	Australia
2000	The Netherlands	Korea	Australia

1896–1906, 1912 and 1924 event not held. * Great Britain had four teams entered. † Tie for third place. ‡ Great Britain represented by the England team.

WOMEN

	Gold	Silver	Bronze
1980	Zimbabwe	Czechoslovakia	Soviet Union
1984	The Netherlands	FRG	United States
1988	Australia	Korea	The Netherlands
1992	Spain	Germany	Great Britain
1996	Australia	Korea	The Netherlands
2000	Australia	Argentina	The Netherlands

1896–1976 event not held

JUDO MEDALS (introduced in 1964)

MEN

HEAVYWEIGHT (Over 80kg – 1964; over 93kg – 1972–6; over 95kg – 1980–96; over 100kg – 2000)

	Gold	Silver	Bronze
1964	Isao Inokuma (JPN)	A Douglas Rogers (CAN)	Parnaoz Chikviladze (URS)
			Anzor Kiknadze (URS)
1972	Willem Ruska (NED)	Klaus Glahn (FRG)	Givi Onashvili (URS)
			Motoki Nishimura (JPN)
1976	Sergei Novrikov (URS)	Gunther Neureuther (FRG)	Sumio Endo (JPN)
			Allen Coage (USA)
1980	Angelo Parisi (FRA)	Dimitar Zaprianov (BUL)	Vladimir Kocman (CZE)
			Radomir Kovacevic (YUG)
1984	Hitoshi Saito (JPN)	Angelo Parisi (FRA)	Cho Yong-Chul (KOR)
			Mark Berger (CAN)
1988	Hitoshi Saito (JPN)	Henry Stöhr (GDR)	Cho Yong-Chul (KOR)
			Grigori Veritchev (URS)
1992	David Khakhaliashvili (EUN)	Naoya Ogawa (JPN)	David Douillet (FRA)
			Imre Csösz (HUN)
1996	David Douillet (FRA)	Ernesto Perez (ESP)	Harry van Barneveld (BEL)
			Frank Moeller (GER)
2000	David Douillet (FRA)	Shinichi Shinohara (JPN)	Indrek Pertelson (EST)
			Tamerlan Timenov (RUS)

1968 event not held

LIGHT HEAVYWEIGHT (Up to 93kg –1972–6; up to 95kg – 1980–96; up to 100kg – 2000)

	Gold	Silver	Bronze
1972	Shoto Chochoshvili (URS)	David Starbrook (GBR)	Chiaki Ishii (BRA)
			Paul Barth (FRG)
1976	Kazuhiro Ninomiya (JPN)	Ramaz Harshiladze (URS)	David Starbrook (GBR)
			Jürg Röthlisberger (SUI)
1980	Robert Van de Walle (BEL)	Tengiz Khubuluri (URS)	Dietmar Lorenz (GDR)
			Henk Numan (NED)
1984	Ha Hyoung-Zoo (KOR)	Douglas Vieira (BRA)	Bjarni Fridriksson (ISL)
			Gunther Neureuther (FRG)
1988	Aurelio Miguel (BRA)	Marc Meiling (FRG)	Robert Van de Walle (BEL)
			Dennis Stewart (GBR)
1992	Antal Kovacs (HUN)	Ray Stevens (GBR)	Dmitri Sergeyev (EUN)
			Theo Meijer (NED)
1996	Pawel Nastula (POL)	Kim Min-Soo (KOR)	Stephane Traineau (FRA)
			Miguel Fernandez (BRA)
2000	Kosei Inoue (JPN)	Nicolas Gill (CAN)	Stephane Traineau (FRA)
			Yuri Stepkin (RUS)

1964–8 event not held

MIDDLEWEIGHT (Up to 80kg – 1964–76; up to 86kg – 1980–96; up to 90kg – 2000)

	Gold	Silver	Bronze
1964	Isao Okano (JPN)	Wolfgang Hofmann (GER)	James Bergman (USA)
			Eui Tae Kim (KOR)
1972	Shinobu Sekine (JPN)	Oh Seung-Lip (KOR)	Brian Jacks (GBR)
			Jean-Paul Coche (FRA)
1976	Isamu Sonoda (JPN)	Valeri Dvoinikov (URS)	Slavko Obadov (YUG)
			Park Youngchul (KOR)
1980	Jürg Röthlisberger (SUI)	Issac Azcuy Oliva (CUB)	Detlef Ultsich (GDR)
			Aleksandr Yatskevitch (URS)
1984	Peter Seisenbacher (AUT)	Robert Berland (USA)	Seiki Nose (JPN)
			Walter Carmona (BRA)
1988	Peter Seisenbacher (AUT)	Vladimir Chestakov (URS)	Ben Spijkers (NED)
			Akinobu Osako (JPN)
1992	Waldemar Legien (POL)	Pascal Tayot (FRA)	Hirotaki Okada (JPN)
			Nicolas Gill (CAN)

	Gold	Silver	Bronze
1996	Jeon Ki-Young (KOR)	Armen Bagdasarov (UZB)	Marko Spittka (GER)
			Mark Huizinga (NED)
2000	Mark Huizinga (NED)	Carlos Honorato (BRA)	Frederick Demontfaucon (FRA)
			Ruslan Mashurenko (UKR)

1968 event not held

LIGHT MIDDLEWEIGHT (Up to 70kg – 1972–6; up to 78kg – 1980–96; up to 81kg – 2000)

	Gold	Silver	Bronze
1972	Toyojazu Nomura (JPN)	Anton Zajkowski (POL)	Dietmar Hötger (GDR)
			Anatoli Novikov (URS)
1976	Vladimir Nevzorov (URS)	Koji Kuramoto (JPN)	Partrick Vial (FRA)
			Marian Talaj (POL)
1980	Shota Khabeleri (URS)	Juan Ferrer La Hera (CUB)	Harald Heinke (GDR)
			Bernard Tchoullouyan (FRA)
1984	Frank Weineke (FRG)	Neil Adams (GBR)	Michel Nowak (FRA)
			Mirces Fratica (ROM)
1988	Waldemar Legien (POL)	Frank Wieneke (FRG)	Torsten Brechot (GDR)
			Bachir Varayev (URS)
1992	Hidehiko Yoshida (JPN)	Jason Morris (USA)	Kim Byung-Joo (KOR)
			Betrand Damaisin (FRA)
1996	Djamel Bouras (FRA)	Toshihiko Koga (JPN)	Soso Liparteliani (GEO)
			Cho in-Chul (KOR)
2000	Makoto Takimoto (JPN)	In-Chul Cho (PRK)	Nuno Delgado (POR)
			Alexei Badolin (EST)

1964–8 event not held

LIGHTWEIGHT (Up to 63kg – 1964–76; up to 71kg – 1980–96; up to 73kg – 2000)

	Gold	Silver	Bronze
1964	Takehide Nakatani (JPN)	Eric Hänni (SUI)	Oleg Stepanov (URS)
			Aron Bogulubov (URS)
1972	Takao Kawaguchi (JPN)	—*	Kim Yong Ik (PRK)
			Jean Jacques Mounier (FRA)
1976	Hector Rodriguez (CUB)	Chang Eun-kyung (KOR)	Felice Mariani (ITA)
			Jozsef Tuncsik (HUN)
1980	Ezio Gamba (ITA)	Neil Adams (GBR)	Karl-Heinz Lehmann (GDR)
			Ravdan Davaadalai (MGL)
1984	Ahn Byeong-Keun (KOR)	Ezio Gamba (ITA)	Luis Onmura (BRA)
			Kerrith Brown (GBR)
1988	Marc Alexandre (FRA)	Sven Loll (GDR)	Michael Swain (USA)
			Guergui Tenadze (URS)
1992	Toshihiko Koga (JPN)	Bertalan Hajtós (HUN)	Chung Hoon (KOR)
			Shay Smadga (ISR)
1996	Kenzo Nakamura (JPN)	Kwak Dae-Sung (KOR)	James Pedro (USA)
			Christophe Gagliano (FRA)
2000	Giuseppe Maddaloni (ITA)	Tiago Camilo (BRA)	Vsevolods Zelanijs (LAT)
			Anatoli Laryukov (BLR)

1968 event not held. * Bakhaavaa Buidaa (MGL) was disqualified after a positive drugs test.

UP TO 66KG (Up to 65kg – 1980–96)

	Gold	Silver	Bronze
1980	Nikolai Solodukhin (URS)	Tsendying Damdin (MGL)	Ilian Nedkov (BUL)
			Janusz Pawlowski (POL)
1984	Yoshiyuki Matsuoka (JPN)	Hwang Jung-Oh (KOR)	Josef Reiter (AUT)
			Marc Alexandre (FRA)
1988	Lee Kyeung-Keun (KOR)	Janusz Pawlowski (POL)	Bruno Carabeta (FRA)
			Yosuke Yamamoto (JPN)
1992	Rogerio Sampaio (BRA)	Jozsef Csák (HUN)	Udo Quellmalz (GER)
			Israel Hernandez (CUB)
1996	Udo Quellmalz (GER)	Yukimasa Nakamura (JPN)	Israel Plana Hernandez (CUB)
			Henrique Guimares (BRA)
2000	Huseyin Ozkan (TUR)	Larbi Benboudaoud (FRA)	Girolamo Giovinazzo (ITA)
			Georgi Vazagashvili (GEO)

1964–76 event not held

UP TO 60KG

	Gold	Silver	Bronze
1980	Thierry Rey (FRA)	Rafael Carbonell (CUB)	Tibor Kinces (HUN)
			Aramby Emizh (URS)
1984	Shinji Hosokawa (JPN)	Kim Jae-Yup (KOR)	Edward Liddie (USA)
			Neil Eckersley (GBR)
1988	Kim Jae-Yup (KOR)	Kevin Asano (USA)	Shinji Hosokawa (JPN)
			Amiran Totikachvili (URS)
1992	Nazim Gousseinov (EUN)	Yoon Hyun (KOR)	Tadamori Koshino (JPN)
			Richard Trautmann (GER)
1996	Tadahiro Nomura (JPN)	Girolamo Giovanazzo (ITA)	Doripalam Narmandakh (MGL)
			Richard Trautmann (GER)
2000	Tadahiro Namura (JPN)	Bu-Kyung Jung (KOR)	Ajdin Smagulov (KGZ)
			Manolo Poulot (CUB)

1964–76 event not held

DISCONTINUED EVENT
OPEN CATEGORY (No Weight Limit)

	Gold	Silver	Bronze
1964	Antonius Geesink (NED)	Akio Kaminaga (JPN)	Theodore Boronovskis (AUS)
			Klaus Glahn (GER)
1972	Willem Ruska (NED)	Vitali Kuznetsov (URS)	Jean-Claude Brondani (FRA)
			Angelo Parisi (GBR)
1976	Haruki Uemura (JPN)	Keith Remfry (GBR)	Shota Chochoshvili (URS)
			Jeaki Cho (KOR)
1980	Dietmar Lorenz (GDR)	Angelo Parisi (FRA)	András Ozsvar (HUN)
			Arthur Mapp (GBR)
1984	Yasuhiro Yamashita (JPN)	Mohamed Rashwan (EGY)	Mihai Cioc (ROM)
			Arthur Schnabel (FRG)

1968 event not held

WOMEN

UP TO 48KG

	Gold	Silver	Bronze
1992	Cecile Nowak (FRA)	Ryoko Tamura (JPN)	Hulya Senyurt (TUR)
			Amarilis Savon (CUB)
1996	Kye Sun (PRK)	Ryoko Tamura (JPN)	Amarilis Savon (CUB)
			Yolanda Soler (ESP)
2000	Ryoko Tamura (JPN)	Lyubov Bruletova (RUS)	Ann Simons (BEL)
			Anna-Maria Gradante (GER)

1964–88 event not held

UP TO 52KG

1992	Almudena Munoz (ESP)	Noriko Mizuguchi (JPN)	Li Zhongyun (CHN)
			Sharon Rendle (GBR)
1996	Marie-Claire Restoux (FRA)	Hyun Sook-Hee (KOR)	Legna Verdecia (CUB)
			Noriko Sugawara (JPN)
2000	Legna Verdecia (CUB)	Noriko Narazaki (JPN)	Sun-Hui Kye (PRK)
			Yuxiang Liu (CHN)

1964–88 event not held

UP TO 57KG   (UP TO 56KG – 1992–6)

1992	Miriam Blasco (ESP)	Nicola Fairbrother (GBR)	Chiyori Tateno (JPN)
			Driulis Gonzalez (CUB)
1996	Driulis Gonzalez (CUB)	Jung Sae-Yong (KOR)	Isabel Fernandez (ESP)
			Liu Chuang (CHN)
2000	Isabel Fernandez (ESP)	Driulis Gonzalez (CUB)	Maria Pekli (AUS)
			Kie Kusakabe (JPN)

1964–88 event not held

UP TO 63KG (UP TO 61KG – 1992–6)

	Gold	Silver	Bronze
1992	Catherine Fleury (FRA)	Yael Arad (ISR)	Zhang Di (CHN)
			Yelena Petrova (EUN)
1996	Yuko Emoto (JPN)	Gella Van De Caveye (BEL)	Jenny Gal (NED)
			Jung Sung-Sook (KOR)
2000	Severine Vandenhende (FRA)	Shufang Li (CHN)	Gella Vandacaveye (BEL)
			Sung-Sook Jung (KOR)

1964–88 event not held

UP TO 70KG (UP TO 66KG – 1992–6)

	Gold	Silver	Bronze
1992	Odalis Reve (CUB)	Emanuela Pierantozzi (ITA)	Kate Howey (GBR)
			Heidi Rakels (BEL)
1996	Min-Sun Cho (KOR)	Aneta Szczepanska (POL)	Claudia Zwiers (NED)
			Xianbo Wang (CHN)
2000	Sibelis Veranes (CUB)	Kate Howey (GBR)	Min-Sun Cho (KOR)
			Ylenia Scapin (ITA)

1964–88 event not held

UP TO 78KG (UP TO 72KG – 1992–6)

	Gold	Silver	Bronze
1992	Kim Mi-jung (KOR)	Yoko Tanabe (JPN)	Laetitia Meignan (FRA)
			Irene de Kok (NED)
1996	Ulla Werbrouck (HUN)	Yoko Tanabe (JPN)	Ylenia Scapin (ITA)
			Diadenis Luna (CUB)
2000	Lin Tang (CHN)	Celine Lebrun (FRA)	Emanuela Pierantozzi (ITA)
			Simona Richter (ROM)

1964–88 event not held

OVER 78KG (OVER 72KG – 1992–6)

	Gold	Silver	Bronze
1992	Zhuang Xiaoyan (CHN)	Estela Rodriguez (CUB)	Yoko Sakuae (JPN)
			Natalia Lupino (FRA)
1996	Sun Fu-Ming (CHN)	Estela Rodriguez (CUB)	Johanna Hagn (GER)
			Christine Cicot (FRA)
2000	Yuan Hua (CHN)	Daima Beltran (CUB)	Seon-Young Kim (KOR)
			Mayumi Yamashita (JPN)

1964–88 event not held

MODERN PENTATHLON MEDALS

MEN
INDIVIDUAL

	Gold	Silver	Bronze
1912	Gösta Lilliehöök (SWE) 27	Gösta Asbrink (SWE) 28	Georg de Laval (SWE) 30
1920	Gustaf Dyrssen (SWE) 18	Erik de Laval (SWE) 23	Gösta Rüno (SWE) 27
1924	Bo Lindman (SWE) 18	Gustaf Dyrssen (SWE) 39.5	Bertil Uggla (SWE) 45
1928	Sven Thofelt (SWE) 47	Bo Lindman (SWE) 50	Helmuth Kahl (GER) 52
1932	Johan Gabriel Oxenstierna (SWE) 32	Bo Lindman (SWE) 35.5	Richard Mayo (USA) 38.5
1936	Gotthard Handrick (SWE) 31.5	Charles Leonard (USA) 39.5	Silvano Abba (ITA) 45.5
1948	Willie Grut (SWE) 16	George Moore (USA) 47	Gösta Gärdin (SWE) 49
1952	Lars Hall (SWE) 32	Gábor Benedek (HUN) 39	István Szondi (HUN) 41
1956	Lards Hall (SWE) 4843	Olavi Nannonen (FIN) 4774.5	Väinö Korhonen (FIN) 4750
1960	Ferenc Németh (HUN) 5024	Imre Nagy (HUN) 4988	Robert Beck (USA) 4981
1964	Ferenc Török (HUN) 5116	Igor Novikov (URS) 5067	Albert Mokeyev (URS) 5039
1968	Björn Ferm (SWE) 4964	András Balczó (HUN) 4953	Pavel Lednev (URS) 4795
1972	András Balczó (HUN) 5412	Boris Onischenko (URS) 5335	Pavel Lednev (URS) 5328
1976	Janusz Pyciak-Peciak (POL) 5520	Pavel Lednev (URS) 5485	Jan Bartu (TCH) 5466
1980	Anatoli Starostin (URS) 5568	Tamás Szombathelyi (HUN) 5502	Pavel Lednev (URS) 5282
1984	Daniel Massala (ITA) 5469	Svante Rasmuson (SWE) 5456	Carlo Massullo (ITA) 5406
1988	János Martinek (HUN) 5404	Carlo Massullo (ITA) 5379	Vakhtang Yagorachvili (URS) 5367
1992	Arkadiusz Skrzypaszek (POL) 5559	Attila Mizsér (HUN) 5446	Eduard Zenovka (EUN) 5361

	Gold	Silver	Bronze
1996	Aleksandr Parygin (KZK) 5551	Eduard Zenovka (RUS) 5530	János Martinek (HUN) 5501
2000	Dimitri Svatkowski (RUS) 5376	Gabor Balogh (HUN) 5353	Pavel Dovgal (BLR) 5338

1896–1908 event not held

TEAM

	Gold	Silver	Bronze
1952	Hungary 116	Sweden 182	Finland 213
1956	Soviet Union 13 690.5	United States 13 482	Finland 13 185.5
1960	Hungary 14 863	Soviet Union 14 309	United States 14 192
1964	Soviet Union 14 961	United States 14 189	Hungary 14 173
1968	Hungary 14 325	Soviet Union 14 248	France 13 289*
1972	Soviet Union 15 968	Hungary 15 348	Finland 14 812
1976	Great Britain 15 559	Czechoslovakia 15 451	Hungary 15 395
1980	Soviet Union 16 126	Hungary 15 912	Sweden 15 845
1984	Italy 16 060	United States 15 568	France 15 565
1988	Hungary 15 886	Italy 15 571	Great Britain 15 276
1992	Poland 16 018	Unified Team 15 924	Italy 15 760

1896–1948 and 1996–2000 event not held. * Sweden finished third but was disqualified when a test indicated that a team member had an excessive blood-alcohol level.

WOMEN

INDIVIDUAL (Introduced in 2000)

	Gold	Silver	Bronze
2000	Stephanie Cook (GBR) 5318pts	Emily de Riel (USA) 5310	Kate Allenby (GBR) 5273

ROWING MEDALS

MEN

SINGLE SCULLS

	Gold	Silver	Bronze
1900	Henri Barrelet (FRA) 7:35.6	André Gaudin (FRA) 7:41.6	St George Ashe (GBR) 8:15.6
1904	Frank Greer (USA) 10:08.5	James Juvenal (USA) 2 lengths	Constance Titus (USA) 1 length
1906	Gaston Delaplane (FRA) 5:53.4	Joseph Larran (FRA) 6:07.2	– *
1908	Harry Blackstaffe (GBR) 9:26.0	Alexander McCulloch (GBR) 1 length	Bernhard von Gaza (GER) d.n.a. Károly Levitsky (HUN) d.n.a.
1912	William Kinnear (GBR) 7:47.6	Potydore Veirman (BEL) 1 length	Everard Butter (CAN) d.n.a. Mikhail Kusik (RUS) d.n.a.
1920	John Kelly (USA) 7:35.0	Jack Beresford (GBR) 7:36.0	Clarence Hadfield d'Arcy (NZL) 7:48.0
1924	Jack Beresford (GBR) 7:49.2	William Garrett-Gilmore (USA) 7:54.0	Josef Schneider (SUI) 8:01.1
1928	Henry Pearce (AUS) 7:11.0	Kenneth Myers (USA) 7:20.8	David Collett (GBR) 7:19.8
1932	Henry Pearce (AUS) 7:44.4	William Miller (USA) 7:45.2	Guillermo Douglas (URU) 8:13.6
1936	Gustav Schäfer (GER) 8:21.5	Josef Hasenöhri (AUT) 8:25.8	Daniel Barrow (USA) 8:28.0
1948	Mervyn Wood (AUS) 7:24.4	Eduardo Risso (URU) 7:38.2	Romolo Catasta (ITA) 7:51.4
1952	Yuri Tyukalov (URS) 8:12.8	Mervyn Wood (AUS) 8:14.5	Teodor Kocerka (POL) 8:19.4
1956	Vyacheslav Ivanov (URS) 8:02.5	Stuart Mackenzie (AUS) 8:07.0	John Kelly (USA) 8:11.8
1960	Vyacheslav Ivanov (URS) 7:13.96	Achim Hill (GER) 7:20.21	Teodor Kocerka (POL) 7:21.26
1964	Vyacheslav Ivanov (URS) 8:22.51	Achim Hill (GER) 8:26.34	Gottfried Kottmann (SUI) 8:29.68
1968	Henri Jan Wienese (NED) 7:47.80	Jochen Meissner (FRG) 7:52.00	Alberto Demiddi (ARG) 7:57.19
1972	Yuri Malishev (URS) 7:10.12	Alberto Demiddi (ARG) 7:11.53	Wolfgang Güldenpfennig (GDR) 7:14.45
1976	Pertti Karpinnen (FIN) 7:29.03	Peter Kolbe (FRG) 7:31.67	Joachim Dreifke (GDR) 7:38.03
1980	Pertti Karpinnen (FIN) 7:09.61	Vasili Yakusha (URS) 7:11.66	Peter Kersten (GDR) 7:14.88
1984	Pertti Karpinnen (FIN) 7:00.24	Peter Kolbe (FRG) 7:02.19	Robert Mills (CAN) 7:10.38
1988	Thomas Lange (GDR) 6:49.86	Peter Kolbe (FRG) 6:54.77	Eric Verdonk (NZL) 6:58.86
1992	Thomas Lange (GER) 6:51.40	Vaclav Chalupa (CZE) 6:52.93	Kajetan Broniewski (POL) 6:56.82
1996	Xeno Mueller (SUI) 6:44.85	Derek Porter (CAN) 6:47.45	Thomas Lange (GER) 6:47.72
2000	Rob Waddell (NZL) 6:48.90	Xeno Müller (SUI) 6:50.55	Marcus Hacker (GER) 6:50.83

1896 event not held. * Only two competitors.

DOUBLE SCULLS

	Gold	Silver	Bronze
1904	United States 10:03.2	United States d.n.a.	United States d.n.a.
1920	United States 7:09.0	Italy 7:19.0	France 7:21.0
1924	United States 7:45.0	France 7:54.8	Switzerland d.n.a.
1928	United States 6:41.4	Canada 6:51.0	Austria 6:48.8
1932	United States 7:17.4	Germany 7:22.8	Canada 7:27.6
1936	Great Britain 7:20.8	Germany 7:26.2	Poland 7:36.2
1948	Great Britain 6:51.3	Denmark 6:55.3	Uruguay 7:12.4
1952	Argentina 7:32.2	Soviet Union 7:38.3	Uruguay 7:43.7
1956	Soviet Union 7:10.66	United States 7:13.16	Australia 7:37.4
1960	Czechoslovakia 6:47.50	Soviet Union 6:50.49	Switzerland 6:50.59
1964	Soviet Union 7:10.66	United States 7:13.16	Czechoslovakia 7:14.23
1968	Soviet Union 6:51.82	The Netherlands 6:52.80	United States 6:54.21
1972	Soviet Union 7:01.77	Norway 7:02.58	GDR 7:05.55
1976	Norway 7:13.20	Great Britain 7:15.26	GDR 7:17.45
1980	GDR 6:24.33	Yugoslavia 6:26.34	Czechoslovakia 6:29.07
1984	United States 6:36.87	Belgium 6:38.19	Yugoslavia 6:39.59
1988	The Netherlands 6:21.13	Switzerland 6:22.59	Soviet Union 6:22.87
1992	Australia 6:17.32	Austria 6:18.42	The Netherlands 6:22.82
1996	Italy 6:16.98	Norway 6:18.42	France 6:19.85
2000	Slovenia 6:16.63	Norway 6:17.98	Italy 6:20.49

1896–1900 and 1906–12 event not held

COXLESS QUADRUPLE SCULLS

	Gold	Silver	Bronze
1976	GDR 6:18.65	Soviet Union 6:19.89	Czechoslovakia 6:21.77
1980	GDR 5:49.81	Soviet Union 5:51.47	Bulgaria 5:52.38
1984	FRG 5:57.55	Australia 5:57.98	Canada 5:59.07
1988	Italy 5:53.37	Norway 5:55.08	GDR 5:56.13
1992	Germany 5:45.17	Norway 5:47.09	Italy 5:47.33
1996	Germany 5:56.93	United States 5:59.10	Australia 6:01.65
2000	Italy 5:45.56	The Netherlands 5:47.91	Germany 5:48.64

1896–1972 event not held

COXLESS PAIRS

	Gold	Silver	Bronze
1904	United States 10:57.0	United States d.n.a.	United States d.n.a.
1908	Great Britain 9:43.0	Great Britain 2.5 lengths	Canada
			Germany
1924	The Netherlands 8:19.4	France 8:21.6	—*
1928	Germany 7:06.4	Great Britain 7:08.08	United States 7:20.4
1932	Great Britain 8:00.0	New Zealand 8:02.4	Poland 8:08.2
1936	Germany 8:16.1	Denmark 8:19.2	Argentina 8:23.0
1948	Great Britain 7:21.11	Switzerland 7:23.9	Italy 7:31.5
1952	United States 8:20.7	Belgium 8:23.5	Switzerland 8:32.7
1956	United States 7:55.4	Soviet Union 8:03.9	Austria 8:11.8
1960	Soviet Union 7:02.01	Austria 7:03.69	Finland 7:03.80
1964	Canada 7:32.94	The Netherlands 7:33.40	Germany 7:38.63
1968	GDR 7:26.56	United States 7:26.71	Denmark 7:31.84
1972	GDR 6:53.16	Switzerland 6:57.06	The Netherlands 6:58.70
1976	GDR 7:23.31	United States 7:26.73	FRG 7:30.03
1980	GDR 6:48.01	Soviet Union 6:50.50	Great Britain 6:51.47
1984	Romania 6:45.39	Spain 6:48.47	Norway 6:51.81
1988	Great Britain 6:36.84	Romania 6:38.06	Yugoslavia 6:41.01
1992	Great Britain 6:27.72	Germany 6:32.68	Slovenia 6:33.43
1996	Great Britain 6:20.09	Australia 6:21.02	France 6:22.15
2000	France 6:32.97	United States 6:33.80	Australia 6:34.26

1896–1906 and 1912–20 event not held. * Only two pairs.

COXED PAIRS

	Gold	Silver	Bronze
1900	The Netherlands 7:34.2	France I 7:34.4	France II 7:57.2
1906*	Italy I 4:23.0	Italy II 4:30.0	France d.n.a.
1906†	Italy 7:32.4	Belgium 8:03.0‡	France 8:08.6
1920	Italy 7:56.0	France 7:57.0	Switzerland d.n.a.
1924	Switzerland 8:39.0	Italy 8:39.1	United States 3m
1928	Switzerland 7:42.6	France 7:48.4	Belgium 7:59.4
1932	United States 8:25.8	Poland 8:31.2	France 8:41.2
1936	Germany 8:36.9	Italy 8:49.7	France 8:54.0
1948	Denmark 8:00.5	Italy 8:12.2	Hungary 8:25.2
1952	France 8:28.6	Germany 8:32.1	Denmark 8:34.9
1956	United States 8:26.1	Germany 8:29.2	Soviet Union 8:31.0
1960	Germany 7:29.14	Soviet Union 7:30.17	United States 7:34.58
1964	United States 8:21.23	France 8:23.15	The Netherlands 8:23.42
1968	Italy 8:04.81	The Netherlands 8:06.80	Denmark 8:08.07
1972	GDR 7:17.25	Czechoslovakia 7:19.57	Romania 7:21.36
1976	GDR 7:58.99	Soviet Union 8:01.82	Czechoslovakia 8:03.28
1980	GDR 7:02.54	Soviet Union 7:03.35	Yugoslavia 7:04.92
1984	Italy 7:05.99	Romania 7:11.21	United States 7:12.81
1988	Italy 6:58.79	GDR 7.00.63	Great Britain 7:01.95
1992	Great Britain 6:49.83	Italy 6:50.98	Romania 6:51.58

1896, 1904, 1908–12 and 1996–2000 event not held. * Over 1000m. † Over 1600m. ‡ Greek cox.

COXLESS FOURS

	Gold	Silver	Bronze
1904	United States 9:05.8	United States d.n.a.	United States d.n.a.
1908	Great Britain 8:34.0	Great Britain 1.5 lengths	The Netherlands
			Canada
1924	Great Britain 7:08.6	Canada 7:18.0	Switzerland 2 lengths
1928	Great Britain 6:36.0	United States 6:37.0	Italy 6:31.6
1932	Great Britain 6:58.2	Germany 7:03.0	Italy 7:04.0
1936	Germany 7:01.8	Great Britain 7:06.5	Switzerland 7:10.6
1948	Italy 6:39.0	Denmark 6:43.5	United States 6:47.7
1952	Yugoslavia 7:16.0	France 7:18.4	Finland 7:23.3
1956	Canada 7:08.8	United States 7:18.4	France 7:20.9
1960	United States 6:26.26	Italy 6:28.78	Soviet Union 6:29.62
1964	Denmark 6:59.30	Great Britain 7:00.47	United States 7:01.37
1968	GDR 6:39.18	Hungary 6:41.64	Italy 6:44.01
1972	GDR 6:24.27	New Zealand 6:25.64	FRG 6:28.41
	Gold	Silver	Bronze
1976	GDR 6:37.42	Norway 6:41.22	Soviet Union 6:42.52
1980	GDR 6:08.17	Soviet Union 6:11.81	Great Britain 6:16.58
1984	New Zealand 6:03.48	United States 6:06.10	Denmark 6:07.72
1988	GDR 6:03.11	United States 6:05.53	FRG 6:06.22
1992	Australia 5:55.04	United States 5:56.68	Slovenia 5:58.24
1996	Australia 6:06.37	France 6:07.03	Great Britain 6:07.28
2000	Great Britain 5:56.24	Italy 5:56.62	Australia 5:57.61

1896–1900, 1906 and 1912–20 event not held

COXED FOURS

	Gold	Silver	Bronze
1900*	Germany 5:59.0	The Netherlands 6:33.0	Germany 6:35.0
1900*	France 7:11.0	France 7:18.0	Germany 7:18.2
1906	Italy 8:13.0	France d.n.a.	France d.n.a
1912	Germany 6:59.4	Great Britain 2 lengths	Norway d.n.a.
			Denmark d.n.a.
1920	Switzerland 6:54.0	United States 6:58.0	Norway 7:02.0
1924	Switzerland 7:18.4	France 7:21.6	United States 1 length
1928	Italy 6:47.8	Switzerland 7:03.4	Poland 7:12.8
1932	Germany 7:19.0	Italy 7:19.2	Poland 7:26.8
1936	Germany 7:16.2	Switzerland 7:24.3	France 7:33.3
1948	United States 6:50.3	Switzerland 6:53.3	Denmark 6:58.6

	Gold	Silver	Bronze
1952	Czechoslovakia 7:33.4	Switzerland 7:36.5	United States 7:37.0
1956	Italy 7:19.4	Sweden 7:22.4	Finland 7:30.9
1960	Germany 6:39.12	France 6:41.62	Italy 6:43.72
1964	Germany 7:00.44	Italy 7:02.84	The Netherlands 7:06.46
1968	New Zealand 6:45.62	GDR 6:48.20	Switzerland 6:49.04
1972	FRG 6:31.85	GDR 6:33.30	Czechoslovakia 6:35.64
1976	Soviet Union 6:40.22	GDR 6:42.70	FRG 6:46.96
1980	GDR 6:14.51	Soviet Union 6:19.05	Poland 6:22.52
1984	Great Britain 6:18.64	United States 6:20.28	New Zealand 6:23.68
1988	GDR 6:10.74	Romania 6:13.58	New Zealand 6:15.78
1992	Romania 5:59.37	Germany 6:00.34	Poland 6:03.27

1896, 1904, 1908 and 1996–2000 event not held. * Two separate finals were held in 1900.

EIGHTS

	Gold	Silver	Bronze
1900	United States 6:09.8	Belgium 6:13.8	The Netherlands 6:23.0
1904	United States 7:50.0	Canada d.n.a.	—
1908	Great Britain I 7:52.0	Belgium 2 lengths	Great Britain
			Canada
1912	Great Britain I 6:15.0	Great Britain II 6:19.0	Germany d.n.a.
1920	United States 6:02.6	Great Britain 6:05.0	Norway 6:36.0
1924	United States 6:33.4	Canada 6:49.0	Italy 0.75 length
1928	United States 6:03.2	Great Britain 6:05.6	Canada 6:03.8
1932	United States 6:37.6	Italy 6:37.8	Canada 6:40.4
1936	United States 6:25.4	Italy 6:26.0	Germany 6:26.4
1948	United States 5:56.7	Great Britain 6:06.9	Norway 6:10.3
1952	United States 6:25.9	Soviet Union 6:31.2	Australia 6:33.1
1956	United States 6:35.2	Canada 6:37.1	Australia 6:39.2
1960	Germany 5:57.18	Canada 6:01.52	Czechoslovakia 6:04.84
1964	United States 6:18.23	Germany 6:23.9	Czechoslovakia 6:25.11
1968	FRG 6:07.00	Australia 6:07.98	Soviet Union 6:09.11
1972	New Zealand 6:08.94	United States 6:11.61	GDR 6:11.67
1976	GDR 5:58.29	Great Britain 6:00.82	New Zealand 6:03.51
1980	GDR 5:49.05	Great Britain 5:51.92	Soviet Union 5:52.66
1984	Canada 5:41.32	United States 5:41.74	Australia 5:42.40
1988	FRG 5:46.05	Soviet Union 5:48.01	United States 5:48.26
1992	Canada 5:29.53	Romania 5:29.67	Germany 5:31.00
1996	Netherlands 5:42.74	Germany 5:44.58	Russia 5:45.77
2000	Great Britain 5:33.08	Australia 5:33.88	Croatia 5:34.85

1896 and 1906 event not held

LIGHTWEIGHT-DOUBLE SCULLS

	Gold	Silver	Bronze
1996	Switzerland 6:23.27	The Netherlands 6:26.48	Australia 6:26.69
2000	Poland 6:21.75	Italy 6:23.47	France 6:24.85

1896–1992 event not held

LIGHTWEIGHT-COXLESS FOURS

	Gold	Silver	Bronze
1996	Denmark 6:09.58	Canada 6:10.13	United States 6:12.29
2000	France 6:01.68	Australia 6:02.09	South Africa 6:03.51

1896–1992 event not held

DISCONTINUED EVENTS
NAVAL ROWING BOATS (200M)

	Gold	Silver	Bronze
1906	Italy 10:45.0	Greece d.n.a.	Greece d.n.a.

COXED 16-MAN NAVAL ROWING BOATS (3000M)

1906	Greece 16:35.0	Greece 17:09.5	Italy d.n.a.

COXED FOURS (INRIGGERS)

	Gold	Silver	Bronze
1912	Denmark 7:47.0	Sweden 7:56.2	Norway d.n.a.

WOMEN

Women's rowing was introduced in 1976 over a course of 1000m. From 1988 it was over 2000m.

SINGLE SCULLS

	Gold	Silver	Bronze
1976	Christine Scheiblich (GDR) 4:05.56	Joan Lind (USA) 4:06.21	Elena Antonova (URS) 4:10.24
1980	Sandra Toma (ROM) 3:40.69	Antonina Makhina (URS) 3:41.65	Martina Schröter (GDR) 3:43.54
1984	Valeria Racila (ROM) 3:40.68	Charlotte Geer (USA) 3:43.89	Ann Haesebrouck (BEL) 3:45.72
1988	Jutta Behrednt (GDR) 7:47.19	Anne Marden (USA) 7:50.28	Magdalene Gueorguivea (BUL) 7:53.65
1992	Elisabeta Lipa (ROM) 7:25.54	Annelies Bredael (BEL) 7:26.64	Silken Laumann (CAN) 7:28.85
1996	Ekaterina Khodotovich (BLR) 7:32.21	Silken Laumann (CAN) 7:35.15	Trine Hansen (DEN) 7:37.20
2000	Ekaterina Khodotovich-Karsten (BLR) 7:28.14	Rumyana Neykova (BUL) 7:28.15	Katrin Rutschow-Stomporowski (GER) 7:28.99

DOUBLE SCULLS

	Gold	Silver	Bronze
1976	Bulgaria 3:44.36	GDR 3:47.86	Soviet Union 3:49.93
1980	Soviet Union 3:16.27	GDR 3:17.63	Romania 3:18.91
1984	Romania 3:26.75	The Netherlands 3:29.13	Canada 3:29.82
1988	GDR 7:00.48	Romania 7:04.36	Bulgaria 7:06.03
1992	Germany 6:49.00	Romania 6:51.47	China 6:55.16
1996	Canada 6:56.84	China 6:58.35	The Netherlands 6:58.72
2000	Germany 6:55.44	The Netherlands 7:00.36	Lithuania 7:01.71

COXED QUADRUPLE SCULLS

	Gold	Silver	Bronze
1976	GDR 3:29.99	Soviet Union 3:32.49	Romania 3:32.76
1980	GDR 3:15.32	Soviet Union 3:15.73	Bulgaria 3:16.10
1984	Romania 3:14.11	United States 3:15.57	Denmark 3:16.02
1988*	GDR 6:21.06	Soviet Union 6:23.47	Romania 6:23.81
1992	Germany 6:20.18	Romania 6:24.34	Unified Team 6:25.07
1996	Germany 6:27.44	Ukraine 6:30.36	Canada 6:30.38
2000	Germany 6:19.62	Great Britain 6:21.64	Russia 6:21.65

*Not coxed.

COXLESS PAIRS

	Gold	Silver	Bronze
1976	Bulgaria 4:01.22	GDR 4:01.64	FRG 4:02.35
1980	GDR 3:30.49	Poland 3:30.95	Bulgaria 3:32.39
1984	Romania 3:32.60	Canada 3:36.06	FRG 3:40.50
1988	Romania 7:28.13	Bulgaria 7:31.95	New Zealand 7:35.68
1992	Canada 7:06.22	Germany 7:07.96	United States 7:08.11
1996	Australia 7:01.39	United States 7:01.78	France 7:03.82
2000	Romania 7:11.00	Australia 7:12.56	United States 7:13.00

COXED FOURS

	Gold	Silver	Bronze
1976	GDR 3:45.08	Bulgaria 3:38.24	Soviet Union 3:49.38
1980	GDR 3:19.27	Bulgaria 3:20.75	Soviet Union 3:20.92
1984	Romania 3:19.30	Canada 3:21.55	Australia 3:23.29
1988	GDR 6:56.00	China 6:58.78	Romania 7:01.13

The 1992–96 and 2000 event not held

COXLESS FOURS

	Gold	Silver	Bronze
1992	Canada 6:30.85	United States 6:31.86	Germany 6:32.34

1976–88 and 1996–2000 event not held

EIGHTS

	Gold	Silver	Bronze
1976	GDR 3:33.32	Soviet Union 3:36.17	United States 3:38.68
1980	GDR 3:03.32	Soviet Union 3:04.29	Romania 3:05.63
1984	United States 2:59.80	Romania 3:00.87	The Netherlands 3:02.92
1988	GDR 6:15.17	Romania 6:17.44	China 6:21.83
1992	Canada 6:02.62	Romania 6:06.26	Germany 6:07.80
1996	Romania 6:19.73	Canada 6:24.05	Belarus 6:24.44
2000	Romania 6:06.44	The Netherlands6:09.39	Canada 6:11.58

LIGHTWEIGHT-DOUBLE SCULLS

	Gold	Silver	Bronze
1996	Romania 7:12.78	United States 7:14.65	Australia 7:16.56
2000	Romania 7:02.64	Germany 7:02.95	United States 7:06.37

1976–1992 event not held

SAILING MEDALS

MEN

OLYMPIC MONOTYPE

	Gold	Silver	Bronze
1920*	The Netherlands (Franciscus Hin) (Johannes Hin)	The Netherlands (Arnoud van der Biesen) (Petrus Beukers)	—
1924†	Léon Huybrechts (BEL)	Henrik Robert (NOR)	Hans Dittmar (FIN)
1928‡	Sven Thorell (SWE)	Henrik Robert (NOR)	Bertil Broman (FIN)
1932§	Jacques Lebrun (FRA)	Adriaan Maas (NED)	Santiago Cansino (ESP)
1936℃	Daniel Kagchelland (NED)	Werner Krogmann (GER)	Peter Scott (GBR)
1948§§	Paul Elvström (DEN)	Ralph Evans (USA)	Jacobus de Jong (NED)
1952**	Paul Elvström (DEN)	Charles Currey (GBR)	Rickard Sarby (SWE)
1956	Paul Elvström (DEN)	André Nelis (BEL)	John Marvin (USA)
1960	Paul Elvström (DEN)	Aleksandr Chuchelov (URS)	André Nelis (BEL)
1964	Willi Kuhweide (GER)	Peter Barrett (USA)	Henning Wird (DEN)
1968	Valentin Mankin (URS)	Hubert Raudaschl (AUT)	Fabio Albarelli (ITA)
1972	Serge Maury (FRA)	Ilias Hatzipavlis (GRE)	Viktor Potapov (URS)
1976	Jochen Schümann (GDR)	Andrei Balashov (URS)	John Bertrand (AUS)
1980	Esko Rechardt (FIN)	Wolfgang Mayrhofer (AUT)	Andrei Balashov (URS)
1984	Russell Coutts (NZL)	John Bertrand (AUS)	Terry Neilson (CAN)
1988	José Luis Doreste (ESP)	Peter Holmberg (ISV)	John Cutler (NZL)
1992	José Maria van der Ploeg (ESP)	Brian Ledbetter (USA)	Craig Monk (NZL)
1996	Mateusz Kuznierewicz (POL)	Sebastian Godefroid (BEL)	Roy Heiner (NED)
2000	Ian Percy (GBR)	Luca Devoti (ITA)	Fredrik Lööf (SWE)

1896–1912 event not held. * 12-foot dinghy (two-handled), no bronze medal awarded. † Meulan Class, 12-foot dinghy.
‡ International 12-foot Class. § Snowbird Class. ℃ International Class. §§ Firefly Class. ** 1952–2000 Finn Class.

SAILBOARD CLASS

	Gold	Silver	Bronze
1984*	Steve Van Den Berg (NED)	Randall Steele (USA)	Bruce Kendall (NZL)
1988†	Bruce Kendall (NZL)	Jan Boersma (AHO)	Michael Gebhardt (USA)
1992†	Franck David (FRA)	Michael Gebhardt (USA)	Lars Kleppich (AUS)
1996‡	Nikolas Kaklamanakis (GRE)	Carlos Espinola (ARG)	Gal Fridman (ISR)
2000	Christoph Sieber (AUT)	Carlos Espinola (ARG)	Aaron McIntosh (NZL)

1896–1980 event were not held. *Windglider. † Lechner ‡ 1996–2000 Mistral.

INTERNATIONAL SOLING

	Gold	Silver	Bronze
1972	United States	Sweden	Canada
1976	Denmark	United States	GDR
1980	Denmark	Soviet Union	Greece
1984	United States	Brazil	Canada
1988	GDR	United States	Denmark

	Gold	Silver	Bronze
1992	Denmark	United States	Great Britain
1996	Germany	Russia	United States
2000	Denmark	Germany	Norway

1896–1968 event not held

INTERNATIONAL 470

	Gold	Silver	Bronze
1976	FRG	Spain	Australia
1980	Brazil	GDR	Finland
1984	Spain	United States	France
1988	France	Soviet Union	United States
1992	Spain	United States	Estonia
1996	Ukraine	Great Britain	Portugal
2000	Australia	United States	Argentina

1896–1972 event held

INTERNATIONAL TORNADO

	Gold	Silver	Bronze
1976	Great Britain	United States	FRG
1980	Brazil	Denmark	Sweden
1984	New Zealand	United States	Australia
1988	France	New Zealand	Brazil
1992	France	United States	Australia
1996	Spain	Australia	Brazil
2000	Austria	Australia	Germany

1896–1972 event not held

INTERNATIONAL STAR

	Gold	Silver	Bronze
1932	United States	Great Britain	Sweden
1936	Germany	Sweden	The Netherlands
1948	United States	Cuba	The Netherlands
1952	Italy	United States	Portugal
1956	United States	Italy	Bahamas
1960	Soviet Union	Portugal	United States
1964	Bahamas	United States	Sweden
1968	United States	Norway	Italy
1972	Australia	Sweden	FRG
1980	Soviet Union	Austria	Italy
1984	United States	FRG	Italy
1988	Great Britain	United States	Brazil
1992	United States	New Zealand	Canada
1996	Brazil	Sweden	Australia
2000	United States	Great Britain	Brazil

1896–1928 and 1976 event not held

FLYING DUTCHMAN

	Gold	Silver	Bronze
1956*	New Zealand	Australia	Great Britain
1960	Norway	Denmark	Germany
1964	New Zealand	Great Britain	United States
1968	Great Britain	FRG	Brazil
1972	Great Britain	France	FRG
1976	FRG	Great Britain	Brazil
1980	Spain	Ireland	Hungary
1984	United States	Canada	Great Britain
1988	Denmark	Norway	Canada
1992	Spain	United States	Denmark

1896–1952 and 1996–2000 event not held. * Sharpie Class.

LASER

	Gold	Silver	Bronze
1996	Robert Scheidt (BRA)	Ben Ainslie (GBR)	Per Moberg (NOR)
2000	Ben Ainslie (GBR)	Robert Scheidt (BRA)	Michael Blackburn (AUS)

1896–1992 event not held

WOMEN

SAILBOARD CLASS

	Gold	Silver	Bronze
1992*	Barbara Kendall (NZL)	Zhang Xiaodong (CHN)	Dorien de Vries (NED)
1996†	Lai-Shan Lee (HKG)	Barbara Kendall (NZL)	Alessandra Sensini (ITA)
2000	Alessandra Sensini (ITA)	Amelie Lux (GER)	Barbara Kendall (NZL)

1896–1988 event not held. * Lechner. † 1996–2000 Mistral.

INTERNATIONAL 470

	Gold	Silver	Bronze
1988	United States	Sweden	Soviet Union
1992	Spain	New Zealand	United States
1996	Spain	Japan	Ukraine
2000	Australia	United States	Ukraine

1896–1984 event not held

EUROPEAN CLASS

	Gold	Silver	Bronze
1992	Linda Andersen (NOR)	Natalia Dufresne (ESP)	Julia Trotman (USA)
1996	Kristine Roug (DEN)	Margriet Matthijsse (NED)	Courtney Becker-Dey (USA)
2000	Shirley Robertson (GBR)	Margriet Matthijsse (NED)	Serena Amoto (ARG)

1896–1988 event not held

DISCONTINUED SAILING EVENTS

SWALLOW

	Gold	Silver	Bronze
1948	Great Britain	Portugal	United States

INTERNATIONAL TEMPEST

1972	Soviet Union	Great Britain	United States
1976	Sweden	Soviet Union	United States

DRAGON

1948	Norway	Sweden	Denmark
1952	Norway	Sweden	Germany
1956	Sweden	Denmark	Great Britain
1960	Greece	Argentina	Italy
1964	Denmark	Germany	United States
1968	United States	Denmark	GDR
1972	Australia	GDR	United States

30 SQUARE METRES

1920	Sweden	—	—

40 SQUARE METRES

1920	Sweden	—	—

5.5 METRES

1952	United States	Norway	Sweden
1956	Sweden	Great Britain	Australia
1960	United States	Denmark	Switzerland
1964	Australia	Sweden	United States
1968	Sweden	Switzerland	Great Britain

6 METRES

1908	Great Britain	Belgium	France
1912	France	Denmark	Sweden

	Gold	Silver	Bronze
1920	Norway	Belgium	–
1924	Norway	Denmark	The Netherlands
1928	Norway	Denmark	Estonia
1932	Sweden	United States	Canada
1936	Great Britain	Norway	Sweden
1948	United States	Argentina	Sweden
1952	United States	Norway	Finland

6 METRES (1907 RATING)

1920	Belgium	Norway	Norway

6.5 METRES

1920	The Netherlands	France	—

7 METRES

1908	Great Britain	—	—
1920	Great Britain	—	—

1912 event not held

8 METRES

1908	Great Britain	Sweden	Great Britain
1912	Norway	Sweden	Finland
1920	Norway	Norway	Belgium
1924	Norway	Great Britain	France
1928	France	The Netherlands	Sweden
1932	United States	Canada	—
1936	Italy	Norway	Germany

8 METRES (1907 RATING)

1920	Norway	Norway	—

10 METRES

1912	Sweden	Finland	Russia

10 METRES (1907 RATING)

1920	Norway	—	—

10 METRES (1919 RATING)

1920	Norway	—	—

12 METRES

1908	Great Britain	Great Britain	—
1912	Norway	Sweden	Finland

12 METRES (1907 RATING)

1920	Norway	—	—

12 METRES (1919 RATING)

1920	Norway	—	—

0.5 TONNES CLASS

1900	France	France	France

0.5–1 TONNES CLASS

1900	France	Great Britain	France

1–2 TONNES CLASS

1900	Switzerland	France	France

2–3 TONNES CLASS

1900	Great Britain	France	France

3–10 TONNES CLASS

	Gold	Silver	Bronze
1900	France	The Netherlands Great Britain	France

10–20 TONNES CLASS

	Gold	Silver	Bronze
1900	France	France	Great Britain

OPEN CLASS

	Gold	Silver	Bronze
1900	Great Britain	Germany	France

OVER-20 TONNES CLASS

	Gold	Silver	Bronze
1900	Great Britain	Great Britain	United States

SHOOTING MEDALS

MEN

FREE PISTOL (50 METRES)

	Gold	Silver	Bronze
1896	Sumner Paine (USA) 442	Holger Nielsen (DEN) 280	Nikolaos Morakis (GRE) d.n.a.
1900	Karl Röderer (SUI) 503	Achille Paroche (FRA) 466	Konrad Stäheli (SUI) 453
1906	Georgios Orphanidis (GRE) 221	Jean Fouconnier (FRA) 219	Aristides Rangavis (GRE) 218
1912	Alfred Lane (USA) 499	Peter Dolfen (USA) 474	Charles Stewart (GBR) 470
1920	Karl Frederick (USA) 496	Afranio da Costa (BRA) 489	Alfred Lane (USA) 481
1936	Torsten Ullmann (SWE) 559	Erich Krempem (GER) 544	Charles des Jammonières (FRA) 540
1948	Edwin Vazquez Cam (PER) 545	Rudolf Schnyder (SUI) 539	Torsten Ullmann (SWE) 539
1952	Huelet Benner (USA) 553	Angel Léon de Gozalo (ESP) 550	Ambrus Balogh (HUN) 549
1956	Pentti Linnosvuo (FIN) 556	Makhmud Oumarov ((URS) 556	Offutt PInion (USA) 551
1960	Alexei Gushkin (URS) 560	Makhmud Oumarov (URS) 552	Yoshihisa Yoshikawa (JPN) 552
1964	Väinö Markkanen (FIN) 560	Franklin Green (USA) 557	Yoshihisa Yoshikawa (JPN) 554
1968	Grigori Kossykh (URS) 562	Heinz Mertem (FRG) 562	Harald Vollmar (GDR) 560
1972	Ragnar Skanakar (SWE) 567	Dan Iuga (ROM) 562	Rudolf Dollinger (AUT) 560
1976	Uwe Potteck (GDR) 573	Harald Vollmar (GDR) 567	Rudolf Dollinger (AUT) 560
1980	Aleksandr Melentyev (URS) 581	Harald Vollmar (GDR) 568	Lubcho Diakov (BUL) 565
1984	Xu Haifeng (CHN) 566	Ragnar Skanaker (SWE) 565	Wang Yifu (CHN) 564
1988	Sorin Babii (ROM) (566+94) 660	Ragnar Skanaker (SWE) (564+93) 657	Igor Bassinki (URS) (570+87) 657
1992	Konstantin Loukachik (EUN) 658	Wang Yifu (CHN) 657	Ragnar Skanaker (SWE) 657
1996	Boris Kokoryev (RUS) 666.4	Igor Basinski (BLR) 662.1	Roberto Di Donna (ITA) 661.8
2000	Tanyu Kiryakov (BUL) 666.0	Igor Basinski (BLR) 663.3	Martin Tenk (CZE) 662.5

1904–08 and 1924–1932 event not held

RAPID-FIRE PISTOL

	Gold	Silver	Bronze
1896	Jean Phrangoudis (GRE) 344	Georgios Orphanidis (GRE)	Holger Nielsen (DEN) d.n.a.
1900	Maurice Larrouy (FRA) 58	Léon Moreaux (FRA) 57	Eugene Balme (FRA) 57
1906	Maurice Lecoq (FRA) 250	Léon Moreaux (FRA) 149	Aristides Rangavis (GRE) 245
1908	Paul van Asbroeck (BEL) 490	Réginald Storms (BEL) 487	James Gorman (USA) 485
1912	Alfred Lane (USA) 287	Paul Palén (SWE) 286	Johan von Holst (SWE) 283
1920	Guilherme Paraense (BRA) 274	Raymond Bracken (USA) 272	Fritz Zulauf (SUI) 269
1924	Paul Bailey (USA) 18	Vilhelm Carlberg (SWE) 18	Lennart Hannelius (FIN) 18
1932	Renzo Morigi (ITA) 36	Heinz Hax (GER) 36	Domenico Matteucci (ITA) 36
1936	Cornelius van Oyen (GER) 36	Heniz Hax (GER) 35	Torsten Ullmann (SWE) 34
1948	Károly Takács (HUN) 580	Carlos Diaz Sáenz Valiente (ARG) 571	Sven Lundqvuist (SWE) 569
1952	Károly Takács (HUN) 579	Szilárd Kun (HUN) 578	Gheorghe Lichiardopom (ROM) 578
1956	Stefan Petrescu (ROM) 587	Evgeni Shcherkasov (URS) 585	Gheorghe Lichiardopom (ROM) 581
1960	William McMillan (USA) 587	Penttii Linnosvuo (FIN) 587	Aleksandr Zabelin (URS) 587
1964	Penttii Linnosvuo (FIN) 592	Ion Tripsa (ROM) 591	Lubomir Nacovsky (TCH) 590
1968	Jozef Zapedzki (POL) 593	Marcel Rosca (ROM) 591	Renart Suleimanov (URS) 591

	Gold	Silver	Bronze
1972	Jozef Zapedzki (POL) 593	Ladislav Faita (TCH) 594	Victor Torshin (URS) 593
1976	Norbert Klaar (GDR) 597	Jürgen Wiefem (GDR) 596	Roberto Ferraris (ITA) 595
1980	Corneliu Ion (ROM) 596	Jürgen Wiefem (GDR) 596	Gerhard Petrisch (AUT) 596
1984	Takeo Kamachi (JPN) 595	Corneliu Ion (ROM) 593	Rauno Bies (FIN) 591
1988	Afanasi Kouzmine (URS) (598+100) 698	Ralf Schumann (GDR) (597+99) 696	Zoltán Kovács (HUN) (594+99) 693
1992	Ralf Schumann (GER) 885	Afanasijs Kuzmins (LAT) 882	Vladimir Vokhmyanin (EUN) 882
1996	Ralf Schumann (GER) 698.0	Emil Milev (BUL) 692.1	Vladimir Vokhmyanin (KAZ) 691.5
2000	Sergei Aliferenko (RUS) 687.6	Michel Ansermet (SUI) 686.1	Iulian Raicea (ROM) 684.6

1904–28 event not held

SMALL-BORE RIFLE (PRONE)*

	Gold	Silver	Bronze
1908	Arthur Carnelm (GBR) 387	Harry Humby (GBR) 386	George Barnes (GBR) 385
1912	Frederick Hird (USA) 194	William Milne (GBR) 193	Harry Burt (GBR) 192
1920	Lawrence Nuesslein (USA) 391	Arthur Rothrock (USA) 386	Dennis Fenton (USA) 385
1924	Pierre Coquelin de Lisle (FRA) 398	Marcus Dinwiddie (USA) 396	Josias Hartmann (SUI) 394
1932	Bertil Rönnmark (SWE) 294	Gustavo Huet (MEX) 294	Zoltán Hradetsky-Soos (HUN) 293
1936	Willy Rögeberg (NOR) 300	Ralph Berzsenyi (HUN) 296	Wladyslaw Karás (POL) 296
1948	Arthur Cook (USA) 599	Walter Tomsen (USA) 599	Jonas Jonsson (SWE) 597
1952	Josif Sarbu (ROM) 400	Boris Andreyev (URS) 400	Arthur Jackson (USA) 399
1956	Gerald Ouellette (CAN) 600†	Vasiliy Borrisov (IURS) 599	GIlmour Boa (CAN) 598
1960	Peter Kohnke (GER) 590	James Hilm (USA) 589	Enrico Pelliccione (VEN) 587
1964	László Hammerm (HUN) 597	Lonas Wigger (USA) 597	Tommy Poom (USA) 596
1968	Jan Kurka (TCH) 598	László Hammerm (HUN) 598	Ian Ballinger (NZL) 597
1972	Li Ho Jun (PRK) 599	Victor Auer (USA) 598	Nicolae Rotaru (ROM) 595
1976	Karlheinz Smieszek (FRG) 599	Ulrich Lind (FRG) 597	Gennadiy Luschikov (URS) 595
1980	Karoly Varga (HUN) 599	Hellfried Helifort (GDR) 599	Petar Zapianov (BUL) 598
1984	Edward Etzem (USA) 599	Michel Bury (FRA) 596	Michael Sullivan (GBR) 596
1988	Miroslav Varga (TCH) (600+103.9) 703.9	Cha Young-Chum (KOR) (598+104.8) 702.8	Attila Zahonyi (HUN) (597+104.9) 701.9
1992	Lee Eun-Chum (KOR) 702.5	Harald Stenvaag (NOR) 701.4	Stefan Pletikosic (IOP) 701.1
1996	Christian Klees (GER) 704.8	Sergei Belyayev (KAZ) 703.3	Jozef Gobci (SLO) 701.9
2000	Jonas Edman (SWE) 701.3	Torben Grimmel (DEN) 700.4	Sergei Martinyov (BLR) 700.3

1896–1906 and 1928 event not held. * In 1908 and 1912 any position was allowed; in 1920 it was a standing position.

† Range found to be marginally short – the record was, therefore, disallowed.

SMALL-BORE RIFLE (Three Positions: Prone, Kneeling and Standing)

	Gold	Silver	Bronze
1952	Erling Kongshaug (NOR) 1164	Viho Ylönen (FIN) 1164	Boris Andreyev (URS) 1163
1956	Anatoliy Bogdanov (URS) 1172	Otakar Horinek (TCH) 1172	Nils Sundberg (SWE) 1167
1960	Viktor Shamburkin (URS) 1149	Marat Niyasov (URS) 1145	Klaus Zähringer (GER) 1139
1964	Lones Wigger (USA) 1164	Velitchko Khristov (BUL) 1152	László Hammerm (HUN) 1151
1968	Bernd Klingner (FRG) 1157	John Writer (USA) 1156	Vitali Parkhimovich (URS) 1154
1972	John Writer (USA) 1166	Lanny Bassham (USA) 1157	Werner Lippoldt (GDR) 1153
1976	Lanny Bassham (USA) 1162	Margaret Murdock (USA) 1162	Werner Seibold (FRG) 1160
1980	Viktor Vlasov (URS) 1173	Bernd Hartstein (GDR) 1166	Sven Johansson (SWE) 1185
1984	Malcolm Cooper (GBR) 1173	Daniel Kipkow (SUI) 1163	Alister Allan (GBR) 1162
1988	Malcolm Cooper (GBR) (1180+99.3) 1279	Alister Allan (GBR) (1181+94.6) 1275.6	Kirill Ivanov (URS) (1173+102) 1275.0
1992	Gratchia Petikiane (EUN) 1267.4	Robert Foth (USA) 1266.6	Ryohei Koba (JPN) 1265.9
1996	Jean-Pierre Amat (FRA) 1273.9	Sergei Belyayev (KAZ) 1272.3	Wolfram Waibem (AUT) 1269.6
2000	Rajmond Debevec (SLO) 1275.1	Juha Hirvi (FIN) 1270.5	Harald Stenvaag (NOR) 1268.6

1896–1948 event not held

RUNNING GAME TARGET

	Gold	Silver	Bronze
1900	Louis Debray (FRA) 20	Pierre Nivet (FRA) 20	Comte de Lambert (FRA) 19
1972	Iakov Zhelezniak (URS) 569	Hanspeter Bellingrodt (COL) 565	John Kynoch (GBR) 562
1976	Aleksandr Gazov (URS) 579	Aleksandr Kedyarov (URS) 576	Jerzy Gresziewicz (POL) 571
1980	Igor Sokolov (URS) 589	Thomas Pfeffer (GDR) 589	Aleksandr Gasov (URS) 587
1984	Li Yuwei (CHN) 587	Helmut Bellingrodt (COL) 584	Shiping Huang (CHN) 581

	Gold	Silver	Bronze
1988	Tor Heiestad (NOR) (591+98) 689	Hunag Shiping (CHN) (589+98) 686	Gennadi Avramenko (URS) (591+95) 685

1896,1904–68 and 1992–2000 event not held

10-METRE RUNNING TARGET

	Gold	Silver	Bronze
1992	Michael Jakosits (GER) 673pts	Anatoli Asrabayev (EUN) 672	Lubos Racansky (TCH) 670
1996	Ling Yang (CHN) 685.8pts	Xiao Jun (CHN) 679.8	Miroslav Janus (CZE) 678.4
2000	Ling Yang (CHN) 681.1	Oleg Moldovan (MOL) 681.0	Zhiyuan Niu (CHN) 677.4

1896–1988 event not held

OLYMPIC TRAP SHOOTING

	Gold	Silver	Bronze
1900	Roger de Barbarin (FRA) 17	René Guyot (FRA) 17	Justinien de Clary (FRA) 17
1906*	Gerald Merlin (GBR) 24	Ioannis Peridis (GRE) 23	Sidney Merlin (GBR) 21
1908†	Sidney Merlin (GBR) 15	Anastasios Metaxas (GRE) 13	Gerald Merlin (GBR) 12
1908	Walter Ewing (CAN) 72	George Beattie (CAN) 60	Alexander Maunder (GBR) 57 Anastasios Metaxas (GRE) 57
1912	James Graham (USA) 96	Alfred Goeldel-Bronikowen (GER) 94	Harry Blau (RUS) 91
1920	Marke Arie (USA) 95	Frank Troeh (USA) 93	Frank Wright (USA) 87
1924	Gyula Halasy (HUN) 98	Konrad Huber (FIN) 98	Frank Hughes (USA) 97
1952	George Généreux (CAN) 192	Knut Holmqvist (SWE) 191	Hans Lijedahm (SWE) 191
1956	Galliano Rossini (ITA) 195	Adam Smelczynski (POL) 190	Alessandro Ciceri (ITA) 188
1960	Ion Dumitrescu (ROM) 192	Galliano Rossini (ITA) 191	Sergei Kalinin (URS) 190
1964	Ennio Mattarelli (ITA) 198	Pavel Senichev (URS) 194	William Morris (USA) 194
1968	Robert Braithwaite (GBR) 198	Thomas Garrigus (USA) 196	Kurt Czekalla (GDR) 196
1972	Angelo Scalzone (ITA) 199	Michel Carrega (FRA) 198	Silvano Basnagi (ITA) 195
1976	Don Haldeman (USA) 190	Armando Marques (POR) 189	Ulbaldesco Baldi (ITA) 189
1980	Luciano Giovanetti (ITA) 198	Rustam Yambulatov (URS) 196	Jörg Damme (GDR) 196
1984	Luciano Giovanetti (ITA) 192	Francisco Boza (PER) 192	Daniel Carlisle (USA) 192
1988	Dmitri Monakov (URS) (197+25) 222	Miloslav Bednarik (TCH) (197+25) 222	Frans Peeters (BEL) (195+24) 219
1992	Petr Hrdilicka (CZE) 219	Kazumi Watanabe (JPN) 219	Marco Venturini (ITA) 218
1996	Michael Diamond (AUS) 149	Josh Lakatos (USA) 147.0	Lance Bade (USA) 147.0
2000	Michael Diamond (AUS) 147	Ian Peel (GBR) 142	Giovanni Pellielo (ITA)140

1896,1904 and 1928–48 event not held. * Single shot. † Double shot.

DOUBLE TRAP

	Gold	Silver	Bronze
1996	Russell Mark (AUS) 189.0	Albano Pera (ITA) 183.0	Zhang Bang (CHN) 183.0
2000	Richard Faulds (GBR) 187	Russell Mark (AUS) 187	Fehaid Al Deehani (KUW) 186

1896–1992 event not held

SKEET

	Gold	Silver	Bronze
1968	Yevgeni Petrov (URS) 198	Romano Garagnani (ITA) 198	Konrad Wirnhier (FRG) 198
1972	Konrad Wirnhier (FRG) 195	Yevgeni Petrov (URS) 195	Michael Buchheim (GDR) 195
1976	Josef Panacek (TCH) 198	Eric Swinkels (NED) 198	Wieslaw Gawlikowski (POL) 196
1980	Hans Kjeld Rasmussen (DEN) 196	Lars-Goran Carlsson (SWE) 196	Roberto Garcia (CUB) 196
1984	Matthew Dryke (USA) 198	Ole Rasmussen (DEN) 196	Luca Scribiani Rossi (ITA) 196
1988	Axel Wegner (GDR) (198+24) 222	Alfonso de Iruarrizaga (CHI) (198+23) 221	Jorge Guardiola (ESP) (196+24) 220
1992	Zhang Shan (CHN) 233*	Juan Jorge Giha (PER) 222	Bruno Rosetti (ITA) 222
1996	Ennio Falco (ITA) 149.0	Miroslav Rzeprkowski (POL) 148.0	Andrea Benelli (ITA) 147.0
2000	Mykola Milchev (UKR) 150	Petr Malek (CZE) 148	James Graves (USA) 147

1896–1964 event not held. * First woman to win an Olympic mixed shooting event.

AIR PISTOL

	Gold	Silver	Bronze
1988	Taniou Kiriakov (BUL) (585+102.9) 687.9	Erich Buljung (USA) (590+97.9) 687.9	Xu Haifeng (CHN) (584+100.5) 684.5

	Gold	Silver	Bronze
1992	Wang Yifu (CHN) 684.8	Sergei Pyzhano (EUN) 684.1	Sorin Babii (ROM) 684.1
1996	Roberto di Donna (ITA) 684.2	Wang Yifu (CHN) 684.1	Tanyu Kiryakov (BUL) 683.8
2000	Franck Dumoulin (FRA) 688.9	Wang Yifu (CHN) 686.9	Igor Basinski (BLR) 682.7

1896–1984 event not held

AIR RIFLE

	Gold	Silver	Bronze
1984	Philippe Herberle (FRA) 589	Andreas Kronthaler (AUT) 587	Barry Dagger (GBR) 587
1988	Goran Maksimovic (YUG) (594+101.6) 685.6	Nicolas Berhtelot (FRA) (593+101.2) 694.2	Johann Riederer (FRG) (592+102) 694.0
1992	Yuri Fedkine (EUN) 695.3	Franck Badiou (FRA) 691.9	Johann Riederer (GER) 691.7
1996	Artem Khadzhibekov (RUS) 695.7	Wolfram Waibem (AUT) 695.2	Jean-Pierre Amat (FRA) 693.1
2000	Yalin Cai (CHN) 696.4	Artem Khadyibekov (RUS) 695.1	Yevgeni Aleynikov (RUS)　693.8

1896–1980 event not held

DISCONTINUED SHOOTING EVENTS
FREE RIFLE (THREE POSITIONS)

	Gold	Silver	Bronze
1896	Georgios Orphanidis (GRE) 1583	Jean Phrangoudis (GRE) 1312	Viggo Jensen (DEN) 1305
1906	Gudbrand Skattebøe (NOR) 977	Konrad Stäheli (SUI) 943	Jean Reich (SUI) 933
1908	Albert Helgerud (NOR) 909	Harry Simon (USA) 887	Ole Saether (NOR) 883
1912	Paul Colas (FRA) 987	Lars Madsen (DEN) 981	Niels Larsen (DEN) 962
1920	Morris Fisher (USA) 996	Niels Larsen (DEN) 989	Östen Östensen (NOR) 980
1924	Morris Fisher (USA) 95	Carl Osburn (USA) 95	Niels Larsen (DEN) 93
1948	Emil Grunig (SUI) 1120	Pauli Janhonen (FIN) 1114	Willy Rögeberg (NOR) 1112
1952	Anatoliy Bogdanov (URS) 1123	Robert Bürchler (SUI) 1120	Lev Vainschtein (URS) 1109
1956	Vasili Borissov (URS) 1138	Allan Erdman (URS) 1137	Vilho Ylönen (FIN) 1128
1960	Hubert Hammerer (AUT) 1129	Hans Spillmann (SUI) 1127	Vasili Borissov (URS) 1127
1964	Gary Anderson (USA) 1153	Shota Kveliashvili (URS) 1151	Martin Gunnarsson (USA) 1136
1968	Gary Anderson (USA) 1157	Vladimir Kornev (URS) 1151	Kurt Müller (SUI) 1148
1972	Lones Wigger (USA) 1155	Boris Melnik (URS) 1155	Lajos Papp (HUN) 1149

1900–1904 and 1928–1936 event not held

FREE RIFLE

1896*	Pantelis Karasevdas (GRE) 2320	Paulas Pavlidis (GRE) 1978	Nicolaos Tricoupes (GRE) 1718
1906†	Marcel de Stadelhofen (SUI) 243	Konrad Stäheli (SUI) 238	Léon Moreaux (FRA) 234
1906‡	Gudbrand Skattebøe (NOR) 339	Louis Richardet (SUI) 332	Konrad Stäheli (SUI) 328
1906§	Konrad Stäheli (SUI) 340	Louis Richardet (SUI) 338	Jean Reich (SUI) 320
1906☾	Gudbrand Skattebøe (NOR) 324	Julius Braathe (NOR) 310	Albert Helgerud (NOR) 305
1908**	Jerry Millner (GBR) 98	Kellogg Casey (USA) 93	Maurice Blood (GBR) 92

1900–1904 event not held. * Over 200m. † Any position. ‡ Prone (300m). § Kneeling (300m). ☾ Standing (300m) ** Over 1000yd

FREE RIFLE (TEAM)

1906	Switzerland 4596	Norway 4534	France 4511
1908	Norway 5055	Sweden 4711	France 4652
1912	Sweden 5655	Norway 5605	Denmark 5529
1920	United States 4876	Norway 4741	Switzerland 4698
1924	United States 676	France 646	Haiti 646

1896–1904 event not held

MILITARY RIFLE

1900*	Emil Kellenberger (SUI) 930	Anders Nielsen (DEN) 921	Ole Östmo (NOR) 917
1900†	Lars Madsen (DEN) 305	Ole Östmo (NOR) 299	Charles du Verger (BEL) 298
1900‡	Konrad Stäheli (SUI) 324	Emil Kellenberger (SUI) 314 Anders Nielsen (DEN) 314	—
1900§	Achille Paroche (FRA) 332	Anders Nielsen (DEN) 330	Ole Östmo (NOR) 329
1906☾	Léon Moreaux (FRA) 187	Louis Richardet (SUI) 187	Jean Reich (SUI) 183
1906§§	Louis Richardet (SUI) 238	Jean Reich (SUI) 234	Raoul de Boigne (FRA) 232
1912*	Sándor Prokopp (HUN) 97	Carl Osburn (USA) 96	Embret Skogen (NOR) 95
1912**	Paul Colas (FRA) 94	Carl Osburn (USA) 94	Joseph Jackson (USA) 93

	Gold	*Silver*	*Bronze*
1920§	Otto Olsen (NOR) 60	Léon Johnson (FRA) 59	Fritz Kuchen (SUI) 59
1920†	Carl Osburn (USA) 56	Lars Madsen (DEN) 55	Lawrence Nuesslein (USA) 54
1920††	Hugo Johansson (SWE) 58	Mauritz Eriksson (SWE) 56	Lloyd Spooner (USA) 56

1904 and 1908 event not held. * Three positions (300m). † Standing (300m). ‡ Kneeling (300m). § Prone (300m). ₵ Standing or kneeling (200m). §§ Standing or kneeling (300m). ** Any Position (600m). †† Prone.
Footnotes follow Military Rifle (Team)

MILITARY RIFLE (TEAM)

1900	Switzerland 4399	Norway 4290	France 4278
1908	United States 2531	Great Britain 2497	Canada 2439
1912	United States 1687	Great Britain 1602	Sweden 1570
1920†	Denmark 266	United States 255	Sweden 255
1920§	United States 289	France 283	Finland 281
1920††	United States 287	South AfricaSouth Africa 287	Sweden 287
1920‡‡	United States 573	Norway 565	Switzerland 563

1896 and 1904 event not held. *Three positions (300m). † Standing (300m). ‡ Kneeling (300m). § Prone (300m). ₵ Standing or kneeling (200m). §§ Standing or kneeling (300m). ** Any Position (600m). †† Prone. ‡‡ Prone (300m and 600m).

SMALL BORE RIFLE

1908*	John Fleming (GBR) 24	M.K. Matthews (GBR) 24	W.B. Marsden (GBR) 24
1908†	William Styles (GBR) 45	H.I. Hawkins (GBR) 45	Edward Amoore (GBR) 45
1912†	Wilhelm Carlberg (SWE) 242	Johan von Holst (SWE) 233	Gustaf Ericsson (SWE) 231

1896–1904 event not held. * Moving target. † Disappearing target.

SMALL BORE RIFLE (TEAM)

1908	Great Britain 771	Sweden 737	France 710
1912*	Sweden 925	Great Britain 917	United States 881
1912†	Great Britain 762	Sweden 748	United States 744
1920	United States 1899	Sweden 1873	Norway 1866

1896–1904 event not held. * Over 25m. †Over 50m.

LIVE PIGEON SHOOTING

1900	Léon de Lunden (BEL) 21	Maurice Faure (FRA) 20	Donald MacIntosh (AUS) 18
			Crittenden Robinson (USA) 18

CLAY PIGEONS (TEAM)

1908	Great Britain 407	Canada 405	Great Britain 372
1912	United States 532	Great Britain 511	Germany 510
1920	United States 547	Belgium 503	Sweden 500
1924	United States 363	Canada 360	Finland 360

RUNNING DEER SHOOTING

1908*	Oscar Swahn (SWE) 25	Ted Ranken (GBR) 24	Alexander Rogers (GBR) 24
1908†	Walter Winans (USA) 46	Ted Ranken (GBR) 46	Oscar Swahn (SWE) 38
1912*	Alfred Swahn (SWE) 41	Ake Lundeberg (SWE) 41	Nestori Toivonen (FIN) 41
1912†	Ake Lundeberg (SWE) 79	Edvard Benedicks (SWE) 74	Oscar Swahn (SWE) 72
1920*	Otto Olsen (NOR) 43	Alfred Swahn (SWE) 41	Harald Natwig (NOR) 41
1920†	Ole Lilloe-Olsen (NOR) 82	Fredrik Landelius (SWE) 77	Einar Liberg (NOR) 71
1924*	John Boles (USA) 40	Cyril Mackworth-Praed (GBR) 39	Otto Olsen (NOR) 39
1924†	Ole Lilloe-Olsen (NOR) 76	Cyril Mackworth-Praed (GBR) 72	Alfred Swahn (SWE) 72

* Single shot. † Double shot.

RUNNING DEER SHOOTING (TEAM)

1908	Sweden 86	Great Britain 85	–
1912	Sweden 151	United States 132	Finland 123
1920*	Norway 178	Finland 159	United States 158
1920†	Norway 343	Sweden 336	Finland 284
1924*	Norway 160	Sweden 154	United States 158
1924†	Great Britain 263	Norway 262	Sweden 250

* Single shot. † Double shot.

RUNNING DEER SHOOTING (SINGLE AND DOUBLE SHOT)

1952	John Larsen (NOR) 413	Per Olof Sköldberg (SWE) 409	Tauno Mäki (FIN) 407
1956	Vitali Romanenko (URS) 441	Per Olof Sköldberg (SWE) 432	Vladimir Sevrugin (URS) 429

MILITARY REVOLVER

	Gold	Silver	Bronze
1896	John Paine (USA) 442	Sumner Paine (USA) 380	Nikolaos Morakis (GRE) 205
1906	Louis Richardet (SUI) 253	Alexandros Theophilakis (GRE) 250	Georgios Skotadis (GRE) 240
1906*	Jean Fouconnier (FRA) 219	Raoul de Boigne (FRA) 219	Hermann Martin (FRA) 215

1900–1904 event not held. * Model 1873.

DUELLING PISTOL

1906*	Léon Moreaux (FRA) 242	Cesare Liverziani (ITA) 233	Maurice Lecoq (FRA) 231
1906†	Konstantinos Skarlatos (GRE) 133	Johann von Holst (SWE) 115	Wilhelm Carlberg (SWE) 115

1896–1904 Event not held. * Over 20m. † Over 25m.

TEAM EVENT

1900	Switzerland 2271	France 2203	The Netherlands 1876
1908	United States 1914	Belgium 1863	Great Britain 1817
1912*	United States 1916	Sweden 1849	Great Britain 1804
1912†	Sweden 1145	Russia d.n.a.	Great Britain d.n.a.
1920*	United States 2372	Sweden 2289	Brazil 2264
1920†	United States 1310	Greece 1285	Switzerland 1270

1904–16 event not held. * Over 50m. † Over 30m.

WOMEN (Introduced in 1984)

SPORT PISTOL

	Gold	Silver	Bronze
1984	Linda Thom (CAN) 585	Ruby Fox (USA) 585	Patricia Dench (AUS) 583
1988	Nino Saloukvadze (URS) (591+99) 690	Tomoko Hasegawa (JPN) (587+99) 686	Jasna Sekaric (YUG) (591+95) 686
1992	Marina Logvinenko (EUN) 684	Li Duihong (CHN) 680	Dorzhsuren Munkhbayar (MGL) 679
1996	Lui Duihong (CHN) 687.9	Diana Yorgova (BUL) 684.8	Marina Logvinenko (RUS) 684.2
2000	Maria Grozdeva (BUL) 690.3	Luna Tao (CHN) 689.8	Lolita Yevlevskaya (BLR) 686.0

SMALL-BORE RIFLE –THREE POSITIONS

	Gold	Silver	Bronze
1984	Wu Xiaoxuan (CHN) 581	Ulrike Holmer (FRG) 578	Wanda Jewelm (USA) 578
1988	Silvia Sperber (FRG) (590+95.6) 685.6	Vessela Letcheva (BUL) (583+100.2) 683.2	Valentina Tcherkasova (URS) (586+95.4) 681.4
1992	Launi Melli (USA) 684.3	Nonka Matova (BUL) 682.7	Malgorzata Ksiazkiewicz (POL) 681.5
1996	Alexandra Ivosev (YUG) 686.1	Irina Gerasimenok (POL) 680.1	Renata Mauer (POL) 679.8
2000	Renata Mauer-Rozanska (POL) 684.6	Tatyana Goldobina (RUS) 680.9	Maria Feklistova (RUS) 679.9

AIR PISTOL

	Gold	Silver	Bronze
1988	Jasna Sekaric (YUG) (389+100.5) 489.5	Nino Saloukvadze (URS) (390+97.9) 487.9	Marina Dobrantcheva (URS) (385+100.2) 485.2
1992	Marina Logvinenko (EUN) 486.4	Jasna Sekaric (IOP) 486.4	Maria Grusdeva (BUL) 481.6
1996	Olga Klochneva (RUS) 490.1	Marina Logvinenko (RUS) 488.5	Maria Grusdeva (BUL) 488.5
2000	Luna Tao (CHN) 488.2	Jasna Sekaric (YUG) 486.5	Annemarie Forder (AUS) 484.0

1984 event not held

AIR RIFLE

	Gold	Silver	Bronze
1984	Pat Spurgin (USA) 393	Edith Gufler (ITA) 391	Wu Xianxuan (CHN) 389
1988	Irina Chilova (URS) (395+103.5) 498.5	Silvia Sperber (FRG) (393+104.5) 497.5	Anna Maloukhina (URS) (394+101.8) 495.8
1992	Yeo Kab-soon (KOR) 498.2	Vesela Letcheva (BUL) 495.3	Aranka Binder (IOP) 495.1
1996	Renata Mauer (POL) 497.6	Petra Horneber (GER) 497.4	Alexandra Ivosev (YUG) 497.2
2000	Nancy Johnson (USA) 497.7	Cho-Hyun Kang (KOR) 497.5	Jing Gao (CHN) 497.2

TRAP

	Gold	Silver	Bronze
2000	Daina Gudzineviciute (LTU) 93	Delphine Racinet (FRA) 92	E. Gao (CHN) 90

1984–96 event not held

DOUBLE TRAP

	Gold	Silver	Bronze
1996	Kim Rhode (USA) 141	Susanne Keirmayer (GER) 139	Deserie Huddleston (AUS) 139
2000	Pia Hansen (SWE) 148	Deborah Gelisio (ITA) 144	Kim Rhode (USA) 139

1984–92 event not held

SKEET

	Gold	Silver	Bronze
2000	Zemfira Meftakhetdinova (AZE) 98	Svetlana Demina (RUS) 95	Diana Igaly (HUN) 93

1984–96 event not held

SOFTBALL MEDALS

WOMEN (Introduced in 1996)

	Gold	Silver	Bronze
1996	United States	China	Australia
2000	United States	Japan	Australia

SWIMMING MEDALS

MEN

50 METRES FREESTYLE

	Gold	Silver	Bronze
1904*	Zóltán Halmay (HUN) 28.0	Scott Leary (USA) 28.6	Charles Daniels (USA) n.t.a.
1988	Matti Biondi (USA) 22.14	Thomas Jager (USA) 22.36	Gennadi Prigoda (URS) 22.71
1992	Aleksandr Popov (EUN) 21.91	Matt Biondi (USA) 22.09	Tom Jager (USA) 22.30
1996	Aleksandr Popov (RUS) 22.13	Gary Hall Jr (USA) 22.26	Fernando Scherer (BRA) 22.29
2000	Anthony Ervin (USA) 21.98	Pieter van den Hoogenband (NED) 22.03	Gary Hall Jr (USA) 21.98

1896–1900 and 1906–84 event not held. * 50 yards. The race was re-swum after the judges disagreed on the result of the first race.

100 METRES FREESTYLE

	Gold	Silver	Bronze
1896*	Alfréd Hajós (HUN) 1:22.2	Efstathios Chorophas (GRE) 1:23.0	Otto Herschmann (AUT) d.n.a.
1904†	Zóltán Halmay (HUN) 1:02.8	Charles Daniels (USA) d.n.a.	Scott Leary (USA) d.n.a.
1906	Charles Daniels (USA) 1:13.4	Zóltán Halmay (HUN) 1:14.2	Cecil Healy (AUS) d.n.a.
1908	Charles Daniels (USA) 1:05.6	Zóltán Halmay (HUN) 1:06.2	Harald Julin (SWE) 1:08.0
1912	Duke Kahanamoku (USA) 1:03.4	Cecil Healy (AUS) 1:04.6	Kenneth Huszagh (USA) 1:05.6
1920	Duke Kahanamoku (USA) 1:01.4	Pua Kealoha (USA) 1:02.2	William Harris (USA) 1:03.0
1924	Johnny Weissmuller (USA) 59.0	Duke Kahanamoku (USA) 1:01.4	Sam Kahanamoku (USA) 1:01.8
1928	Johnny Weissmuller (USA) 58.6	István Bárány (HUN) 59.8	Katsuo Takaishi (JPN) 1:00.0
1932	Yasuji Miyazaki (JPN) 58.2	Tatsugo Kawaishi (JPN) 58.6	Albert Schwartz (USA) 58.8
1936	Ferenc Csik (HUN) 57.6	Masanori Yusa (JPN) 57.9	Shigeo Arai (JPN) 58.0
1948	Walter Ris (USA) 57.3	Alan Ford (USA) 57.8	Géza Kádas (HUN) 58.1
1952	Clarke Scholes (USA) 57.4	Hiroshi Suzuki (JPN) 57.4	Göran Larsson (SWE) 58.2
1956	Jon Hendricks (AUS) 55.4	John Devitt (AUS) 55.8	Gary Chapman (AUS) 56.7
1960‡	John Devitt (AUS) 55.2 (55.16)	Lance Larson (USA) 55.2 (55.10)	Manuel dos Santos (BRA) 55.4
1964	Don Schollander (USA) 53.4	Bobbie McGregor (GBR) 53.5	Hans-Joachim Klein (GER) 54.0
1968	Mike Wenden (AUS) 52.2	Ken Walsh (USA) 52.8	Mark Spitz (USA) 53.0
1972	Mark Spitz (USA) 51.22	Jerry Heidenreich (USA) 51.65	Vladimir Bure (URS) 51.77
1976	Jim Montgomery (USA) 49.99	Jack Babashoff (USA) 50.81	Peter Nocke (FRG) 51.31
1980	Jörg Woithe (GDR) 50.40	Per Holmertz (SWE) 50.91	Per Johansson (SWE) 51.29
1984	Ambrose Gaines (USA) 49.80	Mark Stockwelm (AUS) 50.24	Per Johansson (SWE) 50.31
1988	Matt Biondi (USA) 48.63	Chris Jacobs (USA) 49.08	Stephan Caron (FRA) 49.62

	Gold	Silver	Bronze
1992	Aleksandr Popov (EUN) 49.02	Gustavo Borges (BRA) 49.43	Stephan Caron (FRA) 49.50
1996	Aleksandr Popov (RUS) 48.74	Gary Hall Jr (USA) 48.81	Gustavo Borges (BRA) 49.02
2000	Pieter van den Hoogenband (NED) 48.30	Aleksandr Popov (RUS) 48.69	Gary Hall Jr (USA) 48.73

1900 event not held. * Some confusion exists about the second and third finishers. † 100 yards. ‡ Larson's original manual timing of 55.1 was revised by the judges. (Automatic timings shown were unofficial).

200 METRES FREESTYLE

	Gold	Silver	Bronze
1900	Frederick Lane (AUS) 2:25.2	Zóltán Halmay (HUN) 2:31.4	Karl Ruberi (AUT) 2:32.0
1904*	Charles Daniels (USA) 2:44.2	Francis Gailey (USA) 2:46.0	Emil Rausch (GER) 2:56.0
1968	MIke Wenden (AUS) 1:55.2	Don Schollander (USA) 1:55.8	John Nelson (USA) 1:58.1
1972	Mark Spitz (USA) 1:52.78	Steven Genter (USA) 1:53.73	Werner Lampe (FRG) 1:53.99
1976	Bruce Furniss (USA) 1:50.29	John Naber (USA) 1:50.50	Jim Montgomery (USA) 1:50.58
1980	Sergei Kopliakov (URS) 1:49.81	Andrei Krylov (URS) 1:50.76	Graeme Brewer (AUS) 1:51.60
1984	Michael Gross (FRG) 1:47.44	Michael Heath (USA) 1:49.10	Thomas Fahrner (FRG) 1:49.69
1988	Duncan Armstrong (AUS) 1:47.25	Anders Holmertz (SWE) 1:47.89	Matt Biondi (USA) 1:47.99
1992	Yevgeni Sadovyi (EUN) 1:46.70	Anders Holmertz (SWE) 1:46.86	Antti Kasvio (FIN) 1:47.63
1996	Danyon Loader (NZL) 1:47.63	Gustavo Borges (BRA) 1:48.08	Daniel Kowalski (AUS) 1:48.25
2000	Pieter van den Hoogenband (NED) 1:45.35	Ian Thorpe (AUS) 1:45.83	Massimiliano Rosolino (ITA) 1:46.65

1896 and 1906–64 event not held. * 220 yards.

400 METRES FREESTYLE

	Gold	Silver	Bronze
1896*	Paul Neuman (AUT) 8:12.6	Antonios Pepanos (GRE) 30m	Efstathios Choraphas (GRE) d.n.a.
1904†	Charles Daniels (USA) 6:16.2	Francis Gailey (USA) 6:22.0	Otto Wahle (AUT) 6:39.0
1906	Otto Scheff (AUT) 6:23.8	Henry Taylor (GBR) 6:24.4	John Jarvis (GBR) 6:27.2
1908	Henry Taylor (GBR) 5:36.8	Frank Beaurepaire (AUS) 5:44.2	Otto Scheff (AUT) 5:46.0
1912	George Hodgson (CAN) 5:24.4	John Hatfield (GBR) 5:25.8	Harold Hardwick (AUS) 5:31.2
1920	Norman Ross (USA) 5:26.8	Ludy Langer (USA) 5:29.2	George Vernot (CAN) 5:29.8
1924	Johnny Weismuller (USA) 5:04.2	Arne Borg (SWE) 5:05.6	Andrew Charlton (AUS) 5:06.6
1928	Alberto Zorilla (ARG) 5:01.6	Andrew Charlton (AUS) 5:03.6	Arne Borg (SWE) 5:04.6
1932	Buster Crabbe (USA) 4:48.4	Jean Taris (FRA) 4:48.5	Tautomu Oyokota (JPN) 4:52.3
1936	Jack Medica (USA) 4:44.5	Shumpei Uto (JPN) 4:45.6	Shozo Makino (JPN) 4:48.1
1948	William Smith (USA) 4:41.0	James McLane (USA) 4:43.4	John Marshalm (AUS) 4:47.7
1952	Jean Boiteux (FRA) 4:30.7	Ford Konno (USA) 4:31.3	Per-Olof Ostrand (SWE) 4:35.2
1956	Murray Rose (AUS) 4:27.3	Tsuyoshi Yamanaka (JPN) 4:30.4	Goerge Breen (USA) 4:32.5
1960	Murray Rose (AUS) 4:18.3	Tsuyoshi Yamanaka (JPN) 4:21.4	John Konrads (AUS) 4:21.8
1964	Don Schollander (USA) 4:12.2	Frank Wiegand (GER) 4:14.9	Allan Wood (AUS) 4:15.1
1968	Mike Burton (USA) 4:09.0	Ralph Hutton (CAN) 4:11.7	Allan Mosconi (FRA) 4:13.3
1972	Brad Cooper (AUS) 4:00.27	Steven Genter (USA) 4:01.94	Tom McBeen (USA) 4:02.64
1976	Brian Goodelm (USA) 3:51.93	Tim Shaw (USA) 3:52.54	Vladimir Raskatov (URS) 3:55.76
1980	Vladimir Salnikov (URS) 3:51.31	Andrei Krylov (URS) 3:53.24	Ivan Stukolkin (URS) 3:55.76
1984	George DiCarlo (USA) 3:51.23	John Mykkanen (USA) 3:51.49	Justin Lemberg (AUS) 3:51.79
1988	Uwe Dassler (GDR) 3:46.95	Duncan Armstrong (AUS) 3:47.15	Artur Wojdat (POL) 3:47.34
1992	Yevgeni Sadovyi (EUN) 3:45.00	Kieren Perkins (AUS) 3:45.16	Anders Holmertz (SWE) 3:46.77
1996	Danyon Loader (NZL) 3:47.97	Paul Palmer (GBR) 3:49.00	Daniel Kowalski (AUS) 3:48.39
2000	Ian Thorpe (AUS) 3:40.59	Massimiliano Rosolino (ITA) 3:43.40	Klete Keller (USA) 3:47.00

1900 event not held. * 500m. † 440 yards.

1500 METRES FREESTYLE

	Gold	Silver	Bronze
1896*	Alfréd Hajós (HUN) 18:22.2	Jean Andreou (GRE) 21:03.4	Efstathios Choraphas (GRE) d.n.a.
1900†	John Jarvis (GBR) 13:40.2	Otto Wahle (AUT) 14:53.6	Zóltán Halmay (HUN) 15:16.4
1904‡	Emil Rausch (GER) 27:18.2	Géza Kiss (HUN) 28:28.2	Francis Gailey (USA) 28:54.0
1906‡	Henry Taylor (GBR) 28:28.0	John Jarvis (GBR) 30:31.0	Otto Scheff (AUT) 30.59.0
1908	Henry Taylor (GBR) 22:48.4	Sydney Battersby (GBR) 22:51.2	Frank Beaurepaire (AUS) 22:56.2
1912	George Hodgson (CAN) 22:00.0	John Hatfield (GBR) 22:39.0	Harold Hardwick (AUS) 23:15.4
1920	Norman Ross (USA) 22:23.2	George Vernot (CAN) 22:36.4	Frank Beaurepaire (AUS) 23:04.0
1924	Andrew Charlton (AUS) 20:06.6	Arne Borg (SWE) 20:41.4	Frank Beaurepaire (AUS) 21:48.4

	Gold	Silver	Bronze
1928	Arne Borg (SWE) 19:51.8	Andrew Charlton (AUS) 20:02.6	Buster Crabbe (USA) 20:28.8
1932	Kusuo Kitamura (JPN) 19:12.4	Shozo Makino (JPN) 19:14.1	James Christy (USA) 19:39.5
1936	Noboru Terada (JPN) 19:13.7	Jack Medica (USA) 19:34.0	Shumpei Uto (JPN) 19:34.5
1948	James McLane (USA) 19:18.5	John Marshalm (AUS) 19:31.3	György Mitro (HUN) 19:43.2
1952	Ford Konno (USA) 18:30.0	Shiro Hasizune (JPN) 18:41.4	Tetsuo Okamoto (JPN) 18:51.3
1956	Murray Rose (AUS) 17:58.9	Tsuyoshi Yamanaka (JPN) 18:00.3	George Breen (USA) 18:08.2
1960	John Konrads (AUS) 17:19.6	Murray Rose (AUS) 17:21.7	George Breen (USA) 17:30.6
1964	Bob Windle (USA) 17:01.7	John Nelson (USA) 17:03.0	Allan Wood (AUS) 17:07.7
1968	Mike Burton (USA) 16:38.9	John Kinsella (USA) 16:57.3	Greg Brough (AUS) 17:04.7
1972	Mike Burton (USA) 15:52.58	Graham Windeatt (AUS) 15:58.48	Doug Northway (USA) 16:09.25
1976	Brian Goodelm (USA) 15:02.40	Bobby Hackett (USA) 15:03.91	Steve Holland (AUS) 15:04.66
1980	Vladimir Salnikov (URS) 14:58.27	Aleksandr Chaev (URS) 15:14.30	Max Metzker (AUS) 15:14.49
1984	Michael O'Brien (USA) 15:05.20	George DiCarlo (USA) 15:10.59	Stefan Pfeiffer (FRG) 15:12.11
1988	Vladimir Salnikov (URS) 15:00.40	Stevan Pfeiffer (FRG) 15:02.69	Uwe Dassler (GDR) 15:06.15
1992	Kieren Perkins (AUS) 14:43.48	Glen Housman (AUS) 14:55.29	Jörg Hoffmann (GER) 15:02.29
1996	Kieren Perkins (AUS) 14:56.40	Daniel Kowalski (AUS) 15:02.43	Graeme Smith (GBR) 15:02.48
2000	Grant Hackett (AUS) 14:48.33	Kieren Perkins (AUS) 14:53.59	Chris Thompson (USA) 14:56.81

* 1200m. † 1000m. ‡ One mile.

100 METRES BREASTSTROKE

	Gold	Silver	Bronze
1968	Don McKenzie (USA) 1:07.7	Vladimir Kossinky (URS) 1:08.0	Nikolai Pankin (URS) 1:08.0
1972	Nobutaka Taguchi (JPN) 1:04.94	Tom Bruce (USA) 1:05.43	John Hencken (USA) 1:05.61
1976	John Hencken (USA) 1:03.11	David Wilkie (GBR) 1:03.43	Arvidas Iuozaytis (URS) 1:04.23
1980	Duncan Goodhew (GBR) 1:03.34	Arsen Miskarov (URS) 1:03.92	Peter Evans (AUS) 1:03.96
1984	Steve Lundquist (USA) 1:01.65	Victor Davis (CAN) 1:01.99	Peter Evans (AUS) 1:02.97
1988	Adrian Moorhouse (GBR) 1:02.04	Karoly Guttler (HUN) 1:02.05	Dmitri Volkov (URS) 1:02.20
1992	Nelson Dreibem (USA) 1:01.50	Norbert Rósza (HUN) 1:01.68	Phil Rogers (AUS) 1:01.76
1996	Frederik Deburghgraeve (BEL) 1:00.65	Jeremy Linn (USA) 1:00.77	Mark Warnecke (GER) 1:01.33
2000	Domenico Fioravanti (ITA) 1:00.46	Ed Moses (USA) 1:00.73	Roman Sloudnov (RUS) 1:00.91

1896–1964 Event not held

200 METRES BREASTSTROKE

	Gold	Silver	Bronze
1908	Frederick Holman (GBR) 3:09.2	William Robinson (GBR) 3:12.8	Pontus Hansson (SWE) 3:14.6
1912	Walter Bathe (GER) 3:01.8	Wilhelm Lützow (GER) 3:05.2	Kurt Malisch (GER) 3:08.0
1920	Häken Malmroth (SWE) 3:04.4	Thor Henning (SWE) 3:09.2	Arvo Aaltonen (FIN) 3:12.2
1924	Robert Shelton (USA) 2:56.5	Joseph de Combe (BEL) 2:59.2	William Kirschbaum (USA) 3:01.0
1928	Yoshiyuki Tsuruta (JPN) 2:48.8	Erich Rademacher (GER) 2:50.6	Teofilo Ylidefonzo (PHI) 2:56.4
1932	Yoshiyuki Tsuruta (JPN) 2:45.4	Reizo Koike (JPN) 2:46.4	Teofilo Ylidefonzo (PHI) 2:47.1
1936	Tetsuo Hamuro (JPN) 2:42.5	Erwin Sietas (GER) 2:42.9	Reizo Koike (JPN) 2:44.2
1948	Joseph Verdeur* (USA) 2:39.3	Keith Carter (USA) 2:40.2	Robert Sohm (USA) 2:43.9
1952	John Davies* (AUS) 2:34.4	Bowen Stassforth (USA) 2:34.7	Herbert Klein (GER) 2:35.9
1956	Masaru Furukawa† (JPN) 2:34.7	Masihiro Yoshimura (JPN) 2:36.7	Charis Yunitschev (URS) 2:36.8
1960	William Mulliken (USA) 2:37.4	Yoshihiko Osaki (JPN) 2:38.0	Weiger Mensonides (NED) 2:39.7
1964	Ian O'Brien (AUS) 2:27.8	Georgi Prokopenko (URS) 2:28.2	Chester Jastremski (USA) 2:29.6
1968	Felipe Munoz (MEX) 2:28.7	Vladimir Kossinsky (URS) 2:29.2	Brian Job (USA) 2:29.9
1972	John Hencken (USA) 2:21.55	David Wilkie (GBR) 2:23.67	Nobutaka Taguchi (JPN) 2:23.88
1976	David Wilkie (USA) 2:15.11	John Hencken (USA) 2:17.26	Rick Colella (USA) 2:19.20
1980	Robertas Shulpa (URS) 2:15.85	Alban Vermes (HUN) 2:16.93	Arsen Miskarov (URS) 2:17.28
1984	Victor Davis (CAN) 2:13.34	Glenn Beringen (AUS) 2:15.79	Etienne Dagon (SUI) 2:17.41
1988	József Szabó (HUN) 2:13.52	Nick Gillingham (GBR) 2:14.12	Sergio Lopez (ESP) 2:15.21
1992	Mike Barrowman (USA) 2:10.16	Norbert Rózsa (HUN) 2:11.23	Nick Gillingham (GBR) 2:11.29
1996	Norbert Rózsa (HUN) 2:12.57	Károly Guttler (HUN) 2:13.03	Andrei Korneyev (RUS) 2:13.17
2000	Domenico Fioravanti (ITA) 2:10.87	Terence Parkin (RSA) 2:12.50	Davide Rummolo (ITA) 2:12.73

1896–1906 event not held. * Used the then permissible butterfly stroke. † Used the then permissible underwater technique.

100 METRES BACKSTROKE

	Gold	Silver	Bronze
1904*	Walter Brack (GER) 1:16.8	Georg Hoffmann (GER) 1:18.0	Georg Zacharias (GER) 1:19.6
1908	Arno Bieberstein (GER) 1:24.6	Ludvig Dam (DEN) 1:26.6	Herbert Haresnape (GBR) 1:27.0
1912	Harry Hebner (USA) 1:21.2	Otto Fahr (GER) 1:22.4	Paul Kellner (GER) 1:24.0
1920	Warren Kealoha (USA) 1:15.2	Ray Kegeris (USA) 1:16.2	Gérard Blitz (BEL) 1:19.0
1924	Warren Kealoha (USA) 1:13.2	Paul Wyatt (USA) 1:15.4	Károly Bartha (HUN) 1:17.8
1928	George Kojac (USA) 1:08.2	Walter Laufer (USA) 1:10.0	Paul Wyatt (USA) 1:12.0
1932	Masaji Kiyokawa (JPN) 1:08.6	Toshio Irie (JPN) 1:09.8	Kentaro Kawatsu (JPN) 1:10.0
1936	Adolf Kiefer (USA) 1:05.9	Albert Van de Weghe (USA) 1:07.7	Masaji Kiyokawa (JPN) 1:08.4
1948	Allen Stack (USA) 1:06.4	Robert Cowelm (USA) 1:06.5	Georges Vallerey (FRA) 1:07.8
1952	Yoshinobu Oyakawa (JPN) 1:05.4	Gilbert Bozon (FRA) 1:06.2	Jack Taylor (USA) 1:06.4
1956	David Thiele (AUS) 1:02.2	John Monckton (AUS) 1:03.2	Frank McKinney (USA) 1:04.5
1960	David Thiele (AUS) 1:01.9	FrankMcKinney (USA) 1:02.1	Robert Bennett (USA) 1:02.3
1968	Roland Matthes (GDR) 58.7	Charles Hickox (USA) 1:00.2	Ronnie Mills (USA) 1:00.5
1972	Roland Matthes (GDR) 56.58	Mike Stamm (USA) 57.70	John Murphy (USA) 58.35
1976	John Naber (USA) 55.49	Peter Rocca (USA) 56.34	Roland Matthes (GDR) 57.22
1980	Bengt Baron (SWE) 56.53	Viktor Kuznetsov (URS) 56.99	Vladimir Dolgov (URS) 57.63
1984	Richard Carey (USA) 55.79	David Wilson (USA) 56.35	Mike West (CAN) 56.49
1988	Daichi Suzuki (JPN) 55.05	David Berkoff (USA) 55.18	Igor Polianski (URS) 55.20
1992	Mark Tewksbury (CAN) 53.98	Jeff Rouse (USA) 54.04	David Berkoff (USA) 54.78
1996	Jeff Rouse (USA) 54.10	Rodolfo Cabrera (CUB) 54.98	Neisser Bent (CUB) 55.02
2000	Lenny Krayzelburg (USA) 53.72	Matt Welsh (AUS) 54.07	Stev Theloke (GER) 54.82

1896–1900, 1906 and 1964 event not held. * 100 yards.

200 METRES BACKSTROKE

	Gold	Silver	Bronze
1900	Ernst Hoppenberg (GER) 2:47.0	Karl Ruberm (AUT) 2:56.0	Johannes Drost (NED) 3:01.0
1964	Jed Graef (USA) 2:10.3	Gary Dilley (USA) 2:10.5	Robert Bennett (USA) 2:13.1
1968	Roland Matthes (GDR) 2:09.6	Mitchell Ivey (USA) 2:10.6	Jack Horsley (USA) 2:10.9
1972	Roland Matthes (GDR) 2:02.82	Mike Stamm (USA) 2:04.09	Mitchell Ivey (USA) 2:04.33
1976	John Naber (USA) 1:59.19	Peter Rocca (USA) 2:00.55	Don Harrigan (USA) 2:01.35
1980	Sándor Wladár (HUN) 2:01.93	Zóltán Verraszto (HUN) 2:02.40	Mark Kerry (AUS) 2:03.14
1984	Richard Carey (USA) 2:00.23	Frederic Delcourt (FRA) 2:01.75	Cameron Henning (CAN) 2:02.37
1988	Igor Polianski (URS) 1:59.37	Frank Baltrausch (GDR) 1:59.50	Paul Kingsman (NZL) 2:00.48
1992	Martin Lopez-Zubero (ESP) 1:58.47	Vladimir Selkov (EUN) 1:58.87	Stefano Battistelli (ITA) 1:59.40
1996	Brad Bridgewater (USA) 1:58.54	Tripp Schwenk (USA) 1:58.99	Emanuele Meris (ITA) 1:59.18
2000	Lenny Krayzelburg (USA) 1:56.76	Aaron Piersol (USA) 1:57.35	Matt Welsh (AUS) 1:57.59

1896 and 1904–60 event not held

100 METRES BUTTERFLY

	Gold	Silver	Bronze
1968	Doug Russelm (USA) 55.9	Mark Spitz (USA) 56.4	Ross Wales (USA) 57.2
1972	Mark Spitz (USA) 54.27	Bruce Robertson (CAN) 55.56	Jerry Heidenreich (USA) 55.74
1976	Matt Vogem (USA) 54.35	Joe Bottom (USA) 54.50	Gary Halm (USA) 54.65
1980	Pär Arvidsson (SWE) 54.92	Roger Pyttem (GDR) 54.94	David Lopez (ESP) 55.13
1984	Michael Gross (FRG) 53.08	Pablo Morales (USA) 53.23	Glenn Buchanan (AUS) 53.85
1988	Anthony Nesty (SUR) 53.00	Matt Biondi (USA) 53.01	Andy Jameson (GBR) 53.30
1992	Pablo Morales (USA) 53.32	Rafal Szukala (POL) 53.35	Anthony Nesty (SUR) 53.41
1996	Denis Pankratov (RUS) 52.27	Scott Miller (AUS) 52.53	Vladislav Kulikov (RUS) 52.13
2000	Lars Frölander (SWE) 52.00	Michael Klim (AUS) 52.18	Geoff Huegill (AUS) 52.22

1896–1964 event not held

200 METRES BUTTERFLY

	Gold	Silver	Bronze
1956	William Yorzyk (USA) 2:19.3	Takashi Ishimoto (JPN) 2:23.8	György Tumpek (HUN) 2:23.9
1960	Mike Troy (USA) 2:12.8	Neville Hayes (AUS) 2:14.6	David Gillanders (USA) 2:15.3
1964	Kevin Berry (AUS) 2:06.6	Carl Robie (USA) 2:07.5	Fred Schmidt (USA) 2:09.3
1968	Carl Robie (USA) 2:08.7	Martyn Woodroffe (GBR) 2:09.0	John Ferris (USA) 2:09.3
1972	Mark Spitz (USA) 2:00.70	Gary Halm (USA) 2:02.86	Robin Backhaus (USA) 2:03.23
1976	Mike Bruner (USA) 1:59.23	Steven Gregg (USA) 1:59.54	William Forrester (USA) 1:59.96

	Gold	Silver	Bronze
1980	Sergey Fesenko (URS) 1:59.76	Phil Hubble (GBR) 2:01.20	Roger Pyttem (GDR) 2:01.39
1984	Jon Sieben (AUS) 1:57.04	Michael Gross (FRG) 1:57.40	Rafael Castro (VEN) 1:57.51
1988	Michael Gross (FRG) 1:56.94	Benny Nielsen (DEN) 1:58.24	Anthony Mosse (NZL) 1:58.28
1992	Mel Stewart (USA) 1:56.26	Danyon Loader (NZL) 1:57.93	Franck Esposito (FRA) 1:58.51
1996	Denis Pankratov (RUS) 1:56.51	Tom Malchow (USA) 1:57.44	Scott Miller (AUS) 1:57.48
2000	Tom Malchow (USA) 1:55.35	Denys Sylantyev (UKR) 1:55.76	Justin Norris (AUS) 1:56.17

1896–1952 event not held

200 METRES INDIVIDUAL MEDLEY

	Gold	Silver	Bronze
1968	Charles Hickox (USA) 2:12.0	Greg Buckingham (USA) 2:13.0	John Ferris (USA) 2:13.3
1972	Gunnar Larsson (SWE) 2:07.17	Tim McKee (USA) 2:08.37	Steve Furniss (USA) 2:08.45
1984	Alex Baumann (CAN) 2:01.42	Pablos Morales (USA) 2:03.05	Neil Cochran (GBR) 2:04.38
1988	Tamás Darnyi (HUN) 2:00.17	Patrick Kühm (GDR) 2:01.61	Vadim Yarochtchouk (URS) 2:02.40
1992	Tamás Darnyi (HUN) 2:00.76	Gregory Burgess (USA) 2:00.97	Attila Czene (HUN) 2:01.00
1996	Attila Czene (HUN) 1:59.91	Jani Sievinen (FIN) 2:00.13	Curtis Myden (CAN) 2:01.13
2000	Massimiliano Rosolino (ITA) 1:58.98	Tom Dolan (USA) 1:59.77	Tom Wilkens (USA) 2:00.87

1896–1964 and 1976–80 event not held

400 METRES INDIVIDUAL MEDLEY

	Gold	Silver	Bronze
1964	Richard Roth (USA) 4:45.4	Roy Saari (USA) 4:47.1	Gerhard Hetz (GER) 4:51.0
1968	Charles Hickox (USA) 4:48.4	Gary Halm (USA) 4:48.7	Michael Holthaus (GER) 4:51.4
1972	Gunnar Larsson (SWE) 4:31.98	Tim McKee (USA) 4:31.98	András Hargitay (HUN) 4:32.70
1976	Rod Strachan (USA) 4:23.68	Tim McKee (USA) 4:24.62	Andrei Smirnov (URS) 4:26.90
1980	Aleksandr Sidorenko (URS) 4:22.89	Sergei Fesenko (URS) 4:23.43	Zóltán Verraszto (HUN) 4:24.24
1984	Alex Baumann (CAN) 4:17.41	Ricardo Prado (BRA) 4:18.45	Robert Woodhouse (AUS) 4:20.50
1988	Tamás Darnyi (HUN) 4:14.75	David Wharton (USA) 4:17.36	Stefano Battistelli (ITA) 4:18.01
1992	Tamás Darnyi (HUN) 4:14.23	Erik Namesnik (USA) 4:15.57	Luca Sacchi (ITA) 4:16.34
1996	Tom Dolan (USA) 4:14.90	Eric Namesnik (USA) 4:15.25	Curtis Myden (CAN) 4:16.28
2000	Tom Dolan (USA) 4:11.76	Erik Vendt (USA) 4:14.23	Curtis Myden (CAN) 4:15.33

1896–1960 event not held

4 X 100 METRES FREESTYLE RELAY

	Gold	Silver	Bronze
1964	United States 3:33.2	Germany 3:37.2	Australia 3:39.1
1968	United States 3:31.7	Soviet Union 3:34.2	Australia 3:34.7
1972	United States 3:26.42	Soviet Union 3:29.72	GDR 3:32.42
1984	United States 3:19.03	Australia 3:19.68	Sweden 3:22.69
1988	United States 3:16.53	Soviet Union 3:18.33	GDR 3:19.82
1992	United States 3:16.74	Unified Team 3:17.56	Germany 3:17.90
1996	United States 3:15.41	Russia 3:17.06	Germany 3:17.20
2000	Australia 3:13.67	United States 3:13.86	Brazil 3:17.40

1896–1960 and 1976–80 event not held

4 X 200 METRES FREESTYLE RELAY

	Gold	Silver	Bronze
1906*	Hungary 16:52.4	Germany 17:16.2	Great Britain n.t.a.
1908	Great Britain 10:55.6	Hungary 10:59.0	United States 11:02.8
1912	Australasia† 10:11.6	United States 10:20.2	Great Britain 10:28.2
1920	United States 10:04.4	Australia 10:25.4	Great Britain 10:37.2
1924	United States 9:53.4	Australia 10:02.2	Sweden 10:06.8
1928	United States 9:36.2	Japan 9:41.4	Canada 9:47.8
1932	Japan 8:58.4	United States 9:10.5	Hungary 9:31.4
1936	Japan 8:51.5	United States 9:03.0	Hungary 9:12.3
1948	United States 8:46.0	Hungary 8:48.4	France 9:08.0
1952	United States 8:31.1	Japan 8:33.5	France 8:45.9
1956	Australia 8:23.6	United States 8:31.5	Soviet Union 8:34.7
1960	United States 8:10.2	Japan 8:13.2	Australia 8:13.8

	Gold	Silver	Bronze
1964	United States 7:52.1	Germany 7:59.3	Japan 8:03.8
1968	United States 7:35.78	Australia 7:53.7	Soviet Union 8:01.6
1972	United States 7:35.78	FRG 7:41.69	Soviet Union 7:45.76
1976	United States 7:23.22	Soviet Union 7:27.97	Great Britain 7:32.11
1980	Soviet Union 7:23.50	GDR 7:28.60	Brazil 7:29.30
1984	United States 7:15.69	FRG 7:16.73	Great Britain 7:24.78
1988	United States 7:12.51	GDR 7:13.68	FRG 7:14.35
1992	Unified Team 7:11.95	Sweden 7:15.31	United States 7:16.23
1996	United States 7:14.84	Sweden 7:17.56	Germany 7:17.71
2000	Australia 7:07.05	United States 7:12.64	The Netherlands 7:12.70

1896–1904 event not held. * 4 x 250m. † Composed of three Australians and a New Zealander.

4 X 100 METRES MEDLEY RELAY

	Gold	Silver	Bronze
1960	United States 4:05.4	Australia 4:12.0	Japan 4:12.2
1964	United States 3:38.5	Germany 4:01.6	Australia 4:02.3
1968	United States 3:54.9	GDR 3:57.5	Soviet Union 4:00.7
1972	United States 3:48.16	GDR 3:52.12	Canada 3:52.26
1976	United States 3:42.22	Canada 3:43.23	FRG 3:47.29
1980	Australia 3:45.70	Soviet Union 3:45.92	Great Britain 3:47.71
1984	United States 3:39.30	Canada 3:43.23	Australia 3:43.25
1988	United States 3:36.93	Canada 3:39.28	Soviet Union 3:39.96
1992	United States 3:36.93	Unified Team 3:38.56	Canada 3:39.96
1996	United States 3:34.84	Russia 3:37.55	Australia 3:39.56
2000	United States 3:33.73	Australia 3:35.27	Germany 3:35.88

1896–1956 event not held

DIVING MEDALS

MEN

SPRINGBOARD DIVING

	Gold	Silver	Bronze
1908	Albert Turner (GER) 85.5	Kurt Behrens (GER) 85.3	George Giadzik (USA) 80.8
			Gottlob Walz (GER) 80.8
1912	Paul Günther (GER) 79.23	Hans Luber (GER) 76.78	Kurt Behrens (GER) 73.73
1920	Louis Kuehn (USA) 675.4	Clarence Pinkston (USA) 655.3	Louis Balbach (USA) 649.5
1924	Albert White (USA) 696.4	Pete Desjardins (USA) 693.2	Clarence Pinkston (USA) 653
1928	Pete Desjardins (USA) 185.04	Michael Galitzen (USA) 174.06	Farid Simaika (EGY) 172.46
1932	Michael Galitzen (USA) 161.38	Harold Smith (USA) 158.54	Richard Degener (USA) 151.82
1936	Richard Degener (USA) 163.57	Marshall Wayne (USA) 159.56	Al Greene (USA) 146.29
1948	Bruce Harlan (USA) 163.64	MIller Anderson (USA) 157.29	Samuel Lee (USA) 145.52
1952	David Browning (USA) 205.29	Miller Anderson (USA) 199.84	Robert Clotworthy (USA) 184.92
1956	Robert Clotworthy (USA) 159.56	Donald Harper (USA) 156.23	Joaquin Capilla Pérez (MEX) 162.30
1960	Gary Tobian (USA) 170.00	Samuel Halm (USA) 167.08	Juan Botella (MEX) 162.30
1964	Kenneth Sitzberger (USA) 159.90	Francis Gorman (USA) 157.63	Larry Andreasen (USA) 143.77
1968	Bernard Wrightson (USA) 170.15	Klaus Dibiasi (ITA) 159.74	James Henry (USA) 158.09
1972	Vladimir Vasin (URS) 594.09	F. Giorgio Cagnotto (ITA) 591.63	Craig Lincoln (USA) 577.29
1976	Philip Boggs (USA) 619.05	F. Giorgio Cagnotto (ITA) 570.48	Aleksandr Kosenkov (URS) 567.24
1980	Aleksandr Portnov (URS) 905.025	Carlos Giron (MEX) 892.140	F. Giorgio Cagnotto (ITA) 871.500
1984	Greg Louganis (USA) 754.41	Tan Liangde (CHN) 662.31	Ronald Merriott (USA) 661.32
1988	Greg Louganis (USA) 730.80	Tan Liangde (CHN) 704.88	Li Deliang (CHN) 665.28
1992	Mark Lenzi (USA) 676.530pts	Tan Liangde (CHN) 645.570	Dmitri Sautin (EUN) 627.780
1996	Ni Xiong (CHN) 701.46	Yu Zhoucheng (CHN) 690.93	Mark Lenzi (USA) 686.49
2000	Ni Xiong (CHN) 708.72	Fernando Platas (MEX) 708.42	Dmitri Sautin (RUS) 703.20

1896–1906 event not held

SPRINGBOARD SYNCHRONISED (Introduced in 2000)

	Gold	Silver	Bronze
2000	China 365,58	Russia 329.97	Australia 322.86

PLATFORM DIVING

	Gold	Silver	Bronze
1904*	George Shelton (USA) 12.66	Georg Hoffmann (GER) 11.66	Frank Kehoe (USA) 11.33
			Alfred Braunschweiger (GER) 11.33
1906	Gottlob Walz (GER) 156.00	Georg Hoffmann (GER) 150.20	Otto Satzinger (AUT) 147.40
1908	Hajalmar Johansson (SWE) 83.75	Karl Malmström (SWE) 78.73	Arvid Spangberg (SWE) 74.00
1912	Erik Adlerz (SWE) 73.94	Albert Zürner (GER) 72.60	Gustaf Blomgren (SWE) 69.56
1920	Clarence Pinkston (USA) 100.67	Erik Adlerz (SWE) 99.08	Haig Prieste (USA) 93.73
1924	Albert White (USA) 97.46	David Falm (USA) 97.30	Clarence Pinkston (USA) 94.60
1928	Pete Desjardins (USA) 98.74	Farid Simiaka (EGY) 99.58	Michael Galitzen (USA) 92.34
1932	Harold Smith (USA) 124.80	Michael Galitzen (USA) 124.28	Frank Kurtz (USA) 121.98
1936	Marshall Wayne (USA) 113.58	Elbert Root (USA) 110.60	Hermann Stork (GER) 110.31
1948	Samuel Lee (USA) 130.05	Bruce Harlan (USA) 122.30	Joaquin Capilla Pérez (MEX) 113.52
1952	Samuel Lee (USA) 156.28	Joaquin Capilla Pérez (MEX) 145.21	Günther Haase (GER) 141.31
1956	Joaquin Capilla Pérez (MEX) 152.44	Gary Tobian (USA) 152.41	Richard Connor (USA) 149.79
1960	Robert Webster (USA) 165.56	Gary Tobian (USA) 165.25	Brian Phelps (GBR) 157.13
1964	Robert Webster (USA) 148.58	Klaus Dibiasi (ITA) 147.54	Thomas Gompf (USA) 153.93
1968	Klaus Dibiasi (ITA) 164.18	Alvaro Gaxiola (MEX) 154.49	Edwin Young (USA) 153.93
1972	Klaus Dibiasi (ITA) 504.12	Richard Rydze (USA) 480.75	F. Giorgio Cagnotto (ITA) 475.83
1976	Klaus Dibaisi (ITA) 600.51	Greg Louganis (USA) 576.99	Vladimir Aleynik (URS) 548.61
1980	Falk Hoffmann (GDR) 835.650	Vladimir Aleynik (URS) 819.705	David Ambartsumyan (URS) 817.440
1984	Greg Louganis (USA) 710.91	Bruce Kimbalm (USA) 643.50	Li Kongzheng (CHN) 638.28
1988	Greg Louganis (USA) 638.61	Ni Xiong (CHN) 637.47	Jesus Mena (MEX) 594.39
1992	Sun Shunwei (CHN) 677.310	Scott Donie (USA) 633.630	Ni Xiong (CHN) 600.150
1996	Dmitri Sautin (RUS) 692.34	Jan Hempem (GER) 663.27	Hailiang Xiao (CHN) 658.20
2000	Liang Tian (CHN) 724.53	Jia Hu (CHN) 713.55	Dmitri Sautin (RUS) 679.26

1896–1900 event not held. * Combined springboard and platform event.

PLATFORM SYNCHRONISED (Introduced in 2000)

	Gold	Silver	Bronze
2000	Russia 365.04	China 358.74	Germany 338.88

WOMEN

50 METRES FREESTYLE

	Gold	Silver	Bronze
1988	Kristin Otto (GDR) 25.49	Yang Wenyi (CHN) 25.64	Katrin Meissner (GDR) 25.71 Jill Sterkem (USA) 25.71
1992	Yang Wenyi (CHN) 24.79	Zhuang Yong (CHN) 25.08	Angel Martino (USA) 25.23
1996	Amy van Dyken (USA) 24.87	Le Jingyi (CHN) 24.90	Sandra Volker (GER) 25.14
2000	Inge de Bruijn (NED) 24.32	Therese Alshammar (SWE) 24.51	Dara Torres (USA) 24.63

1896–1984 event not held

100 METRES FREESTYLE

	Gold	Silver	Bronze
1912	Fanny Durack (AUS) 1:22.2	Wilhelmina Wylie (AUS) 1:25.4	Jennie Fletcher (GBR) 1:27.0
1920	Etheda Bleibtrey (USA) 1:13.6	Irene Guest (USA) 1:17.0	Frances Schroth (USA) 1:17.2
1924	Ethel Lackie (USA) 1:12.4	Mariechen Wehselau (USA) 1:12.8	Gertrude Ederle (USA) 1:14.2
1928	Albina Osipowich (USA) 1:11.0	Eleanor Garatti (USA) 1:11.4	Joyce Cooper (GBR) 1:13.6
1932	Helene Madison (USA) 1:06.8	Willemijntje den Ouden (NED) 1:07.8	Eleanor Garatti-Saville (USA) 1:08.2
1936	Henrika Mastenbroek (NED) 1:05.9	Jeanette Campbelm (ARG) 1:06.6	Gisela Arendt (GER) 1:06.6
1948	Greta Andersen (DEN) 1:06.3	Ann Curtis (USA) 1:06.5	Marie-Louise Vaessen (NED) 1:07.6
1952	Katalin Szöke (HUN) 1:06.8	Johanna Termeulen (NED) 1:07.0	Judit Temes (HUN) 1:07.1
1956	Dawn Fraser (AUS) 1:02.0	Lorraine Crapp (AUS) 1:02.3	Faith Leech (AUS) 1:05.1
1960	Dawn Fraser (AUS) 1:01.2	Chris von Saltza (USA) 1:02.8	Natalie Steward (GBR) 1:03.1
1964	Dawn Fraser (AUS) 59.5	Sharon Stouder (USA) 59.9	Kathleen Ellis (USA) 1:00.8
1968	Jan Henne (USA) 1:00.0	Susan Pedersen (USA) 1:00.3	Linda Gustavson (USA) 1:00.3

Gold	Silver	Bronze
1972	Sandra Neilson (USA) 58.59	Shirley Babashoff (USA) 59.02	Shane Gould (AUS) 59.06
1976	Kornelia Ender (GDR) 55.65	Petra Priemer (GDR) 56.49	Enith Brigitha (NED) 56.65
1980	Barbara Krause (GDR) 54.79	Caren Metschuck (GDR) 55.16	Ines Diers (GDR) 55.65
1984	Carrie Steinsiefer (USA) 55.92	Annemarie Verstappen (NED) 56.08	Nancy Hogshead (USA) 55.92
1988	Kristin Otto (GDR) 54.93	Zhuang Yong (CHN) 55.47	Catherine Plewinski (FRA) 55.49
1992	Zhuang Yong (CHN) 54.64	Jenny Thompson (USA) 54.84	Franziska van Almsick (GER) 54.94
1996	Le Jingyi (CHN) 54.50	Sandra Volker (GER) 54.88	Angel Martino (USA) 54.93
2000	Inge de Bruijn (NED) 53.83	Therese Alshammar (SWE) 54.33	Jenny Thompson 54.43
			Dara Torres (USA) 54.43

1896–1908 event not held

200 METRES FREESTYLE

Gold	Silver	Bronze
1968	Debbie Meyer (USA) 2:10.5	Jan Henne (USA) 2:11.0	Jane Barkman (USA) 2:11.2
1972	Shane Gould (AUS) 2:03.56	Shirley Babashoff (USA) 2:04.33	Keena Rothhammer (USA) 2:04.92
1976	Kornelia Ender (GDR) 1:59.26	Shirley Babashoff (USA) 2:01.22	Enith Brigitha (NED) 2:01.40
1980	Barbara Krause (GDR) 1:58.33	Ines Diers (GDR) 1:59.64	Carmela Schmidt (GDR) 2:01.44
1984	Mary Wayte (USA) 1:59.23	Cynthia Woodhead (USA) 1:59.50	Annemarie Verstappen (NED) 1:59.69
1988	Heike Friedrich (GDR) 1:57.65	Silvia Polm (CRC) 1:58.67	Manuela Stellmach (GDR) 1:59.01
1992	Nicole Haislett (USA) 1:57.90	Franziska van Almsick (GER) 1:58.00	Kirsten Kielglass (GER) 1:59.67
1996	Claudia Polm (CRC) 1:58.16	Franziska van Almsick (GER) 1:58.57	Dagmar Hase (GER) 1:59.56
2000	Susie O'Neill (AUS) 1:58.24	Martina Moravcova (SVK) 1:58.32	Claudia Poll (CRC) 1:58.81

1896–1964 event not held

400 METRES FREESTYLE

Gold	Silver	Bronze
1920*	Etheda Bleibtrey (USA) 4:34.0	Margaret Woodbridge (USA) 4:42.8	Frances Schroth (USA) 4:52.0
1924	Martha Norelius (USA) 6:02.2	Helen Wainwright (USA) 6:03.8	Gertrude Ederle (USA) 6:04.8
1928	Martha Norelius (USA) 5:42.8	Marie Braun (NED) 5:57.8	Jospehine McKim (USA) 6:00.2
1932	Helene Madison (USA) 5:28.5	Lenore Kight (USA) 5:28.6	Jennie Maakam (RSA) 5:47.3
1936	Henrika Mastenbroek (NED) 5:26.4	Ragnhild Hveger (DEN) 5:27.5	Lenore Kight-Wingard (USA) 5:29.0
1948	Ann Curtis (USA) 5:17.8	Karen Harup (DEN) 5:21.2	Cathy Gibson (GBR) 5:22.5
1952	Valeria Gyenge (HUN) 5:12.1	Eva Novak (HUN) 5:13.7	Evelyn Kawamoto (USA) 5:14.6
1956	Lorraine Crapp (AUS) 4:54.6	Dawn Fraser (AUS) 5:02.5	Sylvia Ruuska (USA) 5:07.1
1960	Chris von Salza (USA) 4:50.6	Jane Cederquist (SWE) 4:53.9	Catharina Lagerberg (NED) 4:56.9
1964	Virginia Duenkem (USA) 4:43.3	Marilyn Ramenofsky (USA) 4:44.6	Terri Stickles (USA) 4:47.2
1968	Debbie Meyer (USA) 4:31.8	Linda Gustavson (USA) 4:35.5	Karen Moras (AUS) 4:37.0
1972	Shane Gould (AUS) 4:19.04	Novella Calligaris (ITA) 4:22.44	Gudrun Wegner (GDR) 4:23.11
1976	Petra Thuemer (GDR) 4:09.89	Shirley Babashoff (USA) 4:10.46	Shannon Smith (CAN) 4:14.60
1980	Ines Diers (GDR) 4:08.76	Petra Schneider (GDR) 4:09.16	Carmela Schmidt (GDR) 4:10.86
1984	Tiffany Cohen (USA) 4:07.10	Sarah Hardcastle (GBR) 4:10.27	June Croft (GBR) 4:11.49
1988	Janet Evans (USA) 4:03.85	Heike Friedrich (GDR) 4:05.94	Anke Möhring (GDR) 4:06.62
1992	Dagmar Hase (GER) 4:07.18	Janet Evans (USA) 4:07.37	Hayley Lewis (AUS) 4:11.22
1996	Michelle Smith (IRL) 4:07.25	Dagmar Hase (GER) 4:08.30	Kirsten Vlieghuis (NED) 4:08.70
2000	Brooke Bennett (USA) 4:05.80	Diana Munz (USA) 4:07.07	Claudia Poll (CRC) 4:07.83

1896–1912 event not held. * 300m

800 METRES FREESTYLE

Gold	Silver	Bronze
1968	Debbie Meyer (USA) 9:24.0	Pamela Kruse (USA) 9:35.7	Maria Ramirez (MEX) 9:38.5
1972	Keena Rothhammer (USA) 8:53.68	Shane Gould (AUS) 8:56.39	Novella Calligaris (ITA) 8:57.46
1976	Petra Thuemer (GDR) 8:37.14	Shirley Babashoff (USA) 8:37.59	Wendy Weinberg (USA) 8:42.60
1980	Michelle Ford (AUS) 8:28.9	Ines Diers (GDR) 8:32.55	Heike Dähne (GDR) 8:33.48
1984	Tiffany Cohen (USA) 8:24.95	Michele Richardson (USA) 8:30.73	Sarah Hardcastle (GBR) 8:32.60
1988	Janet Evans (USA) 8:20.20	Astrid Strauss (GDR) 8:22.09	Julie McDonald (AUS) 8:22.93
1992	Janet Evans (USA) 8:25.52	Hayley Lewis (AUS) 8:30.34	Jana Henke (GER) 8:30.99
1996	Brooke Bennett (USA) 8:27.89	Dagmar Hase (GER) 8:29.91	Kirsten Vlieghuis (NED) 8:30.84
2000	Brooke Bennett (USA) 8:19.67	Jana Klochkova (UKR) 8:22.66	Kaitlin Sandeno (USA) 8:24.29

1896–1964 event not held

100 METRES BREASTSTROKE

	Gold	Silver	Bronze
1968	Djurdjica Bjedov (YUG) 1:15.8	Galina Prozumenschchikova* (URS) 1:15.9	Sharon Wichman (USA) 1:16.1
1972	Catherine Carr (USA) 1:13.58	Galina Stepanova (URS) 1:14.99	Beverley Whitfield (AUS) 1:15.73
1976	Hannelore Anke (GDR) 1:11.16	Lubov Rusanova (URS) 1:13.04	Marina Kosheveya (URS) 1:13.30
1980	Ute Geweniger (GDR) 1:10.22	Elvira Vasilkova (URS) 1:10.41	Susanne Nielsson (DEN) 1:11.16
1984	Petra Van Staveren (NED) 1:09.88	Anne Ottenbrite (CAN) 1:10.69	Catherine Poirot (FRA) 1:10.70
1988	Tania Dangalakova (BUL) 1:07.95	Antoaneta Frankeva (BUL) 1:08.74	Silke Hörner (GDR) 1:08.83
1992	Yelena Rudkovskaya (EUN) 1:08.00	Anita Nalm (USA) 1:08.17	Samantha Riley (AUS) 1:09.25
1996	Penny Heyns (RSA) 1:07.73	Amanda Beard (USA) 1:08.09	Samantha Riley (AUS) 1:09.18
2000	Megan Quann (USA) 1:07.05	Leisel Jones (AUS) 1:07.49	Penny Heyns (RSA) 1:07.55

1896–1964 event not held. * Later Stepanova.

200 METRES BREASTSTROKE

	Gold	Silver	Bronze
1924	Lucy Morton (GBR) 3:33.2	Agnes Geraghty (USA) 3:34.0	Gladys Carson (GBR) 3:35.4
1928	HIlde Schrader (GER) 3:12.6	Mietje Baron (NED) 3:15.2	Lotte Mühe (GER) 3:17.6
1932	Claire Dennis (AUS) 3:06.3	Hideko Maehata (JPN) 3:06.4	Else Jacobsen (DEN) 3:07.1
1936	Hideko Maehata (JPN) 3:03.6	Martha Genenger (GER) 3:04.2	Inge Sörensen (DEN) 3:07.8
1948	Petronella van Vliet (NED) 2:57.2	Nancy Lyons (AUS) 2:57.7	Eva Novák (HUN) 3:00.2
1952	Eva Székely* (HUN) 2:51.7	Eva Novák (HUN) 2:54.4	Helen Gordon (GBR) 2:57.6
1956	Ursula Happe† (GER) 2:53.1	Eva Székely (HUN) 2:54.8	Eva-Maria ten Elsen (GER) 2:55.1
1960	Anita Lonsbrough (GBR) 2:49.5	Wiltrud Urselmann (GER) 2:50.0	Barbara Göbem (GER) 2:53.6
1964	Galina Prozumenshchikova (URS) 2:46.4	Claudia Kolb (USA) 2:47.6	Svetlana Babanina (URS) 2:48.6
1968	Sharon Wichman (USA) 2:44.4	Djurdjica Bjedov (YUG) 2:46.4	Galina Prozumenshchikova (URS) 2:47.0
1972	Beverley Whitfield (AUS) 2:41.7	Dana Schoenfield (USA) 2:42.05	Galina Stepanova (URS) 2:42.36
1976	Marina Kosheveya (URS) 2:33.35	Marina Yurchenia (URS) 2:36.08	Lubov Rusanova (URS) 2:36.22
1980	Lina Kachushite (URS) 2:29.54	Svetlana Varganova (URS) 2:29.61	Yulia Bogdanova (URS) 2:32.39
1984	Anne Ottenbrite (CAN) 2:30.38	Susan Rapp (USA) 2:31.15	Ingrid Lempereur (BEL) 2:31.40
1988	Silke Hörner (GDR) 2:26.71	Huang Xiaomin (CHN) 2:27.49	Antoaneta Frankeva (BUL) 2:28.34
1992	Kyoko Iwasaki (JPN) 2:26.65	Li Lin (CHN) 2:26.85	Anita Nalm (USA) 2:26.88
1996	Penny Heyns (RSA) 2:25.41	Amanda Beard (USA) 2:25.75	Agnes Kovacs (HUN) 2:26.57
2000	Agnes Kovacs (HUN) 2:24.35	Kristy Kowal (USA) 2:24.56	Amanda Beard (USA) 2:25.35

1896–1920 event not held. * Used then permitted butterfly stroke. † Used then permitted underwater technique.

100 METRES BACKSTROKE

	Gold	Silver	Bronze
1924	Sybil Bauer (USA) 1:23.2	Phyllis Harding (GBR) 1:27.4	Aileen Riggin (USA) 1:28.2
1928	Marie Braun (NED) 1:22.0	Ellen King (GBR) 1:22.2	Joyce Cooper (GBR) 1:22.8
1932	Eleanor Holm (USA) 1:19.4	Philomena Mealing (AUS) 1:21.3	Valerie Davies (GBR) 1:22.5
1936	Dina Senff (NED) 1:18.9	Hendrika Mastenbroek (NED) 1:19.2	Alice Bridges (USA) 1:19.4
1948	Karen Harup (DEN) 1:14.4	Suzanne Zimmermann (USA) 1:16.0	Judy Davies (AUS) 1:16.7
1952	Joan Harrison (RSA) 1:14.3	Geertje Wielema (NED) 1:14.5	Jean Stewart (NZL) 1:15.8
1956	Judy Grinham (GBR) 1:12.9	Carin Cone (USA) 1:12.9	Margaret Edwards (GBR) 1:13.1
1960	Lynn Burke (USA) 1:09.3	Natalie Steward (GBR) 1:10.8	Satoko Tanaka (JPN) 1:11.4
1964	Cathy Ferguson (USA) 1:07.7	Cristine Caron (FRA) 1:07.9	Virginia Duenkem (USA) 1:08.0
1968	Kaye Halm (USA) 1:06.2	Elaine Tanner (CAN) 1:06.7	Jane Swaggerty (USA) 1:08.1
1972	Melissa Belote (USA) 1:05.78	Andrea Gyarmati (HUN) 1:06.26	Susie Atwood (USA) 1:06.34
1976	Ulrike Richter (GDR) 1:01.83	Birgit Treiber (GDR) 1:03.41	Nancy Garapick (CAN) 1:03.71
1980	Rica Reinisch (GDR) 1:00.86	Ina Kleber (GDR) 1:02.07	Petra Reidem (GDR) 1:02.64
1984	Theresa Andrews (USA) 1:02.55	Betsy Mitchelm (USA) 1:02.63	Jolanda De Rover (NED) 1:02.91
1988	Kristin Otto (GDR) 1:00.89	Krisztina Egerszegi (HUN) 1:01.56	Cornelia Sirch (GDR) 1:01.57
1992	Krysztina Egerszegi (HUN) 1:00.68	Tunde Szabo (HUN) 1:01.14	Lea Loveless (USA) 1:01.43
1996	Beth Botsford (USA) 1:01.19	Whitney Hedgepeth (USA) 1:01.47	Marianne Kriem (RSA) 1:02.12
2000	Diana Mocanu (ROM) 1:00.21	Mai Nakamura (JPN) 1:00.55	Nina Schiwanevskaya (ESP) 1:00.89

1896–1920 event not held

200 METRES BACKSTROKE

	Gold	Silver	Bronze
1968	Lillian Watson (USA) 2:24.8	Elaine Tanner (CAN) 2:27.4	Kaye Halm (USA) 2:28.9
1972	Melissa Belote (USA) 2:19.19	Susie Atwood (USA) 2:20.38	Donna Marie Gurr (CAN) 2:23.22
1976	Ulrike Richter (GDR) 2:13.43	Birgit Treiber (GDR) 2:14.97	Nancy Garapick (CAN) 2:15.60
1980	Rica Reinisch (GDR) 2:11.77	Cornelia Polit (GDR) 2:13.75	Birgit Treiber (GDR) 2:14.14
1984	Jolanda De Rover (NED) 2:12.38	Amy White (USA) 2:13.04	Aneta Patrascoiu (ROM) 2:13.29
1988	Krysztina Egerszegi (HUN) 2:09.29	Kathrin Zimmermann (GDR) 2:10.61	Cornelia Sirch (GDR) 2:11.45
1992	Krysztina Egerszegi (HUN) 2:07.06	Dagmar Hase (GER) 2:09.46	Nicole Stevenson (AUS) 2:10.20
1996	Krysztina Egerszegi (HUN) 2:07.83	Whitney Hedgepeth (USA) 2:11.98	Cathleen Rund (GER) 2:12.06
2000	Diana Mocanu (ROM) 2:08.16	Roxana Maracineanu (FRA) 2:10.25	Miki Nakao (JPN) 2:11.05

1896–1964 event not held

100 METRES BUTTERFLY

	Gold	Silver	Bronze
1956	Shelley Mann (USA) 1:11.0	Nancy Ramey (USA) 1:11.9	Mary Sears (USA) 1:14.4
1960	Carolyn Schuler (USA) 1:09.5	Marianne Heemskerk (NED) 1:10.4	Janice Andrew (AUS) 1:12.2
1964	Sharon Stouder (USA) 1:04.7	Ada Kok (NED) 1:05.6	Kathleen Ellis (USA) 1:06.0
1968	Lynette McClements (AUS) 1:05.5	Ellie Daniem (USA) 1:05.8	Susan Shields (USA) 1:06.2
1972	Mayumi Aoki (JPN) 1:03.34	Roswitha Beier (GDR) 1:03.61	Andrea Gyarmati (HUN) 1:03.73
1976	Kornelia Ender (GDR) 1:00.13	Andrea Pollack (GDR) 1:00.98	Wendy Bognoli (USA) 1:01.17
1980	Caren Metschuck (GDR) 1:00.42	Andrea Pollack (GDR) 1:00.90	Christiane Knacke (GDR) 1:01.44
1984	Mary Meagher (USA) 59.26	Jenna Johnson (USA) 1:00.19	Karin Seick (FRG) 1:00.36
1988	Kristin Otto (GDR) 59.00	Birte Weigang (GDR) 59.45	Qian Hong (CHN) 59.52
1992	Qian Hong (CHN) 58.62	Chrissy Ahmann-Leighton (USA) 58.74	Catherine Plewinski (FRA) 59.01
1996	Amy van Dyken (USA) 59.13	Liu Limin (CHN) 59.14	Angel Martino (USA) 59.23
2000	Inge de Bruijn (NED) 56.61	Martina Moravcova (SVK) 57.97	Dara Torres (USA) 58.20

1896–1952 event not held

200 METRES BUTTERFLY

	Gold	Silver	Bronze
1968	Ada Kok (NED) 2:24.7	Helga Lindner (GDR) 2:24.8	Ellie Daniem (USA) 2:25.9
1972	Karen Moe (USA) 2:15.57	Lynn Colella (USA) 2:16.34	Ellie Daniem (USA) 2:26.74
1976	Andrea Pollack (GDR) 2:11.41	Ulrike Tauber (GDR) 2:12.45	Rosemarie Gabriem (GDR) 2:12.86
1980	Ines Geissler (GDR) 2:10.44	Sybille Schönrock (GDR) 2:10.45	Michelle Ford (AUS) 2:11.66
1984	Mary Meagher (USA) 2:06.90	Karen Phillips (AUS) 2:10.56	Ina Beyermann (FRG) 2:11.91
1988	Kathleen Nord (GDR) 2:09.51	Birte Weigang (GDR) 2:09.91	Mary Meagher (USA) 2:10.80
1992	Summer Sanders (USA) 2:08.67	Wang Xiaohong (CHN) 2:09.01	Susie O'Neilm (AUS) 2:09.03
1996	Susie O'Neill (AUS) 2:07.76	Petria Thomas (AUS) 2:09.82	Michelle Smith (IRL) 2:09.91
2000	Misty Hyman (USA) 2:05.88	Susie O'Neill (AUS) 2:06.58	Petria Thomas (AUS) 2:07.12

1896–1964 event not held

200 METRES INDIVIDUAL MEDLEY

	Gold	Silver	Bronze
1968	Claudia Kolb (USA) 2:24.7	Susan Pedersen (USA) 2:28.8	Jan Henne (USA) 2:31.4
1972	Shane Gould (AUS) 2:23.07	Kornelia Ender (GDR) 2:23.59	Lynn Vidali (USA) 2:24.06
1984	Tracy Caulkins (USA) 2:12.64	Nancy Hogshead (USA) 2:15.17	Michele Pearson (AUS) 2:15.92
1988	Daniela Hunger (GDR) 2:12.59	Yelena Dendeberova (URS) 2:13.31	Noemi Ildiko Lung (ROM) 2:14.85
1992	Li Lin (CHN) 2:11.65	Summer Sanders (USA) 2:11.91	Daniela Hunger (GDR) 2:13.62
1996	Michelle Smith (IRL) 2:13.93	Marianne Limpert (CAN) 2:14.35	Lin Li (CHN) 2:14.74
2000	Jana Klochkova (UKR) 2:10.68	Beatrice Caslaru (ROM) 2:12.57	Cristina Teuscher (USA) 2:13.32

1896–1964 and 1976–80 event not held

400 METRES INDIVIDUAL MEDLEY

	Gold	Silver	Bronze
1964	Donna De Varona (USA) 5:18.7	Sharon Finneran (USA) 5:24.1	Martha Randalm (USA) 5:24.1
1968	Claudia Kolb (USA) 5:08.5	Lynn Vidali (USA) 5:22.2	Sabine Steinbach (GDR) 5:25.3
1972	GailNealm (AUS) 5:02.97	Leslie Cliff (CAN) 5:03.57	Novella Calligaris (ITA) 5:03.99
1976	Ulrike Tauber (GDR) 4:42.77	Cheryl Gibson (CAN) 4:48.10	Becky Smith (CAN) 4:50.48

	Gold	Silver	Bronze
1980	Petra Schneider (GDR) 4:36.29	Sharron Davies (GBR) 4:46.83	Agnieszka Czopek (POL) 4:48.17
1984	Tracy Caulkins (USA) 4:39.24	Suzanne Landells (AUS) 4:48.30	Petra Zindler (FRG) 4:48.57
1988	Janet Evans (USA) 4:37.76	Noemi Ildiko Lung (ROM) 4:39.46	Daniela Hunger (GDR) 4:39.76
1992	Krysztina Egerszegi (HUN) 4:36.54	Li Lin (CHN) 4:36.73	Summer Sanders (USA) 4:37.58
1996	Michelle Smith (IRL) 4:39.18	Allison Wagner (USA) 4:42.03	Krysztina Egerszegi (HUN) 4:42.53
2000	Jana Klochkova (UKR) 4:33.59	Yasuko Tajima (JPN) 4:35.96	Beatrice Caslaru (ROM) 4:37.18

1896–1960 event not held

4 X 100 METRES FREESTYLE RELAY

	Gold	Silver	Bronze
1912	Great Britain 5:52.8	Germany 6:04.6	Austria 6:17.0
1920	United States 5:11.6	Great Britain 5:40.8	Sweden 5:43.6
1924	United States 4:58.8	Great Britain 5:17.0	Sweden 5:35.6
1928	United States 4:47.6	Great Britain 5:02.8	South Africa 5:13.4
1932	United States 4:38.0	The Netherlands 4:47.5	Great Britain 4:52.4
1936	The Netherlands 4:36.0	Germany 4:36.8	United States 4:40.2
1948	United States 4:29.2	Denmark 4:29.6	The Netherlands 4:31.6
1952	Hungary 4:24.4	The Netherlands 4:29.0	United States 4:30.1
1956	Australia 4:17.1	United States 4:19.2	South Africa 4:25.7
1960	United States 4:08.9	Australia 4:11.3	Germany 4:19.7
1964	United States 4:03.8	Australia 4:06.9	The Netherlands 4:12.0
1968	United States 4:02.5	GDR 4:05.7	Canada 4:07.2
1972	United States 3:55.19	GDR 3:55.55	FRG 3:57.93
1976	United States 3:44.82	GDR 3:45.50	Canada 3:48.81
1980	GDR 3:42.71	Sweden 3:48.93	The Netherlands 3:49.51
1984	United States 3:43.43	The Netherlands 3:44.40	FRG 3:45.56
1988	GDR 3:40.63	The Netherlands 3:43.39	United States 3:44.25
1992	United States 3:39.46	China 3:40.12	Germany 3:41.60
1996	United States 3:39.29	China 3:40.48	Germany 3:41.48
2000	United States 3:36.61	The Netherlands 3:39.83	Sweden 3:40.30

1896–1908 event not held

4 X 200 METRES FREESTYLE RELAY

	Gold	Silver	Bronze
1996	United States 7:59.87	Germany 8:01.55	Australia 8:05.47
2000	United States 7:57.80	Australia 7:58.52	Germany 7:58.64

1896–1992 event not held

4 X 100 METRES MEDLEY RELAY

	Gold	Silver	Bronze
1960	United States 4:41.1	Australia 4:45.9	Germany 4:47.6
1964	United States 4:33.9	The Netherlands 4:37.0	Soviet Union 4:39.2
1968	United States 4:28.3	Australia 4:30.0	FRG 4:36.4
1972	United States 4:20.75	GDR 4:24.91	FRG 4:26.46
1976	GDR 4:06.95	United States 4:14.55	Canada 4:15.22
1980	GDR 4:06.67	Great Britain 4:12.24	Soviet Union 4:13.61
1984	United States 4:08.34	FRG 4:11.97	Canada 4:12.98
1988	GDR 4:03.74	United States 4:07.90	Canada 4:10.49
1992	United States 4:02.54	Germany 4:05.19	Unified Team 4:06.44
1996	United States 4:02.88	Australia 4:05.08	China 4:07.34
2000	United States 3:58.30	Australia 4:01.59	Japan 4:04.16

1896–1956 event not held

DIVING MEDALS

WOMEN

SPRINGBOARD DIVING

	Gold	Silver	Bronze
1920	Aileen Riggin (USA) 539.9	Helen Wainwright (USA) 534.8	Thelma Payne (USA) 534.1

	Gold	Silver	Bronze
1924	Elizabeth Becker (USA) 474.5	Aileen Riggin (USA) 460.4	Caroline Fletcher (USA) 434.4
1928	Helen Meany (USA) 78.62	Dorothy Poynton (USA) 75.62	Georgia Coleman (USA) 73.78
1932	Georgia Coleman (USA) 87.52	Katherine Rawls (USA) 82.56	Jane Fauntz (USA) 82.12
1936	Majorie Gestring (USA) 89.27	Katherine Rawls (USA) 88.35	Dorothy Poynton-Hilm (USA) 82.36
1948	Victoria Draves (USA) 108.74	Zoe Ann Olsen (USA) 108.23	Patricia Elsener (USA) 101.30
1952	Patricia McCormick (USA) 147.30	Madeleine Moreau (FRA) 139.34	Zoe Ann Jensen (USA) 127.57
1956	Patricia McCormick (USA) 142.36	Jeanne Stunyo (USA) 125.89	Irene MacDonald (CAN) 121.40
1960	Ingrid Krämer (GER) 155.81	Paula Myers-Pope (USA) 141.24	Elizabeth Ferris (GBR) 139.09
1964	Ingrid Krämer-Engem (GER) 145.00	Jeanne Collier (USA) 138.36	Mary Willard (USA) 138.18
1968	Sue Gossick (USA) 150.77	Tamara Pogozheva (URS) 145.30	Keala O'Sullivan (USA) 145.23
1972	Micki King (USA) 450.03	Ulrika Knape (SWE) 434.19	Marina Janicke (GDR) 430.92
1976	Jennifer Chandler (USA) 506.19	Christa Kohler (GDR) 469.41	Cynthia McIngvale (USA) 466.83
1980	Irina Kalinina (URS) 725.910	Martina Proeber (GDR) 698.895	Karin Guthke (GDR 685.245
1984	Sylvie Bernier (CAN) 530.70	Kelly McCormick (USA) 527.46	Christina Seufert (USA) 517.62
1988	Gao Min (CHN) 580.23	Li Qing (CHN) 534.33	Kelly Anne McCormick (USA) 533.19
1992	Gao Min (CHN) 572.400pts	Irina Laschko (EUN) 514.140	Brita Baldus (GER) 503.070
1996	Fu Mingxia (CHN) 547.68	Irina Laschko (RUS) 512.19	Annie Pelletier (CAN) 509.64
2000	Fu Mingxia (CHN) 609.42	Jingjing Guo (CHN) 597.81	Dörte Lindner (GER) 574.35

1896–1912 event not held

SPRINGBOARD SYNCHRONISED (Introduced in 2000)

	Gold	Silver	Bronze
2000	China 345.12	Canada 312.03	Australia 301.50

PLATFORM DIVING

	Gold	Silver	Bronze
1912	Greta Johnson (SWE) 39.9	Lisa Regnelm (SWE) 36.0	Isabelle White (GBR) 34.0
1920	Stefani Fryland-Clausen (DEN) 34.6	Eileen Armstrong (GBR) 33.3	Eva Ollivier (SWE) 33.3
1924	Caroline Smith (USA) 10.5	Elizabeth Becker (USA) 11.0	Hjördis Töpem (SWE) 15.5
1928	Elizabeth Pinkston (USA) 31.6	Georgia Coleman (USA) 30.6	Lala Sjöqvist (SWE) 29.2
1932	Dorothy Poynton (USA) 40.26	Georgia Coleman (USA) 35.56	Marion Roper (USA) 35.22
1936	Dorothy Poynton-Hilm (USA) 33.93	Velma Dunn (USA) 33.63	Käthe Köhler (GER) 33.43
1948	Victoria Draves (USA) 68.87	Patricia Elsener (USA) 66.28	Birte Christoffersen (DEN) 66.04
1952	Patricia McCormick (USA) 79.37	Paula Myers (USA) 71.63	Juno Irwin (USA) 70.49
1956	Patricia McCormick (USA) 84.85	Juno Irwin (USA) 81.64	Paula Myers (USA) 81.58
1960	Ingrid Krämer (GER) 91.28	Paula Myers-Pope (USA) 88.94	Ninel Krutova (URS) 86.99
1964	Lesley Bush (USA) 99.80	Ingrid Krämer-Engem (GER) 98.45	Galina Alekseyeva (URS) 97.60
1968	Milena Duchkova (TCH) 109.59	Natalia Lobanova (URS) 105.14	Ann Peterson (USA) 101.11
1972	Ulrika Knape (SWE) 390.00	Milena Duchkova (TCH) 370.92	Marina Janicke (GDR) 360.54
1976	Elena Vaytsekhovskaya (URS) 406.59	Ulrika Knape (SWE) 402.60	Deborah Wilson (USA) 401.07
1980	Martina Jäschke (GDR) 596.250	Servard Emirzyan (URS) 576.465	Liana Tsotadze (URS) 575.925
1984	Zhou Jihong (CHN) 435.51	Michele Mitchelm (USA) 431.19	Wendy Wyland (USA) 422.07
1988	Xu Yanmei (CHN) 445.20	Michele Mitchelm (USA) 436.95	Wendy Williams (USA) 400.44
1992	Fu Mingxia (CHN) 461.430	Yelena Mirochina (EUN) 411.630	Mary Ellen Clark (USA) 401.910
1996	Fu Mingxia (CHN) 521.58	Annika Walter (GER) 429.22	Mary Ellen Clark (USA) 472.95
2000	Laura Wilkinson (USA)	Li Na (CHN) 542.01	Anne Montminy (CAN) 540.15

1896–1908 event not held

PLATFORM SYNCHRONISED (Introduced in 2000)

	Gold	Silver	Bronze
2000	Russia 332.64	China 321.60	Ukraine 290.34

SYNCHRONISED SWIMMING MEDALS

SOLO

	Gold	Silver	Bronze
1984	Tracie Ruiz (USA) 198.467	Carolyn Waldo (CAN) 195.300	Miwako Motoyoshi (JPN) 187.050
1988	Carolyn Waldo (CAN) 200.150	Tracie Ruiz-Conforto (USA) 197.633	Miwako Motoyoshi (JPN) 191.850
1992	Kristen Babb-Sprague (USA) 191.848	Fumiko Okuno (JPN) 187.056	Sylvia Frechette (CAN) 191.717*

1896–1980 and 1996–2000 event not held. * There was a controversial judging mixup and, belatedly, Frechette was promoted to joint gold medallist.

DUET

	Gold	Silver	Bronze
1984	United States 195.584	Canada 194.234	Japan 187.992
1988	Canada 197.717	United States 197.284	Japan 190.159
1992	United States 192.175	Canada 189.394	Japan 186.868
1996	United States 99.720	Canada 98.367	Japan 97.753
2000	Russia 99.580	Japan 98.650	France 97.437

1896–1980 event not held

TEAM

	Gold	Silver	Bronze
1996	United States 99.720	Canada 98.367	Japan 97.753
2000	Russia 99.146	Japan 98.860	Canada 97.357

1896–1992 event not held

DISCONTINUED SWIMMING EVENTS

100 METRES FREESTYLE (SAILORS)

	Gold	Silver	Bronze
1896	Ioannis Maloknis (GRE) 2:20.4	Spiridon Khasapis (GRE) n.t.a.	Dimitrios Drivas (GRE) n.t.a.

200 METRES OBSTACLE EVENT

1900	Frederick Lane (AUS) 2:38.4	Otto Wahle (AUT) 2:40.0	Peter Kemp (GBR) 2:47.4

400 METRES BREASTSTROKE

1904	Georg Zacharias (GER) 7:23.6	Walter Brack (GER) 20m	Jamison Hardy (USA) d.n.a.
1912	Walter Bathe (GER) 6:29.6	Thor Henning (SWE) 6:35.6	Percy Courtman (GBR) 6:36.4
1920	Hakan Malmroth (SWE) 6:31.8	Thor Henning (SWE) 6:45.2	Arvo Aaltonen (FIN) 6:48.0

880 YARDS FREESTYLE

1904	Emil Rausch (GER) 13:11.4	Francis Gailey (USA) 13:23.4	Géza Kiss (HUN) n.t.a.

4000 METRES FREESTYLE

1900	John Jarvis (GBR) 58:24.0	Zoltán Halmay (HUN) 1:08:55.4	Louis Martin (FRA) 1:13.08.4

UNDERWATER SWIMMING

1900	Charles de Vendeville (FRA) 188.4	André Six (FRA) 185.4	Peder Lykkeberg (DEN) 147.0

PLUNGE FOR DISTANCE

1904	Paul Dickey (USA) 19.05m	Edgar Adams (USA) 17.53m	Leo Goodwin (USA) 17.37m

200 METRES TEAM SWIMMING

1900	Germany 32pts	France 51	France 61

4 X 50 YARDS RELAY

1904	United States (New York AC) 2:04.6	United States (Chicago AC) n.t.a.	United States (Missouri AC) . n.t.a

PLAIN HIGH DIVING

1912	Erik Adlerz (SWE) 40.0	Hjalmar Johansson (SWE) 39.3	John Jansson (SWE) 39.1
1920	Arvid Wallmann (SWE) 183.5	Nils Skoglund (SWE) 183.0	John Jansson (SWE) 175.0
1924	Richmond Eve (AUS) 160.0	John Jansson (SWE) 157.0	Harold Clarke (GBR) 158.0

WATER POLO MEDALS

MEN

	Gold	Silver	Bronze
1900*	Great Britain	Belgium	France
1904*	United States	United States	United States
1908	Great Britain	Belgium	Sweden
1912	Great Britain	Sweden	Belgium
1920	Great Britain	Belgium	Sweden
1924	France	Belgium	United States
1928	Germany	Hungary	France
1932	Hungary	Germany	United States
1936	Hungary	Germany	Belgium
1948	Italy	Hungary	The Netherlands
1952	Hungary	Yugoslavia	Italy
1956	Hungary	Yugoslavia	Soviet Union
1960	Italy	Soviet Union	Hungary
1964	Hungary	Yugoslavia	Soviet Union
1968	Yugoslavia	Soviet Union	Hungary
1972	Soviet Union	Hungary	United States
1976	Hungary	Italy	The Netherlands
1980	Soviet Union	Yugoslavia	Hungary
1984	Yugoslavia	United States	FRG
1988	Yugoslavia	United States	Soviet Union
1992	Italy	Spain	Unified Team
1996	Spain	Croatia	Italy
2000	Hungary	Russia	Yugoslavia

1896–1906 event not held. * Entries were from clubs only, not International teams.

WOMEN (Introduced in 2000)

	Gold	Silver	Bronze
2000	Australia	United States	Russia

TABLE TENNIS MEDALS (Introduced in 1988)

MEN'S SINGLES

	Gold	Silver	Bronze
1988	Yoo Nam-Kyu (KOR)	Kim Ki-Taik (KOR)	Erik Lindh (SWE)
1992	Jan-Ove Waldner (SWE)	Jean-Philippe Gatien (FRA)	Ma Wenge (CHN)
			Kim Taek-Soo (KOR)
1996	Liu Guoliang (CHN)	Wang Tao (CHN)	Jörg Rosskoff (GER)
2000	Linghui Kong (CHN)	Jan-Ove Waldner (SWE)	Guoliang Liu (CHN)

MEN'S DOUBLES

	Gold	Silver	Bronze
1988	China	Yugoslavia	Korea
1992	China	Germany	Korea
			Korea
1996	China	China	Korea
2000	China	China	France

WOMEN'S SINGLES

	Gold	Silver	Bronze
1988	Chen Jing (CHN)	Li Huifen (CHN)	Jiao Zhimin (CHN)
1992	Deng Yaping (CHN)	Qiao Hong (CHN)	Hyung Jung-Hwa (KOR)
			Li Bun-Hui (PRK)
1996	Deng Yaping (CHN)	Jing Chen (TPE)	Qiao Hong (CHN)
2000	Nan Wang (CHN)	Ju Li (CHN)	Jing Chen (TPE)

WOMEN'S DOUBLES

	Gold	Silver	Bronze
			Bronze
1988	Korea	China	Yugoslavia
1992	China	China	Korea
			PRK
1996	China	China	Korea
2000	China	China	Korea

TAE KWON DO MEDALS (Introduced in 2000)

MEN
UP TO 58KG 2000

Gold	Silver	Bronze
Michail Mouroutsos (GRE)	Gabriel Esparza (ESP)	Chi-Hsiung Huang (TPE)

UP TO 68KG

	Gold	Silver	Bronze
2000	Steven Lopez (USA)	Joon-Sik Sin (KOR)	Hadi Saeibonehkohal (IRI)

UP TO 80KG

	Gold	Silver	Bronze
2000	Angel Fuentes (CUB)	Faissal Ebnoutalib (GER)	Victor Garibay (MEX)

OVER 80KG

	Gold	Silver	Bronze
2000	Kyong-Hun Kim (KOR)	Daniel Trenton (AUS)	Pascal Gentil (FRA)

WOMEN
UP TO 49KG

	Gold	Silver	Bronze
2000	Lauren Burns (AUS)	Urdia Rodriguez (CUB)	Shu-Ju Chi (TPE)

UP TO 57KG

	Gold	Silver	Bronze
2000	Jae-Eun Jung (KOR)	Hieu Ngan Tran (VIE)	Hamide Bikcin (TUR)

UP TO 67KG

	Gold	Silver	Bronze
2000	Sun-Hee Lee (KOR)	Trude Gunderesen (NOR)	Yoriko Okamoto (JPN)

OVER 67KG

	Gold	Silver	Bronze
2000	Zhong Cheng (CHN)	Natalya Ivanova (RUS)	Dominique Bosshart (CAN)

TENNIS MEDALS

MEN'S SINGLES

	Gold	Silver	Bronze
1896*	John Boland (GBR)	Dionysios Kasdaglis (GRE)	Momcilló Tapavica (HUN)
			Konstantinos Paspatis (GRE)
1900*	Hugh Doherty (GBR)	Harold Mahoney (GBR)	Reginald Doherty (GBR)
			Arthur Norris (GBR)
1904*	Beals Wright (USA)	Robert LeRoy (USA)	Edgar Leonard (USA)
			Alphonzo Belm (USA)
1906	Max Décugis (FRA)	Maurice Germot (FRA)	Zdenek Zemla (BOH)
1908	Josiah Ritchie (GBR)	Otto Froitzheim (GER)	Wilberforce Eves (GBR)
1908†	Wentworth Gore (GBR)	George Caridia (GBR)	Josiah Ritchie (GBR)
1912	Charles Winslow (RSA)	Harold Kitson (RSA)	Oscar Kreuzer (GER)
1912†	André Gobert (FRA)	Charles Dixon (GBR)	Anthony Wilding (NZL)
1920	Louis Raymond (RSA)	Ichiya Kumagae (JPN)	Charles Winslow (GBR)
1924	Vincent Reynolds (USA)	Henri Cochet (FRA)	Umberto De Morpurgo (ITA)
1988*	Miloslav Mecir (TCH)	Tim Mayotte (USA)	Stefan Edberg (SWE)
			Brad Gilbert (USA)
1992*	Marc Rosset (SUI)	Jordi Arrese (ESP)	Goran Ivanisevic (CRO)
			Andrei Cherkasov (EUN)
1996	Andre Agassi (USA)	Sergi Bruguera (ESP)	Leander Paes (IND)
2000	Yevgeni Kafelnikov (RUS)	Thomas Haas (GER)	Arnaud di Pasquale (FRA)

1928–84 event not held. * Two bronze medals. † Indoor tournaments.

MEN'S DOUBLES

	Gold	Silver	Bronze
1896	GBR/Germany	Greece	Great Britain/Australia
1900*	Great Britain	United States/France	France
			Great Britain
1904*	United States	United States	United States
			United States
1906	France	Greece	Bohemia
1908	Great Britain	Great Britain	Great Britain
1908†	Great Britain	Great Britain	Sweden
1912	South Africa	Austria	France
1912†	France	Sweden	Great Britain
1920	Great Britain	Japan	France
1924	United States	France	France
1988*	United States	Spain	Czechoslovakia
			Sweden
1992*	Germany	South Africa	Croatia
			Argentina
1996	Australia	Great Britain	Germany
2000	Canada	Australia	Spain

1928–84 event not held. * Two bronze medals. † Indoor tournaments.

MIXED DOUBLES

	Gold	Silver	Bronze
1900*	Great Britain	France/GBR	Bohemia/GBR
			United States/GBR
1906	France	Greece	Greece
1912	Germany	Sweden	France
1912†	Great Britain	Great Britain	Sweden
1920	France	Great Britain	Czechoslovakia
1924	United States	United States	The Netherlands

1928–2000 event not held. * Two bronze medals. † Indoor tournaments.

WOMEN'S SINGLES

	Gold	Silver	Bronze
1900*	Charlotte Cooper (GBR)	Hélène Prévost (FRA)	Marion Jones (USA)
			Hedwiga Rosenbaumova (BOH)
1906	Esmee Simiriotou (GRE)	Sophia Marinou (GRE)	Euphrosine Paspati (GRE)
1908	Dorothea Chambers (GBR)	Dorothy Boothby (GBR)	Joan Winch (GBR)
1908†	Gwen Eastlake-Smith (GBR)	Angela Greene (GBR)	Märtha Adlerstrahle (SWE)
1912	Marguerite Broquedis (FRA)	Dora Köring (GER)	Molla Bjurstedt (NOR)
1912†	Ethel Hannam (GBR)	Thora Castenschoid (DEN)	Mabel Parton (GBR)
1920	Suzanne Lenglen (FRA)	Dorothy Holman (GBR)	Kitty McKane (GBR)
1924	Helen Wills (USA)	Julie Vlasto (FRA)	Kitty McKane (GBR)
1988*	Steffi Graf (FRG)	Gabriela Sabatini (ARG)	Zina Garrison (USA)
			Manuela Maleyeva (BUL)
1992*	Jennifer Capriati (USA)	Steffi Graf (GER)	Mary-Jo Fernandez (USA)
			Arantxa Sanchez-Vicario (ESP)
1996	Lindsay Davenport (USA)	Arantxa Sanchez-Vicario (ESP)	Jana Novotna (CZE)
2000	Venus Williams (USA)	Yelena Dementyeva (RUS)	Monica Seles (USA)

1928–84 event not held. * Two bronze medals. † Indoor tournaments.

WOMEN'S DOUBLES

	Gold	Silver	Bronze
1920	Great Britain	Great Britain	France
1924	United States	Great Britain	Great Britain
1988*	United States	Czechoslovakia	Australia
			FRG
1992*	United States	Spain	Australia
			Unified Team
1996	United States	Czech Republic	Spain
2000	United States	The Netherlands	Belgium

1928–84 event not held. * Two bronze medals.

TRAMPOLINING MEDALS (Introduced in 2000 as part of the Gymnastics programme)

MEN

	Gold	Silver	Bronze
2000	Aleksandr Moskalenko (RUS) 41.70	Ji Wallace (AUS) 39.30	Mathieu Turgeon (CAN) 39.10

WOMEN

	Gold	Silver	Bronze
2000	Irina Karavayeva (RUS) 38.90	Oxana Tsyhuleva (UKR) 37.70	Karen Cockburn (CAN) 37.40

TRIATHLON MEDALS (Introduced in 2000; consisting of a 1500m swim, 40km cycle and 10km run)

MEN

	Gold	Silver	Bronze
2000	Simon Whitfield (CAN) 1:48.24	Stephan Vuckovic (GER) 1:48.37	Jan Rehula (CZE) 1:48.46

WOMEN

	Gold	Silver	Bronze
2000	Brigitte McMahon (SUI) 2:00.40	Michellie Jones (AUS) 2:00.42	Magali Messmer (SUI) 2:01.08

VOLLEYBALL MEDALS

MEN

	Gold	Silver	Bronze
1964	Soviet Union	Czechoslovakia	Japan
1968	Soviet Union	Japan	Czechoslovakia
1972	Japan	GDR	Soviet Union
1976	Poland	Soviet Union	Cuba
1980	Soviet Union	Bulgaria	Romania
1984	United States	Brazil	Italy
1988	United States	Soviet Union	Argentina
1992	Brazil	The Netherlands	United States
1996	The Netherlands	Italy	Yugoslavia
2000	Yugoslavia	Russia	Italy

896–1960 event not held

WOMEN

	Gold	Silver	Bronze
1964	Japan	Soviet Union	Poland
1968	Soviet Union	Japan	Poland
1972	Soviet Union	Japan	North Korea
1976	Japan	Soviet Union	South Korea
1980	Soviet Union	GDR	Bulgaria
1984	China	United States	Japan
1988	Soviet Union	Peru	China
1992	Cuba	Unified Team	United States
1996	Cuba	China	Brazil
2000	Cuba	Russia	Brazil

1896–1960 event not held

WEIGHTLIFTING MEDALS

MEN

FLYWEIGHT (Up to 52kg 1972–92; up to 54kg 1996)

	Gold	Silver	Bronze
1972	Zygmunt Smalcerz (POL) 337.5kg	Sándor Holczreitzer (HUN) 330kg	Sándor Holczreitzer (HUN) 327.5kg

	Gold	Silver	Bronze
1976	Aleksandr Voronin (URS) 242.5kg	György Köszegi (HUN) 237.5kg	Mohammad Nassiri (IRI) 235kg
1980	Kanybek Osmonoliev (URS) 245kg	Bong Chol Ho (PRK) 245kg	Gyond Si Han (PRK) 245kg
1984	Zeng Guoqiang (CHN) 235kg	Zhou Peishujn (CHN) 235kg	Kazushito Manabe (JPN) 232.5kg
1988	Sevdalin Marinov (BUL) 270kg	Chun Byung-Kwan (KOR) 260kg	He Zhuogiang (CHN) 257.5kg
1992	Ivan Ivanov (BUL) 265kg	Lin Qisheng (CHN) 262.5kg	Traian Ciharean (ROM) 252.5kg
1996	Halil Mutlu (TUR) 287.5kg	Zhang Xiangsen (CHN) 280.0kg	Sevdalin Minchev (BUL) 277.5kg

1896–1968 and 2000 event not held

BANTAMWEIGHT (Up to 56kg 1948–92; up to 59kg 1996; up to 56kg 2000)

	Gold	Silver	Bronze
1948	Joseph de Pietro (USA) 307.5kg	Julian Creus (GBR) 297.5kg	Richard Tom (GBR) 295kg
1952	Ivan Udolov (URS) 315kg	Mahmoud Namdjou (IRI) 307.5kg	Ali Mirzai (IRI) 300kg
1956	Charles Vinci (USA) 342.5kg	Vladimir Stogov (URS) 337.5kg	Mahmoud Namdjou (IRI) 332.5kg
1960	Charles Vinci (USA) 345kg	Yoshinobu Miyake (JPN) 337.5kg	Esmail Khan (IRI) 330kg
1964	Alexei Vakhonin (URS) 357.5kg	Imre Földi (HUN) 355kg	Shiro Ichinoseki (JPN) 347.5kg
1968	Mohammed Nassiri (IRI) 367.5k	Imre Földi (HUN) 367.5kg	Henryk Trebicki (POL) 357.5kg
1972	Imre Földi (HUN) 377.5kg	Mohammed Nassiri (IRI) 370kg	Gennadi Chetin (URS) 367.5kg
1976	Norair Nurikyan (BUL) 262.5kg	Grzegorz Cziura (POL) 252.5kg	Kenkichi Ando (JPN) 250kg
1980	Daniel Nunez (CUB) 275kg	Yurik Sarkasian (URS) 270kg	Tadeusz Demboncyzk (POL) 265kg
1984	Wu Shude (CHN) 267.5kg	Lai Runming (CHN) 265kg	Masahiro Kotaka (JPN) 252.5kg
1988	Oksen Mirzoyan (URS) 292.5kg*	He Yingqiang (CHN) 287.5kg	Liu Shoubin (CHN) 267.5kg
1992	Chun Byung-kwan (KOR) 287.5kg	Liu Shoubin (CHN) 277.5kg	Luo Jianming (CHN)
1996	Tang Ningsheng (CHN) 307.5kg	Leonidas Sabanis (GRE) 305.0kg	Nikolay Pechalov (BUL) 302.5kg
2000	Halil Mutlu (TUR) 305kg	Wu Wenxiong (CHN) 287.5kg†	Zhang Xiangxiang (CHN) 287.5kg

1896–1936 event not held. * Mitko Grablev (BUL) finished in first place with 297.5kg but subsequently disqualified. † Ivan Ivanov (BUL) finished in second place with 292.5kg but was subsequently disqualified.

FEATHERWEIGHT (Up to 60kg 1920–92; up to 64kg 1996; up to 62kg 2000)

	Gold	Silver	Bronze
1920	Frans de Haes (BEL) 220kg	Alfred Schmidt (EST) 212.5kg	Eugène Ryther (SUI) 210kg
1924*	Pierino Gabetti (ITA) 402.5kg	Andreas Stadler (AUT) 385kg	Arthur Reinmann (SUI) 382.5kg
1928	Franz Andrysek (AUT) 287.5kg	Pierino Gabetti (ITA) 282.5kg	Hans Wölpert (GER) 282.5kg
1932	Raymond Suvigny (FRA) 287.5kg	Hans Wölpert (GER) 282.5kg	Anthony Terlazzo (USA) 280kg
1936	Anthony Terlazzo (USA) 312.5kg	Saleh Mohammed Soliman (EGY) 305kg	Ibrahim Shams (EGY) 300kg
1948	Mahmoud Fayad (EGY) 332.5kg	Rodney Wilkes (TRI) 317.5kg	Jaffar Salmassi (IRI) 312.5kg
1952	Rafael Chimishkyan (URS) 337.5kg	Nikolai Saksonov (URS) 332.5kg	Rodney Wilkes (TRI) 332.5kg
1956	Isaac Berger (USA) 352.5kg	Yevgeni Minayev (URS) 342.5kg	Marian Zielinski (POL) 335kg
1960	Yevgeni Minayev (URS) 372.5kg	Isaac Berger (USA) 362.5kg	Sebastiano Mannironi (ITA) 352.5kg
1964	Yoshinobu Miyake (JPN) 397.5kg	Isaac Berger (USA) 382.5kg	Mieczyslaw Nowak (POL) 377.5kg
1968	Yoshinobu Miyake (JPN) 392.5kg	Dito Shanidze (URS) 387.5kg	Yoshiyuki Miyake (JPN) 385kg
1972	Norair Nurikyan (BUL) 402.5kg	Dito Shanidze (URS) 400kg	Janos Benedek (HUN) 390kg
1976	Nikolai Kolesnikov (URS) 285kg	Georgi Todorov (BUL) 280kg	Kuzumasa Hirai (JPN) 275kg
1980	Viktor Mazin (URS) 290kg	Stefan Dimitrov (BUL) 287.5kg	Marek Seweryn (POL) 282.5kg
1984	Chen Weiqiang (CHN) 282.5kg	Gelu Radu (ROM) 280kg	Tsai Wen-Yee (TPE) 272.5kg
1988	Naim Suleymanoglu (TUR) 342.5kg	Stefan Topourov (BUL) 312.5kg	Ye Huanming (CHN) 287.5kg
1992	Naim Suleymanoglu (TUR) 320kg	Nikolai Peshalov (BUL) 305kg	He Yingqiang (CHN) 295kg
1996	Naim Suleymanoglu (TUR) 357.5kg	Valerios Leonidis (GRE) 332.5kg	Jiangang Xiao (CHN) 322.5kg
2000	Nikolay Pechalov (CRO) 325kg	Leonidis Sabanis (GRE) 317.5kg	Gennadi Oleschuk (BLR) 317.5kg

1896–1912 event not held. * Aggregate of five lifts.

LIGHTWEIGHT (Up to 67.5kg 1920–92; up to 70kg 1996; up to 69kg 2000)

	Gold	Silver	Bronze
1920	Alfred Neuland (EST) 257.5kg	Louis Williquet (BEL) 240kg	Florimond Rooms (BEL) 230kg
1924*	Edmond Décottignies (FRA) 440kg	Anton Zwerina (AUT) 427.5kg	Bohumil Durdis (TCH) 425kg
1928†	Kurt Helbig (GER) 322.5kg Hans Haas (AUT) 322.5kg	—	Fernand Arnout (FRA) 302.5kg
1932	René Duverger (FRA) 325kg	Hans Haas (AUT) 307.5kg	Gastone Pierini (ITA) 302.5kg
1936†	Anwar Mohammed Mesbah (EGY) 342.5kg Robert Fein (AUT) 342.5kg	—	Karl Jensen (GER) 327.5kg
1948	Ibrahim Shams (EGY) 360kg	Attia Hamouda (EGY) 360kg	James Halliday (GBR) 340kg
1952	Tommy Kono (USA) 362.5kg	Yevgeni Lopatin (URS) 350kg	Verne Barberis (AUS) 350kg
1956	Igor Rybak (URS) 380kg	Ravil Khabutdinov (URS) 372.5kg	Chang-Hee Kim (KOR) 370kg
1960	Viktor Bushuyev (URS) 397.5kg	Howe-Liang Tan (SIN) 380kg	Abdul Wahid Aziz (IRQ) 380kg
1964	Waldemar Baszanowksi (POL) 432.5kg	Vladimir Kaplunov (URS) 432.5kg	Marian Zielinski (POL) 420kg
1968	Waldemar Baszanowski (POL) 437.5kg	Parviz Jalayer (IRI) 422.5kg	Marian Zielinski (POL) 420kg
1972	Mukharbi Kirzhinov (URS) 460kg	Mladen Koutchev (BUL) 450kg	Zbigniev Kaczmarek (POL) 437.5kg
1976‡	Pyotr Korol (URS) 305kg	Daniel Senet (FRA) 300kg	Kazimierz Czarnecki (POL) 295kg
1980	Yanko Rusev (BUL) 342.5kg	Joachim Kunz (GDR) 335kg	Mintcho Pachov (BUL) 325kg
1984	Yao Jingyuan (CHN) 320kg	Andrei Socaci (ROM) 312.5kg	Journi Gronman (FIN) 312.5kg
1988	Joachim Kunz (GDR) 340kg	Israil Militossian (URS) 337.5kg	Li Jinhe (CHN) 325kg
1992	Israil Militossian (EUN) 337.5kg	Yoto Yotov (BUL) 327.5kg	Andreas Behm (GER) 320kg
1996	Zhan Xugang (CHN) 357.5kg	Kim Myong-Nam (PRK) 345.0kg	Attila Feri (HUN) 340.0kg
2000	Galabin Bojevski (BUL) 357.5kg	Georgi Markov (BUL) 352.5kg	Sergei Lavrenov (BLR) 340kg

1896–1912 event not held. * Aggregate of five lifts. † Tie-breaker rule relating to bodyweight not yet introduced. ‡ Zbigniew Kaczmarek (POL) finished in first place with 307.5kg but was subsequently disqualified.

MIDDLEWEIGHT (Up to 75kg 1920–92; up to 76kg 1996; up to 77kg 2000)

	Gold	Silver	Bronze
1920	Henri Gance (FRA) 245kg	Pietro Bianchi* (ITA) 237.5kg	Albert Pettersson (SWE) 237.5kg
1924†	Carlo Galimberti (ITA) 492.5kg	Alfred Neuland (EST) 455kg	Jaan Kikas (EST) 450kg
1928	Roger Francois (FRA) 335kg	Carlo Galimberti (ITA) 332.5kg	August Scheffer (NED) 327.5kg
1932	Rudolf Ismayr (GER) 345kg	Carlo Galimberti (ITA) 340kg	Karl Hipfinger (AUT) 337.5kg
1936	Khadr El Thouni (EGY) 387.5kg	Rudolf Ismayr (GER) 352.5kg	Adolf Wagner (GER) 352.5kg
1948	Frank Spellman (USA) 390kg	Peter George (USA) 412.5kg	Sung-Jip Kim (KOR) 380kg
1952	Peter George (USA) 400kg	Gérard Gratton (CAN) 390kg	Sung-Jip Kim (KOR) 382.5kg
1956	Fyodor Bogdanovski (URS) 420kg	Peter George (USA) 412.5kg	Ermanno Pignatti (ITA) 382.5kg
1960	Aleksandr Kurinov (URS) 437.5kg	Tommy Kono (USA) 427.5kg	Gyözö Veres (HUN) 405kg
1964	Hans Zdrazila (TCH) 445kg	Viktor Kurentsov (URS) 440kg	Masashi Ouchi (JPN) 437.5kg
1968	Viktor Kurentsov (URS) 475kg	Masashi Ouchi (JPN) 455kg	Károly Bakos (HUN) 440kg
1972	Yordan Bikov (BUL) 485kg	Mohamed Trabulsi (LIB) 472.5kg	Anselmo Silvino (ITA) 470kg
1976	Yordan Bikov (BUL) 335kg	Vartan Militosyan (URS) 330kg	Peter Wenzem (GDR) 327.5kg
1980	Asen Zlatev (BUL) 360kg	Aleksandr Pervy (URS) 357.5kg	Nedeltcho Kolev (BUL) 345kg
1984	Karl-Heinz Radschinsky (FRG) 340kg	Jaques Demers (CAN) 335kg	Dragomir Cioroslan (ROM) 332.5kg
1988	Borislav Guidikov (BUL) 375kg	Ingo Steinhöfem (GDR) 360kg	Alexander Varbanov (BUL) 357.5kg
1992	Fedor Kassapu (EUN) 357.5kg	Pablo Lara (CUB) 357.5kg	Kim Myong-nam (PRK) 352.5kg
1996	Pablo Lara (CUB) 367.5kg	Yoto Yotov (BUL) 360.0kg	Jon Chol-Ho (PRK) 357.5kg
2000	Zhan Xugang (CHN) 367.5kg	Viktor Mitrou (GRE) 367.5kg	Arsen Melikyan (ARM) 365kg

1896–1912 event not held. * Bianchi and Pettersson drew lots for the silver medal. † Aggregate of five lifts.

LIGHT HEAVYWEIGHT (Up to 82.5kg 1920–92; up to 83kg 1996; up to 85kg 2000)

	Gold	Silver	Bronze
1920	Ernest Cadine (FRA) 290kg	Fritz Hünenberger (SUI) 275kg	Erik Pettersson (SWE) 272.5kg
1924*	Charles Rigoulot (FRA) 502.5kg	Fritz Hünenberger (SUI) 490kg	Leopold Friedrich (AUT) 490kg
1928	Said Nosseir (EGY) 355kg	Louis Hostin (FRA) 352.5kg	Johannes Verheijen (NED) 337.5kg

	Gold	Silver	Bronze
1932	Louis Hostin (FRA) 372.5kg	Svend Olsen (DEN) 360kg	Henry Duey (USA) 330kg
1936	Louis Hostin (FRA) 372.5kg	Eugen Deutsch (GER) 365kg	Ibrahim Wasif (EGY) 360kg
1948	Stanley Stanczyk (USA) 417.5kg	Harold Sakata (USA) 380kg	Gösta Magnussen (SWE) 375kg
1952	Trofim Lomakin (URS) 417.5kg	Stanley Stanczyk (USA) 415kg	Arkadi Vorobyev (URS) 407.5kg
1956	Tommy Kono (USA) 447.5kg	Vassili Stepanov (URS) 427.5kg	James George (USA) 417.5kg
1960	Ireneusz Palinski (POL) 442.5kg	James George (USA) 430kg	Jan Bochenek (POL) 420kg
1964	Rudolf Plukfelder (URS) 475kg	Géza Tóth (HUN) 467.5kg	Gyözö Veres (HUN) 467.5kg
1968	Boris Selitsky (URS) 485kg	Vladimir Belyayev (URS) 485kg	Norbert Ozimek (POL) 472.5kg
1972	Leif Jenssen (NOR) 507.5kg	Norbert Ozimek (POL) 497.5kg	György Horváth (HUN) 495kg
1976†	Valeriy Shary (URS) 365kg	Trendachil Stoichev (BUL) 360kg	Peter Baczako (HUN) 345kg
1980	Yurik Vardanyan (URS) 400kg	Blagoi Blagoyev (BUL) 372.5kg	Dusan Poliacik (TCH) 367.5kg
1984	Petre Becheru (ROM) 355kg	Robert Kabbas (AUS) 342.5kg	Ryoji Isaoka (JPN) 340kg
1988	Israil Arsamokov (URS) 377.5kg	István Messzi (HUN) 370kg	Lee Hyung-Kun (KOR) 367.5kg
1992	Pyrros Dimas (GRE) 370kg	Krzysztof Siemion (POL) 370kg	—‡
1996	Pyrros Dimas (GRE) 392.5kg	Marc Huster (GER) 382.5kg	Andrzej Cofalik (POL) 372.5kg
2000	Pyrros Dimas (GRE) 390kg	Marc Huster (GER) 390kg	George Asanidze (GEO) 390kg

1896–1912 event not held. *Aggregate of five lifts. † Blagoi Blagoyev (BUL) finished in second place with 362.5kg but was subsequently disqualified. ‡ Ibrahim Samadov (EUN) placed third but was subsequently disqualified. No bronze medal was awarded.

MIDDLE HEAVYWEIGHT (Up to 90kg 1952–92; up to 91kg 1996; up to 94kg 2000)

	Gold	Silver	Bronze
1952	Norbert Schemansky (USA) 445kg	Grigori Nowak (URS) 410kg	Lennox Kilgour (TRI) 402.5kg
1956	Arkadi Vorobyev (URS) 462.5kg	David Sheppard (USA) 442.5kg	Jean Debuf (FRA) 425kg
1960	Arkadi Vorobyev (URS) 472.5kg	Trofim Lomakin (URS) 457.5kg	Louis Martin (GBR) 445kg
1964	Vladimir Golovanov (URS) 487.5kg	Louis Martin (GBR) 475kg	Ireneusz Palinski (POL) 467.5kg
1968	Kaarlo Kanganiemi (FIN) 517.5kg	Jan Talts (URS) 507.5kg	Marek Golab (POL) 495kg
1972	Andon Nikolov (BUL) 525kg	Atanas Chopov (BUL) 517.5kg	Hans Bettembourg (SWE) 512.5kg
1976	David Rigert (URS) 382.5kg	Lee James (USA) 362.5kg	Atanas Chopov (BUL) 360kg
1980	Péter Baczakó (HUN) 377.5kg	Rumen Alexandrov (BUL) 375kg	Frank Mantek (GDR) 375kg
1984	Nicu Vlad (ROM) 392.5kg	Dumitru Petre (ROM) 360kg	David Mercer (GBR) 352.5kg
1988	Anatoli Khrapati (URS) 412.5kg	Nail Moukhamediarov (URS) 400kg	Slawomir Zawada (POL) 400kg
1992	Kakhi Kakhiashvili (EUN) 412.5kg	Sergei Syrtsov (EUN) 412.5kg	Serguisz Wolczaniecki (POL) 392.5kg
1996	Alexei Petrov (RUS) 402.5kg	Leonidas Kokas (GRE) 390.0kg	Oliver Caruso (GER) 390.0kg
2000	Akakios Kakiasvilis (GRE) 405kg*	Szymon Kolecki (POL) 405kg	Serguisz Wolczaniecki (POL) 402.5kg

1896–1948 event not held. * Same person as the 1992 winner.

HEAVYWEIGHT (Over 82.5kg 1920–48; over 90kg 1952–68; up to 110kg 1972–92; up to 108kg 1996; up to 105kg 2000)

	Gold	Silver	Bronze
1896*	Launceston Eliot (GBR) 71kg	Viggo Jensen (DEN) 57.2kg	Alexandros Nikolopoulos (GRE) 57.2kg
1896†	Viggo Jensen (DEN) 111.5kg	Launceston Eliot (GBR) 111.5kg	Sotirios Versis (GRE) 90kg
1904‡	Oscar Osthoff (USA) 48pts	Frederick Winters (USA) 45pts	Frank Kungler (USA) 10pts
1904‡	Perikles Kaklousis (GRE) 111.5kg	Oscar Osthoff (USA) 84.36kg	Frank Kungler (USA) 79.83kg
1906*	Josef Steinbach (AUT) 76.55kg	Tullio Camilotti (ITA) 73.75kg	Heinrich Schneidereit (GER) 70.75kg
1906†	Dimitrios Tofalos (GRE) 142.5kg	Josef Steinbach (AUT) 136.5kg	Alexandre Maspoli (FRA) 129.5kg Heinrich Rondm (GER) 129.5kg Heinrich Schneidereit (GER) 129.5kg
1920	Filippo Bottino (ITA) 270kg	Joseph Alzin (LUX) 225kg	Louis Bernot (FRA) 250kg
1924§	Giuseppe Tonani (ITA) 517.5kg	Franz Aigner (AUT) 515kg	Harald Tammer (EST) 497.5kg
1928	Josef Strassberger (GER) 372.5kg	Arnold Luhaäär (EST) 360kg	Jaroslav Skobla (TCH) 375.5kg
1932	Jaroslav Skobla (TCH) 380kg	Václav Psenicka (TCH) 377.5kg	Josef Strassberger (GER) 377.5kg
1936	Josef Manger (GER) 410kg	Václav Psenicka (TCH) 402.5kg	Arnold Luhaäär (EST) 400kg

	Gold	Silver	Bronze
1948	John Davis (USA) 452.2kg	Norbert Schemansky (USA) 425kg	Abraham Charité (NED) 412.5kg
1952	John Davis (USA) 460kg	James Bradford (USA) 437.5kg	Humberto Selvetti (ARG) 432.5kg
1956	Paul Anderson (USA) 500kg	Humberto Selvetti (ARG) 500kg	Alberto Pigaiani (ITA) 452.5kg
1960	Yuriy Vlasov (URS) 537.5k	James Bradford (USA) 512.5kg	Norbert Schemansky (USA) 500kg
1964	Leonid Zhabotinsky (URS) 572.5kg	Yuri Vlasov (URS) 570kg	Norbert Schemansky (USA) 537.5kg
1968	Leonid Zhabotinsky (URS) 572.5kg	Serge Reding (BEL) 555kg	Joseph Dube (USA) 555kg
1972	Jan Talts (URS) 580kg	Alexandre Kraitchev (BUL) 562.5kg	Stefan Grützner (GDR) 555kg
1976Œ	Yuri Zaitsev (URS) 385kg	Krastio Semerdiev (BUL) 385kg	Tadeusz Rutkowski (POL) 377.5kg
1980	Leonid Taranenko (URS) 422.5kg	Valentin Christov (BUL) 385kg	György Szalai (HUN) 390kg
1984	Norberto Oberburger (ITA) 390kg	Stefan Tasnadi (ROM) 380kg	Guy Carlton (USA) 377.5kg
1988	Yuriy Zakharevich (URS) 455kg	József Jacsó (HUN) 427.5kg	Ronny Weller (GDR) 425kg
1992	Ronny Weller (GER) 432.5kg	Artur Akoyev (EUN) 430kg	Stefan Botev (BUL) 417.5kg
1996	Timur Taimazov (UKR) 430.0kg	Sergei Syrtsov (RUS) 420.0kg	Nicu Vlad (ROM) 420.0kg
2000	Hossain Tavakoli (IRI) 425kg	Alan Tsagayev (BUL) 422.5kg	Said Saif Asaad (QAT) 420kg

1900 and 1908–12 event not held. * One-hand lift. † Two-hand lift. ‡ Dumbbell lift. § An aggregate of five lifts. ŒValentin Christov (BUL) finished in first place with 400kg but was subsequently disqualified.

SUPER-HEAVYWEIGHT (Over 110kg 1972–92; over 108kg 1996; over 105kg 2000)

	Gold	Silver	Bronze
1972	Vasili Alexeyev (URS) 640kg	Rudolf Mang (FRG) 610kg	Gerd Bonk (GDR) 572.5kg
1976	Vasili Alexeyev (URS) 440kg	Gerd Bonk (GDR) 405kg	Helmut Losch (GDR) 387.5kg
1980	Sultan Rakhmanov (URS) 440kg	Jürgen Heuser (GDR) 410kg	Tadeusz Rutkowski (POL) 407.5kg
1984	Dinko Lukin (AUS) 412.5kg	Mario Martinez (USA) 410kg	Manfred Nerlinger (FRG) 397.5kg
1988	Aleksandr Kurlovich (URS) 462.5kg	Manfred Nerlinger (FRG) 430kg	Martin Zawieja (FRG) 415kg
1992	Alexander Kurlovich (EUN) 450kg	Leonid Taranenko (EUN) 425kg	Manfred Nerlinger (GER) 412.5kg
1996	Andrei Chemerkin (RUS) 457.5kg	Ronny Weller (GER) 455.0kg	Stefan Botev (AUS) 455.0kg
	Gold	Silver	Bronze
2000	Hossein Rezazadeh (IRI) 472.5kg	Ronny Weller (GER) 467.5kg	Andrei Chemerkin (RUS) 462.5kg*

1896–1968 event not held. * Ashot Danielyan (ARM) finished in third place with 465kg but was subsequently disqualified.

DISCONTINUED WEIGHTLIFTING EVENT
MEN
UP TO 100KG (1980–92; up to 99kg 1996)

	Gold	Silver	Bronze
1980	Ota Zaremba (TCH) 395kg	Igor Nikitin (URS) 392.5kg	Alberto Blanco (CUB) 385kg
1984	Rolf Milser (FRG) 385kg	Vasile Gropa (ROM) 382.5kg	Pekka Niemi (FIN) 367.5kg
1988	Pavel Kuznetsov (URS) 425kg	Nicu Vlad (ROM)* 402.5kg	Peter Immesberger (FRG) 367.5kg
1992	Viktor Tregubov (EUN) 410kg	Timur Taimazov (EUN) 402.5kg	Waldemar Malak (POL) 400kg
1996	Akakios Kakiasvilis (GRE)† 420.0kg	Anatoli Khrapati (KAZ) 410.0kg	Denis Gotfrid (UKR) 402.5kg

1896–1976 event not held. * Andor Szanyi (HUN) finished second with 407.5kg but was subsequently disqualified. † Won the 1992 middle-heavyweight class, representing the Unified Team.

WOMEN (Introduced in 2000)

UP TO 48KG

	Gold	Silver	Bronze
2000	Tara Nott (USA)* 185kg	Raema Lisa Rumbewas (INA) 185kg	Sri Indriyani (INA) 182.5kg

* Izabela Dragneva (BUL) finished in first place with 190kg but was subsequently disqualified.

UP TO 53KG

	Gold	Silver	Bronze
2000	Xia Yang (CHN) 225kg	Feng-Ying Li (TPE) 212.5kg	Winarni Binti Slamet (INA) 202.5kg

UP TO 58KG

	Gold	Silver	Bronze
2000	Soraya Jiminez Mendivil (MEX) 222.5kg	Song Hui (PRK) 220kg	Khassaraporn Suta (INA) 210kg

UP TO 63KG

	Gold	Silver	Bronze
2000	Xiamin Chen (CHN) 242.5kg	Valentina Popova (RUS) 235kg	Ioanna Chatziioannou (GRE) 222.5kg

UP TO 69KG

	Gold	Silver	Bronze
2000	Weining Li (CHN) 242.5kg	Erzsabet Markus (HUN) 242.5kg	Karnam Malleswari (IND) 240kg

UP TO 75KG

	Gold	Silver	Bronze
2000	Maria Urrutia (CUB) 245kg	Ruth Ogbeifo (NGR) 245kg	Yi-Hang Kuo (TPE) 245kg

OVER 75KG

	Gold	Silver	Bronze
2000	Ding Meiyuan (CHN) 300kg	Agata Wrobel (POL) 295kg	Cheryl Haworth (USA) 270kg

WRESTLING MEDALS (Bodyweight classes have changed over time)

FREE-STYLE FLYWEIGHT (Up to 115lb (52.16kg) 1904; up to 52kg 1958–1996; up to 54kg 2000)

	Gold	Silver	Bronze
1904	George Mehnert (USA)	Gustave Bauer (USA)	William Nelson (USA)
1948	Lennart Viitala (FIN)	Halit Balamir (TUR)	Thure Johansson (SWE)
1952	Hasan Gemici (TUR)	Yushu Kitano (JPN)	Mahmoud Mollaghessemi (IRI)
1956	Mirian Tslkalamanidze (URS)	Mohamad-Ali Khojastenpour (IRI)	Hüseyin Akbas (TUR)
1960	Ahmet Bilek (TUR)	Masayuki Matsubara (JPN)	Mohamad Saifpour Saidabadi (IRI)
1964	Yoshikatsu Yoshida (JPN)	Chang-sun Chang (KOR)	Said Aliaakbar Haydari (IRI)
1968	Shigeo Nakata (JPN)	Richard Sanders (USA)	Surenjav Sukhbaatar (MGL)
1972	Kiyomi Kato (JPN)	Arsen Alakhverdyev (URS)	Hyong Kim Gwong (PRK)
1976	Yuji Takada (JPN)	Alexander Ivanov (URS)	Jeon Hae-Sup (KOR)
1980	Anatoli Beloglazov (URS)	Wladyslaw Stecyk (POL)	Nermedin Selimov (BUL)
1984	Saban Trstena (YUG)	Kim Jong-Kyu (KOR)	Yuji Takada (JPN)
1988	Mitsuru Sato (JPN)	Saban Trstena (YUG)	Vladimir Togouzov (URS)
1992	Li Hak-son (PRK)	Larry Lee Jones (USA)	Valentin Jordanov (BUL)
1996	Valentin Jordanov (BUL)	Namik Abdullayev (AZE)	Maulen Mamirov (KAZ)
2000	Namik Abdullayev (AZE)	Samuel Henson (USA)	Amiran Kartanov (GRE)

1896–1900 and 1906–36 event not held

FREE-STYLE BANTAMWEIGHT (Up to 125lb (56.70kg) 1904; 119lb (54kg) 1908; up to 56kg 1924–36; up to 57kg 1948–96; up to 58kg 2000)

	Gold	Silver	Bronze
1904	Isidor Niflot (USA)	August Wester (USA)	Z. B. Strebler (USA)*
1908	George Mehnert (USA)	William Press (GBR)	Aubert Coté (CAN)
1924	Kustaa Pihlajamaki (FIN)	Kaarlo Mäkinen (FIN)	Bryant Hines (USA)
1928	Kaarlo Mäkinen (FIN)	Edmond Spapen (BEL)	James Trifunov (CAN)
1932	Robert Pearce (USA)	Odön Zombori (HUN)	Aatos Jaskari (FIN)
1936	Odön Zombori (HUN)	Ross Flood (USA)	Johannes Herbert (GER)
1948	Nasuk Akar (TUR)	Gerald Leeman (USA)	Charles Kouyov (FRA)
1952	Shohachi Ishii (JPN)	Rashid Mamedbekov (URS)	Kha-Shaba Jadav (IND)
1956	Mustafa Dagistanli (TUR)	Mohamad Yaghoubi (IRI)	Mikhail Chakhov (URS)
1960	Terrence McCann (USA)	Nejdet Zalev (BUL)	Tadeusz Trojanowski (POL)
1964	Yojiro Uetake (JPN)	Hüseyin Akbas (TUR)	Aidyn Ibragimov (URS)
1968	Yojiro Uetake (JPN)	Donald Behm (USA)	Abutaleb Gorgori (IRI)

	Gold	Silver	Bronze
1972	Hideaki Yanagide (JPN)	Richard Sanders (USA)	László Klinga (HUN)
1976	Vladimir Yumin (URS)	Hans-Dieter Brüchert (GDR)	Masao Arai (JPN)
1980	Sergei Beloglazov (URS)	Li Ho Pyong (PRK)	Dugarsuren Ouinbold (MGL)
1984	Hideyaki Tomiyama (JPN)	Barry Davis (USA)	Kim Eui-Kon (KOR)
1988	Sergei Beloglazov (URS)	Askari Mohammadian (IRI)	No Kyung-Sun (KOR)
1992	Alejandro Puerto Díaz (CUB)	Sergei Smal (EUN)	Kim Yong-sik (PRK)
1996	Kendall Cross (USA)	Giga Sissaouri (CAN)	Ri Yong-Sam (PRK)
2000	Alirezas Dabir (IRI)	Yevgeni Buslovich (UKR)	Terry Brands (USA)

1896–1900, 1906 and 1912–20 event not held. * First name often misreported as Zenon.

FREE-STYLE FEATHERWEIGHT Up to 135lb (61.24kg) 1904; up to 133lb (60.30kg) 1908; up to 60kg 1920; up to 61kg 1924–36; up to 63kg 1948–68; up to 62kg 1972–96; up to 63kg 2000)

	Gold	Silver	Bronze
1904	Benjamin Bradshaw (USA)	Theodore McLear (USA)	Charles Clapper (USA)
1908	George Dole (USA)	James Slim (GBR)	William McKie (GBR)
1920	Charles Ackerly (USA)	Samuel Gerson (USA)	P. W. Bernard (GBR)
1924	Robin Reed (USA)	Chester Newton (USA)	Katsutoshi Naito (JPN)
1928	Allie Morrison (USA)	Kustaa Pihlajamäki (FIN)	Hans Minder (SUI)
1932	Hermanni Pihlajamäki (FIN)	Edgar Nemir (USA)	Einar Karlsson (SWE)
1936	Kustaa Pihlajamaki (FIN)	Francis Millard (USA)	Gösta Jönsson (SWE)
1948	Gazanfer Bilge (TUR)	Ivar Sjölin (SWE)	Adolf Müller (SUI)
1952	Bayram Sit (TUR)	Nasser Givétchi (IRI)	Josiah Henson (USA)
1956	Shozo Sasahara (JPN)	Joseph Mewis (BEL)	Erkki Penttilä (FIN)
1960	Mustafa Dagistanli (TUR)	Stantcho Ivanov (BUL)	Vladimir Rubashvili (URS)
1964	Osamu Watanabe (JPN)	Stantcho Ivanov (BUL)	Nodar Khokhashvili (URS)
1968	Masaaki Kanenko (JPN)	Enyu Todorov (BUL)	Shamseddin Seyed-Abbassi (IRI)
1972	Zagalav Abdulbekov (URS)	Vehbi Akdag (TUR)	Ivan Krastev (BUL)
1976	Yang Jung-Mo (KOR)	Zeveg Oidov (MGL)	Gene Davis (USA)
1980	Magomedgasan Abushev (URS)	Mikho Doukov (BUL)	Georges Hadiioannidis (GRE)
1984	Randy Lewis (USA)	Kosei Akaishi (JPN)	Lee Jeung-Keun (KOR)
1988	John Smith (USA)	Stepan Sarkissian (URS)	Simeon Chterev (BUL)
1992	John Smith (USA)	Askari Mohammadian (IRI)	Lazaro Reinoso (CUB)
1996	Thomas Brands (USA)	Jae-Sung Jang (KOR)	Elbrus Tedeyev (UKR)
2000	Murad Oumakhanov (RUS)	Serafim Barzakov (BUL)	Jae-Sung Jang (KOR)

1896–1900, 1906 and 1912 event not held

FREE-STYLE LIGHTWEIGHT (Up to 145lb (65.77kg) 1904; up to 146.75lb (66.60 kg) 1908; up to 67.5kg 1920; up to 66kg 1924–1936; up to 67kg 1948–60; up to 70kg 1964–68; up to 68kg 1972–96; up to 69kg 2000)

	Gold	Silver	Bronze
1904	Otton Roehm (USA)	Rudolph Tesing (USA)	Albert Zirkel (USA)
1908	George de Relwyskow (GBR)	William Wood (GBR)	Albert Gingell (GBR)
1920	Kalle Anttila (FIN)	Gottfried Svensson (SWE)	Peter Wright (GBR)
1924	Russell Vis (USA)	Volmart Wickström (FIN)	Arvo Haavisto (FIN)
1928	Osvald Käpp (EST)	Charles Pacome (FRA)	Eino Leino (FIN)
1932	Charles Pacome (FRA)	Károly Kápáti (HUN)	Gustaf Klarén (SWE)
1936	Károly Kápáti (HUN)	Wolfgang Ehrl (GER)	Hermanni Pihlajamäki (FIN)
1948	Celál Atik (TUR)	Gösta Frandfors (SWE)	Hermanni Pihlajamäki (FIN)
1952	Olle Anderberg (SWE)	Thomas Evans (USA)	Djahanbakte Tovfighe (IRI)
1956	Emamali Habibi (IRI)	Shigeru Kasahara (JPN)	Alimberg Bestayev (URS)
1960	Shelby Wilson (USA)	Viktor Sinyavskiy (URS)	Enyu Dimov (BUL)
1964	Enyu Valtschev (BUL)*	Klaus-Jürgen Rost (GER)	Iwao Horiuchi (JPN)
1968	Abdollah Movahed Ardabili (IRI)	Enyu Valtschev (BUL)*	Sereeter Danzandarjaa (MGL)
1972	Dan Gable (USA)	Kikuo Wada (JPN)	Ruslan Ashuraliev (URS)
1976	Pavel Pinigin (URS)	Lloyd Keaser (USA)	Yasaburo Sagawara (JPN)
1980	Saipulla Absaidov (URS)	Ivan Yankov (BUL)	Saban Sejdi (YUG)
1984	You In-Tak (KOR)	Andrew Rein (USA)	Jukka Rauhala (FIN)
1988	Arsen Fadzayev (URS)	Park Jang-Soon (KOR)	Nate Carr (USA)
1992	Arsen Fadzayev (EUN)	Valentin Getzov (BUL)	Kosei Akaishi (JPN)
1996	Vadim Bogiyev (RUS)	Townsend Saunders (USA)	Zaza Zazirov (UKR)
2000	Daniel Igali (CAN)	Arsen Gitinov (RUS)	Lincoln McIlravy (USA)

1896–1900, 1906 and 1912 event not held. * Valtschev competed as Dimov in 1960.

FREE-STYLE WELTERWEIGHT Up to 158lb (71.67kg) 1904; up to 72kg 1924–36; up to 73kg 1948–60; up to 74kg 1972–96; up to 76kg 2000)

	Gold	Silver	Bronze
1904	Charles Erikson (USA)	William Beckmann (USA)	Jerry Winholtz (USA)
1924	Hermann Gehri (SUI)	Eino Leino (FIN)	Otto Müller (SUI)
1928	Arvo Haavisto (FIN)	Lloyd Appleton (USA)	Maurice Letchford (CAN)
1932	Jack van Bebber (USA)	Daniel MacDonald (CAN)	Eino Leino (FIN)
1936	Frank Lewis (USA)	Ture Andersson (SWE)	Joseph Schleimer (CAN)
1948	Yasar Dogu (TUR)	Richard Garrard (AUS)	Leland Merrill (USA)
1952	William Smith (USA)	Per Berlin (SWE)	Abdullah Modjtabavi (IRI)
1956	Mitsuo Ikeda (JPN)	Ibrahim Zengin (TUR)	Vakhtang Balavadze (URS)
1960	Douglas Blubaugh (USA)	Ismail Ogan (TUR)	Mohammed Bashir (PAK)
1964	Ismail Ogan (TUR)	Guliko Sagaradze (URS)	Mohamad-Ali Sanatkaran (IRI)
1968	Mahmut Atalay (TUR)	Daniel Robin (FRA)	Dagvasuren Purev (MGL)
1972	Wayne Wells (USA)	Jan Karlsson (SWE)	Adolf Seger (FRG)
1976	Jiichiro Date (JPN)	Mansour Barzegar (IRI)	Stanley Dziedzic (USA)
1980	Valentin Raitchev (URS)	Jamtsying Davaajav (MGL)	Dan Karabin (TCH)
1984	David Schultz (USA)	Martin Knosp (FRG)	Saban Sejdi (YUG)
1988	Kenneth Monday (USA)	Adlan Varayev (URS)	Rakhmad Sofiadi (BUL)
1992	Park Jang-soon (KOR)	Kenneth Monday (USA)	Amir Khadem (IRI)
1996	Buvaisa Saityev (RUS)	Park Jang-soon (KOR)	Taykuo Ota (JPN)
2000	Brandon Slay (USA)*	Eui-Jae Moon (KOR)	Adam Bereket (TUR)

1896–1906 and 1912 event not held. * Alexander Leipold (GER) finished in first place but was subsequently disqualified.

FREE-STYLE MIDDLEWEIGHT (Up to 161lb (73kg) 1908; up to 75kg 1920; up to 79kg 1924–60; up to 87kg 1964–68; up to 82kg 1972–96; up to 85kg 2000)

	Gold	Silver	Bronze
1908	Stanley Bacon (GBR)	George de Relwyskow (GBR)	Frederick Beck (GBR)
1920	Eino Reino (FIN)	Väinö Penttala (FIN)	Charles Johnson (USA)
1924	Fritz Hagmann (SUI)	Pierre Ollivier (BEL)	Vilho Pekkala (FIN)
1928	Ernst Kyburz (SUI)	Donald Stockton (CAN)	Samuel Rabin (GBR)
1932	Ivar Johansson (SWE)	Kyösti Luukko (FIN)	József Tunyogi (HUN)
1936	Emile Poilvé (FRA)	Richard Voliva (USA)	Ahmet Kirecci (TUR)
1948	Glen Brand (USA)	Adil Candemir (TUR)	Erik Lindén (SWE)
1952	David Tsimakuridze (URS)	Gholam Reza Takhti (IRI)	György Gurics (HUN)
1956	Nikola Stantchev (BUL)	Daniel Hodge (USA)	Georgi Skhirtladze (URS)
1960	Hasan Güngör (TUR)	Georgi Skhirtladze (URS)	Hans Antonsson (SWE)
1964	Prodan Gardshev (BUL)	Hasan Güngör (TUR)	Daniel Brand (USA)
1968	Boris Mikhailovich Gurevich (URS)	Munkbat Jigjid (MGL)	Prodan Gradshev (BUL)
1972	Leven Tediashvili (URS)	John Peterson (USA)	Vasile Jorga (ROM)
1976	Joh Peterson (USA)	Viktor Novoshilev (URS)	Adolf Seger (FRG)
1980	Ismail Abilov (BUL)	Magomedhan Aratsilov (URS)	István Kovács (HUN)
1984	Mark Schultz (USA)	Hideyuki Nagashima (JPN)	Chris Rinke (CAN)
1988	Han Myung-woo (KOR)	Necmi Gencalp (TUR)	Josef Lohyna (TCH)
1992	Kevin Jackson (USA)	Elmadi Zhabraylov (EUN)	Razul Khadem Azghadi (IRI)
1996	Khadshimurad Magomedov (RUS)	Yang Hyun-Mo (KOR)	Amir Khadem Azghadi (IRI)
2000	Adam Saityev (RUS)	Yoel Romero (CUB)	Mogamed Ibragimov (MKD)

1896–1906 and 1912 event not held

FREE-STYLE LIGHT-HEAVYWEIGHT (Up to 82.5kg 1920; up to 87kg 1924–60; up to 97kg 1964–68; up to 90kg 1972–96; up to 97kg 2000)

	Gold	Silver	Bronze
1920	Anders Larsson (SWE)	Charles Courant (SUI)	Walter Maurer (USA)
1924	Joh Spellman (USA)	Rudolf Svensson (SWE)	Charles Courant (FRA)
1928	Thure Sjöstedt (SWE)	Anton Bögli (SUI)	Henri Lefebre (FRA)
1932	Peter Mehringer (USA)	Thure Sjöstedt (SWE)	Eddie Scarf (AUS)
1936	Knut Fridell (SWE)	August Neo (EST)	Erich Siebert (GER)
1948	Henry Wittenberg (USA)	Fritz Stöckli (SUI)	Bengt Fahlkvist (SWE)
1952	Wiking Palm (SWE)	Henry Wittenberg (USA)	Adil Atan (TUR)
1956	Gholam Reza Tahkti (IRI)	Boris Kulayev (URS)	Peter Blair (USA)
1960	Ismet Atli (TUR)	Gholam Reza Tahkti (IRI)`	Anatoli Albul (URS)
1964	Alexander Medved (URS)	Ahmet Ayik (TUR)	Said Mustafafov (BUL)

	Gold	Silver	Bronze
1968	Ahmet Ayik (TUR)	Shota Lomidze (URS)	József Csatári (HUN)
1972	Ben Peterson (USA)	Gennadi Strakhov (URS)	Károly Bajkó (HUN)
1976	Levan Tediashvili (URS)	Ben Peterson (USA)	Stelica Morcov (ROM)
1980	Sanasar Oganesyan (URS)	Uwe Neupert (GDR)	Aleksandr Cichon (POL)
1984	Ed Banach (USA)	Akira Ota (JPN)	Noel Loban (GBR)
1988	Makharbek Khadartsev (URS)	Akira Ota (JPN)	Kim Tae-Woo (KOR)
1992	Makharbek Khadartsev (EUN)	Kenan Simsek (TUR)	Christopher Campbell (USA)
1996	Rasul Khadem Azghadi (IRI)	Makharbek Khadartsev (RUS)	Eldar Kurtanidze (GEO)
2000	Saghid Murtasaliyev (RUS)	Islam Bairamukov (KAZ)	Yeidar Kurtanidze (GEO)

1896-1912 event not held

FREE-STYLE SUPER-HEAVYWEIGHT (Over 100kg 1972–84; up to 130kg since 1988)

	Gold	Silver	Bronze
1972	Alexander Medved (URS)	Osman Duraliev (BUL)	Chris Taylor (USA)
1976	Soslan Andiev (URS)	Jozsef Balla (HUN)	Ladislau Simon (ROM)
1980	Soslan Andiev (URS)	Jozsef Balla (HUN)	Adam Sandurski (POL)
1984	Bruce Baumgartner (USA)	Bob Molle (CAN)	Ayhan Taskin (TUR)
1988	David Gobedjichvili (URS)	Bruce Baumgartner (USA)	Andreas Schröder (GDR)
1992	Bruce Baumgartner (USA)	Jeff Thue (CAN)	David Gobedjhichvili (EUN)
1996	Mahmut Demir (TUR)	Alexei Medvedev (BUL)	Bruce Baumgartner (USA)
2000	David Mussulbes (RUS)	Artur Taymazov (UZB)	Alexis Rodriguez (CUB)

1896–1968 event not held

GRECO-ROMAN FLYWEIGHT (Up to 52kg 1948–96; up to 54kg 2000)

	Gold	Silver	Bronze
1948	Pietro Lombardi (ITA)	Kenan Olcay (TUR)	Reino Kangasmäki (FIN)
1952	Boris Maksimovich Gurevich (URS)	Iganzio Fabra (ITA)	Leo Honkala (FIN)
1956	Nikolai Solovyov (URS)	Ignazio Fabra (ITA)	Durum Ali Egribas (TUR)
1960	Dumitru Pirvulescu (ROM)	Osman Sayed (UAR)	Mohamad Paziraye (IRI)
1964	Tsutomu Hanahara (JPN)	Angel Kerezov (BUL)	Dumitru Pirvulescu (ROM)
1968	Petar Kirov (BUL)	Vladimir Bakulin (URS)	Miroslav Zeman (TCH)
1972	Petar Kirov (BUL)	Koichiro Hirayama (JPN)	Giuseppe Bognanni (ITA)
1976	Vitali Konstantinov (URS)	Nicu Ginga (ROM)	Koichiro Kirayama (JPN)
1980	Vakhtang Blagidze (URS)	Lajos Racz (HUN)	Mladen Mladenov (BUL)
1984	Atsuji Miyahama (JPN)	Daniel Aceves (MEX)	Bang Dae-Du (KOR)
1988	Jon Ronningen (NOR)	Atsuji Miyahama (JPN)	Lee Jae-Suk (KOR)
1992	Jon Ronningen (NOR)	Alfred Ter-Mkrttchian (EUN)	Min Kyung-Kap (KOR)
1996	Arman Nazaryan (ARM)	Brandon Paulson (USA)	Andrei Kalashnikov (UKR)
2000	Kwon-Ho Sim (KOR)	Lazaro Rivas (CUB)	Yong-Gyun Kang (PRK)

1896–1936 event not held

GRECO-ROMAN BANTAMWEIGHT (Up to 58kg 1924–28; up to 56kg 1932–36; up to 57kg 1948–96; up to 58kg 2000)

	Gold	Silver	Bronze
1924	Eduard Pütsep (EST)	Anselm Ahlfors (FIN)	Väinö Ikonen (FIN)
1928	Kurt Leucht (GER)	Jindrich Maudr (TCH)	Giovanni Gozzi (ITA)
1932	Jakob Brendel (GER)	Marcello Nizzola (ITA)	Louis François (FRA)
1936	Márton Lörincz (HUN)	Egon Svensson (SWE)	Jakob Brendel (GER)
1948	Kurt Pettersén (SWE)	Aly Mahmoud Hassan (EGY)	Habil Kaya (TUR)
1952	Imre Hódos (HUN)	Zakaria Chihab (LIB)	Artem Teryan (URS)
1956	Konstantin Vyrupayev (URS)	Evdin Vesterby (SWE)	Francisco Horvat (ROM)
1960	Oleg Karavayev (URS)	Ion Cernea (ROM)	Petrov Dinko (BUL)
1964	Masamitsu Ichiguchi (JPN)	Vladen Trostiansky (URS)	Ion Cernea (ROM)
1968	János Varga (HUN)	Ion Baciu (ROM)	Ivan Kochergin (URS)
1972	Rustem Kazakov (URS)	Hans-Jürgen Veil (FRG)	Risto Björlin (FIN)
1976	Pertti Ukkola (FIN)	Iván Frgic (YUG)	Farhat Mustafin (URS)
1980	Shamil Serikov (URS)	Jozef Lipien (POL)	Benni Ljungbeck (SWE)
1984	Pasquale Passarelli (FRG)	Masaki Eto (JPN)	Haralambos Holidis (GRE)
1988	Andras Sike (HUN)	Stoyan Balov (BUL)	Haralambos Holidis (GRE)
1992	An Han-Bong (KOR)	Rifat Yildiz (GER)	Sheng Zetian (CHN)
1996	Yovei Melnichenko (KAZ)	Denis Hall (USA)	Sheng Zetian (CHN)

	Gold	Silver	Bronze
2000	Armen Nazarian (BUL)	In-Sub Kim (KOR)	Sheng Zetian (CHN)

1896–1920 event not held

GRECO-ROMAN FEATHERWEIGHT (Up to 60kg 1912–20; up to 62kg 1924–28, 1948–60, 1972–96; up to 61kg 1932–36; up to 63kg 1964–68, 2000)

	Gold	Silver	Bronze
1912	Kaarlo Koskelo (FIN)	Georg Gerstacker (GER)	Otto Lasanen (FIN)
1920	Oskari Friman (FIN)	Hekki Kähkönen (FIN)	Fridtjof Svensson (SWE)
1924	Kalle Antila (FIN)	Aleksanteri Toivola (FIN)	Erik Malmberg (SWE)
1928	Voldemar Väli (EST)	Erik Malmberg (SWE)	Giacomo Quaglia (ITA)
1932	Giovanni Gozzi (ITA)	Wolfgang Ehrl (GER)	Lauri Koskela (FIN)
1936	Yasar Erkan (TUR)	Aarne Reini (FIN)	Einar Karlsson (SWE)
1948	Mehmet Oktav (TUR)	Olle Anderberg (SWE)	Ferenc Tóth (HUN
1952	Yakov Punkin (URS)	Imre Polyák (HUN)	Abdel Rashed (EGY)
1956	Rauno Mäkinen (FIN)	Imre Polyák (HUN)	Roman Dzneladze (URS)
1960	Muzahir Sille (TUR)	Imre Polyák (HUN)	Konstantin Vyrupayev (URS)
1964	Imre Polyák (HUN)	Roman Rurua (URS)	Branko Marttinovic (YUG)
1968	Roman Rurua (URS)	Hideo Fujimoto (JPN)	Simeon Popescu (ROM)
1972	Gheorghi Markov (BUL)	Heniz-Helmut Wehling (GDR)	Kazimierz Lipien (POL)
1976	Kazimierz Lipien (POL)	Nelson Davidian (URS)	László Réczi (HUN)
1980	Stilianos Migiakis (GRE)	István Tóth (HUN)	Boris Kramorenko (URS)
1984	Kim Weon-Kee (KOR)	Kent-Olle Johansson (SWE)	Hugo Dietsche (SUI)
1988	Kamandar Madjidov (URS)	Jivko Vanguelov (BUL)	An Dae-Hyun (KOR)
1992	Akif Pirim (TUR)	Sergei Martynov (EUN)	Juan Luis Maren Delis (CUB)
1996	Wlodzimierz Zawadzki (POL)	Juan Luis Maren Delis (CUB)	Akif Pirim (TUR)
2000	Varteres Samourgachev (RUS)	Juan Luis Maren Delis (CUB)	Akkaki Chachua (GEO)

1896–1920 event not held

GRECO-ROMAN LIGHTWEIGHT (Up to 75kg 1906; up to 47lb (66.6kg) 1908; up to 67.5kg 1912–28; up to 66kg 1932–36; up to 67kg 1948–60; up to 70kg 1964–68; up to 68kg 1972–96; up to 69kg 2000)

	Gold	Silver	Bronze
1906	Rudolf Watzl (AUT)	Karl Karlsen (DEN)	Ferenc Holuban (HUN)
1908	Enrico Porro (ITA)	Nikolav Orlov (URS0	Avid Lindén-Linko (FIN)
1912	Eemil Wäre (FIN)	Gustaf Malmström (SWE)	Edvin Matiasson (SWE)
1920	Eemil Wäre (FIN)	Taavi Tamminen (FIN)	Fritjof Andersen (NOR)
1924	Oskari Friman (FIN)	Lajos Keresztes (HUN)	Kalle Westerlund (FIN)
1928	Lajos Keresztes (HUN)	Eduard Sperling (GER)	Eduard Westerlund (FIN)
1932	Erik Malmberg (SWE)	Abraham Kurland (DEN)	Eduard Sperling (GER)
1936	Lauri Koskela (FIN)	Josef Herda (TCH)	Voldemar Väli (EST)
1948	Gustaf Freij (SWE)	Aage Eriksen (NOR)	Károly Ferencz (HUN)
1952	Shazam Safim (URS)	Gustaf Freij (SWE)	Mikulás Athanasov (TCH)
1956	Kyösti Lentonen (FIN)	Riza Dogan (TUR)	Gyula Tóth (HUN)
1960	Avtandil Koridza (URS)	Branislav Martinovic (YUG)	Gustaf Freij (SWE)
1964	Kazim Avvaz (TUR)	Valeriu Bularca (ROM)	David Gvantseladze (URS)
1968	Munji Mumemura (JPN)	Stevan Horvat (YUG)	Petros Galaktopoulos (GRE)
1972	Shamii Khisamutdinov (URS)	Stoyan Apostolov (BUL)	Gian Matteo Ranzi (ITA)
1976	Suren Nalbandyan (URS)	Stefan Rusu (ROM)	Heinz-Helmut Wehling (GDR)
1980	Stefan Rusu (ROM)	Andrzej Supron (POL)	Lars-Erik Skiold (SWE)
1984	Vlado Lisjak (YUG)	Tapio Sipila (FIN)	James Martinez (USA)
1988	Levon Djoulfalakian (URS)	Kim Sung-Moon (KOR)	Tapio Sipila (FIN)
1992	Attila Repka (HUN)	Islam Dougutchyev (EUN)	Rodney Smith (USA)
1996	Ryzsard Wolny (POL)	Ghani Yalouz (FRA)	Alexander Tretyakov (RUS)
2000	Filberto Azcuy Aguilera (CUB)	Katsuhiko Nagata (JPN)	Alexei Glouchkov (RUS)

1896–1904 event not held

GRECO-ROMAN WELTERWEIGHT (Up to 72kg 1932–36; up to 73kg 1948–60; up to 78kg 1964-68; up to 74kg 1972–96; up to 76kg 2000)

	Gold	Silver	Bronze
1932	Ivar Johansson (SWE)	Väinö Kajander (FIN)	Ercole Gallegatti (ITA)
1936	Rudolf Svedberg (SWE)	Fritz Schäfer (GER)	Eino Virtanen (FIN)
1948	Gösta Andersson (SWE)	Miklós Szilvási (HUN)	Henrik Hansen (DEN)
1952	Miklós Szilvási (HUN)	Gösta Andersson (SWE)	Khalil Taha (LIB)

	Gold	Silver	Bronze
1956	Mithat Bayrak (TUR)	Vladimir Maneyev (URS)	Per Berlin (SWE)
1960	Mithat Bayrak (TUR)	Günther Maritschnigg (GER)	René Schiermeyer (FRA)
1964	Anatoli Kolesov (URS)	Cyril Todorov (BUL)	Bertil Nyström (SWE)
1968	Rudolf Vesper (GDR)	Daniel Robin (FRA)	Károly Bajkó (HUN)
1972	Vitezslav Macha (TCH)	Petros Galaktopoulos (GRE)	Jan Karlsson (SWE)
1976	Anatoli Kykov (URS)	Vitezslav Macha (TCH)	Karlhienz Helbing (FRG)
1980	Ferenc Kocsis (HUN)	Anatoli Bykov (URS)	Mikko Huhtala (FIN)
1984	Jonko Salomaki (FIN)	Roger Tallroth (SWE)	Stefan Rusu (ROM)
1988	Kim Young-Nam (KOR)	Daoulet Tourlykhanov (URS)	Jozef Tracz (POL)
1992	Mnatsakan Iskandaryan (EUN)	Jozef Tracz (POL)	Torbjörn Kornbakk (SWE)
1996	Feliberto Azcuy Aguilera (CUB)	Marko Asell (FIN)	Jozef Tracz (POL)
2000	Murat Kardanov (RUS)	Matt Lindland (USA)	Martio Yli-Hannukselä (FIN)

1896–1928 event not held

GRECO-ROMAN MIDDLEWEIGHT (Up to 85kg 1906; up to 161lb (73kg) 1908; up to 75kg 1912–28; up to 79kg 1932–60; up to 87kg 1964–68; up to 82kg 1972–96; up to 85kg 2000)

	Gold	Silver	Bronze
1906	Verner Weckman (FIN)	Rudolf Lindmayer (AUT)	Robert Bebrens (USA)
1908	Frithiof Märtensson (SWE)	Mauritz Andersson (SWE)	Anders Andersen (DEN)
1912	Claes Johansson (SWE)	Martin Klein (URS)	Alfred Asikainen (FIN)
1920	Carl Westergren (SWE)	Artur Lindfors (FIN)	Matti Perttilä (FIN)
1924	Eduard Westerlund (SWE)	Artur Lindfors (FIN)	Roman Steinberg (EST)
1928	Väinö Kokkinen (FIN)	László Papp (HUN)	Albert Kusnetz (EST)
1932	Väinö Kokkinen (FIN)	Jean Földeák (GER)	Axel Cadier (SWE)
1936	Ivar Johansson (SWE)	Ludwig Schweikert (GER)	József Palotás (HUN)
1948	Axel Grönberg (SWE)	Muhlis Tayfur (TUR)	Ercole Gallegatti (ITA)
1952	Axel Grönberg (SWE)	Kalervo Rauhala (FIN)	Nikolai Belov (URS)
1956	Givi Kartiziya (URS)	Dimiter Dobrev (BUL)	Rune Jansson (SWE)
1960	Dimiter Dobrev (BUL)	Lothar Metz (GER)	Ion taranu (ROM)
1964	Branislav Simic (YUG)	Jiri Kormanik (TCH)	Lothar Metz (GER)
1968	Lothar Metz (GDR)	Valentin Olenik (URS)	Branislav Simic (YUG)
1972	Csaba Hegedus (HUN)	Anatoli Nazarenko (URS)	Milan Nenadic (YUG)
1976	Momir Petkovic (YUG)	Vladimir Cheboksarov (URS)	Ivan Kolev (BUL)
1980	Gennadi Korban (URS)	Jan Polgowicz (POL)	Pavel Pavlov (BUL)
1984	Ion Draica (ROM)	Dimitrios Thanapoulos (GRE)	Soren Claeson (SWE)
1988	Mikhail Mamiachvili (URS)	Tibor Komaromi (HUN)	Kim Sang-Kyu (KOR)
1992	Peter Farkas (HUN)	Piotr Stepien (POL)	Daoulet Tourlykhanov (EUN)
1996	Hamza Yerlikaya (TUR)	Thomas Zander (GER)	Valeri Tsilent (BLR)
2000	Hamza Yerlikaya (TUR)	Sandor Bardosi (HUN)	Muchran Vakhtangadze (GEO)

1896–1904 event not held

GRECO-ROMAN LIGHT-HEAVYWEIGHT (Up to 205lb (93kg) 1908; up to 82.5kg 1912–28; up to 87kg 1932–60; up to 97kg 1964–68, 2000; up to 90kg 1972–1996)

	Gold	Silver	Bronze
1908	Verner Weckman (FIN)	Yrjö Saarala (FIN)	Carl Jensen (DEN)
1912	—*	Anders Ahlgren (SWE)	Béla Varga (HUN)
		Ivor Böhling (FIN)	
1920	Claes Johansson (SWE)	Edil Rosenqvist (SWE)	Johannes Eriksen (DEN)
1924	Carl Westergren (SWE)	Rudolf Svensson (SWE)	Onni Pellinen (FIN)
1928	Ibrahim Moustafa (EGY)	Adolf Rieger (GER)	Onni Pellinen (FIN)
1932	Rudolf Svensson (SWE)	Onni Pellinen (FIN)	Mario Gruppioni (ITA)
1936	Axel Cadier (SWE)	Edwins Bietags (LAT)	August Néo (EST)
1948	Karl-Erik Nilsson (SWE)	Kaelpo Gröndahl (FIN)	Ibrahim Orabi (EGY)
1952	Kaelpo Gröndahl (FIN)	Shalva Shikhladze (URS)	Karl-Erik Nilsson (SWE)
1956	Valentin Nikolayev (URS)	Petko Sirakov (BUL)	Karl-Erik Nilsson (SWE)
1960	Tevfik Kis (TUR)	Krali Bimbalov (BUL)	Givi Kartoziya (URS)
1964	Boyan Radev (BUL)	Per Svensson (SWE)	Heinz Kiehl (GER)
1968	Boyan Radev (BUL)	Nikolai Yakovenko (URS)	Nicolae Martinescu (ROM)
1972	Valeri Rezantsky (URS)	Josip Corak (YUG)	Czeslaw Kwiecinski (POL)
1976	Valeri Rezantsky (URS)	Stoyan Ivanov (BUL)	Czesalw Kwiecinski (POL)
1980	Norbert Nottny (HUN)	Igor Kanygin (URS)	Petre Disu (ROM)
1984	Steven Fraser (USA)	Ilie Matei (ROM)	Frank Andersson (SWE)

	Gold	Silver	Bronze
1988	Atanas Komchev (BUL)	Harri Koskela (FIN)	Vladimir popov (URS)
1992	Maik Bullmann (GER)	Hakki Basar (TUR)	Gogui Kogouachvili (EUN)
1996	Vyachetslav Oleynik (UKR)	Jacek Fafinski (POL)	Maik Bullmann (GER)
2000	Mikael Ljungberg (SWE)	David Saldadze (UKR)	Garrett Lowney (USA)

1896–1906 event not held. * Ahlgren and Böhling were declared equal second after nine hours of wrestling.

GRECO-ROMAN SUPER-HEAVYWEIGHT (Over 100kg 1972–84; up to 130kg 1988–2000)

	Gold	Silver	Bronze
1972	Anatoli Roschin (URS)	Alexandre Tomov (BUL)	Victor Dolipschi (ROM)
1976	Alexander Kolchinsky (URS)	Alexandre Tomov (BUL)	Roman Codreanu (ROM)
1980	Alexander Kolchinsky (URS)	Alexandre Tomov (BUL)	Hassan Bchara (LIB)
1984	Jeffrey Blatnick (USA)	Refik Memisevic (YUG)	Victor Dolipschi (ROM)
1988	Alexander Karelin (URS)	Ranguel Guerovski (BUL)	Tomas Johansson (SWE)
1992	Alexander Karelin (EUN)	Tomas Johansson (SWE)	Ioan Grigoras (ROM)
1996	Alexander Karelin (RUS))	Matt Ghaffari (USA)	Sergei Moureiko (MDA)
2000	Rulon Gardner (USA)	Alexander Karelin (RUS)	Dimitri Debelka (BLR)

1896–1968 event not held

DISCONTINUED WRESTLING EVENTS
FREE-STYLE LIGHT FLYWEIGHT (Up to 48kg)

	Gold	Silver	Bronze
1904	Robert Curry (USA)	John Heim (USA)	Gustav Thiefenthaler (USA)
1972	Roman Dmitriev (URS)	Ognian Nikolov (BUL)	Ebrahim Javadpour (IRI)
1976	Khassan Issaev (BUL)	Roman Dmitriev (URS)	Akira Kudo (JPN)
1980	Claudio Pollio (ITA)	Jang Se Hong (PRK)	Sergei Kornilayev (URS)
1984	Robert Weaver (USA)	Takashi Irie (JPN)	Son Gab-Do (KOR)
1988	Takashi Kobaysahi (JPN)	Ivan Tozorov (BUL)	Sergei Karemtchakov (URS)
1992	Kim Il (PRK)	Kim Jong-shin (KOR)	Vougar Oroudzhov (EUN)
1996	Kim Il (PRK)	Armen Mkrchyan (ARM)	Alexis Vila (CUB)

1896–1900, 1906–68 event not held

FREE-STYLE HEAVYWEIGHT (Over 158lb (71.6kg) 1904; over 73kg 1908; over 82.5kg 1920; over 87kg 1924–60; over 97kg 1964–68; up to 100kg 1972–96)

1904	Bernhuff Hansen (USA)	Frank Kungler (USA)	Fred Warmbold (USA)
1908	George O'Kelly (GBR)	Jacob Gundersen (NOR)	Edmond Barrett (GBR)
1920	Robert Roth (SUI)	Nathan Pendleton (USA)	Ernst Nilsson (SWE)*
			Frederick Meyer (USA)*
1924	Harry Steele (USA)	Henry Wernli (SUI)	Andrew McDonald (GBR)
1928	Johan Richthoff (SWE)	Aukusti Sihovlla (FIN)	Edmond Dame (FRA)
1932	Johan Richthoff (SWE)	Joh Riley (USA)	Nikolaus Hirschl (AUT)
1936	Kristjan Palusalu (EST)	Josef Klapuch (TCH)	Hjalmar Nyström (FIN)
1948	Gyula Bóbis (HUN)	Bertil Antonsson (SWE)	Joseph Armstrong (AUS)
1952	Arsen Mekokishvili (URS)	Bertil Antonsson (SWE)	Kenneth Richmond (GBR)
1956	Hamit Kaplan (TUR)	Hussein Mekhmedov (BUL)	Taisto Kangasniemi (FIN)
1960	Wilfried Dietrich (GER)	Hamit Kaplan (TUR)	Savkus Dzarassov (URS)
1964	Alexander Ivanitsky (URS)	Liutvi Djiber (BUL)	Hamit Kaplan (TUR)
1968	Alexander Medved (URS)	Osman Duraliev (BUL)	Wilfried Dietrich (FRG)
1972	Ivan Yaragin (URS)	Khorloo Baianmunkh (MGL)	József Csatári (HUN)
1976	Ivan Yaragin (URS)	Russell Helickson (USA)	Dimo Kostov (BUL)
1980	Ilya Mate (URS)	Slavtcho Tchervenkov (BUL)	Julius Strnisko (TCH)
1984	Lou Banach (USA)	Joseph Atiyeh (SYR)	Vasile Pascasu (ROM)
1988	Vasile Pascasu (ROM)	Leri Khabelov (URS)	William Scherr (USA)
1992	Leri Khabelov (EUN)	Heiko Balz (GER)	Ali Kayali (TUR)
1996	Kurt Angle (USA)	Abbas Jadidi (IRI)	Arwat Sabejew (GER)

1896–1900, 1906 and 1912 event not held. * Tie for third place.

GRECO-ROMAN LIGHT-FLYWEIGHT (Up to 48kg)

1972	Gheorghe Berceanu (ROM)	Rahim Ahabadi (IRI)	Stefan Anghelov (BUL)
1976	Alexei Shumanov (URS)	Gheorghe Berceanu (ROM)	Stefan Anghelov (BUL)
1980	Zaksylik Ushkempirov (URS)	Constantin Alexandru (ROM)	Ferenc Seres (HUN)
1984	Vincenzo Maenza (ITA)	Markus Scherer (FRG)	Ikuzo Saito (JPN)
1988	Vincenzo Maenza (ITA)	Andrzej Glab (POL)	Bratan Tzenov (BUL)

	Gold	Silver	Bronze
1992	Oleg Kutcherenko (EUN)	Vincenzo Maenza (ITA)	Wiber Sanchez (CUB)
1996	Sim Kwon-Ho (KOR)	Alexander Pavlov (BLR)	Zafar Gulyov (RUS)

1896–1968 event not held

GRECO-ROMAN HEAVYWEIGHT (Open 1896: over 85kg 1906; over 93kg 1908; over 82.5kg 1912–28; over 81kg 1932–60; over 91kg 1964–68; up to 100kg 1972–96)

1896	Carl Schuhmann (GER)	Georgios Tsitas (GRE)	Stephanos Christopoulos (GRE)
1906	Sören Jensen (DEN)	Henri Baur (AUT)	Marcel Dubois (BEL)
1908	Richard Weisz (HUN)	Alexander Petrov (RUS)	Sören Jensen (DEN)
1912	Yrjö Saarela (FIN)	Johan Olin (FIN)	Sören Jensen (DEN)
1920	Adolf Lindfors (FIN)	Poul Hansen (DEN)	Martti Nieminen (FIN)
1924	Henri Deglane (FRA)	Edil Rosenqvist (FIN)	Raymund Badó (HUN)
1928	Rudolf Svensson (SWE)	Hjalmar Nyström (FIN)	Georg Gehring (GER)
1932	Carl Westergren (SWE)	Josef Urban (TCH)	Nikolaus Hirschl (AUT)
1936	Kristjan Palusalu (EST)	John Nyman (SWE)	Kurt Hornfischer (GER)
1948	Ahmet Kireççi (TUR)	Tor Nilsson (SWE)	Guido Fantoni (ITA)
1952	Johannes Kotkas (URS)	Josef Ruzicka (TCH)	Tauno Kovanen (FIN)
1956	Anatoliy Parfenov (URS)	Wilfried Dietrich (GER)	Adelmo Bulgarelli (ITA)
1960	Ivan Bogdan (URS)	Wilfried Dietrich (GER)	Bohumil Kubat (TCH)
1964	István Kozma (HUN)	Anatoliy Roschin (URS)	Wilfried Dietrich (GER)
1968	István Kozma (HUN)	Anatoliy Roschin (URS)	Petr Kment (TCH)
1972	Nicolae Martinescu (ROM)	Nikolai Yakovenko (URS)	Ferenc Kiss (HUN)
1976	Nikolai Bolboshin (URS)	Kamen Goranov (BUL)	Andrzej Skrzylewski (POL)
1980	Gheorghi Raikov (BUL)	Roman Bierla (POL)	Vasile Andrei (ROM)
1984	Vasile Andrei (ROM)	Greg Gibson (USA)	Jozef Tertelje (YUG)
1988	Andrzej Wronski (POL)	Gerhard Himmel (FRG)	Dennis Koslowski (USA)
1992	Hector Milian (CUB)	Dennis Koslowski (USA)	Sergei Demyashkevich (EUN)
1996	Andreas Wronski (POL)	Sergei Lishvan (BLR)	Mikael Ljungberg (SWE)

1900–04 event not held

GRECO-ROMAN ALL-AROUND

1906	Sören Jensen (DEN)	Verner Weckmann (FIN)	Rudolf Watzl (AUT)

DISCONTINUED SPORTS MEDALS

CRICKET

	Gold	Silver	Bronze
1900	Great Britain	France	—

CROQUET
SIMPLE À LA BOULE

	Gold	Silver	Bronze
1900	Aumoitte (FRA)	Johin (FRA)	Waydelich (FRA)

SIMPLE À DEUX BOULES

	Gold	Silver	Bronze
1900	Waydelich (FRA)	Vignerot (FRA)	Sautereau (FRA)

DOUBLES

1900	France	—	—

GOLF
MEN'S SINGLES

	Gold	Silver	Bronze
1900	Charles Sands (USA)	Walter Rutherford (GBR)	David Robertson (GBR)
1904	George Lyon (CAN)	Chandler Egan (USA)	Burt McKinnie (USA)

MEN'S TEAM

1904	United States	United States	—

WOMEN'S SINGLES

	Gold	Silver	Bronze
1900	Margaret Abbott (USA)	Pauline Whittier (USA)	Daria Pratt (USA)

JEU DE PAUME

	Gold	Silver	Bronze
1908	Jay Gould (USA)	Eustace Mills (GBR)	Neville Lytton (GBR)

LACROSSE

	Gold	Silver	Bronze
1904	Canada	United States	Canada
1908	Canada	Great Britain	–

MOTORBOATING
OPEN CLASS

	Gold	Silver	Bronze
1908	France	—	—

60-FOOT CLASS

1908	Great Britain	—	—

8-METRE CLASS

1908	Great Britain	—	—

POLO

	Gold	Silver	Bronze
1900	Great Britain	Great Britain	France
1908	Great Britain	Great Britain	Great Britain
1920	Great Britain	Spain	United States
1924	Argentina	United States	Great Britain
1936	Argentina	Great Britain	Mexico

ROQUE

	Gold	Silver	Bronze
1904	Charles Jacobus (USA)	Smith Streeter (USA)	Charles Brown (USA)

RACKETS
SINGLES

	Gold	Silver	Bronze
1908	Evan Noel (GBR)	Henry Leaf (GBR)	John Jacob Astor (GBR)

DOUBLES

1908	Great Britain	Great Britain	Great Britain

RUGBY UNION

	Gold	Silver	Bronze
1900	France	Germany	Great Britain
1908	Australia	Great Britain	–
1920	United States	France	—
1924	United States	France	Romania

TUG-OF-WAR

	Gold	Silver	Bronze
1900	Sweden/Denmark*	France	—
1904	United States	United States	United States
1906	Germany	Greece	Sweden
1908	Great Britain	Great Britain	Great Britain
1912	Sweden	Great Britain	—
1920	Great Britain	Netherlands	Belgium

1896 event not held. * Combined team.

WINTER

ALPINE SKIING MEDALS

MEN

DOWNHILL

	Gold	Silver	Bronze
1948	Henri Oreiller (FRA) 2:55.0	Franz Gabl (AUT) 2:59.1	Karl Molitor (SUI) 3:00.3
			Rolf Olinger (SUI) 3:00.3
1952	Zeno Colò (ITA) 2:30.8	Othmar Schneider (AUT) 2:32.0	Christian Pravda (AUT) 2:32.4
1956	Anton Sailer (FRA) 2:52.2	Raymond Fellay (SUI) 2:55.7	Andreas Molterer (AUT) 2:56.2
1960	Jean Vuarnet (FRA) 2:06.0	Hans-Peter Lanig (GER) 2:06.5	Guy Périllat (FRA) 2:06.9
1964	Egon Zimmerman (AUT) 2:18.16	Léo Lacroix (FRA) 2:18.90	Wolfgang Bartels (GER) 2:19.48
1968	Jean-Claude Killy (FRA) 1:59.85	Guy Périllat (FRA) 1:59.93	Jean-Daniel Dätwyler (SUI) 2:00.32
1972	Bernhard Russi (SUI) 1:51.43	Roland Collombin (SUI) 1:52.07	Heinrich Messner (AUT) 1:52.40
1976	Franz Klammer (AUT) 1:45.73	Bernhard Russi (SUI) 1:46.06	Herbert Plank (ITA) 1:46.59
1980	Leonhard Stock (AUT) 1:45.50	Peter Wirnsberger (AUT) 1:46.12	Steve Podborski (CAN) 1:46.62
1984	Bill Johnson (USA) 1:45.59	Peter Müller (SUI) 1:45.86	Anton Steiner (AUT) 1:45.95
1988	Pirmin Zurbriggen (AUT) 1:59.63	Peter Müller (SUI) 2:00.14	Franck Piccard (FRA) 2:01.24
1992	Patrick Ortlieb (AUT) 1:50.37	Franck Piccard (FRA) 1:50.42	Günther Mader (AUT) 1:50.47
1994	Tommy Moe (USA) 1:45.75	Kjetil André Aamodt (NOR) 1:45.79	Edward Podivinsky (CAN) 1:45.87
1998	Jean Luc Cretier (FRA) 1:50.11	Lasse Kjus (NOR) 1:50.51	Hannes Trink (AUT) 1:50.63
2002	Fritz Strobl (AUT) 1:39.13	Lase Kjus (NOR) 1:39.35	Stephan Eberharter (AUT) 1:39.41

1924–36 event not held

SLALOM

	Gold	Silver	Bronze
1948	Edi Reinalter (SUI) 2:10.3	James Couttret (FRA) 2:10.8	Henri Oreiller (FRA) 2:12.8
1952	Othmar Schneider (AUT) 2:00.0	Stein Eriksen (NOR) 2:01.2	Guttorm Berge (NOR) 2:01.7
1956	Anton Sailer (FRA) 3:14.7	Chiharu Igaya (JPN) 3:18.7	Stig Sollander (SWE) 3:20.2
1960	Ernst Hinterseer (AUT) 2:08.9	Matthias Leitner (AUT) 2:10.3	Charles Bozon (FRA) 2:10.4
1964	Josef Stiegler (AUT) 2:21.13	William Kidd (USA) 2:21.27	James Hengu (USA) 2:21.52
1968	Jean-Claude Killy (FRA) 1:39.73	Herbert Huber (AUT) 1:39.82	Alfred Matt (AUT) 1:40.09
1972	Francisco Fernández Ochoa (ESP) 1:49.27	Gustavo Thöni (ITA) 1:50.28	Rolando Thöni (ITA) 1:50.30
1976	Piero Gros (ITA) 2:03.29	Gustavo Thöni (ITA) 2:03.73	Willy Frommelt (LIE) 2:04.28
1980	Ingemar Stenmark (SWE) 1:44.26	Phil Mahre (USA) 1:44.76	Jacques Lüthy (SUI) 1:45.06
1984	Phil Mahre (USA) 1:39.21	Steve Mahre (USA) 1:39.62	Didier Bouvet (FRA) 1:40.20
1988	Alberto Tomba (ITA) 1:39.47	Frank Wörndl (FRG) 1:39.53	Paul Frommelt (LIE) 1:39.84
1992	Finn Christian Jagge (NOR) 1:44.39	Alberto Tomba (ITA) 1:44.67	Michael Tritscher (AUT) 1:44.85
1994	Thomas Stangassinger (AUT) 2:02.02	Alberto Tomba (ITA) 2:02.17	Jure Kosir (SLO) 2:02.5
1998	Hans Petter Buraas (NOR) 1:49.31	Ole Christian Furuseth (NOR) 1:50.64	Thomas Sykora (AUT) 1:50.68
2002	Jean-Pierre Vidal (FRA) 1:41.06	Sebastien Amiez (FRA) 1:41.82	Benjamin Raich (AUT) 1:42.41*

1924–36 event not held. * Alain Baxter (GBR) finished in third place but was subsequently disqualified.

GIANT SLALOM

	Gold	Silver	Bronze
1952	Stein Eriksen (NOR) 2:25.0	Christian Pravda (AUT) 2:26.9	Toni Spiss (AUT) 2:28.8
1956	Anton Sailer (AUT) 3:00.1	Andreas Molterer (AUT) 3:06.3	Walter Schuster (AUT) 3:07.2
1960	Roger Staub (SUI) 1:48.3	Josef Stiegler (AUT) 1:48.7	Ernst Hinterseer (AUT) 1:49.1
1964	François Bonlieu (FRA) 1:46.71	Karl Schranz (AUT) 1:47.09	Josef Steigler (AUT) 1:48.05
1968	Jean-Claude Killy (FRA) 3:29.28	WIlly Favre (SUI) 3:31.50	Heinrich Messner (AUT) 3:31.83
1972	Gustavo Thöni (ITA) 3:02.62	Edmund Bruggmann (SUI) 3:10.75	Werner Mattle (SUI) 3:10.99
1976	Heini Hemmi (SUI) 3:26.97	Ernst Good (SUI) 3:27.17	Ingemar Stenmark (SWE) 3:27.41

	Gold	Silver	Bronze
1980	Ingemar Stenmark (SWE) 2:40.74	Andreas Wenzel (LIE) 2:41.49	Hans Enn (AUT) 2:42.51
1984	Max Julen (SUI) 2:41.18	Jure Franko (YUG) 2:41.41	Andreas Wenzel (LIE)
1988	Alberto Tomba (ITA) 2:06.37	Hubert Strolz (AUT) 2:07.41	Pirmin Zurbriggen (SUI) 2:08.39
1992	Alberto Tomba (ITA) 2:06.98	Marc Girardelli (LUX) 2:07.30	Kjetil André Aamodt (NOR) 2:07.82
1994	Markus Wasmeier (GER) 2:52.46	Urs Kälin (SUI) 2:52.48	Christian Mayer (AUT) 2:52.58
1998	Hermann Maier (AUT) 2:38.51	Stephan Eberharter (AUT) 2:39.26	Michael von Grünigen (SUI) 2:39.69
2002	Stephan Eberharter (AUT) 2:23.28	Bode Miller (USA) 2:24.16	Lasse Kjus (NOR) 2:24.32

1924–48 event not held

SUPER GIANT SLALOM

	Gold	Silver	Bronze
1988	Franck Piccard (FRA) 1:39.66	Helmut Mayer (AUT) 1:40.96	Lars-Börje Eriksson (SWE) 1:41.08
1992	Kjetil André Aamodt (NOR) 1:13.04	Marc Girardelli (LUX) 1:13.77	Jan Einar Thorsen (NOR) 1:13.83
1994	Markus Wasmeier (GER) 1:32.53	Tommy Moe (USA) 1:32.61	Kjetil André Aamodt (NOR) 1:32.93
1998	Hermann Maier (AUT) 1:34.82	Hans Knauss (AUT) 1:35.43 Didier Cuche (SUI) 1:35.43	—
2002	Kjetil André Aamodt (NOR) 1:21.58	Stephan Eberharter (AUT) 1:21.68	Andreas Schifferer (AUT) 1:21. 83

1924–84 event not held

ALPINE COMBINATION (DOWNHILL AND SLALOM)

	Gold	Silver	Bronze
1936	Franz Pfnür (GER) 99.25pts	Gustav Lantschner (GER) 96.26	Emile Allais (FRA) 94.69
1948	Henri Orellier (FRA) 3.27pts	Karl Molitor (SUI) 6.44	James Couttet (FRA) 6.95
1988	Hubert Strolz (AUT) 36.55pts	Bernhard Gstrein (AUT) 43.45	Paul Accola (SUI) 48.24
1992	Josef Polig (ITA) 14.58pts	Gianfranco Martin (ITA) 14.90	Steve Locher (SUI) 18.16
1994	Lasse Kjus (NOR) 3:17.53	Kjetil André Aamodt (NOR) 3:18.55	Harald Strand Nielsen (NOR) 3:19.14
1998	Mario Reiter (AUT) 3:08.06	Lasse Kjus (NOR) 3:08.65	Christian Mayer (AUT) 3:10.11
2002	Kjetil André Aamodt (NOR) 3:17.56	Bode Miller (USA) 3:17.84	Benjamin Raich (AUT) 3:18.26

1924–32 and 1952–84 event not held

WOMEN
DOWNHILL

	Gold	Silver	Bronze
1948	Hedy Schlunegger (SUI) 2:28.3	Trude Beiser (AUT) 2:29.1	Resi Hammerer (AUT) 2:30.2
1952	Trude Jochum-Beiser (AUT) 1:47.1	Annemarie Buchner (GER) 1:48.0	Giuliana Mimuzzo (ITA) 1:49.0
1956	Madeleine Berthod (SUI) 1:40.7	Frieda Dänzer (SUI) 1:45.4	Lucile Wheeler (CAN) 1:45.9
1960	Heidi Beibl (GER) 1:37.6	Penelope Pitou (USA) 1:38.6	Traudl Hecher (AUT) 1:38.9
1964	Christl Haas (AUT) 1:55.39	Edith Zimmerman (AUT) 1:56.42	Traudl Hecher (AUT) 1:56.66
1968	Olga Pall (AUT) 1:40.87	Isabelle Mir (FRA) 1:41.33	Christl Haas (AUT) 1:41.41
1972	Marie-Thérèse Nadig (SUI) 1:36.68	Annemarie Pröll (AUT) 1:37.00	Susan Corrock (USA) 1:37.68
1976	Rosi Mittermaier (FRG) 1:46.16	Brigitte Totschnig (AUT) 1:46.68	Cindy Nelson (USA) 1:47.50
1980	Annemarie Moser-Pröll (AUT) 1:37.52	Hanni Wenzel (LIE) 1:38.22	Marie-Thérèse Nadig (SUI) 1:38.36
1984	MIchela Figini (SUI) 1:13.36	Maria Walliser (SUI) 1:13.41	Olga Charvátová (TCH) 1:13.53
1988	Marina Kiehl (FRG) 1:25.86	Brigitte Oertli (SUI) 1:26.61	Karen Percy (CAN) 1:26.62
1992	Kerin Lee-Gartner (CAN) 1:52.55	Hilary Lindh (USA) 1:52.61	Veronika Wallinger (AUT) 1:52.64
1994	Katja Seizinger (GER) 1:35.93	Picabo Street (USA) 1:36.59	Isolde Kostner (ITA) 1:36.85
1998	Katja Seizinger (GER) 1:28.89	Pernilla Wiberg (SWE) 1:29.18	Florence Masnada (FRA) 1:29.37
2002	Carole Montillet (FRA) 1:39.56	Isolde Kostner (ITA) 1:40.01	Renata Götschl (AUT) 1:40.39

1924–36 event not held

SLALOM

	Gold	Silver	Bronze
1948	Gretchen Fraser (USA) 1:57.2	Antoinette Meyer (SUI) 1:57.7	Erika Mahringer (AUT) 1:58.0
1952	Andrea Mead-Lawrence (USA) 2:10.6	Ossi Reichert (GER) 2:11.4	Annemarie Buchner (GER) 2:13.3
1956	Renée Colliard (SUI) 1:52.3	Regina Schöpf (AUT) 1:55.4	Yevgeniya Sidorova (URS) 1:56.7
1960	Anne Heggtveit (CAN) 1:49.6	Betsy Snite (USA) 1:52.9	Barbi Henneberger (GER) 1:56.6
1964	Christine Goitschel (FRA) 1:29.86	Marielle Goitschel (FRA) 1:30.77	Jean Saubert (USA) 1:31.36
1968	Marielle Goitschel (FRA) 1:25.86	Nancy Greene (CAN) 1:26.15	Annie Famose (FRA) 1:27.89
1972	Barbara Cochran (USA) 1:31.24	Danièlle Debernard (FRA) 1:31.26	Florence Steurer (FRA) 1:32.69
1976	Rosi Mittermaier (FRG) 1:30.54	Claudia Giordani (ITA) 1:30.87	Hanni Wenzel (LIE) 1:32.20
1980	Hanni Wenzel (LIE) 1:25.09	Christa Kinshofer (FRG) 1:26.50	Erika Hess (SUI) 1:27.89
1984	Paolette Magoin (ITA) 1:36.47	Perrine Pelen (FRA) 1:37.38	Ursula Konsett (LIE) 1:37.50
1988	Vreni Schneider (SUI) 1:36.69	Mateja Svet (YUG) 1:38.37	Christa Kinshofer-Güthlein (FRG) 1:38.40
1992	Petra Kronberger (AUT) 1:32.68	Annelise Coberger (NZL) 1:33.10	Blanca Fernández-Ochoa (ESP) 1:33.35
1994	Vreni Schneider (SUI) 1:56.01	Elfi Eder (AUT) 1:56.36	Katja Koren (SLO) 1:56.61
1998	Hilde Gerg (GER) 1:32.40	Deboarah Compagnoni (ITA) 1:32.46	Zali Steggall (AUS) 1:32.67
2002	Janica Kostelic (CRO) 1:46.10	Laure Pequegnot (FRA) 1:46.17	Anja Paerson (SWE) 1:47.09

1924–36 event not held

GIANT SLALOM

	Gold	Silver	Bronze
1952	Andrea Mead-Lawrence (USA) 2:06.8	Dagmar Rom (AUT) 2:09.0	Annemarie Buchner (GER) 2:10.0
1956	Ossi Reichert (GER) 1:56.5	Josefine Frandl (AUT) 1:57.8	Dorothea Hochleitner (AUT) 1:58.2
1960	Yvonne Rüegg (SUI) 1:39.9	Penelope Pitou (USA) 1:40.0	Giuliana Chenal-Minuzzo (ITA) 1:40.2
1964	Marielle Goitschel (FRA) 1:52.24	Christine Goitschel (FRA) 1:53.11 Jean Saubert (USA) 1:53.11	—
1968	Nancy Greene (CAN) 1:51.97	Annie Famose (FRA) 1:54.61	Fernande Bochatay (SUI) 1:54.74
1972	Marie-Thérèse Nadig (SUI) 1:29.90	Annemarie Pröll (AUT) 1:30.75	Wiltrud Drexel (AUT) 1:32.35
1976	Kathy Kreiner (CAN) 1:29.13	Rosi Mittermaier (FRG) 1:29.25	Danièlle Debernard (FRA) 1:29.95
1980	Hanni Wenzel (LIE) 2:41.66	Irene Epple (FRG) 2:42.12	Perrine Pelen (FRA) 2:42.41
1984	Debbie Armstrong (USA) 2:20.98	Christin Cooper (USA) 2:21.38	Perrine Pelen (FRA) 2:21.40
1988	Vreni Schneider (SUI) 2:06.49	Christa Kinshofer-Güthlein (FRG) 2:07.42	Maria Walliser (SUI) 2:07.72
1992	Pernilla Wiberg (SWE) 2:12.74	Diann Roffe (USA) 2:13.71 Anita Wachter (AUT) 2:13.71	—
1994	Deborah Compagnoni (ITA) 2:30.47	Martina Ertl (GER) 2:32.19	Vreni Schneider (SUI) 2:32.97
1998	Deborah Compagnoni (ITA) 2:50.59	Alexandra Meissnitzer (AUT) 2:52.39	Katja Seizinger (GER) 2:52.61
2002	Janica Kostelic (CRO) 2:30.01	Anja Paerson (SWE) 2:31.33	Sonja Nef (SUI) 2:31.67

1924–48 event not held

SUPER GIANT SLALOM

	Gold	Silver	Bronze
1988	Sigrid Wolf (AUT) 1:19.03	Michela Figini (SUI) 1:20.03	Karen Percy (CAN) 1:20.29
1992	Deborah Compagnoni (ITA) 1:21.22	Carole Merle (FRA) 1:22.63	Katja Seizinger (GER) 1:23.19
1994	Diann Roffe (USA) 1:22.15	Svetlana Gladisheva (RUS) 1:22.44	Isolde Kostner (ITA) 1:22.45
1998	Picabo Street (USA) 1:18.02	Michaela Dorfmeister (AUT) 1:18.03	Alexandra Meissnitzer (AUT) 1:18.09
2002	Daniela Ceccarelli (ITA) 1:13.59	Janica Kostelic (CRO) 1:13.64	Karen Putzer (ITA) 1:13.86

1924–84 even not held

ALPINE COMBINATION (DOWNHILL AND SLALOM)

	Gold	Silver	Bronze
1936	Christel Cranz (GER) 97.06pts	Käthe Grasegger (GER) 95.26	Laila Schou Nilsen (NOR) 93.48
1948	Trude Beiser (AUT) 6.58pts	Gretchen Fraser (USA) 6.95	Erika Mahringer (AUT) 7.04
1988	Anita Wachter (AUT) 29.25pts	Brigitte Oertli (SUI) 29.48	Maria Walliser (SUI) 51.28
1992	Petra Kronberger (AUT) 2.55pts	Anita Wachter (AUT) 19.39	Florence Masnada (FRA) 21.38
1994	Pernilla Wiberg (SWE) 3:05.16	Vreni Schneider (SUI) 3:05.29	Alenka Dovzan (SLO) 3:06.64
1998	Katja Seizinger (GER) 2:40.74	Martina Ertl (GER) 2:40.92	Hilde Gerg (GER) 2:41.50
2002	Janica Kostelic (CRO) 2:43.28	Renata Götschl (AUT) 2:44.77	Martina Ertl (GER) 2:45.16

1924–32 and 1952–84 event not held

BIATHLON MEDALS

MEN

10,000 METRES

	Gold	Silver	Bronze
1980	Frank Ulrich (GDR) 32:10.69	Vladimir Alikin (URS) 32:53.10	Anatoliy Alyabiev (URS) 33:09.16
1984	Eirik Kvalfoss (NOR) 30:53.8	Peter Angerer (FRG) 31:02.4	Matthias Jacob (GDR) 31:10.5
1988	Frank-Peter Roetsch (GDR) 25:08.1	Valeri Medvedtsev (URS) 25:23.7	Sergei Tchepikov (URS) 25:29.4
1992	Mark Kirchner (GER) 26:02.3	Ricco Gross (GER) 26:18.0	Harri Eloranta (FIN) 26:26.6
1994	Sergei Chepikov (RUS) 28:07.0	Ricco Gross (GER) 28:13.0	Sergei Tarasov (RUS) 28:27.4
1998	Ole Einar Björndalen (NOR) 27:16.2	Frode Andersson (NOR) 28:17.8	Ville Raikkonen (FIN) 28:21.7
2002	Ole Einar Björndalen (NOR) 24:51.3	Sven Fischer (GER) 25:20.2	Wolfgang Perner (AUT) 25:44.4

1924–76 event not held

20,000 METRES

	Gold	Silver	Bronze
1960	Klas Lestander (SWE) 1hr 33:21.6	Antii Tyrväinen (FIN) 1hr 33:57.7	Aleksandr Privalov (URS) 1hr 34:54.2
1964	Vladimir Melyanin (URS) 1hr 20:26.8	Aleksandr Privalov (URS) 1hr 23:42.5	Olav Jordet (NOR) 1hr 24:38.8
1968	Magnar Solberg (NOR) 1hr 13:45.9	Aleksandr Tikhonov (URS) 1hr 14:40.4	Vladimir Gundartsev (URS) 1hr 18:27.4
1972	Magnar Solberg (NOR) 1hr 15:55.5	Hans-Jörg Knauthe (GDR) 1hr 16:07.6	Lars Arvidsson (SWE) 1hr 16:27.03
1976	Nikolai Kruglov (URS) 1hr 14:12.26	Heikki Ikola (FIN) 1hr 15:54.10	Aleksandr Elizarov (URS) 1hr 16:05.57
1980	Anatoli Alyabiev (URS) 1hr 08:16.31	Frank Ullrich (GDR) 1hr 08:27.79	Eberhard Rösch (GDR) 1hr 11:11.73
1984	Peter Angerer (FRG) 1hr 11:52.7	Frank-Peter Roetsch (GDR) 1hr 13:21.4	Eirik Kvalfoss (NOR) 1hr 14:02.4
1988	Frank-Peter Roetsch (GDR) 56:33.3	Valeri Medvedtsev (URS) 56:54.6	Johann Pasler (ITA) 57:10.1
1992	Yevgeni Redkine (EUN) 57:34.4	Mark Kirchner (GER) 57:40.8	Mikael Löfgren (SWE) 57:59.4
1994	Sergei Tarasov (RUS) 57:25.3	Frank Luck (GER) 57:28.7	Sven Fischer (GER) 57:41.9
1998	Halvard Hanevold (NOR) 56:16.4	Pier Carrara (ITA) 56:21.9	Alexei Aidarov (BLR) 56:46.5
2002	Ole Einar Björndalen (NOR) 51:03.3	Frank Luck (GER) 51:39.4	Viktor Maigourov (RUS) 51:40.6

924–56 event not held

COMBINED PURSUIT (Comprising the 10km race noted above, plus a 12.5km race)

	Gold	Silver	Bronze
2000	Ole Einar Björndalen (NOR) 32:34.6	Raphael Poirée (FRA) 33:17.6	Ricco Gross (GER) 33:30.6

1924–96 event not held

BIATHLON RELAY (4 X 7500 METRES)

	Gold	Silver	Bronze
1968	Soviet Union 2hr 13:02.4	Norway 2hr 14:50.2	Sweden 2hr 17:26.3
1972	Soviet Union 1hr 51:44.92	Finland 1hr 54:37.22	GDR 1hr 54:57.67
1976	Soviet Union 1hr 57:55.64	Finland 2hr 01:45.58	GDR 2hr 04:08.61
1980	Soviet Union 1hr 34:03.27	GDR 1hr 34:56.99	FRG 1hr 37:30.26
1984	Soviet Union 1hr 38:51.7	Norway 1hr 39:03.9	FRG 1hr 39:05.1
1988	Soviet Union 1hr 22:30.0	FRG 1hr 23:37.4	Italy 1hr 23:51.5
1992	Germany 1hr 24:43.5	Unified Team 1hr 25:06.3	Sweden 1hr 25:38.2
1994	Germany 1hr 30:22.1	Russia 1hr 31:23.6	France 1hr 32:31.3
1998	Germany 1hr 21:36.2	Norway 1hr 21:56.3	Russia 1hr 22:19.3
2002	Norway 1:23:42.3	Germany 1:24:27.6	France 1:24:36.6

1924–64 event not held

WOMEN (Introduced in 1992)

7500 METRES

	Gold	Silver	Bronze
1992	Anfissa Reztsova (EUN) 24:29.2	Antje Misersky (GER) 24:45.1	Yelena Belova (EUN) 24:50.8
1994	Myriam Bédard (CAN) 26:08.8	Svetlana Paramygina (BLR) 26:09.9	Valentina Tserbe (UKR) 26:10.0
1998	Galina Kukleva (RUS) 23:08.0	Uschi Disl (GER) 23:08.7	Katrin Apel (GER) 23:32.4
2002	Kati Wilhelm (GER) 20:41.4	Uschi Disl (GER) 20:57.0	Magdalena Forsberg (SWE) 21:20.4

15,000 METRES

	Gold	Silver	Bronze
1992	Antje Misersky (GER) 51:47.2	Svetlana Paramygina (EUN) 51:58.5	Myriam Bédard (CAN) 52:15.0
1994	Myriam Bédard (CAN) 52:06.6	Anne Briand (FRA) 52:53.3	Ursula Disl (GER) 53:15.3
1994	Ekaterina Dafovska (BUL) 54:52.0	Yelena Petrova (UKR) 55:09.8	Ursula Disl (GER) 55:17.9
2002	Andrea Henkel (GER) 47:29.1	Liv Grete Poirée (NOR) 47:37.0	Magdalena Forsberg (SWE) 48:08.3

COMBINED PURSUIT (Comprising the 7.5km race noted above, plus a 10km race)

	Gold	Silver	Bronze
2002	Olga Pyleva (RUS) 31:07.7	Kati Wilhelm (GER) 31:13.0	Irina Nikoultina (BUL) 31:15.8

1992–98 event not held

BIATHLON RELAY (4 X 7500 METRES)

	Gold	Silver	Bronze
1992*	France 1hr 15:55.6	Germany 1hr 16:18.4	Unified Team 1hr 16:54.6
1994	Russia 1hr 47:19.5	Germany 1hr 51:16.5	France 1hr 52:28.1
1998	Germany 1hr 40:13.6	Russia 1hr 40:25.2	Norway 1hr 40:37.3
2002	Germany 1hr 27:55.0	Norway 1hr 28:25.6	Russia 1hr 29:19.7

* Only three people per team.

BOBSLEDDING MEDALS

MEN

TWO-MAN BOB

	Gold	Silver	Bronze
1932	United States I 8:14.14	Switzerland II 8:16.28	United States II 8:29.15
1936	United States I 5:29.29	Switzerland II 5:30.64	United States II 5:33.96
1948	Switzerland II 5:29.2	Switzerland I 5:30.4	United States II 5:35.3
1952	Germany I 5:24.54	United States I 5:26.89	Switzerland I 5:27.71
1956	Italy I 5:39.14	Italy II 5:31.45	Switzerland I 5:37.46
1964	Great Britain I 4:21.90	Italy II 4:22.02	Italy I 4:22.63
1968	Italy I 4:41.54*	FRG I 4:41.54	Romania 4:44.46
1972	FRG II 4:47.07	FRG I 4:58.84	Switzerland I 4:59.33
1976	GDR II 3:44.42	FRG I 3:44.99	Switzerland I 3:45.70

	Gold	Silver	Bronze
1980	Switzerland II 4:09.36	GDR II 4:10.93	GDR I 4:11.08
1984	GDR II 3:28.56	GDR I 3:26.04	Soviet Union I 3:26.16
1988	Soviet Union I 3:53.48	GDR I 3:54.19	GDR II 3:54.64
1992	Switzerland I 4:03.26	Germany I 4:03.55	Germany II 4:03.63
1994	Switzerland I 3:30.81	Switzerland II 3:30.86	Italy I 3:31.01
1998	Italy I 3:37.24	—	Germany I 3:37.89
	Canada I 3:27.24		
2002	Germany I 3:10.11	Switzerland I 3:10.20	Switzerland II 3:10.62

1924–28 and 1960 event not held. * Italy had faster single run.

FOUR-MAN BOB*

	Gold	Silver	Bronze
1924	Switzerland I 5:45.54	Great Britain II 5:48.83	Belgium I 6:02.29
1928†	United States II 3:20.5	United States I 3:21.0	Germany II 3:21.9
1932	United States I 7:53.68	United States II 7:55.70	Germany I 8:00.04
1936	Switzerland II 5:19.85	Switzerland I 5:22.73	Great Britain I 5:23.41
1948	United States II 5:20.1	Belgium 5:21.3	United States I 5:21.5
1952	Germany 5:07.84	United States I 5:10.48	Switzerland I 5:11.70
1956	Switzerland I 5:10.44	Italy II 5:12.10	United States I 5:12.39
1964	Canada 4:14.46	Austria 4:15.48	Italy II 4:15.60
1968†	Italy I 2:17.39	Austria I 2:17.48	Switzerland I 2:18.04
1972	Switzerland 4:43.07	Italy I 4:43.83	FRG I 4:43.92
1976	GDR I 3:40.43	Switzerland II 3:40.89	FRG I 3:41.37
1980	GDR I 3:59.92	Switzerland I 4:00.87	GDR II 4:00.97
1984	GDR I 3:20.22	GDR II 3:20.78	Switzerland I 3:21.39
1988	Switzerland I 3:47.51	GDR I 3:47.58	Soviet Union II 3:48.26
1992	Austria I 3:53.90	Germany I 3:53.92	Switzerland I 3:54.13
1994	Germany II 3:27.78	Switzerland I 3:27.84	Germany I 3:28.01
1998‡	Germany II 2:39.41	Switzerland I 2:40.01	Great Britain I 2:40.06
			France 2:40.06
2002	Germany I 3:07.51	United States I 3:07.81	United States II 3:07.86

1960 event not held. * Five-man teams allowed until 1932. † Only two runs. ‡ Three runs.

WOMEN (Introduced in 2002)

TWO-WOMAN BOB

	Gold	Silver	Bronze
2002	United States II 1:37.76	Germany I 1:38.06	Germany II 1:38.29

CURLING MEDALS

MEN

	Gold	Silver	Bronze
1998	Switzerland	Canada	Norway
2002	Norway	Canada	Switzerland

1924–94 event not held

WOMEN

	Gold	Silver	Bronze
1998	Canada	Denmark	Sweden
	Gold	Silver	Bronze
2002	Great Britain	Switzerland	Canada

1924–94 event not held

FIGURE-SKATING MEDALS

MEN

	Gold	Silver	Bronze
1908*	Nikolai Panin (RUS) 219pts	Arthur Cumming (GBR) 164	George Hall-Say (GBR) 104
1908	Ulrich Salchow (SWE) 1886.5pts	Richard Johansson (SWE) 1826.0	Per Thorén (SWE) 1787.0

	Gold	Silver	Bronze
1920	Gillis Grafström (SWE) 2838.5pts	Andreas Krogh (NOR) 2634	Martin Stixrud (NOR) 2561.5
1924	Gillis Grafström (SWE) 2575.25pts	Willy Böckl (AUT) 2518.75	Georges Gautschi (SUI) 2233.5
1928	Gillis Grafström (SWE) 2698.25pts	Willy Böckl (AUT) 2682.50	Robert von Zeebroeck (BEL) 2578.75
1932	Karl Schäfer (AUT) 2602.0pts	Gillis Grafström (SWE) 2514.5	Montgomery Wilson (CAN) 2448.3
1936	Karl Schäfer (AUT) 2959.0pts	Ernst Baier (GER) 2805.3	Felix Kaspar (AUT) 2801.0
1948	Richard Button (USA) 1720pts	Hans Gerschwiler (SUI) 1630.1	Edi Rada (AUT) 1603.2
1952	Richard Button (USA) 1730.3pts	Helmut Seibt (AUT) 1621.3	James Grogan (USA) 1627.4
1956	Hayes Alan Jenkins (USA) 1497.95pts	Ronald Robertson (USA) 1492.1	David Jenkins (USA) 1465.41
1960	David Jenkins (USA) 1440.2pts	Karol Divin (TCH) 141.3	Donald Jackson (CAN) 1401.0
1964	Manfred Schnelldorfer (GER) 1916.9pts	Alain Calmar (FRA) 1876.5	Scott Allen (USA) 1873.6
1968	Wolfgang Schwarz (AUT) 1894.1pts	Tim Woods (USA) 1891.6	Patrick Péra (FRA) 1864.5
1972	Ondrej Nepela (TCH) 2739.1pts	Sergey Tchetveroukhin (URS) 2672.4	Patrick Péra (FRA) 2653.1
1976	John Curry (GBR) 192.74pts	Vladimir Kovalyev (URS) 187.64	Toller Cranston (CAN) 187.38
1980	Robin Cousins (GBR) 189.48pts †	Jan Hoffmann (GDR) 189.72†	Charles Tickner (USA) 187.06
1984	Scott Hamilton (USA) 3.4pl	Brian Orser (CAN) 5.6	Jozef Sabovtchik (TCH) 7.4
1988	Brian Boitano (USA) 3.0pl	Brian Orser (CAN) 4.2	Viktor Petrenko (URS) 7.8
1992	Viktor Petrenko (EUN) 1.5pl	Paul Wylie (USA) 3.5	Petr Barna (TCH) 4.0
1994	Alexei Urmanov (RUS) 1.5pl	Elvis Stojko (CAN) 3.0	Philippe Candeloro (FRA) 6.5
1998	Ilya Kulik (RUS) 1.5pl	Elvis Stojko (CAN) 4.0	Philippe Candeloro (FRA) 4.5
2002	Alexei Yagudin (RUS) 1.5pl	Yevgeni Pluschenko (RUS) 4.0	Timothy Goebel (USA) 4.5

1912 event not held. * Special Figures competition. † Majority of judges in favour of Cousins. Since then, all medals decided by judges' placements.

WOMEN

	Gold	Silver	Bronze
1908	Madge Syers (GBR) 1262.5pts	Elsa Rendschmidt (GER) 1055.0	Dorothy Greenhough-Smith (GBR) 960.0
1920	Magda Mauroy-Julin (SWE) 913.5pts	Svea Norén (SWE) 887.75	Theresa Weld (USA) 898.0pts
1924	Herma Planck-Szabó (AUT) 2094.25pts	Beatrix Loughran (USA) 1959.0	Ethel Muckelt (GBR) 1750.0
1928	Sonja Henie (NOR) 2452.25pts	Fritzi Berger (AUT) 2248.50	Beatrix Loughran (USA) 2254.50
1932	Sonja Henie (NOR) 2302.5pts	Fritzi Berger (AUT) 2167.1	Maribel Vinson (USA) 2158.5
1936	Sonja Henie (NOR) 2971.4pts	Cecilia Colledge (GBR) 2926.8	Vivi-Anne Hultén (SWE) 2763.2
1948	Barbara-Ann Scott (CAN) 1467.7pts	Eva Pawlik (AUT) 1418.3	Jeanette Altwegg (GBR) 1405.5
1952	Jeanette Altwegg (GBR) 1455.8pts	Tenley Albright (USA) 1432.2	Jacqueline du Bief (FRA) 1422.0
1956	Tenley Albright (USA) 1866.30pts	Carol Heiss (USA) 1848.24	Ingrid Wendl (AUT) 1753.91
1960	Carol Heiss (USA) 1490.1pts	Sjoukje Dijkstra (NED) 1424.8	Barbara Roles (USA) 1414.8
1964	Sjoukje Dijkstra (NED) 2018.5pts	Regine Heitzer (AUT) 1945.5	Petra Burka (CAN) 1940.0
1968	Peggy Fleming (USA) 1970.5pts	Gabrielle Seyfert (GDR) 1882.3	Hana Maskova (TCH) 1828.8
1972	Beatrix Schuba (AUT) 2751.5pts	Karen Magnussen (CAN) 2763.2	Janet Lynn (USA) 2663.1
1976	Dorothy Hamill (USA) 193.80pts	Dianne De Leeuw (NED) 190.24	Christine Errath (GDR) 188.16
1980	Anett Pötzsch (GDR) 189.00pts	Linda Fratianne (USA) 188.30	Dagmar Lurz (FRG) 183.04
1984	Katarina Witt (GDR) 3.2pl	Rosalyn Sumners (USA) 4.6	Kira Ivanova (URS) 9.2
1988	Katarina Witt (GDR) 4.2pl	Elizabeth Manley (CAN) 4.6	Debra Thomas (USA) 6.0
1992	Kristi Yamaguchi (USA) 1.5pl	Midori Ito (JPN) 4.0	Nancy Kerrigan (USA) 4.0
1994	Oksana Baiul (UKR) 2.0pl	Nancy Kerrigan (USA) 2.5	Lu Chen (CHN) 5.0
1998	Tara Lipinski (USA) 2.0pl	Michelle Kwan (USA) 2.5	Lu Chen (CHN) 5.0
2002	Sarah Hughes (USA) 3.0pl	Irina Slutskaya (RUS) 3.0	Michelle Kwan (USA) 3.5

1912 event not held

PAIRS

	Gold	Silver	Bronze
1908	Germany 56.0pts	Great Britain 51.5	Great Britain 48.0
1920	Finland 80.75pts	Norway 72.75	Great Britain 66.25
1924	Austria 74.50pts	Finland 71.75	France 69.25
1928	France 100.50pts	Austria 99.25	Austria 93.25
1932	France 76.7pts	United States 77.5	Hungary 76.4
1936	Germany 103.0pts	Austria 102.7	Hungary 97.6
1948	Belgium 123.5pts	Hungary 122.2	Canada 121.0
1952	Germany 102.6pts	United States 100.6	Hungary 97.4
1956	Austria 101.8pts	Canada 101.9	Hungary 99.3
1960	Canada 80.4pts	Germany 76.8	United States 76.2
1964*	Soviet Union 104.4	Germany 103.6	Canada 98.5pts
1968	Soviet Union 315.2pts	Soviet Union 312.3	FRG 304.4
1972	Soviet Union 420.4pts	Soviet Union 419.4	GDR 411.8
1976	Soviet Union 140.54pts	GDR 136.35	GDR 134.57
1980	Soviet Union 147.26pts	Soviet Union 143.80	GDR 140.52
1984	Soviet Union 1.4pl	United States 2.8	Soviet Union 3.8
1988	Soviet Union 1.4pl	Soviet Union 2.8	United States 4.2
1992	Unified Team 1.5pl	Unified Team3.0	Canada 4.5
1994	Russia 1.5pl	Russia 3.0	Canada 4.5
1998	Russia 2.0pl	Russia 3.5	Germany 6.0
2002†	Russia	—	China 4.5
			Canada

1912 event not held. * Marika Kilius/Hansjürgen Bäumler (GER) finished second; were subsequently disqualified, then re-instated. † Canada promoted to equal first place after protests about unfair judging which had placed them second.

ICE DANCE

	Gold	Silver	Bronze
1976	Soviet Union 209.92pts	Soviet Union 204.88	United States 202.64
1980	Soviet Union 205.48pts	Hungary 204.52	Soviet Union 201.86
1984	Great Britain 2.0pl	Soviet Union 4.0	Soviet Union 7.0
1988	Soviet Union 2.0pl	Soviet Union 4.0	Canada 6.0
1992	Unified Team 2.0pl	France 4.4	Unified Team 5.6
1994	Russia 3.4pl	Russia 3.8	Great Britain 4.8
1998	Russia 2.0pl	Russia 4.0	France 7.0
2002	France 2.0pl	Russia 4.0	Italy 6.0

1908–72 event not held

FREESTYLE SKIING MEDALS

MEN

MOGULS

	Gold	Silver	Bronze
1992	Edgar Grospiron (FRA) 25.81pts	Olivier Allamand (FRA) 24.87	Nelson Carmichael (USA) 24.82
1994	Jean-Luc Brassard (CAN) 27.74pts	Sergei Shoupletsov (RUS) 26.90	Edgar Grospiron (FRA) 26.64
1998	Jonny Moseley (USA) 26.93pts	Janne Lahtela (FIN) 26.01	Sami Mustonen (FIN) 25.76
2002	Janne Lahtela (FIN) 27.97pts	Travis Mayer (USA) 27.59	Richard Gay (FRA) 26.91

1924–88 event not held

AERIALS

	Gold	Silver	Bronze
1994	Andreas Schönbächler (SUI) 234.67pts	Phillippe Laroche (CAN) 228.23	Lloyd Langlois (CAN) 222.44
1998	Eric Bergoust (USA) 255.64pts	Sebastien Foucras (FRA) 248.79	Dmitri Daschinsky (BLR) 240.79
2002	Ales Valenta (CZE) 257.02pts	Joe Pack (USA) 251.64	Alexei Grischin (BLR) 252.19

1924–92 event not held

WOMEN

MOGULS

	Gold	Silver	Bronze
1992	Donna Weinbrecht (USA) 23.69pts	Yelizaveta Kozhevnikova (EUN) 23.50	Stine Lise Hattestad (NOR) 23.04
1994	Stine Lise Hattestad (NOR) 25.97pts	Elizabeth McIntyre (USA) 25.89	Yelizaveta Kozhevnikova (EUN) 25.81
1998	Tae Satoya (JPN) 25.06	Tatyana Mittermayer (GER) 24.62	Kari Traa (NOR) 24.09
2002	Kari Traa (NOR) 25.94pts	Shannon Bahrke (USA) 25.06	Tae Satoya (JPN) 24.85

1924–88 event not held

AERIALS

	Gold	Silver	Bronze
1994	Lina Cheryasova (UZB) 166.84pts	Marie Lindgren (SWE) 165.88	Hilde Synnøve Lid (NOR) 164.13
1998	Nikki Stone (USA) 193.00pts	Xu Nannan (CHN) 186.97	Colette Brand (SUI) 171.83
2002	Alisa Camplin (AUS) 193.47pts	Veronica Brenner (CAN) 190.02	Deidra Dionne (CAN) 189.26

1924–92 event not held

ICE HOCKEY MEDALS

MEN

	Gold	Silver	Bronze
1920	Canada	United States	Czechoslovakia
1924	Canada	United States	Great Britain
1928	Canada	Sweden	Switzerland
1932	Canada	United States	Germany
1936	Great Britain	Canada	United States
1948	Canada	Czechoslovakia	Switzerland
1952	Canada	United States	Sweden
1956	Soviet Union	United States	Canada
1960	United States	Canada	Soviet Union
1964	Soviet Union	Sweden	Czechoslovakia
1968	Soviet Union	Czechoslovakia	Canada
1972	Soviet Union	United States	Czechoslovakia
1976	Soviet Union	Czechoslovakia	FRG*
1980	United States	Soviet Union	Sweden
1984	Soviet Union	Czechoslovakia	Sweden
1988	Soviet Union	Finland	Sweden
1992	Unified Team	Canada	Czechoslovakia
1994	Sweden	Canada	Finland
1998	Czech Republic	Russia	Finland
2002	Canada	United States	Russia

* Three-way tie for bronze with the United States and Finland: decided on goal average.

WOMEN

	Gold	Silver	Bronze
1998	United States	Canada	Finland
2002	Canada	United States	Sweden

1924–94 event not held

LUGEING MEDALS

MEN

SINGLES

	Gold	Silver	Bronze
1964	Thomas Köhler (GER) 3:26.77	Klaus Bonsack (GER) 3:27.04	Hans Plenk (GER) 3:30.15
1968	Manfred Schmid (AUT) 2:52.48	Thomas Köhler (GDR) 2:52.66	Klaus Bonsack (GDR) 2:55.33

	Gold	Silver	Bronze
1972	Wolfgang Scheidel (GDR) 3:27.58	Harald Ehrig (GDR) 3:28.39	Wolfram Fiedler (GDR) 3:28.73
1976	Detlef Günther (GDR) 3:27.688	Josef Fendt (FRG) 3:28.196	Hans Rinn (GDR) 3:28.574
1980	Bernhard Glass (GDR) 2:54.796	Paul Hildgartner (ITA) 2:55.372	Anton Winkler (FRG) 2:56.545
1984	Paul Hildgartner (ITA) 3:04.258	Sergey Danilin (URS) 3:04.962	Valeriy Dudin (URS) 3:05.012
1988	Jens Müller (GDR) 3:05.548	Georg Hackl (FRG) 3:05.916	Yuriy Khartchenko (URS) 3:06.274
1992	Georg Hackl (GER) 3:02.363	Markus Prock (AUT) 3:02.669	Markus Schmidt (AUT) 3:02.942
1994	Georg Hackl (GER) 3:21.571	Markus Prock (AUT) 3:21.584	Armin Zöggeler (ITA) 3:21.833
1998	Georg Hackl (GER) 3:18.436	Armin Zöggeler (ITA) 3:18.939	Jens Müller (GER) 3:19.093
2002	Armin Zöggeler (ITA) 2:57.91	Georg Hackl (GER) 2:58.270	Markus Prock (AUT) 2:58.283

1924–60 event not held

TWO-MAN

	Gold	Silver	Bronze
1964	Austria 1:41.62	Austria 1:41.91	Italy 1:42.87
1968	GDR 1:35.85	Austria 1:36.34	FRG 1:37.29
1972	Italy 1:28.35 GDR 1:28.35	—	GDR 1:29.16
1976	GDR 1:25.604	FRG 1:25.889	Austria 1:25.919
1980	GDR 1:19.331	Italy 1:19.606	Austria 1:19.795
1984	FRG 1:23.620	Soviet Union 1:23.660	GDR 1:23.887
1988	GDR 1:31.940	GDR 1:32.039	FRG 1:32.274
1992	Germany 1:32.053	Germany 1:32.239	Italy 1:32.298
1994	Italy 1:36.720	Italy II 1:36.769	Germany 1:36.945
1998	Germany 1:41.105	United States I 1:41.127	United States II 1:41.217
2002	Germany 1:26.082	United States 1:26.216	United States 1:26.220

1924–60 event not held

WOMEN

SINGLES

	Gold	Silver	Bronze
1964	Ortrun Enderlein (GER) 3:24.67	Ilse Geisler (GER) 3:27.42	Helene Thurner (AUT) 3:29.06
1968	Erica Lechner (ITA) 2:28.66	Christa Schmuck (FRG) 2:29.37	Angelika Dünhaupt (FRG) 2:29.56
1972	Anna-Maria Müller (GDR) 2:59.18	Ute Rührold (GDR) 2:59.49	Margit Schumann (GDR) 2:59.54
1976	Margit Schumann (GDR) 2:50.621	Ute Rührold (GDR) 2:50.846	Elisabeth Demleitner (FRG) 2:51.056
1980	Vera Sosulya (URS) 2:36.537	Melitta Sollmann (GDR) 2:37.657	Ingrida Amantova (URS) 2:37.817
1984	Steffi Martin (GDR) 2:46.570	Bettine Schmidt (GDR) 2:46.873	Ute Weiss (GDR) 2:47.248
1988	Steffi Martin-Walter (GDR) 3:03.973	Ute Weiss-Oberhoffner (GDR) 3:04.105	Cerstin Schmidt (GDR) 3:04.181
1992	Doris Neuner (AUT) 3:06.696	Angelika Neuner (AUT) 3:06.769	Susi Erdmann (GER) 3:07.115
1994	Gerda Weissensteiner (ITA) 3:15.517	Susi Erdman (GER) 3:16.276	Andrea Tagwerker (AUT) 3:16.652
1998	Silke Kraushaar (GER) 3:23.779	Barbara Niedernhuber (GER) 3:23.781	Angelika Neuner (AUT) 3:24.253
2002	Sylke Otto (GER) 2:52.464	Barbara Niedernhuber (GER) 2:52:785	Silke Kraushaar (GER) 2:52.865

1924–60 event not held

SKELETON SLED

MEN

	Gold	Silver	Bronze
1928*	Jennison Heaton (USA) 3:01.8	John Heaton (USA) 3:02.8	Earl of Northesk (GBR) 3:05.1
1948†	Nino Bibbia (ITA) 5:23.2	John Heaton (USA) 5:24.6	John Crammond (GBR) 5:25.1
2002	Jim Shea (USA) 1:41.96	Martin Rettl (AUT) 1:42.01	Gregor Stähli (SUI) 1:42.15

1924, 1932–36 and 1952–98 event not held. *Aggregate of three runs. † Aggregate of six runs.

WOMEN

Gold	Silver	Bronze
2002 Tristan Gale (USA) 1:45.11	Lea Ann Parsley (USA) 1:45.21	Alex Coomber (GBR) 1:45.37

1924–98 event not held

NORDIC SKIING MEDALS

MEN

1500 METRES SPRINT (FREESTYLE)

Gold	Silver	Bronze
2002 Tor Arne Hetland (NOR) 2:56.9	Peter Schlickenrieder (GER) 2:57.0	Cristian Zorzi (ITA) 2:57.2

1924–98 event not held

15,000 METRES

	Gold	Silver	Bronze
1924*	Thorleif Haug (NOR)	Johan Gröttumsbraaten (NOR)	Tipani Niku (FIN)
	1hr 14:31.0	1hr 15.51.0	1hr 16:26.0
1928†	Johan Gröttumsbraaten (NOR)	Ole Hegge (NOR)	Reidar Ödegaard (NOR)
	1hr 37:01.0	1hr 39:01.0	1hr 40:11.0
1932‡	Sven Utterström (SWE)	Axel Wikström (SWE)	Veli Saarinen (FIN)
	1hr 23:07.0	1hr 25:07.0	1hr 25:24.0
1936*	Erik-August Larsson (SWE)	Oddbjörn Hagen (NOR)	Pekka Niemi (FIN)
	1hr 14:38.0	1hr 15:33.0	1hr 16:59.0
1948*	Martin Lundström (SWE)	Nils Östensson (SWE)	Gunnar Eriksson (SWE)
	1hr 13:50.0	1hr 14:22.0	1hr 16:06.6
1952*	Hallgeir Brenden (NOR)	Tapio Mäkelä (FIN)	Paavo Lonkila (FIN)
	1hr 1:34.0	1hr 2:09.0	1hr 2:20.0
1956	Hallgeir Brenden (NOR) 49:39.0	Sixten Jernberg (SWE) 50:14.0	Pavel Koltschin (URS) 50:17.0
1960	Haakon Brusveen (NOR) 51:55.5	Sixten Jernberg (SWE) 51:58.6	Veikko Hakulinen (FIN) 52:03.0
1964	Eero Mäntyranta (FIN) 50:54.1	Harald Grönningen (NOR) 51:34.8	SixtenJernberg (SWE) 51:42.2
1968	Harald Grönningen (NOR)	Eero Mäntyranta (FIN)	Gunnar Larsson (SWE)
	47:54.2	47:56.1	48:33.7
1972	Sven-Ake Lundback (SWE)	Fedor Simsachov (URS)	Ivar Formo (NOR)
	45:28.24	46:00.84	46:02.68
1976	Nikolai Bayukov (URS) 43:58.47	Yevgeni Belyayev (URS) 44:01.10	Arto Koivisto (FIN) 44:19.25
1980	Thomas Wassberg (SWE)	Juha Mieto (FIN)	Ove Aunli (NOR)
	41:25.63	41:57.64	452:28.62
1984	Gunde Swan (SWE) 41:25.6	Aki Karvonen (FIN) 41:34.9	Harri Kirvesniemi (FIN) 41:45.6
1988	Michael Deviatyarov (URS)	Pal Mikkelsplass (NOR)	Vladimir Smirnov (URS)
	41:18.9	41:33.4	41:48.5
2002	Andrus Veerpalu (EST) 37:07.4	Frode Estil (NOR) 37:43.4	Jaak Mae (EST) 37:50.8

1992–94 event not held. * Distance was 18km. † Distance was 19.7km. ‡ Distance was 18.2km.

COMBINED PURSUIT*

	Gold	Silver	Bronze
1992	Bjørn Dahlie (NOR)	Vegard Ulvang (NOR)	Giorgio Vanzetta (ITA)
	1hr 05:37.9	1hr 06:31.3	1hr 06:31.2
1994	Bjørn Dahlie (NOR) 1hr 00:08.8	Vladimir Smirnov (KZK) 1hr 00:38.0	Silvio Fauner (ITA) 1hr 01:48.6
1998	Thomas Alsgaard (NOR)	Bjørn Dahlie (NOR)	Vladimir Smirnov (URS)
	1hr 07:01.7	1hr 07:02.8	1hr 07:31.5
2002	Johann Mühlegg (ESP) 49:20.4	Frode Estil (NOR) 49:48.9	—
		Thomas Alsgaard (NOR) 49:48.9	

1924–88 event not held. * From 1992–98 times over 15km (freestyle) were added to those achieved in the 10km (classical) race; in 2002 the second race was a 10km (freestyle)

30,000 METRES (FREESTYLE)

	Gold	Silver	Bronze
1956	Veikko Hakulinen (FIN)	Sixten Jernberg (SWE)	Pavel Koltschin (URS)
	1hr 44:06.0	1hr 44:30.0	1hr 45:45.0
1960	Sixten Jernberg (SWE)	Rolf Rämgard (SWE)	Nikolai Anikin (URS)
	1hr 56:03.9	1hr 51:16.9	1hr 52:28.2

	Gold	Silver	Bronze
1964	Eero Mäntyranta (FIN)	Harald Grönningen (NOR)	Harald Grönningen (NOR)
	1hr 30:50.7	1hr 32:02.3	1hr 32:15.8
1968	Franco Nones (ITA)	Odd Martinsen (NOR)	Odd Martinsen (NOR)
	1hr 35:29.2	1hr 36:28.9	1hr 36:55.3
1972	Vyacheslav Vedenine (URS)	Paal Tyldum (NOR)	Paal Tyldum (NOR)
	1hr 36:31.2	1hr 37:25.3	1hr 37:32.4
1976	Sergei Savelyev (URS)	William Koch (USA)	Ivan Garanin (URS)
	1hr 30:29.38	1hr 30:57.84	1hr 31:09.29
1980	Nikolai Simyatov (URS)	Vassili Rochev (URS)	Vassili Rochev (URS)
	1hr 27:02.80	1hr 27:34.22	1hr 28:03.87
1984	Nikolai Simyatov (URS)	Aleksandr Zavialov (URS)	Gunde Svan (SWE)
	1hr 28:56.3	1hr 24:35.1	1hr 29:35.7
1988	Alexei Prokurorov (URS)	VladimirSmirnov (URS)	Vegard Ulvang (NOR)
	1hr 24:26.3	1hr 24:35.1	1hr 25:11.6
1992	Vegard Ulvang (NOR)	Bjørn Dahlie (NOR)	Terje Langli (NOR)
	1hr 22:27.8	1hr 23:14.0	1hr 23:42.5
1994	Thomas Alsgaard (NOR)	Bjørn Dahlie (NOR)	Mika Myllylä (FIN)
	1hr 12:26.4	1hr 13:13.6	1hr 14:14.0
1998	Mika Myllylä (FIN)	Erling Jeune (NOR)	Silvio Fauner (ITA)
	1hr 33:55.8	1hr 35:27.1	1hr 36:08.5
2002	Johann Mühlegg (ESP)	Christian Hoffman (AUT)	Mikhail Botvinov (AUT)
	1hr 09:28.9	1hr 11:31.0	1hr 11:32.3

1924–52 event not held

50,000 METRES (CLASSICAL)

	Gold	Silver	Bronze
1924	Thorleif Haug (NOR)	Thoralf Strömstad (NOR)	Johan Gröttumsbraaten (NOR)
	3hr 44:32.0	3hr 46:23.0	3hr 47:46.0
1928	Per Erik Hedlund (SWE)	Gustaf Jonsson (SWE)	Volger Andersson (SWE)
	4hr 52:03.0	5h 05:30.0	5h 05:46.0
1932	Veli Saarinen (FIN)	Väinö Likkanen (FIN)	Arne Rustadstuen (NOR)
	4hr 28:00.0	4hr 28:20.0	4hr 31:53.0
1936	Elis Wiklung (SWE)	Axel Wikström (SWE)	Nils-Joel Englund (SWE)
	3hr 30:11.1	3hr 33:20.0	3hr 34:10.0
1948	Nils Karlsson (SWE)	Harald Eriksson (SWE)	Benjamin Vanninen (FIN)
	3hr 47:48.0	3hr 52:20.0	3hr 57:28.0
1952	Veikko Hakulinen (FIN)	Eero Kolehmainen (FIN)	Magnar Estenstad (NOR)
	3hr 33:33.0	3hr 38:11.0	3hr 38:28.0
1956	Sixten Jernberg (SWE)	Veikko Hakulinen (FIN)	Fedor Terentyev (URS)
	2hr 50:27.0	2hr 51:45.0	2hr 53:32.0
1960	Kalevi Hämäläinen (FIN)	Veikko Hakulinen (FIN)	Rolf Rämgard (SWE)
	2hr 59:06.3	2hr 59:26.7	3hr 02:46.7
1964	Sixten Jernberg (SWE)	Assar Rönnlund (SWE)	Arto Tiainen (FIN)
	2hr 43:52.6	2hr 44:58.2	2hr 45:30.4
1968	Olle Ellefsäter (NOR)	Vyacheslav Vedenine (URS)	Josef Haas (SUI)
	2hr 28:45.8	2hr 29:02.5	2hr 29:14.8
1972	Paal Tyldrum (NOR)	Magne Myrmo (NOR)	Vyacheslav Vedenine (URS)
	2hr 43:14.75	2hr 43:29.45	2hr 44:00.19
1976	Ivar Formo (NOR)	Vyacheslav Vedenine (URS)	Vyacheslav Vedenine (URS)
	2hr 37:30.50	2hr 38:13.21	2hr 39:39.21
1980	Nikolai Simyatov (URS)	Juha Mieto (FIN)	Juha Mieto (FIN)
	2hr 27:24.60	2hr 30:20.52	2hr 30:51.52
1984	Thomas Wassberg (SWE)	Juha Mieto (FIN)	Aki Karvonen (FIN)
	2hr 15:55.8	2hr 16:00.7	2hr 17:04.7
1988	Gunde Svan (SWE)	Aki Karvonen (FIN)	Aki Karvonen (FIN)
	2hr 04:30.9	2hr 05:36.4	2hr 06:01.9
1992	Bjørn Dahlie (NOR)	Maurilio De Zolt (ITA)	Maurilio De Zolt (ITA)
	2hr 03:41.5	2hr 04:39.1	2hr 06:42.1
1994	Vladimir Smirnov (KZK)	Myka Myllylä (FIN)	Sture Sivertsen (NOR)
	2hr 07:20.0	2hr 08:41.9	2hr 08:49.0
1998	Bjørn Dahlie (NOR)	Sture Sivertsen (NOR)	Sture Sivertsen (NOR)
	2hr 05:08.2	2hr 05:16.3	2hr 06:01.8

	Gold	Silver	Bronze
2002*	Mikhail Ivanov (RUS) 2hr 06:20.8	Sture Sivertsen (NOR) 2hr 06:44.5	Odd-Björnhjelmeset (NOR) 2hr 08:41.5

* Johann Mühlegg (ESP) finished first in 2hr 06:05.9 but was subsequently disqualified

4X10,000 METRES RELAY

	Gold	Silver	Bronze
1936	Finland 2hr 41:33.0	Norway 2hr 41:39.0	Sweden 2hr 43:03.0
1948	Sweden 2hr 32:08.0	Finland 2hr 41:06.0	Norway 2hr 44:33.0
1952	Finland 2hr 20:16.0	Norway 2hr 23:13.0	Sweden 2hr 24:13.0
1956	Soviet Union 2hr 15:30.0	Finland 2hr 16:31.0	Sweden 2hr 17:42.0
1960	Finland 2hr 18:45.6	Norway 2hr 18:46.4	Soviet Union 2hr 21:21.6
1964	Sweden 2hr 18:34.6	Finland 2hr 18:42.4	Soviet Union 2hr 18:46.9
1968	Norway 2hr 08:33.5	Sweden 2hr 10:13.2	Finland 2hr 10:56.7
1972	Soviet Union 2hr 04:47.94	Norway 2hr 04:57.6	Switzerland 2hr 07:00.06
1976	Finland 2hr 07:59.72	Norway 2hr 09:58.36	Soviet Union 2hr 10:51.46
1980	Soviet Union 1hr 57:03.6	Norway 1hr 58:45.77	Finland 2hr 00:00.18
1984	Sweden 1hr 55:06.3	Soviet Union 1hr 55:16.5	Finland 1hr 56:31.4
1988	Sweden 1hr 43:58.6	Soviet Union 1hr 44:11.3	Czechoslovakia 1hr 45:22.7
1992	Norway 1hr 39:26.0	Italy 1hr 40:52.7	Finland 1hr 41:22.9
1994	Italy 1hr 41:15.0	Norway 1hr 41:15.4	Finland 1hr 42:15.6
1998	Norway 1hr 40:55.7	Italy 1hr 40:55.9	Finland 1hr 42:15.5
2002	Norway 1hr 32:45.5	Italy 1hr 32:45.8	Germany 1hr 33:34.5

1924–32 event not held

WOMEN

1500 METRES SPRINT (FREESTYLE)

	Gold	Silver	Bronze
2002	Yulia Tchepalova (RUS) 3:10.6	Evi Sachenbacher (GER) 3:12.2	Anita Moen (NOR) 3:12.7

1924–98 event not held

10,000 METRES (CLASSICAL)

	Gold	Silver	Bronze
1952	Lydia Wideman (FIN) 41:40.0	Mirja Hietamies (FIN) 42:39.0	Siiri Rantanen (FIN) 42:50.0
1956	Lyubov Kozyryeva (URS) 38:11.0	Radya Yeroschina (URS) 38:16.0	Sonja Edström (SWE) 38:23.0
1960	Maria Gusakova (URS) 39:46.6	Lyubov Baranova-Kozyryeva (URS) 40:04.2	Radya Yeroschina (URS) 40:06.0
1964	Klaudia Boyarskikh (URS) 40:24.3	Yevdokia Mekshilo (URS) 40:26.6	Maria Gusakova (URS) 40:46.6
1968	Toini Gustafsson (SWE) 36:46.5	Berit Mördre (NOR) 37:54.6	Inger Aufles (NOR) 37:59.9
1972	Galina Kulakova (URS) 34:17.8	Alevtina Olunina (URS) 34:54.1	Marjatta Kajosmaa (FIN) 34:56.5
1976	Raisa Smetanina (URS) 30:13.41	Helena Takalo (FIN) 30:14.28	Galina Kulakova (URS) 30:38.61
1980	Barbara Petzold (GDR) 30:31.54	Hilkka Riihivuori (FIN) 30:35.05	Helena Takalo (FIN) 30:45.25
1984	Marja-Liisa Hämäläinen (FIN) 31:44.2	Raisa Smetanina (URS) 32:02.9	Brit Petersen (NOR) 32:12.7
1988	Vida Ventsene (URS) 30:08.3	Raisa Smetanina (URS) 30:17.0	Marjo Matikainen (FIN) 30:20.5
2002	Bente Skari (NOR) 28:05.6	Olga Danilova (RUS) 28:08.1	Yulie Tchepalova (RUS) 28:09.9

1924–48 and 1992–98 event not held

COMBINED PURSUIT

	Gold	Silver	Bronze
1992	Lyubov Yegorova (EUN) 40:07.7	Stefania Belmondo (ITA) 40:31.8	Yelena Välbe (EUN) 40:51.7
1994	Lyubov Yegorova (RUS) 41:38.1	Manuela di Centa (ITA) 41:46.4	Stefania Belmondo (ITA) 42:21.1
1998	Larissa Lazutina (RUS) 46:06.9	Olga Danilova (RUS) 46:13.4	Katerina Neumannova (CZE) 46:14.2
2002†	Olga Danilova (RUS) 24:52.1	Beckie Scott (CAN) 25:09.9	Katerina Neumannova (CZE) 25:10.0

1924–88 event not held. * From 1992–98, times over 10km (freestyle) were added to those achieved in the 5km (classical) race. In 2002 the second race was 5km (freestyle). † Larissa Lazutina (RUS) finished in second place but was subsequently disqualified.

15,000 METRES (FREEESTYLE)

	Gold	Silver	Bronze
1992	Lyubov Yegorova (EUN) 42:20.8	Marjut Lukharinen (FIN) 43:29.9	Yelena Välbe (EUN) 43:42.3
1994	Manuela di Centa (ITA) 39:44.5	Lyubov Yegorova (RUS) 41:03.0	Nina Gavrilyuk (RUS) 41:10.4
1998	Olga Danilova (RUS) 46:55.4	Larissa Lazutina (RUS) 47:01.0	Anita Moen-Guidon (NOR) 47:52.6
2002*	Stefania Belmondo (ITA) 39:54.4	Katerina Neumannova (CZE) 40:01.3	Yulia Tchepalova (RUS) 40:02.1

1924–88 event not held. * Larissa Lazutina (RUS) finished in second place, but was susequently disqualified.

30,000 METRES (CLASSICAL)

	Gold	Silver	Bronze
1992	Stefania Belmondo (ITA) 1hr 22:30.1	Lyubov Yegorova (EUN) 1hr 22:52.0	Yelena Välbe (EUN) 1hr 24:13.9
1994	Manuela di Centa (ITA) 1hr 25:41.6	Marit Wold (NOR) 1hr 25:57.8	Marja-Liisa Hämäläinen (FIN) 1hr 26:13.6
1998	Yulia Chepalova (RUS) 1hr 22:01.5	Stefania Belmondo (ITA) 1hr 22:11.7	Larissa Lazutina (RUS) 1hr 23:15.7
2002*	Gabriella Paruzzi (ITA) 1:30:57.1	Stefania Belmondo (ITA) 1:31:01.6	Bente Skari (NOR) 1:31:36.3

1924–88 event not held. * Larissa Lazutina (RUS) finished first in 1:29:09.0 but was subsequently disqualified.

4 X 5000 METRES RELAY*

	Gold	Silver	Bronze
1956	Finland 1hr 09:01.0	Soviet Union 1hr 09:28.0	Sweden 1hr 09:48.0
1960	Sweden 1hr 04:21.4	Soviet Union 1hr 05:02.6	Finland 1hr 06:27.5
1964	Soviet Union 59:20.2	Sweden 1hr 01:27.0	Finland 1hr 02:45.1
1968	Norway 57:30.0	Sweden 57:51.0	Soviet Union 58:13.6
1972	Soviet Union 48:46.15	Finland 49:19.37	Norway 49:51.49
1976	Soviet Union 1hr 07:49.75	Finland 1hr 08:36.57	GDR 1hr 09:57.95
1980	GDR 1hr 02:11.10	Soviet Union 1hr 03:18.30	Norway 1hr 04:13.50
1984	Norway 1hr 06:49.7	Czechoslovakia 1hr 01:33.0	Finland 1hr 07:36.7
1988	Soviet Union 59:51.1	Norway 1hr 01:33.0	Finland 1hr 01:53.8
1992	Unified Team 59:34.8	Norway 59:56.4	Italy 1hr 00:25.9
1994	Russia 57:12.5	Norway 57:42.6	Italy 58:42.6
1998	Russia 55:33.5	Norway 55:38.0	Italy 56:53.3
2002	Germany 49:30.6	Norway 49:31.9	Switzerland 50:03.6

1924–52 event not held. * Held over three stages prior to 1976.

DISCONTINUED NORDIC SKIING EVENTS

MEN
10,000 METRES (CLASSICAL)

	Gold	Silver	Bronze
1992	Vegard Ulvang (NOR) 27:36.0	Marco Alberello (ITA) 27:55.2	Christer Majbäck (SWE) 27:56.4
1994	Bjørn Dæhlie (NOR) 24:20.1	Vladimir Smirnov (KZK) 24:38.3	Marco Alberello (ITA) 24:42.3
1998	Bjørn Dæhlie (NOR) 27:24.5	Markus Gander (AUT) 27:32.5	Mika Myllylä (FIN) 27:40.1

1924–88 event not held

WOMEN
5,000 METRES (CLASSICAL)

	Gold	Silver	Bronze
1964	Klaudia Boyarskikh (URS) 17:50.5	Mirja Lehtonen (FIN) 17:52.9	Alevtina Koltschina (URS) 18:08.4
1968	Toini Gustafsson (SWE) 16:45.2	Galina Kulakova (URS) 16:48.4	Alevtina Koltschina (URS) 16:51.6
1972	Galina Kulakova (URS) 17:00.50	Marjatta Kajosmaa (FIN) 17:05.50	Helena Sikolova (TCH) 17:07.32
1976	Helena Takalo (FIN) 15:48.69	Raisa Smetanina (URS) 15:49.73	Nina Baldycheva (URS) 16:12.82*
1980	Raisa Smetanina (URS) 15:06.92	Hikka Riihivuori (FIN) 15:11.96	Kvetoslava Jeriová (TCH) 15:23.44
1984	Marja-Liisa Hämäläinen (FIN) 17:04.0	Berit Aunli (NOR) 17:41.1	Kvetoslava Jeriová (TCH) 17:18.3
1988	Marjo Matikainen (FIN) 15:04.0	Tamara Tikhonova (URS) 15:05.3	Vida Ventsene (URS) 15:11.1
1992	Marjut Lukkarinen (FIN) 14:13.8	Lyubov Yegorova (EUN) 14:14.7	Yelena Valbe (EUN) 14:22.7
1994	Lyubov Yegorova (RUS) 14:08.8	Manuela di Centa (ITA) 14:28.3	Marja-Liisa Kirvesniemi (FIN) 14:36.0

	Gold	Silver	Bronze
1998	Larissa Lazutina (RUS) 17:37.9	Katerina Neumannova (CZE) 17:42.7	Bente Martinsen (NOR) 17:49.4

1924–60 event not held. * Galina Kulakova (URS) finished third but was subsequently disqualified.

20,000 METRES (FREESTYLE)

1984	Marja-Liisa Hämäläinen (FIN)	Raisa Smetanina (URS)	Anne Jahren (NOR)
	1hr 01:45.0	1hr 02:26.7	1hr 03:13.06
1988	Tamara Tikhonova (URS) 55:53.6	Anfissa Reztsova (URS) 56:12.8	Raisa Smetanina (URS) 57:22.1

1924–80 event not held

NORDIC COMBINED MEDALS

SPRINT

2002	Samppa Lajunen (FIN)	Ronny Ackermann (GER)	Felix Gottwald (AUT)

1924–98 event not held

INDIVIDUAL*

1924†	Thorleif Haug (NOR)	Thoralf Strömstad (NOR)	Johan Gröttumsbraaten (NOR)
1928†	Johan Gröttumsbraaten (NOR)	Hans Vinjarengen (NOR)	John Snersrud (NOR)
1932	Johan Gröttumsbraaten (NOR)	Ole Stenen (NOR)	Hans Vinjarengen (NOR)
	446.0pts	436.05	434.60
1936	Oddbjörn Hagen (NOR)	Olaf Hoffsbakken (NOR)	Sverre Brodahl (NOR)
	430.30pts	419.80	408.10
1948	Heikki Hasu (FIN) 448.80pts	Martti Huhtala (FIN) 433.65	Sven Israelsson (SWE) 433.40
1952	Simon Slattvik (NOR)	Heikki Hasu (FIN)	Sverre Stenersen (NOR)
	451.621pts	447.50	436.355
1956	Sverre Stenersen (NOR)	Bengt Eriksson (SWE)	Franciszek Gron-Gasienica (POL)
	455.0pts	437.4	436.8
1960	Georg Thoma (GER) 457.952pts	Tormod Knutsen (NOR) 453.000	Nikolai Gusakow (URS) 452.000
1964	Tormod Knutsen (NOR)	Nikolai Kiselyev (URS)	Georg Thoma (GER)
	469.28pts	453.04	452.88
1968	Frantz Keller (FRG) 449.04pts	Alois Kälin (SUI) 447.94	Andreas Kunz (GDR) 444.10
1972	Ulrich Wehling (GDR)	Georg Thoma (GER)	Karl-Heinz Luck (GDR)
	413.34pts	405.55	398.80
1976	Ulrich Wehling (GDR)	Urban Hettich (FRG)	Urban Hettich (FRG)
	423.39pts	418.90	417.47
1980	Ulrich Wehling (GDR) 432.20pts	Jouko Karjalainen (FIN) 429.50	Konrad Winkler (GDR) 425.32
1984	Tom Sandberg (NOR) 422.595pts	Jouko Karjalainen (FIN) 416.900	Jukka Ylipulli (FIN) 410.825
1988	Hippolyt Kempt (SUI)	Klaus Sulzenbacher (AUT)	Allar Levandi (URS)
1992	Fabrice Guy (FRA)	Sylvain Guillaume (FRA)	Klaus Sulzenbacher (AUT)
1994	Fred Børre Lunberg (NOR)	Takanori Kono (JPN)	Bjarte Engen Vik (NOR)
1998	Bjarte Engen Vik (NOR)	Samppa Lajunen (FIN)	Valeri Stolyarov (RUS)
2002	Samppa Lajunen (FIN)	Jaakko Tallus (FIN)	Felix Gottwald (AUT)

* In 1924–52 the distance was 18km; since then it is 15km. † In 1924–28 scoring was on a different basis to that from 1932 onwards.

TEAM

1988	FRG	Switzerland	Austria
1992	Japan	Norway	Austria
1994	Japan	Norway	Switzerland
1998	Norway	Finland	France
2002	Finland	Germany	Austria

1924–84 event not held

SKI-JUMPING MEDALS Normal Hill (1924–88 70m; from 1992 90m)

	Gold	Silver	Bronze
1924*	Jacob Tullin Thams (NOR)	Narve Bonna (NOR)	Anders Haugen (USA)
	18 960pts	18 689	17 916
1928	Alf Andersen (NOR) 19 208pts	Sigmund Ruud (NOR) 18 542	Rudolf Burkert (TCH) 17 937
1932	Birger Ruud (NOR) 228.1pts	Hans Beck (NOR) 227.0	Kaare Wahlberg (NOR) 219.5
1936	Birger Ruud (NOR) 232.0pts	Sven Eriksson (SWE) 230.5	Reidar Andersen (NOR) 228.9

	Gold	Silver	Bronze
1948	Petter Hugsted (NOR) 228.1pts	Birger Ruud (NOR) 226.6	Thorleif Schjeldrup (NOR) 225.1
1952	Arnfinn Bergmann (NOR) 226.0pts	Torbjörn Falkangar (NOR) 221.5	Karl Holmström (SWE) 219.5
1956	Antti Hyvärinen (FIN) 229.9pts	Aulis Kallakorpi (FIN) 225.0	Harry Glass (GER) 224.5
	Gold	Silver	Bronze
1960	Helmut Recknagel (GER) 227.2pts	Niilio Halonen (FIN) 222.6	Otto Leodolter (AUT) 219.4
1964	Veikko Kankkonen (FIN) 229.9pts	Toralf Engan (NOR) 226.3	Torgeir Brandtzäg (NOR) 222.9
1968	Jiri Taska (TCH) 216.5pts	Reinhold Bachler (AUT) 214.2	Baldur Preiml (AUT) 212.6
1972	Yukio Kasaya (JPN) 244.2pts	Akitsuga Konno (JPN) 234.8	Seiji Aochi (JPN) 229.5
1976	Hans-Georg Aschenbach (GDR) 252.0pts	Jochen Danneberg (GDR) 246.2	Karl Schnabl (AUT) 242.0
1980	Toni Innauer (AUT) 266.3pts	Manfred Dekker (GDR) 249.2 Hirokazu Yagi (JPN) 249.2	—
1984	Jens Weissflog (GDR) 215.2pts	Matti Nykänen (FIN) 214.0	Jari Puikkonen (FIN) 212.8
1988	Matti Nykänen (FIN) 229.1pts	Pavel Ploc (TCH) 212.1	Jiri Malec (TCH) 211.8
1992	Ernst Vettori (AUT) 222.8	Martin Höllwarth (AUT) 218.1	Toni Nieminen (FIN) 217.0
1994	Espen Bredesen (NOR) 282.0pts	Lasse Ottesen (NOR) 268.0	Dieter Thoma (GER) 260.5
1998	Jani Soininen (FIN) 234.5pts	Kazuyoshi Funaki (JPN) 233.5	Andreas Wiidhoelz (AUT) 232.5
2002	Simon Ammann (SUI) 269.0pts	Sven Hannawald (GER) 267.5	Adam Malysz (POL) 263.0

* Originally Thorleif Haug (NOR) was placed third due to incorrect calculations at the time. The error was corrected in 1974.

LARGE HILL (1964–88 90m; from 1992 120m)

	Gold	Silver	Bronze
1964	Toralf Engan (NOR) 230.7pts	Veikko Kankkonen (FIN) 228.9	Torgeir Brandtzaeg (NOR) 227.2
1968	Vladimir Belousov (URS) 231.3pts	Jiri Raska (TCH) 229.4	Lars Grini (NOR) 214.3
1972	Wojciech Fortuna (POL) 219.9pts	Walter Steiner (SUI) 219.8	Rainer Schmidt (GDR) 219.3
1976	Karl Schnabl (AUT) 234.8pts	Toni Innauer (AUT) 232.9	Henry Glass (GDR) 221.7
1980	Jouko Törmäinen (FIN) 271.0pts	Hubert Neuper (AUT) 262.4	Jari Puikkonen (FIN) 248.5
1984	Matti Nykänen (FIN) 232.2pts	Jens Weissflog (GDR) 213.7	Pavel Ploc (TCH) 202.9
1988	Matti Nykänen (FIN) 224.0pts	Erik Johnsen (NOR) 207.9	Matjaz Debelak (YUG) 207.7
1992	Toni Nieminen (FIN) 239.5pts	Martin Höllwarth (AUT) 227.3	Heinz Kuttin (AUT) 214.8
1994	Jens Weissflog (GER) 274.5pts	Espen Bredesen (NOR) 266.5	Andreas Goldberger (AUT) 255.0
1998	Kazuyoshi Funaki (JPN) 272.3pts	Jani Soininen (FIN) 260.8	Mashiko Harada (JPN) 258.3
2002	Simon Ammann (SUI) 281.4pts	Adam Malysz (POL) 267.9	Matti Hautamäki (FIN) 256.0

1924–60 event not held

LARGE HILL (TEAM)

	Gold	Silver	Bronze
1988	Finland 634.4pts	Yugoslavia 625.5	Norway 596.1
1992	Finland 644.4pts	Austria 642.9	Czechoslovakia 620.1
1994	Germany 970.1	Japan 956.9	Austria 918.9
1998	Japan 933.0pts	Germany 897.4	Austria 881.5
2002	Germany 974.1pts	Finland 974.0	Slovenia 946.3

1924–84 event not held

SNOWBOARDING MEDALS (Introduced in 1998)

MEN

HALFPIPE

	Gold	Silver	Bronze
1998	Gian Simmen (SUI) 85.2pts	Daniel Franck (NOR) 82.4	Ross Powers (USA) 82.1
2002	Ross Powers (USA) 46.1pts	Danny Kass (USA) 42.5	Jarret Thomas (USA) 42.1

GIANT SLALOM

Gold	Silver	Bronze
1998	Ross Rebagliati (CAN) 2:03.96	Thomas Prugger (ITA) 2:03.98	Ueli Kestenholz (SUI) 2:04.08
2002*	Philip Schoch (SUI)	Richard Richardsson (SWE)	Chris Klug (USA)

* In 2002 two competitors raced in parallel, after an elimination round.

WOMEN

HALFPIPE

Gold	Silver	Bronze
1998	Nicola Thost (GER) 74.6pts	Stine Brun Kjeldaas (NOR) 74.2	Shannon Dunn (USA) 72.8
2002	Kelly Clark (USA) 47.9pts	Dorianne Vidal (FRA) 43.0	Fabienne Reuteler (SUI) 39.7

GIANT SLALOM

Gold	Silver	Bronze
1998	Karine Ruby (FRA) 2:17.34	Heidi Renoth (GER) 2:19.17	Brigitte Koeck (AUT) 2:19.42
2002*	Isabelle Blanc (FRA)	Karine Ruby (FRA)	Lidia Trettel (ITA)

* In 2002 two competitors raced in parallel, after an elimination round.

SPEED-SKATING MEDALS

MEN

500 METRES

	Gold	Silver	Bronze
1924	Charles Jewtraw (USA) 44.0	Oskar Olsen (NOR) 44.2	Roald Larsen (NOR) 44.8
			Clas Thunberg (FIN) 44.8
1928	Clas Thunberg (FIN) 43.4	—	John Farrrell (USA) 43.6
	Bernt Evensen (NOR) 43.4		Roald Larsen (NOR) 43.6
			Jaako Friman (FIN) 43.6
1932	John Shea (USA) 43.4	Bernt Evensen (NOR) 5m	Alexander Hurd (CAN) 8m
1936	Ivar Ballandgrud (NOR) 43.4	Georg Krog (NOR) 43.5	Leo Friesinger (USA) 44.0
1948	Finn Helgesen (NOR) 43.1	Kenneth Bartholomew (USA) 43.2	—
		Thomas Byberg (NOR) 43.2	
		Robert Fitzgerald (USA) 43.2	
1952	Kenneth Henry (USA) 43.2	Donald McDermott (USA) 43.9	Arne Johansen (NOR) 44.0
			Gordon Audley (CAN) 44.0
1956	Yevgeni Grishin (URS) 40.2	Rafael Gratsch (URS) 40.8	Alv Gjestvang (NOR) 41.0
1960	Yevgeni Grishin (URS) 40.2	William Disney (USA) 40.3	Rafael Gratsch (URS) 40.4
1964	Richard McDermott (USA) 40.1	Yevgeni Grishin (URS) 40.6	—
		Vladimir Orlov (URS) 40.6	
		Alv Gjestvang (NOR) 40.6	
1968	Erhard Keller (FRG) 40.3	Richard McDermott (USA) 40.5	—
		Magne Thomassen (NOR) 40.5	
1972	Erhard Keller (FRG) 39.44	Hasse Börjes (SWE) 39.69	Valeri Muratov (URS) 39.80
1976	Yevgeni Kulikov (URS) 39.17	Valeri Muratov (URS) 39.25	Daniel Immerfall (USA) 39.54
1980	Eric Heiden (USA) 38.03	Yevgeni Kulikov (URS) 38.37	Lieuwe de Boer (NED) 38.48
1984	Sergei Fokitchev (URS) 38.19	Yoshihiro Kitazawa (JPN) 38.30	Gaétan Boucher (CAN) 38.39
1988	Uwe-Jens Mey (GDR) 36.45	Jan Ykema (NED) 36.76	Akira Kuriowa (JPN) 36.77
1992	Uwe-Jens Mey (GER) 37.14	Toshiyuki Kuriowa (JPN) 37.18	Junichi Inoue (JPN) 37.26
1994	Aleksandr Golubyev (RUS) 36.33	Sergei Klevchenya (RUS) 36.39	Manabu Horii (JPN) 36.53
1998*	Hiroyasu Shimizu (JPN) 1:11.35	Jeremy Wotherspoon (CAN) 1:11.84	Kevin Overland (CAN) 1:11.86
2002	Casey FitzRandolph (USA) 1:09.23	Hiroyasu Shimizu (JPN) 1:09.26	Kip Carpenter (USA) 1:09.47

* In 1998 the event changed to an aggregate of the times from two races.

1000 METRES

	Gold	Silver	Bronze
1976	Peter Mueller (USA) 1:19.32	Jörn Didriksen (NOR) 1:20.45	Valeri Muratov (URS) 1:20.57
1980	Eric Heiden (USA) 1:15.18	Gaétan Boucher (CAN) 1:16.68	Frode Rönning (NOR) 1:16.91
			Vladimir Lobanov (URS) 1:16.91
1984	Gaétan Boucher (CAN) 1:15.80	Sergei Khlebnikov (URS) 1:16.63	Kai Arne Engelstad (NOR) 1:16.75

	Gold	Silver	Bronze
1988	Nikolai Gulyayev (URS) 1:13.03	Uwe-Jens Mey (GDR) 1:13.11	Igor Gelezovsky (URS) 1:13.19
1992	Olaf Zinke (GER) 1:14.85	Kim Moon-Yan (KOR) 1:14.86	Yukinori Miyabe (JPN) 1:14.92
1994	Dan Jansen (USA) 1:12.43	Igor Zhelezovsky (BLR) 1:12.72	Sergei Klevchenya (RUS) 1:12.85
1998	Ids Postma (NED) 1:10.64	Jan Bos (NED) 1:10.71	Hiroyasu Shimizu (JPN) 1:11.00
2002	Gerard van Velde (NED) 1:07.18	Jan Bos (NED) 1:07.53	Joey Cheek (USA) 1:07.61

1924–72 event not held

1500 METRES

	Gold	Silver	Bronze
1924	Clas Thunberg (FIN) 2:20.8	Roald Larsen (NOR) 2:20.0	Sigurd Moen (NOR) 2:25.6
1928	Clas Thunberg (FIN) 2:21.1	Bernt Evensen (NOR) 2:21.9	Ivar Ballangrud (NOR) 2:22.6
1932	John Shea (USA) 2:57.5	Alexander Hurd (CAN) 5m	William Logan (CAN) 6m
1936	Charles Mathiesen (NOR) 2:19.2	Ivar Ballangrud (NOR) 2:20.2	Birger Wasenius (FIN) 2:20.9
1948	Sverre Farstad (NOR) 2:17.6	Ake Seyffarth (SWE) 2:18.1	Odd Lundberg (NOR) 2:18.9
1952	Hjalmar Andersen (NOR) 2:20.4	Willem van der Voort (NED) 2:20.6	Roald Aas (NOR) 2:21.6
1956	Yevgeni Grischin (URS) 2:08.6	—	Tiovo Salonen (FIN) 2:09.4
	Yuri Mikhailov (URS) 2:08.6		
1960	Roald Aas (NOR) 2:10.4	—	Boris Stenin (URS) 2:11.5
	Yevgeni Grishin (URS) 2:10.4		
1964	Ants Antson (URS) 2:10.3	Cornelis Verkerk (NED) 2:10.6	Villy Haugen (NOR) 2:11.25
1968	Cornelis Verkerk (NED) 2:03.4	Ard Schenk (NED) 2:05.0	—
		Ivar Eriksen (NOR) 2:05.0	
1972	Ard Schenk (NED) 2:02.96	Roar Grönvold (NOR) 2:04.26	Göran Claeson (SWE) 2:05.89
1976	Jan Egil Storholt (NOR) 1:59.38	Yuri Kondakov (URS) 1:59.97	Hans Van Helden (NED) 2:00.87
1980	Eric Heiden (USA) 1:55.44	Kai Stenshjemmet (NOR) 1:56.81	Terje Andersen (NOR) 1:56.92
1984	Gaétan Boucher (CAN) 1:58.36	Sergei Khlebnikov (URS) 1:58.83	Oleg Bogyev (URS) 1:58.89
1988	André Hoffmann (GDR) 1:52.06	Eric Flaim (USA) 1:52.12	Michael Hadschieff (AUT) 1:52.31
1992	Johann-Olav Koss (NOR) 1:54.81	Adne Søndral (NOR) 1:54.85	Leo Visser (NED) 1:54.90
1994	Johann-Olav Koss (NOR) 1:51.29	Rintje Ritsma (NED) 1:51.99	Flako Zandstra (NED) 1:52.38
1998	Ådne Søndrål (NOR) 1:47.87	Ids Postma (NED) 1:48.13	Rintje Ritsma (NED) 1:48.52
2002	Derek Parra (USA) 1:43.95	Jochen Uytdehaage (NED) 1:44.57	Ådne Søndrål (NOR) 1:45.26

5000 METRES

	Gold	Silver	Bronze
1924	Clas Thunberg (FIN) 8:39.0	Julius Skutnabb (FIN) 8:48.4	Roald Larsen (NOR) 2:00.87
1928	Ivar Ballangrud (NOR) 8:50.5	Julius Skutnabb (FIN) 8:59.1	Bernt Evensen (NOR) 9:01.1
1932	Irving Jaffee (USA) 9:40.8	Edward Murphy (USA) 2m	William Logan (CAN) 4m
1936	Ivar Ballangrud (NOR) 8:19.6	Birger Wasenius (FIN) 8:23.3	Antero Ojala (FIN) 8:30.1
1948	Reidar Liaklev (NOR) 8:29.4	Odd Lundberg (NOR) 8:32.7	Göthe Hedlund (SWE) 8:34.8
1952	Hjalmar Andersen (NOR) 8:10.6	Kees Broekman (NED) 8:21.6	Sverre Haugli (NOR) 8:22.4
1956	Boris Schilkov (URS) 7:48.7	Sigvard Ericsson (SWE) 7:56.7	Oleg Gontscharenko (URS) 7:57.5
1960	Viktor Kositschkin (URS) 7:51.3	Knut Johannesen (NOR) 8:00.8	Jan Pesman (NED) 8:05.1
1964	Knut Johannesen (NOR) 7:38.4	Per Moe (NOR) 7:38.6	Anton Maier (NOR) 7:42.0
1968	Anton Maier (NOR) 7:22.4	Cornelis Verkerk (NED) 7:23.2	Petrus Nottet (NED) 7:25.5
1972	Ard Schenk (NED) 7:23.6	Roar Grönvald (NOR) 7:28.18	Sten Stensen (NOR) 7:33.39
1976	Sten Stensen (NOR) 7:24.48	Piet Kleine (NED) 7:26.47	Hans Van Helden (NED) 7:26.54
1980	Eric Heiden (USA) 7:02.29	Kai Stenshjammet (NOR) 7:03.28	Tom Oxholm (NOR) 7:05.59
1984	Tomas Gustafson (SWE) 7:12.28	Igor Malkov (URS) 7:12.30	René Schöfisch (GDR) 7:17.49
1988	Tomas Gustafson (SWE) 6:44.63	Leendert Visser (NED) 6:44.98	Gerard Kemkers (NED) 6:45.92
1992	Geir Karlstad (NOR) 6:59.97	Falko Zandstra (NED) 7:02.28	Leo Visser (NED) 7:04.96
1994	Johann-Olav Koss (NOR) 6:34.96	Kjell Storelid (NOR) 6:42.68	Rintje Ritsma (NED) 6:43.94
1998	Gianni Romme (NED) 6:22.20	Rintje Ritsma (NED) 6:28.24	Bart Veldkamp (BEL) 6:28.31
2002	Jochen Uytdehaage (NED) 6:14.66	Derek Parra (USA) 6:17.98	Jens Boden (GER) 6:21.73

10,000 METRES

	Gold	Silver	Bronze
1924	Julius Skutnabb (FIN) 18:04.8	Clas Thunberg (FIN) 18:97.8	Roald Larsen (NOR) 18:12.2
1928	—*		
1932	Irving Jaffee (USA) 19:13.6	Ivar Ballangrud (NOR) 5m	Frank Stack (CAN) 6m
1936	Ivar Ballangrud (NOR) 17:24.3	Birger Wasenius (FIN) 17:28.2	Max Stiepl (AUT) 17:30.0
1948	Ake Seyffarth (SWE) 17:26.3	Lauri Parkkinen (FIN) 17:36.0	Pentti Lammio (FIN) 17:42.7
1952	Hjalmar Andersen (NOR) 16:45.8	Kees Broekman (NED) 17:10.6	Carl-Erik Asplund (SWE) 17:16.6

	Gold	Silver	Bronze
1956	Sigvard Ericsson (SWE) 16:35.9	Knut Johannesen (NOR) 16:36.9	Oleg Gontscharenko (URS) 16:42.3
1960	Knut Johannesen (NOR) 15:46.6	Viktor Kositschkin (URS) 15:49.2	Kjell Bäckman (SWE) 16:14.2
1964	Jonny Nilsson (SWE) 15:50.1	Anton Maier (NOR) 16:06.0	Knut Johannesen (NOR) 16:06.3
1968	Johnny Höglin (SWE) 15:23.6	Anton Maier (NOR) 15:23.9	Orjan Sandler (SWE) 15:31.8
1972	Ard Schenk (NED) 15:01.35	Cornelis Verkerk (NED) 15:04.70	Sten Stensen (NOR) 15:07.08
1976	Piet Kleine (NED) 14:50.59	Sten Stensen (NOR) 14:53.30	Hans Van Helden (NED) 15:02.02
1980	Eric Heiden (USA) 14:28.13	Piet Kleine (NED) 14:36.03	Tom Oxholm (NOR) 14:36.60
1984	Igor Malkov (URS) 14:39.90	Tomas Gustafson (SWE) 14:39.95	René Schöfisch (GDR) 14:46.91
1988	Tomas Gustafson (SWE) 13:48.20	Michael Hadschieff (AUT) 13:56.11	Leendert Visser (NED) 14:00.55
1992	Bart Veldkamp (NED) 14:12.12	Johann-Olav Koss (NOR) 14:14.58	Geir Karlstad (NOR) 14:18.13
1994	Johann-Olav Koss (NOR) 13:30.55	Kjell Storelid (NOR) 13:49.25	Bart Veldkamp (NED) 13:56.73
1998	Gianni Romme (NED) 13:15.33	Bob de Jong (NED) 13:25.76	Rintje Ritsma (NED) 13:28.19
2002	Jochen Uytdehaage (NED) 12:58.92	Gianni Romme (NED) 13:10.03	Gianni Romme (NED) 13:16.92

* The 1928 Event was abandoned.

WOMEN

500 METRES

	Gold	Silver	Bronze
1960	Helga Haase (GER) 45.9	Natalya Donchenko (URS) 46.0	Jeanne Ashworth (USA) 46.1
1964	Lydia Skoblikova (URS) 45.0	Irina Yegorova (URS) 45.4	Tatyana Sidorova (URS) 45.5
1968	Ludmila Titova (URS) 46.1	Mary Meyers (USA) 46.3 Dianne Holum (USA) 46.3 Jennifer Fish (USA) 46.3	—
1972	Anne Henning (USA) 43.33	Vera Krasnova (URS) 44.01	Ludmila Titova (URS) 44.45
1976	Sheila Young (USA) 42.76	Catherine Priestner (CAN) 43.12	Tatyana Averina (URS) 43.17
1980	Karin Enke (GDR) 41.78	Leah Poulos-Mueller (USA) 42.26	Natalya Petruseva (URS) 42.42
1984	Christa Rothenburger (GDR) 41.02	Karin Enke (GDR) 41.28	Natalya Chive (URS) 41.50
1988	Bonnie Blair (USA) 39.10	Christa Rothenburger (GDR) 39.12	Karin Enke-Kania (GDR) 39.24
1992	Bonnie Blair (USA) 40.33	Ye Qiaobo (CHN) 40.51	Christa Rothenburger-Luding (GER) 40.57
1994	Bonnie Blair (USA) 39.25	Susan Auch (CAN) 39.61	Franziska Schenk (GER) 39.70
1998*	Catriona LeMay Doan (CAN) 1:16.60	Susan Auch (CAN) 1:16.93	Susan Auch (CAN) 1:17.10
2002	Catriona LeMay Doan (CAN) 1:14.75	Monique Garbrecht-Enfieldt (GER) 1:14.94	Sabine Völker (GER) 1:15.19

* In 1998 the event changed to an aggregate of the times from two races.

1000 METRES

	Gold	Silver	Bronze
1960	Klara Guseva (URS) 1:34.1	Helga Haase (GER) 1:34.3	Tamara Rylova (URS) 1:34.8
1964	Lydia Skoblikova (URS) 1:33.2	Irina Yegorova (URS) 1:34.3	Kaija Mustonen (FIN) 1:34.8
1968	Carolina Geijssen (NED) 1:32.6	Ludmila Titova (URS) 1:32.9	Dianne Holum (USA) 1:33.4
1972	Monika Pflug (FRG) 1:31.40	Atje Keulen-Deelstra (NED) 1:31.61	Anne Henning (USA) 1:31.62
1976	Tatyana Averina (URS) 1:28.43	Leah Poulos (USA) 1:28.57	Sheila Young (USA) 1:29.14
1980	Natalya Petruseva (URS) 1:24.10	Leah Poulos-Mueller (USA) 1:25.41	Sylvia Albrecht (GDR) 1:26.46
1984	Karin Enke (GDR) 1:21.61	Andrea Schöne (GDR) 1:22.83	Natalya Petruseva (URS) 1:23.21
1988	Christa Rothenburger (GDR) 1:17.65	Karin Enke-Kania (GDR) 1:17.70	Bonnie Blair (USA) 1:18.31
1992	Bonnie Blair (USA) 1:21.90	Ye Qiaobo (CHN) 1:21.92	Monique Garbrecht (GER) 1:22.10
1994	Bonnie Blair (USA) 1:18.74	Anke Baier (GER) 1:20.12	Ye Qiaobo (CHN) 1:20.22
1998	Marianne Timmer (NED) 1:16.51	Christine Witty (USA) 1:16.79	Catriona Le May Doan (CAN) 1:17.37
2002	Christine Witty (USA) 1:13.83	Sabine Völker (GER) 1:13.96	Jennifer Rodriguez (USA) 1:14.24

1500 METRES

	Gold	Silver	Bronze
1960	Lydia Skoblikova (URS) 2:25.2	Elvira Seroczynska (POL) 2:25.7	Helena Pilejeyk (POL) 2:27.1
1964	Lydia Skoblikova (URS) 2:22.6	Kaija Mustonen (FIN) 2:25.5	Berta Kolokoltseva (URS) 2:27.1
1968	Kaija Mustonen (FIN) 2:22.4	Carolina Geijssen (NED) 2:22.7	Christina Kaiser (NED) 2:24.5
1972	Dianne Holum (USA) 2:20.85	Christina Baas-Kaiser (NED) 2:21.05	Atje Keulen-Deelstra (NED) 2:22.05
1976	Galina Stepanskaya (URS) 2:16.58	Sheila Young (USA) 2:17.06	Tatyana Averina (URS) 2:17.96
1980	Annie Borckink (NED) 2:10.95	Ria Visser (NED) 2:12.35	Sabine Becker (GDR) 2:12.38
1984	Karin Enke (GDR) 2:03.42	Andrea Schöne (GDR) 2:05.29	Natalya Petruseva (URS) 2:05.78
1988	Yvonne Van Gennip (NED) 2:00.68	Karin Enke-Kania (GDR) 2:00.82	Andrea Schöne-Ehrig (GDR) 2:01.49
1992	Jacqueline Börner (GER) 2:05.87	Gunda Niemann (GER) 2:05.92	Seiko Hashimoto (JPN) 2:06.88
1994	Emese Hunyady (AUT) 2:02.19	Svetlana Fedotkin (RUS) 2:02.69	Gunda Niemann (GER) 2:03.41
1998	Marianne Timmer (NED) 1:57.58	Gunda Niemann-Stirnemann (GER) 1:58.86	Christine Witty (USA) 1:58.97
2002	Anni Friesinger (GER) 1:54.02	Sabine Völker (GER) 1:54.97	Jennifer Rodriguez (USA) 1:55.32

3000 METRES

	Gold	Silver	Bronze
1960	Lydia Skobilova (URS) 5:14.3	Valentina Stenina (URS) 5:16.9	Eevi Huttunen (FIN) 5:21.0
1964	Lydia Skobilova (URS) 5:14.9	Valentina Stenina (URS) 5:18.5 Pil-Hwa Han (PRK) 5:18.5	—
1968	Johanna Schut (NED) 4:56.2	Kaija Mustonen (FIN) 5:01.0	Christina Kaiser (NED) 5:01.3
1972	Christina Baas-Kaiser (NED) 4:52.14	Dianne Holum (USA) 4:58.67	Atje Keulen-Deelstra (NED) 4:59.91
1976	Tayana Averina (URS) 4:45.19	Andrea Mitscherlich (GDR) 4:45.23	Lisbeth Korsmo (Nor) 4:45.24
1980	Bjørg Eva Jensen (NOR) 4:32.13	Sabine Becker (GDR) 4:32.79	Beth Heiden (USA) 4:33.77
1984	Andrea Mitscherlich-Schöne (GDR) 4:24.79	Karin Enke (GDR) 4:26.33	Gabi Schönbrunn (GDR) 4:33.13
1988	Yvonne Van Gennip (NED) 4:11.94	Andrea Schöne-Ehrig (GDR) 4:12.09	Gabi Schönbrunn-Zange (GDR) 4:16.92
1992	Gunda Niemann (GER) 4:19.90	Heike Warnicke (GER) 4:22.88	Emese Hunyadi (AUT) 4:24.64
1994	Svetlana Bazhanova (RUS) 4:17.43	Emese Hunyadi (AUT) 4:18.14	Emese Hunyadi (AUT) 4:18.34
1998	Gunda Niemann-Stirnemann (GER) 4:07.29	Claudia Pechstein (GER) 4:08.47	Anna Friesinger (GER) 4:09.44
2002	Claudia Pechstein (GER) 3:57.70	Renate Groenewold (NED) 3:58.94	Cindy Klassen (CAN) 3:58.97

5,000 METRES

	Gold	Silver	Bronze
1988	Yvonne Van Gennip (NED) 7:14.13	Andrea Schöne-Ehrig (GDR) 7:17.2	Gabi Schönbrunn-Zange (GDR) 7:21.61
1992	Gunda Niemann (GER) 7:31.57	Heike Warnicke (GER) 7:37.59	Claudia Pechstein (GER) 7:39.80
1994	Claudia Pechstein (GER) 7:14.37	Gunda Neimann (GER) 7:14.88	Hiromi Yamamoto (JPN) 7:19.68
1998	Claudia Pechstein (GER) 6:59.61	Gunda Niemann-Stirnemann (GER) 6:59.65	Lyudmila Prokasheva (KZK) 7:11.14
2002	Claudia Pechstein (GER) 6:46.91	Gretha Smit (NED) 6:49.22	Clara Hughes (CAN) 6:53.53

1960–84 event not held

DISCONTINUED EVENTS

MEN
ALL-ROUND CHAMPIONSHIP
(Aggregate of placings in 500m, 1500m, 5km and 10km)

	Gold	Silver	Bronze
1924	Clas Thunberg (FIN) 5.5pts	Roald Larsen (NOR) 9.5	Julius Skutnabb (FIN) 11

SPEED-SKATING MEDALS

MEN
500 METRES
Gold	Silver	Bronze
1994	Chae Ji-Hoon (KOR) 43.45	Mirko Vuillermin (ITA) 43.47	Nicky Gooch (GBR) 43.68
1998	Takafuni Nishitani (JPN) 42.862	An Yulong (CHN) 43.022	Hitoshi Uematsu (JPN) 43.713
2002	Marc Gagnon (CAN) 41.802	Jonathan Guilmette (CAN) 41.994	Rusty Smith (USA) 42.027

1924–92 event not held

1000 METRES
1992	Kim Ki-Hoon (KOR) 1:30.76	Frederic Blackburn (CAN) 1:31.11	Lee Joon-Ho (KOR) 1:31.16
1994	Kim Ki-Hoon (KOR) 1:34.57	Chae Ji-Hoon (KOR) 1:34.92	Marc Gagnon (CAN) 1:33.03 *
1998	Kim Dong-Sung (KOR) 1:32.375	Li Jiajun (CHN) 1:32.428	Eric Bedard (CAN) 1:32.661
2002	Steven Bradbury (AUS) 1:29.109	Apolo Anton Uhno (USA) 1:30.160	Mathieu Turcotte (CAN) 1:30.563

1924–88 event not held. * As there was no other finisher in the 'A' final, the winner of the 'B' final was placed third.

1500 METRES
2002*	Apolo Anton Uhno (USA) 2:18.541	Jiajun Li (CHN) 2:18.731	Marc Gagnon (CAN) 2:18.806

1924–98 event not held. * Dong-Sung Kim (KOR) finished first but was subsequently disqualified,

5000 METRES RELAY
1992	South Korea 7:14.02	Canada 7:14.06	Japan 7:18.18
1994	Italy 7:11.74	United States 7:13.37	Australia 7:13.68
1998	Canada 7:32.075	Korea 7:06.776	China 7:11.559
2002	Canada 6:51.579	Italy 6:56.327	China 6:59.633

1924–88 event not held

WOMEN
500 METRES
1992	Cathy Turner (USA) 47.04	Li Yan (CHN) 47.08	Hwang Ok-Sil (PRK) 47.23
1994	Cathy Turner (USA) 45.98	Zhang Yanmei (CHN) 46.44	Amy Peterson (USA) 46.76
1998	Annie Perreault (CAN) 46.568	Yang Yang S (CHN) 46.627	Chun Lee-Kyung (KOR) 46.335*
2002	Yang Yang A (CHN) 44.187	Yevgeniya Radanova (BUL) 44.252	Wang Chunlu (CHN) 44.272

1924–88 event held. * Isabelle Charest (CAN) was disqualified, so the winner of the 'B' final was placed third.

1000 METRES
1994	Chun Lee-Kyung (KOR) 1:36.87	Nathalie Lambert (CAN) 1:36.97	Kim So-Hee (KOR) 1:37.09
1998	Chun Lee-Kyung (KOR) 1:42.776	Yang Yang S (CHN) 1:43.343	Won Hye-Kyung (KOR) 1:43.361
2002	Yang Yang A (CHN) 1:36.391	Gi-Hyun Ko (KOR) 1:36.427	Yang Yang S (CHN) 1:37.008

1924–92 event not held

1500 METRES
2002	Gi-Hyun Ko (KOR) 2:31.581	Eun-Kyung Choi (KOR) 2:31.610	Yevgeniya Radanova (BUL) 2:31.723

1924–98 event not held

3000 METRES RELAY
1992	Canada 4:36.62	United States 4:37.85	Unified Team 4:42.69
1994	Korea 4:26.64	Canada 4:32.04	United States 4:39.34
1998	Korea 4:16.260	China 4:16.383	Canada 4:21.205
2002	Korea 4:12.793	China 4:13.236	Canada 4:15.738

1924–88 event not held

INTERNATIONAL SPORTING ORGANISATIONS

OLYMPIC GAMES
International Olympic Committee (IOC)
Château de Vidy, C.P. 356, 1007 Lausanne, Switzerland
Tel: (41 21) 621 6111
Fax: (41 21) 621 6216
Web: www.olympic.org

ARCHERY
Fédération Internationale de Tir à l'Arc (FITA)
Avenue de Cour 135, CH-1007 Lausanne, Switzerland
Tel: (41 21) 614 3050 Fax: (41 21) 614 3055
Web: www.archery.org

ATHLETICS
International Association of Athletics Federations (IAAF)
17, rue Princesse Florestine, B.P. 359,
98007 Monte Carlo, Monaco Cédex
Tel: (377) 93 10 8888 Fax: (377) 93 15 9515
Web: www.iaaf.org

BADMINTON
International Badminton Federation (IBF)
Manor Park Place, Rutherford Way, Cheltenham,
Gloucestershire GL51 9TU
Tel: (44) 01242 234904 Fax: (44) 01242 221030
Web: www.worldbadminton.net

BASEBALL
International Baseball Federation (IBA)
Avenue Mon-Repos 24, 1005 Lausanne 5, Switzerland
Tel: (41 21) 318 8240 Fax: (41 21) 318 8241
Web: www.baseball.ch

BASKETBALL
Fédération Internationale de Basketball (FIBA)
Boschetsrieder Str. 67, 81379 Münich, Germany
Tel: (49 89) 7481580 Fax: (49 89) 74815833
Web: www.fiba.com

BIATHLON
International Biathlon Union (IBU)
Airport Center-Kasernenstrasse 1, Postfach 1,
5073 Wals Himmelreich,Austria
Tel: (43 662) 85 5050 Fax: (43 662) 85 50508
Web: www.ibu.at

BOBSLEDDING
Fédération Internationale de Bobsleigh et de Tobogganing
(FIBT)
Via Piranesi 44B, 20137 Milan, Italy
Tel: (39 02) 757 3319 Fax: (39 02) 757 3384
Website: www.bobsleigh.com

BOXING
Association Internationale de Boxe Amateur (AIBA)
P.O. Box 76343, Atlanta, Georgia 30358, USA
Tel: (1 770) 455 8350 Fax: (1 770) 454 6467
Web: www.aiba.net

CANOEING
Fédération Internationale de Canoë (FIC)
Callke de la Antracita 7,
4° ES-28045 Madrid, Espagne
Tel: (34 91) 506 1150 Fax: (3491) 506 1155
Web: www.canoeicf.com

CURLING
World Curling Federation (WCF)
74 Tay Street, Perth PH2 8NN, Great Britain
Tel: (44 1738) 45 16 30 Fax: (44 1738) 45 16 41
Web: www.worldcurlingfederation.org

CYCLING
Union Cycliste Internationale (UCI)
CH-1860 Aigle, Switzerland
Tel: (41 24) 468 5811 Fax: (41 24) 468 5812
Web: www.uci.ch

EQUESTRIANISM
Fédération Equestre Internationale (FEI)
Avenue Mon-Repos 24, Case Postale 157,
1000 Lausanne 5, Switzerland
Tel: (41 21) 310 4747 Fax: (41 21) 310 4760
Web: www.horsesort.org

FENCING
Fédération Internationale d'Escrime (FIE)
Avenue Mon-Repos 24, Case Postale 128,
1000 Lausanne 5, Switzerland
Tel: (41 21) 320 3151 Fax: (41 21) 320 3116
Web: www.fie.ch

FIGURE SKATING
International Skating Union (ISU)
Chemin de Primerose 2,
1007 Lausanne, Switzerland
Tel: (41 21) 612 6666 Fax: (41 21) 612 6677
Web: www.isu.org

FOOTBALL (SOCCER)
Fédération Internationale de Football Association (FIFA)
Hitzigweg 11, Case Postale 85, 8030 Zürich, Switzerland
Tel: (41 1) 384 9595 Fax: (41 1) 384 9696
Web: www.fifa.org

GYMNASTICS
Fédération Internationale de Gymnastique (FIG)
Rue des Oeuches 10, Case Postale 359,
2740 Moutier 1, Switzerland
Tel: (41 32) 494 6410 Fax: (41 32) 494 6419
Web: www.fig-gymnastics.com

HANDBALL
Fédération Internationale de Handball (IHF)
Lang Gasse 10, 4052 Basle, Switzerland
Tel: (41 61) 228 9040 Fax: (41 61) 228 9055
Web: www.ihf.info

HOCKEY
Fédération Internationale de Hockey (FIH)
Avenue des Arts 1, Boîte postale 5, 1210 Bruxelles, Belgium
Tel: (32 2) 219 4537 Fax: (32 2) 219 2761
Web: www.fihockey.org

ICE HOCKEY
International Ice Hockey Federation (IIHF)
Parkring 11, 8002 Zürich, Switzerland
Tel: (41 1) 289 8600 Fax: (41 1) 289 8629
Web: www.iihf.com

JUDO
International Judo Federation (IJF)
33rd Floor Doosan Tower, 18-12 Ulchi-ro, 6 Ka,
Chung-Ku, Seoul, Korea
Tel: (82 2) 33 98 10 17 Fax: (82 2) 33 98 10 20
Web: www.ijf.org

LUGEING
Fédération Internationale de Luge de Course (FIL)
Rathausplatz 9, 83471 Berchtesgaden, Germany
Tel: (49 8652) 669 60 Fax: (49 8652) 669 69
Web: www.fil-luge.org

MODERN PENTATHLON
Union Internationale de Pentathlon Moderne (UIPM)
Stade Louis II - Entrance E, 13 avenue des Castelans,
98000 Monaco
Tel: (377) 97 77 8555 Fax: (377) 97 77 8550
Web: www.pentathlon.org

ROWING
Fédération Internationale des Sociétés d'Aviron (FISA)
Avenue de Cour 135, Case Postale 18,
1000 Lausanne 3, Switzerland
Tel: (41 21) 617 8373 Fax: (41 21) 617 8375
Web: www.worldrowing.com

SAILING
International Sailing Federation (ISAF)
Ariadne House, Town Quay, Southampton,
Hampshire SO14 2AQ, Great Britain
Tel: (44 1703) 63 5111 Fax: (44 1703) 63 5789
Web: www.sailing.org

SHOOTING
Fédération Internationale de Tir Sportif (ISSF)
Bavariaring 21, 80336 Münich, Germany
Tel: (49 89) 544 3550 Fax: (49 89) 544 35544
Web: www.issf-shooting.org

SKIING
Fédération Internationale de Ski (FIS)
Blochstrasse 2, 3653 Oberhofen/Thunersee, Switzerland
Tel: (41 33) 244 6161 Fax: (41 33) 244 6171
Web: www.fis-ski.com

SOFTBALL
International Softball Federation (ISF)
1900 South Park Road, US-Plant City, Florida 33566, USA
Tel: (1 813) 864 0100 Fax: (1 813) 864 0105
Web: www.internationalsoftball.com

SWIMMING
Fédération Internationale de Natation Amateur (FINA)
Avenue de l'Avant-Poste 4, 1005 Lausanne, Switzerland
Tel: (41 21) 310 4710 Fax: (41 21) 312 6610
Web: www.fina.org

TABLE TENNIS
International Table Tennis Federation (ITTF)
Avenue Mon-Repos 30, 1005 Lausanne, Switzerland
Tel: (41 21) 340 7090 Fax: (41 21) 340 7099
Web: www.ittf.com

TAEKWONDO
World Taekwondo Federation (WTF)
5th Floor, Sinmunno Bldg, 238 Sinmunno 1-ga,
Jongrogu, Seoul 110-061, Korea
Tel: (82 2) 566 2505 Fax: (82 2) 553 4728
Web: www.wtf.org

TENNIS
International Tennis Federation (ITF)
Bank Lane, Roehampton, London SW15 5XZ, Great Britain
Tel: (44 20) 8878 6464 Fax: (44 20) 8876 7705
Web: www.itftennis.com

TRIATHLON
International Triathlon Union (ITU)
1786 Esquimalt Avenue, Suite 7, West Vancouver,
BC CA-V7V 1R8, Canada
Tel: (1 604) 926 7250 Fax: (1 604) 608 3195
Web: www.triathlon.org

VOLLEYBALL
Fédération Internationale de Volleyball (FIVB)
Avenue de la Gare 12, 1003 Lausanne, Switzerland
Tel: (41 21) 345 3535 Fax: (41 21) 345 3545
Web: www.fivb.ch

WEIGHTLIFTING
International Weightlifting Federation (IWF)
Hold u. 1,1054 Budapest, Hungary
Tel: (36 1) 331 8153 Fax: (36 1) 353 0199
Web: www.iwf.net

WRESTLING
Fédération Internationale de Luttes Associées (FILA)
Avenue Juste-Olivier 17, 1006 Lausanne,Switzerland
Tel: (41 21) 312 8426 Fax: (41 21) 323 6073
Web: www.fila-wrestling.org

INDEX

D

Dæhlie, Bjørn (b. 19 Jun 1967) 53, 58, 107, 110, 113, 117
Daly, John (1880–1972) 12
Danek, Ludvik (1937–1998) 71
Dangalakova, Tonya (b. 30 Jun 1964) 136
Daniels, Charles (1885–1973) 12, 14, 134
Darnyi, Tamás (b. 3 Jun 1967) 136
Daschinsky, Dimitri (b. 9 Nov 1977) 95
Da Silva, Adhemar Ferreira (1927–2001) 70
Davenport, Lindsay (b. 8 Jun 1976) 140
Davenport, Willie (1943–2002) 45, 70
Davenport, Winthrop 140
Davis, Howard (b. 14 Feb 1956) 79
Davis, Pierpoint (1884–1953) 24
Davis, Walt (b. 5 Jan 1931) 30, 139
Day, Jim (b. 7 Jul 1946) 89
Dean, Christopher (b. 27 Jul 1958) 47, 93
Deane, Sir William (b.4 Jan 1943) 59, 113
Deardurff, Deana (b. 8 May 1957) 41
de Bruijn, Inge (b. 24 Aug 1973) 59, 134, 136
de Courbertin, Pierre de Fredi, Baron (1863–1937) 9, 10, 11, 12, 13, 15, 19, 21, 24, 28, 36, 48, 53, 83, 86, 91, 94, 101, 103, 108, 110, 121, 124, 146
Decugis, Marie (1884–1969) 13, 140
Decugis, Max (1882–1978) 13, 139, 140
de Fredi, Baron Pierre *see* de Coubertin
de Gaulle, President Charles (1890–1970) 37, 113
de Kruijff, Gerard (1890–1968) 90
de la Hunty *see* Strickland
Delany, Ronnie (b. 6 Mar 1935) 32
Delecour, Jocelyn (b. 2 Jan 1935) 70
Deleigne, Sebastien 109
Delle-Karth, Werner 42, 112
De Magistris, Gianni (b. 3 Dec 1950) 143
Démanet, Lucien (b. 6 Dec 1874) 97
DeMont, Rick (b. 21 Apr 1956) 41, 88
de Montigny, Fernand (1885–1974) 88
Dench, Patricia (b. 8 Mar 1932) 48
Deng Yaping (b. 5 Feb 1973) 138
Denis, Harry 112
Dennis, Claire (1916–1971) 24
de Pourtalès, Helen, Countess (b. 1869) 11, 146
de Portalès, Hermann, Count (1847–1904) 11
de Riel, Emily (b. 24 Nov 1974) 109
Derbyshire, John (1878–1938) 88
Desborough, Lord (1855–1945) 14
de Seminario, Gladys (b. 18 Sep 1937) 124
Desjardins, Ulise 'Pete' (1907–1985) 21
Desmarteau, Etienne (1873–1905) 12, 44
D'Este, Giliante (1910–1996) 120
Deveric, Stjepan (b. 20 Aug 1961) 129
Devitt, John (b. 4 Feb 1937) 34, 135
Devonish, Arnoldo (1932–1997) 71
Deyna, Kazimiercz (b. 23 Oct 1947) 129
De Zolt, Maurilio (b. 25 Sep 1970) 53, 56,110
de Zubiera, Constantin Henriquez 11
Diaz, Giorge (b. 16 Sep 1970) 74
Dibiasi, Klaus (b. 6 Oct 1947) 43, 86
Dickson, Robert (b. 22 Apr 1931) 29
Didon, Father Henri (1840–1900) 19, 110

Didrikson, Mildred ' babe' (1911–1956) 23, 69
Diem, Carl (1882–1962) 25, 141
Diers, Ines (b. 2 Nov 1963) 46
Diesch, Eckart (b. 1 May 1954) 43
Diesch, Jörg (b. 29 Sep 1951) 43
Diessner, Ullrich (b. 27 Dec 1954) 43, 46
Diessner, Walter (b. 27 Dec 1954) 43, 46
Dietrich, Wilfried (b. 19 Oct 1933) 146
Dijkstra, Sjoukje (b. 28 Jan 1942) 36
Dillard, Harrison (b. 8 Jul 1923) 28, 30
Dimas, Pyrros (b. 13 Oct 1971) 144
Ding Meiyuan 144
Dinwiddie, Marcus (1907–1951) 124
d'Inzeo, Piero (b. 4 Mar 1923) 43, 89
d'Inzeo, Raimondo (b. 2 Feb 1925) 43, 89
Disl, Ursula 'Uschi' (b. 15 Nov 1970) 74, 108
Disney, Walt (1901–1966) 33
Dityatin, Aleksandr (b. 7 Aug 1957) 45, 96, 107, 113
Dixon, Michael (b. 21 Nov 1962) 114
Dixon, Robin (b. 21 Apr 1935) 36
Djemal, Mehmet (b. 1911) 144
Dmitriyev, Artur 94
Dod, Charlotte 'Lottie' (1871–1960) 66
Dod, William (1867–1954) 66
Dodd, Michael (b. 20 Aug 1957) 76
Doe, Charles (b. 4 Sep 1898) 121
Doe Jr, Thomas (1912–1969) 20, 77
Doherty, Laurie (1875–1919) 80, 140
Doherty, Reggie (1872–1910) 80, 140
Dolan, Tom (b. 15 Sep 1975) 134
Dollinger, Marie (1910–1994) 69
Donkova, Yordanka (b. 28 Sep 1961) 68
Doreste Blanco, José-Luis (b. 18 Sep 1956) 54
Doreste Blanco, Luis (b. 7 Mar 1961) 54, 112
d'Oriola, Christian (b. 3 Oct 1928) 92
d'Oriola, Pierre Jonquères (b. 1 Feb 1920) 89
Dorizas, Mikhel (1890–1957) 69, 72
Douglas, John (1882–1930) 78
Doumergue, President Gaston (1863–1937) 19, 112
Downing, Burton (1885–1929) 84
Doyle, Sir Arthur Conan (1859–1930) 15
Dragila, Stacy (b. 25 Mar 1971) 68, 71,
Drapeau, Mayor Jean (b. 1916) 43
Draves, Vicki (b. 31 Dec 1924) 29
Drechsler, Heike (b. 16 Dec 1964) 71
Drobny, Jaroslav (1921–2001) 100
Drummond, Jon (b. 9 Sep 1968) 70
d'Souza, Neville 129
Dubravcic, Sandra (b. 24 Aug 1964) 47, 95
Ducret, Roger (1888–1962) 19, 91
Dunai, Antal (b. 21 Mar 1943) 129
Duncansson, Albert (b. 2 Oct 1911) 23
Dupont, Helena (b. 6 Jul 1939) 90
Duquesne, Lucien (b. 17 Oct 1900) 21
Durack, Fanny (1893–1956) 134
Duvall, Samuel Harding (1836–1908) 12, 67, 11
Dyrssen, Gustaf (1891–1981) 109

E

Eagan, Eddie (1897–1967) 22, 23, 77, 87
Eastlake-Smith, Gladys (1883–1941) 14
Eberhalter, Stephan (b. 24 Mar 1969) 65

H

Q

Notes

Notes

Notes